The Book of

Criminal Minds

Publications International, Ltd.

Contributing writer: Lisa Brooks

Images from Shutterstock.com

Louis Weber, CEO
Publications International, Ltd.
8140 Lehigh Avenue
Morton Grove, IL 60053

ISBN: 978-1-64558-634-0

Manufactured in China.

8 7 6 5 4 3 2 1

Contents

✳ ✳ ✳ ✳

Crime and Punishment

✳ ✳ ✳ ✳

FORGERIES, BANK ROBBERIES, jewel heists, bigamy, crimes of passion, serial killings, mob extortion, assassinations, political corruption, counterfeiting, money laundering, piracy, spying, con artistry, and more—you'll find crimes of all kind described in these pages. Some are funny, some horrific. Some took place centuries ago yet still pique our interest, while others were headline topics within our lifetime.

With 16 chapters divided into different themes, you'll find an assortment of crimes, criminals, and other crime-related topics such as investigations, fingerprints, and famous prison escapes.

Read about:

✳ The thief who hid diamonds from detection in his soup bowl and was drawn to a perfect string of pearls (page 36)

✳ The man who married more than 40 women—many of whom he murdered (page 64)

✳ How H.H. Holmes brought horror to the World's Fair (page 95)

✳ The Ohio serial killer case that Eliot Ness couldn't solve (page 110)

✳ The time when Charlie Chaplin's coffin was stolen for ransom (page 222)

✳ Secrets of "The Body Farm" (page 329)

✳ Outlaws including Billy the Kid, Gregorio Cortez, and Belle Star (page 524)

The Book of Criminal Minds will inform, entertain, and quite possibly scare you. Dive right in.

Chapter 1

Art and Artifacts

Stealing History

Move over, Indiana Jones—the theft of priceless artifacts has been going on for centuries.

✳   ✳   ✳   ✳

IT'S LIKE SOMETHING out of a James Bond movie: An international collector pays big bucks to organized criminals to steal priceless antiquities and smuggle them over international borders. National treasures have been purloined for centuries—taken to distant lands to bring prestige and value to museums, treasuries, and private collections.

A Thief In The Night

Sometimes, looters go straight to the source. Since the days of the earliest pharaohs, Egyptian rulers lived in fear of tomb robbers and went to great lengths to protect the possessions they intended to take into the hereafter.

But thieves were not always cloaked peasants who dug into pyramids in the dark of night; sometimes even Egyptian kings entered the graves of their predecessors to "borrow" goodies for use in the afterlife. King Tutankhamen's tomb included a second inner coffin, four miniature coffins, and some gold bands that had been removed from the tomb of his older brother, Smenkare. The tomb of Pharaoh Pinudjem I included "recycled" sarcophagi from the tomb of Thothmosis I, Egypt's ruler from three dynasties earlier. (Perhaps this sort of grave robbing was simply considered "borrowing from Peter to pay Peter," since every Egyptian king was, in theory, a reincarnation of the falcon god Horus.)

More recently, archaeological sites in the western United States have suffered a rash of thefts by shovel-toting bandits intent on digging up Native and Central American artifacts to sell in thriving legitimate and gray-market art and collectibles markets. In 2003, for instance, one Vanderbilt University professor worked with Guatemalan police, villagers, and even local drug lords to track down a stolen 1,200-year-old monument to a Mayan king.

Museums Robbed and Looted

Museum robberies have become a huge problem, especially for institutions that cannot afford state-of-the-art security systems. In 2001, for example, Russia's Culture Ministry stated that, on average, one Russian museum was victimized by theft each month. In Iraq in April 2003, during the chaos of the U.S.-led invasion of Iraq, some 170,000 items were looted or destroyed in the Iraqi National Museum; many of these artifacts subsequently made their way into private hands.

Authorities are slowly stirring themselves to crack down on a burgeoning traffic in stolen artifacts. In 2005, an Italian court sentenced a Roman antiquities dealer to ten years in prison for receiving and exporting stolen artifacts. The dealer's company sold 110 items through the prestigious auction house Sotheby's and sold another 96 artifacts to ten museums around the world before the operation was shut down.

Government Theft

Conquest and colonization have provided other supply sources for collections. The Israelite temple in Jerusalem was looted by invading armies at least twice: by Babylonian King Nebuchadnezzar around 586 B.C., and again by Roman Emperor Vespasian in A.D. 70. In 480 B.C., when the Persian army sacked Athens, artifacts in the wooden Acropolis temple were carted off to Persepolis as war booty, and during his 1798–99 expedition to Egypt, Napoleon's army uncovered one of the most famous spoils of war, the Rosetta Stone—which was in turn captured by Britain in 1801. Equally famous are the "Elgin Marbles," relief statues from Greece's Parthenon that were brought to London's British Museum in 1816 by the British ambassador to Turkey.

During World War II, the Nazi regime took the pastime of art collecting to a new level. Thousands of priceless paintings, drawings, and sculptures were removed from museums in France and Russia at the behest of senior Nazi leaders. After Europe was liberated in 1945, many works of art were recovered, but others, such as Russia's fabled Amber Room panels, were never recovered at all.

John Myatt, Master Forger

When people hear the word forgery, they usually think of money. But legal currency isn't the only thing that can be faked.

✳ ✳ ✳ ✳

ONET, MONET, MONET. Sometimes I get truly fed up doing Monet. Bloody haystacks." John Myatt's humorous lament sounds curiously Monty Pythonesque, until you realize that he can do Monet—and Chagall, Klee, Le Corbusier, Ben Nicholson, and almost any other painter you can name, great or obscure. Myatt, an artist of some ability, was probably the world's greatest art forger. He took part in an eight-year forgery scam in the 1980s and '90s that shook the foundations of the art world.

Despite what one might expect, art forgery is not a victimless crime. Many of Myatt's paintings—bought in good faith as the work of renowned masters—went for extremely high sums. One "Giacometti" sold at auction in New York for $300,000, and as many as 120 of his counterfeits are still out there, confusing and distressing the art world. But Myatt never set out to break the law.

Initially, Myatt would paint an unknown work in the style of one of the cubist, surrealist, or impressionist masters, and he seriously duplicated both style and subject. For a time, he gave them to friends or sold them as acknowledged fakes. Then he ran afoul of John Drewe.

The Scheme Begins

Drewe was a London-based collector who had bought a dozen of Myatt's fakes over two years. Personable and charming, he ingratiated himself with Myatt by posing as a rich aristocrat. But one day he called and told Myatt that a cubist work the artist had done in the style of Albert Gleizes had just sold at Christies for £25,000 ($40,000)—as a genuine Gleizes. Drewe offered half of that money to Myatt.

The struggling artist was poor and taking care of his two children. The lure of the money was irresistible. So the scheme developed that he would paint a "newly discovered" work by a famous painter and pass it to Drewe, who would sell it and then pay Myatt his cut—usually about 10 percent. It would take Myatt two or three months to turn out a fake, and he was only making about £13,000 a year (roughly $21,000)—hardly worthy of a master criminal.

One of the amazing things about this scam was Myatt's materials. Most art forgers take great pains to duplicate the exact pigments used by the original artists, but Myatt mixed cheap emulsion house paint with a lubricating gel to get the colors he needed. One benefit is that his mix dried faster than oil paints.

The Inside Man

But Drewe was just as much of a master forger, himself. The consummate con man, he inveigled his way into the art world through donations, talking his way into the archives of the Tate

Gallery and learning every trick of *provenance*, the authentication of artwork. He faked letters from experts and, on one occasion, even inserted a phony catalog into the archives with pictures of Myatt's latest fakes as genuine.

As the years went by, Myatt became increasingly worried about getting caught and going to prison, so he told Drewe he wanted out. Drewe refused to let him leave, and Myatt realized that his partner wasn't just in it for the money. He also simply loved conning people.

The Jig Is Up

The scam was not to last, of course. Drewe's ex-wife went to the police with incriminating documents, and when the trail led to Myatt's cottage in Staffordshire, he confessed.

Myatt served four months of a yearlong sentence, and when he came out of prison, Detective Superintendent Jonathan Searle of the Metropolitan Police was waiting for him. Searle suggested that since Myatt was now infamous, many people would love to own a real John Myatt fake. As a result, Myatt and his second wife Rosemary set up a tidy business out of their cottage. His paintings regularly sell for as much as £45,000 ($72,000), and he even has a TV show.

The Museum of Empty Frames

Located in Boston, Massachusetts, the Isabella Stewart Gardner Museum contains paintings, sculptures, tapestries, and other works from Europe, Asia, and America. The museum was named for an American philanthropist and art collector, whose will decreed that her vast collection be permanently displayed to the public. But the museum is not only known for the art that adorns its walls; it is also famous for a brazen unsolved heist.

✳ ✳ ✳ ✳

ISABELLA STEWART GARDNER opened her museum to the public in 1903 and continued to add to her vast collection until her death in 1924. Her will stipulated that no artwork from her collection should ever be sold, and none should be added, and that even the arrangement of the artwork in the museum should remain untouched. In a sense, the museum was frozen in time.

Although Gardner left the museum a $3.6 million endowment, the institution was financially struggling. In 1982, after the FBI uncovered a plot by Boston criminals to rob the museum, the board of trustees decided to use what little funds they had to beef up security. Motion detectors were added, and closed-circuit cameras were placed around the perimeter of the building. The museum also hired more security guards, although it could only afford to pay slightly above minimum wage.

But even with these improvements, there were still flaws and gaps in the museum's security. For one, there were no cameras located inside the building. Also, the police could only be summoned by pushing a button located at a single security desk. By 1988, independent security consultants had warned the board of trustees that their security measures needed improvement; but due to Gardner's insistence that the museum remain unchanged, no more improvements were made.

A Brazen Heist

In the early morning hours of March 18, 1990, two security officers—23-year-old Rick Abath and 25-year-old Randy Hestand—were on duty in the Gardner Museum. At 1:20 A.M., a buzzer for the outside door rang an intercom at Abath's desk. On the closed-circuit television, Abath could see two men dressed as police officers, who told the guard that they were investigating a disturbance and needed to come in.

Once the "police officers" were inside, they asked Abath to summon Hestand, then lured the pair away from the security desk (the location of the only button to call for help), handcuffed them, and wrapped duct tape around their eyes. The thieves took the two guards down to the basement and handcuffed them to a pipe and workbench, their intention to rob the museum now more than obvious.

In just over an hour, the thieves were able to pack thirteen works of art into their car, making two trips back and forth, pilfering works by Rembrandt, Vermeer, Flinck, Degas, and Manet. They also stole an ancient Chinese vase and a bronze eagle finial. At 2:45 A.M., they left the museum, leaving Abath and Hestand still tied up in the basement. The two guards weren't able to get free until the morning guard shift arrived and called the police.

Empty Frames and a Huge Reward

Right off the bat, the heist puzzled art experts. The objects taken were seemingly random and unconnected. Some of the art was extremely valuable, but others had little worth. What's more, the thieves completely bypassed the third floor of the museum, which housed some of the most valuable paintings in the world. All of this would suggest that the thieves were not hired to execute a specific heist.

Regardless, the items the thieves stole still have an estimated value of between $500 and $600 million. One dealer at Sotheby's even puts the estimate at $1 billion. But to this day, no one knows who pulled off the heist or where they hid the art. Sotheby's, along with Christie's auction house, have posted a reward for the return of the art, which now stands at $10 million.

Because of Gardner's insistence that her museum remain unchanged, empty frames now hang where the stolen art was once displayed. Still frozen in time, the museum patiently awaits their return.

Missing Mona Lisa

Leonardo da Vinci's Mona Lisa, *a painting of an enigmatically smiling noblewoman named Lisa Gherardini, is undoubtedly one of the most famous pieces of art in the world. But surprisingly, it took a brazen theft to make it the popular tourist draw it is today.*

✳ ✳ ✳ ✳

Before She Was Famous

PRIOR TO 1911, the *Mona Lisa* was mostly known only throughout the art world, even though Leonardo da Vinci painted the portrait centuries earlier between 1503 and 1517. Later in life, the artist settled in France, where he worked in the service of King Francis I. Da Vinci and the king became close friends, and after da Vinci's death in 1519, the *Mona Lisa* found a new home with the French king. This may explain why an Italian painting created by an Italian artist eventually wound up in the Louvre, Paris's prestigious art museum.

But even in its home amongst some of the most priceless works of art in the world, the *Mona Lisa* remained a lesser-known piece at the museum. Measuring a modest 30 inches by 21 inches, its small footprint and muted colors weren't exactly calling out for attention. But on August 21, 1911, the inconspicuous little painting suddenly drew big attention when it mysteriously disappeared.

Sudden Notoriety

The poor *Mona Lisa* was so neglected and forgotten at the Louvre, that it took more than a day for her absence to be noticed. The museum's own staff hadn't even observed anything out of the ordinary, and the painting's theft may have been ignored far longer had it not been for an amateur artist who set up his easel to paint the *Mona Lisa*'s gallery and noticed something was amiss. After museum guards did a bit of searching and questioning, it was finally understood that the painting was, indeed, stolen.

Overnight, the *Mona Lisa* became a worldwide sensation, as newspapers around the globe reported on the painting's mysterious disappearance. Rumors began to fly as to the motive of the theft: Some believed the pre-World War I tensions between France and Germany had prompted the Germans to steal the painting out of spite. Others thought the United States was behind it, believing the Americans were attempting to pilfer all of France's best art. Investigators even questioned American banker J.P. Morgan about the theft, theorizing that he may have organized the heist.

Ironically, the empty space where the stolen *Mona Lisa* had hung became more popular than the painting had ever been. The Louvre was overrun with curious visitors, all eager to see the vacant spot that became known as Paris's "mark of shame." And for two years, the spot on the wall remained empty, as investigators hit nothing but dead ends in their search for the stolen painting.

Patriotism or Profit?

Then, one day in November 1913, an art dealer in Florence, Italy, named Alfredo Geri received a letter from a man calling himself "Leonardo." The man claimed to have possession of the *Mona Lisa*, and offered it to Geri at a hefty price. Intrigued but suspicious, Geri called in an expert to authenticate the painting. Once it was discovered to be the real deal, he also contacted the authorities. The man calling himself "Leonardo" turned out to be Vincenzo Peruggia, a former employee at the Louvre, and he was immediately arrested for the theft.

Peruggia claimed "patriotic duty" for his actions, stating that the *Mona Lisa* belonged in Italy, not France. But investigators believed his real motive was much more mundane: money. They theorized that Peruggia intended to sell the painting as soon as he stole it, but he never expected the whirlwind of attention his actions caused. So he was forced to hide the painting for two years while he waited for interest to die down.

Perhaps the most interesting part of the story is how Peruggia pulled off his heist: according to his own confession, he simply took the painting off the wall, removed its frame, wrapped it in a smock, and walked right out the door. Thanks to Peruggia's brazen theft of this modest and ignored artwork, the *Mona Lisa* is now the most visited painting in the world.

Norway's Prize Painting

The eerily otherworldly figure in Edvard Munch's The Scream *is instantly recognizable, not only by art enthusiasts, but by casual observers, as well. But the familiar composition has also caught the eye of thieves on more than one occasion.*

✳ ✳ ✳ ✳

Prolific Inspiration

MANY VIEWERS OF *The Scream* understandably believe that the strange, almost alien-like figure at the center of the painting is the one emitting the "scream." But according to Munch, it is not the person screaming, but rather the person's surroundings. He described it as "an infinite scream passing through nature," and originally titled the piece *Der Schrei der Natur (The Scream of Nature)*. Munch's own anxiety was said to be his source of inspiration for the piece, which has since become a symbol for human unease, fear, and depression.

With such profound and serious inspiration, perhaps it is only natural that Munch created not one, but many versions of the scene. In addition to two paintings, he also created two versions in pastels and approximately 45 lithograph prints. But it is the two paintings, both located in museums in Oslo, Norway, that have attracted the most attention.

A Gold Medal in Theft

The version of *The Scream* that most of us are familiar with is the painting that hangs in Oslo's National Gallery. On February 12, 1994, a visit to a museum was the last thing most people were thinking about. The date did, however, draw all eyes to Norway, as the Winter Olympics opened in Lillehammer. While the world was focused on the opening ceremonies and preparing to watch the showdown between Nancy Kerrigan and Tonya Harding, two men broke through a window at the museum, stole *The Scream* in 50 seconds flat, and left a note reading, "Thousand thanks for the bad security!"

Fortunately, the pilfered painting was found only three months later, at a hotel 40 miles south of Oslo. It took investigators another two years to track down the thieves who had left the cheeky note, and although they were convicted for the crime, they were later released due to legal technicalities.

Art Heist, or Diversion?

The second painted version of *The Scream* hangs in the Munch Museum in Oslo and, like its twin at the National Gallery, was also the target of thieves. But its theft, committed ten years after the first on August 22, 2004, came with an unusual twist. On that day, masked gunmen entered the Munch Museum in broad daylight and stole *The Scream* along with another Munch painting entitled *Madonna*.

After two years of searching, Norwegian police were finally able to recover both paintings, although each had sustained damage. *The Scream*, in particular, seemed to have water stains, and investigators theorized that it had been wrapped in something wet. But why would art thieves treat a painting so carelessly, if they were hoping to sell it or return it for ransom?

Police had a theory: the theft of the painting was not about the painting at all—it was a diversion. Around the same time as *The Scream* theft, a Norwegian police officer had been gunned down during an armed robbery, and the authorities were using all their manpower to track down whoever was responsible. Was *The Scream* stolen in an effort to take the heat off of the culprit in this crime? When a criminal named David Toska was arrested for leading the armed robbery, the Norwegian press reported that his lawyer had, indeed, led the authorities to *The Scream* and *Madonna*.

So it would seem that the theft wasn't about the painting at all, but rather a clever way to move the country's attention away from one crime and onto another. By targeting the most famous painting in Norway—and one of the most famous in the entire world—these art thieves gave police, investigators, and art lovers something to "scream" about.

The Antwerp Job

It was one of the largest robberies in history. Shockingly, more than $100 million in diamonds, gold, silver, and world currencies was stolen from what was thought to be an "impenetrable" vault. And had it not been for a simple panic attack, the thieves may have gotten away with it all.

✳ ✳ ✳ ✳

Diamonds Are Forever

IN THE 2003 FILM *The Italian Job*, starring Mark Wahlberg and Charlize Theron, a group of highly skilled thieves pulls off what seems to be an impossible heist. The group of safe-crackers, explosives experts, and computer whizzes manage to expertly pilfer millions of dollars' worth of gold bars, then ride off into the proverbial sunset to begin their new wealthy lives. Of course, those sorts of things only happen in a Hollywood script, right?

Amazingly, sometimes life does imitate art. And that same year, in the early morning hours of February 16, a real-life heist was taking place in the city of Antwerp, Belgium. The city is known for its World Diamond Center, which is home to all of the major diamond mining companies around the globe. In fact, 80 percent of the world's diamonds pass through the Antwerp World Diamond Center at one time or another, making the three-square-block area an obvious target for would-be thieves.

But with such valuable goods in its main vault, the Antwerp World Diamond Center is also equipped with some of the most complicated and state-of-the-art security features found anywhere. In 2003, these included security cameras, motion detectors, seismic sensors, and magnetic field alarms, as well as a three-ton steel vault door that could only be opened with a four-digit combination.

The Heist of the Century

Enter Leonardo Notarbartolo, an Italian thief who had been honing his skills since the age of six, when he stole $8 from a milkman. Notarbartolo often traveled to Antwerp to pawn off stolen jewelry from his homeland, so he was familiar with the area. And his thieving eye was on the Diamond Center. He knew a robbery in such a secure location would be challenging, but not necessarily impossible.

But Notarbartolo knew he couldn't pull off a heist on his own. So he rounded up a crew with nicknames that sounded like they were straight out of the movies: There was "the Genius," who was an electronics expert; "the Monster," an expert lock-picker, mechanic, and driver; "the King of Keys," one of the best key forgers in the world; and finally, "Speedy," one of Notarbartolo's oldest friends.

After eighteen months of planning, surveillance, and surreptitious filming, the crew finally hit their target on February 16. They expertly picked locks, disabled sensors, rerouted alarms, and, using secret footage they'd taken of a guard opening the vault, dialed in the code. Once inside, the group set to work drilling into 109 safety deposit boxes and emptying the contents into duffel bags. At around 5:30 A.M., they hightailed it out of the area before they were discovered, leaving behind zero clues and a baffling mystery for investigators.

A Big Mistake

But no crime is perfect. While the other three group members hid the loot, Notarbartolo and Speedy drove into the countryside to burn a bag of incriminating evidence. But the gravity of the situation began to weigh on poor Speedy, and instead of burning the evidence, he wound up strewing the garbage around in the mud in a panic and having a bit of a nervous breakdown. Notarbartolo quickly ushered him out of the area in an effort to calm him down, leaving behind video-tape, receipts, and envelopes from the Diamond Center. Police were later able to use this evidence to tie the crime back to Notarbartolo and his crafty accomplices.

Notarbartolo was sentenced to ten years in prison, with each of his accomplices— with the exception of "the King of Keys," who was never found—receiving five years. But in one final twist to the story, the expert thief insists that he was set up by a diamond dealer hoping to commit insurance fraud, and that most of the boxes the crew opened were empty. Since most of the reported $100 million stolen has not been recovered, we may never know the truth of what happened in Antwerp.

The Thief of Nova Scotia

Called everything from a "genius" to a "hoarder" to a "psychopath," Canadian John Tillmann was one of the most prolific thieves in the country. But had it not been for a routine traffic stop, the world may have never known his story.

✳   ✳   ✳   ✳

An Early Life of Crime

JOHN TILLMANN WAS born on February 24, 1961, in Halifax, Nova Scotia. Some accounts of his life report that he began stealing by the age of eight, when his grandmother would coerce him into shoplifting from local flea markets. Later in life, he majored in international marketing at Mount Saint Vincent University, and then lived in Moscow for several years, where he learned to speak Russian. Perhaps this was the beginning of Tillmann's fascination with historical artifacts and works of art, but much of his life is shrouded in mystery, so one can only speculate. What is not a mystery is that while in Russia, he met and married university student Katya Anastasia Zhestokova, and soon the couple were living a life of international crime.

Far from shoplifting for his grandmother, Tillmann, with the help of Zhestokova and Zhestokova's brother Vladimir, began traveling throughout Europe, the Middle East, and North and South America, planning and pulling off heists at museums and art houses. Tillmann carefully plotted and organized the thefts. The attractive Zhestokova provided a distraction for any attentive guards, while Vladimir employed his expertise with computer hacking and alarm disabling.

The Letters

Eventually, Tillmann and Zhestokova settled back in Canada, where they continued their life of crime. Tillmann would disguise himself as a maintenance worker, a guard, or a police officer to blend in with his surroundings, then use the sleight of hand skills he'd been perfecting since youth to snatch whatever prize caught his eye. Sometimes he even brought his own mother in on his heists, convincing her to fake chest pains or fainting spells to attract attention while he made off with another treasure. He stole from antique dealers, libraries, museums, and even the Nova Scotia legislature.

Then, late one night, Tillmann and Zhestokova snuck into Dalhousie University in Halifax and hid in a women's bathroom until the night security guard left. Using a duplicate key he'd had made, Tillmann was able to open a vault in the university's library. After a few hours of searching, the pair made an amazing discovery: two letters—the first written by British Army Officer General James Wolfe, the second written by none other than George Washington. The Washington letter alone was worth at least half a million dollars.

Downfall

Tillmann added the letters to his growing collection of stolen items, but he didn't keep everything he purloined. He became a wealthy man by selling much of his loot on the black market, amassing $2 million worth in property, including a house, a Porsche, and a BMW. It was while he was driving one of his cars in July 2012 that police stopped him for a routine traffic violation. But the stop became anything but routine when officers discovered the stolen Wolfe letter in Tillmann's car. The discovery of this hugely valuable stolen item prompted investigators to search the rest of his property, and they were shocked by what they found.

Over the years, Tillmann and his various accomplices had stolen more than 7,000 items, most of which he'd arranged throughout his house as if it were a museum. There were paintings, photographs, books, furniture, and antiques. Some of the more unusual items included a spear, a brass telescope, a gas mask, and a canoe. Tillmann was so efficient and adept at stealing items that many of his victims weren't even aware that anything was missing until the authorities contacted them.

Tillmann was convicted on 40 counts of theft in 2013 and sentenced to nine years in prison. He was paroled in 2016, but the prolific thief died on December 23, 2018, at the age of 57.

The New Master

How did Dutch artist Han van Meegeren manage to fool a Nazi into buying a forged painting? It took a lot of practice, a little bit of plastic, and the help of a pizza oven.

✳   ✳   ✳   ✳

Beginnings in Architecture

WHEN HAN VAN Meegeren was a child, his father once punished him by forcing him to repeatedly write, "I know nothing. I am nothing. I am capable of nothing." This terrible missive was certainly the antithesis of what a parent should tell a child, and van Meegeren, who was born on October 10, 1889, in Deventer, Netherlands, grew up often feeling inadequate.

Young van Meegeren loved art, but his father forbade him from studying the craft, pushing him towards architecture instead. Van Meegeren attended the Delft University of Technology and excelled at his study of architecture, even designing a boathouse for his rowing club which still stands in Delft today. But his heart wasn't in the vocation, and he never took his final exams. Instead, after marrying and having a son, he moved his family to The Hague, where he studied painting at the Royal Academy of Art.

For many years, van Meegeren made a modest living by teaching, sketching, and painting, and his work was reasonably well respected in the Netherlands. But when he tried expanding his repertoire to include paintings in the style of the old masters, he was criticized for his lack of originality. But far from believing his father's words that he was "capable of nothing," van Meegeren was determined to prove that he was capable of so much more. He vowed to create forged paintings so perfect that no one would suspect they weren't genuine.

Planning and Practice

First, van Meegeren had to decide which artist to emulate. He landed on 17th century artist Jan Vermeer, who is only known to have created about 35 paintings. The life of Vermeer is also less well known than many other painters of the time. This gave van Meegeren two advantages: First, since there were only 35 known Vermeers in the world, it wouldn't be unusual if a previously "lost" painting showed up. And second, van Meegeren could paint whatever he wanted, since no one knew exactly how Vermeer chose his subjects.

But there was another problem: how could van Meegeren make a modern painting look as if it had been around for 300 years? He experimented with many paints, canvases, and aging techniques, but his final method was a bit unusual. Van Meegeren bought a pizza oven, dissolved a small amount of plastic into his paint, and then dried his finished painting in the oven.

The plastic prevented the paint from burning up, and the oven resulted in a perfectly dried, aged appearance.

Fooling the Experts (and the Nazis)

With his newfound technique at the ready, van Meegeren began painting his forged Vermeers. And just as he'd hoped, when art experts saw the paintings, they were convinced they'd stumbled onto "lost" paintings. The fake Vermeers were selling for millions of dollars each, allowing van Meegeren to purchase an exclusive home in Amsterdam, jewelry, and works of art.

Then the Nazis, who looted thousands of pieces of art during World War II, occupied the Netherlands. Hermann Göring, one of the most powerful figures in Nazi Germany, had a huge collection of stolen artwork, and in 1942, he bought one of van Meegeren's "Vermeers," believing it would be the prize work in his collection.

When the war ended and Allied forces discovered Göring's artwork, they found paperwork with the "Vermeer" that mentioned van Meegeren's name. Police soon showed up at the door of his Amsterdam mansion, arresting him for collaborating with the Nazis and plundering Dutch cultural property. Faced with the prospect of prison, van Meegeren confessed that the painting was a fake, and hoped the authorities would be lenient on him for swindling a Nazi.

Van Meegeren was sentenced to only one year in prison, but the artist, who had been in poor health for years, died on December 30, 1947, before he'd even served a day. To his fellow countrymen, van Meegeren died a hero—the artist who was so talented he fooled a Nazi.

The Hitler Diaries Hoax

In 1983, Germany's popular magazine Stern *dropped a bomb: It now had access to Adolf Hitler's secret diaries. Experts soon revealed them as phonies authored by a modern crook, leaving prominent historians and major media looking ridiculous.*

✳ ✳ ✳ ✳

Counterfeit Collectibles

THE CROOK WAS Konrad Kujau, a man of numerous aliases and lies. He was born in 1938, and after World War II he lived in East Germany. He moved to West Germany in 1957 and began a life of petty crime, specializing in forgery.

A lifetime Hitler fan, Kujau became a noted Nazi memorabilia "collector." Naturally, he manufactured most of his collection, including authentication documents. He built a favorable reputation as a dealer specializing in ostensibly authentic Hitler stuff: signatures, writing, poetry, and art.

The public display of Nazi anything is illegal in Germany, as is Holocaust denial. Even WWII games sold in modern Germany cannot use the swastika. Nazi memorabilia collections remain strictly on the down low. Modern Germans overwhelmingly repudiate Nazism, and those born post-war also dislike association with a horror they didn't perpetrate. It's a painful subject.

Still, every country has closet Hitler admirers, and Germany is no exception. *Stern* journalist Gerd Heidemann was one—he even bought Hermann Göring's old yacht. In 1979, a collector (Kujau under an alias) invited Heidemann to check out his Nazi collection, including a bound copy of a diary supposedly authored by Hitler. The diary, which covered a period from January to June 1935, had been salvaged from a late-war plane crash in East Germany. The collector also claimed that there were 26 other volumes, each covering a six-month period.

Faulty Fact-Checking

Using his journalistic training, Heidemann went to East Germany and found a backstory that verified a plane crash. Although he didn't dig much deeper, he had a good excuse. At the time, the world thought in terms of East and West Germany. In East Germany, a socialist police state, no one nosed around except where the state approved (which it rarely did). Heidemann and *Stern's* West German homeland was the mainstay of NATO, and the border between East and West Germany bristled with a surprising percentage of the world's military power. *Stern* lacked an easy way to verify anything in East Germany.

So Heidemann basically pitched what he had to *Stern*, and the magazine swung from its heels. Salivating at the "find of a generation," *Stern* authorized Heidemann to offer an advance of $1 million (approximate U.S. equivalent) for the diaries. Kujau played coy, explaining that the other 26 volumes hadn't yet been smuggled out of East Germany. In reality, he needed time to forge them. He finally finished in 1981 and handed over the first volume to Heidemann.

At this point, everyone was too excited to bother with that tedious step called "authentication." *Stern* hadn't even learned Kujau's identity; it was too busy counting its future profit from serialization rights. Anyone who voiced worries about fraud was hushed. Some surprisingly big names entered bids, including *Newsweek*, *Paris Match*, and the *London Times*.

Stretching the Truth

The diaries themselves purported to reveal a kinder, gentler Hitler, a generally okay guy who wasn't even fully aware of the Holocaust. This Hitler is what modern Nazi sympathizers like to imagine existed, not the weird megalomaniac of actual history. But its improbability also spurred skeptics into gear.

In an attempt to deal with the naysayers, *Stern* got a bit hysterical, insisting that noted British historian Hugh Trevor-Roper had pronounced the diaries authentic. But skeptics faulted the diaries' paper, handwriting, and style. After some controversy, West German authorities ran forensics. The testing proved that the paper, ink, and even glue were of post-WWII manufacture. *Stern* had been bamboozled.

Because *Stern* is to Germany what *Time* and *Newsweek* are to the United States, it had a significant amount of credibility to lose. Several *Stern* editors were soon looking for new jobs. To say that the West German government was "annoyed" is an understatement. After *Stern* fired Heidemann, the police charged him with fraud. Heidemann, in his smartest move in a long time, implicated Kujau. When this news was made public in the media, Kujau went into hiding. In May 1983, he decided to turn himself into the police, who were anxiously waiting to arrest him. After several days of intense questioning, the authorities learned that Kujau was a reflexive, perpetual liar who invented falsehoods to cover his fictions.

The High Price of Greed

Kujau and Heidemann were each sentenced to several years in jail. The judge said *Stern* had "acted with such naiveté and negligence that it was virtually an accomplice in the fraud." The roughly $5 million the magazine ultimately gave Heidemann to pay Kujau was never recovered. Heidemann's increasingly lavish lifestyle during the forgeries and subsequent investigations suggests that he spent the majority of the money offshore.

After his release, Kujau tried his hand at politics, replica painting, and (again) forgery. He died of complications from cancer in 2000, but his crime is considered one of the most bold and successful hoaxes of the century.

Declassified East German files later showed that Heidemann had been an East German spy, though it's uncertain whether that had anything to do with the hoax. He claims he was actually a double agent working for West German authorities. With his career prospects impaired, he now keeps a low profile.

The Copycat

A well-known proverb asserts that imitation is the sincerest form of flattery. If that's the case, then English art restorer Tom Keating "flattered" scores of artists throughout his lifetime.

✳ ✳ ✳ ✳

Restoring the Masters

TOM KEATING WAS born on March 1, 1917, in London, England. His parents were not well-off, and a young Keating was forced to work odd jobs to supplement his family's income. Eventually he began working with his father as a house painter, an occupation that foreshadowed his future career.

After serving in World War II, Keating was accepted into the art program at Goldsmith's College, University of London. Although his painting instructors were impressed with his technical artistic abilities, they noted that he lacked originality. Keating dropped out after only two years, but his love of painting led him into the world of art restoration.

After college, Keating began working for an art restorer named Fred Roberts. One day, the two restorers were working on a painting by Frank Moss Bennett, and Keating criticized the British painter's work. Roberts challenged Keating to recreate one of Bennett's paintings, but Keating thought he could do even better: he painted  an original work in Bennett's style, which he then signed with his own name. When Roberts saw the painting, he was amazed by how authentic the work looked. He covered Keating's name and signed it "F.M. Bennett," then sold it to an art gallery. This was Keating's first taste of the world of art forgery.

Revenge for the Starving Artists

Over the next decade, Keating painted many original pieces and exhibited his work in art galleries, but there was little interest in his paintings. He became frustrated with art dealers, believing them to be greedy and disinterested in working with up-and-coming artists. He accused them of taking money from "naïve collectors" while taking advantage of "impoverished artists," and thought it was unfair that his fellow artists often went hungry and even died in poverty while the dealers lived lavish lifestyles.

So, Keating sought vengeance. Since he believed that he was just as good as Rembrandt, or Degas, or Monet, the artist began creating forgeries to fool the "expert" art dealers. His hope was that by flooding the market with forgeries, he could destabilize the whole system. Keating painted forgeries of 100 master artists, including Renoir, Cezanne, Titian, and his personal favorite, Samuel Palmer.

The forger made sure to leave clues within his paintings that would reveal their true nature, such as small flaws or anachronisms. He also used his knowledge as an art restorer to choose his paints and materials carefully. For instance, he would often place a layer of glycerin underneath the oil paint on a canvas, so when a restorer attempted to clean the work, the glycerin would dissolve and the painting would be ruined.

A Forger Revealed

One day in 1970, auctioneers noticed a curious pattern—a large amount of Samuel Palmer watercolors were suddenly for sale. A statistician and journalist who worked at the *Times of London*, Geraldine Norman, decided to look into the anomaly, sending the paintings to a specialist for inspection. The paintings were deemed to be fakes, and Norman published an article about her findings.

After the article was published, she was approached by the brother of Keating's former lover, Jane Kelly, who revealed Keating as the forger.

Norman published a second article soon after which suggested Keating could be an art forger, and Keating, to his credit, made no excuses. "I do not deny these allegations," he said. "In fact, I openly confess to having done them."

He claimed that around 2,000 of his forgeries had been sold, but he refused to provide a list of them, frustrating investigators.

The forger was arrested and put on trial. However, after a motorcycle accident left him in such poor health he wasn't expected to survive, the charges against him were dropped. But Keating surprised everyone by recovering, amazingly escaping punishment for his crimes. In fact, after his trial, the public became so impressed with his talent that he was given his own television show, *Tom Keating on Painters*, in which he demonstrated classic painting techniques.

Keating died in 1984, but his "genuine forgeries" are still out there, some worth tens of thousands of dollars.

Missing in Mexico

It was one of the world's greatest art heists. Scores of priceless pre-Columbian artifacts were stolen out from under the noses of the guards at Mexico's National Museum of Anthropology on Christmas Eve in 1985. But when authorities caught up to the thieves more than three years later, they were in for a surprise.

✳ ✳ ✳ ✳

A Holiday Heist

MOST OF US could be forgiven for imbibing a bit too much on Christmas Eve. It is, after all, a festive time of year filled with food, drink, and merriment. But the eight police guards on duty at the National Museum of Anthropology in Mexico City on Christmas Eve, 1985, should have known better. As they began their holiday celebration at the museum, which was sadly lacking in any other security features, thieves snuck into three different exhibition halls and made off with 124 Mayan, Aztec, Mixtec, and Zapotec artifacts.

Although the guards were supposed to make their rounds through each room in the museum at least once every hour, the theft wasn't noticed until Christmas morning, when they changed shifts.

The stolen items included artifacts made of gold, jade, and turquoise, which museum officials estimated were worth "many millions of dollars." The thieves seemed to have targeted artifacts which were small and concealable, yet also extremely valuable, leading investigators to believe that the culprits were professionals. But museum officials were also confused. They believed that the stolen items were much too famous to be sold on the open market, so what motivated the thieves to pull off the immense heist?

Pointing Fingers

After interrogating the eight museum guards and clearing them of the crime, investigators began their search for the perpetrators. One theory posited that a "psychotic millionaire cultist" had arranged the theft, for the sole purpose of having the artifacts in a private collection. But more common theories placed the blame at the feet of foreign governments, including the KGB and the CIA. The United States, especially, was eyed with suspicion. As Mexican journalist Joel Hernandez Santiago wrote, "It's no secret to anybody that pre-Hispanic pieces stolen from different zones of our country leave Mexico daily, to be taken principally the United States, a country which, lacking its own valuable cultural antecedents, robs or buys others." Ouch.

It took more than three years, until June of 1989, before authorities finally recovered most of the stolen objects from a house in the Mexico City suburb of Satelite. And who were the crafty, devious, "professionals" behind the heist? Their names were Carlos Perches Trevino and Ramon Sardina Garcia, and neither one had ties to a foreign government or a "psychotic millionaire cultist." Rather, they were ordinary men who had dropped out of college and decided to focus on something other than school. Mainly, breaking into the National Museum of Anthropology.

Not-So-Well-Laid Plans

Trevino and Garcia spent six months planning the heist, visiting the museum more than fifty times and making note of details. They photographed the exhibition halls and artifacts, studied the schedules of the security guards, and made sketches of their plans. On the night of the theft, the duo hopped a fence, crawled through the air conditioning ducts, and made their way to the museum's Maya Room, where they spent 30 minutes loading up a canvas bag with items they could easily transport back through the air ducts.

Once they had the loot, the two amateur art thieves were unsure what to do with it. The canvas bag full of priceless artifacts sat on a shelf in Trevino's closet for a year, until he moved to the resort town of Acapulco. There, he made a fatal error: he tried to trade some of the items to a drug trafficker named Salvador Gutierrez in exchange for cocaine. When Gutierrez showed little interest, Trevino took the stash of artifacts back to Mexico City.

But when Gutierrez was arrested on drug charges in 1989, he ratted out Trevino, and authorities closed in. He and Garcia were charged with theft and damage to national treasures, and Trevino was hit with the extra charge of cocaine trafficking and possession due to his dealings with Gutierrez. Far from being professionals, these two would-be art thieves would've been much better off had they stayed in school.

3 Final Art Heists

Some people just can't keep their hands off other people's things—even the world's greatest art. Art thieves take their loot from museums, places of worship, and private residences. Because they would have trouble selling the fruits of their labor on the open market—auction houses and galleries tend to avoid stolen works—art burglars often either keep the art for themselves or try to ransom the hot property back to the original owner. Among the major robberies in the past hundred years are these daring thefts of very expensive art (values estimated at the time of the theft).

❋ ❋ ❋ ❋

1. **Scotland, August 2003: $65 million:** Blending in apparently has its advantages for art thieves. Two men joined a tour of Scotland's Drumlanrig Castle, subdued a guard, and made off with Leonardo da Vinci's *Madonna with the Yarnwinder*. Alarms around the art were not set during the day, and the thieves dissuaded tourists from intervening, reportedly telling them: "Don't worry... we're the police. This is just practice." The painting was recovered in a Glasgow law firm four years later, but the two thieves who escaped in a white Volkswagen Golf have yet to be identified.

2. **Stockholm, December 2000: $30 million:** Caught! Eight criminals each got up to six and half years behind bars for conspiring to take a Rembrandt and two Renoirs—all of

them eventually recovered—from Stockholm's National Museum. You have to give the three masked men who actually grabbed the paintings credit for a dramatic exit. In a scene reminiscent of an action movie, they fled the scene by motorboat. Police unraveled the plot after recovering one of the paintings during an unrelated drug investigation four months after the theft.

3. **Amsterdam, December 2002: $30 million:** Robbers used a ladder to get onto the roof of the Van Gogh Museum, then broke in and stole two of the Dutch master's paintings, *View of the Sea at Scheveningen* and *Congregation Leaving the Reformed Church in Nuenen*, together worth $30 million. Police told the press that the thieves worked so quickly that, despite setting off the museum's alarms, they had disappeared before police could get there. Two men were later caught and convicted of the theft, thanks in part to DNA left at the scene. Both paintings were discovered in 2016 by Italian police investigating suspected Italian mobsters for cocaine trafficking.

Chapter 2

Robberies and Heists

Mailing It In

It was the world's most valuable necklace, said to be worth twice as much as the Hope Diamond. Yet surprisingly, this precious string of pearls was remarkably easy to steal.

※ ※ ※ ※

Stealing for Sport

JOSEPH GRIZZARD HAD a reputation for being a debonair gentleman. The wealthy man often threw lavish parties at his home in Hatton Garden, the neighborhood in London where he claimed to be a jeweler. In reality, Grizzard acquired his wealth through criminal means, although by 1913 he was so well-off that he easily could have retired from his life of heists and thefts.

But money wasn't the only reason Grizzard stole. To him, pulling off a heist was a bit of a game; he enjoyed showing off his winnings. One story credits him with stealing the Ascot Cup, a trophy given to the winner of the Gold Cup horse race. The cup, made of 68 ounces of gold, was stolen in 1907 and never found. But according to those who attended Grizzard's parties, he would serve cocktails from the famous cup for his guests. Another story recounts how Grizzard graciously allowed the police to search his home for stolen diamonds, even though he was hosting dinner guests. The police found nothing and left, at which time Grizzard sat down at the dinner table with his guests and pulled a string of diamonds from the bottom of his soup bowl.

So when Max Mayer, a legitimate jeweler in Hatton Garden, bought a strand of perfect pink pearls, Grizzard took note. The process of culturing pearls was not yet widespread, which meant that all 61 of the blush-pink pearls in the necklace had been plucked from rare oysters. Assembling the entire necklace took ten years, and it was insured by Lloyd's of London for £135,000—an amount that would be equal to around $20 million today.

Postal Pearls

One of the prospective buyers for Mayer's rare necklace was a Parisian jeweler, who wanted to inspect the piece before buying. Amazingly, in the early 20th century it was common practice for jewelers to send expensive jewels through the mail. Mayer simply sent the necklace to Paris and, when the deal fell through, the Parisian jeweler sent it back the same way. This was where Grizzard saw an opportunity.

Grizzard and several accomplices spent weeks eavesdropping on Mayer to find out exactly when the pearls would be in the mail. They also paid close attention to the comings and goings of the mailman on Mayer's mail route. They befriended the unsuspecting man and discovered that he was a heavy drinker who only made a few pounds a week. Seeing an easy target, Grizzard offered him £200, more than his entire year's salary, if he would simply allow Grizzard quick access to a package in his mailbag one day.

When the package arrived, the mailman delivered it to Grizzard, who sliced it open, removed the necklace, and replaced it with a page from a French newspaper and eleven sugar cubes, which weighed the same as the necklace. He then resealed the package and returned it to the mailman. When Mayer received the package that day, he was shocked to find the sugar cubes in place of his priceless necklace.

Cat and Mouse

At first, police believed the necklace must have been stolen in France, as the sugar cubes had been wrapped in a French newspaper. But Alfred Ward, chief inspector of Scotland Yard, wasn't so sure. He suspected the charming Grizzard might have something to do with it, so he assembled a team of undercover operatives to keep an eye on the thief. But Grizzard was just as suspicious of Ward, and had his own team of observers, keeping an eye on the police. The ensuing game of cat and mouse was almost comical.

Eventually, it came down to one weak link within the circle of Grizzard's accomplices, a man named Lesir Gutwirth who just couldn't help but brag about stealing the necklace. Grizzard and his gang were arrested, but even Ward admitted that he liked the affable thief. He frequently visited him in prison, and even advocated for Grizzard's early release. Once Grizzard was out of prison, he acted as a consultant for Ward, helping him out on cases. The two remained unlikely friends until Ward's untimely death in 1916, when a zeppelin bomb hit his home. Grizzard, it is believed, returned to his life of crime; but he surely never accomplished a bigger heist than the Mayer pearls.

The Real Bonnie and Clyde

Bonnie and Clyde, Texas's most notorious outlaws, rose to fame during the Great Depression of the 1930s. The pair gained a mythical, Robin Hood–like status, but the real Bonnie and Clyde were different from the figures portrayed by the popular media.

✳   ✳   ✳   ✳

THE EARLY 1930S was a time when businesses folded at an unprecedented rate and plummeting crop prices forced farmers from their lands in record numbers. Men desperate for work trawled city streets looking for jobs, soup kitchens were swamped, and the value of a dollar plunged. When Bonnie and Clyde began their crime spree, the public viewed them as outsiders fighting back against an uncaring system that had failed the working man.

Where They Started

Bonnie Parker was born on October 1, 1910, in Rowena. When she met Clyde Barrow in 1930, she was already married to a man used to being on the wrong side of the law. However, Bonnie was not a typical gangster's moll. She had been an honor-roll student in high school who excelled in creative writing and even won a spelling championship. After her husband was sentenced to the penitentiary, Bonnie scraped together a living by working as a waitress in West Dallas. Then Clyde Barrow entered her life.

Clyde was born on March 24, 1909, in Telico, just south of Dallas, and spent more of his poverty-stricken youth in trouble with the law than he did in school. He was arrested for stealing turkeys, auto theft, and safecracking. Soon after his romance with Bonnie began, he was sentenced to two years for a number of burglaries and car thefts. Bonnie managed to smuggle a Colt revolver to him, and Clyde was able to escape with his cell mate, William Turner.

A Life on the Run

Clyde and Turner were soon recaptured and sentenced to 14 years at the Texas State Penitentiary. But Clyde was pardoned in February 1932 after his mother intervened and Clyde had had a fellow inmate chop off two of his toes in order to garner sympathy.

After two months of attempting to go straight, Clyde started a crime spree with Bonnie that stretched from Texas to Oklahoma, Missouri, Iowa, New Mexico, and Louisiana. They robbed gas stations, liquor stores, banks, and jewelry stores. They also captured the public imagination by frequently taking hostages as they made their daring escapes and then releasing them unharmed when they were out of danger. Other outlaws came and went from the Barrow Gang, but it was only after several of the robberies culminated in murder that public opinion turned against Bonnie and Clyde.

In total, the Barrow Gang is believed to have murdered at least nine police officers and several civilians during their robberies. While Bonnie posed alongside Clyde clutching a machine gun for photos, many argue that at no time did she ever fire a weapon, let alone kill or injure anyone. Another popular misconception had her dubbed as the cigar-smoking moll of the Barrow Gang. Again, Bonnie was known to smoke only cigarettes, but she once posed with a cigar in what later became a famous photograph.

The Final Showdown

But in January 1934, Clyde made a fatal mistake while carrying out what he called the Eastham Breakout. The plan was to help two Barrow Gang members, Raymond Hamilton and Henry Methvin, break out of jail. The plan worked, but during the escape, a police officer was shot and killed. As a result, an official posse, headed by Frank Hamer, was formed with the sole intent of tracking down Bonnie and Clyde.

Wanted: Dead or Alive

In the month after the Eastham Breakout, Hamer studied Bonnie and Clyde's movements. He discovered that the pair kept to a fairly regular pattern that involved traveling back and forth across the Midwest. Hamer also learned that Bonnie and Clyde used specific locations to meet in the event they were ever separated from the rest of the Barrow Gang. Upon hearing that the pair had recently split off from other gang members during a chase, Hamer checked his maps for the couple's nearest rendezvous point, which turned out to be the Louisiana home of Methvin's father, Ivy. Hamer quickly held a meeting and told the posse they were heading south.

By mid-May, the posse had arrived in the tiny town of Gibsland, Louisiana. Finding that Bonnie and Clyde hadn't arrived yet, Hamer decided to set up an ambush along

Highway 154, the only road into Gibsland. The posse picked a wooded location along the road and began unpacking the dozens of guns and hundreds of rounds of ammunition they had brought with them, which included armor-piercing bullets. The only thing left to figure out was how to get Bonnie and Clyde to stop their car so arrests could be made (or a clear shot could be had if they attempted to run).

Setting the Trap

Hamer came up with a solution: Ivy Methvin's truck was placed on one side of the road as if it had broken down, directly opposite from where the posse was hiding in the trees. Hamer hoped that Bonnie and Clyde would recognize the truck and stop to help Ivy. This would put the pair only a few feet away from the posse's hiding place. As for Methvin's role in all this, some say he willingly helped the posse in exchange for his son getting a pardon. Others claim the posse tied Methvin to a tree and gagged him before stealing his truck. Either way, the truck was put in place, and the posse took its position in the trees along the road on the evening of May 21.

Working in shifts, the posse waited all night and the following day with no sign of Bonnie and Clyde. They were about ready to leave on the morning of May 23 when, at approximately 9:00 A.M., they heard Clyde's stolen car approaching. At that point, Hamer and the other five men present—Texas ranger Manny Gault, Dallas deputy sheriffs Bob Alcorn and Ted Hinton, and Louisiana officers Henderson Jordan and Prentiss Oakley—took cover in the trees.

So Much for a Peaceful Surrender

The official report said that Clyde, with Bonnie in the passenger seat, slowed the car as it neared Methvin's truck. At that point, standard procedure would have been for the posse to make an announcement and give the couple a chance to surrender peacefully. Hamer, however, gave the order to simply fire at will.

The first shot was fired by Oakley, which, by all accounts, fatally wounded Clyde in the head. The rest of the posse members weren't taking any chances, though, and they all fired at the car with their automatic rifles, using up all their rounds before the car even came to a complete stop. The posse members then emptied their shotguns into the car, which had rolled past them and had come to a stop in a ditch. Finally, all of the men fired their pistols at the car until all weapons were empty. In all, approximately 130 rounds were fired.

When it was all over, Bonnie and Clyde were both dead at the respective ages of 23 and 24. Upon examination, it was reported that the bodies each contained 25 bullet wounds, though some reports put that number as high as 50. Unlike Clyde, who died almost instantly, it is believed that Bonnie endured an excruciating amount of pain, and several members of the posse reported hearing her scream as the bullets ripped into her. For this reason, many people to this day question the actions of the posse members and wonder why they never gave the pair a chance to surrender.

The Aftermath

Afterward, members of the posse removed most of the items from Bonnie and Clyde's car, including guns, clothing, and even a saxophone. Later, they supposedly allowed bystanders to go up to the car and take everything from shell casings and broken glass to bloody pieces of Bonnie and Clyde's clothing and locks of their hair. There are even reports that two different people had to be stopped when they attempted to remove parts of Clyde's body (his ear and his finger) as grisly souvenirs.

Despite Bonnie and Clyde's wish to be buried alongside each other, Bonnie's parents chose to bury her alone in the Crown Hill Memorial Park in Dallas. Clyde Barrow is interred at another Dallas cemetery, Western Heights.

Even though it's been more than 70 years since Bonnie and Clyde left this earth, they are still as popular as ever. Every May, the town of Gibsland, Lousiana holds its annual Bonnie and Clyde Festival, the highlight of which is a reenactment of the shootout, complete with fake blood. You can visit the Bonnie and Clyde Ambush Museum any time of the year.

Brazen Armored Car Heists

From Butch Cassidy to John Dillinger, bank robbers have captured the imagination of the American public. Here are some of the most brazen heists of armored cars in American history.

❉ ❉ ❉ ❉

The Great Vault Robbery, Jacksonville, Florida: $22 million

IN MARCH 1997, 33-year-old Philip Johnson, who made $7 an hour as a driver for armored-car company Loomis Fargo, took off with one of the cars he was supposed to be guarding. Johnson pulled off the caper by waiting until the end of the night, when the armored cars returned to the Loomis Fargo vaults. Johnson tied up the two vault employees, loaded an armored car with about $22 million in cash, and took off.

He remained on the lam for more than four months, despite a half-million-dollar reward for his arrest. He was finally arrested crossing into the United States from Mexico in August 1997.

The majority of the money—which had been stashed in a rental storage unit in rural North Carolina—was recovered shortly afterward.

Dunbar Armored, Los Angeles, California: $18.9 million

Though not technically an armored-car robbery, the 1997 heist of $18.9 million dollars from the Dunbar Armored vaults in Los Angeles, is noteworthy for its meticulous planning and the fact that it is considered the largest armed cash robbery in American history.

The mastermind behind the theft was Dunbar Armored employee Allen Pace III, who used his knowledge of the vault's security system, along with his company keys, to gain access to the loot. Pace and his gang were eventually brought down when one of his cohorts, Eugene Hill, paid for something with a stack of bills banded in a Dunbar wrapper. That, plus a shard of taillight that had been the only piece of evidence left at the scene, was enough for investigators to crack the case. Despite the arrest of Pace and several coconspirators, nearly $10 million of the haul still remains unaccounted for.

Armored Motor Service of America, Rochester, New York: $10.8 million

In June 1990, a driver for the Armored Motor Service of America (AMSA) and his female partner stopped for break- fast at a convenience store near Rochester. While the female guard went into the store, a band of armed thieves attacked the driver, waited for the female guard to return, then ordered them to drive the truck to an unnamed location, where the thieves transferred the money to a waiting van, tied up the two guards, and escaped with the money. The total haul of $10.8 million ranked as one the largest heists in history. The robbery was also noteworthy for the fact that it remained unsolved for more than a decade. In 2002, though, the driver of the robbed AMSA truck, Albert Ranieri, admitted to masterminding the whole scheme.

Express Teller Services, Columbia, South Carolina: $9.8 million

In 2007, two young men overpowered an Express Teller Services armored car driver when he and his partners stopped to fuel up. They drove the car to a remote area, where two accomplices waited with another vehicle to transfer the cash. The theft of $9.8 million was one of the biggest in American history, but it wasn't particularly well executed. First, the thieves didn't bring a large enough vehicle or enough bags to take the nearly $20 million that was in the truck. Next, the bandits savagely beat one of the guards, while leaving the other one—who was later arrested as the mastermind—untouched. But the gang really did themselves in by going on a weeklong spending spree involving strippers, tattoos, and Mother's Day gifts. Not surprisingly, just about the entire gang was arrested less than a week later.

The Outlaws

Legends have often portrayed them as romantic, and even heroic, figures, but do Jesse and Frank James deserve such accolades, or have their exploits been exaggerated for dramatic effect?

✳ ✳ ✳ ✳

A Famous Pair

FOR ALMOST AS long as there have been films, there have been films about Jesse and Frank James. In fact, the first two movies to feature stories about Jesse James—*Jesse James Under the Black Flag* and *Jesse James as the Outlaw*, both released in 1921—starred the famous bandit's son, Jesse James Jr. And the flattering fiction doesn't stop at movies; depictions of the brothers have been included in novels, comic books, video games, and songs, including the folk song "Jesse James," which has been recorded by Woody Guthrie, Van Morrison, Bob Seger, Johnny Cash, and Bruce Springsteen, among others.

One thing that many of these cultural depictions have in common is their portrayal of the brothers as almost "Robin Hood-like" figures. The song "Jesse James" even includes the line, "He stole from the rich and he gave to the poor." But history doesn't necessarily agree with this narrative.

War and Crime

Alexander Franklin James and Jesse Woodson James were born, respectively, on January 10, 1843, and September 5, 1847, in Clay County, Missouri. Their family, who were farmers and slaveholders, were sympathetic to the Southern cause when the Civil War broke out in 1861. Young Jesse and Frank each joined bands of Confederate guerrillas during the war, reportedly participating in the murders of dozens of civilians who were loyal to the Union.

After the war, the brothers began their soon-to-be infamous outlaw career. They are believed to be part of a group that robbed the Clay County Savings Association in Liberty, Missouri, on February 13, 1866, the first daylight armed robbery of a bank in the United States during peacetime. This began a years-long string of bank robberies for the brothers, who gradually recruited other criminals to join "the James gang." The James gang robbed banks from Missouri to Iowa to Texas, and in 1873 they branched out their criminal activity to include train robberies, stagecoaches, and stores.

For a decade, as the James gang roamed the South and West, preying upon victims, writers romanticized their exploits for readers in the Northern and Eastern parts of the country, who knew little about the West except for these tales of daring bravery they read in books and magazines. Jesse and Frank James became folk heroes, seemingly forced into their lives of crime by authorities who persecuted them for their loyalties to the South. But although they attained a reputation for being like Robin Hood, there is no evidence that Jesse and Frank ever shared any of their stolen goods with anyone outside their gang. What's more, many of their robberies ended in injured or murdered bank workers, sheriffs, or civilians.

An Ending and a Second Chance

September 7, 1876, was the beginning of the end for the James brothers. After a horribly botched robbery attempt at the First National Bank of Northfield, Minnesota, in which their entire gang was either killed or captured and only Jesse and Frank escaped, the brothers decided to keep a low profile. Jesse moved back to Missouri, while Frank headed east to Virginia. Jesse began the work of building a new gang, by recruiting brothers

Charley and Robert Ford. But unbeknownst to Jesse, Robert had been secretly working with Missouri Governor Thomas T. Crittenden to bring down the outlaw.

On the morning of April 3, 1882, Jesse and the Ford brothers were at the James home preparing to leave for a robbery. In his living room, Jesse turned to rearrange a picture on the wall, and Robert Ford shot the unarmed man in the back of the head, killing him instantly. Although the Ford brothers were charged with first-degree murder, they were immediately pardoned by the governor.

Six months later, Frank James surrendered to Governor Crittenden. He was tried for only two train robberies and one murder, and found not guilty on all charges. He retired from his life of crime and lived the rest of his life a free man. He eventually returned to his family's farm, where he died on February 18, 1915, in the very room where he had been born.

Machine Gun Molly

It's not unusual for single mothers to work odd jobs in order to take care of their children. But single Montreal mom Monica Proietti found a much more lucrative way to provide for her family: robbing banks.

✳ ✳ ✳ ✳

A Lost Childhood

MONICA PROIETTI WAS born on February 25, 1940, in a poor area of Montreal, Quebec, in Canada. With eight siblings, there were few luxuries to go around, and at a young age Proietti began turning to petty crime. Not that it was entirely her own idea; her grandmother, who had spent time in jail for receiving stolen goods, taught her and other neighborhood children the tricks of the trade.

With such an awful role model, it's no wonder Proietti continued down a path of lawlessness. By 13 years old, she had dropped out of school and was arrested for prostitution, which she saw as the only way to make enough money to help her mother support her siblings. But a few years later, she settled down at the age of 17, marrying a 33-year-old Scottish gangster named Anthony Smith. Proietti and Smith had two children together, and for a short time, she relished in her new role as stay-at-home mother.

Loss and Larceny

Her simple life soon turned tragic, however, when a gas leak explosion killed her pregnant mother and three of her siblings in 1958. Proietti was dealt another blow in 1962 when Smith was caught robbing a café and deported to Scotland. With her mother dead and her husband gone, Proietti was left alone to raise her children. She struggled to find work, having no job experience and little education.

But the lonely single mother soon met a new man named Viateur Tessier, who happened to be a proficient bank robber. Like her grandmother years earlier, Tessier became Proietti's teacher in the art of bank robberies. The two began planning robberies together, carrying out heists until 1966, when Tessier was caught and sentenced to 15 years in prison. Proietti was once again a single mother.

This time, however, she knew exactly how she would support her children. In 1967, Proietti began robbing banks with several male accomplices. She started off in minor roles, acting as a lookout and getaway driver, but the men she worked with were so impressed with her calm nerves and the way she handled a gun that soon she was "promoted." Over the next two years Proietti and her crew robbed 20 different banks in Montreal, stealing a total of $100,000.

A Legend Is Born

The public wasn't used to seeing a woman bank robber, so Proietti became a hit in the media. The newspapers dubbed her "Machine Gun Molly," although she never used a machine gun.

She did, however, always carry a gold-plated, semi-automatic M-1 rifle, which she often fired into the ceiling of the banks she robbed. To her credit, she never once shot or injured a person, but she loved to appear intimidating.

Even with her fame, Proietti managed to outwit the authorities for two years. She always dressed as a man when robbing a bank, using wigs and other accessories as disguises, and then dressed in very feminine outfits in her everyday life. But she couldn't hide forever, and her luck would soon run out.

According to some accounts, the robbery that Proietti planned on September 19, 1967, was always meant to be her last. She had finally grown tired of her life of crime and wanted to pull off one last heist before retiring and moving with her children to Florida. That morning, she and two accomplices robbed the Caisse Populaire, stealing around $3,000.

But their getaway didn't go as smoothly as planned. The trio ended up stealing a car and speeding away, but the police quickly found them and chased them down. Proietti lost control of the car and crashed into a bus, and her two accomplices fled the scene. But Proietti, injured in the crash, stayed in the car with her gun, firing at approaching police. They fired back, hitting her in the chest and killing her.

Proietti's death was not the end of her legend. Over the years, "Machine Gun Molly" has been featured in magazine articles, documentaries, books, a musical, and the French-Canadian film *Monica la mitraille*, released in 2004.

Out in 90 Seconds: The Story of the Stopwatch Gang

In the 1970s and '80s, Canada and the United States experienced a whirlwind of unforgettable bank heists pulled by debonair "celebrity" robbers. Even today, their story isn't over.

✳ ✳ ✳ ✳

I N OCTOBER 2005, FBI agents arrested Stephen Duffy, a successful Florida real estate agent, during a security investigation involving passport fraud. They weren't actually looking for the man they found. A fingerprint check showed that Duffy was, in reality, Christopher Clarkson, a fugitive from justice who was once a member of a daring group of bank robbers known as the Stopwatch Gang. As Stephen Duffy, he'd eluded Canadian and American authorities for three decades. Time had finally run out for the last member of the most notorious and resourceful group of bank robbers since the feared Jesse James Gang of the 19th century.

Speed Demons

Speed was the essential ingredient of the Stopwatch Gang. Precision timing and painstaking planning made the thieves so successful. No heist ever exceeded 2 minutes; in most cases the robbers were in and out in 90 seconds. Becoming living legends, they held up more than 100 banks throughout Canada and the United States with panache, precision, and politeness.

The leader of the band was Patrick "Paddy" Michael Mitchell, a Canadian Irishman who, together with his partners Stephen Reid and Lionel Wright, netted somewhere between $8 and $15 million in all. Reid wore a stopwatch around his neck to time the robberies so they wouldn't exceed two minutes in duration—that's how the gang earned its colorful sobriquet. Reid's favorite comment to his intended victims was, "This won't take long, folks."

If they'd stuck to robbing banks, the criminals might still be enjoying the luxury of their posh Arizona hideaway; unfortunately, they decided to branch out into drug smuggling. That's when Clarkson, who had some expertise as a drug runner, joined the gang. Their first attempt at smuggling cocaine into Canada, however, was a disaster, and the group was busted. Clarkson made bail and disappeared. Though he was tried in absentia and found guilty, he would remain free all those years by stealing the identity of a four-year-old California boy, Stephen Duffy, who drowned in the family swimming pool. The fate of the other gang members during those 30 years is the stuff of which legends are made.

Creative Convicts

After they were captured, Mitchell, Reid, and Wright received heavy jail sentences. All three escaped, or as it's known in urban slang, enacted "jackrabbit parole." After recapture, Reid and Wright were sent to Canadian prisons on an inmate exchange.

Mitchell engineered two daring jackrabbit paroles and is believed to be the first fugitive ever to appear on the FBI's Ten Most Wanted List twice. He was arrested for the final time in 1994 after a solo bank heist in Mississippi and sent to Leavenworth Prison. Mitchell's requests for an exchange to Canada so that he could be near his family (he married while on the lam and had a son and two grandchildren) were continually denied by U.S. authorities, who, as Mitchell expressed it, "wanted their pound of flesh."

Mitchell, known as "the gentleman bandit" due to his non-violent approach to robbery, became a successful author and Internet blogger while incarcerated. Mitchell's blog posts were sent via snail mail to a third party who posted them in Mitchell's name on a Canadian Web site, where they became quite popular. As a result, his autobiography, *This Bank Robber's Life*, became a brisk seller online. Because he achieved all this while in custody since 1994, Mitchell never even knew what the Internet was like. He died from lung and brain cancer on January 14, 2007, in a North Carolina prison hospital at age 64. On January 25, his remains returned to his hometown of Ottawa, where hundreds of friends, family members, and admirers turned out for a good old-fashioned Irish wake in honor of this "gentle" bandit who loved robbing banks but never harmed a soul.

Stephen Reid, who was serving a 14-year sentence, also made good use of his time behind bars, writing a semi-fictional novel entitled *Jackrabbit Parole*. A copy of Reid's manuscript was sent to critically acclaimed Canadian poet and editor Susan Musgrave, writer-in-residence at the University of Waterloo. Susan agreed to edit Reid's novel, leading to a string of correspondence that resulted in her proposal of marriage to him. They were married in 1986, the same year that Reid's best-selling novel was published. It was Musgrave's third marriage, yet her first in the confines of a penitentiary, where the couple also spent their honeymoon. In 1987, Reid was paroled, and the couple settled down in a seaside tree house near Victoria, British Columbia, with Susan's daughter from a previous marriage, Charlotte. In 1989, the couple's daughter, Sophie, was born. It seemed like a modern fairy tale, if a little rough around the edges.

For quite some time, Stephen trod the straight and narrow. Life appeared blissful. However, as Susan's literary career continued to blossom, Reid's began to flounder. Struggling with the stress of trying to complete his second novel, Reid turned to the overriding demon in his life—heroin. He'd been addicted to the drug since his early teens and hadn't kicked the habit. This time his addiction would have dire consequences, shattering the near-idyllic family life of the ex-con and the writer.

During the process of building a new home, Reid met Allan McCallum, a recovering drug addict. On June 9, 1999, while doing heroin and cocaine, the two men became fairly strung out and decided to rob a bank—a bad idea that ended in a worse fate. A total disaster, the heist was a careless, sloppy, ill-planned attempt and very uncharacteristic for a former member of the Stopwatch Gang. The men were captured after a chase and five-hour standoff. Reid was charged with ten counts, including attempted murder for shooting at pursuing police officers. On December 22, 1999, the 49-year-old was sentenced to 18 years in prison. After serving more than eight years, Reid was granted day parole in January 2008. This allowed him freedom during the day but required him to spend his nights at a halfway house.

Speeding Along the Straight and Narrow

It seems the only member of the Stopwatch Gang to remain outside of prison and really go straight was Lionel Wright, who cut off all contact with his former cohorts. Wright is said to be working as an accountant for Correctional Service of Canada, a division of the criminal justice system. A richer irony may be hard to find.

D. B. Cooper: Man of Mystery

D. B. Cooper is perhaps the most famous criminal alias since Jack the Ripper. Although the fate of the infamous hijacker remains a mystery, the origins of the nom de crime "D. B. Cooper" is a matter that's easier to solve.

✳   ✳   ✳   ✳

The Crime

A T PORTLAND (OREGON) International Airport the night before Thanksgiving in 1971, a man in a business suit, reportedly in his mid-40s, boarded Northwest Orient Airlines flight 305 bound for Seattle, Washington. He had booked his seat under the name Dan Cooper. Once the flight was airborne, Cooper informed a flight attendant that his briefcase contained an explosive device. In the days before thorough baggage inspection was standard procedure at airports, this was a viable threat. The flight attendant relayed the information to the pilots, who immediately put the plane into a holding pattern so that Cooper could communicate his demands to FBI agents on the ground.

When the Boeing 727 landed at Seattle–Tacoma Airport, the other passengers were released in exchange for $200,000 in unmarked $20 bills and two sets of parachutes. FBI agents photographed each bill before handing over the ransom and then scrambled a fighter plane to follow the passenger craft when Cooper demanded that it take off for Mexico City via Reno, Nevada. At 10,000 feet, Cooper lowered the aft stairs of the aircraft and, with the ransom money strapped to his chest, parachuted into the night, still dressed in his business suit. The pilot noted the area as being near the Lewis River, 25 miles north of Portland, somewhere over the Cascade Mountains.

The mysterious hijacker was never seen again. The FBI found a number of fingerprints on the plane that didn't match those of the other passengers or members of the crew, but the only real clue that Cooper left behind was his necktie. On February 10, 1980, an eight-year-old boy found $5,800 in decaying $20 bills along the Columbia River, just a few miles northwest of Vancouver, Washington. The serial numbers matched those included in the ransom. Other than that, not a single note of the ransom money has turned up in circulation.

Origins of the Name

The FBI launched a massive hunt for the man who had hijacked Flight 305. This included checking the rap sheets of every known felon with the name Dan Cooper, just in case the hijacker had been stupid enough to use his real name. When Portland agents interviewed a man by the name of D. B. Cooper, the story was picked up by a local reporter. This D. B. Cooper was cleared of any involvement in the case, but the alias stuck and was adopted by the national media.

Who was Dan Cooper?

Countless books, TV shows, and even a movie have attempted to answer this question. The FBI has investigated some 10,000 people, dozens of whom had at some point confessed to family or friends that they were the real D. B. Cooper. In October 2007, the FBI announced that it had finally obtained a partial DNA profile of Cooper with evidence lifted from the tie he left on the plane. This has helped rule out many of those suspected of (or who have confessed to) the hijacking.

The author of one book about the case, a retired FBI agent, offered a $100,000 reward for just one of the bills from the ransom money. He's never had to pay out. Officially, the FBI does not believe that Cooper survived the jump. However, no evidence of his body or the bright yellow and red parachute he used to make the jump has ever been found. On December 31, 2007, more than 36 years after the man forever known as D. B. Cooper disappeared into the night sky, the FBI revived the case by publishing never-before-seen sketches of the hijacker and appealing for new witnesses.

Masks Only a Robber Could Love

Do bank robbers actually wear Richard Nixon masks? Or is that just something we see in the movies? You might be surprised.

✳   ✳   ✳   ✳

Laughing on the Inside

HOLLYWOOD GAVE US *Quick Change* in 1990, in which Bill Murray dresses as a clown to rob a bank. In 2008's *Batman* movie *The Dark Knight*, the Joker and his gang dress in clown masks to rob a bank of their own.

In real life, a gang of six thieves, some of whom dressed in clown costumes, robbed a jewelry store in the Mexican city of Guadalajara in July 2009. They got away with at least 1.2 million pesos worth—about $900,000 USD—of stolen goods.

Police, though, got the last laugh: In October, prosecutors filed robbery charges against two alleged members of the gang.

I'm Not a Crook. Well . . .

Patrick Swayze and company robbed a bank while wearing the masks of former presidents in *Point Break* (1991). One of the robbers wore a Richard Nixon mask, while the others wore masks of Jimmy Carter, Lyndon Johnson, and Ronald Reagan.

In October 2009, a robber wearing his own Richard Nixon mask held up a Dunn County, Wisconsin, bank at gunpoint. No word on whether he declared "I am not a crook," before he fled the scene.

He's Not Really Going Skiing

Countless bank robbers in movies and television shows have worn ski masks. In January 2009, a robber in Stow, Ohio, followed suit. Obviously having been taught the value of good manners, Feliks Goldshtein waited in line at the National City Bank branch behind several other customers. When he finally reached a teller, though, his good manners disappeared. He refused to take off his mask when asked and instead pointed a gun at the teller. The police caught Goldshtein after a chase.

Restaurant Heists

Some go to a fast food or fast casual restaurant for a quick, easy meal. Other people go for other purposes.

✳   ✳   ✳   ✳

Macaroni Salad for Three

EVEN THOUGH YOU break into a restaurant to steal its cash register and surveillance system, it doesn't mean that there is no evidence leading back to you. Mt. Morris, New York, restaurant Build-A-Burger received justice when three burglars— who stole various electronics, cash, and a big bowl of macaroni salad—were arrested after their trail of evidence led the cops straight to them.

The cops arrived on the scene of the restaurant to begin their investigation when they discovered a trail of cash register parts, rubber gloves, and macaroni salad along the pedestrian trail behind the restaurant. After following the evidence for a short time, the trail of evidence led to the hungry burglars' hideout.

Arrested for the offense was M. Sapetko, thirty-four, J. Marullo, thirty-five, and T. Walker, twenty-three, who were later charged with fourth-degree grand larceny, third-degree burglary, and third-degree criminal mischief. According to the police report, the three men passed around the bowl of macaroni salad to eat as they escaped, leaving a mess of evidence behind them.

Although all of the other merchandise was returned to the restaurant, the macaroni salad had to be thrown away. That night, the three men were able to fall asleep in jail with their bellies full of their last meal as free men for many years to come.

Miami Ice

Miami Police arrested a man who held up a local Checkers restaurant for cash and customers' jewelry. Early that morning as the restaurant was opening, the Florida man jumped out of the storage freezer and began his heist. The customers ran outside to safety, calling 911 in hopes that the police would get there in time. They did, and the man was arrested for third-degree burglary.

The puzzling thing for the cops working the case is how long the man waited in the freezer before he began his heist. It could have been an hour or a few, but it certainly wasn't all night because it is likely the man would have frozen to death before he had a chance to make his move.

Hamburglars Foiled by the King

Two men from Stockton, California, attempted to rob a Burger King but had trouble finding their get-away car afterwards. The two criminals, J. Lovitt and G. Gonzales, entered the burger joint with their guns out and loaded at 9:45 P.M. The two men focused on one crew member and the manager to get their loot as—unbeknownst to them—the third employee snuck out the back entrance of the restaurant.

Lovitt and Gonzales packed their sacks with cash as quickly as possible in order to get back to their running getaway car parked out back, but what they didn't realize was that their car wouldn't be waiting for them. As the third employee snuck out back to call the cops, he noticed a running car that he figured belonged to the burglars. The quick-thinking employee jumped in the car and drove it around the corner, leaving the ham-burglars without a fast-food escape route.

The two came running outside only to realize that their plan had been foiled. They ran around the parking lot frantically, looking for their car, but to no avail. Lovitt and Gonzales fled on foot but were soon apprehended by the Stockton Police and taken to San Joaquin County Jail. Maybe they'll be smart enough to use Grimace as a getaway driver the next time they decide to mess with the king of burgers.

When Homeowners Strike Back

Could you handle being robbed with panache? Perhaps these stories will serve as inspiration...

✳   ✳   ✳   ✳

Never Lose Sleep Over Guilt

A MAN FROM MANCHESTER, New Hampshire, woke up to a strange sight one morning in the home he shared with his wife. Walking into the hallway after a quiet night's sleep, John Terrell found a random pair of shoes outside of an unoccupied bedroom.

A little shocked by the confusing placement of a pair of shoes he had never seen before, he peeked through the open door to find a man sleeping in the bed with a large hunting knife stick-ing out of his back pocket.

John grabbed the pair of shoes and quietly walked back to the bedroom where his wife was still sleeping. He woke her, and she couldn't believe what he told her until she saw the pair of shoes. It was startling, but they were calm as Elinor Terrell called the police and John held the man at gunpoint.

Apparently, the burglar, Renaud Plaisir, had been on an all-night spree and was pretty tired by time he got to the Terrell's home. Plaisir cut a hole in the screen door on the first floor, searched through the downstairs cabinetry, scavenged some leftover hot wings from the fridge, made his way upstairs, and fell into bed for a little cat nap.

Plaisir missed his alarm though. When the police arrived, they found a backpack full of merchandise from homes he had hit earlier in the night. Plaisir had apparently made it through the whole house perusing it for valuables, but he was never able to make it out. He woke in the morning—not knowing where he was—to police officers swarming around him. Plaisir was taken in and charged with burglary.

One-Armed Bandit Brawls With a Boxer

A one-armed burglar attempted to rob a home in Florida one afternoon, but didn't realize that the homeowner was a Crossfit coach and boxer.

Albert Thompson broke into a home in Santa Rosa Beach when the homeowner was asleep, attempting to steal $80. But when the woman awoke to find him in her home, she was able to subdue him and keep him at the scene until police arrived.

While the fact that Thompson only has one arm may have given him less of an advantage, it's never a good idea to challenge someone who is used to lifting weights and throwing hooks and jabs.

Thompson was arrested and charged with burglary of an occupied dwelling, misdemeanor petit theft, and obstruction by a disguised person.

Chapter 3

Weddings Gone Wrong and Murderous Marriages

Wedding Police Blotter

In these real-life examples of weddings-gone-wild, there's plenty of fodder for front page headlines. When police arrived at these nuptials, they encountered all sorts of disturbances, from fistfights to shouting matches.

※ ※ ※ ※

Outspoken Ex-Girlfriend: When Marie Salomon attended the Bridgeport, Connecticut, wedding ceremony of her ex-boyfriend, the minister uttered the weighted phrase: "Speak now or forever hold your peace." Salomon stood and yelled her objections in the middle of the ceremony. Eventually, police were called to the scene, and Salomon was charged with breaching the peace and trespassing.

Crowbar Crasher: If you think that was bad…when Lisa Coker showed up at her ex-boyfriend's wedding reception, she didn't come empty-handed. Coker brought a crowbar and a razor blade to the Tampa, Florida, affair. After fighting with the mother of the groom, who then required 16 stitches, Coker was arrested.

Groom vs. Fashion Police: John Lucas, age 53, was arrested during his own wedding reception when a police officer working the event attempted to enforce the venue's dress code. According to police, Lucas's nephew appeared at the Kenner, Louisiana, reception dressed in sagging pants. (The nephew denied the charge to newspapers.) A police officer told the teenager to pull up his pants, and he refused. The situation escalated quickly, and when the groom and his brother defended the 19-year-old, the police all three men for disturbing the peace.

Attack of the Bride's Sister: Annmarie Bricker wasn't invited to her sister's Hebron, Indiana, wedding reception, but she went anyway. Bricker wanted to talk out a few family problems, and by the time police arrived, the 23-year-old had wrestled the bride to the ground and pulled out clumps of the woman's hair. Bricker was arrested on a misdemeanor battery charge and later resigned from her job as a 9-1-1 dispatcher.

Newlyweds Cash In: Brian Dykes and Mindy McGhee wed at a quaint chapel in Sevierville, Tennessee, then promptly robbed the place. After the wedding, the couple waited until the cover of darkness and then stole a cash-filled lockbox from the chapel. They were later found at a local restaurant where they confessed to the $500 theft and were jailed on $10,000 bonds.

Right in the Kisser: How can a prenuptial party go wrong? When the groom kisses the bride's friend, for starters. Apparently, the bride's 12-year-old son reported that her fiancé smooched one of the female attendees. The bride-to-be tackled the groom, punched him in the face, threw his watch in the bushes, and broke his glasses. The Poulsbo, Washington, woman was jailed on assault charges.

Bride and Groom Brawl: Pittsburgh, Pennsylvania, newlyweds David and Christa Wielechowski spent the night in jail after duking it out in a hotel hallway. The couple insisted they were joking when the groom kicked his vociferous bride squarely in the rear. When hotel guests came to the bride's rescue and restrained the groom, the bride attacked them. The brawl then moved into an elevator and to the hotel lobby, drawing more guests to the fracas. The groom—a local dentist—was booked into the county jail with a black eye and only one shoe. His bride, still wearing her wedding gown, was in a separate holding cell.

Makin' It Rain: In Tampa, Florida, in 2009, groom Markeith Brown finished off his wedding reception by tossing dollar bills onto the dance floor while the younger guests snatched them up. Apparently, this didn't go over so well with one of the other guests, who made that fact known. An all-out brawl followed: More guests got involved; non-guest reinforcements were called in; a policeman got punched; and the groom's grandma ended up with hands around her throat. Fortunately, the groom managed to avoid arrest, and he and his bride (who was none too happy about the whole thing) were able to go on their (hopefully uneventful) honeymoon cruise.

Brazen Bigamists

Some people really like the institution of marriage. In fact, some like it so much they get married again and again. Most of them get divorced between weddings— but a few went another route.

✳   ✳   ✳   ✳

BIGAMY IS A felony in 37 states, carrying a sentence of up to ten years in prison. The problem? Prosecutions are not that common, and many times, offenders come away with a slap on the wrist.

Making (Serial) Marriages Work

Anthony Glenn Owens was a man of God, pious and devoted to his church. At least that's what one Texas woman thought when he proposed to her in 2002. He even traveled all the way to Mississippi to ask her father for permission for her hand. Maybe her dad would have said no if he'd known what the new bride discovered. Owens was already married—to seven other women. Apparently he didn't believe in divorce.

After the couple established a new life and a church in Georgia, a female pastor told the woman that she'd seen Owens with seven other women over the years. She said he had cheated on them and stolen from them. The newest Mrs. Owens began to investigate her husband's past. She found several marriages and no divorces. So she took her findings to the police. Four of the wives came forward, claiming that Owens had used them and left them broke.

Owens was sentenced to two years in prison and four more years of probation. His defense? He never meant to hurt anyone, and as a man of God, he was misled by teachings of the Mormon faith (although he was not Mormon himself). He was released in 2005 but was back in jail by 2007 for parole violations. What did he do with his free time in those 18 months of freedom? He proposed to four more women.

When You Love Love Too Much

Ed Hicks is another man who just can't get enough of a good thing. In fact, his profile on an Internet dating site claimed he was "in love with love." When the law caught up to him in 2005, he was married to two women and had been married to at least five others. In three cases, he didn't bother with divorce between the ceremonies. Unlike the devious Owens, who stole from his many wives before moving on, Hicks appeared to be a sweet-talking romantic who is handy around the house. In short, the wives liked the guy. "He could be a real nice husband," explained Sharon Hicks Pratt, wife number two. "But he had to have more than just one woman."

What was once a problem for the women turned into a problem for Hicks when the ladies began to find out, and the dominoes began to fall. The last three wives even formed an unofficial support group—and are committed to warning future wives about his secret past. Even after his arrest, Hicks began an online relationship with at least four other women. The wives must know his type by now, because three of those "pen pals" were fictional women created by wife number six to see if he'd take the bait. He did.

Equality of the Sexes

Lest you get the idea that women are constant victims, and only men can cheat in the name of love, consider the case of Kyle McConnell (a woman) from Roseville, Michigan. She was charged with felony bigamy and sentenced to 22 months to ten years in prison.

The popular McConnell had a talent for finding lonely men, marrying them, and stealing their money, according to sheriff's Detective Tim Donnellon. Apparently, her pattern was to drain their bank accounts and move on to the next guy by the time the current husband found out.

It worked pretty well, too. All in all, she managed to marry about 15 men. Isn't love grand?

Bluebeard in the Flesh

"All of the women for Johann go crazy!"

✳   ✳   ✳   ✳

IN 1905, WHEN the police finally caught up with Johann Hoch, he had already proposed to what would have been his 45th wife. His habit was to meet a lonely middle-aged woman, propose, marry her, and take her money in the space of about a week. Depending on Johann's mood, about a third of the women were murdered; the others were simply abandoned.

Hoch was born John Schmidt in 1855 in the Grand Duchy of Hesse in what is now Germany. He allegedly married one wife while still living in Europe, and they immigrated to the United States around 1890. There, he began using a pseudonym and marrying—and burying—more women. He went by numerous aliases over the years, including Jacob Erdoff, C.A. Calford, Jacob Huff, Joseph Hoch, Dr. G.L. Hart, Jacob Hock, Adolf Hoch, Fred Doess, Martin Dose, Henry Hartman, Henry Bartells, H. Ireck, John Healey, William Frederick Bessing, and Count Otto van Kurn.

Along with changing his name, he changed his location. Hoch moved from place to place, including but not limited to Chicago, San Francisco, Baltimore, Ohio, Indiana, and several cities in New York state.

Hoch's method of murder was slipping his new bride some arsenic, which was a perfect crime in those days. Arsenic was used in embalming fluid, so the minute an undertaker came into the house, convicting someone of arsenic poisoning was basically impossible.

When the story came to light, the press was fascinated—how could an ugly man who spoke like a comedian with a German accent convince so many women to marry him? Why, his last Chicago wife (his 44th overall) had agreed to marry him while her sister (wife #43) was lying dead on her bed! *The Herald American,* which could be counted on to print the wildest rumors in town, claimed that Hoch used hypnosis on the women and that he had learned all he knew about murdering from the infamous H. H. Holmes.

Hoch's power over women made it seem as though he *must* have had access to some sort of magic spell. As his trial continued, wife #44, the woman who had first reported him to authorities, came to his cell daily to bring him money and beg him to forgive her. He received numerous letters containing marriage proposals while in prison. Any marriage would have been a short one—Johann was hanged in 1906 and buried in a potter's field.

Legend has it that as Hoch was about to be hanged, he said to the guards, "I don't look like a monster now, do I?" After the deed was done, one of the guards replied, "Well, not anymore."

Testimony from the Other Side

When Zona Heaster Shue of Greenbrier County, West Virginia, died suddenly at age 23, her doctor attributed her passing to natural causes. But when Zona's mother encountered her ghost, a shocking tale of murder was revealed. Would testimony from the Other Side help to nab Zona's killer?

✳ ✳ ✳ ✳

Gone Too Soon

ON JANUARY 23, 1897, a boy who was doing chores at the Shue home discovered Zona's limp body lying at the bottom of the stairs. He ran to tell her husband—Edward Stribbling "Trout" Shue—and then he summoned a doctor. When Dr. George W. Knapp arrived, Shue escorted him to the bedroom where he'd moved Zona's lifeless body. Although Shue had already dressed Zona for burial, Knapp examined her body. As the doctor went about his duties, Shue became noticeably distressed, so Knapp cut the examination short. Suspecting natural causes as the reason for Zona's passing and not wishing to upset her husband any further, Knapp reported her cause of death as "everlasting faint" but later changed the finding to "childbirth." Although Zona hadn't told anyone that she was pregnant, the doctor surmised that complications from a pregnancy must have been the culprit because he'd recently treated her for "female trouble." During his hasty examination, Knapp noticed a few bruises on Zona's neck but quickly passed them off as unrelated.

Whirlwind Courtship

Little is known about her life, but it is believed that Zona Heaster was born in Greenbrier County, West Virginia, around 1873. In October 1896, she met Shue, a drifter who had recently moved to the area to work as a blacksmith.

Only months after they met, Zona Heaster and Edward Shue married. But for reasons that she couldn't quite explain, Zona's mother—Mary Jane Heaster—had taken an instant disliking to her son-in-law. Despite her concerns, the newlyweds seemed to get along until that tragic day when Zona was found dead. In an instant, Mary Jane's world was turned upside down. She grieved, as would any mother who must bury a child, but she sharply disagreed with Dr. Knapp's determination of her daughter's cause of death. In her mind, there was only one way that her daughter could have died at such a young age: Shue had killed her and had covered it up.

It All Comes Out in the Wash

At Zona's wake, those who came to pay their respects noticed Shue's erratic behavior. He continued to openly mourn his wife's passing, but something seemed odd about the way he grieved. His mood alternated between extreme sadness and sudden manic energy. He tended to his wife's body like a man possessed, allowing no one to get close to it. He also tied a large scarf around his wife's neck for no apparent reason, and even stranger, he placed a pillow on one side of Zona's head and a rolled-up cloth on the other; he told puzzled onlookers that they would help her "rest easier." And when Zona's body was moved to the cemetery for burial, several people noticed a strange looseness to her neck as they transported her. Not surprisingly, people began to talk.

Mary Jane Heaster did not have to be convinced that Shue was acting suspiciously about Zona's death. She had always hated him and wished that her daughter had never married him. She had a sneaking suspicion that something wasn't right, but she didn't know how to prove it. After the funeral, Mary Jane Heaster washed the sheet that had lined her daughter's coffin. To her horror, the water inside the basin turned red. Then, even more shockingly, the sheet turned pink and the water again turned clear. Mary Jane was convinced that this was a sign, so she began praying that her daughter would come to her to reveal the truth. A few weeks later, her prayers were answered.

Ghostly Visions

According to Mary Jane, Zona's apparition came to her over the course of four nights. It described how abusive Shue had been throughout their marriage and stated that he was responsible for her death. The tragedy occurred because Shue thought that Zona hadn't cooked meat for supper; he went into a rage, strangled her, and broke her neck. To demonstrate the brutality of Shue's attack, Zona's ghost rotated her head completely around. This horrified Mary Jane, but it also brought her some relief; her beloved daughter had returned from the grave to seek the justice that she deserved. Armed with the unbridled power of a mother's love, Mary Jane was determined to avenge her daughter's death.

Please Believe Me!

Mary Jane immediately told local prosecutor John Alfred Preston of her ghostly visit, and begged him to investigate. Whether or not he took Mary Jane at her word is open to debate, but Preston did agree to interview Knapp and others associated with the case.

After learning that Dr. Knapp's examination had been cursory at best, Preston and Knapp agreed that an autopsy would help to clear things up, so Zona's body was exhumed. A local newspaper reported that Edward Shue "vigorously complained" about the exhumation but was forced to witness the proceedings. When Dr. Knapp proclaimed that Zona's neck was indeed broken, Shue was arrested and charged with his wife's murder.

While Shue awaited trial, tales of his unsavory past started coming to light. It was revealed that he'd been married twice before. His first marriage (to Allie Estelline Cutlip) had ended in divorce in 1889, while Shue was incarcerated for horse theft. In their divorce decree, Cutlip claimed that Shue had frequently beaten her. In 1894, Shue married Lucy Ann Tritt; however, the union was short-lived—Tritt died just eight months into their marriage under "mysterious" circumstances.

In the autumn of 1896, Shue moved to Greenbrier County, where he met Zona Heaster. Was there a pattern of violence with this lethal lothario?

Trial

Shue's trial began on June 22, 1897. Both the prosecution and the defense did their best to discredit each other. For every witness who spoke of Shue's ill temper, another likened him to an altar boy. After Shue took the stand, many agreed that he handled himself skillfully. Then it was Mary Jane Heaster's turn. When questioned by the prosecution, her ghostly encounter with her daughter was not mentioned. But when she was cross-examined by Shue's attorney, Mary Jane recalled in great detail how Zona's spirit had fingered Shue as her abuser and killer. The defense characterized Mary Jane's "visions" as little more than a grieving mother's ravings, assuming that the jury would agree. They were wrong. When the trial concluded, the jury quickly rendered a guilty verdict. Not only had they believed Mary Jane's supernatural tale, they fell just short of delivering the necessary votes to hang Shue for his evil deeds; instead, he was sentenced to life in prison. And as it turned out, that wouldn't be very long.

Epilogue

In July 1897, Shue was transferred to the West Virginia Penitentiary in Moundsville, where he lived out the rest of his days. The convicted murderer died on March 13, 1900, of an epidemic that was sweeping the prison. But his name lives on, as does the ghostly legend of Zona Heaster Shue. A historical marker located beside Route 60 in Greenbrier County reads: "Interred in nearby cemetery is Zona Heaster Shue. Her death in 1897 was presumed natural until her spirit appeared to her mother to describe how she was killed by her husband Edward. Autopsy on the exhumed body verified the apparition's account. Edward, found guilty of murder, was sentenced to the state prison. Only known case in which testimony from ghost helped convict a murderer."

The Woodchipper Murder

It's rare for a murderer to be convicted without a body to help prove guilt. But the murder of Helle Crafts, whose body was not recovered, not only ended with a conviction, but inspired a chilling scene in a Hollywood movie.

* * * *

Sudden Disappearance

IT WAS A match that seemed made in heaven. Danish-born flight attendant Helle Nielsen married airline pilot Richard Crafts in 1979, and the couple settled in Newtown, Connecticut, with their three children. But their happy married life didn't last long. Within seven years of marrying, Helle discovered that her husband was having affairs and hired a private investigator to expose the infidelity. She also contacted a divorce lawyer. It was clear that the scorned woman was planning to leave her husband and start a new life.

On the snowy night of November 18, 1986, after working on a long international flight, Helle was dropped off at her home but one of her friends. That was the last time anyone—except Richard—saw her. Over the next few weeks, he told several stories that attempted to explain her whereabouts, telling some people that she was visiting her parents in Denmark, while telling others that she was on vacation with a friend in the Canary Islands. He even told some of her friends that she had simply left with no warning, and he had no idea where she was.

Evidence of Foul Play

Helle's friends were understandably suspicious. She was finally reported missing on December 1, but it took weeks for authorities to look at the case with more detail. By Christmas, they had a warrant to search the Crafts house. While Richard and his kids were vacationing in Florida for the holiday, police went through the house with a fine-tooth comb, searching for evidence. What they discovered was disturbing: pieces of carpet had been removed from the bedroom floor and there was a blood smear on the bed. But perhaps most damning were Richard's credit card records, which showed that around the time of Helle's disappearance, he had bought a freezer and new bedding, and rented a woodchipper.

As the circumstantial evidence mounted, a local man named Joseph Hine came forward with some new information. Hine drove a snowplow in the winter, and on the night that Helle disappeared he was plowing the road and noticed a rental truck with an attached woodchipper parked next to an area lake. Investigators also discovered a receipt for a chainsaw, which could not be found in the house. Armed with the new information, authorities began searching in and around the lake, where they discovered small amounts of human tissue, a tooth crown, a fingernail, bone chips, blond hairs, and blood that matched the same type as Helle's. The chainsaw was found in the lake, where it was still covered in hair and blood that matched Helle's DNA.

Murder and a Movie

While investigators were certain that Richard had killed his wife, they could not charge him with the crime until she was officially recorded as dead. This is difficult to do without the identification of a body, but a forensic dentist was able to positively identify the tooth crown as belonging to Helle, and a death certificate was issued. Richard was immediately arrested. Authorities theorized that he struck Helle in the head in their bedroom, causing blood stains on the carpet and bedding, which he disposed of. He then froze her body in the freezer, cut her apart with the chainsaw, and ran the pieces through the woodchipper, believing he'd committed the perfect murder.

After a trial that ended with a hung jury, a second trial found Richard guilty on November 21, 1989, and he was sentenced to 50 years in prison. Richard's own sister, who took custody of his children, urged the judge to impose the maximum sentence, citing the fact that he never showed remorse. The horrific nature of his crime eventually caught the attention of film directors Joel and Ethan Coen, who used it as inspiration for the famous "woodchipper" scene in their 1996 film *Fargo*.

Operation Royal Charm: A Wedding Bust

Undercover FBI agents spent several years watching their targets, members of an international counterfeiting and smuggling ring, and developing a relationship with them. Then the ultimate wedding sting operation just fell into place.

❋ ❋ ❋ ❋

Nice Day for a Fake Wedding

Two of the agents, who had gained the trust of the criminals, posed as bride and groom, with a fake wedding that was months in the making. A date was set, and invitations were sent out. The wedding was planned for 2 P.M. on a Sunday afternoon in August 2005, just off the coast of New Jersey. A luxury yacht named *Operation Royal Charm* was docked outside of Atlantic City, and guests started arriving from far and wide. No detail was forgotten; guests and the bridal party were decked out in wedding finery befitting the high rollers that they were. There were even wedding presents, including a pair of Presidential Rolex watches.

But when the guests boarded a boat that they thought would take them out to the yacht, they got a bit of a surprise. There was no wedding! And instead of a cruise on a luxury boat, eight wedding guests got caught in an FBI sting that led to the arrest of about 60 other residents of Asia and the United States, all involved in a variety of international trafficking crimes.

Quite the Wedding Gifts

Authorities seized $4.4 million in counterfeit $100 bills, $42 million worth of counterfeit cigarettes, $700,000 worth of fake U.S. postage stamps and blue jeans, and very real quantities of Viagra, ecstasy, and methamphetamine. The criminals were also charged with conspiracy to ship $1 million of automatic rifles, silenced pistols, submachine guns, and rocket launchers—none of which were delivered.

Bad Brides

These ladies may have gone a little over the top on their wedding days. And we don't mean with the decorations...

✳ ✳ ✳ ✳

Married Mugshot

IN MARCH OF 2009, newlyweds Jade and Billy Puckett left their wedding reception, only to be caught in a "March Madness" DUI sting that was being conducted by deputies in Harris County, Texas. When Billy was charged with driving under the influence, Jade became belligerent and was charged with public intoxication. But it didn't end there! Jade claimed she was not allowed to change clothing and was humiliated when an unidentified male in the courtroom took photos of her in her wedding dress—photos that wound up on the Internet. She filed a complaint with the Harris County Precinct 8 Constable's office just days after her arrest.

Bridezilla Indeed!

Mark Allerton and Teresa Brown were friends for 16 years before they got hitched in a 2007 fairy-tale wedding at a castle in Aberdeen, Scotland. The castle is used in the popular British soap opera *Monarch of the Glen,* but the fight Mark and Teresa got into after the ceremony was even more dramatic than the show. According to police, Teresa attacked Mark with one of her stiletto heels, leaving him with a bleeding puncture wound on his head. Teresa spent two days in jail, but Mark stood by her, saying they had no plans to split. The bride said her freakout was caused by a reaction to an antidepressant. Note: Might want to adjust those meds before the wedding.

Breaking up the Band

Elmo Fernadez and his wife Fabiana had been married in a civil ceremony long before, but in 2008, they decided to renew their vows in a religious ceremony in Port Chester, New York. Everything was going swimmingly until the reception, when the band explained that they could only play music when the DJ was not playing. Fabiana didn't care for that excuse and went on a rampage, knocking over a set of $600 conga drums and destroying other equipment valued at $350. Girlfriend just wanted her money's worth! The cops hauled in Fabiana, her husband, and her daughter that night.

Celebrity Wedding Ruckus

In 2007, groom Carlos Barron and bride Tara Hensley were arrested on their wedding night after partying at a Huntington, South Carolina, nightclub called Envy. Police said they had no choice but to arrest the couple and three other members of the wedding party after they received a report of shots fired, and the crowd refused to disperse. But when it was revealed that one of the arrestees was Cincinnati Bengals running back Quincy Wilson, the boys in blue had a little more explaining to do.

Two Birds with One Threat

Diane Carnes did something not-too-bright on the day before her March 2008 wedding. It seems Diane thought it would be convenient to schedule her wedding at the Scotts Bluff County, Nebraska, courthouse while she was already there taking care of a pesky suspended license violation problem. Her license had been revoked after a DUI, but she got caught driving again. At her trial, Diane threatened one of the jurors, but no matter—she scheduled her wedding for the next day and went on home. The thing is, threatening a juror is a little bit illegal, so when Diane showed up the next day for her wedding, she was arrested. What a way to start a new, married life!

Real-life Wedding Crashers

Sure, 2005's Wedding Crashers, *starring Owen Wilson and Vince Vaughn, was a hit. In real life, however, the premise is not quite as funny.*

✳ ✳ ✳ ✳

Crash Like No Other

IN SEPTEMBER 2007, a reception hall in quiet Idaho Falls, Idaho, was home to one of the most audacious attempts to crash a wedding ever recorded. Throughout the evening, one of the female guests dined, danced, and snatched a bite of wedding cake before the bride and groom even had a chance to cut the first piece. The woman signed the guest book, chatted with the wedding party, posed for photographs, and helped decorate the couple's getaway car.

But, as newlyweds Sciara and Charles Dougherty would later discover, Kimberly Cooper was not on the guest list. Cooper, with her 12-year-old daughter in tow, stole hundreds of dollars in wedding gifts. When police discovered several wedding presents and gift cards from the wedding in Cooper's home, she blamed her daughter for the crime.

Cooper was also accused of crashing another wedding, just hours after the Doughertys' reception ended. Newlyweds Courtney and Josh Van Tress became suspicious after gift cards went missing, and no one seemed to be able to explain Cooper's presence as a "mystery guest." When the couple saw Cooper the next day during a chance encounter at a local Target store, they confronted her—as she was busy paying for purchases with gift cards from their wedding.

Dress the Part . . . or Not

Unfortunately, there are a number of accounts of wedding crashers helping themselves to more than prime rib and cake. In August 2007, Anthony and Jennifer Smith of Garden Grove,

California, returned from their honeymoon to discover a guest stole money-filled envelopes from their cache of wedding gifts. The well-dressed guest wore blue and burgundy clothing—just like the rest of the wedding party—and made off with about $1,500 in cash.

But not every crasher blends in as seamlessly. In September 2009, police in Seymour, Indiana, reported that a man wearing a baseball cap and T-shirt appeared uninvited at Aaron and Margaret Thompson Brown's wedding, where he swiped a large wire birdcage. That doesn't sound so bad, unless you know that the birdcage was meant to feather the newlywed's nest. It was filled with checks, gift cards, and cash worth about $5,000.

Lawrencia Bembenek: Run, Bambi, Run!

"Bambi." Laurie Bembenek would be the first to tell you she hates that nickname. It's all part of the image portrayed by the prosecution when she was on trial for murder. They suggested that she was a materialistic second wife—and a cold-blooded, calculating murderer.

❋　❋　❋　❋

A Murder in Beer City

MILWAUKEE ISN'T TYPICALLY known as a hotbed of crime. Maybe that's why Lawrencia Bembenek's case garnered such a following—from the murder to her conviction, to her escape and ultimate release. It all began on May 28, 1981, when Christine Schultz was found murdered in bed in her Milwaukee home. The victim was the ex-wife of Fred Schultz, a detective for the Milwaukee Police Department. Laurie was his second wife—and the only one with motive, means, and opportunity to commit the crime, according to the district attorney.

Although all of the evidence was circumstantial, it still mounted against Bembenek. Fred Schultz had an alibi for the time of the murder, while Laurie did not. There was no sign of a break-in at the Schultz home, but Laurie had access to Fred's key. Even more incriminating, she had access to Fred's off-duty revolver. As a former police officer, she knew how to use the gun. And finally, a wig with fibers similar to those found at the crime scene was found in the plumbing system of Laurie's apartment building.

The case drew national attention. It had all the hallmarks of a steamy crime drama—a love triangle gone wrong, a second wife fighting for what should have been hers, and a former Playboy bunny and model turned vindictive.

Presumed Guilty

With no alibi, Bembenek's best defense was the eyewitness testimony of her 11-year-old stepson, who said the murderer was a heavyset, wig-wearing man with broad shoulders. There was also the matter of possible police retribution. Laurie had been fired from her position on the police force. The police said it was for possession of marijuana while she said she had stood up to sexual harassment.

None of that seemed to matter. The jury had heard enough. Laurie Bembenek was found guilty in March 1982 and sentenced to life in prison at the Taycheedah Correctional Institution.

For years she maintained her innocence but was unable to get her conviction overturned. She eventually met and became engaged to Nick Gugliatto, the brother of a fellow inmate. In July 1990, she escaped with Gugliatto's help and they ran to Thunder Bay, Ontario, Canada, where they lived secret lives for three months. At that point, the couple was featured on an episode of *America's Most Wanted*, and people recognized them, leading to a quick arrest. Back in Wisconsin, Laurie pleaded no contest to second-degree murder and was sentenced to time served. She was free.

Life After Prison

Since that time, more evidence has been found that exonerates Laurie. For starters, there was semen at the scene, making it likely that Christine was raped and the murderer was male. Also, the bullets recovered didn't match the service revolver Laurie was thought to have used. Finally, her husband had prior contact with a criminal who later told friends that he committed the crime.

Since her release, Laurie has found it hard to adjust to the outside world. She's had problems with drugs and alcohol and has had difficulty finding work. Scheduled to appear on the *Dr. Phil Show* in 2002, she felt claustrophobic in her hotel room and jumped from a window. Her leg was injured so badly that it had to be amputated.

Laurie has written a book and been the subject of a made-for-TV movie. But despite the infamy, Laurie's most fervent desire is still elusive—that her conviction be overturned.

The Ghost of the Sausage Vat Murder

The story of Louisa Luetgert, the murdered wife of "Sausage King" Adolph Luetgert, is a gruesome tale of betrayal, death, and a lingering specter. It is also one of the greatest stories in Chicago lore. According to legend, each year on the anniversary of her death, Louisa appears on the corner of Hermitage Avenue where it once crossed Diversey Parkway. But her ghost not only haunts her old neighborhood; allegedly, she also coaxed her treacherous husband into an early grave.

✳   ✳   ✳   ✳

Land of Opportunity

ADOLPH LUETGERT WAS born in Germany and came to America after the Civil War. He arrived in Chicago around

1865 and worked in tanneries for several years before opening his first business—a liquor store—in 1872. Luetgert married his first wife, Caroline Roepke, that same year. She gave birth to two boys, only one of whom survived childhood. Just two months after Caroline died in November 1877, Luetgert quickly remarried a much younger woman, Louisa Bicknese, and moved to the northwest side of the city. As a gift, he gave her an unusual gold ring that had her initials inscribed inside the band. Little did Luetgert know that this ring would prove to be his downfall.

Trouble for the "Sausage King"

In 1892, Luetgert built a sausage factory at the southwest corner of Hermitage and Diversey. But just a year later, sausage sales declined due to an economic depression. Luetgert had put his life's savings into the factory, along with plenty of borrowed money, so when his business suffered, creditors started coming after him.

Instead of trying to reorganize his finances, however, Luetgert answered a newspaper ad posted by an English millionaire who made a deal with him to buy out the majority of the sausage business. The Englishman proved to be a conman, and Luetgert ended up losing even more money in the deal. Luetgert eventually laid off many of his workers, but a few remained as he attempted to keep the factory out of the hands of creditors for as long as possible.

Luetgert's business losses took a terrible toll on his marriage. Friends and neighbors frequently heard the Luetgerts arguing, and things became so bad that Luetgert eventually started sleeping in his office at the factory. He carried on with several mistresses and even became involved with a household servant who was related to his wife. When Louisa found out about his involvement with her relative, she became enraged.

Luetgert soon gave the neighbors even more to gossip about. One night, during another shouting match with Louisa, he allegedly took his wife by the throat and began choking her. After noticing alarmed neighbors watching him through the parlor window, Luetgert reportedly calmed down and released his wife before she collapsed. A few days later, Luetgert was seen chasing his wife down the street, shouting at her and waving a revolver.

Vanishing Louisa

Louisa disappeared on May 1, 1897. When questioned about it days later, Luetgert stated that Louisa had left him and was possibly staying with her sister or another man. When Louisa's brother, Dietrich Bicknese, asked Luetgert why he had not informed the police of Louisa's disappearance, the sausage maker told him that he'd hired a private investigator to find her because he didn't trust the police.

When Bicknese informed the police of his sister's disappearance, Captain Herman Schuettler and his men began to search for Louisa. They questioned neighbors and relatives, who detailed the couple's violent arguments. Schuettler summoned Luetgert to the precinct house on a couple of occasions and each time pressed him about his wife's disappearance. Luetgert stated that he did not report Louisa's disappearance because he could not afford the disgrace and scandal.

During the investigation, a young German girl named Emma Schimke told police that she had passed by the factory with her sister at about 10:30 P.M. on May 1 and remembered seeing Luetgert leading his wife down the alleyway behind the factory.

Police also questioned employees of the sausage factory. Frank Bialk, a night watchman at the plant, told police that when he arrived for work on May 1, he found a fire going in one of the boilers. He said Luetgert asked him to keep the fire going and then sent him on a couple of trivial errands while Luetgert stayed in the basement. When Bialk returned to the factory, he went back to the boiler fire and heard Luetgert finishing his work at around 3:00 A.M.

Later that morning, Bialk saw a sticky, gluelike substance on the floor near the vat. He noticed that it seemed to contain bits of bone, but he thought nothing of it. After all, Luetgert used all sorts of waste meats to make his sausage, so he assumed that's what it was.

On May 3, Luetgert asked another employee, Frank Odorofsky, to clean the basement and told him to keep quiet about it. Odorofsky put the slimy substance into a barrel and scattered it near the railroad tracks as Luetgert had requested.

A Gruesome Discovery

On May 15, the police search was narrowed to the factory basement and a vat that was two-thirds full of a brownish, brackish liquid. Using gunnysacks as filters, officers drained the greasy paste from the vat and began poking through the residue with sticks. Officer Walter Dean found several bone fragments and two gold rings—one a heavy gold band engraved with the initials "L. L."

Luetgert, proclaiming his innocence, was questioned again shortly after the search and was subsequently arrested for the murder of his wife several days later. Despite the fact that Louisa's body was never found and there was no real evidence to link her husband to the crime, the police and prosecutors believed they had a solid case against Luetgert. He was indicted for Louisa's murder, and the details of the crime shocked the city. Even though he had been charged with boiling Louisa's body, rumors circulated that she had actually been ground up into sausage that was sold to local butcher shops and restaurants. Not surprisingly, sausage sales dropped dramatically in Chicago in 1897.

Hounded to the Grave?

Luetgert's trial ended in a hung jury on October 21. The judge threw out the case, and prosecutors had to try the whole thing again. A second trial was held in 1898, and this time Luetgert was convicted and sentenced to a life term at Joliet Prison.

While in prison, Luetgert continued to maintain his innocence and was placed in charge of meats in the cold-storage warehouse. Officials described him as a model prisoner. But by 1899, Luetgert began to speak less and less and often quarreled with other convicts. He soon became a shadow of his former, blustering self, fighting for no reason and often babbling incoherently in his cell at night. But was he talking to himself or to someone else?

Legend has it that Luetgert claimed Louisa haunted him in his jail cell, intent on having revenge for her murder. Was she really haunting him, or was the ghost just a figment of his rapidly deteriorating mind? Based on the fact that neighbors also reported seeing Louisa's ghost, one has to wonder if she did indeed drive Luetgert insane.

Luetgert died in 1900, likely from heart trouble. The coroner who conducted the autopsy also reported that his liver was greatly enlarged and in such a condition of degeneration that "mental strain would have caused his death at any time."

Perhaps Louisa really did visit him after all.

The Ghost of Louisa Luetgert

Regardless of who killed Louisa, her spirit reportedly did not rest in peace. Soon after Luetgert was sent to prison, neighbors swore they saw Louisa's ghost inside her former home, wearing a white dress and leaning against the fireplace mantel.

The sausage factory stood empty for years, looming over the neighborhood as a grim reminder of the horrors that had taken place there. Eventually, the Library Bureau Company purchased the factory for a workshop and storehouse for library furniture and office supplies. During renovations, they discarded the infamous vats in the basement.

On June 26, 1904, the old factory caught on fire. Despite the damage done to the building's interior, the Library Bureau reopened its facilities in the former sausage factory. In 1907, a contracting mason purchased the old Luetgert house and moved it from behind the factory to another lot in the neighborhood, hoping to dispel the grim memories—and ghost—attached to it.

Hermitage Avenue no longer intersects with Diversey, and by the 1990s, the crumbling factory stood empty. But in the late '90s, around the 100th anniversary of Louisa's death, the former sausage factory was converted into condominiums and a brand-new neighborhood sprang up to replace the aging homes that remained from the days of the Luetgerts. Fashionable brick homes and apartments appeared around the old factory, and rundown taverns were replaced with coffee shops.

But one thing has not changed. Legend has it that each year on May 1, the anniversary of her death, the ghost of Louisa can still be spotted walking down Hermitage Avenue near the old sausage factory, reliving her final moments on this earth.

Chapter 4

Murder Most Foul

Mass Murderers vs. Serial Killers

Serial killers are made of sugar and spice and everything nice, and mass murderers are…wait, that's not right. The distinction between the two is actually very simple.

※　※　※　※

The Mass Murderer

A MASS MURDERER KILLS four or more people during a short period of time, usually in one location. In most cases, the murderer has a sudden mental collapse and goes on a rampage, progressing from murder to murder without a break. About half the time, these outbreaks end in suicides or fatal standoffs with the police.

Various school shootings over the years have been instances of mass murder, as have been famous cases of postal workers, well, "going postal." A case in which someone murders his or her entire family is a mass murder. Terrorists are lumped into this category as well, but they also make up a group of their own.

The Serial Killer

A serial killer usually murders one person at a time (typically a stranger), with a "cooling off" period between each transgression. Unlike mass murderers, serial killers don't suddenly snap one day—they have an ongoing compulsion (usually with a sexual component) that drives them to kill, often in very specific ways. Serial killers may even maintain jobs and normal relationships while going to great lengths to conceal their killings. They may resist the urge to kill for long periods, but the compulsion ultimately grows too strong to subjugate. After the third victim, an aspiring killer graduates from plain ol' murderer to bona fide serial killer.

The Rest

In between these two groups, we have the spree killer and the serial spree killer. A spree killer commits murder in multiple locations over the course of a few days. This is often part of a general crime wave. For example, an escaped convict may kill multiple people, steal cars, jaywalk, and litter as he tries to escape the police. As with a mass murderer, a spree killer doesn't plan each murder individually.

The serial spree killer, on the other hand, plans and commits each murder separately, serial-killer style. But he or she doesn't take time off between murders or maintain a double life. It's all killing, all the time. One of the best-known examples is the Washington, D.C.-area beltway snipers who killed ten people within three weeks in October 2002.

Of course, if you see any of these types of killer in action, don't worry about remembering the right term when you call the police. They're all equally bad.

The Butcher and the Thief

Meet the two charming fellows who inspired the children's rhyme: "Burke's the Butcher, Hare's the Thief, Knox the boy that buys the beef."

✳ ✳ ✳ ✳

The Cadaver Crunch

IN THE 1820s, Edinburgh, Scotland, was suffering from a "cadaver crunch." Considering the city was regarded as a center of medical education, the lack of bodies for students to dissect in anatomy classes posed a problem. At the time, the only legal source of corpses for dissection in Britain was executed criminals. Interestingly, at the same time that enrollment in medical schools was rising (as well as the need for cadavers), the number of executions was decreasing. This was due to the repeal of the so-called "Bloody Code," which by 1815 listed more than 200 capital offenses.

The growing need for corpses created a grisly new occupation. "Resurrection Men" dug up the newly buried dead and sold the bodies to medical schools. William Burke and William Hare decided to cut out the middleman: Over the course of a year, they murdered at least 15 people in order to sell their bodies.

A Grisly Business

The pair fell into the cadaver supply business on November 29, 1827. At the time, Hare was running a cheap boarding house in an Edinburgh slum. Burke was his tenant and drinking buddy. When one of Hare's tenants died still owing four pounds, Hare and Burke stole the tenant's corpse from his coffin and sold it to recover the back rent. Dr. Robert Knox, who taught anatomy to 500 students at Edinburgh Medical College, paid more than seven pounds for the body.

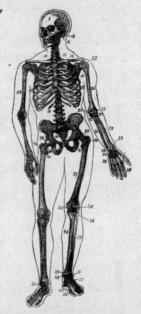

Encouraged by the profit, Burke and Hare looked for other bodies to sell to Knox. Their first victim was another tenant at the boarding house, who fell ill a few days later. Burke and Hare "comforted" the sick man with whiskey until he passed out, and then smothered him. The result was a body that looked like it had died of drunkenness, with no obvious marks of foul play.

Over the course of the next year, Burke and Hare lured more victims into the lodging house. They sold the bodies to Knox, who not only accepted them without question, but increased the pair's payment to ten pounds because of the "freshness" of the bodies they provided.

Their initial targets were strangers to Edinburgh, but Burke and Hare soon began to take more risks, murdering local prostitutes and "Daft Jamie," a well-known neighborhood character. People began to talk about the disappearances, and Knox's students began to recognize the bodies brought to them for dissection.

The End of Burke and Hare

Burke and Hare's mercenary killings ended on October 31, 1828, when Burke lured an old Irish woman named Mary Docherty to the house. James and Ann Gray, who were also boarders at the time, met Docherty there. Docherty was invited to spend the night, and arrangements were made for the Grays to board elsewhere. The next morning, the Grays returned and found the old woman's body under the bed. Although they were offered a bribe of ten pounds a week to keep quiet, the Grays ran for the police.

Hare testified against Burke in exchange for immunity. He was released in February 1829 and disappeared from the historical record, though popular legend claims he ended his life a blind beggar on the streets of London. Burke was tried for murder, found guilty, and hung. Although there was no evidence that Knox had any knowledge of the murders, angry crowds appeared at his lectures and tore his effigy to shreds. He eventually moved to London.

Fittingly, Burke's corpse was turned over to the Edinburgh Medical College for "useful dissection." A bit more oddly, skin from his body was used to bind a small book.

The murders eventually led to the passage of the Anatomy Act of 1832, which provided new legal sources for medical cadavers and eliminated the profit motive that drove Burke and Hare to murder.

More Than a Minor Contribution

How a Civil War surgeon-turned-madman helped shape our understanding of the English language.

* * * *

An Unlikely Contributor

THE OXFORD ENGLISH DICTIONARY (OED) is widely considered the definitive record of the English language. For more than a century, readers have turned to it to understand and pronounce millions of words.

Less well known, however, is the fact that one of its earliest and most important contributors was William Chester Minor, a Civil War surgeon who murdered a man in England, sliced off his own penis, and wrote all his contributions for the world-renowned dictionary while locked inside the padded walls of an insane asylum.

The son of Congregational Church missionaries, Minor was born in Ceylon (now Sri Lanka) in June 1834. At age 14, he was sent to the United States to attend medical school at Yale. After graduation, he enlisted in the U.S. Army, where he served as a physician during some of the Civil War's fiercest skirmishes, including the bloody Battle of the Wilderness in 1864.

The Definition of Madness

Though he had admitted to previously having had "lascivious thoughts" in Ceylon, there is some speculation that exposure to the brutality of war hastened Minor's descent into madness. Whatever the case, he wound up in New York City shortly after the war. While there he developed an unhealthy taste for prostitutes and other assorted "pleasures" found in the city's less savory areas.

By 1868, his erratic behavior landed him in St. Elizabeth's asylum in Washington, D.C. Soon after his release, Minor was relieved of his military commission. He eventually settled overseas in London. If the move to England was intended to halt his increasing insanity, it failed—a year after his relocation, Minor shot and killed George Merrett, whom he suspected of breaking into his home. After a subsequent jury found Minor not guilty by reason of insanity, he was marched off to England's Broadmoor asylum in Berkshire.

A New Hobby

Because of his military pension he was afforded comfortable quarters at Broadmoor, including two rooms, one of which he constructed into a library to house his growing collection of books. Shortly after his "incarceration," a public request was released, asking for volunteers to contribute to the OED. With plenty of free time on his hands and a large collection of books at his disposal, Minor began enthusiastically contributing entries to the fledgling dictionary—a pastime that would take up most of the remainder of his life.

For the next two decades Minor pored through his library, finding quotations for thousands of words in the dictionary by keeping lists of recurring words that matched the current needs of the OED. Minor's lists became so prolific that the editors of the OED eventually just sent Minor their lists of words they needed filled.

Minor's contributions, said to have numbered more than 10,000 entries, were so frequent and numerous that he eventually developed a friendship with the OED's editor, Dr. James Murray, who made the trip to Broadmoor to visit the institutionalized contributor. Murray would later say that Minor's contribution to the OED was so enormous that it "could easily have illustrated the last four centuries [of words] from his quotations alone."

Further Descent

Whatever satisfaction Minor took from his meaningful work on the OED, it did nothing to stop his lunacy, which had grown to such a state that he amputated his own penis in 1902. Still,

Murray helped guarantee Minor's release from Broadmoor, which was approved by Home Secretary Winston Churchill in 1910. Upon his liberation from the asylum, Minor returned to America, where he would remain until his death in 1920.

Jack the Ripper's Eerie Austin Connection

Could America's first serial killer be one of Austin's best-kept and most grisly secrets?

* * * *

BEFORE JACK THE Ripper made his bloody trail through London, Austin experienced a similar murder spree. The Ripper-like murders began on New Year's Eve, 1884. Someone killed Mollie Smith, a servant girl, and put a large hole in her head. Two more women were butchered in similar attacks a few months later.

A Trail of Blood

The killings weren't limited to servants, however. As the Austin murder spree continued, victims became more upscale. Each death was a little more gory. The final murders recorded occurred on Christmas Eve, 1885, almost a full year after they had begun. The victims included Mrs. Eula Phillips, a wealthy woman who—for amusement—worked as a prostitute.

To stop the binge of killing, Austin police began questioning men on the streets after dark. The city erected "moonlight towers" to illuminate the streets. Seventeen of those towers still light downtown Austin and are listed in the National Register of Historic Places. The city's efforts were apparently successful, as the slaughter ended.

The Whitechapel Murders

Jack the Ripper began killing women in London as early as the day after Christmas in 1887. It could be coincidence, but the Ripper's physical description, style of killing, and victims seemed eerily similar to the Austin murders. Possible killers included a man called "the Malay Cook," who left Austin late in January 1886 and was interviewed in London in 1888. According to that interview, he said he'd been robbed by a woman "of bad character." Unless he recovered his money, he planned to murder and mutilate women in London's Whitechapel area.

No one knows if Austin was the training ground for Jack the Ripper, of course, but the possibility is chilling.

The Lizzie Borden Murder Mystery

Most people know the rhyme that begins, "Lizzie Borden took an axe and gave her mother 40 whacks…" In reality, approximately 20 hatchet chops cut down Abby Borden, but no matter the number, Lizzie's stepmother was very much dead on that sultry August morning in 1892. Lizzie's father, Andrew, was killed about an hour later. His life was cut short by about a dozen hatchet chops to the head. No one knows who was guilty of these murders, but Lizzie has always carried the burden of suspicion.

✳ ✳ ✳ ✳

Andrew Borden, an American "Scrooge"

ANDREW JACKSON BORDEN had been one of the richest men in Fall River, Massachusetts, with a net worth of nearly half a million dollars. In 1892, that was enormous wealth. Andrew was a shrewd businessman: At the time of his death, he was the president of the Union Savings Bank and director of another bank plus several profitable cotton mills.

Despite his wealth, Andrew was miserly. Though some of his neighbors' homes had running hot water, the three-story Borden home had just two cold-water taps, and there was no water available above the first floor. The Bordens' only latrine was in the cellar, so they generally used chamber pots that were either dumped onto the lawn behind the house or emptied into the cellar toilet. And, although most wealthy people used gas lighting by that point in time, the Bordens lit their house with inexpensive kerosene lamps.

Worst of all, for many years, Andrew was an undertaker who offered some of the lowest prices in town. He worked on the bodies in the basement of the Borden home, and allegedly, he bent the knees of the deceased—and in some cases, cut off their feet—to fit the bodies into smaller, less expensive coffins in order to increase his business.

So, despite the brutality of Andrew's murder, it seems few people mourned his loss. The question wasn't why he was killed, but who did it.

Lizzie vs. William

In 1997, when psychic Jane Doherty visited the murder site, she uncovered several clues about the Lizzie Borden case. Doherty felt that the real murderer was someone named "Willie." There is no real evidence to support this claim, but some say Andrew had an illegitimate son named William, who may have spent time as an inmate in an insane asylum. His constant companion was reportedly his hatchet, which he talked to as though it were a friend. Also, at least one witness reportedly saw William at the Borden house on the day of the murders. William was supposedly there to challenge Andrew about his new will.

Was William the killer? A few years after the murders, William took poison and then hung himself in the woods. Near his swinging body, he'd reportedly left his hatchet on the ground. So with William dead and Lizzie already acquitted, the Borden murder case was put to rest.

Lizzie's Forbidden Romance

One of the most curious explanations for the murder involves the Bordens' servant Bridget Sullivan. Her participation has always raised questions. Like the other members of the Borden household, Bridget had suffered from apparent food poisoning the night before the murders. She claimed to have been ill in the backyard of the Borden home.

During the time Abby was being murdered, Bridget was apparently washing windows in the back of the house. Later, when Andrew was killed, Bridget was resting in her room upstairs. Why didn't she hear two people being butchered?

According to some theories, Lizzie and Bridget had been romantically involved. In this version of the story, their relationship was discovered shortly before the murders. Around this same time, Andrew was reportedly rewriting his will. His wife was now "Mrs. Borden," to Lizzie, not "Mother," as Lizzie had called her stepmother for many years. The reason for the estrangement was never clear.

Lizzie also had a strange relationship with her father and had given him her high school ring, as though he were her sweetheart. He wore the ring on his pinky finger and was buried with it.

Just a day before the murders, Lizzie had been attempting to purchase prussic acid—a deadly poison—and the family came down with "food poisoning" that night. Some speculate that Bridget was Lizzie's accomplice in the murders and helped clean up the blood afterward.

This theory was bolstered when, a few years after the murders, Lizzie became involved with actress Nance O'Neil. For two years, Lizzie and the statuesque actress were inseparable. This prompted Emma Borden, Lizzie's sister, to move out of their shared home.

At the time, the rift between the sisters sparked rumors that either Lizzie or Emma might reveal more about the other's role in the 1892 murders. However, neither of them said anything new about the killings.

Whodunit?

Most people believe that Lizzie was the killer. She was the only one accused of the crime, with good reason. Lizzie appeared to be the only one in the house at the time, other than Bridget. She showed no signs of grief when the murders were discovered. During questioning, Lizzie changed her story several times. The evidence was entirely circumstantial, but it was compelling enough to go to trial.

Ultimately, the jury accepted her attorney's closing argument, that the murders were "morally and physically impossible for this young woman defendant." In other words, Lizzie had to be innocent because she was petite and well bred. In 19th-century New England, that seemed like a logical and persuasive defense. As a consequence, Lizzie went free, and no one else was charged with the crimes.

But Lizzie wasn't the only one with motive, means, and opportunity. The most likely suspects were family members, working alone or with other relatives. Only a few had solid alibis, and—like Lizzie—many changed their stories during police questioning. But there was never enough evidence to officially accuse anyone other than Lizzie.

So whether or not Lizzie Borden truly "took an ax" and killed her parents, she's the one best remembered for the crime.

Lizzie Borden Bed & Breakfast

The Borden house has been sold several times over the years, but today it is a bed-and-breakfast—the main draw, of course, being the building's macabre history. The Victorian residence has been restored to reflect the details of the Borden home at the time of the murders, including the couch on which Andrew lay, his skull hideously smashed.

As a guest, you can stay in one of six rooms, even the one in which Abby was murdered. Then, after a good night's sleep, you'll be treated to a breakfast reminiscent of the one the

Bordens had on their final morning in 1892. That is, if you got to sleep at all. (They say the place is haunted.)

As with all good morbid attractions, the proprietors at the Lizzie Borden B&B don't take themselves too seriously. Before you leave, you can stop by the gift shop and pick up a pair of hatchet earrings, an "I Survived the Night at the Lizzie Borden Bed & Breakfast" T-shirt, or an ax-wielding Lizzie Borden bobble-head doll.

Come into My Parlor

H. H. Holmes has secured a place in history as one of the most horrifyingly prolific killers the world has ever seen.

✳   ✳   ✳   ✳

BORN IN MAY 1860 in New Hampshire, Herman Webster Mudgett was a highly intelligent child, but he was constantly in trouble. Charming, handsome, and charismatic, he nonetheless displayed traits of detachment and dispassion from an early age. As a teen, he became abusive to animals—a classic sign of a sociopath.

Fascinated with skeletons and the human body, Mudgett decided to pursue a medical degree. After marrying Clara Lovering, he enrolled in medical school. There, he had access to skeletons and cadavers. He came up with a scheme to fleece insurance companies by taking out policies for family members or friends, using stolen cadavers to fake their deaths, and collecting the insurance money.

When authorities became suspicious, he abandoned Clara and their newborn baby, moving from city to city and taking on various jobs, most likely scheming and manipulating everyone he crossed. In 1886, the charming liar and thief with murderous intentions surfaced in Chicago with a new name: H. H. Holmes. The city would become the site of his deadliest swindle of all.

A "Castle" with a Most Intriguing Floor Plan

If you lived in Chicago in the late 1800s, you were likely consumed with thoughts of the World's Columbian Exposition. Planners hoped it would make America a superstar country and put Chicago on the map as an A-list city. The Great Fire of 1871 had demolished the town, but the fair would bring the city back—and in a big way.

With new people flooding into the city every day looking to nab one of the world's fair jobs, Chicago was experiencing a population boom that made it very easy for people to simply vanish. The handsome and charismatic Holmes recognized this as an opportunity to lure women into his clutches while most people had their focus elsewhere.

He married his second wife, Myrta, in 1887, without ever securing a divorce from Lovering. Holmes quickly shipped Myrta off to live in suburban Wilmette, while he took up residence in Chicago, free to do as he pleased. He secured a position as a pharmacist at a drugstore in Englewood. He worked for the elderly Mrs. Holden, who was happy to have a handsome young doctor to help out at her store. When Mrs. Holden suddenly disappeared, Holmes told people she had moved to California, and he purchased the store.

Next, Holmes purchased a vacant lot across the street from the drugstore and began constructing a house with a floor plan he designed himself. The three-story house at 63rd and Wallace would have more than 60 rooms and 50 doors, secret passageways, gas pipes with nozzles that piped noxious fumes into windowless rooms, chutes that led down to the basement, and an airtight vault.

To add insult to inury, Holmes hired and fired construction crews on a regular basis; it was said that his swindler's streak got him out of paying for most of the materials and labor used to create this "Murder Castle."

Up & Running

Advertised as a lodging for world's fair tourists, the building opened in 1892. Holmes placed ads in the newspaper to rent rooms, but also listed classified ads calling for females interested in working for a start-up company. Of course, there was no start-up company, and Holmes hired the prettiest women or those who could offer him some sort of financial gain. One by one, they inevitably succumbed to his charm. He made false promises to woman after woman, luring them deeper into his confidence. He took advantage of their naïveté to gain their trust and steal their money.

When he was done with a woman, either because she became suspicious of him or because he had gotten what he needed from her, Holmes got rid of her—without remorse or emotion. Sometimes he piped gas into a victim's room to kill her in her sleep; other times he locked her in his airtight vault and listened as she slowly suffocated. Evidence shows he tortured some of them before killing them. After he had brutalized the unfortunate soul, he destroyed the evidence in a vat of acid or a kiln he had built expressly for that purpose, often selling his victims' bones and organs to contacts in the medical field.

The End of "Doctor Death"

After the world's fair ended, creditors put pressure on Holmes, and he knew it was time to flee. Strange as it seems, when Holmes was finally brought to justice, it wasn't initially for homicide; it was for one of his many financial swindles. But as clues about missing women emerged, investigators became suspicious of him for other reasons.

Detective Frank Geyer began to follow the trail of this mysterious man whose identity changed with the weather. Geyer had traced many missing world's fair women back to Holmes's lodging house. He was particularly interested in the whereabouts of three children—Howard, Nellie, and Alice Pietzel. Geyer followed their tracks across the Midwest and into Canada. In Toronto he finally found a house where Holmes had allegedly stayed with several children in tow. Buried in a shallow grave in the backyard, stuffed in a single traveling trunk, he discovered the bodies of the two Pietzel girls. Geyer found the boy's remains several months later in an oven in a home in Indianapolis, Indiana.

When the evidence was brought back to court, Geyer got full clearance to investigate every inch of Holmes's Chicago dwelling. The investigation turned up a lot more than detectives anticipated, and one of America's most chilling stories of murder and crime officially broke.

Inside his heavily guarded cell, Herman Webster Mudgett admitted his crimes. He officially confessed to 27 murders, six attempted murders, and a whole lot of fraud. What he didn't confess to, however, were any feelings of remorse. Holmes was executed by hanging in 1896. He was buried in Holy Cross Cemetery near Philadelphia in a coffin lined with cement, topped with more cement, and buried in a double grave—per his own request. Was he ready to rest eternally after a life of such monstrosity? Or was he afraid that someone would conduct experiments on him as he had done to so many of his hapless victims?

"I was born with the devil in me. I could not help the fact that I was a murderer, no more than the poet can help the inspiration to sing."

—H. H. HOLMES

Chicago Killers

Holmes was far from Chicago's only infamous killer. Some of the most notorious names in American crime were born and bred in the city and its surrounding suburbs.

✳ ✳ ✳ ✳

Not the Superhero Black Widow

I LOVE YOU—REALLY, I do: Chicagoan Tillie Klimek poisoned her husband, remarried, and then did the same thing three more times, collecting life insurance and claiming that she'd foreseen her husbands' deaths in her dreams. Earning her the monikers "Black Widow" and "Mrs. Bluebeard," Klimek is also suspected of having murdered a handful of her children, cousins, and a boyfriend who didn't take the bait. She was sentenced to life in prison in 1922 and died in 1936.

"Supermen" They Weren't

Richard Loeb and Nathan Leopold grew up in the Kenwood neighborhood. Loeb's father was a Sears, Roebuck & Co. vice president, Leopold's was a wealthy box manufacturer. Loeb was obsessed with crime novels, and Leopold was obsessed with Loeb—and with the idea of Nietzsche's superman, a superior individual who was above the law and could do as he pleased. Leopold believed that a superman could even commit murder. When Loeb conceived of the idea to attempt a perfect crime—one for which they would never be caught—Leopold was his willing accomplice.

In 1924—when Loeb was 18 and Leopold was 19—the two lured Loeb's 14-year-old cousin Bobby Franks into a car and beat the unsuspecting child to death. They attempted to hide the body near Wolf Lake; they did a poor job, however, and a passerby found the body the next day. Investigators then discovered Leopold's glasses in the area where the body was found, and the boys were quickly apprehended.

The trial was a sensation; because the boys had pleaded guilty, the main point of the trial was to determine if the boys would go to prison or be hanged. Defense attorney Clarence Darrow claimed that both boys were mentally unstable because they had been abused by their governesses; using this defense among others, Darrow persuaded the judge to spare the boys' lives, much to prosecutor Robert Crowe's chagrin.

Loeb was killed in prison in 1936. Leopold was a model prisoner and was released in 1958. Even prosecutor Robert Crowe had become convinced of Leopold's reform and considered writing a letter to the parole board on his behalf. Leopold lived most of the rest of his life in Puerto Rico. He died in 1971.

Bobby Franks is buried in Rosehill Cemetery. Some cemetery workers claimed to see a young boy wandering the cemetery at times; when they approached him, he would disappear, however. The workers claimed the ghost did not rest until Leopold's death in 1971.

Keep Your Windows Locked

A raging alcoholic and a sociopath, Richard Speck sneaked into a dorm through an unlocked window and brutally murdered eight nurses in 1966. The systematic killings of the students shocked the nation. The Chicago Police Department sent 60 officers on a hunt for Speck. After listening to the testimony of Corazon Amurao (the sole surviving nurse), the jury at his trial deliberated for only 49 minutes and sentenced him to death. The death penalty was declared unconstitutional in 1972 (while Speck was on death row), and Speck was sentenced to eight consecutive terms of 50 to 150 years each.

Speck's bizarre, cold-blooded persona became the subject of much clinical and popular debate throughout his years in prison. As a child, Speck was abused by his stepfather and suffered several serious falls; he had the IQ of a ten-year-old, and many specialists believe he had undiagnosed brain damage. Speck died of a heart attack in 1991. After no one claimed the body, Speck was cremated, and his ashes were scattered in an undisclosed location.

Beyond Our Reach

A brilliant but tormented mathematician, Ted Kaczynski (aka "the Unabomber") traded his position at Berkeley for a life in Montana, where he read philosophy and became one of the country's most infamous domestic terrorists. Kaczynski, who was raised on Chicago's Southwest Side, was the subject of a massive FBI manhunt after nearly 20 years of mailing bombs to academics and businessmen—as well as attempting to blow up a plane in 1979. The fact that Kaczynski's preferred targets were universities and airlines led FBI agents to dub him the "Unabomber."

Kaczynski has intense suspicions about technological progress and the effect it has on human beings and nature. One prison psychiatrist diagnosed Kaczynski with paranoid schizophrenia in 1998, but others are not convinced. Specialists will likely be studying his case for years to come to determine the root of his psychological distress; conjecture lays blame across the spectrum, from an illness he contracted as an infant to psychological experiments he underwent while he was a Harvard undergrad. Investigators still are not sure how he chose his specific targets. Kaczynski was sentenced to life in prison and is currently in a maximum-security lockup in Colorado. It was reported that he became friends with Timothy McVeigh, who committed the Oklahoma City bombing, until the other man's execution.

"I wonder now, Nathan, whether you think there is a God or not. I wonder whether you think it is pure accident that this disciple of Nietzsche's philosophy dropped his glasses or whether it was an act of Divine Providence to visit upon your miserable carcasses the wrath of God."

—STATE'S ATTORNEY ROBERT CROWE,
IN HIS SUMMATION DURING THE LEOPOLD & LOEB CASE

Murder at the Garden

The world was fascinated when a skirt-chasing Gilded Age architect died atop the landmark he designed.

✳ ✳ ✳ ✳

Concerts by superstars the likes of Jimi Hendrix, Elvis Presley, John Lennon, Michael Jackson, Frank Sinatra, and Barbra Streisand; legendary boxing matches featuring Joe Louis, Rocky Marciano, Sugar Ray Robinson, Joe Frazier, and Muhammad Ali; home games of basketball's New York Knicks and ice hockey's New York Rangers. These are just some of the events that have taken place at Madison Square Garden since the first of its four incarnations was constructed in 1879. Yet, perhaps the most notorious Garden event was the cold-blooded murder of the man who designed the second Garden, located like its predecessor at 26th Street and Madison Avenue.

That man's name was Stanford White, and his 1906 Garden shooting in front of a high-society audience led to the "Trial of the Century." (A somewhat premature title? It would subsequently be shared with court cases starring, among others, Leopold and Loeb, John Scopes, Gloria Vanderbilt, the Nazis at Nuremberg, and O. J. Simpson). Indeed, the aforementioned witnesses were not only elevated in terms of their social status but also in terms of their location, since the crime took place at the venue's rooftop theater during the premiere of the saucy musical *Mam'zelle Champagne*. Soon, the general public was abuzz with gossip about the sex and jealousy that gave rise to the murder.

Mirrors and a Swing

Stanford White was not only the esteemed architect of numerous neoclassical New York City public buildings and private mansions, he was also a notorious (and married) womanizer who enjoyed assignations at a downtown loft apartment where he had installed a red velvet swing so that his girls could "entertain" him. A standout among them was Evelyn Nesbit, a beautiful artists' model and chorus girl who had met "Stanny" shortly after relocating from Pittsburgh to New York in 1901. At the time, she was 16; he was 47. As Nesbit would later recall, it was during their second rendezvous at the apartment on West 24th Street, where some walls and ceilings were covered in mirrors, that the redhead "entered that room as a virgin," and, she attested, lost consciousness after a glass of champagne and was sexually assaulted. They subsequently had a relationship that lasted several months, though White continued to dally with other women during that time as well.

Thereafter, while White continued treating girls and young women to his swing and mirrors, Nesbit embarked on a relationship with—and was twice impregnated by—young actor John Barrymore. Yet, it was the details of her affair with White that tormented Harry Kendall Thaw, the man whom Nesbit married in 1905. The son of a Pittsburgh coal and railroad tycoon, Thaw was a violent, drug-addicted ne'er-do-well who also had a taste for chorus girls. When he met Nesbit, the stage was set for a tragic showdown.

White's first bad move was to make less-than-complimentary remarks about Thaw to some ladies they both were pursuing. When Thaw learned about these cracks, he wasn't exactly delighted. His annoyance turned to jealous rage when, after he somehow turned on the charm to woo Nesbit, she admitted that she kept declining his proposals of marriage because "Stanny" had taken her virginity. This only made Thaw more determined, and after forcing his marriage proposals—and himself—on the social-climbing Nesbit, the chorus beauty finally relented.

A Pistol in His Pocket

According to Nesbit, she was continually brutalized by Thaw, and his preoccupation with her deflowering at the hands of "The Beast" finally exploded in violence on the night of June 25,

1906. It was on that evening that the Thaws happened to dine at the Café Martin where White, his son, and a friend were also eating. Like White, the Thaws were planning to attend the play's premiere at the Madison Square Roof Garden, and at some point Harry must have learned about this. After dropping Evelyn off at their hotel so that he could arm himself, he reappeared in a black overcoat (despite the summer heat), whisked his young wife off to the show, and paced nervously up and down between the dinner-theater tables before White arrived at around 10:50 P.M. Thaw continued to hover for the next 15 minutes, until an onstage rendition of a song unfortunately titled "I Could Love a Million Girls" inspired him to approach the seated architect and shoot him three times from point-blank range.

One bullet entered White's left eye, killing him instantly; the other two grazed his shoulders as he fell off his chair. However, since two stage performers had just engaged in a dueling dialogue, most audience members thought the shooting was all part of the fun—until several witnesses screamed. At that point, according to the following day's *Times*, the theater manager leapt onto a table and demanded that the show must go on. Yet, when "the musicians made a feeble effort at gathering their wits" and "the girls who romped on the stage were paralyzed with horror," the manager informed his audience that an accident had occurred and they should leave quietly.

Arrested near the venue's elevators, Thaw asserted that White "deserved it . . . I can prove it. He ruined my life and then deserted the girl." According to a different witness quoted in the *Times*, Thaw claimed that White had ruined his *wife*, not his life.

Either way, after the jury at this first "Trial of the Century" was deadlocked, Thaw's plea of insanity at the second resulted in his imprisonment at a state hospital for the criminally insane. Released in 1913 and judged sane in 1915—the year he granted Evelyn a divorce—he was again judged insane and sentenced to an asylum two years later for assaulting and horse-whipping a teenage boy.

An Ongoing Story

The 1955 movie *The Girl in the Red Velvet Swing*, starring Joan Collins as Evelyn Nesbit, Ray Milland as Stanford White, and Farley Granger as Harry Kendall Thaw, recounts the love-triangle murder. An even more fictionalized account was provided in James Cagney's final feature film, *Ragtime* (1981) with Norman Mailer as White and Elizabeth McGovern as Nesbit.

Following the first two incarnations of the Garden that were constructed at 26th Street and Madison Avenue in 1879 and 1890, Madison Square Garden III opened at 50th Street and Eighth Avenue in 1925. The current version of the indoor arena, located at Eighth Avenue and 33rd Street, opened in 1968.

The Great Plains Butcher

In many cold cases, the victims are known while the killer is a cipher. In the case of Eugene Butler, we know he murdered six people and buried them on his property. Their identities, however, remain unknown.

✳ ✳ ✳ ✳

BORN IN 1849 in New York, Eugene Butler moved out west to North Dakota in the 1880s. He bought a farm in Niagara, North Dakota, where he lived alone. He was reportedly something of a recluse, minimizing contact with his neighbors. When he visited the nearby town, it was to hire farmhands for busy times.

In 1906, Butler came more prominently to his neighbors atten-tion when he began to visibly suffer from hallucinations and paranoid delusions. He would ride through the countryside at night screaming. Because of this behavior, he was admitted to the North Dakota State Hospital, an asylum for the mentally ill, where he lived relatively quietly until his death in 1913. His neighbors, and staff at the hospital, did not know that in his years at the farm, he had also committed several grisly murders.

It was not until after his death that the bodies of his victims were found, when workmen sent by his relatives to renovate the property discovered a series of skeletons under the cellar. They were young men, probably itinerant farmhands hired by Butler who were not missed when they disappeared. Butler killed them by crushing their skulls; he even built a trap door to more easily dispose of the remains. Money left at the house led some to speculate that Butler became paranoid and thought the men were stealing from him.

None of the victims have ever been identified, and some of the bones were even stolen, probably by people looking for grisly souvenirs of a case that captured the public's imagination.

The Butcher Was a Wienie

So, the mugger is dead, your wife is dead, but you made it out unscathed? Something doesn't quite add up…

✳   ✳   ✳   ✳

IN 1920, BUTCHER Carl Wanderer, a veteran of World War I, approached a drifter in a bar and offered him the princely sum of $10 to pretend to rob him. Wanderer explained that he was in the doghouse with his wife, but that if he punched a mugger in front of her, he'd look like a hero. The drifter agreed to the deal.

The next day, as Wanderer and his wife (who was due to deliver the couple's first child the following month) returned home from the movies, the drifter attacked them in the entryway of their apartment building. Wanderer pulled out a gun, shot the drifter to death, then turned and shot his wife to death too. Wanderer told police that his wife had tragically been killed during the ruckus. For a couple of days, Wanderer was hailed as a hero. But the police—and, more importantly, the newspaper reporters—had an uneasy feeling about Wanderer's story. They were especially suspicious of the fact that he and the drifter had exactly the same model of pistol.

Reporters soon discovered that Wanderer had a girlfriend— a 16-year-old who worked across the street from Wanderer's butcher shop. Within weeks, Wanderer's story had fallen apart, and he broke down and confessed to the murders.

Initially put on trial only for the murder of his wife, Wanderer was sentenced to 25 years in prison. The newspapers were out-raged that he hadn't been sentenced to hang and published the names and addresses of the jurors so that people could harass them. Eventually, Wanderer was rushed back into court to stand trial for the death of the drifter. This time, he was sen-tenced to death.

At his hanging, he entertained the reporters by singing a popu-lar song of the day, "Old Pal Why Don't You Answer Me," just before his execution. One reporter said, "He shoulda been a song plugger." Another, however, said, "He should have been hanged just for his voice!" All were thankful Wanderer would sing no more.

Murderess

It was the "trial of the century"—for what may well have been the most poorly executed murder of the time.

✳ ✳ ✳ ✳

IT WAS A terrible thing to wake up to on that March morning in 1927. Nine-year-old Lorraine Snyder found her mother Ruth, her hands and feet bound, begging for help in the hall outside her bedroom. The girl rushed to her neighbors in the New York City suburb, and they called the police.

What the police found was more terrible still. Ruth Snyder's husband Albert lay dead in the bedroom—his skull smashed, wire strung around his neck, and a chloroform-soaked cloth shoved up his nose. His 32-year-old widow told the police that a large Italian man had knocked her out, stolen her jewelry, and assaulted her husband.

But the police found her jewels under a mattress; they also discovered a bloody pillowcase and a bloody, five-pound sash weight in a closet. As if this evidence wasn't damning enough, police located a check Ruth had written to Henry Judd Gray in the amount of $200. Gray's name was found in her little black book—along with the names of 26 other men.

To cinch the matter, Lorraine told the cops that "Uncle Judd" had been in the home the previous night. A tie clip with the initials HJG was found on the floor.

A Marriage on the Rocks

Ruth Brown met Albert Snyder—14 years her senior—in 1915. He was an editor of *Motor Boating* magazine, and Ruth was a secretary. She and Albert married and had Lorraine, but their union was flawed from the start. Albert was still enthralled with his former fiancée of ten years ago, who had died; he named his boat after her and displayed her photograph in his and Ruth's home.

In the meantime, Ruth haunted the jazz clubs of Roaring Twenties Manhattan, drinking and dancing 'til the wee hours of the morning without her retiring spouse, whom she had dubbed "the old crab."

In 1925, the unhappy wife went on a blind date and met Judd Gray, a low-key corset salesperson. Soon the duo was meeting for afternoon trysts at the Waldorf Astoria—leaving Lorraine to play in the hotel lobby. Eventually, Ruth arranged for her unsuspecting husband to sign a life insurance policy worth more than $70,000.

The Jig Is Up

At the murder scene, the police questioned Ruth about Gray. "Has he confessed?," she blurted. It wasn't long before she had spilled her guts, though she claimed it was Gray who'd actually strangled Albert.

Meanwhile, 33-year-old Gray—not exactly the sharpest knife in the drawer—was found at a hotel in Syracuse, New York. It didn't take police long to locate him; after leaving Ruth's house, he had actually stopped to ask a police officer when he could catch the next bus to New York City. Gray quickly confessed but claimed it was Ruth who'd strangled Albert. Ruth had mesmerized him, he stated, through alcohol, sex, and threats.

A month after the arrest of the murderous duo, a brief trial ensued. For three weeks, the courtroom was jammed with 1,500 spectators. In attendance were such luminaries as songwriter Irving Berlin and the producers of the Broadway play Chicago. Also on hand was novelist James M. Cain, who drew on the case for his novel *Double Indemnity*, later turned into a film noir classic by director Billy Wilder and writer Raymond Chandler. The media frenzy over the courtroom drama even exceeded coverage of the execution of anarchist-bombers Sacco and Vanzetti. Miming the fevered reporting of city tabloids such as the *Daily News*, the stodgy *New York Times* carried page-one stories on the crime for months.

Guilty!

Ruth and Gray were pronounced guilty after a 100-minute deliberation by an all-male jury. When their appeal failed and their plea for clemency to Governor Al Smith was denied, the deadly pair was driven 30 miles "up the river" to Sing Sing Prison's death row. En route, excited onlookers hung from rooftops to catch a glimpse of the doomed couple.

Robert Elliott, the man slated to execute the pair, professed angst over putting a woman to death; Ruth would be the first female executed since 1899. "It will be something new for me to throw the switch on a woman," he told reporters, "and I don't like the job." The former electrical contractor received threats because of his role as hangman. He asked the warden for a raise to help salve the stress. Yet, Elliott would long continue his grim work, sending a total of 387 convicts to the next world.

The End

On January 12, 1928, at 11 P.M., 20 witnesses—chosen from the 1,500 who'd applied—watched Ruth enter the execution chamber. The Blonde Butcher, as she had been dubbed, was strapped weeping into a wooden chair, a leather cap clamped on her head. "Jesus, have mercy on me," she moaned, "for I have sinned."

In a room close by, Elliott threw a switch, and 2,000 volts surged through Ruth's body. At that instant, a reporter for the *Daily News* triggered a camera hidden in his pants. A garish photo of the murderess's last moment would appear on the paper's front page the next day. The headline read, "DEAD." Minutes later, it was Gray's turn. Although his feet caught fire during the execution, for most witnesses it was Ruth's final moments that were stamped indelibly in their minds.

Ohio's Greatest Unsolved Mystery

From 1935 until 1938, a brutal madman roamed the Flats of Cleveland. The killer—known as the Mad Butcher of Kingsbury Run—is believed to have murdered 12 men and women. Despite a massive manhunt, the murderer was never apprehended.

❋ ❋ ❋ ❋

I N 1935, THE Depression had hit Cleveland hard, leaving large numbers of people homeless. Shantytowns sprang up on the eastern side of the city in Kingsbury Run—a popular place for transients—near the Erie and Nickel Plate railroads.

It is unclear who the Mad Butcher's first victim was. Recent research suggests it may have been an unidentified woman found floating in Lake Erie—in pieces—on September 5, 1934; she would be known as Jane Doe I but dubbed by some as the "Lady of the Lake." The first official victim was found in the Jackass Hill area of Kingsbury Run on September 23, 1935. The unidentified body, labeled John Doe, had been dead for almost a month. A mere 30 feet away from the body was another victim, Edward Andrassy. Unlike John Doe, Andrassy had only been dead for days, indicating that the spot was a dumping ground. Police began staking out the area.

After a few months passed without another body, police thought the worst was over. Then on January 26, 1936, the partial remains of a new victim, a woman, were found in downtown Cleveland. On February 7, more remains were found at a separate location, and the deceased was identified as Florence Genevieve Polillo. Despite similarities among the three murders, authorities had yet to connect them—serial killers were highly uncommon at the time.

Tattoo Man, Eliot Ness, and More Victims

On June 5, two young boys passing through Kingsbury Run discovered a severed head. The rest of the body was found near the Nickel Plate railroad police station. Despite six distinctive tattoos on the man's body (thus the nickname "Tattoo Man"), he was never identified and became John Doe II.

At this point, Cleveland's newly appointed director of public safety, Eliot Ness (fresh off his Prohibition-era successes), was officially briefed on the case. While Ness and his men hunted down leads, the headless body of another unidentified male was found west of Cleveland on July 22, 1936. It appeared that the man, John Doe III, had been murdered several months earlier. On September 10, the headless body of a sixth victim, John Doe IV, was found in Kingsbury Run.

Ness officially started spearheading the investigation. Determined to bring the killer to justice, Ness's staff fanned out across the city, even going undercover in the Kingsbury Run area. As 1936 drew to a close, no suspects had been named nor new victims discovered. City residents believed that Ness's team had run the killer off. But future events would prove that the killer was back ... with a vengeance.

The Body Count Climbs

A woman's mutilated torso washed up on the beach at 156th Street on February 23, 1937. The rest would wash ashore two months later. (Strangely, the body washed up in the same location as the "Lady of the Lake" had three years earlier.)

On June 6, 1937, teenager Russell Lauyer found the decomposed body of a woman inside of a burlap sack under the Lorain-Carnegie Bridge in Cleveland. With the body was a newspaper from June of the previous year, suggesting a timeline for the murder. An investigation indicated the body might belong to one Rose Wallace; this was never confirmed, and the victim is sometimes referred to as Jane Doe II. Pieces of another man's body (the ninth victim) began washing ashore on July 6, just below Kingsbury Run. Cleveland newspapers were having a field day with the case that the "great" Eliot Ness couldn't solve. This fueled Ness, and he promised justice.

Burning of Kingsbury Run

The next nine months were quiet, and the public began to relax. When a woman's severed leg was found in the Cuyahoga River on April 8, 1938, however, people debated its connection to the Butcher. But the rest of Jane Doe III was soon found inside two burlap sacks floating in the river (*sans* head, of course).

On August 16, 1938, the last two confirmed victims of the Butcher were found together at the East 9th Street Lakeshore Dump. Jane Doe IV had apparently been dead for four to six months prior to discovery, while John Doe VI may have been dead for almost nine months.

Something snapped inside Eliot Ness. On the night of August 18, Ness and dozens of police officials raided the shantytowns in the Flats, ending up in Kingsbury Run. Along the way, they interrogated or arrested anyone they came across, and Ness ordered the shanties burned to the ground. There would be no more confirmed victims of the Mad Butcher of Kingsbury Run.

Who Was the Mad Butcher?

There were two prime suspects in the case, though no one was ever charged. The first was Dr. Francis Sweeney, a surgeon with the knowledge many believed necessary to mutilate the victims the way the killer did. (He was also a cousin of Congressman Martin L. Sweeney, a known political opponent of Ness.)

In August 1938, Dr. Sweeney was interrogated by Ness, two other men, and the inventor of the polygraph machine, Dr. Royal Grossman. By all accounts, Sweeney failed the polygraph test (several times), and Ness believed he had his man, but he was released due to lack of evidence.

Two days after the interrogation, on August 25, 1938, Sweeney checked himself into the Sandusky Veterans Hospital. He remained institutionalized at various facilities until his death in 1965. Because Sweeney voluntarily checked himself in, he could have left whenever he desired.

The other suspect was Frank Dolezal, who was arrested by private investigators on July 5, 1939, as a suspect in the murder of Florence Polillo, with whom he had lived for a time. While in custody, Dolezal confessed to killing Polillo, although some believe the confession was forced. Either way, Dolezal died under mysterious circumstances while incarcerated at the Cuyahoga County Jail before he could be charged.

As for Eliot Ness, some believe his inability to bring the Butcher to trial weighed on him for the rest of his life. Ness went to his grave without getting a conviction.

To this day, the case remains open.

Backwoods Butcher: Ed Gein

To find the story of one of the most gruesome killers in American history, you don't have to look far from Wisconsin. The terrifying tale of Ed Gein unfolded in the town of Plainfield.

✳   ✳   ✳   ✳

ED GEIN WAS the son of an overbearing mother who taught him that sex was sinful. When she died in 1945, he was a 39-year-old bachelor living alone in a rundown farmhouse in rural Plainfield.

After his mother's death, Gein developed a morbid fascination with the medical atrocities performed by the Nazis during World War II. This fascination led him to dig up female corpses from cemeteries, take them home, and perform his own experiments on them, such as removing the skin from the body and draping it over a tailor's dummy. He was also fascinated with female genitalia, which he would fondle and, on occasion, stuff into women's panties and wear around the house.

He soon tired of decomposing corpses and set out in search of fresher bodies. Most of his victims were women around his mother's age. He went a step too far, however, when he abducted the mother of local sheriff's deputy Frank Worden. Learning that his missing mother had been seen with Gein on the day of her disappearance, Worden went to the Gein house to question the recluse. What he found there defied belief. Human heads sat as prize trophies in the living room along with a belt made from human nipples and a chair completely upholstered in human skin. But for Worden, the worst sight was in the woodshed. Strung up by the feet was the headless body of his mother. Her torso had been slit open, and her heart was found on a plate in the dining room.

Gein confessed but couldn't recall how many people he'd killed. He told detectives that he liked to dress up in the carved-out torsos of his victims and pretend to be his mother. He spent ten years in an insane asylum before he was judged fit to stand trial. He was found guilty, but criminally insane, and died in 1984, at age 77.

The Black Dahlia Murder Mystery

One of the most baffling murder mysteries in U.S. history began innocently enough on the morning of January 15, 1947. Betty Bersinger was walking with her young daughter in the Leimert Park area of Los Angeles, when she spotted something lying in a vacant lot that caused her blood to run cold. She ran to a nearby house and called the police. Officers Wayne Fitzgerald and Frank Perkins arrived on the scene shortly after 11:00 A.M.

✳ ✳ ✳ ✳

A Grisly Discovery

LYING ONLY SEVERAL feet from the road, in plain sight, was the naked body of a young woman. Her body had numerous cuts and abrasions, including a knife wound from ear to ear that resembled a ghoulish grin. Even more horrific was that her body had been completely severed at the midsection, and the two halves had been placed as if they were part of some morbid display. That's what disturbed officers the most: The killer appeared to have carefully posed the victim close to the street because he wanted people to find his grotesque handiwork.

Something else that troubled the officers was that even though the body had been brutally violated and desecrated, there was very little blood found at the scene. The only blood evidence recovered was a possible bloody footprint and an empty cement package with a spot of blood on it. In fact, the body was so clean that it appeared to have just been washed.

Shortly before removing the body, officers scoured the area for a possible murder weapon, but none was recovered. A coroner later determined that the cause of death was from hemorrhage and shock due to a concussion of the brain and lacerations of the face, probably from a very large knife.

Positive Identification

After a brief investigation, police were able to identify the deceased as Elizabeth Short, who was born in Hyde Park, Massachusetts, on July 29, 1924. At age 19, Short had moved to California to live with her father, but she moved out and spent the next few years moving back and forth between California, Florida, and Massachusetts. In July 1946, Short returned to California to see Lt. Gordon Fickling, a former boyfriend, who was stationed in Long Beach. For the last six months of her life, Short lived in an assortment of hotels, rooming houses, and private homes. She was last seen a week before her body was found, which made police very interested in finding out where and with whom she spent her final days.

The Black Dahlia Is Born

As police continued their investigation, reporters jumped all over the story and began referring to the unknown killer by names such as "sex-crazed maniac" and even "werewolf." Short herself was also given a nickname: the Black Dahlia. Reporters said it was a name friends had called her as a play on the movie *The Blue Dahlia*, which had recently been released. However, others contend Short was never called the Black Dahlia while she was alive; it was just something reporters made up for a better story. Either way, it wasn't long before newspapers around the globe were splashing front-page headlines about the horrific murder of the Black Dahlia.

Still Unknown

As time wore on, hundreds of police officers were assigned to the Black Dahlia investigation. They combed the streets, interviewing people and following leads. Although police interviewed thousands of potential suspects—and dozens even confessed to the murder—to this day, no one has ever officially been charged with the crime. More than 60 years and several books and movies after the crime, the Elizabeth Short murder case is still listed as "open." We are no closer to knowing who killed Short or why than when her body was first discovered.

There is one bright note to this story. In February 1947, perhaps as a result of the Black Dahlia case, the state of California became the first state to pass a law requiring all convicted sex offenders to register themselves.

Partners in Murder

Some will tell you that people are just born bad, while others think society is responsible. In the case of 24-year-old Murl Daniels, his turn for the worst came from a chance encounter inside an institution meant to rehabilitate him: the Mansfield Reformatory in Ohio.

❋ ❋ ❋ ❋

IN 1948, WHILE serving time at Mansfield Reformatory for a robbery conviction, Murl Daniels was introduced to another inmate, John West, who was incarcerated for stealing an automobile. The two quickly became friends and started discussing all the robberies they could commit together once they were released. According to legend, Daniels and West also made a pact to hunt down and kill all the prison guards and officials they felt had done them wrong.

The Rampage Begins

By July, both Daniels and West had been released. They wasted no time getting started on their new partnership in crime, beginning by holding up Columbus-area bars and taverns. While the two men always carried guns with them, for the first few robberies, they never fired a shot. That all changed when Daniels and West burst into a Columbus tavern owned by Earl Ambrose and shot him to death duringtheir robbery attempt.

Perhaps it was that first taste of blood that set them off. Regardless, after the Ambrose murder, Daniels and West continued their murderous spree and headed north to Mansfield. It is believed the duo's first target was to be a Mansfield guard named Harris, but they didn't know where he lived. They intended to get the address from Harris's supervisor and the superintendent of the prison's farm, John Niebel. Since Niebel also lived on that farm, Daniels and West knew just how to get there.

Cold-Blooded Murder

On the evening of July 21, 1948, Harris and West snuck into the farmhouse and dragged Niebel, his wife, and his 20-year-old daughter from their beds. After forcing the entire family to strip naked, the pair led them out into a field, where all three were shot to death. Daniels and West then fled, abandoning their plan to track down Harris.

The following day, neighbors discovered the bodies of the Niebel family. It didn't take long for authorities to determine that Daniels and West were the men they were looking for. They began the largest manhunt in Ohio history up to that time.

Surprisingly, the killers didn't immediately try to flee Ohio for a more anonymous environment. Rather, they only headed as far north as Cleveland, where they continued their rampage, stealing cars and often shooting and killing the owners in the process. Local newspapers quickly got wind of the pair's crime spree, nicknaming them the Mad Dog Killers.

The End of the Road

When Daniels and West finally decided to get the heck out of Ohio, it was too late. On July 24, the pair were met by a police roadblock as they closed in on the state line. While Daniels was willing to give up quietly, West would not go down without a fight. He opened fire on the officers lining the roadblock and was finally shot dead. Daniels was arrested without incident, thus ending a two-week killing spree that claimed the lives of six innocent victims.

Daniels was put on trial for the murders of the Niebel family, found guilty on all counts, and sentenced to death. He met the Ohio State Penitentiary electric chair on January 3, 1949. He was only 24 years old.

Writing What You Know

In 1994, fans of novelist Anne Perry's Victorian murder mysteries were shocked to learn that the best-selling writer knew her topic a little too well.

✳ ✳ ✳ ✳

Best Friends

IT STARTED OUT innocently enough: Juliet Hulme arrived in New Zealand in 1948, where she met Pauline Parker. Sixteen-year-old Parker and fifteen-year-old Hulme quickly became best friends, bonding particularly over their shared experience of serious illness and its related isolation. As a young girl, Parker had suffered from osteomyelitis, an infection of the bone marrow that required several painful surgeries. Hulme, meanwhile, had recurring bouts of respiratory ailments, culminating with tuberculosis.

Intelligent and imaginative, the two girls created an increasingly violent fantasy life they called the "Fourth World," which was peopled with fairy-tale princes and Hollywood stars they dubbed the "saints." They wrote constantly, sure their stories were their ticket to the Hollywood of their imagination. At night, the girls would sneak outside to act out stories about the characters they had created.

No Matter What

In 1954, Hulme's parents separated. As her father prepared to return to England, Hulme's parents decided to send Juliet to live with relatives in South Africa. Not only would the climate be better for her health, they reasoned, but also the move would bring an end to a relationship that both girls' parents felt had grown too intense. Ever fantasizing, Hulme and Parker convinced themselves that Parker was also moving to South Africa with Hulme. Not surprisingly, Mrs. Parker refused to allow it. Determined to stay together, the girls decided to kill Parker's mother and flee to America, where they planned to sell their writing and work in the movies that played such an important role in their fantasy life.

On June 22, the girls went on what they described as a farewell outing to Victoria Park with Mrs. Parker. There, they bludgeoned Mrs. Parker to death with half a brick tied in a stocking. The girls expected the woman to die after a single blow so they could blame the death on a fall, but they were horrifyingly wrong—it took 45 blows to kill her. The hysterical girls then ran back to a park kiosk, screaming and covered in blood. The girls' story that Mrs. Parker had slipped and fallen rapidly disintegrated after the police arrived and found the murder weapon in the surrounding woods.

"Incurably Bad"

The trial, with its titillating accusations of lesbianism and insanity, grabbed international headlines, not only because of the brutality of the murder, but also because of the excerpts from Parker's diary that were used as evidence. The diary revealed the intensity of the relationship between the two girls and the fantasy world they inhabited. The diary also made it clear that the murder, flippantly described in its pages as "moider," was premeditated. The entry for June 22 was titled "The Day of the Happy Event."

Parker and Hulme were found guilty following a six-day trial during which the Crown Prosecutor described them as "not incurably insane, but incurably bad." Because they were under 18 and considered juveniles, they could not be given a capital sentence. Instead, they were sentenced to separate prisons for an unspecified term. After five years, they were released on the condition that they never contact each other again.

Hulme returned to England and later took her stepfather's name, Perry. She also changed her first name; as Anne Perry, she went on to write dozens of popular mysteries, many of them falling into the detective fiction and historical murder-mystery genres. Parker, meanwhile, lives in obscurity in an English village.

The murders were fairly forgotten, at least for a time. Years later, Perry's true identity was uncovered as a result of the publicity surrounding the 1994 release of the movie *Heavenly Creatures*, directed by Peter Jackson. The film, starring Kate Winslet as Hulme, focused on the events leading to the murder.

Perry was upset about the film. "It's like having some disfigurement and being stripped naked and set up in the High Street for everybody to walk by and pay their penny and have a look," she told *The New York Times*. "I would like to put my clothes on and go home, please, be like anybody else."

Crime and Punishment

This tale of greed and mass murder ushered in a new era of forensic science.

✳ ✳ ✳ ✳

Love's Labor Lost

JACK GRAHAM'S MOTHER, Daisie King, knew her only son was no angel, but she must have hoped he'd change his ways: Barely into his 20s, Graham had little patience for lawful employment, and he'd already been convicted of running illegal booze and check forgery. It's thought that King paid for her son's lawyer and anted up $2,500 in court-ordered restitution on the forgery convictions. By 1953, however, it seemed that Graham was settling down. He married and by 1955 had two children. His mother, a successful businesswoman, bought a house in Colorado for the young couple, built a drive-in restaurant, and installed Graham as its manager.

But the drive-in lost money. Graham blamed his mother's meddling in the management for the loss, but he later admitted he had skimmed receipts. He also confessed to vandalizing the place twice, once by smashing the front window and the second time by rigging a gas explosion to destroy equipment he'd used as security for a personal loan. A new pickup truck Graham bought himself mysteriously stalled on a railway track with predictable results. This too proved to be an attempt at insurance fraud.

Flight to Doom

In the fall of 1955, King wanted to see her daughter in Alaska, and she prepared for her trip there via Portland and Seattle. On November 1, Graham saw her off on United Air Flight 629. Eleven minutes after takeoff, the plane exploded in the sky. Forty-four people died, including King.

Within 24 hours FBI fingerprint experts were at the crash site to help identify bodies. The painstaking task of gathering wreckage from over a three-mile trail of scraps started. By November 7, Civil Aeronautics investigators concluded sabotage was the probable cause of the disaster.

Criminal investigators joined the FBI technical teams. Families of passengers and crew members were interviewed while technicians reassembled the plane's midsection where the explosion likely occurred. In the course of sifting through wreckage, bomb fragments and explosives residue were identified.

Avalanche of Evidence

Inevitably, investigators took an interest in Graham. Not only would he receive a substantial inheritance from his mother's estate, he had also taken out a $37,500 travel insurance policy on her. Moreover, he had a criminal record, and according to witnesses, a history of heated arguments with his mother.

Graham was first interviewed on November 10, and again over the following two days. In a search of his property on

November 12, agents discovered a roll of primer cord in a shirt pocket and a copy of the travel insurance policy secreted in a small box. Circumstantial evidence contradicted his statements, including that provided by his wife, half-sister, and acquaintances.

Finally, Graham admitted he'd built a bomb and placed it in his mother's luggage. On November 14, he was arraigned on charges of sabotage. At the time the charge did not carry a death penalty, so he was brought into court on November 17 and charged with first-degree murder.

A Case of Firsts

Notwithstanding the confession, investigators continued to gather forensic evidence, putting together what may have been the most scientifically detailed case in U.S. history up to that date. The case had other firsts as well. It was the first case of mass murder in the United States via airplane explosion. Graham's trial, which began on April 16, 1956, also marked the first time TV cameras were permitted to air a live broadcast of a courtroom trial.

On May 5, 1956, the jury needed only 69 minutes to find Graham guilty. On January 11, 1957, he was executed at Colorado State Penitentiary, remorseless to the end.

Murder in the Heartland

If you ever find yourself in northwestern Kansas looking for the village of Holcomb, don't blink or you'll miss it. It's the kind of place where nothing ever seems to happen. And yet, back in 1959, Holcomb became one of the most notorious locations in the history of American crime.

✳   ✳   ✳   ✳

"Everyone Loved the Clutters..."

IN THE 1940S, successful businessman Herb Clutter built a house on the outskirts of town and started raising a family with his wife, Bonnie. The Clutters quickly became one of the most popular families in the small village, due largely to their friendly nature. People would be hard-pressed to find someone who had a bad word to say about them.

On the morning of Sunday, November 15, 1959, Clarence Ewalt drove his daughter Nancy to the Clutter house so she could go to church with the family as she did every week. She was a good friend of the Clutters' teenage daughter, who was also named Nancy. Nancy Ewalt knocked on the door several times but got no response. She went around to a side door, looked around and called out, but no one answered. At that point, Mr. Ewalt drove his daughter to the Kidwell house nearby and picked up Susan Kidwell, another friend. Susan tried phoning the Clutters, but no one answered. So the three drove back to the Clutter house. The two girls entered the house through the kitchen door and went to Nancy Clutter's room, where they discovered her dead body.

Unspeakable Acts

Sheriff Robinson was the first officer to respond. He entered the house with another officer and a neighbor, Larry Hendricks. According to Nancy Ewalt, the three men went first to Nancy Clutter's room, where they found the teenager dead of an apparent gunshot wound to the back of the head. She was lying on her bed facing the wall with her hands and ankles bound. Down the hallway in the master bedroom, the body of Bonnie Clutter was discovered. Like her daughter, Bonnie's hands and feet were also bound, and she appeared to have been shot point-blank in the head.

In the basement of the Clutter home, police found the bodies of Herb Clutter and his 15-year-old son, Kenyon. Like his mother and sister, Kenyon had been shot in the head; his body was tied to a sofa.

As atrocious as the other three murders were, Herb Clutter appeared to have suffered the most. Like the others, he had been shot in the head, but there were slash marks on his throat, and his mouth had been taped shut. And although his body was lying on the floor of the basement, there was a rope hanging from the ceiling suggesting that, at some point, he may have been hung from the rope.

Dewey's Task Force

Alvin A. Dewey of the Kansas City Bureau of Investigation (KBI) was put in charge of the investigation. Even though Dewey was a police veteran and had seen his fair share of violent murders, the Clutter murders hit him hard. Herb Clutter was a friend, and their families had attended church together.

At his first press conference after the bodies were discovered, Dewey announced that he was heading up a 19-man task force that would not rest until they found the person or persons responsible for the horrific murders. But he knew it was going to be a tough case. For one, the amount of blood and gore at the scene suggested that revenge might have been the motive. But the Clutters were upstanding members of the community and loved by all, as evidenced by the nearly 600 mourners who showed up for the family's funeral service. The idea that the murders were the result of a robbery gone bad was also being pursued, but Dewey had his doubts about that, as well. For him, it just didn't fit that the entire Clutter family would have walked in on a robbery and then been killed the way they had. For that reason, Dewey began to believe that there had been more than one killer.

A Secret Clue

There was not a lot of evidence left behind at the crime scene. Not only was the murder weapon missing, but whoever pulled the trigger had taken the time to pick up the spent shells. However, Dewey did have an ace up his sleeve, and it was something not even the press was made aware of. Herb Clutter's body had been found lying on a piece of cardboard. On that cardboard were impressions from a man's boot. Both of the victims found in the basement, Herb and Kenyon Clutter, were barefoot, which meant the boots may have belonged to the killer. It wasn't much to go on, but for Dewey, it was a start. Still, as Christmas 1959 crept closer, the case was starting to come to a standstill. Then, finally, a big break came from an unlikely place: Lansing Prison.

A Break in the Case

The man who would break the case wide open was Lansing Prison inmate Floyd Wells. Earlier in the year, Wells had been sentenced to Lansing for breaking and entering. His cellmate was a man named Richard Hickock. One night, the two men were talking, and Hickock mentioned that even though he was going to be released from prison soon, he had nowhere to go. Wells told him that back in the late 1940s, he had been out looking for work and stumbled across a kind, rich man named Clutter who would often hire people to work around his farm. Once he mentioned Herb Clutter, Hickock seemed obsessed with the man. He wouldn't stop asking Wells to tell him everything he knew about Clutter. How old was he? Was he strong? How many others lived in the house with him?

One night, Hickock calmly stated that when he was released, he and his friend Perry Smith were going to rob the Clutters and murder anyone in the house. Wells said that Hickock even went so far as to explain exactly how he would tie everyone up and shoot them one at a time. Wells further stated that he never believed Hickock was serious until he heard the news that the Clutters had been murdered in exactly the way Hickock had described.

Captures and Confessions

On December 30, after attempting to cash a series of bad checks, Hickock and Smith were arrested in Las Vegas. Among the items seized from the stolen car they were driving was a pair of boots belonging to Hickock. When confronted with the fact that his boots matched the imprint at the crime scene,

Hickock broke down and admitted he had been there during the murders. However, he swore that Perry Smith had killed the whole family and that he had tried to stop him.

When Smith was informed that his partner was putting all the blame on him, he decided it was in his best interest to explain his side. Smith gave a very detailed version of how Hickock had devised a plan to steal the contents of a safe in Herb Clutter's home office. The pair had arrived under cover of darkness at approximately 12:30 A.M. Finding no safe in the office, the pair went up into the master bedroom, where they surprised Herb Clutter, who was sleeping alone in bed. When told they had come for the contents of the safe, Herb told them to take whatever they wanted, but he said there was no safe in the house. Not convinced, Smith and Hickock rounded up the family and tied them up, hoping to get one of them to reveal the location of the safe. When that failed, Smith and Hickock prepared to leave. But when Hickock started bragging about how he had been ready to kill the entire family, Smith called his bluff, and an argument ensued. At that point, Smith said he snapped and stabbed Herb Clutter in the throat. Seeing the man in such pain, Smith said he then shot him to end his suffering. Smith then turned the gun on Kenyon. Smith ended his statement by saying that he'd made Hickock shoot and kill the two women.

The Verdict

The murder trial of Richard Hickock and Perry Smith began on March 23, 1960, at Finney County Courthouse. Five days later, the case was handed over to the jury, who needed only 40 minutes to reach their verdict: Both men were guilty of all charges. They recommended that Hickock and Smith be hanged for their crimes.

Sitting in the front row when the verdicts were read was Truman Capote, who had been writing a series of articles about the murders for *The New Yorker*. Those articles would later inspire his best-selling novel *In Cold Blood*.

After several appeals, both men were executed at Lansing Prison, one right after the other, on April 14, 1965. Richard Hickock was the first to be hanged, with Perry Smith going to the same gallows roughly 30 minutes later. Agent Alvin Dewey was present for both executions.

Several years after the murders, in an attempt to heal the community, a stained-glass window at the First Methodist Church in Garden City, Kansas, was posthumously dedicated to the memory of the Clutter family. Despite an initial impulse to bulldoze the Clutter house, it was left standing and today is a private residence.

The Moors Murderers: Britain's Most Hated Couple

A killing spree fascinated and horrified England in the 1960s. Saddleworth Moor had always had an ominous air to it, but tensions suddenly got much, much worse.

✳ ✳ ✳ ✳

BURYING A BODY in highly acidic soil is smart—the flesh decays faster, making it harder for police to tell exactly what happened to the victim. That's what Ian Brady and Myra Hindley were counting on when they buried their victims in an acidic grassy moor.

Normal and Abnormal Childhoods

Myra Hindley was born in 1942 just outside of Manchester. She was a normal, happy girl and even a popular babysitter among families in her neighborhood. At age 15, she left school. Three years later, she secured a job as a typist for a small chemical company. There she met Ian Brady, a 23-year-old stock clerk, and her future partner in life and crime.

Born to a single mother, Brady was given to a nearby family at a young age when his mom, a waitress, could no longer afford to take care of him. In school, he was an angry loner who bullied younger children and tortured animals.

At the chemical company, Hindley became enamored with Brady, an intense young man fascinated with Nazis and capable of reading *Mein Kampf* in German. In her diary, Hindley gushed that she hoped he would love her, although Brady was decidedly distant. It wasn't until a year after they met that he asked her on a date—at the company's Christmas party.

An Off-kilter Romance

Brady's preoccupation with Nazism, torture philosophies, and sadomasochism didn't bother Hindley, and as the couple became closer, they began to photograph themselves in disturbing poses. It became evident that Brady had found a companion to help turn his twisted fantasies into reality: Between 1963 and 1965, the pair murdered five children and buried their bodies in the Saddleworth Moors, leading the gruesome acts to be called the "Moors Murders."

The Murders Begin

Their first victim, 16-year-old Pauline Reade, was on her way to a dance on July 12, 1963, when a young woman offered her a ride. Presumably assuming that it was okay to take a ride from a fellow female—Myra Hindley—Reade accepted. Along the way, Hindley suddenly pulled the car over to look for a missing glove; Reade helpfully joined Hindley in looking. Meanwhile, Brady had followed the car on his motorcycle. He snuck up behind Reade as she was looking for the glove and smashed her skull with a shovel. Reade's body was later found with her throat slashed so deeply that she was nearly decapitated. Unfortunately, hers wasn't nearly the grisliest death in the Moors Murders.

Four months later, on November 23, 1963, at a small-town market, Hindley asked 12-year-old John Kilbride to escort her home with some packages. He agreed. Brady was hidden in the backseat, and Kilbride became victim number two.

Keith Bennett had turned 12 only four days before June 16, 1964, when he encountered Hindley. Walking to his grandmother's house, he accepted a ride from Hindley, who again claimed to need help finding a glove. This time, instead of waiting in the car, she watched as Brady murdered the boy.

As the murderous couple stalked their fourth victim, their bloodlust swelled. On Boxing Day, an English holiday that falls on December 26, the couple lured ten-year-old Lesley Ann Downey to their home. Sadly, their youngest victim suffered the most gruesome and memorable fate. The couple took pornographic photos of the gagged child and recorded 16 minutes of audio of Downey crying, screaming, vomiting, and begging for her mother.

Expanding the Circle

But their treacherous ways reached a pinnacle when, perhaps bored with each other, they tried to get Hindley's 17-year-old brother-in-law, David Smith, in on the act. Like Brady, Smith was a hoodlum, not at all liked by Hindley's family. Smith and Brady had previously bonded by bragging about doing bad things, including murder. Until October 6, 1965, however, Smith assumed it was all a joke.

The couple invited Smith to their house, and he waited in the kitchen while Hindley went to fetch Brady. Upon hearing a scream, he ran to the living room to see Brady carrying an ax and what he perceived to be a life-size doll. It wasn't a doll, of course, but 17-year-old Edward Evans. Smith watched as Brady hacked the last bit of life out of the boy. Afraid that he would be next, Smith helped the couple clean up the mess as if nothing had happened. He waited, terrified, until early the next morning and then snuck out and went to the police.

Facing the Consequences

This wretched crime spree shook Great Britain. The trial of Myra Hindley and Ian Brady lasted 14 days, during which dozens of photos were submitted as evidence, including pictures of the couple in torturous sexual poses. Hindley claimed that she was unconscious when most of the photos were taken and that Brady had used them to blackmail her into abetting his crimes. That claim was quickly dismissed, as police investigators who examined the photos testified that she appeared to be fully aware of what was going on and seemed to be enjoying herself.

At the time of the trial, the bodies of Lesley Ann Downey, John Kilbride, and Edward Evans had been discovered, all buried in the moor. Great Britain had just revoked the death penalty, so Ian Brady was sentenced to three sequential life sentences for the murders. Myra Hindley was charged with two of the murders as well as aiding and abetting. She was sentenced to life in prison.

The couple suffered miserably behind bars. After serving nearly 20 years, Brady was declared insane and committed to a mental hospital. Hindley was so viciously attacked that she had to have plastic surgery on her face. In the 1980s, the couple admitted to the murders of Pauline Reade and Keith Bennett and led police to Reade's grave. Hindley claimed remorse and appealed many times for her freedom. She received an open degree from a university, found God in prison, and even enlisted the help of a popular, devout Roman Catholic politician, Lord Longford, in her bid for release. But the high court of England denied her requests. Although she fought for her freedom up until her death in 2002, perhaps Hindley knew deep down that she'd never be free—she even called herself Britain's most hated woman. The BBC agreed and ran the quote, along with her infamous mug shot and jail photos, as her obituary.

Death from on High

When a troubled man exacted revenge from a lofty perch, a stunned nation watched in horror and disbelief. What could cause a man to kill indiscriminately? Why hadn't anyone seen it coming? Could such a thing happen again? Decades later the mystery continues.

✳ ✳ ✳ ✳

IN AN AMERICA strained by an escalating war in Vietnam, the 1966 headline still managed to shock the senses. The "Texas Tower Sniper" had killed his mother and wife before snuffing out the lives of 13 innocents on the University of Texas (UT) campus at Austin. At least the Vietnam conflict offered up motives. Like most wars, battle lines had been drawn, and a steady buildup of threats and tensions had preceded the violence. But here, no such declarations were issued. Bullets came blazing out of the sky for no apparent reason. After the victims breathed their last and the nightmare drew to a close, a stunned populace was left with one burning question: Why?

Undercurrents

Charles Whitman appeared to have enjoyed many of life's advantages. He hailed from a prominent family in Lake Worth, Florida, and from outside appearances the future was Whitman's to make or break. But friction with his abusive father found Whitman seeking escape. After a brutal incident in which he returned home from a party drunk only to be beaten—and nearly drowned in a swimming pool—by his father, the 18-year-old Whitman enlisted in the U.S. Marines. He served for five years, distinguishing himself with a Sharpshooters Badge. After that he attended college at UT. During that period, Whitman also married his girlfriend, Kathy Leissner.

Whitman's life plan appeared to be straightforward. After obtaining a scholarship, he would seek an engineering degree, hoping to follow it up with acceptance at officer's candidate school. But things didn't go as planned.

Opportunity Lost

After leaving the military, Whitman worked toward a variety of goals in and out of school. Unfortunately, the ex-Marine's efforts were fraught with failure, and his frustrations multiplied. In the spring of 1966, Whitman sought the help of UT psychiatrist Dr. Maurice Dean Heatly. In a moment of ominous foretelling, Whitman remarked that he fantasized "going up on the [campus] tower with a deer rifle and shooting people." The doctor, having heard similar threats in the past, was mostly unimpressed. Since Whitman hadn't previously exhibited violent behavior, Heatly took his statement as nothing more than an idle threat.

Surprise Assault

During the wee hours of August 1, 1966, Whitman's demons finally won out, and his killing spree began. For reasons still uncertain, the murderer kicked off his blood quest by first stabbing his mother in her apartment and his wife while she slept. Both died from the injuries.

Whitman then made his way to the UT campus and ascended the soon-to-be infamous tower. At his side he had enough provisions, weapons, and ammo to hole up indefinitely. Just before noon, he lifted a high-powered rifle and began shooting. He picked off victims one by one from the observation deck of the 307-foot-tall tower. Whitman's sharpshooting prowess (he once scored 215 points out of a possible 250 in target practice) added to the danger. By the time people finally realized what was happening, quite a few had already been cut down.

Lives Cut Short

As the attacks progressed, Austin police hatched a plan. Officers Ramiro Martinez and Houston McCoy snuck into the tower, surprising Whitman. Both sides exchanged fire. The 96-minute attack ended with two fatal shots to Whitman's head, compliments of McCoy's 12-gauge shotgun. The horror was over. In its ultimate wake lay 16 dead and 31 wounded. An autopsy performed on Whitman revealed a brain tumor that may have caused him to snap.

The authorities later found a note at his home. Its matter-of-fact tone is chilling to this day: "I imagine it appears that I brutaly [sic] kill [sic] both of my loved ones. I was only trying to do a quick thorough job. If my life insurance policy is valid... please pay off all my debts... Donate the rest anonymously to a mental health foundation. Maybe research can prevent further tragedies of this type."

Who Was the Zodiac Killer?

On the evening of December 20, 1968, 17-year-old David Faraday and 16-year-old Betty Lou Jensen headed out on their first date in Benicia, California. Late that night, a passing motorist noticed two lifeless bodies lying next to a car at a "lover's lane" parking spot. It was Faraday and Jensen, who had both been shot to death. The unwitting couple became the first official victims of the Zodiac Killer, who would spend the next six years taunting the police and frightening the public.

✳   ✳   ✳   ✳

Senseless Killings

THE MURDERS OF Faraday and Jensen stumped investigators. There appeared to be no motive, and forensic data of the time yielded few clues. Why would someone gun down two teenagers who were merely out having fun? No leads developed, and the case quickly grew cold.

Months later, just before midnight on July 4, 1969, another young couple, Michael Mageau and Darlene Ferrin, were in their car at Blue Rock Springs Park in Vallejo, about four miles from where Faraday and Jensen were murdered. As they sat in the car, another car pulled up behind them and the driver exited, approaching their car with a flashlight. The stranger shined the bright light in their faces, and then, without warning, began shooting. When it was all over, Ferrin was dead; but Mageau, despite being shot three times, somehow survived to speak to what had happened.

About an hour later, at 12:40 A.M. on July 5, a man called the Vallejo Police Department saying he wanted to "report a murder," giving the dispatcher the location of Mageau and Ferrin's car. Using a calm, low voice, he also confessed that he had "killed those kids last year." It was the first contact anyone had with the killer, but it wouldn't be the last.

Clues and Codes

Mageau was able to describe his attacker as a white male with curly brown hair, around 200 pounds, 5 feet 8 inches tall, in his late 20s. It was little to go on, but it was a start. Then, on August 1, three Northern California newspapers, the *Vallejo Times Herald*, *San Francisco Chronicle*, and *San Francisco Examiner* all received virtually identical handwritten letters that contained crime details that only the killer could know. Each newspaper also received one third of a three-part coded cipher that the writer claimed would reveal his identity. The letters all ended with the same symbol: a circle with a cross through it.

The killer demanded that the ciphers be published on the front pages of each paper, otherwise he threatened to go on another killing spree. But investigators were not convinced that the letters came from the actual killer, so the *Chronicle* published its part of the code on page four, along with a quote from the Vallejo chief of police asking for more proof.

The promised killing spree never materialized, and all three sections of the cipher were published over the next week. Then, on August 7, the *Examiner* received another letter that began with, "Dear Editor This is the Zodiac speaking." The killer now had a nickname which would soon become infamous. In the letter, the Zodiac Killer described details of the crimes known only to police, and taunted them for not yet solving his code, saying that once they did, they "will have me."

The very next day, a high school teacher named Donald Harden and his wife, Bettye, solved the cipher. The disturbing message began with the words "I like killing people because it is so much fun." The Zodiac then said that he was killing people to act as his "slaves" in the afterlife, in a rambling message full of misspellings and typos. Despite the killer's previous taunt, nowhere did the note reveal, or even hint, at the killer's identity.

A Killer Unchecked

On September 27, 1969, the Zodiac Killer struck again. A man wearing a black hood with a circle and cross symbol on his chest attacked college students Bryan Hartnell and Cecelia Shepard as they were picnicking at Lake Berryessa, tying them up and then stabbing them repeatedly. The attacker then drew the circle and cross symbol on Hartnell's car, along with the dates of each murder. Once again, he called the police—this time the Napa County Sheriff's Office—to report his own crime. And once again, the killer left behind a witness, when Hartnell survived the attack. Police were able to lift a palm print from the pay phone where the killer had called the police, but were unable to match it to a perpetrator.

Even with two witnesses, a description of the attacker, fingerprints, and handwritten letters, the identity of the Zodiac Killer remained frustratingly elusive. The last confirmed Zodiac Killer murder occurred on October 11, 1969, when he shot taxi driver Paul Stine in the head and then ripped off part of Stine's bloodstained shirt. The Zodiac Killer then sent another letter to the *Chronicle*, along with a piece of Stine's shirt, in which he mocked police for failing to catch him and threatened to shoot school children on a bus.

More Letters, But No Answers

Over the next few years, the Zodiac Killer kept up a strange correspondence with Bay Area newspapers, hinting at numerous other victims, making bomb threats, and demanding that people begin wearing buttons featuring his circle and cross symbol. Some of the letters included codes or strange references, including a 340-character cipher sent to the *Chronicle* on November 8, 1969, that has never been solved. He would often end his letters with a "score" claiming "SFPD = 0" while the Zodiac's "score" continued to climb, suggesting he continued his killing spree.

The final letter thought to be from the Zodiac Killer was sent on January 29, 1974; the killer then simply seemed to disappear. But the investigation into his identity continues to this day. More than 2,500 suspects have been considered, including the "Unibomber," Ted Kaczynski, but no one has ever been arrested. Law enforcement agencies hope that modern DNA testing may one day yield clues to his identity. Until then, the closing line of the Zodiac's final letter still haunts investigators: "Me – 37; SFPD – 0."

The Guru

He is one of the most notorious criminals the country has ever seen. But surprisingly, although Charles Manson spent most of his life in prison, he never actually killed anyone with his own hands; he simply convinced others to do his bidding.

❋ ❋ ❋ ❋

A Troubled Childhood

CHARLES MANSON HAD it rough right from the start. He was born Charles Milles Maddox on November 12, 1934, in Cincinnati, Ohio, to his 16-year-old mother, Kathleen Maddox. His biological father was nowhere to be found, so his mother married William Eugene Manson just before his birth. But his teenage mother wasn't ready to settle down with a baby and husband, and she often left her young son with various babysitters while she went out to binge drink.

When Manson was five years old, his mother was arrested for assault and robbery, and spent the next three years in prison. Manson was sent to live with an aunt and uncle until his mother's release from prison, then moved with her to West Virginia, where she continued to drink and run into trouble with the law. With such a tumultuous childhood, perhaps it's no surprise that Manson's first serious offense occurred when he was only nine years old. Known for his frequent truancy, the young Manson set his school on fire. This resulted in a stint at a boarding school for delinquent boys, which did nothing to stop his newfound criminal streak.

A Need for Attention

Over the next decade, Manson lived a life of lawlessness, first engaging in petty theft and then moving on to more serious offenses including car thefts and armed robberies. He received his first prison sentence—three years for stealing a car and failing to appear in court—in 1956. Another prison sentence followed in 1960, after Manson attempted to cash a forged check and then later took two women to New Mexico for the purpose of prostitution. While in prison, authorities noted that he had a "tremendous drive to call attention to himself." They would soon discover that their assessment was correct.

When Manson was released from prison in 1967, he moved to San Francisco and rented an apartment with a female acquaintance. Over the next few months, he allowed more and more women to join them, until 19 women were living in the apartment with Manson. The group, often under the influence of LSD and other hallucinogenic drugs, considered him their "guru," and he began teaching his followers disturbing prophecies and implying that he was Jesus.

Dysfunctional "Family"

At he continued to gain followers, Manson moved "the Manson Family" to Spahn Ranch, a Los Angeles movie set that was no longer in use. He continued to prophesy to his followers, telling them that a race war would soon occur in the United States, and Armageddon was imminent. Even more unnerving, Manson began to believe that he himself was the key to unleashing the apocalypse.

Manson's plan was to purposely trigger the prophesied race war by killing white celebrities and pinning their murders on blacks. On August 8, 1969, he set his plan in motion. Four of Manson's followers were ordered to go to the house that actress Sharon Tate was renting, and to kill everyone inside. The resulting murders horrified the nation, as did the Manson-ordered murders of Leno and Rosemary LaBianca the next day.

Over the next few months, evidence pointing to many of Manson's Family members mounted, and on December 1, several of his followers were arrested. Manson was already in custody on suspicion of car theft, and the "guru" would never go free again. During the trial, neither Manson nor any of his followers showed remorse for their actions, and on January 25, 1971, Manson was convicted of first-degree murder and sentenced to death. His sentence would later be commuted to life in prison when California abolished the death penalty in 1972. The leader of the murderous Manson Family died on November 19, 2017, at the age of 83, having spent four decades behind bars.

7 Grisly Crimes

Our TV screens are saturated with crime. Every night we witness more bizarre slayings and mayhem than the night before. Makes you wonder how far-fetched those scriptwriters will get. After all, real people don't commit those types of crimes, right? Wrong. In fact, the annals of history are crammed with crimes even more gruesome than anything seen on television. Here are some of the 20th century's wildest crimes.

✳ ✳ ✳ ✳

1. **Ed Kemper:** Ed Kemper had a genius IQ, but his appetite for murder took over at age 15 when he shot his grandparents because he wanted to see what it felt like. Nine years later, he'd done his time for that crime, and during 1972 and 1973, Kemper hit the California highways, picking up pretty students and killing them before taking the corpses back to his apartment, having sex with them, then dissecting them. He killed six women in that manner and then took an ax to his own mother, decapitating and raping her, then using her body as a dartboard. Still not satisfied, he killed one of his mother's friends as well. Upset that his crimes didn't garner the media attention he thought they warranted, Kemper confessed to police. He gleefully went into detail about his penchant for necrophilia and decapitation. He asked to be executed, but because capital punishment was suspended at the time, he got life imprisonment and remains incarcerated in California.

2. **Andrei Chikatilo:** Andrei Chikatilo was Russia's most notorious serial killer. The Rostov Ripper, as he came to be called, began his rampage in 1978 in the city of Shakhty, where he started abducting teenagers and subjecting them to unspeakable torture before raping and murdering them, and, often, cannibalizing their bodies. Authorities gave the crimes little attention, but as the body count grew, police

were forced to face the facts—Russia had a serial killer. Chikatilo was actually brought in for questioning when the police found a rope and butcher knife in his bag during a routine search, but he was released and allowed to continue his killing spree. In the end, he got careless and was arrested near the scene of his latest murder. Under interrogation, he confessed to 56 murders. During the trial, he was kept in a cage in the middle of the court, playing up the image of the deranged lunatic. It didn't help his cause, though. He was found guilty and executed with a shot to the back of the head on February 14, 1994.

3. **Cameron Hooker:** With the assistance of his wife, Janice, in May 1977 Cameron Hooker snatched a 20-year-old woman who was hitchhiking to a friend's house in northern California. He locked her in a wooden box that was kept under the bed he shared with Janice, who was well aware of what lay beneath. During the next seven years, Hooker repeatedly tortured, beaten, and sexually assaulted the young woman. Eventually, she was allowed out of the box to do household chores, but she was forced to wear a slave collar. As time went by, Hooker allowed his prisoner more and more freedom, even letting her get a part-time job. Janice's conscience finally got the best of her, and she helped the young woman escape. After seven years of hell, the prisoner simply got on a bus and left. Hooker was convicted and sentenced to 104 years in a box of his own.

4. **Andras Pandy:** Andras Pandy was a Belgian pastor who had eight children by two different wives. Between 1986 and 1989, his former wives and four of the children disappeared. Pandy tried to appease investigators by faking papers to show that they were living in Hungary. He even coerced other children into impersonating the missing ones. Then, under intense questioning, Pandy's daughter Agnes broke down. She told authorities that she had been held by her father as a teenage sex slave and then was forced to join

him in killing her family members, including her mother, brothers, stepmother, and stepsister. The bodies were chopped up, dissolved in drain cleaner, and flushed down the drain. Pandy was sentenced to life in prison, while Agnes received 21 years as an accomplice. Until his death in 2013, he still claimed that all of the missing family members are alive and well in Hungary.

5. **Harold Shipman:** The most prolific serial killer in modern history was British doctor Harold Shipman, who murdered up to 400 of his patients between 1970 and 1998. Shipman was a respected member of the community, but in March 1998, a colleague became alarmed at the high death rate among his patients. She went to the local coroner, who in turn went to the police. They investigated, but found nothing out of the ordinary. But when a woman named Kathleen Grundy died a few months later, it was revealed that she had cut her daughter Angela out of her will and, instead, bequeathed £386,000 to Shipman. Suspicious, Angela went to the police, who began another investigation. Kathleen Grundy's body was exhumed and examined, and traces of diamorphine (heroin) were found in her system. Shipman was arrested and charged with murder. When police examined his patient files more closely, they realized that Shipman was overdosing patients with diamorphine, then forging their medical records to state that they were in poor health. Shipman was found guilty and sentenced to 15 consecutive life sentences, but he hung himself in his cell in January 2004.

6. **Fred and Rose West:** In the early 1970s, a pattern developed in which young women were lured to the home of Fred and Rose West in Gloucester, England, subjected to sexual depravities, and then ritually slaughtered in the soundproof basement. The bodies were dismembered and disposed of under the cellar floor. As the number of victims increased, the garden became a secondary burial plot.

This became the final resting place of their own daughter, 16-year-old Heather, who was butchered in June 1983.

Police became increasingly concerned about the whereabouts of Heather. One day they decided to take the family joke that she was "buried under the patio" seriously. When they began excavating the property in June 1994, the number of body parts uncovered shocked the world. With overwhelming evidence stacked against him, Fred West committed suicide while in custody in 1995. Rose received life imprisonment.

7. **John Wayne Gacy:** In the mid-1960s, John Wayne Gacy was, by all outward appearances, a happily married Chicago-area businessman who doted on his two young children. But when Gacy was convicted of sodomy in 1968, he got ten years in jail, and his wife divorced him. Eighteen months later, Gacy was out on parole. He started a construction company, and in his spare time, he volunteered as a clown to entertain sick children. He also began picking up homeless male prostitutes. After taking them home, Gacy would beat, rape, and slaughter his victims before depositing the bodies in the crawl space underneath his house.

In 1978, an investigation into the disappearance of 15-year-old Robert Piest led police to Gacy, following reports that the two had been seen together on the night the boy disappeared. Suspicions were heightened when detectives uncovered Gacy's sodomy conviction, and a warrant was issued to search his home. Detectives found a piece of jewelry belonging to a boy who had disappeared a year before. They returned to the house with excavating equipment and they made a gruesome discovery.

Gacy tried to escape the death penalty with a tale of multiple personalities, but it didn't impress the jury. It took them only two hours to convict him of 33 murders. On May 10, 1994, he was put to death by lethal injection.

The Clean-Cut Killer

One of the most notorious serial killers in history, Ted Bundy confessed to killing 36 women, but the true number may be even higher. His murderous rampage spanned the country, from Seattle to Tallahassee.

✳ ✳ ✳ ✳

A Bright Future

AT THE TIME Ted Bundy was born, on November 24, 1946, having a child out of wedlock was often considered shameful. So his single mother, Eleanor Louise Cowell, gave birth to him at a home for unwed mothers in Burlington, Vermont, then allowed her parents to raise him as their son while she was considered his "sister." Cowell never admitted to the identity of Bundy's biological father, but when he was about three years old, she moved with him to Tacoma, Washington, and married his new stepfather, Johnny Bundy.

While Bundy showed some unusual behavior from an early age, such as a fascination with knives, he was also a good student with a seemingly bright future ahead of him. He had a few false starts after high school, bouncing between several universities and working minimum-wage jobs, but Bundy eventually settled at the University of Washington, where he became an honor student who earned a degree in psychology. He even worked at Seattle's Suicide Crisis Hotline Center, where coworkers described him as "empathetic."

A Serial Killer Is Born

Whether that "empathy" was a façade or not, one thing is certain: eventually, it disappeared altogether. Investigators were never able to pinpoint exactly when Bundy went from a promising honor student to a cold-blooded killer, but many believe it was around 1974. In January of that year, he snuck into a University of Washington student's apartment as she slept and viciously bludgeoned her with a metal bedframe. Although she survived, she was in a coma for ten days and sustained permanent physical and mental damage.

Frighteningly, over the next few months, female university students in Washington and Oregon began vanishing. Several witnesses described a man who always seemed to turn up in the area of the disappearances. He was young, had dark hair, drove a tan Volkswagen Beetle, and often had an arm in a sling or a cast on his leg. He would lure women by asking for help carrying books or loading boxes in his car. Police were able to create a composite sketch thanks to witness descriptions, and several people came forward with Bundy's name. His reign of terror might have ended there, but authorities simply thought the young man seemed too "clean cut" to be their perpetrator.

Stopping the Monster

By August 1974, the disappearances in the Pacific Northwest ended, but the same thing began to occur in Utah, Colorado, and Idaho when Bundy started attending the University of Utah Law School. A year later, Utah police caught a break when they stopped a tan Volkswagen Beetle suspiciously cruising a neighborhood early one morning. Inside, Bundy had a veritable "kidnapping kit," complete with ski mask, handcuffs, rope, crowbar, and ice pick. Bundy perfectly fit the description of the offender in a recent kidnapping case, and he was arrested. He was tried, convicted, and sentenced to 15 years in prison for kidnapping, but escaped after only a few months.

Now on the run, Bundy made his way across the country to Tallahassee, where he broke into a sorority house in the middle of the night, killing two women and leaving two others with terrible injuries. His final victim, a week later, was only 12 years old when she was murdered by Bundy. Police closed in on the serial killer, who had left a trail of evidence and witnesses throughout Florida, and who had no money, no car, and nowhere to run.

Bundy was tried in 1979 and 1980 for several murders and kidnappings, and sentenced to death by electrocution. Before his death, he confessed to dozens of murders and described how he not only killed the women, but would often return to their dead bodies, to bathe them, dress them, and, most disturbingly, engage in necrophilia. In accordance with his will, after he was executed on January 24, 1989, Bundy's ashes were scattered in the Cascade Mountains—the same area where he confessed to killing several women. In death, as in life, Ted Bundy continues to haunt his victims.

A Voice from Beyond the Grave

After the murder of Teresita Basa in the late 1970s, another woman began to speak in Basa's voice—saying things that only Teresita could have known—to help solve the mystery of her murder.

✳ ✳ ✳ ✳

IN FEBRUARY 1977, firemen broke into a burning apartment on North Pine Grove Avenue in Chicago. Beneath a pile of burning clothes, they found the naked body of 47-year-old Teresita Basa, a hospital worker who was said to be a member of the Filipino aristocracy. There were bruises on her neck and a kitchen knife was embedded in her chest. Her body was in a position that caused the police to suspect that she had been raped.

However, an autopsy revealed that she hadn't been raped; in fact, she was a virgin. Police were left without a single lead: They had no suspects and no apparent motive for the brutal murder. The solution would come from the strangest of all possible sources—a voice from beyond the grave.

"I Am Teresita Basa"

In the nearby suburb of Evanston, shortly after Teresita's death, Remibios Chua started going into trances during which she spoke in Tagalog in a slow, clear voice that said, "I am Teresita Basa." Although Remibios had worked at the same hospital as Teresita, they worked different shifts, and the only time they are known to have even crossed paths was during a new-employee orientation. Remibios's husband, Dr. Jose Chua, had never heard of Basa.

While speaking in Teresita's voice, Remibios's accent changed, and when she awoke from the trances, she remembered very little, if anything, about what she had said. However, while speaking in the mysterious voice, she claimed that Teresita's killer was Allan Showery, an employee at the hospital where both women had worked. She also stated that he had killed her while stealing jewelry for rent money.

Through Remibios's lips, the voice pleaded for them to contact the police. The frightened couple initially resisted, fearing that the authorities would think that *they* should be locked away. But when the voice returned and continued pleading for an investigation, the Chuas finally contacted the Evanston police, who put them in touch with Joe Stachula, a criminal investigator for the Chicago Police Department.

Lacking any other clues, Stachula interviewed the Chuas. During their conversation, Remibios not only named the killer, but she also told Stachula exactly where to find the jewelry that Showery had allegedly stolen from Teresita. Prior to that, the police were not even aware that anything had been taken from the apartment.

Remarkably, when police began investigating Showery, they found his girlfriend in possession of Teresita's jewelry. Although the authorities declined to list the voice from beyond the grave as evidence, Showery was arrested, and he initially confessed to the crime. When his lawyers learned that information leading to his arrest had come from supernatural sources, they advised him to recant his confession.

The Surprise Confession

Not surprisingly, the voice became a focal point of the case when it went to trial in January 1979. The defense called the Chuas to the witness stand in an effort to prove that the entire case against Showery was based on remarks made by a woman who claimed to be possessed—hardly the sort of evidence that would hold up in court.

But the prosecution argued that no matter the origin of the voice, it had turned out to be correct. In his closing remarks, prosecuting attorney Thomas Organ said, "Did Teresita Basa come back from the dead and name Showery? I don't know. I'm a skeptic, but it doesn't matter as to guilt or innocence. What does matter is that the information furnished to police checked out. The jewelry was found where the voice said it would be found, and Showery confessed."

Detective Stachula was asked if he believed the Chuas: "I would not call anyone a liar," he said. "...Dr. and Mrs. Chua are educated, intelligent people...I listened and acted on what they told me...[and] the case was wrapped up within three hours."

Showery told the jury that he was "just kidding" when he confessed to the crime; he also claimed that the police had coerced him into an admission of guilt. Nevertheless, after 13 hours of deliberation, the jury reported that they were hopelessly deadlocked and a mistrial was declared.

A few weeks later, in a shocking development, Allan Showery changed his plea to "guilty" and was eventually sentenced to 14 years in prison. Some say that Teresita's ghost had visited him and frightened him into confessing.

Obviously shaken by the experience, the Chuas avoided the press as much as possible. In 1980, in her only interview with the press, Remibios noted that during the trial, people were afraid to ride in cars with her, but she said that she was never afraid because the voice said that God would protect her family. Still, she hoped that she would never have to go through such an experience again. "I've done my job," she said. "I don't think I will ever want to go through this same ordeal."

Having attracted national attention, the case quickly became the subject of a best-selling book and countless magazine articles, a TV movie, and a 1990 episode of *Unsolved Mysteries*. The case is often cited as "proof" of psychic phenomena, possession, and ghosts, but it's simply another mystery of the paranormal world. Exactly what it proves is impossible to say; after all, the ghost of Teresita Basa is no longer talking.

Berkowitz's Reign of Terror

For one year, a murderous madman who called himself the Son of Sam held New York City hostage. Terrified residents stopped going outside, and some women even changed their appearance for fear of provoking the mysterious serial slayer. At its height, the police effort to catch the killer involved more than 200 determined detectives.

❋   ❋   ❋   ❋

BETWEEN JULY 1976 AND July 1977, New Yorkers couldn't pick up a newspaper or turn on the television without hearing about the notorious serial killer who referred to himself in cryptic letters only as the Son of Sam. He struck seemingly at random, primarily attacking young women, and by the time he was finally captured on August 10, 1977, six people were dead and seven gravely wounded.

The Son of Sam turned out to be a troubled loner named David Berkowitz, who told investigators upon his capture that demons in the form of howling dogs had instructed him to kill.

The Seeds Are Planted

Berkowitz had led a distressed life almost from the beginning. Abandoned as a baby, he was adopted by Nathan and Pearl

Berkowitz, a middle-class couple who gave him a loving home. But Berkowitz grew up feeling scorned and unwanted because he was adopted. He made few friends, was viewed by neighbors as a bully, and did poorly in school.

When Pearl Berkowitz died of breast cancer in 1967, her son fell into a deep depression, and his emotional problems steadily worsened. His father remarried in 1971, and the animosity Berkowitz expressed toward his new stepmother eventually caused the newlywed couple to flee to Florida. Berkowitz, just 18, found himself alone in New York.

On Christmas Eve 1975, Berkowitz's internal rage reached the boiling point, and he stalked the streets with a knife, looking for someone to kill. He later told police that he stabbed two women that night, though police could locate only one, a 15-year-old girl named Michelle Forman who survived multiple stab wounds.

Berkowitz fled the Bronx and moved into a two-family home in Yonkers, where his mental state continued to decline. Barking dogs kept him awake at night, and Berkowitz eventually perceived their howls as demonic commands to kill. He moved out of the house and into a nearby apartment, where he became convinced that his neighbor's black Labrador retriever was also possessed. After shooting the dog, Berkowitz came to believe that its owner, a man named Sam Carr, also harbored demons.

The Shootings

The voices in his head eventually encouraged Berkowitz to once again seek victims on the street. On July 29, 1976, he shot Jody Valenti and Donna Lauria as they sat chatting in a car outside of Lauria's apartment. Lauria died instantly from a shot to the throat; Valenti survived.

In the months that followed, Berkowitz continued his nocturnal attacks, using a distinctive .44 Bulldog revolver to dispatch his victims.

October 23, 1976: Carl Denaro and Rosemary Keenan were shot while sitting in a parked car. Denaro was struck in the head, but both survived.

November 26, 1976: Donna DeMasi and Joanne Lomino were attacked by Berkowitz as they walked home from a late movie. DeMasi survived with minor injuries; Lomino was left paralyzed.

January 30, 1977: Christine Freund and her fiancé, John Diel, were shot as they sat in a parked car. Freund was killed, Diel survived.

March 8, 1977: College student Virginia Voskerichian was shot and killed while walking home from class.

April 17, 1977: Valentina Suriani and her boyfriend, Alexander Esau, were shot and killed. Police found a note signed "Son of Sam."

June 26, 1977: Judy Placido and Sal Lupu were shot in their car after a night of dancing at a local disco. Both survived.

July 31, 1977: Bobby Violante and Stacy Moskowitz were both shot while sitting in a parked car. Moskowitz was killed, and Violante lost the vision in one eye and partial vision in the other.

Sam Speaks Up

At the scene of the Suriani-Esau shootings in April, police found a rambling, handwritten letter from Berkowitz in which he referred to himself as "Son of Sam." In the note, Berkowitz revealed that he felt like an outsider and was programmed to kill. He told police that to stop his murderous rampage, they'd have to shoot him dead. Forensic psychiatrists used the letter to develop a psychological profile of "Son of Sam" and concluded that he likely suffered from paranoid schizophrenia and thought himself a victim of demonic possession.

As the daily papers splashed gruesome details of each new killing across their front pages, New Yorkers began to panic. Women with dark hair cut their locks short or bought blond wigs because the killer seemed to have a penchant for brunettes. Many New Yorkers simply refused to go outside after dark.

A ticket for parking too close to a fire hydrant finally led to David Berkowitz's capture. Two days after the Violante/Moskowitz shootings, a woman named Cacilia Davis, who lived near the murder scene, called police to report seeing a strange man, later identified as Berkowitz, loitering in the neighborhood for several hours before snatching a parking ticket off the windshield of his car and driving away.

New York police detectives, working with the Yonkers police, decided to pay a visit to Berkowitz. They examined his car, parked outside his apartment, and spotted a rifle on the back seat. A search of the vehicle also revealed a duffel bag containing ammunition, maps of the crime scenes, and a letter to a member of the police task force charged with finding the Son of Sam.

Arrest and Aftermath

Berkowitz was arrested later that evening as he started his car. He immediately confessed to being the Son of Sam, telling the arresting officers, "You got me. What took you so long?"

In court, David Berkowitz admitted to six murders and received six life sentences, though he later recanted his testimony and claimed to have pulled the trigger in only two of the killings. The others, he said, had been committed by members of a Satanic cult to which he belonged. Despite his claims, no one else was ever charged in association with the Son of Sam killings.

Jeffrey Dahmer: "The Milwaukee Monster"

The Oxford Apartments in Milwaukee are gone. The seedy complex at 924 North 25th Street was torn down in 1992 to prevent the site from becoming a ghoulish tourist attraction. But the empty lot still attracts visitors hoping to see a remnant of Apartment 213 and "The Milwaukee Monster." The small one-bedroom apartment was reputed to be tidy, clean, and home to charming serial killer Jeffrey Dahmer, his pet fish, and his collection of dismembered corpses.

✳   ✳   ✳   ✳

Once Upon a Time

JEFFREY DAHMER WAS born in Milwaukee on May 21, 1960, and his family later moved to Ohio. He attended Ohio State University for one semester, then enlisted in the army in 1979. After being discharged for chronic drunkenness, he eventually moved back to Wisconsin, where he lived with his grandmother.

According to his parents, Dahmer started off as a sweet boy but became increasingly withdrawn during adolescence. They noticed his preoccupation with death, but they dismissed it. Friends knew he liked to dissect roadkill. Once he even impaled a dog's head on a stick. Another time, when his father noticed foul smells coming from the garage, Jeffrey told his dad he was using acid to strip the flesh from animal carcasses. Later, his stepmother realized that he might actually have been cleaning human bones.

There's a First Time for Everything

Dahmer committed his first murder in June 1978, at age 18. While still living with his parents in Ohio, he picked up a young male hitchhiker. The two had sex, then Dahmer beat the man to death, dismembered his body, and buried him in the woods. Later, Dahmer exhumed the body, crushed the bones with a mallet, and scattered them throughout the woods. His next three victims were all men Dahmer met at gay bars and brought back to a hotel or to his grandmother's house, where he seduced, drugged, and strangled them before sexually assaulting their corpses and cutting them up.

Bad Moves

In September 1988, Dahmer's grandmother kicked him out because he and his friends were too loud and drank too much. The day after he moved into his own apartment, Dahmer was arrested for fondling, drugging, and propositioning a 13-year-old Laotian boy. He was sentenced to a year in prison but was released after ten months. No one knew that he had already murdered four men.

After being released on probation for the assault, Dahmer moved back in with his grandmother. But as a stipulation of his early release, he had to find his own apartment. Thus, in May 1990, Dahmer moved to his now infamous home at the Oxford Apartments.

Modus Operandi

Living on his own, Dahmer stepped up his killing spree. Between May and July 1991, he killed an average of one person each week, until he had committed a total of 17 known murders. With few exceptions, the victims were poor, gay, nonwhite men. He would meet them in gay bars or bathhouses, drug them, strangle them, have sex with them, and then dismember them with an electric saw. He saved some parts to eat, and some skulls he cleaned and kept as trophies. He even experimented with creating "zombies" by drilling holes into his victims' heads and injecting acid into their brains while they were still alive. For the most part, he was unsuccessful, as only one man survived for more than a few hours.

On May 27, 1991, a 14-year-old Laotian boy escaped Dahmer's apartment and ran into the streets, half-naked, drugged, and groggy. Neighbors called the police, who escorted the boy back to Dahmer's apartment. Sweet-spoken Dahmer convinced the police that it was merely a lover's spat and that the boy was an adult. The police left without conforming the boy's age or doing a background check on Dahmer. If they had, they would have discovered that he was a convicted child molester still on probation. After the police left, the boy, who was the brother of the boy Dahmer had been imprisoned for molesting, became his latest victim. The next week, when neighbors saw reports of a missing boy who looked like Dahmer's "boyfriend," they contacted the police and FBI but were told that he was an adult and with his lover.

The One that Got Away

Tracy Edwards was the lucky one. On July 22, police saw him running down the street with a handcuff on his wrist and stopped him for questioning. Edwards said a man was trying to kill him. He led the police back to Dahmer's apartment, where they found a human head in the refrigerator, an array of skulls in the closet, a barrel of miscellaneous body parts, a pot full of hands and penises, a box of stray bones, a freezer full of entrails, and snapshots of mutilated bodies in various stages of decay arranged in sexual poses. The police arrested Dahmer on the spot, ending his 13-year killing spree.

Crazy Like a Fox

At his trial, Dahmer's lawyer tried to convince the jury that his client was insane, emphasizing the heinousness of the crimes. Still, Dahmer was found sane and guilty of all 15 charges against him and was sentenced to 936 years in prison—15 consecutive life sentences.

And So We Come to the End

Dahmer was fairly infamous when he entered the Columbia Correctional Institute in Portage. He was kept out of the main prison population to protect him from other inmates. Even so, on November 28, 1994, he was assigned to a work detail with two convicted killers: Jesse Anderson and Christopher Scarver. When the guards checked in on them after a while, Anderson and Dahmer were dead; Dahmer's skull had been crushed.

Connecticut River Valley Killer

A serial killer went unpunished and his murders unsolved.

＊　＊　＊　＊

THE MURDERS ATTRIBUTED to the serial killer nicknamed the Connecticut River Valley Killer between 1978 and 1987 did not actually take place in Connecticut, but in New Hampshire and Vermont. (The Connecticut River flows through Massachusetts, Vermont, and New Hampshire in addition to Connecticut.)

The assumed first victim, Cathy Millican, died in 1978. Her body was found at the New Hampshire wetland preserve where she had been photographing birds. She had been stabbed about 30 times. The body of a second woman was found in 1981. At the time, police did not connect the two cases. Then, in the mid-1980s three women disappeared. The condition of their bodies when they were found pointed towards stab wounds. Looking back at previous cases, investigators began to establish connections that pointed to a serial killer. At least seven women were believed to have been killed.

In 1988, a woman named Jane Boroski stopped at a convenience store in New Hampshire, where she was approached by the driver of the vehicle next to hers. He dragged her from her car and stabbed her repeatedly before driving away. Amazingly, Boroski managed to get back in her car and reach her friend's home, even though she saw her assilant's car on the road. While Boroski was able to work with the police to provide a composite sketch of her assailant, he was never found.

No further murders happened, and the case went cold.

Literary Superstar/Murderer

Norman Mailer is widely held to be one of the 20th century's greatest (and most controversial) writers. But it was his involvement with criminal Jack Henry Abbott that wound up being one of the more contentious episodes of his career.

✳   ✳   ✳   ✳

Author/Prisoner

BORN ON A U.S. Army base in Michigan in 1944 to a soldier and an Asian prostitute, Jack Henry Abbott bounced around foster homes as a young child. He became a regular attendee of juvenile detention centers until finally entering a reformatory at age 16. Five years later, while in prison, he stabbed a fellow inmate to death. In 1971, he escaped lock-up and robbed a bank in Colorado. Abbott was recaptured and had additional years added on to his sentence.

In 1977, Abbott heard that famed author Norman Mailer was working on a book called *The Executioner's Song*. The plot was about convict Gary Gilmore, who was scheduled to be executed—the first example of capital punishment to occur in the United States in years.

Abbott began writing to Mailer, offering to help the writer understand the mind-set of a convict. In particular, Abbott— who had been in jail his entire adult life (save nine and a half months)—offered an insight into the mind of the "state-reared" long-term convict. "The model we emulate is a fanatically defiant and alienated individual," Abbott wrote, "who cannot imagine what forgiveness is, or mercy or tolerance, because he has no experience of such values."

Mailer, who admitted that he knew little about prison violence, began corresponding with Abbott. As the men communicated, Mailer realized that the convict was a powerful and entirely self-taught writer.

The Beast on Broadway

The Executioner's Song won the 1980 Pulitzer Prize for fiction. Mailer continued to correspond with Abbott. In June 1980, Mailer's friend Robert Silvers, editor of *The New York Review of Books*, published some of Abbott's letters. The missives created a sensation, and publisher Random House offered Abbott a $12,500 advance for a book. Titled *In the Belly of the Beast*, the book was to be published in the summer of 1981.

As the countdown to the book's release continued, a surprising thing happened: Its author came up for parole in late spring 1981. Despite Abbott's own admission that "I cannot imagine how I can be happy in American society," and even though he had spent virtually his entire adult life locked up, Abbott was indeed paroled. It's possible the parole board was influenced by a letter from Mailer offering Abbott a job as a research assistant at $150 per week. On June 5, Abbott flew to New York City where he met Mailer and moved into a halfway house.

"Exceptional Man"

In early July, *In the Belly of the Beast* was published to over-whelming acclaim. *The New York Times Book Review* found Abbott "an exceptional man." The convict had become a bit of a celebrity.

This lasted about three weeks. Little did anyone know that Abbott was rapidly spinning out of control. He hated the city, and he got increasingly paranoid. Even something as basic as buying toothpaste sent him into a panic. Mailer tried to get Abbott to hang on until August, when he could accompany the family to Maine. But it was not to be. Early on the morning of July 18, Abbott went to a small café, where he argued with a 22-year-old waiter named Richard Adan. Abbott stabbed Adan to death with the knife that he had bought almost as soon as he had been paroled.

The next day, the Sunday *Times* unwittingly ran a glowing review of *In the Belly of the Beast*.

Afterword

Abbott fled the city, but he was eventually caught and brought back to stand trial for murder. The trial was stormy, with the press demonizing Mailer for his part in getting Abbott released, in particular for Mailer's initial claim that "Culture is worth a little risk."

The jury didn't agree and convicted Abbott of manslaughter. In February 2002, Abbott hung himself in his prison cell.

The Redhead Murders

In the 1980s, a string of murders of redheaded women along U.S. highways began to baffle investigators. It would take 30 years before any breaks would come in the cases, with one arriving from a very unlikely source.

✳ ✳ ✳ ✳

The Victims

ON FEBRUARY 13, 1983, an elderly couple driving down Route 250 in Wetzel County, West Virginia, saw what they thought was a store mannequin lying in the snow. But they soon realized, to their horror, that what they were seeing was not a plastic figure, but rather a dead body.

The woman was white, about five feet six inches tall, and had brown eyes and reddish-brown auburn hair. Beyond those cursory characteristics, investigators were unable to identify her.

A year later, the body of a victim later identified as 28-year-old Lisa Nichols was found along Interstate 40 in West Memphis, Arkansas. She had been strangled to death, and like the Jane Doe found in West Virginia, had reddish hair. It took investigators nine months to identify Nichols, because she had been estranged from her family for some time. Since she hadn't spoken to them in so long, no one was looking for her or noticed when she disappeared.

Over the next year, half a dozen more bodies were found along highways in Tennessee and Kentucky. Some of the victims were strangled or suffocated; some were too highly decomposed to determine a cause of death. Although they all shared a similar reddish hair color, the bodies were found hundreds of miles from each other and each case was handled by a different police department, so the connection wasn't immediately noted. And like Nichols, many of the victims seemed to be drifters without many family contacts. With no one searching for them or wondering about their fate, authorities weren't pressured to solve the cases.

Amateur Sleuths

Even though some began to consider the possibility of a serial killer early on, the Redhead Murders (as they came to be known) were a low priority, eventually growing cold altogether. Until, that is, an unlikely group of investigators—a high school sociology class—began shining a new light on the murders. In 2018, students at Elizabethton High School in Tennessee studied the Redhead Murders for a class project, contacting police agencies and the FBI to create a profile of the likely killer or killers of the victims in each case. They concluded that the cases likely were connected, and the Redhead Murders were the work of a serial killer. Their profile theorized that the killer was a truck driver based in or near Knoxville, Tennessee, who would lure hitchhikers or prostitutes into his truck before killing them and dumping their bodies along the road.

It would be easy to dismiss the work of high school students without investigative experience, but authorities close to the cases were impressed by their theories. And the students' work was awarded even more validity after one of the victims, a woman who had been found dead along a Kentucky highway, was finally identified after 30 years as Espy Pilgrim. Pilgrim had last been seen at a truck stop in Kentucky, asking for a ride to North Carolina.

A Killer Found?

But even more chilling is the fact that the killer in the Redhead Murder cases may have already been found. In 1985, a trucker named Jerry Leon Johns attempted to strangle a redheaded woman named Linda Schacke, throwing her on the side of Interstate 40 when he thought she was dead. Miraculously, Schacke survived the attack and Johns was arrested. Despite the obvious similarities to the Redhead Murders, he claimed to be innocent of the killings, and had airtight alibis that seemed to exclude him. But 30 years later, after Johns died in prison at the age of 67, his DNA was positively matched to one of the Redhead Murder victims. What's more, at the time of the killings, Johns lived in Cleveland, Tennessee, just southwest of Knoxville. Exactly as the students in the Elizabethton High School class had predicted.

Was Johns the Redhead Murder serial killer? We may never know for sure. But the story of the Redhead Murders investigation reminds us to never overlook a good idea or theory, even if it comes from the most unlikely source.

Double Murder and DNA

We take many forensic technologies for granted today, but some are relatively recent in origin. In the 1980s, genetic fingerprinting solved two murders and changed investigation.

✳   ✳   ✳   ✳

THE CASES IN question were those of Lynda Mann and Dawn Ashworth. They were murdered in Leicestershire, England, in 1983 and 1986. Police suspected the same person committed both crimes. The girls were both 15 when they died. Both were raped and strangled. And in both investigations, police found semen of the same type.

Police arrested 17-year-old Richard Buckland in 1986. He had facts about Dawn's crime scene that were not public knowledge, and he kept confessing to Dawn's murder. He kept retracting this confession, however, and he consistently denied murdering Lynda Mann.

To strengthen the case against Richard, investigators turned to a brand-new technology: genetic fingerprinting. Experts found that the crime scene samples matched each other, but neither matched Richard. He was innocent.

Police still had to find their murderer. In 1987, Officials collected DNA samples from more than 5,000 local men. Not one matched. Then local Ian Kelly was overheard bragging that he had submitted his own DNA sample in place of a friend's. Police questioned Kelly, who quickly named the friend: Colin Pitchfork.

Police brought in Pitchfork, and he almost immediately confessed to both murders. To double check, experts compared his DNA to the crime scene samples—and everything matched. Pitchfork pleaded guilty the following January, ending the first murder investigation ever to use genetic fingerprinting.

Terror in Ukraine

With nicknames like "The Beast of Ukraine" and "The Terminator," it's obvious that Soviet-Ukrainian Anatoly Yuryovych Onoprienko was not a model citizen. His reign of murderous terror only lasted six years, but in that short time he killed dozens of victims.

✳ ✳ ✳ ✳

Abandoned

WHEN ANATOLY YURYOVYCH Onoprienko was finally apprehended, he told investigators that murdering people was pretty much his destiny. After all, according to statistics he'd read, around 70 percent of children who are brought up in orphanages grow up to engage in lives of crime. Onoprienko was one of those unlucky children; but surprisingly, he wasn't even an orphan.

Onoprienko was born on July 25, 1959, in the Ukrainian village of Lasky. He was the younger of two sons; his older brother, Valentin, was already 13 years old when he was born. When Onoprienko was four years old, his mother died. His grandparents began caring for him, even though his father, a decorated World War II veteran, was still alive. But soon after, Onoprienko's father turned him over to an orphanage, while the teenaged Valentin was free to continue living with their father. This may have been the beginning of a building resentment in the young Onoprienko.

Targeting Families

Little is known about Onoprienko's younger adult life, although he is believed to have grappled with mental problems for years and struggled to hold a job. It was not until 1989, when he was 30 years old, that he decided to carry out his first murder. And, unlike the tentative first crimes of some serial killers, he carried it out in terrifying fashion.

According to Onoprienko's confession, he enlisted the help of a friend, Sergei Rogozin, to break into a house with the intent of burglarizing it. But while they were robbing the house, the family of ten who lived there came home to find the intruders. Onoprienko and Rogozin killed all of them—two adults and eight children—using weapons they were carrying for "self-defense." After this first murder spree, Onoprienko cut ties with his friend and began working alone.

What followed was a string of murders straight out of a nightmare.

Onoprienko was deliberate in choosing his victims, searching for families who lived in isolated houses so there would be as few observers as possible. He would lure the occupants outside, or sometimes simply break down the door, then would systematically kill everyone in the home: first the male head of the household, followed by his wife, then lastly the children, who had just seen the horrifying murders of their parents.

Onoprienko would then steal any valuables in the house before burning it down to destroy evidence. In several instances, he also killed random neighbors or people simply passing by, to eliminate the possibility of witnesses.

Apprehension

By 1996, police were alarmed by the number of unsolved murders in Ukrainian villages, and began to mobilize their forces in an effort to hunt down the killer. They eventually arrested a man named Yury Mozola, certain they had their murderer, and even tortured him in an effort to get him to confess. But Mozola refused to confess to anything, and ultimately died due to the brutal torture.

Several weeks later, Onoprienko was finally apprehended, discovered hiding out at his girlfriend's house. The evidence was fairly clear: She was wearing a ring that he'd taken from one of his victims, and Onoprienko was in possession of a gun that was linked to many of the murders.

Many investigators believe that Onoprienko's motives stemmed from his childhood abandonment. Perhaps the sight of happy families, something he never experienced, was more than he could bear. But Onoprienko offered another explanation, saying he was guided by "voices" who urged him to kill. Whatever the reason, "The Beast of Ukraine" would never again see freedom: the killer, who confessed to 52 murders, died in prison of heart failure in 2013, at the age of 54.

The Monster of Florida

The tenth woman to be executed in the United States after the 1976 reinstatement of capital punishment, Aileen Wuornos was a confessed killer who shot at least seven men. But was she a cold-blooded murderer, a victimized woman who was forced to defend herself, or some mixture of both?

✳ ✳ ✳ ✳

Trouble from the Start

BY ALL ACCOUNTS, Aileen Wuornos had a deeply troubled life right from the start. Born to teenaged parents on February 29, 1956, in Rochester, Michigan, she was the older of two siblings. She never met her father, who was in prison when she was born, serving time for child molestation. Just before Wuornos' fourth birthday, her mother abandoned her and her brother, leaving them with their grandparents.

It may have seemed like this arrangement would provide stability for Wuornos and her brother, but the truth was much less ideal. Although her grandparents legally adopted the siblings in 1960, they were alcoholics and terrifyingly violent. Wuornos later stated that her grandfather sexually assaulted her and often beat her, and, after her grandmother died of liver failure in 1971, he threw her out of the house.

With nowhere to turn, Wuornos lived in the woods and relied on prostitution to support herself. She soon settled into a life of criminal activity, and was arrested numerous times for charges including theft, armed robbery, and disorderly conduct. She lived the life of a vagabond, eventually making her way to Florida, where she met and married a wealthy yacht club president named Lewis Fell in 1976.

Instead of seeing her marriage as a ticket to a better life, Wuornos caused trouble in their well-to-do neighborhood, where she was arrested for assault after starting a bar fight. She even attacked 69-year-old Fell with his own cane, prompting him to file a restraining order against her. Their marriage was annulled after only nine weeks.

Over the next decade, Wuornos perpetrated a string of crimes that spanned the Sunshine State, from armed robbery in Edgewater to forging checks in Key West. Then, in 1986, she met hotel maid Tyria Moore at a lesbian bar in Daytona Beach. The two began a relationship and moved in together, Wuornos continuing her work as a prostitute to support them.

Murder or Self-Defense?

In late 1989, Wuornos' prostitution work took a deadly turn. On November 30 that year, she had an encounter with 51-year-old Richard Charles Mallory, an electronics store owner from Clearwater. Police found Mallory's abandoned vehicle two days later, and on December 13, they discovered his body several miles away. He had been shot several times. Six more victims followed, all of them middle aged men who had been shot and left along the highway.

Witnesses began reporting two women, whose descriptions matched Wuornos and Moore, driving the victims' cars. After the pair abandoned one of the cars, police were able to lift fingerprints from it, which they matched to the two women. Wuornos and Moore were arrested, and Moore agreed to elicit a confession from her girlfriend in order to avoid prosecution.

Wuornos did confess to the crimes, but she claimed she had acted in self-defense. Mallory was a convicted rapist, so many of her supporters believed her claim that he violently attacked her and she was protecting herself; however, she was convicted of his murder and sentenced to death. She was also convicted of five other murders, and received six death sentences in total. She later provided a conflicting account of the killings, saying she murdered the men in order to rob them, not to defend herself, and said she "would kill again" if given the chance.

When Wuornos was executed on October 9, 2002, her supporters said she died a heroic and independent woman who was punished for defending herself from male aggression. Others believe her life of pain and violence led to uncontrollable anger and psychosis. Either way, her life has been repeatedly depicted in documentaries, literature, songs, and, perhaps most famously, in the 2003 Oscar-winning film, *Monster*.

The Juice Is Loose

Once a celebrated football player, actor, and spokesperson, O.J. Simpson is now much more likely to be remembered for his arrest in the murder of his ex-wife, and the "Trial of the Century" that ended in a surprising verdict.

✳   ✳   ✳   ✳

Career and Family

IN THE 1970s and 80s, Orenthal James Simpson, born on July 9, 1947, was enjoying fame, fortune, and the admiration of the American people. A running back who played with the Buffalo Bills and the San Francisco 49ers, he gained 11,236 rushing yards throughout his career and earned the nickname "The Juice," a play on both his initials and his electric presence on the football field. He also appealed to fans of Hollywood, appearing in dramatic productions including *Roots* and *The Towering Inferno*, and demonstrating his comedic chops in *The Naked Gun* trilogy. He seemed to lead a relatively charmed life.

In 1977, while still married to his first wife, Marguerite Whitley, Simpson began dating 18-year-old nightclub waitress Nicole Brown. Whitley and Simpson divorced in 1979, and in 1985, he and Brown were married. The couple had two children, but their relationship was plagued with conflict. Brown confided in friends and family about her unhappiness, claiming that Simpson was abusive. After one particularly nasty fight in 1989, in which Simpson allegedly threatened to kill his wife, he pleaded "no contest" to a spousal abuse charge. Unsurprisingly, the pair divorced in 1992, citing irreconcilable differences.

Death and the Dream Team

But sadly, that wasn't the end of their story. On June 12, 1994, Brown and a friend, Ron Goldman, were found stabbed to death outside her condo, with police listing Simpson as a person of interest in the murder. So Simpson did what any reasonable innocent person would do: he ran. On June 17, he made a call from a cell phone on the Santa Ana Freeway, and police were able to track his location to a now-famous white Ford Bronco driven by his friend Al Cowlings. The surreal low-speed chase that followed was widely broadcast and seen by around 95 million viewers, with Simpson finally surrendering outside his home. He swore that he "wasn't running," although the gun, passport, large amount of cash, and disguise he had with him seemed to suggest otherwise.

Simpson's murder trial began on January 24, 1995, and quickly became one of the most highly publicized trials in American history. He assembled a "dream team" of defense attorneys who were used to high-profile cases, including Johnnie Cochran, Robert Kardashian, Robert Shapiro, and F. Lee Bailey. With her work cut out for her, Marcia Clark was the lead prosecutor for the State of California.

An Open and Shut Case?

Clark seemed to have a reasonable amount of evidence to win the case, including Brown's complaints of abuse, DNA at the crime scene that matched Simpson, a bloody glove found at Simpson's home that contained DNA from Brown and Goldman, and the fact that Simpson had no alibi for the time of the murder. But the defense claimed that investigators had been careless when collecting DNA from the scene, compromising the evidence, and even alleged that police had planted the bloody glove. In perhaps the most famous moment of the trial, Simpson was asked to try on the gloves used in the murder, and appeared to have trouble fitting them on his hands. Cochran's quip, "If it doesn't fit, you must acquit" has become infamous.

Apparently jurors took Cochran's words to heart, because on October 3, 1995, Simpson was found not guilty of the murders. More than 100 million people tuned in to hear the verdict, many watching in disbelief that the former athlete was acquitted. But two years later, after Goldman's family filed a civil suit, Simpson was found liable for wrongful death and battery against Goldman and Brown and ordered to pay $33,500,000 in damages.

The once-revered football player and entertainer has seen nothing but trouble since his murder acquittal, running into even more trouble with the law. In 2007, he was arrested again after robbing two sports memorabilia dealers at gunpoint in Las Vegas. Simpson claimed the items had been stolen from him; but this time, a jury found him guilty and he spent nine years in prison. Now in his 70s, Simpson lives in Las Vegas, where he continues to claim he is an innocent man.

The Deaths of Tupac and The Notorious B.I.G.

Tupac Shakur—known as Tupac—and Christopher Wallace—known as The Notorious B.I.G.—were two of the biggest rappers in the 1990s and arguably in history. Onetime friends, the young rappers later become rivals. Sadly, both would end up dead following drive-by shootings just six months apart. And more than 20 years after the slayings, both murders remain unsolved.

✳ ✳ ✳ ✳

Difficult Upbringings, Big Successes

BORN IN 1971, Tupac Shakur came from a family of Black Panthers and radical politics. He grew up in challenging homes and homeless shelters, but his creative chops landed him at the Baltimore School for the Arts, where he studied ballet, poetry, and acting. His family later moved from Baltimore to the San Francisco Bay Area; there, Shakur joined a rap group and signed a record deal. In 1991, Shakur released his debut solo album, *2Pacalypse Now*, which caused controversy with its biting social commentaries.

One year younger than his contemporary, Christopher Wallace grew up in Brooklyn. He was an accomplished student who, by age 15, was selling drugs. Wallace also began rapping as a teenager, at that time for fun. An editor at a rap scene national magazine got hold of one of Wallace's rap tapes, and the young rapper subsequently appeared in the magazine.

Shakur and Wallace would later meet in the early 1990s. When they met, Shakur was already an accomplished artist, while Wallace was working on his first album, *Ready to Die*, which would go on to sell millions of copies. The two struck up a friendship, and Wallace even asked Shakur to become his manager, an offer Shakur declined.

But a feud ultimately developed between their dueling record labels, and this feud turned personal in 1994 when Shakur was shot five times during a robbery at a New York City recording studio. Shakur—who miraculously survived—believed Wallace was behind the shooting.

Unsolved Mysteries

On September 7, 1996, Shakur attended a Mike Tyson boxing match in Las Vegas. After leaving the event with Suge Knight, the then-CEO of Death Row Records, Shakur got into a brawl with Orlando Anderson, a Crips gang member, in the MGM Grand casino's lobby. Shortly after the fight, a white Cadillac pulled up beside Shakur's vehicle at a traffic light, and an occupant in the Cadillac fired into Shakur's vehicle, striking the rapper four times. Six days later, Shakur died at a Las Vegas hospital.

A 2002 investigation carried out by *Los Angeles Times* suggested that the gang Southside Crips carried out Shakur's killing in retaliation for the brawl in the MGM Grand lobby hours before the attack on Shakur's vehicle. The story also said that Wallace supplied the weapon for Shakur's murder, and he agreed to pay the gang $1 million for Shakur's killing. Orlando Anderson—a suspect involved in MGM Grand brawl—later died in a drug-related shooting.

Meanwhile, Wallace was shot dead on March 9, 1997 in Los Angeles, after leaving a music industry party. A dark-colored Chevrolet Impala pulled up next to his vehicle and an occupant fired into Wallace's side of his vehicle. An unsealed autopsy later revealed that a single bullet that pierced several vital organs killed Wallace.

Though speculation swirled about the role of corrupt police officers in Wallace's killing, the FBI ended its inquiry in 2005 after prosecutors concluded that there was scant evidence to pursue a case. That year, a federal judge concluded that a Los Angeles police detective intentionally withheld evidence in a wrongful death lawsuit filed against the city by Wallace's family; the lawsuit, however, was dismissed in 2010. Kevin McClure, 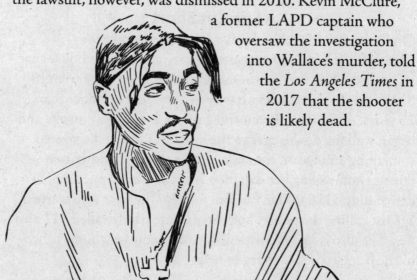 a former LAPD captain who oversaw the investigation into Wallace's murder, told the *Los Angeles Times* in 2017 that the shooter is likely dead.

A Beauty and a Beast

A murdered child beauty queen, more than 1,600 persons of interest, two false confessions, and still no answers: the heartbreaking case of JonBenét Ramsey has confounded investigators for decades.

✳ ✳ ✳ ✳

Beauty Queen

BORN ON AUGUST 6, 1990, JonBenét Ramsey's unusual moniker was a French-styled take on her father's first and middle name, John Bennett. John had three adult children from a marriage that ended in divorce in 1978. After he married his second wife, Patsy, who was thirteen years his junior, the couple had two more children, Burke, born in 1987, and JonBenét.

By the time she was in kindergarten, JonBenét was competing in the controversial world of child beauty pageants in the family's hometown of Boulder, Colorado. Blond-haired, blue-eyed, and with a sweet smile, the little girl won titles with names like "Little Miss Colorado" and "National Tiny Miss Beauty." At only six years old, JonBenét seemed destined for a bright future.

A Life Cut Short

On December 25, 1996, JonBenét received a bike for Christmas. The family attended a party at a friend's house that night, and when they got home, JonBenét and Burke went to bed. What happened next has been a mystery for more than 25 years. At 5:30 on the morning of the 26th, Patsy awoke and began walking downstairs to the kitchen, but she discovered something strange on the stairs. It was a long, handwritten ransom note saying her daughter had been kidnapped and demanding $118,000 in ransom money. The note also warned against calling the police, but Patsy immediately called 911 anyway. She also called family and friends, many of whom rushed to the Ramsey house to try to help.

When the police arrived minutes later, they cordoned off JonBenét's bedroom, assuming they were dealing with a kidnapping. Meanwhile, family, friends, police, and the Ramseys were free to roam the rest of the house. Investigators first focused on the ransom note, which was unusually long and referenced an amount of money that exactly matched John's Christmas bonus. But by 1:00 P.M., after no one had tried to claim the ransom, police asked John to search the house for anything amiss. He started his search in the basement, where, behind a latched door, he found the body of JonBenét.

In an unusual move, John picked up his daughter and carried her upstairs, which instantly contaminated the crime scene. The little girl was found with duct tape over her mouth, and cords wrapped around her wrists and neck. An autopsy revealed that she'd been hit over the head and strangled, with cause of death listed as asphyxia and craniocerebral trauma.

Suspects and Confessions

Almost immediately, investigators began focusing on the Ramseys themselves, theorizing that someone in the house had killed JonBenét and then staged the ransom note to cover it up. The media, as well, looked to the Ramseys, categorizing Patsy as an obnoxious "pageant mother" and questioning John's tampering of the crime scene. Even nine-year-old brother Burke was eyed with suspicion. But there was little evidence to support these theories, and no one in the family was ever officially considered a suspect.

Others believed that an intruder killed JonBenét, citing a boot print that was found near the body that did not match anyone in the house, and a broken basement window that could've been a point of entry. In later years, investigators were able to extract DNA from blood spots and skin cells that were found on the girl's clothes, which was found to belong to an unknown male. As of today, the DNA has still not been matched to anyone. Strangely, two different men—John Karr and Gary

Oliva—both confessed to the murder at different times, but neither confession was supported by the evidence and investigators consider them to be false confessions.

Patsy Ramsey died of ovarian cancer in 2006, her daughter's murder case still open and unsolved. Despite the lack of new leads, the little girl's remaining family hopes that one day, her killer will be found.

Teresa Halbach's Justice

In 1985, Steven Allan Avery was wrongfully convicted of sexual assault and attempted murder. After 18 years in prison, DNA evidence exonerated him; but two years later he once again found himself in hot water, accused of a heinous murder. But was he the right man this time? Or was he once again facing prison for a crime he didn't commit?

✳   ✳   ✳   ✳

The Budding Photographer

TERESA HALBACH WAS born in 1980 and grew up on a dairy farm in Green Bay, Wisconsin. Described by friends as "outgoing," "brave," and "spontaneous," Halbach took the opportunity to see some of the world during her college years, traveling to Spain, Mexico, and Australia, where she learned to scuba dive. After graduating from the University of Wisconsin, Halbach moved back to Green Bay to be near her parents, and began working as a photographer.

According to one of Halbach's old boyfriends, "photography was her life." But getting started in the photography business meant taking some odd jobs and less-than-glamorous assignments to get a foot in the door. Halbach went to work for *Auto Trader* magazine, photographing cars to be listed for sale. On October 31, 2005, Halbach had three appointments booked for the magazine, the last being at Avery's Auto Salvage, where she went and met with Steven Avery.

A Troubled and Difficult Life

Steven Avery was born in 1962 in Manitowoc County, Wisconsin. His mother once said that he attended a school for "slower kids," and school records showed that his intelligence quotient was somewhere around 70. He began running into trouble at an early age, spending 10 months in prison when he was 18 for breaking into a bar. He was jailed again in 1982, after two friends came forward and said that Avery poured gasoline on his cat and threw it in a bonfire, something he later said he did because he was "young and stupid."

So perhaps it seemed only a matter of time before he was accused of something more serious, which is exactly what happened in 1985. On July 29 that year, a woman jogging alone on the shores of Lake Michigan in Two Rivers, Wisconsin, was attacked, sexually assaulted, and beaten. When the woman later described her attacker, police thought he sounded a lot like Steven Avery. And when shown a picture of Avery, the woman identified him as her attacker.

But Avery insisted that he'd been 40 miles away in Green Bay at the time of the attack, a claim that he backed up with a time-stamped store receipt and the testimony of 16 eyewitnesses. However, this was not enough evidence to convince a jury, and Avery was convicted and sentenced to 32 years in prison. After 18 years of claiming his innocence, DNA evidence, along with the confession of the real rapist, finally freed Avery in 2003. Ready to get on with his life, Avery moved to Gibson, Wisconsin, where his family has owned and operated a salvage yard since 1965.

The Search for Teresa

It was the salvage yard where Halbach met up with Avery on Halloween, her last stop of the day. Avery was selling his sister's minivan, and wanted to list it on *Auto Trader*. The young photographer arrived in her dark-green Toyota RAV4, ready to snap pictures of Avery's car. But later that day, it became evident that something was wrong: Teresa Halbach never returned home.

Search parties were soon sent out, with one group searching the area that Halbach was last known to have visited: Avery's Auto Salvage. On November 5, her car was found on the property, covered with tree branches and plywood, the license plates removed. Inside, police discovered bloodstains, which prompted an immediate search of the salvage yard. By the next day, 200 officers were on the property, combing through the yard, garage, and the trailer where Avery lived.

Within days, investigators had found the missing license plates from Halbach's car hidden in an abandoned station wagon on the property. They also found a spare key to her RAV4 in Avery's bedroom. And most disturbing of all, charred human bones were discovered in a burn pit near his trailer. When the blood from Halbach's car was tested, the DNA matched Avery. It seemed clear that Avery had something to do with Halbach's disappearance, and on November 15, he was arrested for Halbach's murder.

An Open and Shut Case?

In a January 17, 2006, hearing, Avery pled not guilty. Two days later, an FBI crime lab announced that the charred bone fragments, were, in fact, from Halbach, putting to rest any question that she might still be alive. And on March 3, Avery's nephew, Brendan Dassey, confessed to helping his uncle kill Halbach and dispose of her body. It seemed that prosecutors had an open and shut case.

But Avery's lawyers weren't so sure. First, Dassey recanted his confession, saying he'd been coerced. Then there was the matter of the blood in Halbach's car: Avery's lawyers discovered an unsealed evidence box which contained a vial of Avery's blood collected in 1996 which appeared to have a puncture hole in the stopper. Could Avery's blood have been planted in the RAV4? An FBI crime technician said the blood in the car lacked a specific acid that would've been used to preserve the blood in the vial, but an expert for the defense said the test could be inconclusive. And what about the key that was found in Avery's bedroom? Defense lawyers contended that it was planted by the two police officers who claimed to have found it.

But all of this raises the question: Why would investigators want to pin a murder on Avery if he wasn't guilty? After he was released from prison in 2003, Avery filed a $36 million wrongful conviction lawsuit against Manitowoc County. His lawyers allege that sheriff's officers were so angry about the lawsuit that they planted evidence to make Avery seem guilty.

Avery was sentenced to life in prison in 2007, still protesting his innocence. The case became the topic of the true crime documentary on Netflix, *Making a Murderer*, that began airing in 2015. One thing is certain: No matter who is guilty, Teresa Halbach was the victim of a terrible crime and deserves justice. If Steven Avery is not responsible, who is? Why were her bones found on Avery's property? Since many of Avery's family members also worked at the salvage yard, could one of his relatives be the culprit? Whatever the answer is, investigators owe it to Halbach to see her story through to the truthful end.

The Jennings 8

The population of Jennings, Louisiana, is less than 10,000. This quiet parish seat of Jefferson Davis Parish was never known for much beyond its proximity to Louisiana's bayous. But then it became famous for the worst of reasons.

✳ ✳ ✳ ✳

Disturbing Discoveries

THE FIRST BODY was found floating in a canal on May 20, 2005. She was identified as 28-year-old Loretta Lynn Chaisson Lewis, who was known to engage in prostitution and drug use. Investigators were unable to determine a cause of death, but toxicology results revealed cocaine and alcohol in her system. Perhaps it seemed reasonable to assume that her death was the result of her lifestyle, but investigators would soon discover that Lewis's case was not an isolated incident.

Over the next four years, seven more women turned up dead. A month after Lewis was found, Ernestine Marie Daniels Patterson was discovered five miles from where Lewis had turned up. Although she also had drugs in her system, the examination of her body revealed that her throat had been cut. Two years later, in 2007, Kristen Gary Lopez and Whitnei Dubois were found, Lopez in a body of water and Dubois on the side of a road. Cause of death could not be determined for either one. In 2008, Laconia "Muggy" Brown was found on the roadside with a slit throat, the obvious victim of a homicide. But the cause of death of two others who were found the same year, Crystal Shay Benoit Zeno and Brittney Gary, remains a mystery. The last body, that of Necole Guillory, was found by highway workers in 2009. Once again, investigators could not determine a cause of death.

The Jefferson Davis Parish Sherriff's Office created a task force made up of local, state, and federal agencies to investigate the murders, and set up a reward for information leading to the killer. At first, it seemed like the murders must have been the work of a serial killer, and police even had a suspect: a local strip club owner and drug dealer named Frankie Richard. But investigators were unable to piece together enough evidence to charge him with anything.

Startling Similarities

As the investigation continued, authorities were noticing many similarities between the eight victims. All of the women struggled with drug addiction, and all were from the south side of Jennings, known to be the home of the poorer working-class residents in the town. What's more, the victims all knew each other, some very well. For instance, Lopez and Gary were cousins, Gary and Zeno were once roommates, and Dubois' boyfriend was the brother-in-law of Lewis.

And the women all shared another similarity: they were all police informants. This fact has led some of the family members of the Jennings 8 (also known as the Jeff Davis 8) to believe that the police themselves are responsible for the murders. New Orleans-based investigative journalist Ethan Brown even looked into this allegation when he began researching a book on the case in 2011. He discovered that one of the victims, Lopez, was present when the police shot and killed a drug dealer named Leonard Crochet in 2005. Although Crochet was unarmed, the shooting was deemed justifiable; but the Jennings 8 families continue to wonder if the women were "silenced" because of what they knew.

Ultimately, although four different people have been arrested in connection with the killings, the evidence has not been enough to support charges. The frustrated families believe that the women's lower socioeconomic standing, as well as their histories with drug use and prostitution, have quelled the authorities' interest in the case. For now, they can only continue to remind the public of the loss of their loved ones, and hope that one day, their killer—or killers—will be found.

The Case of Samuel Little

Who was Samuel Little? For decades, he killed with impunity.

✳ ✳ ✳ ✳

BORN IN 1940, Samuel Little spent most of his life as a nomad, shoplifting to support himself as he moved around. He had run-ins with the police—for stealing, drugs, solicitation, and even a couple of accusations of murder—but spent little time in jail.

Then in 2012, police arrested him at a homeless shelter in Kentucky. He was wanted for a narcotics charge in California.

When he arrived in Los Angeles, the LAPD took a DNA sample for their records. It had three unexpected matches to cold cases from the 1980s. All of them were homicide. Little swore he was innocent, but by 2014, he was serving three life sentences for murdering three women in California.

Fast forward four years. The FBI had reviewed Little's murders and noticed similarities to other cold cases, especially one in Texas. Texas Rangers interviewed Little in May 2018 and got a waterfall of revelations. Little confessed in detail to more than 90 murders in 14 states. He even drew pictures of his victims. Over the next year, investigators across the country confirmed 34 of the murders, then 60. The number kept growing. The more they learned, the more Little looked like the most prolific serial killer in U.S. history.

The Golden State Killer

A DNA database solved the case of a cop who killed and covered his tracks.

✳ ✳ ✳ ✳

CALIFORNIA'S SACRAMENTO COUNTY area was wracked with a series of violent rapes in the 1970s. The rapist planned each incident meticulously, even breaking into houses ahead of time to prepare for his entry later. The crimes ended in 1979 with no suspects.

Later that year, the area around Santa Barbara County experienced a terrifying series of murders. The killer often targeted couples, tying up the man, raping the woman, and murdering both. The killer stopped in 1986 without being caught.

It was not until 2001 that officials connected the rapist to the murderer. Entered into the criminal database, DNA from both crime sprees matched each other. Two big investigations become one massive one. This "Golden State Killer" had committed more than 50 rapes and at least 12 murders. But

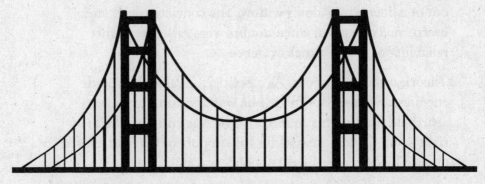

the DNA didn't match any person in the database, so there was still no suspect.

Then investigators turned from criminal DNA databases to genealogical ones. Investigators looked for familial matches to the killer's DNA in the open-source database GEDmatch. In 2018, they narrowed their results down to a solid suspect: Sacramento resident and one-time cop Joseph James DeAngelo. Officials compared the Golden State Killer's DNA to items taken from DeAngelo's trash and there it was, a perfect match.

The Golden State Killer was finally caught.

A Cold Case Closed

On February 28, 1986, Swedish Prime Minister Olof Palme was gunned down on a Stockholm street as he and his wife strolled home from the movies unprotected around midnight. The prime minister was fatally shot in the back. His wife was seriously wounded but survived.

✳   ✳   ✳   ✳

BORN IN 1927, Sven Olof Joachism Palme served two terms as prime minister of Sweden, from 1969–1976 and again from 1982–1986. His second term was cut short by his assassination, which rocked Scandavania.

In 1988, a petty thief and drug addict named Christer Petterson was convicted of the murder because he was picked out of a lineup by Palme's widow. The conviction was later overturned on appeal when doubts were raised as to the reliability of Mrs. Palme's evidence.

Theories were numerous. As a politician, Palme had made enemies, and some speculated he was assassinated by pro-apartheid South African forces, as he was anti-apartheid; by right-wing Chilean fascists for his support of Chilean leftists; or even by extremist Swedish police forces.

In 2020, Swedish prosecutors announced that they were finally closing the case. They said there was "reasonable evidence" that the murder was the work of a man named Stig Engström. A graphic designer, he had been interviewed by police as an eyewitness at the scene. At the time, several of his statements seemed to contradict other witness testimony. Engström portrayed himself as speaking to Palme's wife and talking to police; other witnesses did not remember him being as involved as he claimed. He was believed to be a publicity-seeker.

Two authors who wrote accounts of the crime focused on him as a suspect. In 2020, a Swedish prosecutor at a press conference said it was the current theory. As Engström had committed suicide in 2000, no motive was explained.

Chapter 5

In the World of Sports

Baseball's Darkest Hour

Baseball's Golden Age was preceded by its darkest hour: the 1919 World Series–fixing scandal.

※ ※ ※ ※

THE CHICAGO HERALD AND EXAMINER described him as "a little urchin," the young lad who emerged from the crowd outside a Chicago courthouse on that September day in 1920 and was said to have grabbed Joe Jackson by the coat sleeve. The newspaper's report of the exchange went like this:

"It ain't true, is it?" the lad said.

"Yes, kid, I'm afraid it is," Jackson replied.

"Well, I'd never have thought it," the boy exclaimed.

Nowhere did the newspaper report that the boy demanded, "Say it ain't so, Joe," although this version of the story was passed down through the generations. A few years before his 1951 death, Jackson told *Sport Magazine* that the story was made up by a sportswriter. He said the only words exchanged on the way out of the courthouse that day were between him and a law enforcement officer.

What *is* so is this: Members of the 1919 Chicago White Sox committed baseball's cardinal sin, deliberately losing the World Series to the Cincinnati Reds for pay.

Ripe for a Fix

Two years after their 1917 world championship, the White Sox took the American League pennant. The White Sox were favored to defeat Cincinnati in the World Series—heavily favored, in some gambling circles. By all accounts, Sox infielder Chick Gandil made contact with gamblers and indicated that the Series could be thrown. He immediately involved 29-game-winner Eddie Cicotte, and others followed: Jackson, pitcher Claude Williams, infielders Buck Weaver and "Swede" Risberg, outfielder Oscar "Happy" Felsch, and utility man Fred McMullin. Some of the players would play lead parts in the fixing of games. Others, notably Weaver and some say Jackson, knew about the plan but were not active participants.

When the Series began, the players were promised a total of $100,000 to throw the games. By the time the Reds won the Series in eight games, the payout was considerably less, and whispers about what had taken place began swelling to a roar. Sportswriters speculated about a possible fix even before Cincinnati wrapped up the Series, but nobody wanted to believe it could be true.

Conspiracy to Defraud the Public

The 1920 season began with rumors about gambling in other big-league dugouts. In September a grand jury convened to examine instances of gambling in the game, and the jury soon looked at the 1919 World Series. Eight White Sox players were called to testify, and several admitted knowledge of the fix. All eight were indicted for conspiracy to defraud the public and injure "the business of Charles Comiskey and the American League." Although the group was acquitted due to lack of evidence, the damage had been done.

Bring in the Judge

The Black Sox were not as fortunate on the scales of baseball justice, as Judge Kenesaw Mountain Landis, baseball's first commissioner, suspended all eight players for life. It was a crushing blow for Chicago, and for Weaver and Jackson in particular. While Gandil had received $35,000 and Cicotte $10,000 for the fix, Weaver received nothing. Actually, it was proven that he had *turned down* an invitation to participate in the scam. And Jackson, considered one of the greatest outfielders and hitters in the history of the game, hit .375 with six RBI in the 1919 Series while playing errorless defense.

Many still clamor for Shoeless Joe to be enshrined in the Hall of Fame, arguing that his numbers support the claim that he did nothing to contribute to the fixing of the 1919 World Series. However, the $5,000 he accepted from the gamblers sealed his fate as a tragic figure in baseball's most infamous 20th-century scandal.

Say it ain't so, Joe.

Too bad it was.

Michael Vick's Dog Fighting Shenanigans

A promising career was cut short—by a player's own actions.

✳ ✳ ✳ ✳

QUARTERBACK MICHAEL VICK spent 13 seasons with the NFL, spending most of his career with the Philadelphia Eagles and the Atlanta Falcons. He was the number one draft pick in the 2001 NFL draft, and it was easy to see why: Vick was known for his rushing abilities, and he broke records for the most rushing yards by a quarterback in a season with 1,039, and the most career rushing yards by a quarterback with 6,109. It's safe to say that at the beginning of his career, the football star was well on his way to a life of comfortable prosperity, provided he didn't do anything stupid.

And then he did something stupid.

Finding Trouble

Vick was born in Newport News, Virginia, on June 26, 1980. His family lived in a public housing project in a crime-ridden area of the city, where drug dealing and drive-by shootings were a way of life. But Vick and his second cousin, Aaron Brooks, spent a lot of time at their local Boys and Girls Club learning the ins and outs of football. "Sports kept me off the streets," Vick would later tell *Sporting News* magazine.

Sports would not, however, keep him out of trouble forever. Vick maintained property in rural Surry County, Virginia, just across the James River from his hometown. On April 25, 2007, a search warrant was issued for the property resulting from a drug investigation of Vick's cousin, Davon Boddie. But instead of drugs, investigators found something even more disturbing. More than 70 dogs, some with signs of injuries, were discovered on the property, with evidence that they were used in an interstate dog fighting ring.

Unsettling Evidence

As state and federal authorities looked into the evidence, the details that emerged were upsetting—not only to animal rights activists, but to anyone who believes the axiom that dogs are man's best friend. Vick and his partners–Purnell Peace, Quanis Phillips, and Tony Taylor–created a dog fighting ring known as "Bad Newz Kennels," where spectators placed bets on the outcome and owners of winning dogs could collect tens of thousands of dollars. The dogs were also taken to locations in six other states to participate in fights.

But the worst of the allegations concerned those dogs who were considered "underperformers"–if Vick and his partners weren't satisfied with a dog's fighting abilities, that dog would be killed by terribly inhumane methods including drowning, strangling, and shooting. Vick personally participated in killing at least eight dogs himself.

Prison, Bankruptcy, and a Comeback

In July, Vick and his partners were indicted on state and federal charges, and by August, all had pled guilty under plea bargain agreements. On December 10, Vick was sentenced for the federal charges to 23 months in prison, with Judge Henry E. Hudson questioning his remorse over "promoting, funding, and facilitating this cruel and inhumane sporting activity" and saying he didn't believe Vick had taken full responsibility for his actions. Vick was later sentenced on the state charges to three years in prison, which was suspended on condition of good behavior. He also deposited $1 million into an escrow account, which his attorneys used to help cover the costs of caring for the confiscated dogs and moving them into adoptive homes.

Before the dog fighting scandal, Vick's yearly income was estimated to be around $25 million. But due to his poor choices, he was forced to file for bankruptcy protection in July 2008. After he was released from prison, coach Tony Dungy took him under his wing and helped him with his return to the NFL. In 2010, while playing for the Philadelphia Eagles, he earned the Comeback Player of the Year award and was named the Eagle's starting quarterback. He later played for the New York Jets and the Pittsburgh Steelers before officially retiring from football in 2017.

He has lobbied for H.R. 2492—the Animal Fighting Spectator Prohibition Act—which would establish penalties for spectators of illegal animal fights and make it a felony for adults to bring children to such fights. One can only hope that he has learned his lesson.

Anything but a Shining Example

College football has produced some notable coaches throughout the history of the game, like Pop Warner, Barry Switzer, and of course the incomparable Bear Bryant. But in 2011, the football program at Pennsylvania State University came under scrutiny for a disturbing and horrifying reason, and the names of Jerry Sandusky and Joe Paterno would be remembered for deeds that were anything but an innocent game.

✳   ✳   ✳   ✳

A Shining Example

JERRY SANDUSKY MARRIED his wife, Dottie, in 1966. The couple adopted six children, and also occasionally served as foster parents. By all appearances a man who cared for troubled kids, Sandusky founded "The Second Mile," a charity that helped children in need and provided care for foster children, in 1977. The charity provided services to 100,000 kids every year, and donors included major companies like Walmart, Bank of America, and PepsiCo. President George H.W. Bush even praised The Second Mile, calling it a "shining example" of charity work.

Professionally, Sandusky was an assistant coach for the Penn State Nittany Lions from 1969 until 1999, and after he retired he became a coach emeritus, with an office at Penn State and access to all the football facilities. He also remained active in The Second Mile, hosting summer football camps every year.

Disturbing Allegations

Then, in 2008, almost a decade after his retirement, a student at Central Mountain High School in Mill Hall, Pennsylvania, made an allegation of abuse against Sandusky. The student claimed that he and Sandusky had met through The Second Mile program, and Sandusky had been molesting him since he was 12 years old. When the Pennsylvania attorney general's office looked into the claim, they began to discover an unsettling number of new complaints against the former coach and revealed the shocking truth about Sandusky's image as a fatherly caretaker.

Over the next three years, Pennsylvania Attorney General Linda Kelly gathered enough evidence to indict Sandusky on 52 counts of sex crimes against boys, with some of the victims being as young as seven years old. As details came to light, the public was sickened by the manipulative, deviant actions of a man who took advantage of children he supposedly cared for. Sandusky would choose his victims from The Second Mile charity, looking for boys who lacked a father figure in their life. He would then employ a tactic common with pedophiles called "grooming," where he would buy the children gifts and take them to football games to earn their trust, all the while engaging in increasingly inappropriate touching and behavior.

Locked Away for Life

In addition to Sandusky's crimes, an independent investigation by former FBI director Louis Freeh concluded that several Penn State school officials—including coach Joe Paterno, athletic director Tim Curley, school president Graham Spanier, and school vice president Gary Schultz—knew about the abuse and did nothing to stop it. Paterno's contract was immediately terminated, and Curley, Spanier, and Schultz were found guilty of child endangerment.

The Penn State football program was also punished, with the NCAA imposing a $60 million fine, a four-year postseason ban, scholarship reductions, and a forfeit of all victories between 1998 and 2011. The Big Ten Conference also imposed an additional $13 million fine. As for Sandusky, he was found guilty on 45 of the charges against him and sentenced to a minimum of 30 years in prison. Because of Sandusky's age, the judge who presided over the case was satisfied that the disgraced football coach would be imprisoned for the rest of his life.

Pete Rose: From Highest-Paid to Prison

The name Pete Rose is synonymous with the Cincinnati Reds, the team he managed and played with throughout most of his career. It's also synonymous with record-breaking feats: Rose holds Major League Baseball records for most career hits, singles, games played, at-bats, and plate appearances. He also earned three World Series rings, three batting titles, two Gold Glove awards, and 17 All-Star appearances. But there's one other word often associated with Pete Rose: gambling. And unfortunately, this is the legacy that frequently overshadows the player's athletic accomplishments.

✳   ✳   ✳   ✳

A Stellar Career

PETE ROSE PLAYED his first professional season with the Cincinnati Reds in 1963, when he was voted the National League Rookie of the Year. He was batting .312 by the 1965 season, and he spent 16 seasons batting at least .300. In 1979 he became the highest-paid athlete in team sports when the Philadelphia Phillies signed him to a four-year, $3.2 million contract, and in 1984 he briefly joined the Montreal Expos. It was during his stint with the Expos, on April 13, 1984, that Rose got his 4000th career hit.

After only 95 games with the Expos, Rose was traded back to the Reds, where he was named player-manager. He retired from playing in 1986, but he continued to manage the Reds for another three years, ending with a career managerial record of 412 wins and 373 losses.

A Career Gamble

In February 1989, Commissioner of Baseball Peter Ueberroth and National League President Bart Giamatti began questioning Rose about rumors that he had made bets on baseball.

Rose denied the allegations, but in March of that year, *Sports Illustrated* published a detailed account of the unfolding scandal, and soon lawyer John M. Dowd was hired to conduct a formal investigation into the matter.

On June 27, 1989, the *Dowd Report*, a 225-page summary of the lawyer's findings, was published.

Along with the report, Dowd submitted bank and telephone records, betting records, expert testimony, and transcripts of interviews with Rose and other witnesses to Giamatti, who had replaced Ueberroth as Commissioner of Baseball. The report detailed Rose's alleged gambling activities between 1985 and 1987, including 52 games in 1987 where Rose bet between $2,000 and $10,000 a day. Even after the report's release, Rose continued to deny any wrongdoing; however, on August 24, he agreed to be placed on baseball's ineligible list. In return, the MLB agreed not to issue a formal finding regarding the gambling allegations. Tommy Helms replaced Rose as Reds manager, and soon after he began therapy for treatment of a gambling addiction.

One year later, Rose found himself in hot water again, this time for tax evasion. Rose was charged with filing false income tax returns that did not report income from selling autographs and memorabilia and from horse racing winnings. The ex-MLB star was sentenced to five months in prison and fined $50,000.

Coming Clean

It wasn't until Rose published his autobiography, *My Prison Without Bars*, that he finally admitted what seemed to be clear all along: he bet on baseball games while playing with and managing the Reds. He emphasized that he never bet *against* his team—he only bet for the Reds to win. Some fans felt that this was excusable; after all, he wasn't trying to throw games like the 1919 White Sox World Series scandal. He only wanted his team to win. But experts point out that even betting on a team to win can damage the integrity of the game. Especially since Rose did not bet on every single game—he bet on games in which he had the most confidence. This meant that when he didn't bet on a game, it was a signal to other gamblers to bet against the Reds. And when he did bet on his team, he was more apt to change his managerial style for that particular game, in order to give himself the best chance of winning.

Over the years, Rose has made repeated attempts to be reinstated into MLB, but he so far has been denied. And because he is on the permanent ineligible list, he may not be inducted into the Baseball Hall of Fame, despite his many records. He was, however, inducted into the Cincinnati Reds Hall of Fame in 2016.

Southern Methodist University's "Death" Penalty

In the early 1980s, the Southern Methodist University Mustangs were a football powerhouse. Between 1981 and 1984, they had an impressive record of 41 wins, five losses, and one tie. This feat would've been admirable for any school, but it was especially notable for SMU, a tiny private school in Dallas with a total enrollment of less than 10,000 students. The university was seemingly undeterred by its small stature, holding its own against Southwest Conference giants like Texas and Arkansas. But the football world was about to find out that SMU's prowess wasn't created by chance, but rather by deliberate—and illegal—action.

✳   ✳   ✳   ✳

IN THE 1970S, SMU was popular enough—they attracted plenty of fans to their games, but the team wasn't taken as seriously as they wanted to be. So they hired Ron Meyer, the previous coach at the University of Nevada, Las Vegas. While at UNLV, Meyer had accrued a respectable 27–8 win-loss record. He was also determined and flashy, which SMU hoped would work in their favor.

The J.R. Ewing of Football

It certainly did: Meyer's aggressive recruiting strategy helped him procure some of the best football players in Texas. His brash but charming manner earned him many comparisons to *Dallas*'s J.R. Ewing, and one after another, talented players signed on to the unassuming SMU. Former quarterback Lance McIlhenny has stated that Meyer was the "greatest salesman" he ever knew. But the best college players in the state weren't necessarily signing up for SMU because of great sales tactics. Meyer's recruiting staff would often pay players, while Meyer looked the other way. Small incentives of $10 or $20 soon turned into hundreds of dollars, with some recruiters handing prospective players $100 dollar bills when meeting them for the first time.

Payments and Probation

In 1982, Meyer moved on to coach the New England Patriots, but his recruiting tactics were well established within the school by then. Eventually, the fact that unusually good players were signing on to SMU did not go unnoticed, and by 1985, investigations into recruiting practices resulted in three years' probation for the Mustangs. Probation was nothing new for the team: SMU had faced probation seven times—more than any other school in their division.

But the worst was yet to come: Two former Mustangs players—Sean Stopperich and David Stanley—came forward with information about SMU's recruiting methods, claiming that not only had they both been paid large sums of money but also that SMU maintained a "slush fund" to quietly pay players. The National Collegiate Athletic Association (NCAA) launched an investigation and discovered that between 1985 and 1986, while the school was in the midst of a three-year probation, SMU paid 13 players a total of $61,000 from this fund. The athletic department was well aware of this fund, but it allowed it to continue unabated, planning to secretly phase it out once the 13 players graduated.

Laying Down the Law

Due to SMU's repeat violations, they were shown no mercy by the NCAA, which instituted the "death penalty": this harsh penalty bans a school from competing in a sport for at least one year. The university's entire 1987 season was cancelled, and all of SMU's home games for 1988 were cancelled. In addition, their probation was extended until 1990, and the team was banned from bowl games and live television until 1989.

The scandal—and its death penalty—greatly damaged SMU's football program, leading to years of repairing and reworking the once mighty Mustangs. In 2009, the school won its first bowl game since 1984, with a 45–10 victory over the University of Nevada, Reno, in the Hawaii Bowl. Since then, they've appeared in a handful of bowl games over the years, as the modest little school slowly and steadily tries to rebuild itself to its former glory.

A Plot for Naught

January 6, 1994 started out as a normal day for figure skater Nancy Kerrigan. Preparing to skate at the U.S. Figure Skating Championships in Detroit, she put in some practice time on the rink at Cobo Arena and then left, walking out through a corridor. Suddenly, her "normal" day was anything but: an attacker viciously hit her in the leg with a metal baton, leaving her on the floor clutching her knee and wailing, "why?" And it was a good question: Why would anyone want to attack America's favorite skating sweetheart?

✳ ✳ ✳ ✳

Fierce Rivals

KERRIGAN WASN'T THE only top skater in 1994. Her main rival was Tonya Harding, who'd been climbing the ranks in the skating world since the mid-1980s. Her defining year was 1991, when she became the first woman to land a triple axel in competition. Over the next few years, she developed a fierce rivalry with Kerrigan, and by 1994, the two were favored to be chosen for the Olympic team set to compete in Lillehammer, Norway. Was the attack on Kerrigan an attempt to knock her out of Olympic contention?

What Did Harding Know?

It didn't take long for investigators to find Kerrigan's attacker. He was identified as Shane Stant, who had followed Kerrigan to Detroit and waited for her in the arena corridor, ready to ambush. Soon after, it was discovered that Harding's ex-husband, Jeff Gillooly, and her bodyguard, Shawn Eckhardt, had hired Stant to carry out the attack on Kerrigan. At first, Harding insisted that she knew nothing about her ex-husband's plans, but Gillooly had another story to tell. He claimed that Harding was in on the plot from the beginning, and she even helped to schedule the attack. He showed authorities a scrap of paper on which Harding had written some of Kerrigan's practice times and locations, presumably to help Stant know exactly where he needed to go.

Even after the information came to light, Harding denied involvement in the attack. She did, however, change her story to say that she found out about Gillooly's actions *after* the fact and failed to report anything to authorities. On March 16, 1994, she pleaded guilty to conspiring to hinder prosecution of the attackers, and she received three years' probation, a $100,000 fine, and 500 hours of community service. She was also forced to resign from the U.S. Figure Skating Association, which banned her for life.

A Foiled Plot

After the investigation, one thing was clear: the attack on Kerrigan was meant to remove her from competition. Kerrigan's doctor told the *New York Times* that Stant "was clearly trying to debilitate her." Years after the attack, Stant was interviewed for sports site *Bleacher Report*, where he described how bodyguard Eckhardt's original plan involved cutting

Kerrigan's Achilles tendon. Fortunately, Stant—who apparently had a bit of a conscience—refused to cut her, and instead decided on the "whack heard 'round the world."

While Kerrigan recovered from the attack, Harding won the U.S. Figure Skating Championships. And because the investigation into the Kerrigan attack was still ongoing at the time, she secured a spot to the Olympics and was allowed to compete. But Kerrigan, who suffered only bruising to her knee, recuperated in time to take the second spot, and she ultimately won the silver medal that year. And Harding? A disappointing eighth place. What's more, she was forced to give up her 1994 U.S. Champion title. The entire plot, it turned out, was all for naught.

Bountygate

For sports stars, it's bad enough to cheat during games and events; using performance-enhancing drugs, illegal equipment, or running shady plays that escape the notice of referees can end up ruining careers and disappointing loyal fans. But between 2009 and 2011, the New Orleans Saints took cheating to a much more sinister level.

✳ ✳ ✳ ✳

A Bounty of Suspicion

IN THE NFL, non-contract bonuses are referred to as "bounties"; but paying them out is frowned upon, and the NFL constitution specifically forbids bounties that are paid for on-field misconduct or any actions against individual players or teams. Supposedly, however, many teams maintain bounty programs anyway. Former NFL players claim that these programs have been around for decades, with anywhere from 30 to 40 percent of players participating at any given time. But for the most part, the players themselves maintain these bounty programs—a sort of informal betting system to which team coaches turn a blind eye.

But in 2009, after the
Saints defeated the
Minnesota Vikings in
the National Football
Conference (NFC)
Championship game,
Vikings players and
coaches began voicing
concerns that Saints
players were deliberately
attempting to injure
Vikings quarterback Brett
Favre. In fact, Vikings

coach Brad Childress recalled at least 13 instances where he felt
that Saints players had hit Favre harder than necessary. There
was also some concern that the same thing had happened to
Arizona Cardinals quarterback Kurt Warner a week earlier.
The Saints went on to win the Super Bowl that year, but seeds
of suspicion about the team's integrity had been planted.

Cheaters Never Win

During the 2010 offseason, an anonymous source contacted
NFL officials and revealed that the suspicions were well-
founded. Not only had the Saints players been targeting Favre
and Warner, but their attempts to knock the quarterbacks out
of the game were part of a bounty program organized by Saints
defensive coordinator Gregg Williams.

After a yearlong investigation, the NFL concluded that
Williams had, in fact, created a bounty program when he
joined the Saints in 2009, in an effort to make the team's
defense more aggressive. There was also evidence that head
coach Sean Payton knew about the program and tried to cover
it up.

The details of the program were disturbing: Williams and 22 of
27 Saints players took part, by pooling cash into a pot that was

doled out depending on each player's performance. Knocking down a kick returner could earn a player $100. Causing an injury that resulted in an opposing player being carted off or carried away by a stretcher was worth $1,000. And if a player was so injured that they were unable to return for the rest of the game, whoever caused the injury was awarded $1,500. In a memo sent by the NFL to all 32 teams in the league, it was even revealed that Saints linebacker Jonathan Vilma offered $10,000 cash to any player who could knock Brett Favre out of the NFC Championship game. And Favre and Warner weren't the only specific players targeted: others included Green Bay Packers quarterback Aaron Rodgers and Seattle Seahawks quarterback Matt Hasselbeck.

Williams eventually issued a statement calling the bounty program "a terrible mistake," and he was indefinitely suspended. Payton was suspended for the entire 2012 season. And the New Orleans Saints were fined $500,000, hopefully convincing other teams to avoid negative controversy in the future.

※ **Chapter 6**

Crime and the Stars

When Celebs Go Bad!

Back in the day, celebrities were publicly pilloried for their bad behavior. Sometimes, anyway. As you'll read later in this chapter, a little bit of scandal could ruin some careers but help others. Today, a well-publicized arrest and a (brief) stint in (a cushy) jail might actually seem like a smart career move. Here are just a few of the rich and famous who have had brushes with the law.

※   ※   ※   ※

Ozzy Osbourne

IN 1982, THE Black Sabbath front man and reality TV superstar angered Texans everywhere by drunkenly urinating on a wall at the Alamo. Osbourne was banned from the city of San Antonio for a decade but later made amends by donating $20,000 to the Daughters of the Republic of Texas to help restore the fabled landmark.

Matthew McConaughey

In October 1999, following a noise complaint, McConaughey was found by police sitting naked in his home playing the bongos. The cops also found the actor's stash, which led to McConaughey being arrested for marijuana possession and resisting arrest. The drug charges were later dropped, and McConaughey was simply fined $50 for violating a municipal noise ordinance.

Winona Ryder

In December 2001, Ryder was nabbed for shoplifting merchandise at the ritzy Saks Fifth Avenue store in Beverly Hills. She was convicted of grand theft and vandalism but received a relatively light sentence: three years probation and 480 hours of community service and restitution.

Nicole Richie

In February 2003, the daughter of singer Lionel Richie was charged with heroin possession and driving with a suspended license. Three years later, she was arrested again for driving under the influence. Her sentence: four days in jail. Actual time served: 82 minutes.

Natasha Lyonne

Known for such films as *Slums of Beverly Hills* (1998) and *American Pie* (1999), Lyonne was arrested in December 2004 after verbally attacking her neighbor, breaking the neighbor's mirror, and threatening to harm the neighbor's dog. A warrant was issued against the troubled actress in April 2005 for failure to appear before a judge, and a second warrant was issued in January 2006. In December 2006, Lyonne was finally sentenced to a conditional discharge. She later went to rehab, and would go on to became known for her role in *Orange Is the New Black* and her lead role in Netflix's *Russian Doll*.

Paris Hilton

Over the years, media personality and socialite Paris Hilton has been charged with a variety of crimes, including driving under the influence of alcohol and driving with a suspended license (twice). In June 2007, the hard-partying hotel heiress finally received her due when she was sentenced to 45 days in jail, though she was quickly released because of an undisclosed medical condition. Instead of doing her time in the slammer, Hilton was given 40 days house arrest with a monitoring device. In 2010, she was arrested for cocaine possession. Her lawyers argued that the purse where the drugs were found was not hers—it simply wasn't up to the star's fashion standards! Ultimately she pled guilty to two misdemeanors, resulting in a fine, a year of probation, community service, and a drug-treatment program. Hilton has also been the victim of crime—she has dealt with multiple stalkers and a case of identity theft.

Lindsay Lohan

In July 2007, the former child star was found by police in a Santa Monica parking garage engaged in a heated argument with a former assistant. She failed a sobriety test, and police also found a small amount of cocaine on her person. Lohan pleaded guilty to cocaine possession and driving under the influence and was sentenced to one day in jail, community service, and three years probation. Actual time spent behind bars: 84 minutes.

Bill Murray

In 2007, during a trip to Sweden, the former *Ghostbusters* and *Saturday Night Live* funnyman was charged with driving under the influence—while driving a golf cart. He refused to take a breath test but signed a document saying he had been driving drunk. He was allowed to leave the country without punishment.

Lori Loughlin and Felicity Huffman

In 2019, a number of wealthy people were implicated in a conspiracy to get their children into the colleges of their choice by faking exam scores and outright bribery. Two of those people were well-known actresses Lori Loughlin, of *Full House* fame, and Felicity Huffman, known for her work on *Desperate Housewives* and other shows. Loughlin and her husband were accused of conspiracy to commit honest services mail fraud. She was fined and sentenced to two months in prison. Felicity Huffman ultimately served about ten days in prison and was fined; she was accused of trying to bribe someone to falsify her daughter's SAT results. Her husband, everyman actor William Macy, was never charged.

1924 Murder Mystery

Who's at the heart of the cloaked-in-secrets demise of Thomas Ince? Who, of the loads of lovelies and gallons of gents on the infamous Oneida yacht that night, was the killer? Curious minds demand to know.

✳ ✳ ✳ ✳

THE NIGHT IS November 15, 1924. The setting is the *Oneida* yacht. The principal players are: Thomas H. Ince, Marion Davies, Charlie Chaplin, and William Randolph Hearst.

The Facts

✳ By 1924, William Randolph Hearst had built a huge newspaper empire; he dabbled in filmmaking and politics; he owned the *Oneida*. Thomas H. Ince was a prolific movie producer. Charlie Chaplin was a star comedian. Marion Davies was an actor. The web of connections went like this: Hearst and Davies were lovers; Davies and Chaplin were rumored to be lovers; Hearst and Ince were locked in tense business negotiations; Ince was celebrating a birthday.

✳ For Ince's birthday, Hearst planned a party on his yacht. It was a lavish one—champagne all around. In the era of Prohibition, this was not just extravagant, it was also illegal. But Hearst had ulterior motives: He'd heard rumors that his mistress, Davies, was secretly seeing Chaplin, and so he invited Chaplin to the party. The *Oneida* set sail from San Pedro, California, headed to San Diego on Saturday, November 15.

✳ An unfortunate but persistent fog settled over the events once the cast of characters were onboard the yacht. What is known definitively is that Ince arrived at the party late, due to business, and that he did not depart the yacht under his own power. Whether he was sick or dead depends on which version you believe, but it's a fact that Ince left the yacht on a stretcher on Sunday, November 16. What happened? Various scenarios have been put forward over the years.

* Possibility 1: Hearst shoots Ince. Hearst invites Chaplin to the party to observe his behavior around Davies and to verify their affair. After catching the two in a compromising position, he flies off the handle, runs to his stateroom, grabs his gun, and comes back shooting. In this scenario, Ince tries to break up the trouble but gets shot by mistake.

* Possibility 2: Hearst shoots Ince. It's the same end result as possibility 1, but in this scenario, Davies and Ince are alone in the galley after Ince comes in to look for something to settle the queasiness caused by his notorious ulcers. Entering and seeing the two people together, Hearst assumes Chaplin—not Ince—is with Davies. He pulls out his gun and shoots.

* Possibility 3: Chaplin shoots Ince. Chaplin, a week away from marrying a pregnant 16-year-old to avoid scandal and the law, is forlorn to the point where he considers suicide. While contemplating his gun, it accidentally goes off, and the bullet goes through the thin walls of the ship to hit Ince in the neighboring room.

* Possibility 4: An assassin shoots Ince. In this scenario, a hired assassin shoots Ince so Hearst can escape an unwanted business deal with the producer.

* Possibility 5: Ince dies of natural causes. Known for his shaky health, Ince succumbs to rabid indigestion and chronic heart problems. A development such as this would not surprise his friends and family.

Aftermath

Regardless of which of the various scenarios might actually be true, one fact is that Ince was wheeled off Hearst's yacht. But what happened next?

That's not so clear, either. The facts of the aftermath of Ince's death are as hazy as the facts of the death itself. All reports agree that Ince did, in fact, die. There was no autopsy, and his body was cremated. After the cremation, Ince's wife, Nell, moved to Europe. But beyond those matters of record, there are simply conflicting stories.

Self-protection Reigns

The individuals involved had various reasons for wanting to protect themselves from whatever might have happened on the yacht. If an unlawful death did indeed take place, the motivation speaks for itself. But even if nothing untoward happened, Hearst was breaking the Prohibition laws. The damage an investigation could have caused was enough reason to make Hearst cover up any attention that could have come his way from Ince's death. As a result, he tried to hide all mention of any foul play. Although Hearst didn't own the *Los Angeles Times*, he was plenty powerful. Rumor has it that an early edition of the paper after Ince's death carried the screaming headline, "Movie Producer Shot on Hearst Yacht." By later in the day, the headline had disappeared.

For his part, Chaplin denied being on the *Oneida* in the first place. In his version of the story, he didn't attend the party for Ince at all. He did, however, claim to visit Ince—along with Hearst and Davies—later in the week. He also stated that Ince died two weeks after that visit. Most reports show that Ince was definitely dead within 48 hours of the yacht party.

Davies agreed that Chaplin was never aboard the *Oneida* that fateful night. In her version, Ince's wife called her the day after Ince left the yacht to inform her of Ince's death. Ince's doctor claimed that the producer didn't die until Tuesday, two days after the yacht party.

So, what really happened? Who knows? Most of the people on the yacht never commented on their experience. Louella Parsons certainly didn't. The famed gossip columnist was reportedly aboard the *Oneida* that night (although she denied it as well). She had experienced some success writing for a Hearst newspaper, but shortly after this event, Hearst gave her a life-time contract and wide syndication, allowing her to become a Hollywood power broker.

Coincidence? No one can say for certain.

Trouble for the Prince of Noir

Robert Mitchum was the original offscreen bad boy—before James Dean ever appeared on the scene. He defined cool before Hollywood knew the hip meaning of the word. He was rugged, handsome, and jaunty. A hobo turned actor, he was the antithesis of the typical movie hero—and he was on his way to becoming a star, primarily in film noir. Then it happened: A drug bust with a buxom blonde, and Mitchum was in the headlines in a way he never intended. Ironically, this incident accelerated his stardom.

✳   ✳   ✳   ✳

IN AUGUST 1948, Hollywood tabloids were emblazoned with headlines proclaiming the scandalous drug bust (for possession of marijuana) of actor Robert Mitchum, who was in the company of 20-year-old aspiring actress Lila Leeds. This was the era of the marijuana frenzy: The government was at war with cannabis users, and propaganda, entrapment, blatant lies, and excessive punishments were just a few of the weapons they used. Mitchum was the perfect whipping boy. The actor was no stranger to pot and hashish, having experimented with both as a teenage hobo riding the rails. He was also a fugitive from the law, having escaped from a Georgia chain gang after being arrested for vagrancy in Savannah at age 16. Despite hiring Jerry Giesler, Hollywood's hottest defense attorney, Mitchum was found guilty and was sentenced to 60 days on a prison farm. His "I don't give a damn" smirk when his sentence was pronounced would define the attitude of the drug culture that burst upon the scene as the '40s came to a close.

A Career Ruined?

When Mitchum was sentenced, he was earning $3,000 a week—a princely sum at the time. He was married to his childhood sweetheart, Dorothy Spence, and was in the midst of a seven-year contract with RKO studios. When the tabloids ran a picture of inmate 91234 swabbing the jail corridors in prison attire, Mitchum anticipated it would be "the bitter end" of his career and his marriage.

In reality, the publicity had the opposite effect. With the exception of causing a small embarrassment to the studio and causing the cancellation of a speech Mitchum was scheduled to deliver to a youth group, the actor's offscreen bad-boy persona had little negative effect on his career or personal life. If anything, it only added verisimilitude to his counterculture, tough-guy, antihero image.

Great PR

While Mitchum served his 60-day sentence on the honor farm (which he described as "Palm Springs without the riff-raff"), RKO released the already-completed film *Rachel and the Stranger* (1948). Not only did movie audiences stand and cheer when Mitchum appeared on the screen, the low-budget movie also became the studio's most successful film of the year.

In 1950, another judge reviewed Mitchum's conviction and reversed the earlier court decision because the arrest smelled of entrapment: Leeds's Laurel Canyon bungalow had been bugged by two overly ambitious narcotics agents. The judge changed Mitchum's plea to not guilty and expunged the conviction from his records—not that Mitchum appeared to care one way or the other. By then, he was a bona fide Hollywood star.

A Long and Successful Livelihood

Mitchum enjoyed an illustrious career, making more than 70 films, some to critical acclaim. He also enjoyed success as a songwriter and singer, with three songs hitting the best-seller charts. His marriage remained intact for 57 years, possibly a

Hollywood record. He earned a star on the Hollywood Walk of Fame along with several other prestigious industry awards. Not a bad lifetime of achievements for a pot-smoking vagabond fugitive from a chain gang. Often seen with a cigarette dangling from his sensual lips, Mitchum died of lung cancer and emphysema on July 1, 1997, at his home in Santa Barbara, California. He was 79 years old.

The Rise and Fall of Fatty Arbuckle

As the saying goes, "The bigger they are, the harder they fall." And when it comes to early Hollywood scandals, no star was bigger or fell harder than Roscoe "Fatty" Arbuckle.

✳ ✳ ✳ ✳

THE SCURRILOUS AFFAIR that engulfed Roscoe "Fatty" Arbuckle (1887–1933) in 1921 remains one of the biggest Hollywood scandals of all time because of its repercussions on the film industry. (It was instrumental in the creation of organized film censorship in Hollywood.) The Fatty Arbuckle scandal rocked the world when it broke, and though few people today know the details, in 2007, *Time* magazine ranked it fourth on its list of the Top 25 crimes of the past 100 years.

As one of Hollywood's first headline-grabbing scandals, it contained all the elements that make a scandal juicy—drunkenness, debauchery, and death. But what made the tawdry tale big was Arbuckle, who himself was big in size (nearly 300 pounds), big in popularity, and, as Tinseltown's highest paid comedian, one of the biggest stars in the Hollywood galaxy at the time.

The Rise

Arbuckle began his career as a child, performing in minstrel shows and sing-alongs. The young entertainer already carried a noticeable girth, but his remarkable singing voice, acrobatic agility, and knack for comedy made him a rising star on the vaudeville circuit.

In 1913, Arbuckle got his big break in film when Mack Sennett hired him on at Keystone Film Company. Arbuckle initially rollicked as one of Sennett's Keystone Cops, but he was soon developing his unique comic persona as the lovable fat man and honing his own slapstick specialties based on the seeming contradiction between his size and graceful agility.

By 1914, Arbuckle was teamed with comedienne Mabel Normand for the extremely successful "Fatty and Mabel" shorts, in which the pair offered humorous interpretations of romantic rituals. Arbuckle's charming persona ensured that he always got the girl. He became so adept at working out the duo's physical gags for the camera that he soon took over direction of the films.

In 1917, Arbuckle formed Comique Film Corporation with Hollywood mogul Joseph Schenck, who offered Arbuckle creative control and an astounding paycheck. At Comique, Arbuckle launched the screen career of the great Buster Keaton, who played the rotund actor's sidekick in classic silent comedies such as *Coney Island* (1917), *Good Night, Nurse!* (1918), and *The Garage* (1920).

In 1919, Arbuckle reached unprecedented heights when Paramount Pictures handed him a monstrous three-year $3 million contract to make several feature-length films. But Hollywood's first million-dollar man would have to work like a dog to meet production schedules. So on Labor Day weekend in 1921, a worn out Arbuckle headed to San Francisco for some rest and relaxation.

The Scandal

For the large-living, heavy-drinking Arbuckle, R & R meant a weekend-long bash at the St. Francis Hotel. On September 5, several people joined Arbuckle for a party, including a 26-year-old actress named Virginia Rappe and her friend Maude Delmont. Much has been exaggerated about the sexual exploits of Rappe, but her bad reputation was largely the product of the sensationalized press of the day. However, Delmont was a convicted extortionist known for her penchant for blackmail.

Around 3:00 A.M., Arbuckle left the party for his suite. Shortly thereafter, screams emanated from his room. According to press accounts of the day, several guests rushed in to find Rappe's clothing torn. She hysterically shouted at Arbuckle to stay away from her, supposedly uttering, "Roscoe did this to me." Though very dramatic, Rappe's accusation was most likely untrue and was probably invented to sell newspapers.

The story goes that the shaken Rappe was placed in a cold bath to calm her down and was later put to bed when a doctor diagnosed her as intoxicated. The next day, the hotel doctor gave her morphine and catheterized her when Delmont mentioned that Rappe hadn't urinated in some time.

Delmont later called a doctor friend to examine Rappe, saying that Arbuckle had raped her. He found no evidence of rape but treated Rappe to help her urinate. Four days later Delmont took Rappe to the hospital, where she died of peritonitis caused by a ruptured bladder. Delmont called the police, and on September 11, Arbuckle was arrested for murder.

The Fall

Arbuckle told police—and would contend all along—that he entered his room and found Rappe lying on the bathroom floor. He said he picked her up, placed her on the bed, and rubbed ice on her stomach when she complained of abdominal pain.

Delmont told police that Arbuckle used the ice as a sexual stimulant, and years later, rumors circulated that Arbuckle had raped Rappe with a soda or champagne bottle. Yet, there was no mention of this in the press during the arrest and trial. Instead, police alleged that Arbuckle's immense weight caused Rappe's bladder to rupture as he raped her. But contemporary research speculates that Rappe was probably struck hard in the abdomen, not raped. Whatever the cause, the public—enraged by the extremely sensationalized reports in the newspapers—wanted Arbuckle hanged.

Over the next seven months, Arbuckle was tried three times for the death of Virginia Rappe. The first two ended with hung juries. In the final trial, the jury deliberated for six minutes before declaring Arbuckle not guilty and offering a written apology for the injustice placed upon him.

Arbuckle was exonerated, but the damage was done. In April 1922, the Hays Office, the motion picture industry's censorship organization, which was established in the wake of the scandal, banned Arbuckle's movies and barred him from filmmaking. Although the blacklisting was lifted in December 1922, it would be several years before Arbuckle resumed his Hollywood career. A few years after his acquittal, Arbuckle began directing under the name William Goodrich, and in the early 1930s, RKO hired him to direct a series of comic shorts. In 1933, Vitaphone—part of Warner Bros.— hired Arbuckle to appear in front of the camera again in a series of six sync-sound shorts shot in Brooklyn.

But his revitalized career was short-lived. On June 29, 1933, one day after finishing the sixth film and signing a long-term contract with Warner Bros., Arbuckle died of a heart attack at age 46. Nearly eight decades later, Arbuckle is sadly remembered more for a crime that he *didn't* commit than as the comedic genius he was.

Albert Dekker's Gruesome Demise

When a veteran actor is found dead in his apartment, compromised circumstances unleash a wave of speculation.

✳ ✳ ✳ ✳

Sex-O-Rama

IF YOU ENTER "kinky Hollywood sex" into an Internet search engine (we don't recommend this idea, by the way), you probably won't find a reference to Albert Dekker. Yet, when Dekker, the star of *Doctor Cyclops* (1940) and *The Killers* (1946), died tragically more than 40 years ago, his body was found in a state that greatly pushed the envelope of accepted sexual mores of the time. When the seasoned thespian took his final bow at age 62, he left even the most jaded observers slack-jawed in disbelief.

Who Was Albert Dekker?

Born in Brooklyn, New York, in 1905, Albert Dekker was a highly respected character actor who had been trained for the stage. After a solid career on Broadway, in which he appeared in *Grand Hotel* and *Parnell* in the early 1930s, he moved to Hollywood. Interested in politics, Dekker held the Democratic seat in the California State Assembly from 1944 to 1946. However, his life was not without tragedy. In the early 1950s, Dekker was one of many victimized by the accusations of Joseph McCarthy, which resulted in the actor's return to the stage. Also, his son John died from an accidental gunshot wound. But by the 1960s, Dekker had returned to Hollywood.

Macabre Discovery

On May 5, 1968, when Dekker's fiancée Geraldine Saunders was unable to reach him by telephone, she drove to his Hollywood apartment and found a number of notes left on his door by concerned friends. After summoning the building's manager, Saunders entered the residence. What she saw sprawled before her was enough to make her lose consciousness. Dekker was dead, that was for certain, but the way that he had died was most disturbing. Kneeling nude in his bathtub, the actor wore a hangman's noose around his neck and sported a hypodermic needle in each arm. Suggestive words such as *whip* and *slave* were scrawled on his body in red lipstick, and a rubber-ball bit was stuffed in his mouth, with the metal chains from the bit tied behind his head. Blindfolded by a scarf, Dekker was attached to three leather straps that terminated in a hitch. These, in turn, were hooked to a strap that was held in

Dekker's hand. Completing the bizarre picture were a pair of handcuffs around each wrist (with keys inserted) and obscene drawings on his abdomen.

All Choked Up

After a brief investigation, detectives concluded that Dekker had committed suicide. However, finding little evidence to support that theory, Los Angeles County Coroner Thomas Noguchi ruled the death an "accidental death, not a suicide." Some of Dekker's friends rejected both findings. They suspected murder even though the death scene showed no signs of forced entry or a struggle, although according to some reports, some camera equipment and cash were missing. Dekker's fiancée also insisted that the actor was murdered. She guessed that the killer was "someone he knew and let into the apartment." But coroner Noguchi rejected the idea of foul play in favor of accidental strangulation by "autoerotic asphyxia." The coroner explained that this solitary sexual act often features blindfolds, cross-dressing, and handcuffs. This appeared to be the case with Dekker.

A Sexual Pioneer

After his death, Albert Dekker became even more famous, but unfortunately, his heightened fame was for all the wrong reasons. Dekker's last film, *The Wild Bunch*, was released posthumously in 1969. The Western featured a group of desperados who had little use for conformity or rules. The film, directed by Sam Peckinpah, is now considered a masterpiece of editing and one of Hollywood's most provocative revisionist Westerns. It was a notable final film and a fitting epitaph considering the mode of Dekker's death.

In 2009, actor David Carradine was found dead in a similar embarrassing state. The circumstances surrounding Carradine's death invited speculation along the same lines as Dekker's demise. Sadly, both actors' deaths overshadowed their talents and accomplishments.

Little Rascals with Big Troubles

Our Gang was a popular prepubescent posse of rogues, rascals, and scamps that appeared in more than 200 short films over the course of 20 years. During the 1950s, the series was sold to television and rechristened The Little Rascals, *and it ran in syndication for decades. Most of the 41 actors who portrayed the troublesome tykes went on to live rich and resourceful lives. However, for some of the motley mites, tragedy, turmoil, and tribulation marked their adult years.*

Matthew "Stymie" Beard

BEARD COSTARRED IN numerous Our Gang shorts in the 1930s, but he started using drugs in adulthood and eventually spent time in jail for possession and dealing. He finally kicked his heroin habit in the 1960s and enjoyed a minor comeback as an actor, appearing on television shows such as *Starsky and Hutch,* and in small roles in several critically acclaimed miniseries. He died in 1981.

Scott "Scotty" Beckett

A prodigious talent who joined the Rascals in 1934, Beckett became one of Hollywood's top child actors after leaving the Our Gang family in 1936. Beckett appeared in such notable films as *Dante's Inferno* (1935), *Charge of the Light Brigade* (1936), and *King's Row* (1942). But his childhood success didn't translate into adult employment, and he spent the last ten years of his life in a self-destructive spiral. He died of an apparent drug overdose in 1968 at age 38.

Robert Blake

One of the most famous and successful members of the Our Gang clan, Robert Blake appeared in 40 episodes of the series from 1939 to 1944 under the name Mickey Gubitosi. Later, he appeared as a regular in the Red Ryder film series. After serving in the U.S. Army, Blake became a noted movie actor, starring in such well-regarded films as *In Cold Blood* (1967) and *Tell Them Willie Boy Is Here* (1969). He also played the title character on the TV series *Baretta* from 1975 to 1978. But his career and personal integrity suffered a serious blow when he was arrested and charged with murdering his wife in 2001. Although he was acquitted of murder, he was found responsible for her death in a civil trial and was ordered to pay $30 million in damages to her children.

Jay R. "Freckle Face" Smith

Freckle Face was a steady contributor to the Our Gang series until 1929. At age 14, he retired from acting and later served in the U.S. Army and ran a retail paint business in Hawaii. In 2002, Smith was murdered by a transient that he'd befriended. His body was discovered in the desert near Las Vegas.

Carl "Alfalfa" Switzer

Carl Switzer was among the most popular and fondly regarded Our Gang alumni. A staple of the group from 1935 until 1940, he forged a fortuitous and formidable career as an adult character actor, appearing in such notable films as *It's a Wonderful Life* (1946), *Pat and Mike* (1952), and *The Defiant Ones* (1958). Despite that success, he also had difficulty dismantling his demons. In January 1959, he was shot and killed in a bizarre argument over an unpaid $50 debt and a missing hunting dog. He was just 31 years old.

Billie "Buckwheat" Thomas

Buckwheat, who was a member of Our Gang from 1934 until the series' demise in 1944, was one of the few African American members of the group. He appeared in 97 productions, including all 52 of the Our Gang films produced by MGM, the studio that assumed control of the series in 1938. After leaving the show, Thomas worked as a film technician until his death of a heart attack in 1980 at age 49. Ten years later, he was the subject of an odd controversy when the investigative program *20/20* aired an interview with an imposter—a grocery store clerk in Arizona—who claimed to be the "real" Buckwheat.

Thelma Todd: Suicide or Murder?

During her nine-year film career, Thelma Todd costarred in dozens of comedies with the likes of Harry Langdon, Laurel and Hardy, and the Marx Brothers. Today, however, the "Ice Cream Blonde," as she was known, is best remembered for her bizarre death, which remains one of Hollywood's most enduring mysteries. Let's explore what could have happened.

❋　❋　❋　❋

Sins Indulged

TODD WAS BORN in Lawrence, Massachusetts, in 1906 and arrived in Hollywood at age 20 via the beauty pageant circuit. Pretty and vivacious, she quickly became a hot commodity and fell headlong into Tinseltown's anything-goes party scene. In 1932, she married Pasquale "Pat" DiCicco, an agent of sorts who was also associated with gangster Charles "Lucky" Luciano. Their marriage was plagued by drunken fights, and they divorced two years later.

For solace, Todd turned to director Roland West, who didn't approve of her drinking and drug use, but he could not stop her. With his help, Todd opened a roadhouse called Thelma Todd's Sidewalk Café, located on the Pacific Coast Highway, and the actress moved into a spacious apartment above the restaurant. Shortly after, Todd began a romantic relationship with gangster "Lucky" Luciano, who tried to get her to let him use a room at the Sidewalk Café for illegal gambling. Todd repeatedly refused.

On the morning of December 16, 1935, Todd was found dead in the front seat of her 1934 Lincoln Phaeton convertible, which was parked in the two-car garage she shared with West. The apparent cause of death was carbon monoxide poisoning, though whether Todd was the victim of an accident, suicide, or murder remains a mystery.

Little evidence supports the suicide theory, outside the mode of death and the fact that Todd led a fast-paced lifestyle that sometimes got the better of her. Indeed, her career was going remarkably well, and she had purchased Christmas presents and was looking forward to a New Year's Eve party. So suicide does not seem a viable cause, though it is still mentioned as a probable one in many accounts.

The Accident Theory

However, an accidental death is also a possibility. The key to her car was in the "on" position, and the motor was dead when Todd was discovered by her maid. West suggested to investigators that the actress turned on the car to get warm, passed out because she was drunk, and then succumbed to carbon monoxide poisoning. Todd also had a heart condition, according to West, and this may have contributed to her death.

Nonetheless, the notion of foul play is suggested by several incongruities found at the scene. Spots of blood were discovered on and in Todd's car and on her mouth, and her nose was broken, leading some to believe she was knocked out then placed in the car to make it look like a suicide. (Police attributed the injuries to Todd falling unconscious and striking her head on the steering wheel.) In addition, Todd's blood-alcohol level was extremely high—high enough to stupefy her so that someone could carry her without her fighting back—and her high-heeled shoes were clean and unscuffed, even though she would have had to ascend a flight of outdoor, concrete stairs to reach the garage, which was a 271-step climb behind the restaurant. Investigators also found an unidentified smudged handprint on the left side of the vehicle.

Two with Motive

If Todd was murdered, as some have suggested, who had motive? Because of her wild lifestyle, there are several potential suspects, most notably Pasquale DiCicco, who was known to have a violent temper, and "Lucky" Luciano, who was angry at

Todd for refusing to let him use her restaurant for his shady and illegal activities.

Despite the many questions raised by the evidence found at the scene, a grand jury ruled Todd's death accidental. The investigation had been hampered by altered and destroyed evidence, threats to witnesses, and cover-ups, making it impossible to ever learn what really happened. An open-casket service was held at Forest Lawn Memorial Park, where the public viewed the actress bedecked in yellow roses. After the service, Todd was cremated, eliminating the possibility of a second autopsy. Later, when her mother, Alice Todd, died, the actress's ashes were placed in her mother's casket so they could be buried together in Massachusetts.

The Sex-sational Trial of Errol Flynn

When a handsome leading man was charged with rape, his status in Hollywood was in doubt. But rather than signaling his end in the business, his popularity soared ever higher.

✳ ✳ ✳ ✳

THE SAYING "IN like Flynn" means little these days, but during the 1940s, it was used to compliment one who was doing exceedingly well. More to the point, it usually referred to sexual conquests made by a lucky "man about town."

The saying originated with Hollywood heartthrob Errol Flynn (1909–1959), the swashbuckling star of *Captain Blood* (1935) and *The Adventures of Robin Hood* (1938). A "man's man" in the most cocksure sense, Flynn was known for his barroom brawls and trysts both on camera and off, which became part of his star image.

He wore this colorful mantle like a badge of honor, but he did suffer a hit to his reputation when he was charged with two counts of statutory rape.

Swashbuckling Seductor

The alleged crimes took place during the summer of 1942. In one instance, 17-year-old Betty Hansen claimed that Flynn had seduced her after she became ill from overimbibing at a Hollywood party. In the other, 15-year-old Peggy Satterlee insisted that Flynn took advantage of her on his yacht, *The Sirocco*, during a trip to Catalina Island. Both women claimed that he referred to them by the nicknames "S.Q.Q." (San Quentin Quail) and "J.B." (Jail Bait), thereby suggesting that Flynn knew that they were underage. Flynn was arrested that fall and charged with two counts of rape. Proclaiming his innocence, he hired high-powered attorney Jerry Giesler, who called the girl's motives and pasts into question and stacked the jury with nine women in the hopes that Flynn's considerable charm might win them over. The move would prove prophetic.

Questionable Character?

When the defense presented its case, Giesler went directly for the jugular. His cross-examination revealed that both girls had engaged in sexual relations *before* the alleged incidents with Flynn and that Satterlee had even had an abortion. More damning, Satterlee admitted to frequently lying about her age and was inconsistent in a number of her answers. Sadly, then and now, many girls and women who have been sexually active are no longer seen as worthy of protection or respect.

There was also Satterlee's claim that Flynn had taken her below deck to gaze at the moon through a porthole. Giesler challenged the expert testimony of an astronomer hired by the prosecution, getting the man to admit that, given the boat's apparent course, such a view was physically impossible through the porthole in Flynn's cabin.

The Verdict

By the time Flynn took the stand, the members of the all-female jury were half won over by his charm. By the time he finished arguing his innocence, their minds were made up. The effect was not at all surprising for a man whom actress and eight-time costar Olivia de Havilland once described as "...the handsomest, most charming, most magnetic, most virile young man in the entire world."

When a verdict of "not guilty" was read, women in the court-room applauded and wept. Afterward, the jury forewoman noted: "We felt there had been other men in the girls' lives. Frankly, the cards were on the table and we couldn't believe the girls' stories."

Continued Fortune in a Man's World

Cleared of all charges, Errol Flynn continued to make movies, resumed his carousing ways, and grew even more popular in the public eye. Many felt that, despite the verdict, Flynn had indeed had sexual relations with the young women, but most were willing to forgive the transgression because the liaisons seemed consensual and the allegations of rape looked like a frame job.

Young men would regard the amorous actor as an ideal to emu-late, and women would continue to swoon as always. But years of hard living eventually took their toll on Flynn. By the time he reached middle age, his looks had all but vanished. At the premature age of 50, Flynn suffered a massive heart attack and died. Death only served to cement Flynn's legendary status.

A Reckoning: Harvey Weinstein, #MeToo, and Time's Up

In Hollywood, everyone knew Harvey Weinstein's name. By the end of 2017, however, his reputation would wind up in tatters.

✳ ✳ ✳ ✳

ADMIRED—AND FEARED—BY MUCH of the film industry, the movie producer's career took off in the late 1970s and early 1980s when Weinstein and his brother Bob created a film production company called Miramax.

By the late 1980s and early 1990s, Miramax produced a number of hits, including *The Thin Blue Line* (1988), *Sex, Lies, and Videotape* (1989), *Tie Me Up! Tie Me Down!* (1990), and *Pulp Fiction* (1994). The company won its first Academy Award for Best Picture in 1997 for *The English Patient*. Weinstein himself took home an Oscar for *Shakespeare in Love* in 1999.

As Weinstein's clout among the industry's best and brightest grew, the movie mogul developed a reputation as a notorious executive who called for his films to be fundamentally restructured or reedited prior to release. He earned and proudly wore the moniker "Harvey Scissorhands"; for example, fellow producer Scott Rudin infamously fought Weinstein over the music and final cut of *The Hours* (2002).

Weinstein and his brother left Miramax to form their own production company, The Weinstein Company, in 2005. He became increasingly active in politics and outspoken on issues like gun control and health care. And his colleagues continued to praise him: an analysis found that, between 1966 and 2016, Weinstein tied with God as the second-most thanked person during Academy Award acceptance speeches.

A Reckoning

Exposes by the *New York Times* and the *New Yorker*, each published days apart in early October 2017, painted a startling picture of the alleged harassment by the powerful producer.

The stories found that Weinstein harassed, assaulted, or raped more than a dozen women throughout his life and career. A number of prominent actresses, including Ashley Judd and Rose McGowan, described how Weinstein would appear in hotel rooms in nothing but a bathrobe and ask for a massage. A published audiotape from a 2015 New York Police Department sting found Weinstein pressuring model Ambra Battilana Gutierrez to come into his hotel room. In the tape, Weinstein admitted to groping Gutierrez.

Weinstein issued an apology and acknowledged "a lot of pain" but disputed the allegations. He said he was working with a therapist and was preparing to sue the *New York Times*. But Weinstein's leave of absence was short-lived: three days after the first story broke about his misconduct, his company's board announced his ouster.

The accusations against Weinstein piled up, and within months, more than 80 women came forward to accuse Weinstein of a host of inappropriate behavior. Police in Los Angeles, New York, and the United Kingdom separately confirmed investigations into allegations involving Weinstein. New York state prosecutors filed a lawsuit against the Weinstein Company in February 2018.

The Academy of Motion Picture Arts and Sciences voted overwhelmingly to expel Weinstein. Institutions across the United States and the United Kingdom took similar actions to revoke honors or memberships in Weinstein's name. Weinstein's legacy was eroding before his eyes, and the entertainment industry, alongside workplace culture across the nation, was undergoing rapid change.

#MeToo and Time's Up

Despite Weinstein's laundry list of allegations, the movie producer's behavior prompted a pair of wide-reaching campaigns. In 2006, activist Tarana Burke had created the phrase "Me Too" in an attempt to bring awareness to sexual assault victims. After the explosive allegations, Burke's 12-year-old phrase was coopted by actress Alyssa Milano when she encouraged people to reply to a tweet about sexual harassment or assault with the words "me too." Immediately, Milano's call lit social media abuzz, and thousands of women—young, old, and from different backgrounds—shared their own stories.

"In many regards Me Too is about survivors talking to survivors," Burke told the *Boston Globe*." ... It was about survivors exchanging empathy with each other."

And on January 1, 2018, a group of 300 women in the film, television, and theater industries launched a complementary initiative called Time's Up, a manifesto and coalition aimed at providing a wealth of resources for victims of assault, harassment, and inequality in the workplace. A legal fund developed to assist victims amassed $21 million in two months.

Chaplin's Coffin Held for Ransom

In the silent era, he entertained millions without ever uttering a single word. During his career, he produced and starred in nearly 100 movies, making him a millionaire at an early age. Perhaps that's why after his death, two men thought Charlie Chaplin's casket was worth more than half a million dollars in ransom.

✳ ✳ ✳ ✳

The Life and Death of a Silent Star

BORN IN LONDON on April 16, 1889, Charles Spencer Chaplin had his first taste of show business at age 5 when his mother, a failing music hall entertainer, could not continue her act, and little Charlie stepped up and finished her show. After years of moving back and forth between his separated parents, workhouses, and school, he officially entered show business in 1898 (at age 9) when he became one of the Eight Lancashire Lads, a musical comedy act that worked the lower-class music halls in London. After a couple of years, he was seeking employment in various offices, factories, and households to support his mentally ill and sick mother. Finally, around age 12, he reentered the music hall scene, joining Fred Karno's London Comedians, a traveling music hall act.

Chaplin continued working with traveling shows until he signed his first contract with the legendary Keystone Studio, in late 1913, at age 24. In February 1914, Chaplin's first movie, *Making a Living*, premiered. It would be the first of more than 30 shorts that Chaplin made in 1914 alone. In fact, from 1915 until the end of his career, Chaplin was featured in nearly

100 movies, mostly shorts. No small feat considering that he wrote, starred in, directed, produced, and even scored all of his own movies. All of this not only made Charlie Chaplin a household name but also a very rich man.

Public Success, Private Mess

But not everything was wine and roses for Chaplin. After three failed marriages, the 54-year old actor caused quite a stir in 1943 when he married his fourth wife, Oona O'Neill, who was just 17 at the time. More scandal found Chaplin in the early 1950s when the U.S. government began to suspect that he and his family might be Communist sympathizers. There seemed to be very little to support their suspicions other than the fact that Chaplin had simply chosen to live in the United States while not declaring U.S. citizenship. Regardless, Chaplin soon tired of what he deemed harassment and moved to Switzerland, where he lived with his wife and their eight children until his death on Christmas Day 1977. Shortly thereafter, perhaps the strangest chapter in Charlie Chaplin's story began.

Grave Robbers

On March 2, 1978, visitors to Charlie Chaplin's grave were shocked to discover a massive hole where the actor's coffin had been. It soon became clear that sometime overnight, someone had dug up and stolen Chaplin's entire casket. But who would do such a thing? And why? It didn't take long to find the answer. Several days later, Oona began receiving phone calls from people claiming to have stolen the body and demanding a portion of Chaplin's millions in exchange for the casket. Oona dismissed most of the callers as crackpots, with the exception of one. This mysterious male caller seemed to know an awful lot about what Chaplin's coffin looked like. But because he was demanding the equivalent of $600,000 U.S. dollars in exchange for the coffin's safe return, Oona told the caller she needed more proof. Several days later, a photo of Chaplin's newly unearthed casket arrived in her mailbox, and Oona alerted Swiss police.

The Arrests

When Oona Chaplin first met with Swiss authorities, she could only show them the photo and tell them that the caller was male and that he spoke with a Slavic accent. She also told them that she had no intention of paying the ransom. But the police convinced Oona that the longer she pretended to be willing to pay the ransom, the better chance they had of catching the thief. Oona was emotionally unable to deal with the fiasco, so Chaplin's daughter Geraldine complied with the investigators' request.

During the next few weeks, Geraldine did such a convincing job that she talked the caller's ransom price down from $600,000 to $250,000, though the Chaplin family still did not plan to pay it. In the meantime, Swiss police were desperately trying to trace the calls. Their first big break came when they established that the calls were coming from a local Lausanne pay phone. However, there were more than 200 pay phones in the town. Undaunted, police began staking out all of them. Their hard work paid off when they arrested 24-year-old Roman Wardas, who admitted to stealing Chaplin's coffin, stating that he had gotten the idea after reading about a similar body "kidnapping" in an Italian newspaper. Based on information Wardas provided police, a second man, 38-year-old Gantcho Ganev, was also arrested. Like Wardas, Ganev admitted to helping take the casket but claimed that it was all Wardas's idea and that he just helped out.

So Where's the Body?

Of course, once the two suspects were in custody, the question on everyone's minds was the location of Chaplin's casket. Ganev and Wardas claimed that after stealing the casket from the cemetery, they drove it to a field and buried it in a shallow hole.

Following directions provided by both suspects, Swiss police descended upon a farm about 12 miles from the Chaplin estate. Spotting a mound of what appeared to be freshly moved dirt, they began digging, and on May 17, 1978, in the middle of a cornfield, Chaplin's unopened coffin was recovered.

Once word got out, people began flocking to the farm, so the farmer placed a small wooden cross, ornamented with a cane, over the hole where the casket had been buried. For several weeks, people brought flowers and paid their respects to the empty hole.

The Aftermath

After a short trial, both men were convicted of extortion and disturbing the peace of the dead. As the admitted mastermind of the crime, Wardas was sentenced to nearly five years of hard labor. Ganev received only an 18-month suspended sentence.

As for Chaplin's unopened casket, it was returned to Corsier-Sur-Vevey Cemetery and was reburied in the exact spot where it had originally been interred. Only this time, to deter any future grave robbers, Oona ordered it buried under six feet of solid concrete. And when she passed away 14 years later, her will stipulated that she also be buried under at least six feet of concrete. She was.

Anything but Splendor: Natalie Wood

The official account of Natalie Wood's tragic death is riddled with holes. For this reason, cover-up theorists continue to run hog-wild with conjecture. Here's a sampling of the questions, facts, and assertions surrounding the case.

✳ ✳ ✳ ✳

A Life in Pictures

THERE ARE THOSE who will forever recall Natalie Wood as the adorable child actress from *Miracle on 34th Street* (1947) and those who remember her as the sexy but wholesome grown-up star of movies such as *West Side Story* (1961),

Splendor in the Grass (1961), and Bob & Carol & Ted & Alice (1969). Both groups generally agree that Wood had uncommon beauty and talent.

Wood appeared in her first film, Happy Land (1943), in a bit part alongside other people from her hometown of Santa Rosa, California, where the film was shot. She stood out to the director, who remembered her later when he needed to cast a child in another film. Wood was uncommonly mature and professional for a child actress, which helped her make a relatively smooth transition to ingenue roles.

Although Wood befriended James Dean and Sal Mineo—her troubled young costars from Rebel Without a Cause (1955)—and she briefly dated Elvis Presley, she preferred to move in established Hollywood circles. By the time she was 20, she was married to Robert Wagner and was costarring with Frank Sinatra in Kings Go Forth (1958), which firmly ensconced her in the Hollywood establishment. The early 1960s represent the high point of Wood's career, and she specialized in playing high-spirited characters with determination and spunk. She added two more Oscar nominations to the one she received for Rebel and racked up five Golden Globe nominations for Best Actress. This period also proved to be personally turbulent for Wood, as she suffered through a failed marriage to Wagner and another to Richard Gregson. After taking time off to raise her children, Wood remarried Wagner and returned to her acting career.

Shocking News

And so, on November 29, 1981, the headline hit the newswires much like an out-of-control car hits a brick wall. Natalie Wood, the beautiful, vivacious 43-year-old star of stage and screen, had drowned after falling from her yacht the Splendour, which was anchored off California's Santa Catalina Island. Wood had been on the boat during a break from her latest film, Brainstorm, and was accompanied by Wagner and Brainstorm costar Christopher Walken. Skipper Dennis Davern was at the helm. Foul play was not suspected.

In My Esteemed Opinion

After a short investigation, Chief Medical Examiner Dr. Thomas Noguchi listed Wood's death as an accidental drowning. Tests revealed that she had consumed "seven or eight" glasses of wine, and the coroner contended that in her intoxicated state Wood had probably stumbled and fallen overboard while attempting to untie the yacht's rubber dinghy. He also stated that cuts and bruises on her body could have occurred when she fell from the boat.

Doubting Thomases

To this day, many question Wood's mysterious demise and believe that the accidental drowning theory sounds a bit too convenient. Pointed questions have led to many rumors: Does someone know more about Wood's final moments than they're letting on? Was her drowning really an accident, or did someone intentionally or accidentally *help* her overboard? Could this be why she sustained substantial bruising on her face and the back of her legs? Why was Wagner so reluctant to publicly discuss the incident? Were Christopher Walken and Wood an item as had been rumored? With this possibility in mind, could a booze-fueled fight have erupted between the two men? Could Wood have then tried to intervene, only to be knocked overboard for her efforts? And why did authorities declare Wood's death accidental so quickly? Would such a hasty ruling have been issued had the principals involved not been famous, wealthy, and influential?

Ripples

At the time of Wood's death, she and Wagner were seven years into their second marriage to each other. Whether Wood was carrying on an affair with Walken, as was alleged, may be immaterial, even if it made for interesting tabloid fodder. But Wagner's perception of their relationship could certainly be a factor. If nothing else, it might better explain the argument that ensued between Wagner and Walken that fateful night.

Case Closed?

Further information about Wood's death is sparse because no eyewitnesses have come forward. However, a businesswoman whose boat was anchored nearby testified that she heard a woman shouting for help, and then a voice responding, "We'll be over to get you," so the woman went back to bed. Just after dawn, Wood's body was found floating a mile away from the *Splendour*, approximately 200 yards offshore. The dinghy was found nearby; its only cargo was a stack of lifejackets.

In 2008, after 27 years of silence, Robert Wagner recalled in his autobiography, *Pieces of My Heart: A Life*, that he and Walken had engaged in a heated argument during supper after Walken had suggested that Wood star in more films, effectively keeping her away from their children. Wagner and Walken then headed topside to cool down. Sometime around midnight, Wagner said he returned to his cabin and discovered that his wife was missing. He soon realized that the yacht's dinghy was gone as well. In his book, he surmised that Wood may have gone to secure the dinghy that had been noisily slapping against the boat. Then, tipsy from the wine, she probably fell into the ocean and drowned. Walken notified the authorities.

Was Natalie Wood's demise the result of a deadly mix of wine and saltwater as the coroner's report suggests? This certainly could be the case. But why would she leave her warm cabin to tend to a loose rubber dinghy in the dark of night? Could an errant rubber boat really make such a commotion?

Perhaps we'll never know what happened that fateful night, but an interview conducted shortly before Wood's death proved prophetic: "I'm frightened to death of the water," said Wood about a long-held fear. "I can swim a little bit, but I'm afraid of water that is dark."

Lana Turner and the Death of a Gangster

On the evening of April 4, 1958, Beverly Hills police arrived at the home of actress Lana Turner to discover the dead body of her one-time boyfriend Johnny Stompanato, a violent gangster with underworld ties. He had been stabbed to death, but the exact circumstances of his demise were muddied by the sensational reporting of the tabloid press.

✳   ✳   ✳   ✳

Sweater Girl

LANA TURNER'S FIRST credited film role came in 1937 with *They Won't Forget*, which earned her the moniker "Sweater Girl," thanks to the tight-fitting sweater her character wore. Turner went on to star in hits such as *Honky Tonk* (1941), *The Postman Always Rings Twice* (1946), and *Peyton Place* (1957).

Hanging with the Wrong Crowd

Offscreen, Turner was renowned for her many love affairs. During her lifetime, she amassed eight marriages to seven different husbands. It was shortly after the breakup of her fifth marriage to actor Lex Barker in 1957 that Turner met Johnny Stompanato. When she discovered that his name was not John Steele (as he had told her) and that he had ties to underworld figures such as Mickey Cohen, she realized the negative publicity that those ties could bring to her career, so she tried to end the relationship. But Stompanato incessantly pursued her, and the pair engaged in a number of violent incidents, which came to a head on the night of April 4.

Turner's 14-year-old daughter, Cheryl Crane, rushed to her mother's defense after hearing Stompanato threaten to "cut" Turner. Fearing for her mother's life, the girl grabbed a kitchen knife, then ran upstairs to Turner's bedroom. According to Crane's account, Turner opened the door and Cheryl saw

Stompanato with his arms raised in the air in a fury. Cheryl then rushed past Turner and stabbed Stompanato, killing him. Turner called her mother, who brought their personal physician to the house, but it was too late. By the time the police were called, much time had passed and evidence had been moved around. According to the Beverly Hills police chief, who was the first officer to arrive, Turner immediately asked if she could take the rap for her daughter.

At the crime scene, the body appeared to have been moved and the fingerprints on the murder weapon were so smudged that they could not be identified. The case sparked a media sensation, especially among the tabloid press, which turned against Turner, essentially accusing her of killing Stompanato and asking her daughter to cover for her. Mickey Cohen, who paid for Stompanato's funeral, publicly called for the arrests of both Turner and Crane. For years, ugly rumors surrounding the case persisted.

"The Performance of a Lifetime"?

During the inquest, the press described Turner's testimony as "the performance of a lifetime." But police and authorities knew from the beginning that Turner did not do it. At the inquest, it took just 20 minutes for the jury to return a verdict of justifiable homicide, so the D.A. decided not to bring the case to trial. However, Turner was convicted of being an unfit mother, and Crane was remanded to her grandmother's care until she turned 18, further tainting Turner's image. There was an aura of "guilt" around Turner for years, though she was never seriously considered a suspect in the actual murder.

As fate would have it, Turner's film *Peyton Place*, which features a courtroom scene about a murder committed by a teenager, was still in theaters at the time of the inquest. Ticket sales skyrocketed as a result of the sensational publicity, and Turner parlayed the success of the film into better screen roles, including her part in a remake of *Imitation of Life* (1959), which would become one of her most successful films. She appeared in romantic melodramas until the mid-1960s, when age began to affect her career. In the '70s and '80s, she made the transition to television, appearing on shows such as *The Survivors, The Love Boat,* and *Falcon Crest.*

William Desmond Taylor

The murder of actor/director William Desmond Taylor was like something out of an Agatha Christie novel, complete with a handsome, debonair victim and multiple suspects, each with a motive. But unlike Christie's novels, in which the murderer was always unmasked, Taylor's death remains unsolved nearly 100 years later.

✳   ✳   ✳   ✳

O N THE EVENING of February 1, 1922, Taylor was shot in the back by an unknown assailant; his body was discovered the next morning by a servant, Henry Peavey. News of Taylor's demise spread quickly, and several individuals, including officials from Paramount Studios, where Taylor was employed, raced to the dead man's home to clear it of anything incriminating, such as illegal liquor, evidence of drug use, illicit correspondence, and signs of sexual indiscretion. However, no one called the police until later in the morning.

Numerous Suspects

Soon an eclectic array of potential suspects came to light, including Taylor's criminally inclined former butler, Edward F. Sands, who had gone missing before the murder; popular movie comedienne Mabel Normand, whom Taylor had entertained the evening of his death; actress Mary Miles Minter, who had a passionate crush on the handsome director who was 28 years her senior; and Charlotte Shelby, Minter's mother, who often wielded a gun to protect her daughter's honor, tarnished though it might be in other people's views.

Taylor's murder was the last thing Hollywood needed at the time, coming as it did on the heels of rape allegations against popular film comedian Fatty Arbuckle. Scandals brought undue attention on Hollywood, and the Arbuckle story had taken its toll. Officials at Paramount tried to keep a lid on the Taylor story, but the tabloid press had a field day. A variety of personal foibles were made public in the weeks that followed, and both Normand and Minter saw their careers come to a screeching halt as a result. Taylor's own indiscretions were also revealed, such as the fact that he kept a special souvenir, usually lingerie, from every woman he bedded.

Little Evidence

Police interviewed many of Taylor's friends and colleagues, including all potential suspects. However, there was no evidence to incriminate anyone specifically, and no one was formally charged.

Investigators and amateur sleuths pursued the case for years. Sands was long a prime suspect, based on his criminal past and his estrangement from the victim. But it was later revealed that on the day of the murder, Sands had signed in for work at a lumberyard in Oakland, California—some 400 miles away—and thus could not have committed the crime. Coming in second was Shelby, whose temper and threats were legendary. Shelby's own acting career had fizzled out early, and all of her hopes for stardom were pinned on her daughter. She threatened many men who tried to woo Mary.

In the mid-1990s, another possible suspect surfaced—a long-forgotten silent-film actress named Margaret Gibson. According to Bruce Long, author of *William Desmond Taylor: A Dossier*, Gibson confessed to a friend on her deathbed in 1964 that years before she had killed a man named William Desmond Taylor. However, the woman to whom Gibson cleared her conscience didn't know who Taylor was and thought nothing more about it.

The Mystery Continues

Could Margaret Gibson (aka Pat Lewis) be Taylor's murderer? She had acted with Taylor in Hollywood in the early 1910s, and she may even have been one of his many sexual conquests. She also had a criminal past, including charges of blackmail, drug use, and prostitution, so it's entirely conceivable that she was a member of a group trying to extort money from the director, a popular theory among investigators. But according to an earlier book, *A Cast of Killers* by Sidney D. Kirkpatrick, veteran Hollywood director King Vidor had investigated the murder as material for a film script and through his research believed Shelby was the murderer. But out of respect for Minter, he never did anything about it.

Ultimately, however, we may never know for certain who killed William Desmond Taylor, or why. The case has long grown cold, and anyone with specific knowledge of the murder is likely dead. Unlike a Hollywood thriller, in which the killer is revealed at the end, Taylor's death is a macabre puzzle that likely will never be solved.

Long Live the Crime-Fighting King

If a chubby, jumpsuit-wearing Elvis came karate-kicking out of a limo, what would you do?

✳   ✳   ✳   ✳

BACK IN 1977, shortly before Elvis ended his reign as the King of Rock and Roll, you would run, which is just what two trouble-making teens did when Presley gave them the scare of their lives.

Around midnight on June 23, The King arrived in Madison, Wisconsin, for a show. En route to his hotel from the airport, Presley's limousine, a 1964 Cadillac, hit a red light at the intersection of Stoughton Road and East Washington Avenue. Peering out the window to the right, Presley was watching a young man reading the gas meters at the corner Skyland Service Station, when two teenage misfits charged at the employee and began beating him up.

With a penchant for helping others, Presley, wearing his trademark aviator sunglasses and a dark blue Drug Enforcement Agency jumpsuit over his sequined outfit, busted out of the limousine, despite his bodyguards' requests. He ran toward the scene, kicking karate-style and saying, "I'll take you on."

The hoodlums ran off. As it turned out, the young attendant's father owned the service station and one of the attackers had recently been fired. Getting back in the limousine, Presley reportedly laughed and said, "Did you see the looks on their faces?"

With a caravan of fans in pursuit having just witnessed Presley's crime-prevention skills, the King's entourage continued on to the hotel. The next day, Presley gave a lackluster concert, prompting one local reviewer to write: "So, long live the King. His reign is over. But that is no reason for us not to remember him fondly."

Presley died 51 days later, on August 16, 1977, yet as the reviewer said, many remember his Madison exploits fondly. While Skyland closed years ago, the lot was most recently the site of a used car store, which paid homage to Elvis and Madison's famed gas station altercation with a marble plaque.

Bugsy Siegel's "Screen Test"

When mobster Bugsy Siegel acted out a scene at the behest of actor pal George Raft, the results proved eye-opening. Much to the surprise of all, the gangster could really act. Unfortunately, Siegel never pursued acting, choosing instead to remain on his murderous course. This begs the obvious question: "What if?"

✳ ✳ ✳ ✳

IN THE ANNALS of the underworld, there was perhaps no one more dapper, or more ruthless, than Benjamin "Bugsy" Siegel (1906–1947). Nearly six feet tall, with piercing blue eyes that melted the heart of many a woman, Siegel had movie-star looks and savoir faire that disguised a temperament that could easily be described as hair-triggered. During his hard-lived life, Siegel committed nearly every crime in the book and was implicated by the FBI for more than 30 murders.

Born Benjamin Hymen Siegelbaum, the up-and-coming mobster picked up the nickname "Bugsy" (the slang term *bugs* means "crazy") for his high level of viciousness. Siegel hated the tag, considering it a low-class connection to his hardscrabble youth, and threatened to kill anyone who used it in his presence. Still, the mobster was said to be a natural born charmer who never seemed at a loss for companionship, female or otherwise.

One of Siegel's closest friends was Hollywood actor George Raft, who was known for such memorable films as *Scarface* (1932), *I Stole a Million* (1939), and *They Drive by Night* (1940). The two had both grown up on the gritty streets of New York City's Lower East Side. Throughout their lives, the pair would engage in a form of mutual admiration. For example, Raft's movie career featured many mob-related roles. So, when he needed the proper tough-guy "inspiration," the actor would mimic mannerisms and inflections that he picked up from his real-life mobster pals. Siegel, on the other hand, made no secret of the fact that he was starstruck by Hollywood and sometimes wished that he too had become an actor. He viewed Raft as the Real McCoy in this arena and gave him due respect. Hoping to get ever closer to the Hollywood action, while at the same time expanding his "operations," Siegel moved to California in 1937.

A Natural Born ... Actor?

In no time, Siegel was hobnobbing with major celebrities even as his deadly business dealings escalated. In 1941, Raft was shooting *Manpower* with the legendary Marlene Dietrich, when Siegel showed up on the set to observe. After watching Raft go through a few takes before heading off to his dressing room, Siegel told his buddy that he could do the scene better. An amused Raft told his friend to go ahead and give it a shot. Over the course of the next few minutes, the smirk would leave Raft's face.

Siegel reenacted Raft's scene perfectly. He had not only memorized the dialogue line for line, but he interpreted Raft's nuanced gestures as well. This was no small feat given the fact that Siegel had absolutely no training as an actor. A stunned Raft told Siegel that he just might have what it takes to be an actor.

A Dream Unfulfilled

But such Tinseltown dreams were not to be. Despite his demonstrated talent, moviemakers probably wouldn't have used him. And who could blame them? What if Siegel decided to go "Bugsy" on them for not awarding him a role, for critiquing his performance, or for changing his lines? Temperamental actors are one thing; homicidal ones, quite another.

History shows that Siegel played it fast and loose from that point forward, putting most of his energies into creating the Flamingo Hotel and, along with it, the gaming capital of the world—Las Vegas. Siegel's mob associates from the East Coast put him in charge of construction of the opulent hotel. Siegel envisioned an extravegent hotel and, at least for him, money was no object. But when costs soared to $6 million—four times the original budget—Siegel's associates became concerned.

On June 20, 1947, Siegel's dreams of a life on the silver screen came to an abrupt end when a number of well-placed rounds from an M-1 Carbine sent the Hollywood gangster into the afterworld at age 41. It is believed that Siegel was killed by his own mob associates who were convinced that he was pilfering money from the organization. Siegel's life and grisly end are grand pieces of mob drama that got their due on the silver screen in the 1991 flick *Bugsy*, which starred Warren Beatty as the doomed mobster.

More Stars Behind Bars!

Most actors have done their time working their way up the ladder through roles in B-movies, television, or theater. But a surprising number of actors have literally done time—as in prison time. Here's a sample:

Lillo Brancato

BRANCATO PLAYED ROBERT De Niro's son in *A Bronx Tale* (1993) and a bumbling mobster on *The Sopranos*. But drug addiction took its toll on his career. In December 2005, Brancato and a friend broke into an apartment looking for drugs. In the process, an off-duty policeman was shot and killed. Brancato was charged with second-degree murder and attempted burglary. He was acquitted on the murder charges in 2008 but served time for attempted burglary.

Rory Calhoun

A popular leading man who appeared in numerous Westerns, Calhoun was a petty criminal as a teenager and served three years in a federal reformatory for car theft. Reformed by a priest, he was a blue-collar worker until a chance meeting with star Alan Ladd led to a career in the movies, including two Marilyn Monroe films.

Stacy Keach

In the mid-1980s, the star of the acclaimed Western *The Long Riders* (1980) served six months in prison for smuggling cocaine into England.

Paul Kelly

Paul Kelly played lead roles in many B-films, mostly crime melodramas. In the late 1920s, he killed his best friend, actor Ray Raymond, in a fistfight over Raymond's wife, actress Dorothy MacKaye. He served two years for manslaughter, then went on to a successful film and stage career, receiving a Tony Award in 1948 for his role in *Command Decision*.

Tommy Rettig

As a child actor, Rettig gained lasting fame as Lassie's master in the popular 1950s TV series. But in 1972, he was arrested for growing marijuana, and in the mid-1970s, he was sentenced to five and a half years in prison for smuggling cocaine into the U.S. The charges were dropped after an appeal, as was another drug charge five years later.

Christian Slater

In 1989, Slater was involved in a drunken car chase that ended when he crashed into a telephone pole and kicked a policeman while trying to escape. He was charged with evading police, driving under the influence, assault with a deadly weapon (his boots), and driving with a suspended license. In 1994, Slater was arrested for trying to bring a gun onto a plane. In 1997, he was sentenced to 90 days in jail for cocaine abuse, battery, and assault with a deadly weapon.

Mae West

In 1926, Mae West, one of Hollywood's most iconic sex symbols, was sentenced to ten days in jail when her Broadway show, *Sex*, was declared obscene.

Chapter 7

Gangsters, Mobsters, and the Mafia

Who Founded the Mafia?

To be honest, we really didn't want to answer this question. But then our editors made us an offer we couldn't refuse.

✳ ✳ ✳ ✳

THIS IS LIKE asking, "Who founded England?" or "Who founded capitalism?" The Mafia is more of a phenomenon than an organization—it's a movement that rose from a complicated interaction of multiple factors, including history, economics, geography, and politics. Hundreds of thousands of pages have been written by historians, sociologists, novelists, screenwriters, and criminologists who have attempted to chart the history and origins of the Mafia, so it's doubtful that we'll be able to provide any real revelations in five hundred words. But we're a hardy bunch, and we'll do our best.

By all accounts, the Mafia came to prominence in Sicily during the mid-nineteenth century. Given Sicily's history, this makes sense—the island has repeatedly been invaded and occupied, and has generally been mired in poverty for thousands of years. By the mid-nineteenth century, Italy was in total chaos due to the abolition of feudalism and the lack of a central government or a semblance of a legitimate legal system.

As sociologists will confirm, people who live in areas that fall victim to such upheaval tend to rely on various forms of self-government. In Sicily, this took the form of what has become known as the Mafia. The fellowship, which originated in the rural areas of the Mediterranean island, is based on a complicated system of respect, violence, distrust of government, and the code of *omertà*—a word that is synonymous with the group's code of silence and refers to an unspoken agreement to never cooperate with authorities, under penalty of death. Just as there is no one person who founded the Mafia, there is no one person who runs it. The term "Mafia" refers to any group of organized criminals that follows the traditional Sicilian system of bosses, *capos* ("chiefs"), and soldiers. These groups are referred to as "families."

In the United States

Although the Mafia evolved in Sicily during the nineteenth century, most Americans equate it to the crime families that dominated the headlines in Chicago and New York for much of the twentieth century. The American Mafia developed as a result of the huge wave of Sicilian immigrants that arrived in the United States in the late nineteenth and early twentieth centuries. These newcomers brought with them the Mafia structure and the code of *omertà*.

These Sicilian immigrants often clustered together in poor urban areas, such as Park Slope in Brooklyn and the south side of Chicago. There, far from the eyes of authorities, disputes were handled by locals. By the 1920s, crime families had sprung up all over the United States and gang wars were prevalent. In the 1930s, Lucky Luciano—who is sometimes called the father of the American Mafia—organized "The Commission," a faux-judiciary system that oversaw the activities of the Mafia in the United States.

Though Mafia families have been involved in murder, kidnapping, extortion, racketeering, gambling, prostitution, drug dealing, weapons dealing, and other crimes over the years, the phenomenon still maintains the romantic appeal that it had when gangsters like Al Capone captivated the nation. Part of it, of course, is the result of the enormous success of the *Godfather* films, but it is also due, one presumes, to the allure of the principles that the Mafia supposedly was founded upon: self-reliance, loyalty, and *omertà*.

So there you have it: a summary of the founding of the Mafia. Of course, we could tell you more, but then we'd have to . . . well, you know.

Spin Mobsters

In times past, the Mafia's PR machine went into overdrive during the holidays.

✳   ✳   ✳   ✳

MEMBERS OF THE Mafia always claimed to outsiders that "the Mafia" didn't even exist, but they weren't dumb enough to believe that anyone was buying that line. They knew that the general public was aware that La Cosa Nostra controlled everything from gambling to prostitution to garbage pickup in some cities across America. Throughout the 20th century, New York, Chicago, Las Vegas, and every major metropolitan area in the United States had an active mob presence, and the leaders of these criminal gangs were eager to pacify the "little people" in the communities they controlled. What better time to present a kinder, gentler face of the Mafia than during the Christmas season?

A Turkey You Can't Refuse

New York gangster Joe Colombo tried denying the Mafia's existence by founding such groups as the Italian-American Civil Rights League (first called the Italian American Defamation League), which fought the stereotyping of Italians as mobsters and even sent members to picket the offices of the FBI. But

Chicago mob boss Al Capone took a more practical approach to community relations. When the holidays rolled around, he'd roll his troops into the poor Italian, Irish, and Jewish neighborhoods he controlled. Their trucks were piled high with booze, turkeys, and toys. Compared to the money they were making on their nefarious dealings, what they spent on these Christmas handouts was just a drop in the bucket, but to the poverty-stricken residents of the ghettos, it looked like a fortune.

Why wasn't the mob prevented from manipulating the poor in this deceitful manner? The truth is, many in law enforcement turned a blind eye because they, too, were being paid off. It would be many years before the Mafia was pressured to end such public displays during the Christmas season.

The Real Gangs of New York

New York's gang history reflects the city's global diversity.

✳ ✳ ✳ ✳

✳ Amberg Gang (Jewish, Brooklyn, ca. 1920–35). Run by Joseph, Hyman, and Louis "Pretty" Amberg. Was mostly involved in labor/protection racketeering in Brooklyn.

✳ Bonanno Family (Italian, all boroughs, 1931–present). Born from the post-Castellammarese War truce of 1931. The only Family still bearing its original name. Diverse criminal activity.

✳ Bowery Boys (Anglo-Saxon, Manhattan, ca. 1850–63). Mostly political in nature, specifically anti-Irish Catholic, plus other ethnic violence and petty crime.

✳ Broadway Mob (Sicilian, Manhattan and Brooklyn, ca. 1921–33). A Joe "Adonis" Doto, "Lucky" Luciano, and Frank Costello operation, precursor to the Five Families. Created to violate Prohibition.

* Brownsville Boys (Italian/Jewish, Brooklyn, ca. 1927–57). Tagged by media as "Murder, Inc." Mainly enforcement and murder for hire.

* Bug & Meyer Mob (Jewish, various boroughs, ca. 1920–35). Benjamin "Bugsy" Siegel and Meyer Lansky, sometimes called the "La Kosher Nostra;" gambling, bootlegging, and murder for hire.

* Colombo Family (Italian, mainly Brooklyn, 1931-present—in diluted form). They began as the Profaci Family after the Castellammarese War truce; diverse criminal activity.

* Dead Rabbits (Irish, Manhattan, 1850s). Partly political in focus, they were the Bowery Boys' rivals (especially during the famed 1857 riot). Mostly petty crime.

* East Harlem Purple Gang (Mostly Italian, Manhattan, 1970s). Including some very famous names, later amalgamated into the Mafia families. Drugs and murder for hire.

* Five Percenters (African American, Manhattan/Brooklyn, 1963–present). An offshoot of the Nation of Islam that smokes and drinks. On the cusp between street gang and church.

* Five Points Gang (Italian, Manhattan, ca. 1890–1910s). Prep school for Johnny Torrio and Al Capone centered on the famously poor Victorian district. Diverse petty crime: strong-arming, loansharking, and robbery.

* Gambino Family (Italian, all boroughs, 1920s–present). Began as the Mangano Family after the Castellammarese War truce. Led by Albert Anastasia, later John Gotti. Diverse criminal activity.

* Genovese Family (Italian, all boroughs, ca. 1900–present). Started as the Luciano Family under "Lucky" Luciano after the Castellammarese War truce. Perhaps the most powerful Family today; diverse criminal activity.

* Hip Sing Tong (Chinese, Manhattan, 1890s–present). Fought the On Leong for control of Chinatown in the early 1900s. Some legit activities plus gambling, loansharking, and drugs.

* Jolly Stompers (African American, Bronx/Brooklyn, ca. 1960s–1970s). Recruited a young Mike Tyson into their ranks. Very violent, mostly into robbery.

* Latin Kings (Hispanic, various boroughs, 1986–present). Came from Chicago. Strong in hierarchy and philosophy but also strong in arson, theft, drugs, and murder.

* Lucchese Family (Italian, various boroughs, ca. 1917–present). Grew out of the Reina gang after the Castellammarese truce. Diverse criminal activity.

* Mau Maus (Mostly Puerto Rican, Brooklyn, 1954–62). A particularly ruthless gang, they engaged in some petty crime and drug dealing but mostly violence for its own sake.

* Monk Eastman Gang (Mainly Jewish, Manhattan, ca. 1890s–1917). Fierce rival to the Five Points Gang. Pimping, political violence at Tammany's behest, petty crime.

* On Leong Tong (Chinese, Manhattan, 1893–present). Fought the early 1900s Tong Wars. Many legitimate endeavors; have also dealt in racketeering, drugs, gambling, and human trafficking.

* Whyos (Irish, Manhattan, 1860s–90s). Dominated Manhattan underworld until crushed by the Monk Eastman Gang. Extortion, prostitution, intimidation for hire.

Bloody Angle: The Most Violent Place in New York?

If you're looking for some NYC history but don't feel like hitting a museum, take a trip over to Chinatown and check out Bloody Angle. This infamous area at the bend in Doyers Street was the site of untold bloodshed for years.

✳ ✳ ✳ ✳

LOWER MANHATTAN TODAY is quite the place to be. The East Village is full of restaurants and boutiques; SoHo offers high-end shopping and crowds of tourists; the Lower East Side is hipster central, and, of course, the crocodiles that inhabit Wall Street keep that area bustling. But not so long ago, the southern end of the island was rife with gangs, prostitution rings, corruption, and general debauchery.

Chinatown, a neighborhood that became "official" (and ghettoized) around 1882 with ratification of the Chinese Exclusion Act, was particularly active in terms of violence and chaos. Secret societies called "tongs" were formed to protect and support Chinese American residents, but before long the groups were simply gangs that spent their time dealing in criminal activity—and they weren't afraid to use violence against anyone who didn't like it. Many different tong gangs existed, and they didn't all get along. Unrest grew, and by the end of the 19th century and beginning of the 20th, the Tong Wars were on. Few participants made it through alive.

Doyers Street: A Bad Part of Town

Running more or less north and south between Pell Street and the Bowery, Doyers Street is just one block long. Halfway down the block, Doyers turns sharply—hence the "angle" part of Bloody Angle's name. This turn provided a great spot for ambush, and the battling gangs knew it. In 1909, the bloodiest tong war in Chinatown history began when a gang that called themselves the Hip Sings killed an On Leong comedian for being disrespectful. The ensuing war was ruthless, and its locus was the bend in Doyers Street. From then on, the spot would be known as the Bloody Angle.

Herbert Asbury, whose book *The Gangs of New York* was later made into a hit movie by Martin Scorsese, wrote, "The police believe, and can prove it as far as such proof is possible, that more men have been murdered at the Bloody Angle than at any other place of like area in the world." The tongs were vicious and showed no mercy: If you got in their way, you were a goner.

Adding to the danger of the area was a warren of underground tunnels. Connecting buildings and adjacent streets, the tunnels were frequented by gang members who used them to facilitate their dastardly deeds. An assassin would ambush and kill a victim and then disappear down into the tunnels. Several minutes later the killer would emerge, far from the scene of the crime.

Plenty of places near Bloody Angle offered killers opportunities to calm their nerves with a drink—and nail down an alibi. Gang hangouts included The Dump, The Plague, The Hell Hole, and McGuirck's Suicide Hall.

New Violence, and a Cleanup

Eventually, the Tong Wars quieted down, at least for protracted periods of time. By 1930, it was mostly safe to take Doyers if you were passing through Chinatown. But then in the late 1980s, crack cocaine gripped New York, and as a result, gangs grew once again. Bloody Angle returned to being the most dangerous block in the city as the Chinese Flying Dragon gang launched a turf war against the Vietnamese Born to Kill (or BTK) gang.

Anticrime crusades in the 1990s and 2000s cleaned up much of New York. Today, Bloody Angle is more likely to be called "Hair Alley" because of the multitude of salons and barbershops located there.

As for the hidden tunnels, most have either been closed up or repurposed by locals. A tunnel once used by criminals to escape capture in the 1900s is now a belowground shopping arcade— and don't worry, it's safe to shop there.

All about Al

If you took three pushpins and stuck them into a map of the United States in the three places Al Capone spent most of his time, you'd have a triangle spanning New York, Chicago, and Florida. Considering the size of the globe, this triangle wouldn't look like much. And yet, Capone is one of the world's most notorious criminals.

✳   ✳   ✳   ✳

H E'S THE RACKET guy everyone's heard of, and most people associate him with Chicago. But Al Capone was a native Brooklynite. Alphonse Gabriel Capone entered the world January 17, 1899, in Brooklyn. Papa Capone came from a town just south of Naples, while Mama hailed from a smaller town farther south, near Salerno. Alphonse was the fourth child (and fourth son) for Gabriele and Teresina Capone; three more boys and two girls (one survived infancy) would follow. Gabriele was a barber, while Teresina made dresses.

They initially lived near the Navy Yard and then moved to Park Slope. By all accounts, Capone's childhood was a normal, if rather harsh, one. The neighborhood by the Brooklyn Navy Yard was tough. But soon, Capone's father moved the family to an apartment over his barbershop. The new neighborhood had a greater diversity of nationalities than the one in which they had previously lived. Capone was a typical child, hanging out with friends.

Fourteen-year-old Alphonse was a promising student, but he was naturally foul tempered. One day, after his sixth-grade teacher hit him, he swiftly retaliated against her with a punch.

Not surprisingly, such behavior was frowned upon. The principal whaled the daylights out of Alphonse, who had had enough and quit school.

Street Education

Shortly after these events, the family moved again, and the new neighborhood would have quite an effect on the young Capone. He met the people who would have the most influence on him throughout his life. Because Alphonse was drawn to the action, he began hanging out near the John Torrio Association. Torrio's Five Points Gang had begun in Manhattan's notorious neighborhood of that name and expanded into Brooklyn. Now, Torrio was a prominent local racketeer and pimp, and he'd occasionally hire Alphonse to carry out errands.

The "gentleman gangster" taught him how to have what seemed like an outwardly respectable life while simultaneously conducting business in the numbers racket and brothels. Torrio came to trust Alphonse immensely over time, and he and Frankie Yale, another notorious Brooklyn thug and loan shark, mentored young Alphonse in crime. Frankie was a muscle guy who used aggression and strong-arm tactics to build a successful criminal business. Another early Brooklyn associate was Salvatore Lucania, who, after a slight name change, became world famous as "Lucky" Luciano.

In the midst of all this lawless learning, Capone met Mae Coughlin, a middle-class Irishwoman. They had a son in 1918 and married shortly after. Capone made an attempt to earn a legitimate living—moving to Baltimore after he was married and doing well as a bookkeeper. But when his father died in 1920, Capone followed Torrio to Chicago to start the career that would make him infamous.

Chicago

Torrio had taken over the underworld business in Chicago, and with the coming of Prohibition in 1920, he ended up controlling an empire that included brothels, speakeasies, and gambling clubs. Torrio brought Capone on board as partner. Capone moved his family into a house on Chicago's Far South Side. But after a reform-minded mayor was elected in the city, Torrio and Capone moved their base of operations southwest to suburban Cicero, where the pair essentially took over the town. Frank Capone, Al's brother, was installed as the front man of the Cicero city government and was fatally shot by Chicago police in 1924.

Rivalries and Threats

By this point, Capone had made a name for himself as a wealthy and powerful man. He was also a target. When gangland rival Dion O'Bannon was killed, Capone and Torrio easily took over O'Bannon's bootlegging territory—but they also set themselves up for a lifelong war with the remaining loyalists in O'Bannon's gang.

Capone and Torrio survived many assassination attempts. In 1925, when Hymie Weiss and Bugs Moran attempted to kill Torrio outside the crime boss's own home, Capone's partner finally decided to retire. He handed the empire over to Capone. Capone adapted to his role as the head honcho very easily. He actively cultivated a public persona, showing up at the opera, Chicago White Sox games, and charity events. He played politics with the smoothest politicians. And he dressed impeccably.

From 1925 to '29, Capone simultaneously polished his public persona and meted out violence to retain his superior gangland status. In New York in 1925, he orchestrated the Adonis Club Massacre, killing a rival gang leader and establishing his influence outside of Chicago. In 1926, he is believed to have had Billy McSwiggin, a public prosecutor, killed. When public perception turned against him, Capone stepped up his community involvement. He frequently told the press that his motto was "public service." In fact, because he provided jobs for hundreds of Italian immigrants through his bootlegging business, he genuinely considered himself a public servant.

When it came to his employees, Capone could be generous to a fault. He also cultivated relationships with jazz musicians who appeared in his Cicero nightspot, The Cotton Club. In 1926, Capone even organized a peace conference to try to stop the violence among gangs.

The crime boss was wildly successful in creating his public image—so successful, in fact, that he caught the attention of the president of the United States. After the St. Valentine's Day Massacre in Chicago (see the next page for details) in February 1929, in which seven members or associates of a rival gang were killed, the government initiated a focused attempt to put Capone behind bars. In 1930, Capone was listed as Public Enemy Number One. Knowing PR is everything, he was also running a soup kitchen that provided free meals. In 1931, he was convicted on multiple counts of tax evasion and was sentenced to 11 years behind bars. He was ultimately transferred to Alcatraz, where he was unable to use money or personal influence to carve out the kind of pampered life he expected to live while in prison.

Florida

Because of intense media scrutiny in Chicago, Capone bought an estate in Palm Island, Florida, in 1928. Though the residents of the town were chilly to his family's arrival, the Capones established a home and a retreat in this small community. It was to this estate that Capone would return when looking to avoid the glare of his public profile in Chicago, and it was at this estate that he eventually died. While in prison, Capone suffered from neurosyphilis and was confused and disoriented. He was released from prison in 1939 and had a brief stay in a Baltimore hospital, but he returned to Palm Island, where he slowly deteriorated until his death on January 25, 1947. The man who took the world by storm with his organized and brutal approach to crime was survived by his wife, son, and four grandchildren. Though he occupied only a small corner of the world, Al Capone left a huge mark on it.

My Bloody Valentine

The episode is infamous in American history. Almost no one dared to stand up to Capone and his men, including the police, because that meant possibly winding up on the wrong end of a gun. Still, one man was determined to dethrone Capone—George "Bugs" Moran. For a few years, Moran and his North Side Gang had been slowly muscling their way into Chicago in an attempt to force Capone and his men out. As 1929 began, rumors started to fly that Capone was fed up and was planning his revenge. As the days turned into weeks and nothing happened, Moran and his men began to relax and let their guard down. That would prove to be a fatal mistake.

✳ ✳ ✳ ✳

Gathering for the Slaughter

ON THE MORNING of February 14, 1929, six members of the North Side Gang—James Clark, Frank Gusenberg, Peter Gusenberg, Adam Heyer, Reinhart Schwimmer, and Al Weinshank—were gathered inside the SMC Cartage Company at 2122 North Clark Street in the Lincoln Park neighborhood on Chicago's north side. With them was mechanic John May, who was not a member of the gang but had been hired to work on one of their cars. May had brought along his dog, Highball, and had tied him to the bumper of the car while he worked. Supposedly, the men were gathered at the warehouse to accept a load of bootleg whiskey. Whether that is true or not remains unclear. What is known for certain is that at approximately 10:30 A.M., two cars parked in front of the Clark Street entrance of the building. Four men—two dressed as police officers and two in street clothes—got out and walked into the warehouse.

Murderers in Disguise

Once the men were inside, it is believed they announced that the warehouse was being raided and ordered everyone to line up facing the back wall. Believing the armed men were indeed police officers, all of Moran's men, along with John May, did as they were told. Suddenly, the four men began shooting, and, in a hail of shotgun fire and more than 70 submachine-gun rounds, the seven men were brutally gunned down.

When it was over, the two men in street clothes calmly walked out of the building with their hands up, followed by the two men dressed as police officers. To everyone nearby, it appeared as though there had been a shootout and that the police had arrived and were now arresting two men.

"Nobody Shot Me"

Minutes later, neighbors called police after reportedly hearing strange howls coming from inside the building. When the real police arrived, they found all seven men mortally wounded. One of the men, Frank Gusenberg, lingered long enough to respond to one question. When authorities asked who shot him, Gusenberg responded, "Nobody shot me." The only survivor of the massacre was Highball the dog, whose howls first alerted people that something was wrong.

When word of the massacre hit the newswire, everyone suspected Al Capone had something to do with it. Capone stood strong, though, and swore he wasn't involved. Most people, however, felt that Capone had orchestrated the whole thing as a way to get rid of Moran and several of his key men. There was only one problem—Bugs Moran wasn't in the warehouse at the time of the shooting. Some believe that Moran may have driven up, seen the cars out front, and, thinking it was a raid, driven away. One thing is for certain: February 14, 1929, was Moran's lucky day.

Police launched a massive investigation but were unable to pin anything on Capone, although they did arrest two of his gunmen, John Scalise and Jack "Machine Gun" McGurn, and charged them with the murders. Scalise never saw the inside of the courthouse—he was murdered before the trial began.

Charges against McGurn were eventually dropped, although he was murdered seven years later, on Valentine's Day, in what appeared to be retaliation for the 1929 massacre.

Al Capone Haunted by the Truth

Publicly, Al Capone may have denied any wrongdoing, but it appears that the truth literally haunted him until his dying day. In May 1929, Capone was incarcerated at Philadelphia's Eastern State Penitentiary, serving a one-year stint for weapons possession. Such a span was considered "easy time" by gangster standards, but Capone's time inside would be anything but. Haunted by the ghost of James Clark—who was killed in the St. Valentine's Day Massacre—Capone was often heard begging "Jimmy" to leave him alone.

The torment continued even after Capone was released. One day, Capone's valet, Hymie Cornish, saw an unfamiliar man in Capone's apartment. When he ordered the man to identify himself, the mysterious figure slipped behind a curtain and vanished. Capone insisted that Cornish, like himself, had seen the ghost of Clark. Some say that Clark didn't rest until Capone passed away on January 25, 1947.

Ghosts Still Linger

The warehouse at 2122 North Clark Street, where the bloody massacre took place, was demolished in 1967. The wall against which the seven doomed men stood, complete with bullet holes, was dismantled brick by brick and sold at auction. A businessman bought the wall and reassembled it in the men's room of his restaurant. However, the business failed and the owner, believing the wall was cursed, tried getting rid of it to recoup his losses.

He sold the individual bricks and was successful in getting rid of many of them, but they always seemed to find their way back to him. Sometimes they would show up on his doorstep along with a note describing all the misfortune the new owner had encountered after buying the brick.

At the former site of the warehouse, some people report hearing the sounds of gunfire and screams coming from the lot. People walking their dogs near the lot claim that their furry friends suddenly pull on their leashes and try to get away from the area as quickly as possible. Perhaps they sense the ghostly remnants of the bloody massacre that happened more than 75 years ago.

Gangster's Paradise

Throughout the 1920s and '30s, Wisconsin's Northwoods were the place for bad guys looking to escape the heat—literally and figuratively—of Chicago. After the Chicago & North Western Railroad expanded due north into Wisconsin's wooden hinterlands, Chicagoland's elite came to vacation on the crystal-clear lakes. But they didn't come alone. For gangsters and their henchmen, the Northwoods were both a summer playground and a year-round hideout. Today, numerous communities have their own stories of gangster legend and lore. Here's a lineup of the most memorable.

✳   ✳   ✳   ✳

The Capones

BIG AL CAPONE turned 21 the day after the Volstead Act, the legislation that made alcohol illegal, went into effect. This seems like an ironic twist for someone who would go down in history known as a bootlegger, gangster, and criminal mastermind.

The Northwoods wasn't a temporary escape for Big Al, as it served as his permanent getaway. He didn't even try to cover up this fact, dubbing his Couderay retreat "The Hideout." His home on the shores of Cranberry Lake came complete with a gun turret alongside the driveway, openings in the stone walls for machine guns, and a personal jail. Booze runners from Canada would land their planes on the lake, and Capone's gang then took care of the distribution.

Al's older brother, Ralph "Bottles" Capone, was the director of liquor sales for the mob and covered his tracks by operating Waukesha Waters, a distribution company for Waukesha Springs mineral water. But Ralph had another passion: bookmaking. Ralph was less vicious than his brother, but bookmaking got him into trouble. He landed in prison in the early 1930s for tax evasion, coincidentally the same charge that sent Al to Alcatraz, where he was imprisoned for seven-and-a-half years. When Big Al was released in November 1939, he was so stricken with syphilis that he was unseated as leader of the criminal underworld. He died seven years later.

Later, Ralph lived in Mercer, from 1943 until his death on November 22, 1974. He managed the Rex Hotel and Billy's Bar and owned a house that had previously belonged to his brother. Ralph sponsored community Christmas parties, donated food and gifts to the needy, contributed to churches, and financed high school class trips. Despite his criminal history, locals remember him mostly for his kindness and charity. He also earned at least $20,000 a year from an Illinois cigarette vending machine business and was repeatedly investigated by the Internal Revenue Service. After 1951, Ralph Capone didn't even bother to file tax returns. At the time of his death he owed $210,715 in back taxes.

The Most Vicious

Few gangster aficionados know the story of John Henry Seadlund, dubbed "The World's Most Vicious Criminal" by FBI director J. Edgar Hoover. A loafer from Minnesota, Seadlund turned to crime after a chance meeting with Tommy

Carroll, a veteran of John Dillinger's gang. To make fast cash as a new criminal, Seadlund considered kidnapping wealthy Chicagoans vacationing in the Northwoods and demanding ransom. But after joining with a new lowlife, James Atwood Gray, Seadlund's kidnapping plot expanded to include a professional baseball player. The plan was to kidnap the St. Louis Cardinals' star pitcher Dizzy Dean, but Seadlund gave up when he realized how exactly hard it might be to get ransom from Dean's ballclub.

Kidnapping ballplayers didn't pan out, so Seadlund abducted a retired greeting card company executive while heading out of Illinois in September 1937. After getting ransom, he exacted a kidnapping and murder scheme on the retiree, leaving him and accomplice Gray dead in a dugout near Spooner. He was caught when marked bills from the ransom were used at a race-track the following January.

Beyond Bigwigs

Northwoods legend and lore extends beyond the mob's biggest names. During Prohibition, federal agents found and confiscated major gang-run stills in towns across Wisconsin's northern third. Elcho was the purported home to a mob doctor who traded bullet removal for booze, and Hurley was a gangster hot spot, as it was a "wide-open" town that flouted Prohibition and laws against prostitution. Wisconsin's Northwoods mob stories are as big as its fish tales.

Public Enemy No. 1

After serving eight-and-a-half years for robbery and assault, John Dillinger took off on a ten-month crime spree that earned him the title "Public Enemy No. 1." He and his gang rampaged across the Upper Midwest, busting cronies out of the slammer, robbing banks, murdering lawmen, and escaping from the FBI each time. Possibly needing a quiet vacation, Dillinger and accomplices headed to northern Wisconsin in 1934. For that story, read on...

Shoot-out at Little Bohemia

Infamous gangster John Dillinger was something of a media darling during his long, terrorizing reign. He was also the force behind one of the most embarrassing federal mishaps of all time.

✳ ✳ ✳ ✳

BORN JUNE 22, 1903, John Dillinger was in his early thirties when he first caught the FBI's eye. They thought they were through with him in January 1934, when he was arrested after shooting a police officer during a bank robbery in East Chicago, Indiana. However, Dillinger managed to stage a daring escape from his Indiana jail cell using a wooden gun painted with black shoe polish.

In an era known for its long list of public enemies, John Dillinger and his crew stood out more like endeared celebrities than the convicted killers and robbers they were known to be. Historians attribute this strange awe to the gang's Robin Hood–like appeal during a stressful time for the public.

Robbing the Rich

The public, demoralized by the ongoing Depression, lacked financial and bureaucratic faith after suffering devastating losses at what they saw to be the hands of irresponsible government and financial institutions. When the dashing, physically graceful Dillinger and his equally charismatic crew began tearing through banks, they not only provided an exciting and dramatic media distraction, they also destroyed banks' potentially devastating mortgage paperwork in their wake. The masses seemed eager to clasp onto the real-life drama and connect it to their own plight. The public was more than willing to forgive the sins of outlaws such as Dillinger's crew in favor of the payback they provided to financial institutions.

Law officials, however, weren't so keen on the criminals. J. Edgar Hoover and his newly formed Federal Bureau of

Investigation were weary of gangsters' soft public perception and crafted a series of hard-hitting laws meant to immobilize them. Those found guilty of crimes such as robbing banks would now face stiffer penalties. Dillinger, one of the most prominent, popular, and evasive of the lot, was at the top of Hoover's hit list. However, keeping the gangster in jail and strapped with a sufficient sentence seemed like more work than Hoover could handle.

Hiding Out

Dillinger, always hard to contain, had fled the supposedly escape-proof county jail in Crown Point, Indiana, in March 1934. A month and a few bank robberies later, Dillinger and company ended up hiding out in a woodsy Wisconsin lodge called Little Bohemia, so named because of the owner's Bohemian ethnic roots. Tipped off by the lodge owner's wife, Hoover and a team of federal investigators from Chicago responded with an ill-fated ambush that would go down in history as one of the greatest federal fiascoes of all time.

The Dillinger gang, including well-known characters such as Harry Pierpont and "Baby Face" Nelson, plus gang members' wives and girlfriends, had planned only a short layover at the wilderness retreat. Although owner Emil Wanatka and wife Nan had befriended an outlaw or two during the days of Prohibition, the Dillinger crew was a notch or two above the types they had known. The couple didn't share the public's glorified view of these men.

So, upon discovering that their new slew of guests were members of the notorious gang, Wanatka made a bold move and confronted them. Dillinger assured him that they would be of no inconvenience and would not stay long. Apparently bank robbers are not the most trustworthy folks, because in the several days of their stay the bunch proved to be much more than an inconvenience. Wanatka and his wife were basically held hostage at their humble hostel for the entire length of the

Dillinger gang's stay. Telephone calls were monitored, lodge visitors were subject to scrutiny at both arrival and departure, and anyone, including Emil and Nan themselves, who went into town for supplies was forced to travel with a Dillinger escort. Even beside that, the sheer fear of housing sought-after sociopaths was too much for the Wanatka couple and their young son to handle. A plan for relief was soon hatched.

Knowing that any lodge departure would be surveyed closely, the Wanatkas decided to plant a note on Nan to pass to police. They would convince the gangsters that she and their ten-year-old son were merely departing for a nephew's birthday party and then would find a way to transmit their cry for help.

Although Dillinger gave permission for the pair's trip, the frightened mother soon discovered "Baby Face" Nelson hot on their trail and ready to jump at the first sight of suspicious activity. Still, Nan managed to pass word to her family, who then contacted the authorities. At the birthday party for her nephew, Nan provided details that were ultimately shared with law enforcement. Officials planned a siege.

The Heat Is On

Seizing the opportunity to make an example of Dillinger and his exploits, FBI agents Hugh Clegg and Melvin Purvis plotted an ambush at the lodge under Hoover's guidance. Unfortunately for the agents and innocent bystanders, Dillinger and company were not so easily taken.

As the agents approached, the lodge's watchdogs indeed barked at the strangers, but only after a series of miscalculated gunshots did the Dillinger gang stir. Clegg and Purvis had mistakenly fired at three patrons leaving the lodge's bar. This was the first tragedy of Little Bohemia that day: One of the patrons was killed instantly, and the other two were brutally wounded.

The Dillinger gang had long grown weary of the watchdogs' random yelps, but when they heard these unfortunate shots they knew their hideout had been discovered. They made a hasty escape. Nelson, in a nearby cabin, escaped along the shoreline of Star Lake. Both parties forced nearby neighbors to provide getaway cars.

The agents didn't have the same knowledge of the land's lay and fell victim to a nearby ditch and a wall of barbed wire. Wounded and entangled, the agents were sitting ducks. Their suspects were free to flee and take their turn at gunfire now that they had the upper hand.

Unhappy Ending

A premature and somewhat pompous notion had Hoover pledging a significant story to the press in anticipation of the planned attack. Unluckily for him, with the unintentional victims and their families involved, the story would be a hellish one. The ambush resulted in not a single loss for the Dillinger gang. On the other side were two injured law officers, two wounded bystanders, and the death of a complete innocent.

Both Dillinger and Nelson were killed within the year. But Little Bohemia Lodge remains on Highway 51, the main thoroughfare to and through the Northwoods. It still serves breakfast, lunch, and dinner, with a heaping helping of history.

The Death of John Dillinger... or Someone Who Looked Like Him

After the botched trap at Little Bohemia, the public was in an uproar and the FBI was under close scrutiny. To everyone at the FBI, the message was clear: Hoover wanted Dillinger, and he wanted him ASAP.

✳   ✳   ✳   ✳

ON JULY 22, 1934, outside the Biograph Theater on Chicago's north side, John Dillinger passed from this world into the next in a hail of bullets. Or did he? Conspiracy theorists believe that FBI agents shot and killed the wrong man and covered it all up when they realized their mistake. So what really happened that fateful night?

The Woman in Red

The FBI's big break came in July 1934 with a phone call from a woman named Anna Sage. Sage was a Romanian immigrant who ran a Chicago-area brothel. Fearing that she might be deported, Sage wanted to strike a bargain with the feds. Her proposal was simple: In exchange for not being deported, Sage was willing to give the FBI John Dillinger. According to Sage, Dillinger was dating Polly Hamilton, one of her former employees. Melvin Purvis personally met with Sage and told her he couldn't make any promises but he would do what he could about her pending deportation.

Several days later, on July 22, Sage called the FBI office in Chicago and said that she was going to the movies that night with Dillinger and Hamilton. Sage quickly hung up but not before saying she would wear something bright so that agents could pick out the threesome in a crowd. Not knowing which movie theater they were planning to go to, Purvis dispatched several agents to the Marbro Theater, while he and another group of agents went to the Biograph. At approximately 8:30 P.M., Purvis believed he saw Dillinger, Sage, and Hamilton enter the Biograph. As she had promised, Sage indeed wore something bright—an orange blouse. However, under the marquee lights, the blouse's color appeared to be red, which is why Sage was forever dubbed "The Woman in Red."

Purvis tried to apprehend Dillinger right after he purchased tickets, but he slipped past Purvis and into the darkened theater. Purvis went into the theater but was unable to locate Dillinger in the dark. At that point, Purvis left the theater, gathered his men, and made the decision to apprehend Dillinger as he was exiting the theater. Purvis positioned himself in the theater's vestibule, instructed his men to hide outside, and told them that he would signal them by lighting a cigar when he spotted Dillinger. That was their cue to move in and arrest Dillinger.

"Stick 'em up, Johnny!"

At approximately 10:30 P.M., the doors to the Biograph opened and people started to exit. All of the agents' eyes were on Purvis. When a man wearing a straw hat, accompanied by two women, walked past Purvis, the agent quickly placed a cigar in his mouth and lit a match. Perhaps sensing something was wrong, the man turned and looked at Purvis, at which point Purvis drew his pistol and said, "Stick 'em up, Johnny!" In response, the man turned as if he was going to run away, while at the same time reaching for what appeared to be a gun. Seeing the movement, the other agents opened fire. As the man ran away, attempting to flee down the alleyway alongside the theater, he was shot four times on his left side and once in the back of the neck before crumpling on the pavement. When Purvis reached him and checked for vitals, there were none. Minutes later, after being driven to a local hospital, John Dillinger was pronounced DOA. But as soon as it was announced that Dillinger was dead, the controversy began.

Dillinger Disputed

Much of the basis for the conspiracy stems from the fact that Hoover, both publicly and privately, made it clear that no matter what, he wanted Dillinger caught. On top of that, Agent Purvis was under a lot of pressure to capture Dillinger, especially since he'd failed with a previous attempt. Keeping that in mind, it would be easy to conclude that Purvis, in his haste to capture Dillinger, might have overlooked a few things. First, it was Purvis alone who pointed out the man he thought to be Dillinger to the waiting agents. Conspiracy theorists contend that Purvis fingered the wrong man that night, and an innocent man ended up getting killed as a result. As evidence, they point to Purvis's own statement: While they were standing at close range, the man tried to pull a gun, which is why the agents had to open fire. But even though agents stated they recovered a .38-caliber Colt automatic from the victim's body (and even had it on display for many years), author Jay Robert Nash discovered that that particular model was not even available until a good five months after Dillinger's alleged death! Theorists believe that when agents realized they had not only shot the wrong man, but an unarmed one at that, they planted the gun as part of a cover-up.

Another interesting fact that could have resulted in Purvis's misidentification was that Dillinger had recently undergone plastic surgery in an attempt to disguise himself. In addition to work on his face, Dillinger had attempted to obliterate his fingerprints by dipping his fingers into an acid solution. On top of that, the man who Purvis said was Dillinger was wearing a straw hat the entire time Purvis saw him. It is certainly possible that Purvis did not actually recognize Dillinger but instead picked out someone who merely looked like him. If you remember, the only tip Purvis had was Sage telling him that she was going to the movies with Dillinger and his girlfriend. Did Purvis see Sage leaving the theater in her orange blouse and finger the wrong man simply because he was standing next to Sage and resembled Dillinger? Or was the whole thing a setup orchestrated by Sage and Dillinger to trick the FBI into executing an innocent man?

So Who Was It?

If the man shot and killed outside the theater wasn't John Dillinger, who was it? There are conflicting accounts, but one speculation is that it was a man named Jimmy Lawrence, who was dating Polly Hamilton. If you believe in the conspiracy, Lawrence was simply in the wrong place at the wrong time. Or possibly, Dillinger purposely sent Lawrence to the theater hoping FBI agents would shoot him, allowing Dillinger to fade into obscurity. Of course, those who don't believe in the conspiracy say the reason Lawrence looked so much like Dillinger is because he was Dillinger using an alias. Further, Dillinger's sister, Audrey Hancock, identified his body. Finally, they say it all boils down to the FBI losing or misplacing the gun Dillinger had the night he was killed and inadvertently replacing it with the wrong one. Case closed.

Not really, though. It seems that whenever someone comes up with a piece of evidence to fuel the conspiracy theory, some-one else has something to refute it. Some have asked that Dillinger's body be exhumed and DNA tests be performed, but nothing has come of it yet. Until that happens, we'll probably never know for sure what really happened on that hot July night back in 1934. But that's okay, because everyone loves a good mystery.

Entrepreneurs of Death: The Story of the Brownsville Boys

Following the rise of the National Crime Syndicate, or what people now call the Mafia, a group of enterprising killers formed an enforcement arm that the press dubbed "Murder, Incorporated." Officially, they were known as "The Combination" or "The Brownsville Boys," since many of them came from Brooklyn's Brownsville area.

* * * *

THE COMBINATION BEGAN their mayhem-for-money operation around 1930 following the formation of the National Crime Syndicate. Until their demise in the mid-1940s, they enforced the rules of organized crime through fear, intimidation, and murder. Most of the group's members were Jewish and Italian gangsters from Brooklyn; remorseless and bloodthirsty, murder for money was their stock-in-trade. The number of murders committed during their bloody reign is unknown even today, but estimates put the total at more than a thousand from coast to coast. The title "Murder, Incorporated" was the invention of a fearless *New York World-Telegram* police reporter named Harry Feeney; the name stuck.

Filling a Need

The formation of the group was the brainchild of mob over-lords Johnny Torrio and "Lucky" Luciano. The most high-profile assassination credited to the enterprise was the murder of gang lord Dutch Schultz, who defied the syndicate's orders to abandon a plan to assassinate New York crime-buster Thomas Dewey. The job went to one of the Combination's top-echelon gunsels, Charles "Charlie the Bug" Workman, whose bloody prowess ranked alongside such Murder, Inc., elite as Louis "Lepke" Buchalter, the man who issued the orders; Albert Anastasia, the lord high executioner; Abe "Kid Twist" Reles, whose eventual capitulation led to the group's downfall; Louis Capone (no relation to Al); Frank Abbandando; Harry "Pittsburg Phil" Strauss, an expert with an ice pick; Martin "Buggsy" Goldstein; Harry "Happy" Maione, leader of the Italian faction; Emanuel "Mendy" Weiss, who is rumored to have never committed murder on the Sabbath; Johnny Dio; Albert "Allie" Tannenbaum; Irving "Knadles" Nitzberg, who twice beat a death sentence when his convictions were over-turned; Vito "Socko" Gurino; Jacob Drucker; Philip "Little Farvel" Cohen; and Sholom Bernstein, who like many of his cohorts turned against his mentors to save his own life. It was an era of infamy unequaled in mob lore.

Loose Lips

Though many of the rank and file of Murder, Inc., appeared to enjoy killing, Reles, a former soda jerk, killed only as a matter of business. Known as "Kid Twist," Reles may not have been as bloodthirsty as some of his contemporaries, but he was cursed with a huge ego and a big mouth, and he wasn't shy about doing his bragging in front of cops, judges, the press, or the public at large. The little man with the big mouth would eventually lead to the unraveling of the Combination and greatly weaken the power of the National Crime Syndicate. When an infor-mant fingered Reles and "Buggsy" Goldstein for the murder of a small-time hood, both men turned themselves in, believing they could beat the rap just as they had a dozen times before, but this one was ironclad. Reles sang loud and clear, implicating his peers and bosses in more than 80 murders and sending several of them to the electric chair, including the untouchable Buchalter. He also revealed the internal secret structure of the National Syndicate. Reles was in protective custody when he "fell" to his death from a hotel room on November 12, 1941, while surrounded by police. By the mid-1940s, Murder, Inc., was a thing of the past, and the National Crime Syndicate was in decline.

When it came to singing like a canary, only Joe Valachi would surpass the performance of Reles, once the most trusted member of the Brownsville Boys.

Albert Anastasia

A gun; an ice pick; a rope; these were some of the favorite tools of Albert Anastasia, notorious mob assassin. When he wasn't pulling the trigger himself, this head of Murder, Inc. was giving the orders to kill, beat, extort, and rob on the mob-controlled waterfronts of Brooklyn and Manhattan.

✳ ✳ ✳ ✳

BORN IN ITALY in 1902 as Umberto Anastasio, Anastasia worked as a deck hand before jumping ship in New York, where he built a power base in the longshoremen's union. Murder was his tool to consolidate power. Arrested several times in the 1920s, his trials were often dismissed when witnesses would go missing. It wasn't long before he attracted the attention of mob "brain" Lucky Luciano and subsequently helped whack Joe "the Boss" Masseria in 1931, an act that opened the way for Luciano to achieve national prominence within the organization.

Luciano put Anastasia, Bugsy Siegel, and Meyer Lanksy in charge of what became known as Murder, Inc. With his quick temper and brutal disposition, Anastasia earned the nickname "Lord High Executioner."

A History of Violence

After Reles began singing like a canary and had his mysterious "fall," Anastasia climbed the next rung in the mob ladder by ordering the violent 1951 deaths of the Mangano brothers and ultimately taking over the Mangano family. Eventually, however, he alienated two powerful rivals, Vito Genovese and Meyer Lansky. On October 25, 1957, as Albert Anastasia dozed in a barber's chair at New York's Park Sheraton Hotel, he was riddled by two masked gunmen (possibly Larry and Joe Gallo), who acted on orders from Genovese.

Anastasia had evaded justice for decades, but he couldn't escape the violence he himself cultivated in organized crime.

The Mayfield Road Mob

Cleveland's most notorious criminal gang kept the streets of Little Italy safe while turning the city into one of America's most notorious Mafia towns.

✳ ✳ ✳ ✳

O N JULY 5, 1930, the two biggest players in the Cleveland criminal underworld met to negotiate a new power-sharing arrangement. One was Joe Porrello, head of the Porrello family gang and reigning Cleveland mob boss. The other was Frank Milano, leader of the Mayfield Road Mob, which ran most of Cleveland's illegal rackets from the city's Little Italy district.

The meeting was held at Milano's Venetian Restaurant at the corner of Mayfield and Murray Hill roads in the heart of Little Italy. The mood was friendly until the upstart Milano demanded a piece of the Porrello clan's lucrative corn sugar business (corn sugar was a key ingredient for making bootleg whiskey). When Porrello balked, Milano's henchman gunned him down—leaving the Mayfield Road Mob to take over the corn sugar business and Milano to step in as the new Cleveland don.

The Reign of Quiet

Once in control, Milano moved the Mayfield Road Mob into gambling, loan sharking, and labor union racketeering—its main operation once Prohibition had ended—and eventually molded the Cleveland crime syndicate into one of the top Mafia organizations in the United States. Ironically, Milano's boys kept Mayfield Road and surrounding neighborhood streets crime-free. Burglars, muggers, and punks knew that misbehaving in Little Italy meant swift and severe retribution from Milano's crew. Milano's run as boss ended in 1934 after he fled to Mexico to avoid charges of tax evasion, and his lieutenant that succeeded him, Alfred Polizzi, retired from the racket in 1944. Leadership of the Cleveland Mafia passed to a faction headed by John Scalish, thus ending the Mayfield Road Mob's magnanimous reign.

Cold and Clammy

Gangster "Crazy" Joe Gallo went about his underworld business with style and panache. If there was limelight to be sampled, chances are Gallo would be standing directly beneath it. Unfortunately for the crime boss, such flamboyance would trigger his early demise.

✳ ✳ ✳ ✳

Wise Guy of Note

IN SOME WAYS, Joe Gallo was a gangster ahead of his time. He certainly viewed himself that way. Here was a dutiful, workaday mobster who, for all of his limitations, saw opportunity in areas of criminal activity where others saw only strife. Before long, Gallo pioneered alliances with non-Mafia gangs that proved profitable all around. These unlikely but shrewd couplings of rival groups were masterful strokes.

But there was another side to Gallo that wasn't nearly as good for business: his public side. Much like Benjamin "Bugsy" Siegel before him, Gallo had a sense of flair, a taste for the good life, and plenty of celebrity friends.

Gallo and his boys were well- known for their keen sense of style. The wise guys looked like they had come straight from central casting in their black suits, narrow black ties, and darker-than-pitch sunglasses. Tabloids often ran covers of the boys done up in such "gangster chic." The public seemed to love it. The mob, not so much.

Gallo simply couldn't resist being the center of attention. And he liked to talk. In an enterprise that conducts its business well beneath the radar, this was *not* the preferred path.

Wild Child

Born on April 7, 1929, in the tough Red Hook section of Brooklyn, Gallo quickly rose from street criminal to key enforcer in the Profaci Crime Family. With help from brothers Albert and Larry—as well as mobsters Frank Illiano, Nicholas Bianco, and Vic Amuso—no tactic seemed too ruthless or too bloody. In 1957, after allegedly rubbing out gangster Albert Anastasia in a barber chair at New York's Park Sheraton Hotel, Gallo (perhaps not unreasonably) asked mob boss Joseph Profaci for a bigger slice of the pie. The don's refusal sparked a turf war between the Gallo gang and the Profacis. The bloody feud continued into the 1960s, ultimately working to the favor of the Profacis.

Can't Win for Trying

After Joe Profaci died of cancer in 1962, power was transferred to his underboss, Joseph Magliocco, then later to Joseph Colombo. Due to Gallo's inability to achieve the exalted seat—as well as his ten-year incarceration for extortion—the mobster's leadership skills were placed in question. It wasn't that the Gallo boys didn't try. They had even gone so far as kidnapping Magliocco (during the Profaci-Gallo wars) in hopes that a human bargaining chip would bring them better profits. It didn't. In the long run nothing seemed to work out for the gang. The huge cash tributes that Profaci demanded of the Gallos prior to the kidnapping were suspended—but only for a brief period. After Magliocco was returned, the fees were reinstated. In the bloody dream of big-time money, Gallo and his crew had been effectively squeezed out of the action.

The Gang That Couldn't Shoot Straight

The gang's big ideas and general ineptitude caught the eye of *New York Post* columnist Jimmy Breslin, who lampooned them in his bestselling 1969 novel, *The Gang That Couldn't Shoot Straight*. A movie would follow with the buffoonish lead role (loosely based on Gallo's life) given to actor Jerry Orbach.

Things got interesting after the movie's release when Gallo, fresh out of prison, approached Orbach to set history straight. Oddly, the two men took to each other and became friends. Orbach was astonished by Gallo's grasp of art and literature and introduced him to his circle of friends. Soon, Gallo was hobnobbing with Hollywood figures and members of the literary set. Everybody, it seemed, wanted to meet this real-life *Mafioso* with the cultural dexterity to quote from such figures as Camus and Sartre. After rotting for ten long years behind bars and suffering countless indignities as Profaci's underpaid soldier, could Gallo's star finally be on the rise?

Stars in His Eyes

Although suspected in the recent assassination of boss Joe Colombo, Gallo announced that he was "turning legit" in 1972. The purportedly reformed mobster planned to write a book about his life and perhaps even try his hand at acting. This might explain why Gallo found himself in the company of Jerry Orbach, comedian David Steinberg, and columnist Earl Wilson at New York's Copacabana one night before his 43rd birthday. It may also explain why the mob no longer wanted Gallo around. In the eyes of syndicate members, they didn't come much riskier than a starstruck, publicity-mad mobster who invited the scrutiny of federal agents bent on destroying La Cosa Nostra. In fact, the only thing that might trump such an actionable offense would be a gangster who had taken the oath of *omertà*, only to go straight and announce plans to write a tell-all book.

Bad Clams

During the wee hours of April 7, 1972, the unlikely group disbanded. Gallo, his bodyguard Pete Diapoulas, and four women made their way to Umberto's Clam House on Mulberry Street. While mobsters regarded this popular Little Italy location as Mafia holy ground, a hit was nevertheless in the making. As Gallo and his bodyguard pondered menu choices with their backs to the door, one or two gunmen barged in. Hearing the danger, Gallo and Diapoulas instinctively rose and made a run for it. Despite their maneuvers, both men were hit. Diapoulas took a bullet to his hip (he would later recover) and Gallo caught no less than five slugs. The mortally wounded mobster wobbled out the front door, making it as far as his Cadillac before collapsing in a lifeless heap.

While it wasn't quite the Hollywood ending that the mobster had hoped for, it was a Hollywood ending of sorts. The death of "Crazy" Joe Gallo had been every bit as flamboyant as his existence. To live in the limelight, to die in the limelight— maybe it was all somehow equal.

Bombs Away

A modern-day Robin Hood and a calculated killer, Danny Greene's dual roles made him the most notorious celebrity in Cleveland, Ohio—or, as it was called during Greene's time, Bomb City, U.S.A.

✳ ✳ ✳ ✳

NORTHEAST OHIO HAS a history of colorful locals, and Cleveland is no exception. During the 1960s and 1970s, one legendary gangster made his mark as a modern-day Robin Hood, befriending poor families and blowing up his competition.

Cleveland's Other Nickname

Irish American gangster Danny Greene was part of a headline-making underworld fueled by bullets and bombs. In fact, Greene's penchant for homemade incendiaries helped earn Cleveland's nickname: Bomb City, U.S.A. In 1976 alone, 36 bombs ripped through the cityscape. Most of them were either made by—or aimed at—Greene.

Greene's hard-knocks childhood in Cleveland ended when he left school to join the Marines in 1951. When his years in the service ended, Greene circled back to Cleveland where he worked the docks and became president of the local International Association of Longshoremen. He reportedly used green ink to write union bylaws, but his tactics were anything but whimsical. Greene issued a 25-percent dues increase and expected members to "voluntarily" work extra hours and donate the proceeds—or suffer the consequences.

Unwanted Attention

It wasn't long before Greene's dealings with other union leaders captured the attention of the FBI. Greene became an informant but only shared information about his competition. In 1964, his heavy-handed management style fueled an old-fashioned exposé by the *Cleveland Plain Dealer*. Greene laughed off the story, but the IRS didn't find it funny. Neither did the U.S. attorney's office, local prosecutors, or the U.S. Department of Labor. The verdict: Greene had emptied the union's coffers and lined his pockets with the money.

Although Greene escaped jail time, his days as a union boss were over. He found work offering "protection" to area businesses. He enforced his own bomb- or bullet-ridden version of the law and became a modern-day Robin Hood. He paid Catholic school tuition for children from poor families and had more than two dozen turkeys delivered to neighborhood homes for Thanksgiving.

Unsavory Connections

Greene also teamed with local mobster Alex "Shondor" Birns. The partnership soured when more than $60,000 of Birns's money went missing on Greene's watch. The feud between Greene and Birns ended only when both players were blown to bits. In 1975, Birns was fatally sent through the roof of his own car. Even after Birns's death, Greene's life was still on the line. Reportedly, the dead man had left a $25,000 reward on Greene's head.

Next, Greene's home exploded, but he survived with only minor injuries. In the ensuing months, Greene was shot at, returned fire, lost his "assistant" (who blew up in a car bombing), and detected a bomb in his car that failed to detonate. He also found a bomb that wasn't wired effectively and another that would have worked—had the hit men been within range to detonate it. When Greene traveled out of state, assassins followed but got lost before they could kill him. Shots were fired at Greene as he strolled down a sidewalk, but he wasn't hit.

The Bombs Catch Up

When Greene went to the dentist on October 6, 1977, however, his charmed life was soon to be over. Rival mobsters stuffed a vehicle with explosives, parked next to Greene's vehicle, and waited for him to return. This time it was a successful hit. The bomb blew Greene's left arm 100 feet from his body, but his emerald-encrusted ring stayed on his finger. His back was ripped open during the fatal attack, and his clothing was torn away, except for his ankle-high boots and socks. Next to Greene, untouched, was a gym bag containing a loaded gun and a printed prayer to the Virgin Mary.

What Happened to Jimmy Hoffa?

James Riddle Hoffa was born on February 14, 1913, in Brazil, Indiana, but his family moved to Detroit in 1924. It was here that a teenaged Hoffa became active in unions, after working for a grocery chain that paid poorly and offered substandard conditions for its employees. Hoffa eventually became a powerful figure in the Teamsters union, and he spent the rest of his life working with unions in Detroit. At least, that's the assumption. In truth, no one knows where Hoffa spent the end of his life, because in 1975, he simply disappeared.

❋　❋　❋　❋

A Poor Career Choice

IN A 2004 EPISODE of the popular Discovery Channel show *MythBusters*, the show's hosts, Adam Savage and Jamie Hyneman, traveled to Giants Stadium in East Rutherford, New Jersey, for a reason that had nothing to do with football. The curious television hosts were exploring an oft-told urban legend claiming that the body of Jimmy Hoffa had been encased in concrete and buried in the end zone of the stadium. Using ground-penetrating radar, Savage and Hyneman searched the field for anything unusual beneath the surface, but ultimately found nothing. Their findings were later confirmed when Giants Stadium was demolished to make way for a new sports complex in 2010.

The *MythBusters* search was just one of many investigations into Hoffa's disappearance, which is rife with unknowns. But here's what we do know: Hoffa began to rise to power in the International Brotherhood of Teamsters (IBT) union in the 1940s, eventually becoming president of the IBT in 1957. While it seems like a respectable career path, the union was heavily influenced by organized crime, and Hoffa spent much of his time with the IBT making deals and arrangements with gangsters to strengthen and expand its power in the region.

By the 1960s, Hoffa's corrupt dealings began to catch up with him, and in 1967, he was sentenced to 13 years in prison for bribery and fraud.

A Struggle to Regain Power

Hoffa's sentence was commuted by President Richard Nixon in 1971, under the condition that he not seek "direct or indirect management of any labor organization" until 1980. But, with newfound freedom and a thirst for the power he once had, Hoffa ignored this term. Within two years, he was once again vying for presidency of the IBT. But if Hoffa thought he'd be welcomed back with open arms, he was wrong. His attempts to regain power were met with strong resistance, not only by IBT members, but also many of the gangsters he had once worked with. On July 30, 1975, Hoffa was invited to attend a "peace meeting" between him and two of his organized crime contacts, Anthony Provenzano and Anthony Giacalone, presumably to smooth out tensions between the groups.

The Meeting, the Mob, and the Mystery

Several witnesses saw Hoffa at the location of the meeting, which was set for 2:00 P.M. in the afternoon. At 2:15 P.M., he called his wife from a pay phone to impatiently say that Provenzano and Giacalone hadn't shown up yet. What happened next has been the subject of countless speculation. Hoffa simply vanished, leaving behind his unlocked car and very few other clues. Provenzano and Giacalone denied ever setting up a meeting, and both had alibis that placed them away from the meeting location that afternoon.

Many theories have circulated about Hoffa's fate, but he was officially declared legally dead in 1982. Over the years, various Teamsters and mobsters have alleged to "know the truth" about what happened to him, but none of these claims have panned out. The FBI has investigated scores of tips, searching for traces of Hoffa in the homes of gangsters, backyard sheds, horse farms, landfills, and even the Florida Everglades.

A particularly creative theory posits that Hoffa's body was dismembered and the pieces were added to steel in a Detroit auto factory, which were then exported to Japan. The real story is probably much more mundane. But until we know for sure, the mysterious fate of Jimmy Hoffa will no doubt continue to inspire macabre tales.

Crime and Punishment: When Mobsters Screw Up

Not everything goes off without a hitch. In fact, it rarely does. Here are some examples of some of the most-botched crime jobs in history.

✳   ✳   ✳   ✳

ORGANIZED CRIME IS serious business. After all, it usually involves violence, weapons, other people's money, the law, and prison. With those pieces loose on the chessboard, it's really easy to mess up. Take the two New York mobsters who agreed to do a little job: hit Al Capone. They had a nice trip on the Twentieth Century Limited, but in Chicago they were met at the train, taken someplace quiet, and beaten to death. Pieces of them were sent back with a note: "Don't send boys to do a man's job."

Don't Mess with the Wrong Guy

There's also the mistake of not knowing who you're dealing with. Faced with debts in his electrical business, Florida businessperson George Bynum borrowed $50,000 from a mob loan shark. He was able to make $2,500 payments on the interest, but he couldn't pay off the principal, so he decided to go into the crime business himself. He tipped off a burglary gang about a house that he had wired, in exchange for a cut of the take. The burglars broke in, but the home owner was there, and they beat him up. The owner was Anthony "Nino" Gaggi, a Gambino family mobster. Gaggi found out that Bynum had planned the burglary. On July 13, 1976, John Holland called Bynum from the Ocean Shore Motel and pitched a lucrative wiring contract. When Bynum arrived at the motel, Gaggi and some friends were waiting, and that was the last anyone heard from Bynum.

If You're Laying Low, Lay Low!

Often the bungling of criminals is much more humorous. Enrico "Kiko" Frigerio was a Swiss citizen, and when the famed Pizza Connection—a scheme to push heroin through pizza parlors in New York—was broken by the FBI in 1984, he fled to Switzerland. Frigerio stayed there for years, until a documentary film crew decided to do a movie about his life. As technical advisor, he decided to give them a tour of his old New York haunts, but when he stepped off a plane onto U.S. soil, he was immediately arrested. Frigerio hadn't realized that he was still under indictment. Oops!

A Continuing Comedy of Errors

Jimmy Breslin once wrote a comic novel called *The Gang That Couldn't Shoot Straight*. He must have been thinking about New Jersey's DeCavalcante crime family, the only one never given a seat on the Mafia's ruling commission. Vincent "Vinnie Ocean" Palermo ruled the DeCavalcante family like a bad Marx Brothers movie. Once, Palermo's men were given a supply of free cell phones—supplied by the FBI to tap their conversations. Another time, Palermo put a .357 Magnum to the head of a boat mechanic to force him to admit that he'd ruined the motor on Palermo's speedboat. "I was so mad, I bit his nose," Palermo said.

Then there was the time that Palermo and the missus went on vacation, and he decided to hide the family jewelry—$700,000 worth—in the bottom of a trash bag. "My wife took the garbage out for the first time in 20 years, and that was the end of the jewelry."

Finally, in 1999, Palermo was arrested and agreed to turn informant in exchange for leniency in sentencing. He helped to put away such stalwarts as Frankie the Beast, Anthony Soft-Shoes, and Frank the Painter. Palermo himself admitted to four murders, including that of newspaper editor Frank Weiss. He said that it was a good career move: "I shot him twice in the head. They made me a captain." He will not be missed.

Valachi Speaks

On June 22, 1962, in the federal penitentiary in Atlanta, Georgia, a man serving a sentence of 15 to 20 years for heroin trafficking picked up a steel pipe and murdered another convict. The killer was Joseph "Joe Cargo" Valachi; the intended victim was Joseph DiPalermo—but Valachi got the wrong man and killed another inmate, Joe Saupp. This mistake touched off one of the greatest criminal revelations in history.

✳ ✳ ✳ ✳

JOE VALACHI, A 59-year-old Mafia "soldier," was the first member of the Mafia to publicly acknowledge the reality of that criminal organization—making *La Cosa Nostra* (which means "this thing of ours") a household name. He opened the doors to expose an all-pervasive, wide-ranging conglomerate of crime families, the existence of which was repeatedly denied by J. Edgar Hoover and the FBI. By testifying against his own organization, Valachi violated *omertà*, the code of silence.

The Boss's Orders

Vito Genovese was the boss of New York's powerful Genovese crime family. Valachi had worked for the family for much of his life—primarily as a driver, but also as a hit man, enforcer, numbers runner, and drug pusher. When Valachi was on his way to prison after having been found guilty of some of these activities, Genovese believed the small-time operator had betrayed him to obtain a lighter sentence for himself. So Genovese put a $100,000 bounty on Valachi's head. He and Valachi were actually serving sentences in the same prison when Valachi killed Joe Saupp—mistaking him for Joseph DiPalermo, whom he thought had been assigned by Genovese to murder him. Whether or not Valachi had broken the code of silence and betrayed Genovese before the bounty was placed on his head, he certainly did it with a vengeance afterward.

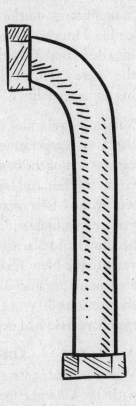

But why did Valachi turn informer? The answer to that question isn't entirely clear. Most speculate that Valachi was afraid of a death sentence for killing Saupp and agreed to talk to the Feds in exchange for a lighter sentence.

The Cat Is Out of the Bag

Valachi was a barely literate, street-level miscreant whose knowledge of the workings of the organization was limited. However, when he was brought before John L. McClellan's Senate Permanent Investigations Subcommittee in October 1963, he began talking beyond his personal experience, relaying urban legends as truth, and painting a picture of the Mafia that was both fascinating and chilling.

All in all, Joe Valachi helped identify 317 members of the Mafia. His assistance gave Attorney General Robert Kennedy

"a significant addition to the broad picture of organized crime."
Unlike Hoover, Bobby Kennedy had no problem acknowledging the Mafia. (One theory about Hoover's denials is that they were a result of long-term Mafia blackmail regarding his homosexuality.)

Valachi's revelations ran the gamut from minor accuracies to babbling exaggerations, as well as from true to false, but the cat was out of the bag. Americans became fascinated with crime families, codes of honor, gang wars, hit killings, and how widely the Mafia calamari had stretched its tentacles. Very private criminals suddenly found their names splashed across headlines and blaring from televisions. During the next three years in the New York–New Jersey–Connecticut metropolitan area, more organized criminals were arrested and jailed than in the previous 30 years. Whatever safe conduct pass the Mafia may have held had expired.

On-screen and in Print

When journalist Peter Maas interviewed Valachi and came out with *The Valachi Papers*, the U.S. Department of Justice first encouraged but then tried to block its publication. Regardless, the book was released in 1968. This work soon became the basis of a movie that starred Charles Bronson as Joe Valachi. The novel *The Godfather* was published in 1969, and in the film *The Godfather: Part II*, the characters of Willie Cicci and Frank Pentangeli were reportedly inspired by Valachi.

The $100,000 bounty on the life of Joseph Valachi was never claimed. In 1966, Valachi unsuccessfully attempted to hang himself in his prison cell using an electrical cord. Five years later, he died of a heart attack at La Tuna Federal Correctional Institution in Texas. He had outlived his chief nemesis, Genovese, by two years.

Chapter 8

Politics and Government

6 Political Scandals

Political scandals and corruption in the United States have been around since the birth of the nation and don't show any signs of going away, much to the satisfaction of late-night comedians and talk show hosts. Who needs soap operas when real life in Washington is so scandalous? Check out these accounts of infamous political scandals.

✳   ✳   ✳   ✳

1. **Teapot Dome Scandal:** The Teapot Dome Scandal was the largest of numerous scandals during the presidency of Warren Harding. Teapot Dome is an oil field reserved for emergency use by the U.S. Navy located on public land in Wyoming. Oil companies and politicians claimed the reserves were not necessary and that the oil companies could supply the Navy in the event of shortages. In 1922, Interior Secretary Albert B. Fall accepted $404,000 in illegal gifts from oil company executives in return for leasing the rights to the oil at Teapot Dome to Mammoth Oil without asking for competitive bids. The leases were legal but the gifts were not. Fall's attempts to keep the gifts secret failed, and, on April 14, 1922, *The Wall Street Journal* exposed the bribes. Fall denied the charges, but an investigation revealed a $100,000 no-interest loan in return for leases that Fall had forgotten to cover up. In 1927, the

Supreme Court ruled that the oil leases had been illegally obtained, and the U.S. Navy regained control of Teapot Dome and other reserves. Fall was found guilty of bribery in 1929, fined $100,000, and sentenced to one year in prison. He was the first cabinet member imprisoned for his actions while in office. President Harding was not aware of the scandal at the time of his death in 1923, but it contributed to his administration being considered one of the most corrupt in history.

2. **Chappaquiddick:** After being elected to the Senate in 1962, Edward M. "Ted" Kennedy became known as a liberal who championed causes such as education and health care, but his actions created a shadow over his reputation. On July 18, 1969, Kennedy attended a party on Chappaquiddick Island in Massachusetts. He left the party with 29-year-old Mary Jo Kopechne, who had campaigned for Ted's late brother Robert. Soon after the two left the party, Kennedy's car veered off a bridge and Kopechne drowned. An experienced swimmer, Kennedy said he tried to rescue her but the tide was too strong. He swam to shore, went back to the party, and returned with two other men. Their rescue efforts also failed, but Kennedy waited until the next day to report the accident, calling his lawyer and Kopechne's parents first, claiming the crash had dazed him. There was speculation that he tried to cover up that he was driving under the influence, but nothing was ever proven. Kennedy pleaded guilty to leaving the scene of an accident, received a two-month suspended jail sentence, and lost his driver's license for a year. The scandal may have contributed to his failed presidential bid in 1980, but Kennedy's powerful political career continued for decades.

3. **Watergate:** Watergate is the name of the scandal that caused Richard Nixon to become the only U.S. president to resign from office. On May 27, 1972, concerned that Nixon's bid for reelection was in jeopardy, former CIA

agent E. Howard Hunt, Jr., former New York assistant district attorney G. Gordon Liddy, former CIA operative James W. McCord, Jr., and six other men broke into the Democratic headquarters in the Watergate Hotel in Washington, D.C. They wiretapped phones, stole some documents, and photographed others. When they broke in again on June 17 to fix a bug that wasn't working, a suspicious security guard called the Washington police, who arrested McCord and four other burglars. A cover-up began to destroy incriminating evidence, obstruct investigations, and halt any spread of scandal that might lead to the president. On August 29, Nixon announced that the break-in had been investigated and that no one in the White House was involved. Despite his efforts to hide his involvement, Nixon was done in by his own tape recordings, one of which revealed that he had authorized hush money paid to Hunt. To avoid impeachment, Nixon resigned on August 9, 1974. His successor, President Gerald Ford, granted him a blanket pardon on September 8, 1974, eliminating any possibility that Nixon would be indicted and tried. *Washington Post* reporters Bob Woodward and Carl Bernstein helped expose the scandal using information leaked by someone identified as Deep Throat, a source whose identity was kept hidden until 2005, when it was finally revealed to the public that Deep Throat was former Nixon administration member William Mark Felt.

4. **Wilbur Mills:** During the Great Depression, Wilbur Mills served as a county judge in Arkansas and initiated government-funded programs to pay medical and prescription drug bills for the poor. Mills was elected to the House of Representatives in 1939 and served until 1977, with 18 of those years as head of the Ways and Means Committee. In the 1960s, Mills played an integral role in the creation of the Medicare program, and he made an unsuccessful bid for president in the 1972 primary. Unfortunately for Mills,

he's best known for one of Washington's juiciest scandals. On October 7, 1974, Mills' car was stopped by police in West Potomac Park near the Jefferson Memorial. Mills was drunk and in the back seat of the car with an Argentine stripper named Fanne Foxe. When the police approached, Foxe fled the car. Mills checked into an alcohol treatment center and was reelected to Congress in November 1974. But just one month later, Mills was seen drunk onstage with Fanne Foxe. Following the incident, Mills was forced to resign as chairman of the Ways and Means Committee and did not run for reelection in 1976. Mills died in 1992, and despite the scandal, several schools and highways in Arkansas are named for him.

5. **The Iran-Contra Affair:** On July 8, 1985, President Ronald Reagan told the American Bar Association that Iran was part of a "confederation of terrorist states." He failed to mention that members of his administration were secretly planning to sell weapons to Iran to facilitate the release of U.S. hostages held in Lebanon by pro-Iranian terrorist groups. Profits from the arms sales were secretly sent to Nicaragua to aid rebel forces, known as the contras, in their attempt to overthrow the country's democratically-elected government. The incident became known as the Iran-Contra Affair and was the biggest scandal of Reagan's administration. The weapons sale to Iran was authorized by Robert McFarlane, head of the National Security Council (NSC), in violation of U.S. government policies regarding terrorists and military aid to Iran. NSC staff member Oliver North arranged for a portion of the $48 million paid by Iran to be sent to the contras, which violated a 1984 law banning this type of aid. North and his secretary Fawn Hall also shredded critical documents. President Reagan repeatedly denied rumors that the United States had exchanged arms for hostages, but later stated that he'd been misinformed. He created a Special Review Board to inves-

tigate. In February 1987, the board found the president not guilty. Others involved were found guilty but either had their sentences overturned on appeal or were later pardoned by George H. W. Bush.

6. **The Keating Five:** After the banking industry was deregulated in the 1980s, savings and loan banks were allowed to invest deposits in commercial real estate, not just residential. Many savings banks began making risky investments, and the Federal Home Loan Bank Board (FHLBB) tried to stop them, against the wishes of the Reagan administration, which was against government interference with business. In 1989, when the Lincoln Savings and Loan Association of Irvine, California, collapsed, its chairman, Charles H. Keating, Jr., accused the FHLBB and its former head Edwin J. Gray of conspiring against him. Gray testified that five senators had asked him to back off on the Lincoln investigation.

These senators—Alan Cranston of California, Dennis DeConcini of Arizona, John Glenn of Ohio, Donald Riegle of Michigan, and John McCain of Arizona—became known as the Keating Five after it was revealed that they received a total of $1.3 million in campaign contributions from Keating. While an investigation determined that all five acted improperly, they all claimed this was a standard campaign funding practice. In August 1991, the Senate Ethics Committee recommended censure for Cranston and criticized the other four for "questionable conduct." Cranston had already decided not to run for reelection in 1992. DeConcini and Riegle served out their terms but did not run for reelection in 1994. John Glenn was reelected in 1992 and served until he retired in 1999. John McCain continued his work in the Senate until his death in 2018, when he was honored by fond remembrances from both sides of the political aisle.

They Helped Kill Lincoln: Booth's Co-Conspirators

John Wilkes Booth is well known for his assassination of President Abraham Lincoln at Ford's Theatre on April 14, 1865, but he wasnt a lone wolf. The rather lengthy list of his coconspirators has not been quite so memorable.

✳ ✳ ✳ ✳

A POPULAR SHAKESPEAREAN STAGE actor who traveled the country performing, John Wilkes Booth could have kept busy enjoying his notoriety and fame. Instead, inspired by the secession of the Southern states that set off the Civil War, he was firmly entrenched in his racist, whie supremecist beliefs and loyalty to the Confederacy. Once Lincoln freed the enslaved people in the rebelling states, a conviction took hold in Booth's mind branding the abolitionist president his arch-enemy. Dead set on bringing down Lincoln and preserving the Confederacy and the institution of slavery, Booth began to plot his attack. Initially, he planned to kidnap Lincoln and then ransom him for captive Confederate soldiers, but the conspiracy evolved, of course, into the first presidential assassination in U.S. history.

The Accomplices

Booth, who was charismatic and persuasive, had no trouble forming a gang of like-minded conspirators. Samuel Arnold, George Atzerodt, David Herold, Lewis Powell, John Surratt, and Michael O'Laughlen all joined with Booth to design various plots that would achieve victory for the South and cause trouble for Lincoln and his backers.

Meeting regularly at a boardinghouse run by Mary Surratt, the mother of one of the conspirators, the club decided to kidnap Lincoln in early 1865. They would simply snatch him from his box at a play and then ransom him for a few imprisoned Confederate soldiers. It would be a twofold victory, as they would cause grievance for their nemesis and bring the Confederacy closer to victory. Their plan was thwarted, though, when Lincoln failed to appear at the scheduled event. Similar plans were hatched, but for various reasons, none of the kidnapping plots came to fruition. Frustrated with his inability to capture Lincoln and spurred by Lincoln's continued attempts to dismantle the system of slavery, Booth determined that kidnapping was simply not enough: Lincoln must die!

Arnold, John Surratt, and O'Laughlen later swore that they knew nothing of the plot to commit murder, but Atzerodt, Herold, and Powell most certainly did. They each had their own assigned roles in the grand assassination plot, unsuccessful though they were in carrying out those parts. Atzerodt was slated to assassinate Vice President Andrew Johnson, while Powell and Herold were scheduled to kill Secretary of State William Seward. All three assassinations were planned for the same time on the evening of April 14.

Going into Action

Only Booth found complete success in the mission, however. Atzerodt apparently backed down from his assignment in fear. Powell cut a path of carnage through the Seward mansion, stabbing the secretary of state in the face and neck and wounding two of Seward's sons, a daughter, a soldier guarding Seward, and a messenger, although no one was killed. Herold had been with Powell but ran away when the mission didn't seem to be going smoothly. Booth shot Lincoln in the back of the head. The president died on the morning of April 15.

Booth immediately fled the scene, injuring a leg in his mad dash. He met up with Herold, and the pair was on the run for two weeks before finally being discovered on a small farm. The fugitives were holed up in a barn—Herold surrendered, but when Booth refused to do the same, soldiers set the barn on fire. In the ensuing melee, Booth was shot in the neck; he died a few hours later. Atzerodt, Herold, and Powell were hanged for their crimes, as was one more purported coconspirator, Mary Surratt. She ran the boardinghouse in which much of this plot was hatched, a plot which definitely included her son at various times. Her specific involvement and knowledge of the affair, however, has frequently been challenged.

The rest of the original coconspirators, as well as others with suspicious acquaintance to the group, were sentenced to jail time for their involvement.

The Guy Who Killed the Guy Who Killed Abraham Lincoln

What's it take to bring down an assassin? Sharp-shooting skills and a story of your own.

✳ ✳ ✳ ✳

The Mad Hatter

YOU MIGHT FIGURE that a guy who takes down a presidential assassin is a stand-up sort of fellow. But according to legend, Thomas "Boston" Corbett, the man who shot Lincoln's assassin, John Wilkes Booth, was a few bullets shy of a full round.

Born in London in 1832, Thomas Corbett moved with his parents to Troy, New York, in 1839. As a young man, he became a hat maker and was exposed to the dangerous chemicals involved, included mercurious nitrate, which was used in curing felt. Long-term exposure would more than likely turn him into a certified "mad" hatter. After losing his first wife and child during childbirth, Corbett turned to the bottle. Later, however, he turned to Jesus Christ and moved to Boston. It was here that he rechristened himself as "Boston."

An account from a Massachusetts hospital states that Corbett, described as a religious fanatic, cut off his own testes after reading from the Bible the book of Matthew chapters 18 and 19 (which discuss removing offending body parts) and being approached by prostitutes on the city streets. After removing his offending body part, he apparently attended church and ate dinner at home before calling the doctor.

A Bullet for Booth

In 1861, Corbett enlisted as a private in Company I, 12th New York Militia. After several years in service, he found himself with a group on the hunt for the infamous assassin John Wilkes Booth. And though the cavalry was instructed to bring Booth in alive, it's generally accepted that Corbett shot him while Booth was surrounded in a burning barn. Given the chaos, the distance, and the smoke, it's surprising that the bullet even hit Booth.

Fifteen Minutes of Fame

Corbett wasn't punished for shooting Booth. In fact, he received a share of the reward money, totaling $1,653.85. For a short period of time, Corbett was considered a hero and even signed autographs for his fans.

Afterward, Corbett moved around for a few years and eventually settled in Concordia, Kansas, where, in 1887, he was elected as the assistant doorkeeper to the Kansas House of Representatives. He lived as a bit of a hermit, but he preached at the Methodist Episcopal Church and became known as something of an evangelist. People still came from other towns to see the famed gunman who took down Booth. Then one day in the winter of 1887, Corbett threatened to shoot people over an argument on the floor of the House of Representatives. He was quickly arrested, determined to be unstable, and booked for a permanent vacation to a psych hospital.

Loose Ends

That wasn't the last America would hear from Boston Corbett. He escaped from the hospital on his second attempt in May 1888, stole a pony that was tied up in front of the hospital, and high-tailed it out of there. He reappeared one week later in Neodesha, Kansas, and was said to have later headed down to Mexico.

Corbett seemed to have disappeared, though sightings were reported far and wide. As with everything surrounding the Lincoln assassination, there are plenty of conspiracy theories regarding Corbett: There are some who say that Corbett wasn't the one who shot Booth. Others say that it was not actually Booth who Corbett shot, and that Corbett later traveled to Enid, Kansas, to meet a man claiming to be Booth.

What is known about Corbett is that before he disappeared, he made a dugout home near Concordia, Kansas. Today, a stone marker between two trees in the middle of a pasture stands as a monument to the guy who killed the guy who killed the 16th president of the United States.

Stealing the President

While he was alive, President Abraham Lincoln was loved and admired by many. Perhaps his popularity was the reason why in 1876, a group of men decided that people would be willing to pay a lot of money to see the 16th president of the United States— even if he was dead.

✳ ✳ ✳ ✳

Breaking Out Boyd

THE PLOT WAS hatched in 1876, 11 years after President Lincoln's assassination by John Wilkes Booth. Illinois engraver Benjamin Boyd had been arrested on charges of creating engraving plates to make counterfeit bills. Boyd's boss, James "Big Jim" Kinealy, a man known around Chicago as the King of the Counterfeiters, was determined to get Boyd out of prison in order to continue his counterfeiting operation.

Kinealy's plan was to kidnap Lincoln's corpse from his mausoleum at the Oak Ridge Cemetery in Springfield, Illinois, and hold it for ransom—$200,000 in cash and a full pardon for Boyd. Not wanting to do the dirty work himself, Kinealy turned to two men: John "Jack" Hughes and Terrence Mullen, a bartender at The Hub, a Madison Street bar frequented by Kinealy and his associates.

Kinealy told Hughes and Mullen that they were to steal Lincoln's body on Election Night, November 7, load it onto a cart, and take it roughly 200 miles north to the shores of Lake Michigan. They were to bury the body in the sand, to stow it until the ransom was paid. The plan seemed foolproof until Hughes and Mullen decided they needed a third person to help steal the body—a fellow named Lewis Swegles. It was a decision Hughes and Mullen would come to regret.

The Plan Backfires

The man directly responsible for bringing Boyd in was Patrick D. Tyrrell, a member of the Secret Service in Chicago. Long before their current role of protecting the president of the United States, one of the main jobs for members of the Secret Service was to track down and arrest counterfeiters. One of Tyrrell's informants was a small-time crook by the name of Lewis Swegles. Yes, the same guy who agreed to help Hughes and Mullen steal the president's body. Thanks to the stool pigeon, everything the duo was planning was being reported back to the Secret Service.

On the evening of November 7, 1876, Hughes, Mullen, and Swegles entered the Lincoln Mausoleum, unaware of the Secret Service lying in wait. The hoods broke open Lincoln's sarcophagus and removed the casket, and Swegles was sent to get the wagon. Swegles gave the signal to make the arrest, but once the Secret Service men reached the mausoleum, they found it to be empty. In all the confusion, Hughes and Mullen had slipped away, leaving Lincoln's body behind. Unsure what to do next, Tyrrell ordered Swegles back to Chicago to see if he could pick up the kidnappers' trail. Swegles eventually found them in a local Chicago tavern, and on November 16 or 17 (sources vary), Hughes and Mullen were arrested without incident.

Lincoln Is Laid to Rest (Again)

With no laws on the books at the time pertaining to the stealing of a body, Hughes and Mullen were only charged with attempted larceny of Lincoln's coffin and a count each of conspiracy. After a brief trial, both men were found guilty. Their sentence for attempting to steal the body of President Abraham Lincoln: One year in the Illinois state penitentiary in Joliet.

As for Lincoln's coffin, it remains at its home in Oak Ridge Cemetery; it has been moved an estimated 17 times and opened 6 times. On September 26, 1901, the Lincoln family took steps to ensure Abe's body could never be stolen again: It was buried 10 feet under the floor of the mausoleum, inside a metal cage, and under thousands of pounds of concrete.

Pulling the Wool Over The Eyes of New York City

Throughout the 1860s and 1870s, a man named William "Boss" Tweed controlled New York City politics—and, subsequently, New York City itself. Graft, payoffs, cheating, and a healthy dose of high-quality corruption were the order of the day.

✳ ✳ ✳ ✳

It All Started with Tammany Hall

A S THE UNITED States struggled to stand on its own following the American Revolution, political organizations began to spring up across the East Coast. The biggest and most influential was the Tammany, named after Native American Chief Tamanend. Founded on May 12, 1789, it was first a social and political organization. Then, under the leadership of Aaron Burr, the group embraced the politics of Thomas Jefferson and began supporting candidates. It was no small coincidence that Burr was elected vice president in 1800.

The strength of Tammany continued to grow, aiding the presidential election of Andrew Jackson in 1828 and 1832. By then, the powerful Democratic faction literally ran all of the politics in New York City, based out of their huge headquarters called "Tammany Hall." The organization became known by the same name.

Tammany Hall soon became a tool of the Irish Catholic community, which had quickly formed in New York City after the potato famine in Ireland drove its inhabitants to the shores of Manhattan in the mid-1840s. By the mid-1850s, Tammany Hall controlled the outcome of mayoral races, as well as other elected offices. Skilled in the art of politics, the leaders of this political machine kept New York City running—and their pockets filled.

Who's the Boss?

In New York City, a young Scottish-Irish bookkeeper and volunteer firefighter named William Tweed used his municipal position to become elected as an alderman in New York City in 1851. He soon became a member of Congress and, in 1857, became the leader of Tammany Hall.

The next 14 years became a swirl of voting fraud, judge-buying, and contract kickbacks for "Boss" Tweed and his cronies. In one instance, a carpenter received more than $360,000 for work done in a building that had very little wood in it. A furniture dealer was paid nearly $180,000 for three conference tables and 40 chairs. A plasterer received more than $130,000 for a mere two days of work.

Tweed orchestrated the construction of the New York County Courthouse—a task that took nearly 20 years (2 years past his death, in fact) and cost $13 million. It was estimated that the project's price tag should have been half that figure. When an investigation was conducted into the excessive amount, the resulting report cost nearly $8,000 to print. The owner of the printing company was William Tweed.

Getting Tweed Off

The "Tweed Ring," which included the mayor and city comp-
troller, profited to the tune of an estimated $100 million to
$200 million by the time the illegal activities were exposed in
1871. New York newspapers and magazines, featuring unflat-
tering political cartoons of Tweed by illustrator Thomas Nast
(see the next article for a profile of the man who took him
down), revealed the graft under the Tweed Ring, and the "Boss"
was brought to trial in 1874. Found guilty of embezzlement, he
was sentenced to 12 years in prison, but served only a year
on appeal.

Arrested the next year on a separate charge, Tweed escaped to
Cuba but was found and held by Cuban officials. Before U.S.
marshals could claim Tweed, however, he bolted to Spain. The
Spanish government immediately grabbed him as he landed.

William Tweed was returned to a New York City jail (a jail that
he may very well have had built under his regime), where he
died two years later in April 1878. He was only 55.

The Mighty Pen!

*Thomas Nast was one of the most important editorial cartoonists
of his day—and an unrelenting foe of political corruption.*

✳ ✳ ✳ ✳

WHEN HE PICKED up his pen, he drew beautifully. He
invented Santa Claus as we know him today, created the
Republican elephant and the Democratic donkey, and used his
skilled pen to fan the fires of patriotism during the Civil War.
But it was his efforts to draw attention to New York City's corrupt political system for which cartoonist Thomas Nast is best
known today.

Nast was born in Landau, Germany, in 1840 and emigrated
to New York City with his mother and sister at the age of six.
(His father followed three years later.) A natural talent, Nast

studied art, and at age 15 he was hired as a reportorial artist for *Frank Leslie's Illustrated Newspaper*. He later went to work for the *New York Illustrated News*, which sent him to Europe to cover, among other things, Giuseppe Garibaldi's military campaign in Sicily.

A National Audience

In 1862, Nast accepted a full-time position with the prestigious *Harper's Weekly*, for whom he had previously freelanced. The magazine sent him to the battlefields of the Civil War, where his artistic talent shone. An avowed Union supporter, Nast unabashedly used his pen to criticize, with dramatic flair, the Confederate war effort and rouse support for the North.

His gig with *Harper's Weekly* made Nast nationally famous, and after the war he was solicited to illustrate books. Nast enjoyed such work and accepted numerous illustration jobs while he continued to work for *Harper's Weekly*. It is estimated that over the course of his career, Nast provided drawings for more than 100 volumes.

Tweed in the Crosshairs

In 1868, Nast turned his pen against William Magear "Boss" Tweed. Tweed used his influence to put almost all of city government and much of the state legislature in his pocket. Tweed was the worst kind of political crook, and Nast was unrelenting in his artistic attacks against Tweed's administration. The cartoonist's campaign in *Harper's Weekly* and the *New York Times* lasted nearly three years.

Tweed and his cronies quickly felt the effects of Nast's drawings, which depicted the politician and his followers as sleazy scum with their hands in the public till. Legend has it that Tweed became so incensed over Nast's illustrations that he told his underlings, "Stop them damn pictures. I don't care what the papers write about. My constituents can't read. But, damn it, they can see the pictures."

At one point, intermediaries for Tweed visited Nast and offered him a $100,000 "gift" to study art in Europe. Naturally, Nast realized he was being bribed, so he played along, upping the payoff amount until it reached $500,000—which Nast then declined.

Nast's cartoons helped bring an end to Tweed's culture of corruption. In 1871, Tweed was kicked out of office by angry voters and eventually jailed. However, he managed to escape in 1876 and tried to flee to Spain. In an ironic twist, he was recognized and arrested by a customs official who could not speak English but who recognized Tweed from Nast's dead-on caricatures!

Nast's Later Life

In the years that followed, Nast's relationship with *Harper's Weekly* began to sour. Nast left the magazine in 1886. He free-lanced for various magazines until 1892, when he established his own, *Nast's Weekly*. Unfortunately, the publication lasted only six months. Nast had difficulty finding substantial illustration work in the years that followed, and in 1902 he accepted an appointment from President Theodore Roosevelt as consul general to Ecuador. In a sad irony, Nast contracted yellow fever while abroad and died on December 7, 1902.

To this day, Thomas Nast is revered as one of the most influential political cartoonists who ever lived, demonstrating every time he put ink on paper that the pen really is mightier than the sword.

"Gentleman" Jimmy Walker

The 1920s, a time of easy money, easy virtue, and even easier vice, established a corrupt but colorful mayor as the "Beau James" of the Jazz Age.

✳ ✳ ✳ ✳

AMERICAN MAYORS HOLD one of the most important political executive offices in the nation. While the best of all time in New York City was arguably Fiorello H. La Guardia, the Republican "fusionist" reformer who fought the Mob and read children the funnies over the radio during a newspaper strike, Gotham has also had more than its fair share of mayoral villains and scoundrels.

These include Fernando Wood, whose vote rigging and criminal affiliations made him the standard bearer for 19th-century institutionalized corruption, and Abraham Oakey Hall, known as "Boss Tweed's mayor" because of the role he played in defrauding taxpayers out of between $40 million and $200 million during his 1868–72 tenure. But these crooks and scam artists aside, New York's worst mayor has to be Jimmy Walker, a skirt-chasing, former Tin Pan Alley composer. His affairs with chorus girls and official lack of interest in around 32,000 Prohibition speakeasies (some of which he owned) endeared him to many voters, but his involvement with kickbacks and public extortion led to his downfall.

A Large and Crooked Role

Like Wood and Hall, James John Walker was a product of the Tammany Hall Democratic machine that, concurrent with the political rise of Irish-Americans, played a large and often crooked role in New York City politics from the late 18th century to the early 1960s. The son of an Irish-born assemblyman and alderman from Greenwich Village, Walker, too, was a member of the New York state assembly, as well as the New York state senate, before defeating the incumbent John Hylan in 1925 to become mayor in 1926. His electoral platform ballyhooed legalized beer and a five-cent subway fare, as well as legalized Sunday boxing, baseball, and movies. You could safely say that Walker was going for the "common-person" vote.

Hoping, as he said during his inauguration speech, that "the people of this city would not look upon their public servants as antagonistic, but... as their servants and friends," Walker quickly befriended plenty of females at the clubs he frequented. This allowed him to add the sobriquets of "Beau James" and the "Night Mayor" to that of "Gentleman Jimmy," which had come courtesy of his dandified demeanor and custom-made clothes.

Jimmy got off to a flying start during his first two years in office, spending 143 days out of the office for vacation trips to Palm Beach, Palm Springs, Europe, and the Caribbean. Then, when he was publicly brought to task for giving himself a pay raise from $25,000 annually to $40,000, he characteristically quipped, "Why, that's cheap. Think what it would cost if I worked full-time."

A Little Fireside Chat

Walker continually laughed off accusations of corruption. He won reelection easily in 1929, defeating the highly ethical La Guardia, but his dismissive attitude toward his troubles became more difficult to maintain after the onset of the Great Depression. In 1931, the New York state legislature commenced an investigation into his administration's misdeeds, including the extortion of money from innocent citizens who had been accused of bogus crimes. Just a year later, Walker was charged with extorting and accepting several hundred thousand dollars in kickbacks from business executives who had been handed sweet city contracts.

At that point, Governor Franklin Roosevelt suggested he and Jimmy have a little fireside chat. Governor Roosevelt was not a man to be trifled with, and on September 1, 1932, Walker resigned as mayor and absconded to France, where he married his longtime mistress, the English actress Betty Compton, after divorcing his former-chorus-girl wife.

The Walkers returned to New York City in 1935. Jimmy became the head of Majestic Records, and in 1940, just before he and Betty received their own divorce, the irrepressible "Beau James" bounced back from his public disgrace with an appointment as municipal arbiter to the garment industry. Mayor La Guardia made the appointment.

Jimmy Walker passed from this realm of pleasure on November 18, 1946, at the age of 65.

You Can't Take Down a Bull Moose

During a 1912 Milwaukee political speech, Teddy Roosevelt took a lickin' (or rather, a bullet) but kept on tickin'.

✳ ✳ ✳ ✳

A Four-Way Race

AMERICAN POLITICS WERE in a state of chaos during the presidential election season of 1912. Ex-President Theodore Roosevelt had broken with the Republicans and established the Progressive Party, which then nominated the "Bull Moose" himself as its candidate. Incumbant President (and Republican) William Howard Taft was running for a second term, Woodrow Wilson waged a high-minded campaign on behalf of the Democrats, and Eugene Debs was running as a Socialist. Roosevelt needed every vote in this contentious four-way race. In particular, he needed to win over Progressives allied with Wisconsin senator Bob LaFollette, who had expected to receive the Progressive Party's nomination and was increasingly critical of Roosevelt. To this end, Roosevelt included Milwaukee at the end of an extensive speaking tour.

Milwaukee Turns Deadly

On the evening of October 14, a large crowd gathered to see the Bull Moose leave from his Milwaukee hotel for a speech at the auditorium. Roosevelt stepped into a waiting car where Henry F. Cochems, Chairman of the National Speakers' Bureau of the Progressive Party, was seated. As Roosevelt stood waving to the crowd from the open car, John Schrank, a New York City saloonkeeper who had followed Roosevelt across the country, stepped forward and fired a Colt revolver into Roosevelt's chest.

Roosevelt's stenographer leapt upon the shooter. The Bull Moose's knees buckled at first, but he straightened and raised his hat to the crowd. Roosevelt barked to a crowd of people looking to do harm to Schrank, "Don't hurt him; bring him to me here!" Schrank, still struggling for possession of the weapon, was dragged to Roosevelt who studied him while Cochems secured the revolver.

Later Roosevelt admitted that he had no curiosity concerning Schrank: "His name might be Czolgosz or anything else as far as I'm concerned," he said referring to the assassin who felled President McKinley in 1901 (giving Vice President Roosevelt the presidency). Later, Schrank said he was convinced by a dream that Roosevelt was responsible for McKinley's death, and that he believed no president should be allowed to serve three terms.

Saved by a Speech (and Some Suspenders)

Though he was bleeding steadily from a hole below his right nipple, Roosevelt refused to be taken to the hospital. He could tell that the bullet, slowed first by his heavy overcoat, then his folded 50-page speech, his metal glasses case, and finally his thick suspenders, had not penetrated his lung. At the auditorium, in front of a crowd of 9,000–12,000 people, Roosevelt's first words were: "Ladies and gentlemen, I don't know whether you fully understand that I have just been shot; but it takes more than that to kill a Bull Moose." Someone yelled, "Fake!" but Roosevelt smiled and opened his vest to reveal his blood-stained shirt. The room went silent.

Roosevelt vs. LaFollette

Instead of collapsing, Roosevelt spoke for 90 minutes. When aides tried to cut short his speech, he quipped: "I am all right and you cannot escape listening to the speech either." When a woman near the stage said, "Mr. Roosevelt, we all wish you would be seated;" the candidate quickly replied: "I thank you, madam, but I don't mind it a bit." LaFollette supporters yelled protests at each mention of their beloved senator's name, but Roosevelt ignored their outbursts.

After speaking, Roosevelt was rushed to the hospital where exploratory surgery revealed that the bullet was inoperable. Roosevelt later admitted that he never believed the wound fatal. "Anyway... if I had to die," he laughed, "I thought I'd rather die with my boots on." During his weeklong hospital recovery, both Wilson and Taft suspended their campaigns. Still, Schrank got his wish in the end: Although Roosevelt's Milwaukee speech was sensational, it failed to impress the LaFollette Progressives, who voted overwhelmingly against Roosevelt, denying him the third term.

The Plot to Assassinate President Truman

Puerto Ricans have sought independence from the United States for decades. In 1950, two ardent nationalists took matters into their own hands as part of a campaign to win independence through violent means. Their target? President Harry Truman.

✳ ✳ ✳ ✳

MEMBERS OF THE Puerto Rican Nationalist Party were spoiling for a fight. They had tried—and failed—to reach their goal of independence through electoral participation. By the 1930s, party leader Dr. Pedro Albuzu Campos was advocating a campaign of violent revolution. Throughout the 1930s and 1940s, the Nationalist Party was involved in one confrontation after another. In 1936, Albuzu was charged with conspiring to overthrow the government and was incarcerated. He spent the next six years in jail in New York. When he finally returned to Puerto Rico in 1947, the tinder of *nacionalismo puertorriqueño* was bone-dry and smoldering.

The Match Is Lit

On October 30, 1950, Nationalists seized the town of Jayuya. With air support, the Puerto Rico National Guard crushed the rebellion. Griselio Torresola and Oscar Collazo, two *nacionalistas*, decided to retaliate at the highest level: the president of the United States. They had help from natural wastage. The White House, which looks majestic from the outside, has been quite the wretched dump at many points in its history. By 1948, it was physically unsound, so the Truman family moved to Blair House. It would be a lot easier to whack a president there than it would have been at the White House.

The Attempt

At 2:20 P.M. on November 1, 1950, Torresola approached the Pennsylvania Avenue entrance from the west with a 9mm Luger pistol. Collazo came from the east carrying the Luger's cheaper successor, the Walther P38. White House police guarded the entrance. Truman was upstairs taking a nap.

Collazo approached the Blair House steps, facing the turned back of Officer Donald Birdzell, and fired, shattering Birdzell's knee. Nearby Officers Floyd Boring and Joseph Davidson fired at Collazo through a wrought-iron fence but without immediate effect. Birdzell dragged himself after Collazo, firing his pistol. Then bullets from Boring and Davidson grazed Collazo in the scalp and chest—seemingly minor wounds. Out of ammo, Collazo sat down to reload his weapon.

Officer Leslie Coffelt staffed a guard booth at the west corner as Torresola took him unaware. Coffelt fell with a chest full of holes. Next, Torresola fired on Officer Joseph Downs, who had just stopped to chat with Coffelt. Downs took bullets to the hip, then the back and neck. He staggered to the basement door and locked it, hoping to deny the assassins entry. Torresola advanced on Birdzell from behind as the officer engaged Collazo and fired, hitting his other knee. Birdzell lost consciousness as Torresola reloaded.

Weapon recharged, Oscar Collazo stood, then collapsed from his wounds. At that moment, a startled Truman came to the window to see what was the matter. Torresola was 31 feet away. If he had looked up at precisely the right moment, the Puerto Rican nationalist would have achieved his mission.

Officer Coffelt had one final police duty in life. Despite three chest wounds, he forced himself to his feet, took careful aim, and fired. A bullet splattered the brain matter of Griselio Torresola all over the street. Coffelt staggered back to the guard shack and crumpled.

Collazo survived and was sentenced to death. Before leaving office, President Truman commuted Collazo's sentence to life imprisonment. Officers Downs and Birdzell recovered. Officer Leslie Coffelt died four hours later. The Secret Service's day room at Blair House is now named the Leslie W. Coffelt Memorial Room.

'Sconsin Scandals

Every state has its scandals. Over the years, many a Wisconsin politician has been caught being naughty. From drunken driving and assault to lots of campaign violations, Wisconsin has a sordid history of lawmakers being bad.

✳   ✳   ✳   ✳

The Great Caucus Scandal

CORRUPTION. MISCONDUCT. FALSIFICATION. Extortion. The biggest political scandal in Wisconsin history went down in 2001. Madison's Capitol Hill made embarrassing national headlines when five bigwig lawmakers were brought up on multiple criminal felony charges. The case was cracked open by *Wisconsin State Journal* investigative journalist Dee J. Hall. The ace reporter's suspicions were substantiated when a key former Republican Assembly caucus staffer finally agreed to blow the whistle. Brian Burke (D-Milwaukee), Senate Majority Leader Chuck Chvala (D-Madison), Assembly Majority Leader Steven Foti (R-Oconomowoc), Assistant Assembly Majority Leader Bonnie Ladwig (R-Mount Pleasant), and Assembly Speaker Scott Jensen (R-Waukesha) all pleaded guilty or were convicted of several counts of campaign violations. Apparently, illegal campaigning is one thing state Democrats and Republicans could agree upon.

Repeat Offender

Representative David Plombon's long entanglement with Johnny Law started in 1994. He was in a car with his estranged wife and assaulted her. He pleaded no contest to disorderly conduct and received a year of probation. That same year, his driver's license was revoked after an OWI (operating while intoxicated). Months later, this busy lawbreaker was caught green-handed and arrested for possession of marijuana. The following year, he landed a spot in prison for violating conditions of his probation. He served 12 days.

I Saw that Parking Spot First!

Road-raging Representative Robert Behnke pleaded no contest to disorderly conduct in 1982. Why the disorder? A heated argument over a State Capitol parking space! He was fined $25 plus $13 for court fees. For Behnke, 1982 was a banner year. He was also accused of second-degree sexual assault. That case was dismissed when the alleged victim was deemed an incompetent witness.

Wily Wally

In 1980, Representative Walter Ward pleaded guilty to two election law violations for misuse of campaign funds and was sentenced to jail. By the next year, the shameful bad boy was convicted of misdemeanor and felony sexual assault stemming from an incident with a legislative aide. He was sentenced to four years of incarceration. To no one's surprise but his own, Wally was not reelected.

If He Builds It...
Senator Bruce Peloquin was charged with a mysterious misdemeanor theft in 1978. What did he allegedly try to steal? Bricks! However, he was subsequently found to be not guilty of the crime.

Bad Credit
Misusing credit cards must have been popular in 1978. Representatives R. Michael Ferrall and Joseph Looby, along with Senator Henry Dorman, were all charged with their own dubious charges.

Ethically Challenged
A more recent scandal concerns Wisconsin Supreme Court Justice Annette Ziegler. During her stint in the Washington County Circuit Court, she ruled in multiple cases involving West Bend Savings Bank. The problem was that she failed to disclose a pesky conflict of interest: Her husband was a paid director on the bank's board.

The Biggest Texas Political Scandals

Next to football, politics may be the most popular sport in Texas. But with politics often comes scandal, and Texas has had more than its fill of that.

✳ ✳ ✳ ✳

Johnson Wins by a Nose
CONTROVERSY DOGGED LYNDON Johnson in his first two runs for the U.S. Senate. In 1941, the member of Congress and future president ran for a vacant Senate seat

in a special election against Texas governor W. Lee "Pappy" O'Daniel. Johnson initially appeared to be the winner but lost when some questionable returns were counted. He ran again in 1948, finishing second in a three-way Democratic primary to Coke Stevenson, but a runoff was forced when Stevenson failed to win a majority. Johnson won the runoff by 87 votes amidst accusations of fraud, including one that involved votes brought in by campaign manager (and future governor) John B. Connally that appeared to have been cast in alphabetical order. After a friendly judge struck down Stevenson's appeal, Johnson went on to win the general election.

Estes Donates Soiled Money

Billy Sol Estes was both a friend and an enemy of Lyndon Johnson. As a wealthy fertilizer salesman, Estes contributed to Johnson's campaigns for the Senate and the vice presidency. Unbeknownst to Johnson, much of Estes's wealth came from sources as odorous as his fertilizer. In the late 1950s, Estes lied about buying cotton from local farmers to obtain bank loans for nonexistent cotton and fertilizer he claimed was in storage. After his accountant and a government investigator died under suspicious circumstances, Estes and three associates were indicted on 57 counts of fraud. Two of these indicted associates also died suspiciously. Estes was found guilty of fraud and sentenced to eight years in prison, with an additional 15 years tacked on for other charges. His association with Johnson nearly caused President Kennedy to dump his vice president. Estes's conviction was ultimately overturned by the U.S. Supreme Court in 1965, however, on the grounds that having TV cameras and reporters in the courtroom (uncommon at that time) deprived him of a fair trial. After Johnson's death, Estes accused his one-time friend of involvement in a conspiracy behind the Kennedy assassination.

Bribery Makes Real Estate Deals Easier

The Texas Sharpstown Scandal is named for the Sharpstown master-planned community near Houston and its backer, banker and insurance company manager Frank Sharp. Sharp made loans of $600,000 from his bank to state officials, who then bought stock in his insurance company. They next passed legislation to inflate the value of the insurance company, which allowed the officials to sell their stock profitably. The huge profits aroused the suspicions of the Securities and Exchange Commission in 1971, and charges were filed against Sharp and others. The governor, lieutenant governor, and House speaker, among other state officials, were accused of bribery. Sharp received three years' probation and a $5,000 fine. One victim of the fraud, Strake Jesuit College Preparatory, lost $6 million.

Questionable Congressional Ethics

Democrat Jim Wright represented Texas in Congress for 34 years, serving as Speaker of the House from 1987 to '89. In 1988, Republican Newt Gingrich led an investigation by the House Ethics Committee into charges that Wright used bulk purchases of his book to get around congressional limits on speaking fees and that his wife had been given a job to get around a limit on political gifts. Wright was forced to resign from Congress in 1989, and Gingrich eventually became Speaker of the House with his own subsequent ethics violations.

Corruption as a Lifestyle

George Parr was a political force in Duval County from the 1920s to the '60s. Replacing his brother in 1926 as county judge, Parr used legal and illegal tactics to convince the county's majority Mexican American population to support the Democratic Party. Parr was convicted of income-tax evasion in 1934 and served nine months with little effect on his influence as the "Duke of Duval County." He found questionable votes to help Lyndon Johnson win the 1948 Democratic senatorial primary and was linked to but never accused of at least three murders of political opponents. While appealing a conviction and five-year sentence for federal income tax evasion in 1975, Parr committed suicide.

John Edwards's Serious Error

In the world of the rich and famous—whether they are actors, sports stars, or politicians—affairs are so commonplace we barely bat an eye. It's certainly not unheard of for a famous name to publicly offer vehement denials and then later, fallen from grace, to come forward with apologies for their indiscretions. But the story of John Edwards adds even more drama: a wife fighting cancer, a baby with questionable paternity, and an expensive cover-up.

❋　❋　❋　❋

Presidential Aspirations

JOHN EDWARDS BEGAN his career as a lawyer, making a name for himself in his home state of North Carolina, where he was eventually considered the top plaintiff's lawyer in the state. He was elected to the U.S. Senate in 1998, having had no political experience before winning the seat. By 2003, he had decided to run for president, later dropping out of the race as John Kerry took the lead. But Kerry chose him as his vice-presidential running mate, and Edwards was right back in the fray. Although Kerry/Edwards conceded to Bush/Cheney, Edwards was ready to throw his hat back in the ring a few years later, when he announced he would be running for president in 2008.

To gear up for what would be a long fight, the Edwards campaign hired a filmmaker named Rielle Hunter to produce a series of webisodes about life on the campaign trail. Edwards had met Hunter at a bar in New York when he was in town attending a business meeting. And soon after their professional relationship began, the *New York Post* hinted that there could be more to their pairing than met the eye: a gossip item in the paper claimed that a married political candidate had a girlfriend in New York, who he promised to marry "when his current wife is out of the picture." Although no names were mentioned, the story led some to believe that it was referring to Edwards and Hunter.

Tabloid Fodder

On October 10, 2007, the *National Enquirer* published a story that did, in fact, name Edwards. The *Enquirer* claimed that Edwards was having an affair with a campaign worker. On the same day, the *Huffington Post* published an article about Hunter, giving her name and listing some of the films she'd worked on. Finally, the next day, *New York* magazine published a story that linked Edwards and Hunter.

Edwards and Hunter both denied the allegations, with Edwards insisting he only had eyes for his wife, Elizabeth, who had been fighting breast cancer since 2004 and was "an extraordinary human being." And Hunter claimed that the story was a lie and "completely unfounded and ridiculous." The *Enquirer* fought back, saying their story was "100 percent accurate," and on December 19, 2007, they published another story, this time with a twist: the article included a photo of a visibly pregnant Hunter, with an anonymous source claiming that Edwards was the father of the child.

Lies and Admissions

A month later, Edwards suspended his race for the presidency, with many speculating that the affair rumors hurt his campaign and may have ruined his chances for a vice presidential bid. On February 27, 2008, Hunter's daughter, Frances Quinn, was born, but no father was listed on the birth certificate, fueling more suspicion. As late as July 23, Edwards was still denying the affair, but on August 8, he finally issued a statement admitting he "made a serious error in judgment" and that he had already told his wife about the affair and asked for forgiveness. But he continued to claim that Hunter's child was not his.

More allegations were starting to arise: A member of Edwards's campaign team, Andrew Young, stated that Edwards asked him to "get a doctor to fake the DNA results" of a paternity test. Young even publicly claimed that he was the child's father, but later recanted that claim.

What's more, a grand jury began investigating whether any of Edwards's campaign funds had been used to cover up the affair. As more facts came to light, it was discovered that Young had solicited funds from wealthy socialite Rachel Lambert Mellon (often known as Bunny Mellon). Mellon had paid $725,000 to Edwards's personal accounts, which had been used to support Hunter. On January 21, 2010, Edwards finally admitted that he was the father of Frances Quinn. And on June 3, 2011, he was indicted by a North Carolina grand jury on six felony charges, including conspiracy, issuing false statements, and violating campaign contribution laws. The trial ended with one not guilty verdict and five deadlocks, and a mistrial was declared.

Moving On

Sadly, Elizabeth Edwards succumbed to cancer on December 7, 2010. It was discovered that the affair between her husband and Hunter had been ongoing much longer than anyone realized, including during the time she was undergoing treatment for the disease. She had stated that she tried to forgive Edwards for his indiscretions, but it became more difficult as he continued to lie about the situation. Elizabeth intended to divorce her husband after a mandatory one-year separation.

After the scandal settled down, Edwards decided to return to his original career: law. He founded the law firm Edwards Kirby Attorneys at Law in Raleigh, North Carolina, and went on to be considered one of the leading personal injury lawyers in the state.

A Senator's Lewd Bathroom Behavior

There are few things more private than a person's bathroom habits. This generally falls into the "none of your business" category. But for one United States Senator, a trip to the bathroom proved to be anything but private, and it ultimately led to his downfall.

✳ ✳ ✳ ✳

Can I Have Some Privacy?

ON JUNE 11, 2007, U.S. Senator from Idaho Larry Craig was passing through the Minneapolis-St. Paul International Airport when he stopped for a bathroom. A short while later, he was led out by a police officer and arrested on suspicion of lewd conduct. So, what exactly happened in that bathroom?

On the day of Craig's arrest, police had planned an undercover operation after receiving complaints of sexual activity in the airport bathroom. An undercover officer waited in one of the stalls, and after about 15 minutes, he noticed Craig loitering just outside, occasionally peeking through the partition between doors. The senator then went into the adjacent stall, and after a few moments, began tapping his foot. This tapping gesture was, according to the arresting officer, "a signal used by persons wishing to engage in lewd conduct." Craig then slid his foot over until it was touching the officer's foot in the next stall, and then waved his hand under the stall divider several times.

Wide Stance

Craig's actions were allegedly well-known signals that implied a solicitation for anonymous sex. But instead of agreeing to a rendezvous, the officer in the next stall showed Craig his police identification and escorted him out of the bathroom. He was interviewed in the airport police station, and he denied that his actions had any particular meaning. When asked about moving his foot into the next stall, he said, "I'm a fairly wide guy," and Craig claimed that he had merely "positioned" himself in the stall. As for the hand underneath the partition, Craig insisted that he was simply reaching down to the floor to pick up a piece of paper, but the arresting officer stated that "there was not a piece of paper on the bathroom floor."

Accusations and Denials

On August 8, Craig pleaded guilty to disorderly conduct and paid a $500 fine; but he later stated that he regretted ever pleading guilty. "At the time of this incident, I complained to the police that they were misconstruing my actions. I was not involved in any inappropriate conduct," he asserted. But after the scandal broke, several men came forward claiming to have had sexual contact with the senator. Again, Craig vehemently denied the accusations, telling a reporter for the *Idaho Statesman* that "I don't go around anywhere hitting on men, and by God, if I did, I wouldn't do it in Boise, Idaho!"

The senator stated that his reasons for pleading guilty stemmed from being "relentlessly and viciously harassed" by the *Idaho Statesman*, which began inves-  tigating claims of Craig's homosexuality shortly after his arrest. He stated that he made the "poor decision" to plead guilty "in hopes of making it go away." Unfortunately for the senator however, things just got worse: Craig resigned from Mitt Romney's 2008 presidential campaign, with Romney stating, "He's disappointed the American people." Members of Craig's Republican Party began demanding that he resign, and a complaint was filed with the Senate Ethics Committee.

On September 1, 2007, Craig announced that he would resign at the end of the month; however, within a few weeks he'd changed his mind, saying that he would serve out his term in an effort to "clear my name in the Senate Ethics Committee. He left office on January 3, 2009, and did not run for reelection, bringing his political career to an end. He unsuccessfully attempted to get his guilty plea reversed several times, which led to one more giant misstep for the former senator: to pay for all of his appeals, Craig dipped into his campaign funds, and he was subsequently ordered to pay back $242,000 to the U.S. Treasury Department.

Rod Blagojevich: Another Corrupt Illinois Politician

It's not difficult to find corrupt politicians in any corner of the world. Perhaps it's a hunger for power and a desperation for votes that drives some people to unethical and illegal behavior. And in America, one state has developed a notorious reputation for producing more than its share of crooked political figures; in fact, Illinois's famous political corruption scandals have been around as long as the state itself. But while some names—like Governor Len Small, who defrauded the state a million dollars, or state official Orville Hodge, who embezzled more than $6 million in state funds—may not sound familiar, no doubt the name Rod Blagojevich rings a bell.

✳   ✳   ✳   ✳

A Quick Rise to the Top

BLAGOJEVICH WAS BORN in Chicago, and he spent much of his childhood and teenage years working odd jobs to help support his family. After high school, he earned a bachelor of arts in history from Northwestern University, and he then went to the Pepperdine University School of Law. In 1990, he married Patricia Mell, who is the daughter of influential former Chicago alderman Richard Mell. With the help of his father-in-law, Blagojevich was elected to the Illinois House of Representatives in 1992. Four years later, he became a U.S. congressman, representing Illinois's 5th Congressional District. And in 2002, with his powerful father-in-law once again providing campaign assistance, Blagojevich was elected governor of Illinois. He was reelected four years later, seemingly at the top of his political game.

Mistakes and Media

And then, in 2008, Blagojevich's political career began to collapse. A complaint from the U.S. Department of Justice alleged the governor was engaging in "pay to play" schemes—using his position of power to demand favors in exchange for gubernatorial appointments or legislation. In particular, the Justice Department was concerned with the seat recently vacated by Barack Obama, as he resigned to begin his presidency. According to the complaint, Blagojevich was offering up Obama's empty seat to "the highest bidder."

An FBI wiretap recorded the governor expressing his desire to get something in return for the senate seat, calling it "golden" and saying he would not fill the position for "nothing." Federal agents arrested Blagojevich at his home on December 9. Authorities charged him with conspiracy to commit mail and wire fraud and solicitation of bribery.

Within a month, the Illinois House and Senate voted to impeach the governor, and lieutenant governor Pat Quinn succeeded him. With his trial not set until June 3, 2010, Blagojevich hired a publicist named Glenn Selig, who founded the crisis management public relations firm "The Publicity Agency."

Selig prompted the disgraced governor to go on a media tour to proclaim his innocence, and Blagojevich was soon popping up everywhere: He had appearances on *Today*, *Good Morning America*, and *The View*, as well as multiple programs on news channels like CNN and MSNBC. He stopped by *Late Show with David Letterman*, where he insisted that his impeachment was politically motivated revenge for his refusal to raise taxes.

He even managed to publish an autobiography entitled *The Governor: The Truth Behind the Political Scandal That Continues to Rock the Nation*.

Conviction

At the trial in 2010, Blagojevich was indicted on 24 federal charges. Strangely, his defense team never called a single witness, believing that the prosecution could not prove their case. This may have resulted in some confusion for the jury, who were unable to agree on 23 of the 24 charges: Blagojevich was convicted on only one charge, but a mistrial was declared for the other charges. Not content with the outcome, the prosecution called for a retrial. While three of the charges were eventually dropped, on June 27, 2011, Blagojevich was found guilty of 17 charges pertaining to extortion and bribery, and he was sentenced to 14 years in prison. Blagojevich was released from prison in 2020 when President Donald Trump commuted his sentence. Later that same year, he began a politics-themed podcast.

Investigation, Forensics and Detection

Top Ten Crime Scene Traces

Have people learned nothing from TV crime shows? Here's a hint: Just walk through a room, let alone commit a crime, and you'll leave a trace that will detail your every action.

✳ ✳ ✳ ✳

1. **Tool marks:** If you use any sort of physical object to commit your crime—a pickax on a door lock, a ladder to reach a window, a knife or a rag (for any purpose)—it will be traceable. Tools used in any capacity create tiny nicks that can be detected, identified, and tracked by a crime-scene investigator.

2. **Paint:** A simple paint chip left at a crime scene reveals volumes. If it's from the vehicle you used in committing the crime, it indicates the make and model. If paint is found on the tool you used to break into a house, it could place you at the scene. Think it's too hard for investigators to distinguish specific paint colors? There are 40,000 types of paint classified in police databases.

3. **Dust and dirt:** Even if you're a neat-and-tidy sort of criminal, dust and dirt are often missed by the most discerning eye. These particles can reveal where you live and work

and if you have a pet (and what kind). If you've trudged through fields or someone's backyard, researchers can use palynology—the science that studies plant spores, insects, seeds, and other microorganisms—to track you down.

4. **Broken glass:** Microscopic glass fragments cling to your clothes and can't be laundered out easily. Crime labs examine tint, thickness, density, and refractive index of the fragments to determine their origins.

5. **Fibers:** The sources include clothing, drapes, wigs, carpets, furniture, blankets, pets, and plants. Using a compound microscope, an analyst can determine if the fibers are manufactured or natural, which often indicates their value as evidence. The more specific the fiber, the easier it will be to identify (consider the differences between fibers from a white cotton T-shirt and those from a multicolored wool sweater). There are more than a thousand known fibers, as well as several thousand dyes, so if an exact match is found, you will be too.

6. **Blood:** A victim's blood tells investigators a lot, but they're also looking for different kinds of blood—including yours if you were injured at the scene—and the patterns of blood distribution. Detectives are well trained in collecting blood evidence to estimate when the crime occurred and who was involved. By the way, don't think it's enough just to clean up any blood, because investigators use special lights that reveal your efforts.

7. **Bodily fluids:** Saliva, urine, vomit, and semen are a crime-scene investigator's dream, providing DNA evidence that will implicate even the most savvy criminal. Saliva is commonly found left behind by a criminal who took time out for a beverage, a snack, or a cigarette.

8. **Fingerprints:** One of the best ways to identify a criminal is through fingerprints left at the scene. But you kept track of

what you touched and then wiped everything down, right? It doesn't matter: You still left smeared prints that can be lifted and analyzed. Investigators enter fingerprint evidence into national databases that can point directly to you.

9. **Shoe prints:** If you have feet (and assuming you're not a "barefoot burglar"), you left behind shoe prints. They could be in soil or snow or perhaps on a carpet or across a bare floor. The particular treads on the soles of shoes make them easy to trace, and the bottoms of most shoes have nicks or scratches that make them easy to identify.

10. **Hair:** Humans shed a lot of hair from all parts of their bodies, so bald bandits have no advantage. Hairs as tiny as eyelashes and eyebrows have unique characteristics that reveal a lot about a person, including race, dietary habits, and overall health. And don't forget: While your hair is dropping all over the crime scene, the victim's hair is clinging to your clothing.

The Thief of Police

Some say that the best way to catch a criminal is to think like a criminal. Eugene Francois Vidocq took that idea to heart.

✳   ✳   ✳   ✳

From the Circus to the Army

BORN ON JULY 24, 1775, in Arras, France, Eugene Francois Vidocq wasted no time in embracing a life of petty crime. His father owned a bakery and a general store, where he dealt in corn and turned a decent profit, making his family reasonably wealthy and privileged. But that didn't stop a young, teenaged Vidocq from getting into fights and stealing money from his own family's bakery. After several such incidents, his father had him thrown in prison for two weeks, hoping the experience would discourage Vidocq from engaging in crime; unfortunately, the plan didn't work.

Vidocq decided to board a ship to America, stealing a large amount of money to help him get started in his new life. But before he could set off for the new continent, he himself was the victim of a theft, waking up one morning to find his (stolen) money had been, ironically, stolen. Now penniless, Vidocq was forced to join a circus to make ends meet, although he was not a gifted performer. And when he was caught kissing the wife of a puppeteer, his circus career was over.

In 1791 Vidocq joined the army, which turned out to be a much better fit for his talents. Already well-versed in the art of fighting, the teenager gained a reputation for challenging other soldiers to duels, earning the nickname "Reckless." But when he challenged a superior officer to a duel, Vidocq was arrested for insubordination. This didn't sit well with him: he deserted and enlisted in a different army under a false identity.

Master of Escape

In 1793 Vidocq left the army and returned to his hometown of Arras. The next few years were restless and troubled for the young adult. He began to wander around France and Belgium, committing frauds and thefts to support himself. In Lille, France, he fell in love with a woman named Francine Longuet, but she left him for another man. Vidocq attacked and beat him, for which Vidocq was sent to prison.

This began a pattern of arrests, prison, and prison breaks for Vidocq. He became quite adept at slipping away from the authorities who were supposed to be keeping him under lock and key. One time he escaped dressed as a sailor; another time he escaped wearing a nun's habit. He even jumped out a window into a river during one prison break. He spent years on the run, at one point being sentenced to death due to his constant crime sprees.

A U-Turn

By July 1809, Vidocq realized he was up against the proverbial wall. He needed a way out of the crime-filled hole he had dug for himself. So instead of continuing to run from the police, he offered them his services as an informant. The police agreed, and Vidocq began providing information about the many criminals he had worked with over the years. His spying resulted in so many arrests and convictions that in 1811 he officially became a member of the police force. He developed and founded a plainclothes unit of officers called the Brigade de la Sûreté, or the Security Brigade, and in 1813, Napoleon Bonaparte declared it a state security force with authority over all of France.

Vidocq resigned from the police force in 1832 and pioneered another idea: He began the first private police agency. Although authorities eventually suppressed the organization, Vidocq's *Bureau des Renseignements* (Office of Information), was the precursor to the modern detective agency.

Vidocq became well-known all over France, where he befriended authors like Victor Hugo, Honore de Balzac, and Alexandre Dumas. His exploits were believed to have inspired some of their stories, including the characters of both the escaped convict Valjean and the policeman Javert in Hugo's *Les Miserables*. Vidocq died on May 11, 1857, at the age of 81, leaving behind a legacy that is a curious mix of criminality and law enforcement.

No Two Fingerprint Readers Are Alike

Even if you're innocent, you may get fingered falsely by a fingerprint. They're not as reliable as people think.

✳ ✳ ✳ ✳

✳ Until DNA testing came along, fingerprint identification was considered the gold standard of evidence. But it turns out that fingerprint identification is far from foolproof.

* A *Chicago Tribune* investigative study on forensics found that fingerprint analysis is subjective and that even the most experienced examiners make egregious mistakes. *Tribune* reporters reviewed 200 cases of DNA and death row exonerations nationwide over a 20-year period and found that more than 25 percent had been based on flawed forensic testing or testimony.

* Another *Tribune* study examined the "science" of fingerprinting. When researchers sifted through the findings culled by an independent proficiency tester, they learned that crime lab examiners often got things wrong. In fact, nearly a quarter of the U.S. labs cited in the study returned false positives.

* Fingerprint identification is far from an exact "science." Analysts look for points of similarity, but there are no universal standards, and no research dictates the number of points that establish a match with certainty. A complete fingerprint is rarely lifted from a crime scene, and yet no research determines how much of a latent (partial) fingerprint is sufficient to create a match.

* A study published in the *Journal of Forensic Sciences* found error rates at or above 2 percent, while another study found the rate could be as low as 0.8 percent or as high as 4 percent. Obviously, there's more than perception and numbers at stake. A false positive at the 2 percent rate would mean that there are approximately 4,800 false convictions or guilty pleas every year.

Leave No Trace?

Movie bad guys are always trying to sand or burn off their fingerprints, but can it really be done?

* * * *

An Ancient Art

THE USE OF fingerprints as identifiers or signatures dates back thousands of years, when different ancient civilizations used fingerprints on official documents. By the 1300s, someone had already noted, in surviving documents, that all the fingerprints he had seen in his life were unique. Scientists now know that fingerprints emerge during the first trimester of human embryo development and last in the same form for the entire human lifetime. Older people can naturally have very shallow fingerprints that are hard to read, but the shapes of these fingerprints are still the same.

People who work in certain fields are more likely to sand their fingerprints off during their regular daily routines. Construction workers who build with brick, stone, concrete, and other abrasive materials can end up losing their fingerprints. So can people who handle a lot of paper or cardboard. These changes are temporary: since only the topmost layer of skin is abraded, it will come back with the same pattern.

A Modern Problem

In the 21st century, people noticed a new form of fingerprint annihilation. A small number of cancer patients being treated with a chemotherapy drug called capecitabine found that they no longer had fingerprints. In the past, people easily went entire lifetimes without ever noticing their fingerprints, but modern banking and security often require them, and fingerprint technology is now showing up in the protection of personal devices like smartphones and laptops. Patients have been questioned in banks, locked out of their own computers, and stopped in security lines—as if being treated for cancer wasn't hard enough.

Researchers aren't sure whether or not these cancer patients' damaged or obliterated fingerprints will eventually grow back. But how could it be ambiguous like this? The answer is in the makeup of our fingerprints, which grow up into the topmost layer of skin *from* the layer beneath. If you trimmed down your rose bushes for the winter, would you expect tulips the next spring? Without doing major damage to your fingertips, you simply can't get rid of your fingerprints.

The Imperfect Solution

Villains of the past have tried a lot of superficial ways to scrub off their identities. The first known and famous case was a gangster in the 1930s named Handsome Jack, who made cuts to disrupt his fingerprints. His case made a splash in the press, but his mutilated prints were even easier to spot than they had been. Most documented attempts to change fingerprints fall into this category, where the actions taken to obscure the fingerprints create a new, more identifiable, scarred fingerprint.

To truly distort and alter your fingerprints, you would need to disrupt the connection between the two layers of skin where fingerprints root and grow. As of yet, there's no reasonable way to do this. Criminals and other wannabe disappearers may have more luck in the future.

Exposed to Poison

Long a favorite of mystery-novel writers and opportunistic bad guys, poison has an ancient and infamous relationship with people. Some poisons occur naturally and others are manufactured, but all of them spell bad news if you're the unlucky recipient of a dose.

✳ ✳ ✳ ✳

Poison Plants

Deadly Nightshade, aka belladonna: Every part of this perennial herb is poisonous, but the berries are especially dangerous.

The poison attacks the nervous system instantly, causing a rapid pulse, hallucinations, convulsions, ataxia, and coma.

Wolfsbane: This deadly plant was used as an arrow poison by the ancient Chinese, and its name comes from the Greek word meaning "dart." Wolfsbane takes a while to work, but when it does, it causes extreme anxiety, chest pain, and death from respiratory arrest.

Meadow Saffron: This tough little plant can be boiled and dried, and it still retains all of its poisonous power. As little as seven milligrams of this stuff could cause colic, paralysis, and heart failure.

Hemlock: This plant is probably the best known of the herbaceous poisons: It was used to knock off the Greek philosopher Socrates. Hemlock is poisonous down to the last leaf and will often send you into a coma before it finishes you for good.

Plans of Attack

There are five ways a person can be exposed to poison: ingestion (through the mouth), inhalation (breathed in through the nose or mouth), ocular (in the eyes), dermal (on the skin), and parenteral (from bites or stings).

Helpful Poison Stats

More than half of poison exposures occur in children under the age of six, and most poisonings involve medications and vitamins, household and chemical personal-care products, and plants. Eighty-nine percent of all poisonings occur at home. If you or someone in your house ingests something poisonous, stay calm and call 911 (if the person has collapsed or is not breathing) or your local poison control center (three-quarters of exposures can be treated over the phone with guidance from an expert).

Good Old Arsenic

Mystery novels are filled with stories of characters choosing to off their enemies with arsenic. Colorless and odorless, this close relative of phosphorous exists in a variety of compounds, not all of which are poisonous. Women in Victorian times used to rub a diluted arsenic compound into their skin to improve their complexions, and some modern medications used to treat cancer actually contain arsenic. When certain arsenic compounds are concentrated, however, they're deadly; arsenic has been blamed for widespread death through groundwater contamination.

The Dubiously Poisoned

Napoleon Bonaparte: Many historians believe that Napoleon died of arsenic poisoning while imprisoned, because significant traces of arsenic were found in his body by forensics experts 200 years after his death. It has been argued, however, that at that time in history, wallpaper and paint often contained arsenic-laced pigments, and that Napoleon was simply exposed to the poison in his everyday surroundings.

Vincent Van Gogh: Emerald green, a color of paint used by Impressionist painters, contained an arsenic-based pigment. Some historians suggest that Van Gogh's neurological problems had a great deal to do with his use of large quantities of emerald green paint.

Food Poisoning

Unfortunately, this is a form of poisoning most of us know something about. When food is spoiled or contaminated, bacteria such as salmonella breed quickly. Because we can't see or taste these bacteria, we chomp happily away and don't realize we're about to become really sick. The Centers for Disease Control and Prevention estimates that in the United States alone, food poisoning causes about 76 million illnesses, 325,000 hospitalizations, and up to 5,000 deaths each year.

Blood Poisoning

This form of poisoning occurs when an infectious agent or its toxin spreads through the bloodstream. People actually have a low level of bacteria in their blood most of the time, but if nasty bacteria are introduced, they can cause sepsis, a life-threatening condition. The bacteria can enter the bloodstream through open wounds or from the bite of a parasite.

Snakebites

Because snakes' venom is injected, snakes themselves are considered "venomous" rather than "poisonous." Still, an estimated 8,000 snakebites occur in the United States every year. Poisonous snakes found in North America include rattlesnakes, copperheads, cottonmouths, and coral snakes. While most of these reptiles won't bite unless provoked, if you are bitten you have to take the antivenin fast. Arthur Conan Doyle's Sherlock Holmes story, "The Adventure of the Speckled Band," famously involves the use of a live snake as a murder weapon.

Skull and Crossbones

When pirates sailed the high seas, they flew a flag emblazoned with a skull-and-crossbones symbol. When seafarers saw this Jolly Roger flag, they knew trouble was on its way. Bottles that contain poisons or other toxic substances often bear this symbol to warn anyone against drinking or even touching the contents with bare hands. Murder mysteries have revolved around a character removing a warning label or switching it to confuse something benign wtih something poisonous.

Allan Pinkerton—Spying for the Union Cause

The exploits of Allan Pinkerton during the Civil War helped pave the way for the modern Secret Service.

✳ ✳ ✳ ✳

IN A LETTER to President Lincoln dated April 21, 1861, detective Allan Pinkerton offered his services and commented on one of the traits that would make him an icon of law enforcement for generations. "Secrecy is the great lever I propose to operate with," he wrote.

Establishing the Eye

Born in Scotland in 1819, Pinkerton came to the United States in 1842. He originally was a barrel builder by trade, but his skills at observation and deduction led him to a career fighting crime. By age 30, he'd joined the sheriff's office of Cook County, Illinois, and been appointed Chicago's first detective. He later joined attorney Edward Rucker to form the North-Western Police Agency, forerunner of the Pinkerton Agency. As his corporate logo, Pinkerton chose an open eye, perhaps to demonstrate that his agents never slept. Clients began calling him "The Eye." Pinkerton and his operatives were hired to solve the growing number of train robberies, which became more and more of a problem as railroads expanded across the nation. George B. McClellan, president of the Ohio and Mississippi Railroad, took particular notice.

Wartime Duties

In 1861, Pinkerton's agency was hired to protect the Philadelphia, Wilmington, and Baltimore Railroad. In the course of their duties, Pinkerton and his agents learned of a preinaugural plot to kill President-elect Lincoln. The detectives secretly took Lincoln into Washington before he was scheduled to arrive, thwarting the conspirators. Lincoln was inaugurated without incident.

When the war began, Pinkerton was given the duty of protecting the president as a forerunner of today's Secret Service. He was also put in charge of gathering intelligence for the army, now run by his old railroad boss, McClellan. The detective and his operatives infiltrated enemy lines. Using surveillance and undercover work, both new concepts at the

time, agents gathered vital information. Pinkerton tried to get details any way he could. His people interviewed escaped slaves and tried to convince literate former slaves to return to the South to spy. He used female spies, and he even infiltrated the Confederacy himself several times using the alias Major E. J. Allen.

Uncertain Information

While much of this was invaluable, his work was tarnished by a seeming inability to identify enemy troop strengths. His reports of enemy troops were detailed, including notes on morale, supplies, movements, and even descriptions of the buttons on uniforms. Yet the numbers of troops he provided were highly suspect.

In October 1861, as McClellan was preparing to fight, Pinkerton reported that Confederate General Joseph Johnston's troops in Virginia were "not less than 150,000 strong." In reality, there were fewer than 50,000. The next year he reported the strength of Confederate General John Magruder at Yorktown, putting troop numbers at about 120,000 when the true number was closer to 17,000.

After the true strength of these forces was discovered, Pinkerton was ridiculed. Some historians believe that Pinkerton was unaware of the faulty information, but others insist he intentionally provided inflated figures to support McClellan's conservative battle plans. The truth will likely never be known, as all of Pinkerton's records of the war were lost in the Great Chicago Fire of 1871.

Return to Civilian Life

After McClellan, one of Pinkerton's staunchest supporters, was relieved of his command by Lincoln, Pinkerton limited his spying activities and shifted his work back toward criminal cases, which included the pursuit of war profiteers. He ultimately returned to Chicago and his agency, working until his death in 1884.

Life on the Body Farm

When Mary Scarborough wrote the lyrics to "Old MacDonald Had a Farm," she probably didn't have a research facility in mind. In fact, one won't find cows, chickens, or pigs that go "oink" at the Body Farm—just scores of rotting human bodies.

✳ ✳ ✳ ✳

E-I-E-I-Oh, Gross

THE BODY FARM (officially known as the University of Tennessee Forensic Anthropology Facility) was the brainchild of Dr. William Bass, a forensic anthropologist from Kansas. Its purpose, however nauseating, is to help law enforcement agencies learn to estimate how long a person has been dead. After all, determining the time of death is crucial in confirming alibis and establishing timelines for violent crimes.

After 11 years of watching and learning about human decomposition, Bass realized how little was actually known about what happens to the human body after death. With this in mind, he approached the University of Tennessee Medical Center and asked for a small plot of land where he could control what happens to a post-mortem body and study the results. The facility was established in the 1980s.

A Creepy Joint

Just outside of Knoxville, the eerie three-acre wooded plot that Bass claimed for his scientific studies—which is surrounded by a razor wire fence (lest the dead bodies try to escape?)—is where an unspecified number of cadavers in various states of decomposition are kept.

While some hang out completely in the open, others spend their time in shallow graves or entombed in vaults. Others dip their toes and other body parts in ponds. And a few spend eternity inside sealed car trunks.

Body Snatchers

If you're going to start a body farm, it doesn't take a forensic anthropologist to realize that there might be a problem
in obtaining bodies. One way is to use bodies that have been
donated for medical studies. Another focuses on cadavers that
rot away each year at medical examiners offices, with nary a
soul to claim them. Enter Bass and his associates. Like "pods"
from *Invasion of the Body Snatchers*, these scientists grab every
body they can lay their hands on. (Legally, of course. For a story
of illegal body acquisition, see page 85 of chapter 4.)

Reading the Body

According to Bass, two things occur when a person dies. At
the time of death, digestive enzymes begin to feed on the body,
"liquefying" the tissues. If flies have access to it, they lay eggs in
the body. Eventually, the eggs hatch into larvae that feast on the
remaining tissues. By monitoring and noting how much time
it takes for maggots to consume the tissues, authorities can
estimate how long a person has been dead. Scientists can also
compare the types of flies that are indigenous to the area with
the types that have invaded the body to determine whether
the body has been moved. "People will have alibis for certain
periods," says Bass. "If you can determine that the death happened at another time or location, it makes a big difference in
the outcome of the court case."

But the farm isn't all tissue decomposition—scientists also
learn about the normal wear-and-tear that a human body goes
through. For instance, anthropologists look at the teeth of the
victim to try to determine their age at the time of death. The
skull and pelvic girdles are helpful in determining a person's
sex, and scientists can also estimate how tall the person was
by measuring the long bones of the legs or even a single finger.
Other researchers watch what happens to the five types of fatty
acids leaking from the body into the ground. By analyzing the
profiles of the acids, scientists can determine the time of death
and how long it has been at its current location.

Simulations and Defenses

The prestigious FBI uses the Body Farm as a real-world simulator to help train its agents. Every February, representatives visit the site to dig for bodies that farm hands have prepared as simulated crime scenes. "We have five of them down there for them," explains Bass. "They excavate the burials and look for evidence that we put there."

Stranger Than Fiction

Bass's Body Farm drew the attention of readers when popular crime novelist Patricia Cornwell featured it in her 1994 book, *The Body Farm*. In it, Cornwell describes a research facility that stages human corpses in various states of decay and in a variety of locations—wooded areas, the trunk of a car, underwater, or beneath a pile of leaves—all to determine how bodies decay under different circumstances.

Unfortunately, the real perps are catching on. Some criminals try to confuse investigators by tampering with the bodies and burial sites, spraying the victim with insecticides that prevent insects (such as maggots) from doing their job.

Further Afield

At another facility at the University of New Mexico, scientists have collected over 500 human skeletons and store them as "skeletal archives" to create biological profiles based on what happens to bones over time. And in Germany, the Max Planck Institute for Computer Science has been working on a 3-D graphics program based on forensic data to produce more accurate likenesses of the victims. Although many other proposed farms never got off the ground due to community protest, since the inception of Bass's original Body Farm, another farm has been established at Western Carolina University. Ideally, Bass would like to see body farms all over the nation. Since decaying bodies react differently depending on their climate and surroundings, says Bass, "It's important to gather information from other research facilities across the United States."

The Clairvoyant Crime-Buster

Before there were TV shows like Ghost Whisperer *and* Medium, *which make the idea of solving crimes through ESP seem almost commonplace, there was psychic detective Arthur Price Roberts. And his work was accomplished in the early 1900s, when high-tech aids like electronic surveillance and DNA identification were still only far-fetched dreams. Police in those times often used purported psychics to help solve many cases.*

✳ ✳ ✳ ✳

"I See Dead People"

A MODEST MAN BORN in Wales in 1866, Roberts deliberately avoided a formal education because he believed too much learning could stifle his unusual abilities. He moved to Milwaukee, Wisconsin, as a young man where, ironically, the man who never learned to read was nicknamed "Doc."

One of his earliest well-known cases involved a baffling missing person incident in Peshtigo, a small town about 160 miles north of Milwaukee. A man named Duncan McGregor had gone missing in July 1905, leaving no clue as to his whereabouts. The police searched for him for months, and finally his desperate wife decided to go to the psychic detective who had already made a name for himself in Milwaukee. She didn't even have to explain the situation to Roberts; he knew immediately upon meeting her who she was.

Roberts meditated on the vanished husband, then sadly had to tell Mrs. McGregor that he'd been murdered and that his body was in the Peshtigo River, caught near the bottom in a pile of timber. Roberts proved correct in every detail.

Mystery of the Mad Bombers

Roberts solved numerous documented cases. He helped a Chicago man find his brother who had traveled to Albuquerque and had not been heard from for months;

Roberts predicted that the brother's body would be found in a certain spot in Devil's Canyon, and it was.

After coming up with new evidence for an 11th hour pardon, Roberts saved a Chicago man named Ignatz Potz, who had been condemned to die for a murder he didn't commit. But his most famous coup came in 1935 when he correctly predicted that the city of Milwaukee would be hit by six large dynamite explosions, losing a town hall, banks, and police stations. People snickered; such mayhem was unheard of in Milwaukee. Roberts made his prediction on October 18 of that year. In little more than a week, the Milwaukee area entered a time of terror.

First, a town hall in the outlying community of Shorewood was blasted, killing two children and wounding many other people. A few weeks later, the mad bombers hit two banks and two police stations. Federal agents descended upon the city, and several local officers were assigned to work solely on solving the bombings. Finally, the police went to Roberts to learn what was coming next. Roberts told them one more blast was in the works, that it would be south of the Menomonee River, and that it would be the final bomb. Police took him at his word and blanketed the area with officers and sharpshooters.

And sure enough, on November 4, a garage in the predicted area blew to smithereens in an explosion that could be heard as far as eight miles away. The two terrorists, young men 18 and 21 years old, had been hard at work in the shed assembling 50 pounds of dynamite when their plan literally backfired. Few people argued with Roberts's abilities after that.

His Final Fortune

Roberts's eeriest prediction, however, may have been that of his own death. In November 1939, he told a group of assembled friends that he would be leaving this world on January 2, 1940. And he did, passing quietly in his own home on that exact date. Many of his most amazing accomplishments will probably never be known because a lot of his work was done secretly for various law enforcement agencies. But "Doc" Roberts had an undeniable gift, and he died secure in the knowledge that he had used it to help others as best he could.

Psychic Detectives

"Doc" Roberts wasn't the only person with a reputation for unusual abilities. When the corpse just can't be found, the murderer remains unknown, and the weapon has been stashed in some secret corner, law enforcement agencies may tap their secret weapons.

✳ ✳ ✳ ✳

"Reading" the Ripper: Robert James Lees

WHEN THE PSYCHOTIC murderer known as Jack the Ripper terrorized London in the 1880s, the detectives of Scotland Yard consulted a psychic named Robert James Lees who said he had glimpsed the killer's face in several visions. Lees also claimed he had correctly forecasted at least three of the well-publicized murders of women. The Ripper wrote a sarcastic note to detectives stating that they would still never catch him. Indeed, the killer proved right in this prediction.

Feeling Their Vibes: Florence Sternfels

As a psychometrist—a psychic who gathers impressions by handling material objects—Florence Sternfels was successful enough to charge a dollar for readings in Edgewater, New Jersey, in the early 20th century. Born in 1891, Sternfels believed that her gift was a natural ability rather than a supernatural one, so she never billed police for her help in solving crimes. Some of her best "hits" included preventing a man from blowing up an army base with dynamite, finding two missing boys alive in Philadelphia, and leading police to the body of a murdered young woman. She worked with police as far away as Europe to solve tough cases but lived quietly in New Jersey until her death in 1965.

The Dutch Grocer's Gift: Gerard Croiset

Born in the Netherlands in 1909, Gerard Croiset nurtured a growing psychic ability from age six. In 1935, he joined a Spiritualist group, began to hone his talents, and within two years had set up shop as a psychic and healer. After a touring lecturer discovered his abilities in 1945, Croiset began assisting law enforcement agencies around the world, traveling as far as Japan and Australia. He specialized in finding missing children but also helped authorities locate lost papers and artifacts. At the same time, Croiset ran a popular clinic for psychic healing that treated both humans and animals. His son, Gerard Croiset, Jr., was also a professional psychic and parapsychologist.

Accidental Psychic: Peter Hurkos

As one of the most famous psychic detectives of the 20th century, Peter Hurkos did his best work by picking up vibes from victims' clothing. Born in the Netherlands in 1911, Hurkos lived an ordinary life as a house painter until a fall required him to undergo brain surgery at age 30. The operation seemed to trigger his latent psychic powers, and he was almost immediately able to mentally retrieve information about people and "read" the history of objects by handling them.

Hurkos assisted in the Boston Strangler investigation in the early 1960s, and in 1969, he was brought in to help solve the grisly murders executed by Charles Manson. He gave police many accurate details including the name Charlie, a description of Manson, and that the murders were ritual slayings.

The TV Screen Mind of Dorothy Allison

New Jersey housewife Dorothy Allison broke into the world of clairvoyant crime solving when she dreamed about a missing local boy as if seeing it on television. In her dream, the five-year-old boy was stuck in some kind of pipe. When she called police, she also described the child's clothing, including the odd fact that he was wearing his shoes on the opposite feet.

When Allison underwent hypnosis to learn more details, she added that the boy's surroundings involved a fenced school and a factory. She was proven correct on all accounts when the boy's body was found about two months after he went missing, floating close to a pipe in a pond near a school and a factory with his little shoes still tied onto the wrong feet. Allison, who began having psychic experiences as a child, considered her gift a blessing and never asked for pay. One of her more famous cases was that of missing heiress Patty Hearst in 1974. Although Allison was unable to find her, every prediction she made about the young woman came true, including the fact that she had dyed her hair red.

Like a Bolt Out of the Blue: John Catchings

While at a Texas barbeque on an overcast July 4, 1969, 22-year-old John Catchings was hit by a bolt of lightning. He survived but said the electric blast opened him to his life's calling as a psychic. He then followed in the footsteps of his mother, Bertie, who earned her living giving "readings."

Catchings often helped police solve puzzling cases but he became famous after helping police find a missing, 32-year-old Houston nurse named Gail Lorke. She vanished in late October 1982, after her husband, Steven, claimed she had stayed home from work because she was sick. Because Catchings worked by holding objects that belonged to victims, Lorke's sister, who was suspicious of Steven, went to Catchings with a photo of Gail and her belt. Allegedly, Catchings saw that Lorke had indeed been murdered by her husband and left under a heap of refuse that included parts of an old, wooden fence. He also gave police several other key details. Detectives were able to use the information to get Steven Lorke to confess his crime. Among many other successes, Catchings also helped police find the body of Mike Dickens in 1980 after telling them the young man would be found buried in a creek bed near a shoe and other rubbish, including old tires and boards. Police discovered the body there just as Catchings had described it.

Lock-Picking Know-How

Regardless of what is portrayed in cops-and-robbers flicks, you need at least two tools to pick a lock.

✳ ✳ ✳ ✳

WHETHER YOU'RE A wannabe ruffian or a forgetful home-owner, you should know that it is nearly impossible to pick a lock with only one paper clip, one bobby pin, or one of anything else. Although you can certainly accomplish the task with simple tools, you will need two of them—one to act as a pick and a second one to serve as a tension wrench.

The simple pin-and-tumbler locks on most doors contain a cylinder and several small pins attached to springs. When the door is locked, the cylinder is kept in place by the pins, which protrude into the cylinder. When a matching key is inserted into the lock, the pins are pushed back and the cylinder turns. The key to lock-picking, then, is to push the pins back while simultaneously turning the cylinder. This is why two items are required—a pick to push the pins and a tension wrench to turn the cylinder. Professional locksmiths often use simple lock-picking techniques to avoid damaging the offending lock.

Common household items that can serve as tension wrenches include small screwdrivers and bent paper clips. Items you can use as picks include safety pins, hair fasteners, and paper clips. The determined apprentice may be happy to learn that there is a situation in which one paper clip may suffice in picking a lock: Small, inexpensive padlocks sometimes succumb to large paper clips that are bent in such a way that one end is the pick and the other end is the tension wrench. Even so, the process involves more than just jamming something into the lock and turning the doorknob. Seasoned lock-pickers rely on their senses of hearing and touch to finish the job success-fully. They're anticipating a vibration accompanied by a distinct "click" that means each pin is in alignment.

One List You Don't Want to Be On

With the Most Wanted List, the FBI came to rely on the vigilance of good citizens for its most dangerous work.

✳ ✳ ✳ ✳

DURING THE MIDDLE part of the 20th century, nothing was cooler than a G-man. Tough, dogged, honest, and dedicated to rounding up America's most dastardly criminals, agents of the FBI enjoyed wide and largely unwavering public support. This approval stemmed as much from the agents' heroic efforts as from the notorious reputations of the outlaws they hunted: criminals such as Pretty Boy Floyd, John Dillinger, and Bonnie and Clyde.

In 1949, a reporter for the International News Service capitalized on the public's interest in the agency's work by writing a wire story on the "toughest guys" the FBI was pursuing at the time. The article became wildly popular, and Bureau Director J. Edgar Hoover, a master of public relations, created the Ten Most Wanted Fugitives List in response.

When the list first appeared in 1950, it included bank robbers and car thieves, but over time, the nature of the criminals who made the list changed. The 1970s saw a focus on organized crime figures; more recently, emphasis has shifted to terrorists and drug dealers.

Criminals must meet two criteria in order to become candidates for the world's most famous rogues gallery. First, they must have an extensive record of serious criminal activity or a recent criminal history that poses a particular threat to public safety. Second, there must be a reasonable likelihood that publicity from their presence on the list will aid in their capture. Criminals are only removed from the list for three reasons: They are captured, the charges against them are dropped, or they no longer fit the criteria for the list.

Over the years, the program has proved remarkably effective. Nearly 500 criminals have appeared on the list, and more than 90 percent of them have been captured. About a third of these former fugitives were caught as a direct result of public tips.

Long-Standing Fugitives of the Ten-Most Wanted List

Here are the criminals who have spent the most time on the list.

✳ ✳ ✳ ✳

1.   Donna Jean Willmott spent close to eight years on the Top Ten list before surrendering on December 6, 1994.
In 1985, Willmott purchased 36 pounds of explosives from an undercover FBI agent. She planned to use the material to free the leader of a Puerto Rican leftist terrorist group from prison.

2.   Claude Daniel Marks appeared on the list the same number of years as Willmott, down to the day.
The two were partners in the prison-escape plan, purchasing the explosives and eventually surrendering together.

3.   Benjamin Hoskins Paddock spent eight years on the list.
A bank robber who escaped from a Texas prison, Paddock is one of only a few fugitives to be removed from the list without being captured, found dead, or surrendering. The FBI removes fugitives from the list under three conditions: They are captured, the federal process against them is dismissed, or they no longer fit the Top Ten criteria. Paddock made the list on June 10, 1969, and was removed for no longer fitting the criteria in May 1977.

4.   Glen Stewart Godwin was on the Top Ten list since December 7, 1996, for crimes and prison escapes.
In 1987, he escaped from Folsom State Prison in California, where he was serving time for murder. He was arrested later

that year for drug trafficking in Mexico. He was convicted and sent to prison in Guadalajara, where he allegedly murdered a fellow inmate and escaped five months later. He remains at large, though he was removed from the list in 2016 in the belief that the publicity was not helping with his capture.

5. Arthur Lee Washington spent 11 years on the Top Ten list before being removed on December 27, 2000.

He officially remains at large, wanted for the attempted murder of a New Jersey state trooper during a traffic stop. He may, however, be deceased.

6. Leo Joseph Koury spent 12 years on the list before being found dead on June 16, 1991.

Koury, who was placed on the list on April 20, 1979, was wanted for murder, extortion, mail fraud, and attempted kidnapping.

7. Katherine Anne Power was on the list for close to 14 years before being removed on June 15, 1984.

As a student at Brandeis University in 1970, Power was part of a group that fire-bombed and stole arms from a national Guard armory before robbing a bank. A police officer was shot during the bank robbery, prompting Power to go into hiding for 23 years. In 1993, she turned herself in, pled guilty to manslaughter, and was sentenced to 8 to 12 years in prison.

8. Charles Lee Herron racked up 18 years 4 months, and 9 days of Top Ten status.

He stood accused of the 1968 murder of two Tennessee police officers when he was placed on the list on February 9, 1968. He was captured on June 18, 1986, at home in Jacksonville, Florida.

9. Victor Manuel Gerena was on the list for 32 years, wanted in connection with the 1983 armed bank robbery.

He has been linked to Los Macheteros, a Puerto Rican terrorist group that advocates for independence from the United States. After making off with $7 million, Gerena disappeared and is thought to be living in Cuba. His 32 years on the list gives him the current record.

10.   Donald Eugene Webb was on the list for 25 years.
In 1980, Webb was being sought as a suspect in a burglary when he was pulled over for running a stop sign in Saxonburg, Pennsylvania. A fight ensued, and Webb allegedly shot and killed the police officer. Webb was also shot during the incident, leading the FBI to believe that he may have died from his injuries. He was removed from the list in 2007.

Miranda Warning

The violation of one man's rights becomes a warning to us all.

✳   ✳   ✳   ✳

MOST OF US have never heard of Ernesto Miranda. Yet in 1963, this faceless man would prompt the passage of a law that has become an integral part of all arrests. Here's how it came to pass.

You Have the Right to Remain Silent

In 1963, following his arrest for the kidnapping and rape of an 18-year-old woman, Ernesto Miranda was placed in a Phoenix, Arizona, police lineup. When he stepped down from the gallery of suspects, Miranda asked the officers about the charges against him. His police captors implied that he had been positively identified as the kidnapper and rapist of a young woman. After two hours of interrogation, Miranda confessed.

Miranda signed a confession that included a typed paragraph indicating that his statement had been voluntary and that he had been fully aware of his legal rights.

But there was one problem: At no time during his interrogation had Miranda actually been advised of his rights. The wheels of justice had been set in motion on a highly unbalanced axle.

Anything You Say Can and Will Be Used Against You in a Court of Law

When appealing Miranda's conviction, his attorney attempted to have the confession thrown out on the grounds that his client hadn't been advised of his rights. The motion was over-ruled. Eventually, Miranda would be convicted on both rape and kidnapping charges and sentenced to 20 to 30 years in prison. It seemed like the end of the road for Miranda—but it was just the beginning.

You Have the Right to an Attorney

Miranda requested that his case be heard by the U.S. Supreme Court. His attorney, John J. Flynn, submitted a 2,000-word petition for a writ of *certiorari* (judicial review), arguing that Miranda's Fifth Amendment rights had been violated. In November 1965, the Supreme Court agreed to hear Miranda's case. The tide was about to turn.

A Law Is Born

After much debate among Miranda's attorneys and the state, a decision in Miranda's favor was rendered. Chief Justice Earl Warren wrote in his *Miranda v. Arizona* opinion, "The person in custody must, prior to interrogation, be clearly informed that he has the right to remain silent, and that anything he says will be used against him in court; he must be clearly informed that he has the right to consult with a lawyer and to have the law-yer with him during interrogation, and that, if he is indigent, a lawyer will be appointed to represent him."

Aftermath

In the wake of the U.S. Supreme Court's ruling, police depart-ments across the nation began to issue the "Miranda warn-ing." As for Miranda himself, his freedom was short-lived. He would be sentenced to 11 years in prison at a second trial that did not include his prior confession as evidence. Miranda was released in 1972, and he bounced in and out of jail for various offenses over the next few years. On January 31, 1976, Miranda was stabbed to death during a Phoenix bar fight. The suspect received his Miranda warning from the arresting police officers and opted to remain silent. Due to insufficient evidence, he would not be prosecuted for Ernesto Miranda's murder.

What It's Like: Crime Scene Decontamination Crew

The next time the big television executives sit around the conference table to decide which new shows will air in the fall, chances are one that will never make the lineup is CSD: Miami *(Crime Scene Decontamination). Call us cynical, but it's unlikely that viewers would want to rush home to watch cleanup crews swab up buckets of blood while they eat their dinner. This is a job that's not for the weak of stomach.*

✻ ✻ ✻ ✻

The Worst of the Worst

DEATH ISN'T THE most pleasant thing to think about, but cleaning up after someone dies is no picnic, either. This is particularly true if that person died in a violent way, say, a murder or suicide. Blood has pooled through the mattress and soaked into the floor below, bits of bone and brain matter are everywhere—that mess doesn't go away by itself. That's when Crime Scene Decontamination units (also called CTS— Crime/Trauma Scene–Decon crews) are called in.

CTS decon crews handle the worst of the worst. Hours or even days after a violent crime has occurred or a methamphet-amine lab has been busted, CTS decon crews are contracted to come in and clean up. Sorry crime-show fans: You won't find a slightly-grizzled-but-still-handsome detective tiptoeing through this scene in an Armani suit—this is dirty work that would make most people sick to their stomachs.

The Task at Hand

By the time the decontamination crew is called to the trauma scene, the police, fire department, and crime scene investigators have all done their jobs and left (*these* are the people you see on TV). A decontamination lead will be appraised of the situation and alerted to the risks involved. Some are worse than others, such as decomposing bodies. Bodies that are discovered hours, days, or even months after death are considered to be in a state of decomposition or "decomp." During decomp, the body swells, the skin liquefies, and maggots move in to feed off the body. But this all pales in comparison to the smell as ammonia gas from the body fills the room. And if this doesn't make you contemplate a new line of work, consider that all of the creepy-crawlies that made the body their home must be rounded up and destroyed to eliminate any biohazard threat.

Dressing for Success

After putting on disposable head-to-toe biohazard suits, cleaners will don filtered respirators, rubber gloves, and booties before entering the crime scene. They'll also bring tools of their trade. There are no microscopes, centrifuges, or fingerprinting kits; instead, there are 55-gallon plastic containers, mops, sponges, enzyme solvents, putty knives, and shovels.

Once the contaminated material has been cleaned off of the room's surfaces and the site has been returned to normal, the cleaners must properly dispose of the hazardous waste material. Since federal regulations deem even the smallest drop of blood or bodily fluid to be biohazardous waste, the cleaners must transport all matter in specially designed containers to medical waste incinerators—all, of course, at an additional cost to the client.

The Big Business of Violence

To date, there are more than 300 companies that provide professional decontamination of crime scenes. Each one of these companies typically handles up to 400 cases a year and is on call around the clock. Decontamination companies are contracted through police departments, insurance companies, or by the deceased's relatives. And there's big money to be made: Companies charge between $1,000 and $6,000 to clean up a crime scene and return it to its original condition. In addition to cleaning houses, decon crews often clean car interiors and busted meth labs. In the case of the meth labs, virtually all of the carpeting, furniture, cabinets, and fixtures—basically, anything that can absorb dangerous chemicals such as methanol, ammonia, benzene, and hydrochloric acid—must be removed and destroyed.

The TV executives will probably never glamorize decontaminating crews. However, for those families in need of a CTS decon team, they provide a valuable service in helping them get their lives back to normal. It is important, sensitive work and in most cases, worth every penny the cleaners charge.

A Few Good Men (and Women)

A crime scene decontamination company is hardly going to have a booth at the local job fair. So, who on earth would get into this kind of work? Some decon workers find their way into the field from medical backgrounds (say, as an emergency room nurse) or the construction industry. The latter, in particular, proves helpful when dealing with jobs that require walls torn into or taken down. This is often the case in clean-ups that take place in meth labs.

And then there's the paycheck. Depending on the company and its location, decontamination cleaners can make as much as $35,000 to $60,000 a year and sometimes more. In metropolitan cities where caseloads are high, cleaners can earn as much as $100,000 a year—and that's without a college education. Of course, few actually see that much money; the average career of a decontamination cleaner is less than eight months.

One of the requirements for becoming a decontamination cleaner is a strong stomach and the ability for the cleaner to detach themselves from their environment but still have empathy for family members and friends of the deceased. If the thought of picking up dog poo grosses you out, this is not the job for you. It's also not for you if you are easily depressed or internalize human suffering. Decontamination cleaners must be able to handle the worst-case scenario as "just part of the job." Before crew members are sent on their first job, cleaners must go through training that includes performing heavy physical labor while wearing a biohazard suit, watching videos of prior crime scenes, or cleaning up a room strewn with animal remains—all without tossing their cookies.

On second thought, maybe it's time to check the online job listings again.

Primed to Be a Private Eye

Think being a PI is all high-speed chases and sultry suspects? Actually, for the most part, working as a private investigator can be a lot like any job—you stare blankly at a computer screen in a dimly lit cubicle for eight hours a day—only for less money than many other jobs. But the good news is that working in the private investigation field can be just about anything you make of it—just look at Thomas Magnum!

✳   ✳   ✳   ✳

Questionable Origins

THE FIRST PRIVATE eye on record was the French criminal and privateer named Eugene Francois Vidocq, whom we highlighted earlier in this chapter, who founded a private investigation firm in 1833. Most of his investigators were his friends who were ex-convicts and other citizens of questionable character. Vidocq was periodically arrested by the police on a series of trumped-up charges, but he was always released after they failed to produce enough evidence to support their claims. Despite his questionable background, Vidocq made a number of significant contributions to the field of investigation, including record keeping, ballistics, indelible ink, and unalterable bond paper.

The Modern PI

Fast forward to recent statistics from the U.S. Department of Labor, which state that in 2019, there were approximately 36,000 working gumshoes. While more than a third of working private investigators have college degrees, many have only high school diplomas or Associate degrees, and some have neither. Those with college degrees come from varied backgrounds, such as accounting, computer science, business administration, or the dozens of other majors whose curriculum lends itself to specific types of investigative work. Interestingly, most private investigators do not have a degree in criminal justice.

The Nature of the Work

Talk to anyone who's knowledgeable about the private investigation business and they'll tell you that the prerequisites for success are an unquenchable thirst for answers and the ability to root out details after everyone else has come up empty handed. Superior communication skills and a special area of expertise, say, in computers, also come in handy. The most successful private eyes are people who can think logically, apply their unique knowledge to a problem, and consistently come up with creative means to their ends.

A Day in the Life

Depending on their background, private investigators can end up working for a variety of employers: individuals, professional investigative firms, law firms, department stores, or bail bondsmen. Many set up their own private practice. One place they can count on *never* working is for the local police department or the FBI. Government agencies rarely interface with private investigation firms. Unfortunately, that nixes the dramatic movie image of a lone-wolf PI getting a call in the middle of the night because the police are stumped and desperately need help.

The type of work private investigators do is largely dependent on the type of company they work for, the types of cases they take, and what their clients ask of them. The majority of cases have to do with locating lost or stolen property, proving that a spouse has been unfaithful, finding missing friends or relatives, conducting background investigations, or proving that a business associate absconded with the company cash.

Much of the work that private investigators do involves long hours sitting behind the wheel of their car doing surveillance with binoculars and cameras with telephoto lenses. Only the highest-profile cases involving investigative firms with large operating budgets can afford sophisticated surveillance vans loaded with high-tech equipment. Other cases require collecting facts the old-fashioned way: by interviewing suspects, witnesses, and neighbors in person. Facts that can't be collected that way are often obtained by perusing public records by computer, or researching tax records, business licenses, DMV records, real estate transactions, court records, and voter registrations.

The PI Paycheck

But how much can a private eye expect to make? Fortunately (or unfortunately, whatever the case may be), the entertainment industry has painted a rather broad picture of the private investigation business. For every television show about a PI living on a Hawaiian estate, there's another show about a PI living in a dilapidated trailer house on the beach. The truth is, the median salary for private investigators in 2019 was $50,510 per year, or 24.28 an hour. The lowest 10 percent earned less than $30,390, while the highest 10 percent earned more than $89,760. Not too shabby, but probably not the lap of luxury, either.

Still Want to Be a Private Eye?

For those who remain undaunted by the proposition of drinking their dinner out of a thermos and spending ten hours a day in a car or cubicle, here's some insight on how to pursue a career in private investigation: Many private investigators have retired early from military, police, or fire department careers. Having pensions or retirement funds can help with "getting over the hump" until the earnings as a PI increase.

Some states require specific schooling while others require new investigators to spend time completing on-the-job training before applying for their license. Most states have licensing requirements for becoming a PI, so it's important to look into what's required and how long it takes before one can expect to begin to make a decent living. If the type of work requires that private investigators carry a firearm, a private eye will need to look into the local ordinances for carrying a concealed weapon.

If nothing else, private investigation can certainly be a fascinating and challenging career choice that promises a break from the ordinary job doldrums. So grab that Beretta, rev up that Ferrari, and get ready for your new life as a gumshoe!

A New Twist on Turning Yourself In

It's highly unlikely that a criminal could collect a reward on himself, but it's not entirely outside the realm of possibility.

✳   ✳   ✳   ✳

He Who Offers the Reward Doles It Out

ANYONE CAN OFFER a reward: the family of a crime victim, a concerned citizens' group, a corporation, and a nonprofit organization such as Crime Stoppers, which pays for anonymous tips. And some local government bodies even offer rewards in certain criminal investigations. But there are no uniform laws or regulations regarding how these rewards are disbursed.

In point of fact, whoever offers the reward gets to determine who can collect the money. Nonetheless, it's difficult to imagine a provision that would allow the perpetrator of the crime to pocket the dough.

The business of rewards can be tricky. A well-publicized, big-money offer sometimes works against an investigation by attracting greedy tipsters who provide useless leads to overworked detectives. Law enforcement agencies generally don't discourage reward offers, but they do try to use them strategically. Often, they won't publicize a reward until an investigation nears a dead end, the hope being that it'll renew interest in the crime and jog the memories of legitimate tipsters.

Money's Not Always the Issue

Many police officials concede that offers of rewards rarely lead to successful investigations. Most useful tips, they say, come from honest citizens with good intentions that go beyond monetary recompense.

And the existence of a reward doesn't necessarily mean the tipsters will know how to collect it. In July 2008, the FBI offered a $25,000 reward in its search for Nicholas Sheley, a suspect in a series of killings. Sheley, it seems, walked into a bar in Granite City, Illinois, to get a drink of water. The bar's patrons had seen his face on the TV news. One called the police; another ran outside and flagged down a squad car. Sheley was quickly taken into custody. Four months later, an FBI spokesman said that nobody had stepped forward to collect the 25 grand.

Never mind the bad guys. Sometimes even the good guys don't get the money.

Wanted Criminals Win Free Cases of Beer

A criminal might try to claim a reward and end up in the hands of the police. They might also try to claim free prizes...

✳   ✳   ✳   ✳

THE DERBYSHIRE POLICE Department of England had quite a few fugitives they couldn't get a grip on. The fugitives had evaded all of the law enforcement's previous tactics to bring them into custody, but there was one thing the fugitives couldn't resist: free beer.

Takin' Names

Although it seemed far-fetched, calling these wanted criminals and saying they won a case of free beer with a fake sweepstakes ploy was the detectives' only hope to bring these fugitives to justice. Undercover agents called the criminals with the faux news and arranged a time and a place in which they could come and pick up their free case of beer. Many were intrigued, but not all of them fell for the trap.

All in all, nineteen thirsty fugitives arrived and were then brought in to the station, realizing that the free beer they were promised would never come to materialize. One thing that did materialize in Derbyshire that day was the swift and cunning stratagems of law enforcement.

Role Playing: The Non-Suspects in Police Lineups

Appropriately enough, these "fillers" (also known as "distractors") are mostly criminals or suspected criminals. Who better to act as possible perps?

✳ ✳ ✳ ✳

IN THE TRADITIONAL "live" police lineup, in which a witness picks out the bad guy from behind a one-way mirror, the police typically present one actual suspect and four or five similar-looking inmates from the local jail. The lineup can be either simultaneous (with the suspect and fillers standing together) or sequential (with the possible perps coming out one by one). When there aren't enough suitable inmates, police officers and other station staff may participate. Occasionally, the police will even recruit people with the right look off the street and pay them a small fee for their trouble.

Nevertheless, it can be difficult to come up with five people who closely match the description of a suspected perpetrator. And even when such fillers can be found, the very nature of using people who bear similarities to the culprit can lead to false identifications—if one filler resembles the suspect much more closely than the other participants, he stands a pretty good chance of being identified by the witness as the perp. Furthermore, if the police choose fillers who don't closely match the description of the suspect, a judge might later rule that the lineup was unfair.

For this reason, many police departments have switched from using traditional lineups to utilizing photo arrays, also known as virtual lineups. With this method, the police select a series of mug shots that closely match the description of the suspected perpetrator. In the United States, the conventional virtual lineup includes two rows of three pictures and has been dubbed the "six pack." As with the live lineup, some police departments prefer to use a sequential virtual lineup, showing the witness only one picture at a time.

Some departments utilize software that automatically picks suitable faces from a large database of police pictures. So if you ever get arrested, be sure to smile for your mug shot—you never know who will be checking you out later.

Mafia Buster!

Joseph Petrosino was one of the first New York cops to take on the Mafia. He was clever, fearless—and effective.

✳   ✳   ✳   ✳

Takin' Names

THE NAME JOSEPH Petrosino means nothing to most New Yorkers—unless they're police officers, who regard the guy as a legend. In the first decade of the 20th century, Petrosino established himself as one of the toughest, most effective detectives in NYPD history. His beat was Little Italy, and he spent much of his career going toe-to-toe with the Mafia. It was a war that ultimately cost him his life.

Petrosino was brought into the department by Captain Alexander Williams, who had watched Petrosino tangle with local thugs on the city streets. Petrosino didn't meet the police height requirement, but in addition to being tough as nails, he spoke fluent Italian and was familiar with the local culture. Williams quickly realized that Petrosino could be an invaluable asset to the force.

The NYPD put Petrosino to work as a sergeant in 1883. He wasted no time making his presence known within the city's Italian community. Strong and fearless, Petrosino became a brawler when necessary, but he also knew the value of quiet detective work. (Dedication and fearlessness eventually elevated him to the rank of lieutenant.) To gather intelligence, for instance, Petrosino routinely disguised himself as a tunnel "sandhog" laborer, a blind street beggar, and other urban denizens who can slip around unnoticed.

Petrosino solved plenty of crimes during his career, but it was his labor to eliminate the vicious gangs preying on Italian immigrants that made him famous. Italian gangsters started setting up shop in the city around 1900, bringing murder, theft, and extortion with them. Petrosino made it his mission to end their reign of terror.

Unspeakable Violence

Foremost among Petrosino's gangland foes was Vito Cascio Ferro, whom some consider one of the inspirations for Mario Puzo's *The Godfather*. Ferro arrived in New York from Sicily in 1901, already a mob boss to be feared and respected. Petrosino made no secret of his desire to implicate Ferro in the gruesome murder in which a body had been dismembered and stuffed in a barrel. As Petrosino closed in, Ferro fled to Sicily, vowing his revenge.

Meanwhile, Petrosino continued to battle the various gangs plaguing Little Italy. Kidnapping and murder were on the rise, as was the use of bombs. (In one terrifying incident, Petrosino managed to extinguish a bomb's fuse with his *fingers* just seconds before the bomb was set to explode.) Determined to stay ahead of the criminals, Petrosino established the nation's first bomb squad, teaching himself and his crew how to dismantle the deadly devices.

In 1908, Vito Ferro again attempted to reach into New York, this time through an intermediary—a murderous Sicilian named Raffaele Palizzolo. At first, clueless city officials embraced Palizzolo, who claimed to want to eliminate the Black Hand, as the Mafia was also called. But Petrosino was skeptical and tailed Palizzolo everywhere. This forced Palizzolo to return to Sicily, much to Ferro's anger.

All the News That's Fit to Blab

Petrosino's boss, Police Commissioner Theodore Bingham, was eager to eliminate New York's Mafia menace once and for all. Early in 1909 he sent Petrosino on a clandestine trip to Italy to meet with law enforcement officials there and gather intelligence. Because the underworld had put a price on his head, Petrosino made the trip disguised as a Jewish merchant named Simone Velletri. Unfortunately, his mission didn't remain a secret for long: While Petrosino was still in transit, the *New York Herald* ran a story that he was on his way to Italy specifically to gather information on Italian gangsters. The source? Bingham, who had stupidly confided in a reporter.

By the time Petrosino arrived in Italy, news of his mission had spread throughout the local underworld. Ferro ordered a hit. On March 12, 1909, two gunmen cut down Petrosino. The detective's funeral was one of the largest in New York history. Police officers and citizens lined the streets as the procession traveled through the city. The journey took five and a half hours—a fitting journey for a man who died for the rule of law.

The Royal Canadian Mounted Police

Is there an icon as visibly Canadian as the red-serge-and-Stetson uniform of the famous Royal Canadian Mounted Police?

✳ ✳ ✳ ✳

✳ The RCMP's legal establishment began in 1873 as the North-West Mounted Police (NWMP), assigned to bring law and order to western Canada. Their motto is French: *Maintiens le droit* ("Maintain the right"). A big job for a big place!

✳ One of the Mounties' first jobs was to banish troublemakers. By 1874, whiskey peddlers from the United States had infested southern Alberta. The Mounties believed that the native First Peoples had suffered enough without rotgut booze, and most whiskey men abandoned their fort well ahead of the arrival of the NWMP.

✳ Along with a force of civilian volunteers from Prince Albert, the Mounties lost a battle in the snow to the Metis at Duck Lake, Saskatchewan, in March 1885 during the Northwest Rebellion. The government forces were lucky not to be encircled and wiped out—a decision for which they could thank Metis leader Louis Riel, who urged against further bloodshed.

✳ The NWMP began to operate in the Yukon in 1895. Good timing, considering the characters coming up from the United States to pan, hack, dig, and sift for gold. Skagway arrivals were surprised to find NWMP constables at the Canadian border, turning back undesirables and making sure the rest brought enough food to avoid famine in Dawson.

✳ They became the Royal North-West Mounted Police in 1904, receiving that designation from King Edward VII.

* The RNWMP became the RCMP with the absorption of the Dominion Police, with law enforcement authority in every square yard of Canada (later every square meter).

* The Depression years were a time of modernization for the RCMP. The marine division was created in 1932. Police dogs became part of the force in 1935, and it began using aircraft in 1937.

* The RCMP schooner *St. Roch* was the first vessel to navigate the entire Northwest Passage in one season (1944).

* An era ended in 1966. Universal RCMP training in horseback riding and horse care was discontinued, though the Musical Ride carries on those traditions in ceremonial fashion. This ceremonial equestrian drill team shows off all over Canada from spring to fall. The 32 members of the Musical Ride perform in uniform (red serge and Stetson) and are armed with white lances.

* Only in 1969 did the RCMP discontinue use of dogsled patrols in the North.

* The first women became uniformed Mounties in 1974.

* Until 1984, the Mounties were responsible for Canada's internal counterintelligence function. The agent of change was the revelation of some unlawful covert operations concerning Quebec separatists.

* Canada has about half a million Sikh citizens and residents. Male Sikhs wear turbans, not Stetsons or billed police caps. In 1990, after a national controversy, Sikh RCMP constables were allowed to wear their turbans in uniform.

* Though a police force, the RCMP was also a regiment of dragoons (mounted rifles). It had a guidon with battle honors from the Northwest Rebellion, South Africa, and World Wars I and II.

Odd Ordinances and Ludicrous Laws

Legally Speaking

Every day, in addition to the thousands of people who deliberately and maliciously perform illegal acts, there are thousands more who inadvertently break laws and statutes that are outdated, outlandish, and somewhat amusing—but still on the books. These are America's forgotten laws.

✳ ✳ ✳ ✳

WHAT'S NOT SO funny is that most are still enforceable. In 2020, an old San Diego law got some new attention. The 1918 city law said that police could charge someone for "seditious behavior" if they said rude things out loud. While the U.S. Supreme Court has ruled that people can only be charged in cases where "seditious language" is tied to an actual imminent crime, San Diego police were using the archaic law to issue tickets for things like overhearing someone quoting rap lyrics that were less than complimentary to the police, or using profanity in the presence of the cops.

Because the tickets were handled at a low level, people were just paying them as they would speeding tickets, and no one was looking at the matter from the perspective of the Constitution and free speech.

In 2020, reporters dug up more than 80 instances of the statute being used since 2013. In addition, an examination showed that Black San Diegans were issued these tickets at a higher proportion than white San Diegans. The law went under review.

In this chapter, we'll look at some other strange and unusual laws and statutes. Many make you wonder just what incident triggered its passing...

Strange and Unusual U.S. Laws

General

* Carrying a set of wooden teeth across state lines is illegal in the United States—unless you are a dentist.

* Several states have laws that only allow sex between heterosexuals—and only in the missionary position.

* Imitating the mascots Smokey the Bear or Woodsy the Owl is not legally allowed anywhere in the United States.

* Having sexual relations while unmarried is against the law in Virginia and Oklahoma.

* In the states of Kentucky and Tennessee, heckling public speakers is within the bounds of civility, but throwing eggs at them can draw a year in jail.

Alabama

* Driving a motorboat down a street is illegal in Brewton, Alabama.

* Trains are not allowed to move faster than an average person can walk in the city of Andalusia, Alabama.

* Get your peanuts early if you're shopping in Lee County, Alabama. It's illegal to buy a bag of peanuts there on Wednesdays between sunset and sunrise.

* Putting salt on a railroad track could get you the death penalty in Alabama.

* In Alabama, you can't play dominos on Sunday.

* Better wear shoes if you're getting behind the wheel in Alabama. Driving barefoot or in slippers is illegal.

Alaska

* In Alaska, you can't look at a moose from an airplane.

* In Anchorage, Alaska, you may not tie your dog to the roof of a car.

* It's perfectly legal to shoot a bear in Alaska. However, it is against the law to wake a sleeping bear to take a picture.

Arizona

* Women are not legally allowed to wear pants in Tucson, Arizona.

* It's not so surprising that it's illegal to cut down a Saguaro cactus in Arizona—but a 25-year prison sentence?

* It's against the law to manufacture imitation cocaine in Arizona.

* Whatever you do in Arizona, don't ride your horse up the stairs of the county courthouse.

Arkansas

* Blindfolding cows on highways in Arkansas is illegal.

* Bring your reading glasses and have your mind made up, because you only have five minutes to vote in Arkansas.

* Dogs are prohibited from barking after 6:00 P.M. in Fayetteville, Arkansas. Good luck enforcing that!

* Well, that's thoughtful: While it is legal for a man to beat his wife in Arkansas, the limit is one time per month.

* Flirting with a member of the opposite sex on the streets of Little Rock, Arkansas, can earn you a 30-day jail sentence.

California

* In Los Angeles, it's unlawful to bathe two babies in the same bathtub simultaneously.

* It's illegal for infants to dance in a public hall in Los Angeles.

* You can't kill a moth under a streetlight in Los Angeles.

* Crying on the witness stand is against the law in Los Angeles.

* It's illegal to mail a complaint about a hotel having cockroaches in Los Angeles.

* Horses are under no circumstances allowed to wear cowbells in Tahoe City, California.

* All public vehicles are required to have spittoons—those old-fashioned receptacles for spitting out your chewing tobacco refuse—in the city of San Francisco.

* Ontario, California, will not tolerate any roosters crowing.

* Bothering a butterfly will result in a $500 fine in California.

* Prostitutes in San Francisco are not required to make change for bills over $50.

* In Chico, California, you'll be fined $500 if you set off a nuclear device within city limits.

* The city of Pasadena, California, made it illegal for secretaries to be alone with their bosses.

* Women are not allowed to bathe in business offices in Carmel, California.

Colorado

* Swimming is allowed only at night in Durango, Colorado.

* Kissing a woman while she's asleep is a crime in Logan County, Colorado.

* If you have the itch to rip those tags off your pillows and mattresses (that clearly say "Do Not Remove"), Colorado is the place for you. It's legal there to do so.

* It's illegal to offer to loan your neighbor your vacuum cleaner in Denver.

Connecticut

* Hartford, Connecticut, has made it illegal for dogs to go to school.

* For a good evening view in Devon, Connecticut, you'd better walk west—it's illegal to walk backward after sunset.

* Moms might rejoice at this law: Silly string is prohibited in Southington, Connecticut.

* Keep the speed down when biking in Connecticut. You aren't allowed to exceed 65 mph.

* Kissing your wife is a Sunday no-no in Hartford, Connecticut.

* Playing Scrabble in the moments before a politician's speech is against the law in Atwoodville, Connecticut.

Delaware

* Laws in Delaware prohibit you from flying over a body of water unless you are carrying ample supplies of food and drink.

* In Whitesville, Delaware, women aren't allowed to propose to men.

Florida

* Breaking more than three dishes a day isn't allowed in Florida.

* It is illegal to go "underneath a sidewalk" while in the state of Florida.

* It's illegal to imitate an animal in Miami.

* It's illegal to hunt or kill a deer if you're in the midst of swimming in Florida.

* In case you wondered: It's not legal to sell your children in Florida.

* Horses in Fort Lauderdale, Florida, are required to wear horns and headlights.

Georgia

* It's illegal to tie a giraffe to a telephone pole in Atlanta.

* Mannequins can only be dressed behind closed shades in Atlanta.

* Happy Hour is not quite as happy in Athens-Clarke County, Georgia. Selling two beers for the price of one is outlawed.

Hawaii

* Hawaii prohibits placing coins in one's ear.

* Until the early 1800s, Hawaiian law forbade women from eating bananas—under penalty of death.

* Residents of Hawaii can receive a fine for not owning a boat.

Idaho

* Best idea ever or worst? In Idaho, it's illegal for a man to give a woman a box of candy that weighs less than 50 pounds.

* In Boise, Idaho, you cannot fish from a giraffe's back.

* Grin and bear it: By law, anyone out in public in Pocatello, Idaho, must have a smile on their face.

Illinois

* Until the 1970s, it was illegal in Chicago to "indecently exhibit any stud horse or stud bull" in a public place.

* A bill introduced in 1901 would have made it mandatory that assistance be given to anyone too drunk to mark a ballot at a polling place.

* In 1893 in Chicago, it was determined by the courts that there was no law on the books prohibiting "disorderly conduct." A judge ordered all prisoners being held on such charges freed—and there were more than 1,000 such prisoners in custody at the time!

* In Chicago, *garbage* goes in a *garbage can*; It is illegal to "dump garbage, slop, or kitchen waste down a privy."

* In Chicago, a $5 penalty may be levied against anyone who "throws a rock or casts a stone" in public.

* The Chicago building ordinance specifies that buildings may not be taller than 130 feet. By the time this law went into effect in 1893, there were already a handful of buildings much taller than that!

* As of 1896, laws stated that visitors to Lincoln Park, Chicago, were to keep off the grass.

* It is technically illegal to fly a kite downtown Chicago.

* If you have less than a dollar, you can be arrested for vagrancy in Chicago.

* But be careful where you go to *get* a dollar... It is also illegal to be caught "prowling about banks or brokerage houses."

* No one is allowed to gamble on presidential elections in Chicago.

* In Kenilworth, Illinois, a rooster must be 300 feet from a residence in order to crow.

Indiana

* In South Bend, Indiana, it's illegal for monkeys to smoke cigarettes. Apparently cigars are okay, but only if the monkey goes outside.

* Winter must get long in Indiana. Bathing is prohibited from October through March.

* Fishing tackle isn't allowed in cemeteries in Muncie, Indiana.

* Liquor stores cannot sell milk in Indiana.

* Not wanting to deal with decimals, Indiana law declared that Pi would be equal to 4 rather than 3.1415. However, due to mathematical confusion, this law was repealed.

Iowa

* Kissing someone for more than five minutes is a crime in Iowa.

* In Iowa, one-armed pianists may not charge for their performances.

* Firefighters in Fort Madison, Iowa, will be well prepared to fight fires—that is, if the building doesn't burn down first. They are required to practice fire fighting for 15 minutes before answering a fire call.

Kansas

* Throwing a knife at anyone wearing a striped suit is illegal in Natoma, Kansas.

* Politicians are never allowed to hand out cigars on an election day in Kansas (any other day is fine).

* Serving wine in a teacup is against the law in Topeka, Kansas.

Kentucky

* Kentucky's 100-year-old "Infidel" law effectively bans any non-Christian religious publication from public schools—and most public schools across the state have reinforced the ban in their policy manuals.

* If "cleanliness is close to godliness," Kentuckians are among the blessed, provided they abide a state law ordering that people must have a bath once a year.

* In Kentucky, remarrying the same man four times is a crime.

* Any man who comes face-to-face with a cow has to remove his hat in Fruithill, Kentucky.

* Women in Owensboro, Kentucky, must have their husband's permission to buy a hat.

Louisiana

* Leaving puddles of rain on your lawn for more than 12 hours is against the law in Lake Charles, Louisiana.

* Bank tellers in Louisiana have reason to feel safe: It is against the law to rob a bank and shoot the teller with a water pistol.

* Prisoners in Louisiana could receive an additional two years in jail if they attempt to hurt themselves.

Maine

* You may not use a feather duster to tickle a girl under the chin in Portland, Maine.

* It is illegal to own an armadillo in the state of Maine.

* In Maine, you are open to getting a fine if you leave your Christmas decorations up after January 14.

* Ads are banned from cemeteries in Wells, Maine.

* The town of Rumford, Maine, has made it illegal to bite your landlord under any circumstances.

Maryland

* Be kind to bivalves: In Maryland, it's illegal to mistreat oysters.

* Sorry, Simba: In Maryland, it's not legal to take a lion to the movies.

* It's illegal to swim in public fountains within the city limits of Rockville, Maryland.

Massachusetts

* In Boston, Massachusetts, it's illegal to take a bath unless one has been ordered by a physician to do so.

* In Boston, it's okay to kiss in public—as long as it isn't in front of a church or on Sunday: That's the day when all displays of public affection are against the law.

* You can't even cross the street on Sunday in Marblehead, Massachusetts.

* Selling suntan oil after noon on Sunday is a crime in Provincetown, Massachusetts.

Michigan

* Clawson, Michigan, found it necessary to pass a law that farmers can't sleep with their pigs, cows, horses, goats, or chickens.

* Putting a skunk in a boss's desk is a crime in Michigan.

* It's illegal to tie animals to fire hydrants in Michigan.

* In Harper Woods, Michigan, it's illegal to sell sparrows painted as parakeets.

* It's illegal to fall asleep in a bathtub in Detroit.

Minnesota

* In Minnesota, women may face 30 days in jail for impersonating Santa Claus.

* You cannot cross the Minnesota state line with a duck on top of your head.

* In St. Cloud, Minnesota, it is illegal to eat a hamburger on Sunday.

* Don't even think about parking your elephant on Main Street in Virginia, Minnesota.

Mississippi

* In Tylertown, Mississippi, it is illegal to shave in the middle of Main Street.

* Disturbing a church service in Mississippi may result in a citizen's arrest.

Missouri

* Carrying a bear on a Missouri highway is illegal, unless it's in a cage.

* Playing hopscotch on a sidewalk is forbidden on Sundays in Missouri.

* A milkman cannot run while on the job in St. Louis.

* Minors in Kansas City, Missouri, better have their own matches—it's legal for them to buy papers and tobacco, but not a lighter.

Montana

* You can't buy a lollipop without a doctor's note while church services are in session if you live in Kalispell, Montana.

* It is a felony in Montana if a woman opens her husband's mail.

* Sports must not be big in Excelsior Springs, Montana—it is illegal to throw a ball within the city limits.

Nebraska

* Selling doughnut holes is absolutely against the law in Lehigh, Nebraska.

* Barbers aren't allowed to eat onions in Waterloo, Nebraska, between 7 A.M. and 7 P.M.

Nevada

* Don't get too friendly at happy hour in Nyala, Nevada—buying drinks for more than three people in a single round is against the law.

* Swearing around dead people is illegal at funeral homes in Nevada.

* In Elko, Nevada, they are prepared for pandemics! The law states that everyone must wear a mask while on the street. (In ordinary times, that must make it easy for bank robbers.)

New Hampshire

* Picking seaweed from the beach is not considered legal in New Hampshire.

* In New Hampshire, you cannot pay off your gambling debts by selling the clothes you are wearing.

New Jersey

* In Cresskill, New Jersey, cats must wear not one but three bells so that birds are forewarned of their whereabouts.

* There's no steak tartare in Ocean City, New Jersey—the selling of raw hamburger is prohibited.

* In Newark, New Jersey, it's against the law to sell ice cream after 6 P.M.—unless the customer has a note from his or her doctor.

New Mexico

* *Merriam-Webster's Dictionary* was once banned in Carlsbad, New Mexico, because it was believed to contain obscene words.

* It is illegal to hunt in Mountain View Cemetery in Deming, New Mexico.

New York

* Swimming nude is allowed only between 8:30 P.M. and 5 A.M. in Spring Valley, New York.

* New York City has outlawed any entertainment-based acts of throwing a ball at someone's head.

* New Yorkers can be fined $25 for flirting.

* Arresting a dead man for debt is a crime in the state of New York.

* In Brooklyn, people can sleep in tubs—but donkeys cannot.

North Carolina

* In Hornytown, North Carolina, don't open a massage parlor.

* A law in North Carolina forbids the use of an elephant to plow cotton fields.

* It's a crime to swim with a deer in water higher than its knees in North Carolina.

* It's illegal for kids under the age of seven to attend college in Winston-Salem, North Carolina (sorry, Doogie).

North Dakota

* In Fargo, North Dakota, it's illegal to lie down and fall asleep with your shoes on.

* North Dakota has outlawed the serving of beer with pretzels at public restaurants and bars.

Ohio

* Hey, I'm talking here... Anyone can be nailed for a $25 fine in Ohio if they blatantly ignore a public speaker on Decoration Day by playing croquet or pitching horseshoes within one mile of the speaker's stand.

* No more flushing money down the toilet... An ordinance in Bexley prohibits the installation and usage of slot machines in outhouses.

* It is forbidden for anyone to hold office in Ohio who has participated in or conducted a duel.

* No seriously, I was just holding it up... Leaning against a public building can earn you a fine in Clinton County.

* In Ohio, it's illegal for more than five women to live in one house.

* In Akron, no person is allowed to solicit sex from another person of the same gender if it offends the second person.

* No person can be arrested on a Sunday or on the Fourth of July in Ohio.

* It's a crime to post a sign at a swimming pool in Akron, or on any public building, for that matter.

Oklahoma

* In Oklahoma, people who make ugly faces at dogs can be fined or jailed. Apparently, it's okay for bulldogs to make ugly faces at people because they can't help it.

* Giving booze to fish is illegal in Oklahoma.

* Hitting a baseball out of the park is a crime in Muskogee, Oklahoma.

* It is illegal to fish for whales on land in Oklahoma but legal to hunt them off the "coast."

Oregon

* Women can't drink coffee after 6 P.M. in Corvallis, Oregon.

* In Oregon, you can be fined up to $6,250 and face up to a year in jail if you adopt an endangered animal.

* Making a dead person serve on a jury is a crime in Oregon.

Pennsylvania

* In Morrisville, Pennsylvania, women need a permit to wear makeup.

* Sleeping in the fridge is illegal in Pittsburgh.

* Drivers in Pennsylvania who encounter multiple horses coming toward them are required to pull off the road and cover their cars with blankets until the animals pass.

* In Danville, Pennsylvania, all fire hydrants must be inspected one hour before a fire.

Rhode Island

＊ In Providence, Rhode Island, you can buy toothpaste and mouthwash on a Sunday, but you can't buy a toothbrush.

＊ A dentist who pulls the wrong tooth from a patient in South Foster, Rhode Island, can be required to have the same tooth removed from his own mouth by a blacksmith.

＊ It's illegal to smoke a pipe after sunset in Newport, Rhode Island.

＊ It's not legal to wear transparent clothes in Providence, Rhode Island. Spoilsports.

South Carolina

＊ Eating nuts on a city bus in Charleston, South Carolina, could cost you a $500 fine or even 60 days in jail.

＊ A Spartanburg, South Carolina, law forbids people from eating watermelon in the Magnolia Street Cemetery.

＊ No runaway grooms: If a man promises to marry a woman in South Carolina, he is bound by law to do so.

＊ You cannot fire a missile without a permit in South Carolina.

South Dakota

＊ In South Dakota, it's illegal to lie down and fall asleep in a cheese factory.

＊ Movies that depict police officers as being beaten or treated badly are banned in South Dakota.

Tennessee

＊ At restaurants in Memphis, Tennessee, all pie must be eaten on the premises, as it is illegal to take unfinished pie home.

＊ It is not legal to use a lasso to catch a fish in Tennessee. Though good luck trying.

Texas

* Texas has a law preventing people from carrying concealed ice cream cones.

* Criminals in Texas must give their victims written or verbal notice 24 hours in advance, explaining what crime is about to be committed.

* You may not dust any public place with a feather duster in Clarendon, Texas.

* When two trains meet each other at a railroad crossing, each shall come to a full stop, and neither shall proceed until the other has gone.

* A citizen cannot work for the state government if his supervisor has "reasonable grounds to believe that the person is a communist."

* It is illegal to sell a secondhand watch without an invoice that clearly states the watch is used "in letters larger than any other letters on the invoice."

* It is illegal to carry wire cutters in your pocket in the city of Austin.

* People wanting to enjoy a nice, cold beer had better be sitting down. They can take as many as three sips while standing up, but if they draw that fourth one, they're crossing the line into criminality.

* Speaking of beer, the authorities really don't want anyone making it without proper authorization. In fact, the *Encyclopedia Britannica* has been banned in Texas because it contains instructions for how to brew your own. Yep, not just *B*, but every single volume of it.

* Gun Barrel City protects its citizens against cotton fires by prohibiting the storage of cotton within 50 feet of a house or building where fire is kept or used.

* An Odessa city ordinance prohibits anyone riding in a parade vehicle or on a parade float or animal from throwing, dropping, or handing out candy, food, toys, souvenirs, or similar items to persons along the parade route.

* Houston also does not allow its citizens to light candles in or on the grounds of certain public and government buildings, including the Sam Houston Coliseum, the Jesse H. Jones Center for the Performing Arts, the Albert Thomas Convention Center and its underground parking garages, City Hall, the Police Administration Building, the Municipal Court, and the Public Library.

* The city of Galveston does, however, allow partiers to get drunk in its parks. Any alcoholic beverages may be consumed in a city park or even on a city playground, as long as written permission is obtained from the director of parks and recreation.

* A parent or person who has the duty of control and reasonable discipline of a child is liable for any property damage caused by the child. Hotels and inns may seek up to $25,000 in damages for the malicious conduct of a child between the ages of 10 and 18.

Utah

* Calling a girl a "slut" could land you a $1,000 fine and six months in jail in Utah.

* Snowball throwers can expect a $50 fine in Provo, Utah.

Vermont

* No atheists allowed in Vermont—it is illegal to deny that God exists.

* Not taking a bath on a Saturday night is against the law in Barre, Vermont.

* Restaurant owners can't offer margarine in Vermont unless they have a public notice posted.

Virginia

* A Virginia law states that bribery or corrupt practices are forbidden—unless you are a political candidate.

* Hunting is illegal in Virginia on Sundays. That is, except for raccoons—you can hunt them until 2 A.M.

* It's against the law to tickle a woman in Virginia.

* Having sex with the lights on is illegal in Virginia.

* In Virginia, children may not trick-or-treat on Halloween.

Washington

* Carrying a concealed weapon in Seattle is illegal if it's more than six feet long. Spears don't tuck into coats very well.

* Playing baseball in any public place is against the law in Wentachee, Washington.

* The state of Washington has made it illegal to pretend your parents are rich.

West Virginia

* Adultery is subject to a $20 fine in West Virginia.

* It's perfectly legal to take home roadkill for dinner in West Virginia.

* No one other than a baby is allowed to ride in a baby carriage in Roderfield, West Virginia.

Wisconsin

* In Madison, Wisconsin, divorcing couples must be aware that joint custody is not allowed for family pets. Custody is awarded to the party who is in possession of the animal at the time of the divorce.

* In Wisconsin, there are ordinances, statutes, and regulations restricting every possible contingency—even, for example, legally blind people who want to hunt deer with a rifle or crossbow. It is permitted by law.

* Instead of deer hunting, why not go after goats? By law, anyone who catches a stray goat under four months of age in Wisconsin is required to be paid $5 by its owner.

* During your hunt, whether you're looking for deer tracks or goat tracks, stay away from train tracks! Besides rail employees, it's Wisconsin law that only newspaper reporters are allowed to walk by railroad tracks.

* Speaking of trians, whenever two trains meet at an intersection, neither may proceed until the other has. That's the law, though it could take all day waiting for the first move.

* And if you and a sweetheart happen to be riding one of those trains, keep the funny business to a minimum; in Wisconsin it's illegal to kiss on a train. Maybe that's why in old Hollywood films there's so much kissing at depots.

* Does all this make the prospect of rail travel sound like too much trouble? If you're upset, we don't blame you. But whatever you do, as you depart the train, don't throw stones. Wisconsin outlaws throwing rocks at rail cars.

* Perhaps you would rather travel by old-fashioned wagon instead. Hitch up your horse, but be careful: In Wisconsin, if you camp in a wagon on any public highway, you risk a fine of up to $10.

* If you want live on the edge, and risk that whopping penalty by setting up house on the road, don't leave anything outside after dark. It is illegal to leave any material on a state highway after sundown—unless you mark it with a lantern that has enough oil to burn until daylight. It's the law.

Wyoming

* In Wyoming, you need an official permit to take a picture of a rabbit at certain times of the year.

Animal Crime and Punishment

Rats declared public enemies, pigs hung in the town square, wolves tried and executed…it's hard to imagine animals held criminally responsible for their actions, but it has happened!

✳ ✳ ✳ ✳

Ox Murderers

PERHAPS THE EARLIEST recorded mention of legal prosecution of an animal is an Old Testament verse in Exodus chapter 21, verse 28: "When an ox gores a man or a woman to death, the ox shall be stoned, and its flesh shall not be eaten; but the owner of the ox shall not be liable."

It's unknown how many Israelite oxen were actually stoned and left uneaten after jabbing unwary citizens, but it's clear that such events were backed by ancient Biblical edict.

The Case of the Reticent Rats

In medieval France, rats were legally charged with the crime of eating barley. But it was extremely difficult to get the rats to appear in court, as villagers of Autun discovered in 1522. The village judge appointed a defense lawyer for the rats and waited for them to show up. The lawyer argued that his clients inhabited many towns so one summons was insufficient to reach them all. The rats were given more time, and villagers were advised to keep their cats from eating any court-bound rats. Eventually, the case was dismissed.

Marauding Mice

Perhaps the people of Autun had heard about a similar action taken in 1519 in Glurns, Switzerland. A farmer asked the court to charge area field mice with damage to his hay. But he was careful to request counsel for the mice so they would receive a fair trial. The farmer claimed he had observed mice eating area hay fields for at least 18 years and found corroborating testimony from a field worker and another farmer.

The defense counsel asserted that the mice were also helpful, assisting in insect control in the fields. He asked for a safe field for the mice to live in and for relocation assistance for any pregnant mice. The sentence allowed the mice two weeks to move out of the damaged fields and banned them for eternity. In a show of leniency, pregnant mice and infants were allowed an extra 14 days to relocate.

Insect Indictments

Rats were not the only creatures to prey upon barley and other staple crops. Weevils, locusts, and worms were regularly charged by formal courts during the Middle Ages. Because most courts were administered by the church, insect pests could even be excommunicated or formally barred from services and the Lord's Supper.

One famous case again occurred in France. In 1546, a massive population of weevils that threatened the barley crop was miraculously decimated when the villagers practiced some extreme religion and performed many penitent acts.

The weevils stayed away for four decades but returned with a vengeance in 1586. This time a full trial was held, defense counsel was hired for the weevils, and a settlement was attempted. The peasants offered the weevils their own tract of land if they would just stay there, but the defense persuaded the court that the land in question was not fertile enough to support his clients. Ironically, insects ate the final record of judgments in the case, leaving the fate of the barley weevils unknown.

Prosecuting Porky

In ancient times, livestock were often left to roam village streets and squares, foraging for garbage and other "found" food. Accidents were bound to happen, and pigs attacked children and other vulnerable humans from time to time. Records of pig prosecution exist in a number of European countries and show that they were by far the most common species brought to trial for murder of humans. Suspected pigs were usually kept in the same jail as human criminals and were sometimes tortured for "evidence," their frantic grunts and screams accepted as confessions. Execution methods included hanging or live burial.

In 1457, a sow and her six piglets were accused of killing a five-year-old boy and were sentenced to death. The sow was hung by her hind legs on a gallows, but the piglets were forgiven due to their youth and the fact that they were, it was claimed, corrupted by their mother.

Kitty Kriminals

The old wives' tale that cats smother infants dates back at least to 1462 when a cat was tried for just such a crime. It was found guilty and hanged. During the great witch trials of the Middle Ages, cats were often thought to be spirit companions of accused witches and were often killed with their owners.

Beasts of the Burden of Proof

Bulls, horses, oxen, and goats were often tried as humans, especially in cases of bestiality. However, in 1750, a female donkey was found not guilty in a case in France because a group of respectable citizens all signed a document testifying that they had been acquainted with the animal for her entire life and she had never acted scandalously. The creature's human assaulter, however, was sentenced to death.

Beavers in Contempt

A resident of Pierson, Michigan, received a letter from the state government in December 1997, threatening to charge the "unauthorized" contractors building two wood dams in nearby Spring Pond $10,000 a day if they did not stop.

The government was informed by the resident's landlord that the illegal builders were a couple of beavers and that if these two animals were forced to pay fines, beavers all over the state would have to be treated similarly.

The state dropped its case.

Interesting Animal Laws

From pet dogs to bears, animals have been subject to some of the strangest laws out there. Check out our list to make sure you and your pets are living within the law.

✳ ✳ ✳ ✳

✳ Oftentimes, a homeowner's insurance premiums will increase if they decide to adopt an exotic or unusual pet.

✳ Choose your exotic pets well: Zoos will usually refuse to accept pets, and in most places it's against the law to release animals into the wild. Now *what* are you going to do with that pet panther?

✳ In French Lick Springs, Indiana, there was once a law requiring black cats to wear bells around their necks on Friday the 13th.

✳ In most villages, towns, and cities, it's illegal to take in a wild animal as a pet.

✳ In most jurisdictions, keeping a deer in your backyard is illegal.

✳ Many states, including Minnesota, Wyoming, Georgia, California, and Kentucky, ban the private ownership of primates as pets.

✳ Punching a bull in the nose is illegal in Washington, D.C.

✳ In Florida, it is illegal to have sexual relations with a porcupine. But...why does this need to be said?

✳ A frog—yes, a frog—can be arrested for keeping a person awake with its "ribbit" noises in Memphis, Tennessee.

✳ In Arizona, you can't shoot a camel.

✳ You can't take your French poodles to the opera in Chicago.

* Training a seal to balance a ball on its nose is illegal in Sweden.

* Giving a lit cigar to a pet is against the law in Zion, Illinois.

* In Carlsbad, New Mexico, if you artificially color a baby chick, duckling, gosling, or rabbit, you are no longer legally allowed to sell it, raffle it off, display it in a shop, or give it away as a prize.

* Cats and dogs can't fight in the town of Barber, North Carolina. Not legally, anyway.

* Catching a mouse without a hunting license isn't allowed in Cleveland, Ohio.

* In Ohio, it is against the law to get a fish drunk.

* Ohioans need a license to keep a bear.

* Here kitty, kitty... In Canton, Ohio, people are required to notify authorities within one hour of losing their pet tiger or any other dangerous animal.

* Put away the chicken paint... It is against the law in Ohio to sell any rabbit or baby poultry, including, but not limited to, chicks and ducklings, that have been colored with dye.

* It sounds a little fishy to me... It is illegal in Ohio to fish for whales on a Sunday. It is also illegal to get a fish drunk, no matter what day of the week it is.

* In Paulding, Ohio, police officers are permitted to bite a dog in order to quiet the animal.

* Other waterfowl are permitted... It's against the law to parade your duck down Ohio Avenue in McDonald, Ohio.

* It's a public offense in Toledo, Ohio, to throw a snake at someone. Other reptiles are permitted?

* Milking someone else's cow is a crime anywhere in Texas.

* In Corpus Christi, Texas, you can't raise alligators in your home.

* Shooting a buffalo is prohibited from the second story of a hotel in Texas.

* It is illegal to sell, purchase, or possess an alligator in the great state of Texas. But that's not all—monitor lizards, anacondas, cobras, crocodiles, cougars, lions, tigers, chimpanzees, gorillas, elephants, bears, weasels, dingos, and jackals are not considered pets in the Lone Star State.

Monsters and More

Planning to bag Bigfoot? Want to capture yourself a Yeti? Or net yourself a sea monster? Better think again. Because believe it or not, there are laws on the books protecting these creatures from harm—even though they may not even exist (the creatures, not the laws). Check it out:

✳   ✳   ✳   ✳

* In 1969, the board of commissioners in Washington state's Skamania County passed an ordinance making it illegal to kill a Bigfoot. The punishments for violating this law are quite severe: a $10,000 fine and a prison sentence of five years. Was Bigfoot on that board of commissioners?

* The law's text cites the high number of purported Bigfoot sightings in the county as justification. The law also covers its bases by mandating protection not only for creatures called "Bigfoot," but also for those called "Yeti," "Sasquatch," and "Giant Hairy Ape." Of course, it's hard to tell how serious commissioners were about this law: It was originally passed on April 1.

* Some monsters are more beloved than others. Champ, a twisty sea monster rumored to live under the surface of Lake Champlain, is protected by law in not just one state but two.

* In the 1980s, both Vermont and New York passed resolutions that made it illegal to harm Champ in any way. The sea serpent is held in such high esteem in the region that the community of Port Henry, New York, celebrates Champ Day each summer. During this festival, vendors flock to the streets of Port Henry to hawk elephant ears, folk art, and lots of T-shirts with Champ appliqués.

* Champ isn't the only sea monster who's earned protection from hunters and poachers. In 1973, the Arkansas state senate passed a resolution sponsored by Senator Robert Harvey naming certain sections of the White River a safe refuge for a sea monster called Whitey. Whitey is a household name for many Arkansans. Sightings of the creature, described by one witness as a gray-skinned beast as wide as a car and three car lengths long, began in 1915. The creature has been a part of Arkansas folklore ever since.

* In the summer of 1937, inventive monster hunters began building a giant rope net to capture Whitey after a sighting. Whitey escaped capture, though, when hunters ran out of money and materials to build their net.

* U.S. residents aren't the only ones obsessed with protecting undiscovered creatures. In Bhutan the government set up the Sakteng Wildlife Sanctuary in 2001 to protect the mythical migoi. The migoi is a version of the United States' Yeti. The beasts are rumored to tower eight feet tall and boast reddish-brown fur. Legends say that the migoi are clever enough to walk backward to mislead trackers. If hunters get too close, the creatures can even render themselves invisible—at least according to legend.

* The Sakteng Wildlife Sanctuary encompasses 253 square miles of land set aside as protected land for the migoi. Again, though, it's difficult to tell just how serious the Bhutan government was when creating the sanctuary. The Sakteng Wildlife Sanctuary also provides a home for snow leopards,

tigers, and other wildlife that actually do exist. The "migoi habitat" angle may be a way to attract additional tourists to the region.

Sounds and Smells

Laws having to do with speech, song, snores, sneezes, and stinky smells.

✳   ✳   ✳   ✳

✳ It's against the law to whisper in church in Rehoboth Beach, Delaware.

✳ In Georgia, watch your tongue around dead people. It's unlawful to swear in front of a dead body in a funeral home or coroner's office.

✳ You aren't allowed to ride public transportation in Atlanta if you have bad body odor.

✳ Mispronouncing the city name is illegal in Joliet, Illinois.

✳ Chicagoans, next time a tourist asks you for directions; Make sure you know what you are talking about! It is illegal to give "misleading information about . . . the location of restaurants or hotels."

✳ A 1923 declaration stated that, since we have cut all ties from England, the official language of the State of Illinois would be referred to as "American," not "English."

✳ Humming on the street on Sunday is illegal in Cicero, Illinois.

✳ If you're planning on going to a movie in Gary, Indiana, watch what you eat. It's illegal to go to a theater within four hours of eating garlic.

✳ In New Orleans, Louisiana, it's against the law to gargle in public.

* Preschoolers better do their learning during daytime hours in Topeka, Kansas, because singing the alphabet on the streets at night is forbidden.

* Better not blow your nose in public if you're in Waterville, Maine; it's illegal.

* Talking on the phone without a parent on the line is a crime in Blue Earth, Minnesota.

* Public sneezing is never allowed in the state of Nebraska.

* The town of Tryon, North Carolina, has made it illegal to play the piccolo between 11 P.M. and 7:30 A.M.

* Snoring so loudly that your neighbors can hear you is illegal in Dunn, North Carolina.

* In Marion, Oregon, ministers are forbidden from eating garlic or onions before delivering a sermon.

* In Port Arthur, Texas, it's against the law to emit any obnoxious odor in an elevator.

* Whistling underwater is not legal in Vermont. It's also just plain difficult to do.

* In Nicholas County, West Virginia, no clergy member may tell jokes or humorous stories from the pulpit during church services.

* It was once illegal to sneeze on a train in the state of West Virginia.

* Put that flute and drum away! It is illegal to play them on Milwaukee streets. Trombones, tubas, and steam calliopes apparently remain legal.

* Watch your mouth! Swearing is forbidden by law in public places in Salem, Wisconsin.

Hairy Laws

Haircuts and hairstyles...all subject to the law.

※ ※ ※ ※

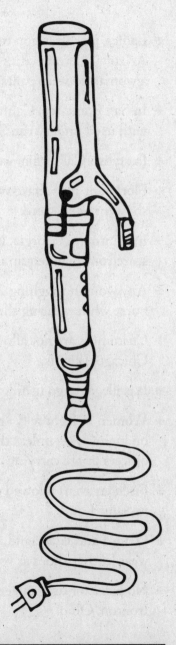

* You're a criminal if you use hair curlers without a license in Oklahoma.

* Alabama strictly forbids wearing a fake moustache in church if it could cause laughter.

* In Florida, snoozing under the hair dryer is prohibited.

* Goatees are illegal in Massachusetts.

* Michigan law states that a woman's hair is technically owned by her husband.

* Men are required to grow beards in Brainerd, Minnesota.

* Any man shaving his chest is breaking the law in Omaha, Nebraska.

* Mothers in Nebraska are prohibited from giving their daughters a perm without a state license.

* Men with mustaches are not allowed to kiss women in Eureka, Nevada.

* It's illegal to fall asleep during a haircut in Erie, Pennsylvania.

What You Wear

*Watch out when you're getting dressed...you might become
a lawbreaker without realizing it.*

✳ ✳ ✳ ✳

✳ Ladies, pay attention to your wardrobe choices when in
Arizona. Certain cities still have laws that make it illegal for
a woman to wear pants.

✳ In San Francisco, California, it is illegal to wipe your car
with used underwear. So, is it okay to use clean underwear?

✳ In stylish California, women may not drive in a housecoat.

✳ Floridians must have very clean clothes—it's illegal to
shower naked there.

✳ In Quitman, Georgia, it's illegal to change the clothes on a
storefront mannequin unless the shades are down.

✳ Any woman weighing 200 pounds is forbidden from riding a
horse while wearing shorts in the town of Gurnee, Illinois.

✳ Customers are not allowed to sleep at any Laundromat in
Chicago, Illinois.

✳ It is illegal to go fishing in your pajamas in Chicago, Illinois.

✳ Women in Kentucky aren't allowed to be in swimsuits while
on highways—unless they are either being escorted by two
officers or are carrying clubs.

✳ Firemen aren't allowed to rescue women wearing nightgowns
in Saint Louis.

✳ Oxford and Cleveland, Ohio, made it illegal for women to
wear leather shoes at voting polls.

✳ No place for drag queens...Cross-dressing is prohibited in
Ironton, Ohio.

* In Oxford, Ohio, it is illegal for a woman to disrobe in front of a man's picture. We're curious as to whether it's legal if his eyes are closed in the photo?

* It's no reflection on you, ma'am . . . The wearing of patent leather shoes in public by women is prohibited in Cleveland, Ohio, in order to prevent men from using the reflection as a way to peer up a woman's skirt.

* A little modesty, please . . . In Oxford, Ohio, it's illegal for a woman to strip off her clothes while standing in front of a photo of a man.

* In Fountain Inn, South Carolina, horses were once required to wear pants when in public.

* In St. Croix, Wisconsin, women are not allowed to wear anything red in public.

* Wearing a hat in a theater could cost you in Wyoming, but only if it happens to block anyone else's view of the show.

On the Road

Unusual laws about vehicles and roads? We've got them here.

✳ ✳ ✳ ✳

* Stepping out of a plane while flying over Maine is strictly against the law.

* Drivers may not be blindfolded while operating a motor vehicle in Alabama.

* In Glendale, Arizona, it is illegal to drive a car in reverse, so virtually everyone in a mall parking lot is breaking the law.

* California law strictly forbids hunting animals from a moving vehicle—unless your target is a whale.

* Here's a law that might be easier said than done: In Sterling, Colorado, cats that run free must be fitted with a taillight.

* Driving livestock on a school bus is illegal in Florida.

* In the 1930s, laws were passed prohibiting the parking of automobiles in Chicago's Loop during business hours. More than 200 police officers were dispatched to ticket all cars parked, "regardless of political connections."

* In Chicago, it is still on the books that you must contact city officials before entering the city in an "automobile." This dates back to the days when automobiles were still quite a novelty—and terribly dangerous.

* Shooting rabbits from motorboats is illegal in Kansas.

* If two trains come together in one spot on the same track in Kansas, neither one may proceed until the other has passed. So . . . how does that work?

* It is against Maine law to step out of a plane while it's in flight.

* Maine has a law that bans the sale of cars on Sunday.

* It is illegal for an ambulance to go faster than 20 mph in Port Huron, Michigan.

* In Montana, it is against the law for a sheep to ride in the cab of a truck without a chaperone.

* In Nevada, camels are not to be driven on the highway.

* It is against the law to lie down on a sidewalk in Reno, Nevada.

* Farmers, do you know where your cows are? Any cattle crossing New Hampshire state roads must be wearing a device that collects their feces.

* It's illegal to drive a car if you're blind in New York.

* In Youngstown, Ohio, it is illegal to ride on the roof of a taxi cab.

* Don't try this at home... In Marion, Ohio, it is against the law to eat a doughnut and walk backwards on a city street.

* In Oxford, Ohio, it is against the law to drive around the town square more than 100 times in a single session.

* In Cleveland, Ohio, it is illegal to drive while someone sits in your lap.

* Because roller skaters are nothing but trouble... It's perfectly legal to go roller skating in North Canton, Ohio, but you are required by law to first notify the police before doing so.

* In Youngstown, Ohio, it's against the law to run out of gasoline.

* It is illegal to throw pickle juice on a trolley in Rhode Island.

* It is illegal to drive while sleeping in Tennessee.

* In Memphis, Tennessee, a law was passed to prohibit women from driving unless they have a man walking in front of the car while waving a red flag.

* Galveston, Texas, doesn't allow camels to wander the streets unattended.

* Littering is never a good idea, but throwing garbage out of a plane might land one in jail in Galveston, Texas.

* In Galveston don't even think about landing an airplane on the beach or what is commonly known as Seawall Boulevard.

* Riding a horse at night can be dangerous. That's why Texarkana requires horses to be equipped with tail lights after dark.

* In Houston, Texas, no one may drive cattle, horses, mules, hogs, sheep, or goats over public streets without written permission from the chief of police.

* Utah drivers must beware: Birds have the right of way on all public highways.

* In Seattle, Washington, women who sit on men's laps on buses or trains without placing a pillow between them face an automatic six-month jail term.

* Riding an ugly horse on a public street in Wilbur, Washington, is a crime.

* In Milwaukee, Wisconsin, you can't park a car for more than two hours unless a horse is tied to it.

Food and Drink

Eat, drink, be merry, and....commit a crime? Maybe!

❋ ❋ ❋ ❋

* You cannot give a moose any alcoholic beverages in Fairbanks, Alaska.

* Peeling an orange in a hotel room in California is a crime.

* In Arizona, it is illegal to refuse a person a glass of water. Aimed primarily at businesses, this law is meant to cut down on dehydration deaths among homeless people.

* It's illegal to eat chicken with a fork in Gainesville, Georgia.

* In Chicago, serving whiskey to a dog is against the law.

* How hungry are you? It is against the law in Chicago to eat in a restaurant that is on fire.

* Horses are not allowed to eat fire hydrants in Marshalltown, Iowa. Well, they're not very tasty.

* In Kentucky, it's illegal to have an ice cream cone in your back pocket. Thank goodness cargo pants have side pockets!

* Massachusetts law prohibits giving beer to hospital patients.

- Massachusetts takes its clam chowder seriously—people there are legally forbidden to put tomatoes in it.

- Don't give a baby coffee in Lynn, Massachusetts—it's illegal.

- Presumably, it's all right to drink beer from a bucket in St. Louis, Missouri. Just don't do it while sitting on the curb—that's against city law.

- Slurping soup is against the law in New Jersey.

- It's illegal to offer someone a glass of water without a permit in Walden, New York.

- That's a bit corny… It's against the law to sell corn flakes on Sunday in Columbus, Ohio.

- You can go to jail for taking a bite out of someone else's hamburger in Oklahoma.

- Bristow, Oklahoma, mandates that all restaurants serve customers one peanut per every glass of water.

- In Houston, Texas, it's illegal to sell Limburger cheese on Sundays.

Northern Justice

Canada is one of the world's most peaceful and underpopulated countries, so naturally one would think it would be easy to keep the citizens in line. So why are all these strange laws still on the books? Eh, why not?

* * * *

Penny Pummeling

WHEN KIDS LEAVE coins on the railway tracks to be flattened by trains, they could be facing a year in juvenile jail or a $250 (that is, a 25,000-penny) fine. This is because they are defacing the currency of the country and the law clearly states that it is illegal to "melt down" or "break up" money.

Scamming the Queen

Canada is still technically a constitutional monarchy, so when Her Royal Highness visits, you'd best show some respect! For instance, it's a severe offense to sell the queen shoddy or defective merchandise.

No Fake Witches

Canada has complete freedom of religion, so if you're claiming to be a witch, you better be the real thing. Genuine witches, or wiccans, are considered fine, but should you grab a broom and a pointy hat and pretend to be a witch, you are violating the Criminal Code of Canada. Those who "pretend to exercise or use any kind of witchcraft, sorcery, enchantment, or conjuration" can be punished. Makes you wonder whether the jails are filled to capacity on Halloween.

No Yellow Margarine

While the rest of Canada can enjoy yellow margarine with impunity, Quebec's dairy industry has successfully lobbied the provincial government to pass a law that all margarine sold to the public must be a color other than yellow (so that the consumer doesn't mistake it for butter). Plans for blue and pink bread spreads were quickly abandoned in favor of the blander-hued off-white.

The Cow: Queen of Beasts

Canada's animal cruelty laws impose a penalty of two years on anyone who tortures or mistreats any animal. But woe to the soul who abuses a cow—inflicting harm on Bessie can result in up to five years behind bars.

Trick, Treat, or Be Eaten

Polar bears may be an endangered species but not in the Far North town of Churchill, Manitoba. Visits from the snowy bruins present so much of a problem in this community (people must huddle in their houses as the large predators rumble through) that the municipal government has banned furry Halloween costumes for fear of attracting the bears.

Crime Comics

Canada has notoriously vague obscenity laws—one problematic prohibition takes a stand against images showing the "commission of crimes, real or fictitious." At least that stops super villains in Canadian comic books from dressing as polar bears or bothering cows.

Carousing in Calgary

Calgary, Alberta, is cracking down on horseplay after closing time, as shown in its system of bylaws. Spitting can cause you to be $115 out of pocket, and relieving yourself in public carries a price tag of $300. Curiously enough, brawling and beating the wazoo out of one other will result in only a $250 penalty. Better to punch than to pee!

Simple Skill Testing Questions

No one can simply be given a prize in a Canadian raffle, draw, or sweepstakes. Instead, Canadians are required to "earn" the prize, usually by answering a "skill-testing question," which often takes the form of a simple arithmetic problem. So if you're not up on your basic math, there's a chance that jet-ski's not coming home with you.

Just Say "Boo!"

Canadian law specifically states that it is a criminal act to frighten a child or a sick person to death. Apparently, it's just peachy to pop out of a laundry hamper while wearing a hockey mask—as long as your victim is a healthy adult!

One in Five Songs

Non-Canadians have a difficult time understanding Canadian Content laws or "Can-Con," which require a substantial portion of television and radio programming be filled with homegrown Canadian talent. Basically, it's an attempt to keep Canadian culture from being overwhelmed by Hollywood and Nashville.

Outlandish Laws around the World

North America is not alone in passing laws that sound a bit strange to the modern ear...

✳ ✳ ✳ ✳

✳ Close the blinds! In Singapore, walking around in your house while nude is against the law—it's considered pornographic.

✳ Be careful how you break your eggs in England. Anyone caught breaking a boiled egg on the pointed end can be thrown in the "village stocks" for a day. This ordinance was put in place by King Edward VI and has yet to be overturned.

✳ Have a duel planned in Paraguay? If you're not a legal blood donor, you could be arrested.

✳ Cursing in French may sound elegant, but it's illegal in Montreal. Swearing in English is okay, though.

✳ Dressing in a hurry has its hazards in Thailand, where it's illegal to leave your house unless you're wearing underwear.

✳ British law mandates that if you are driving a car, you must be in the front seat.

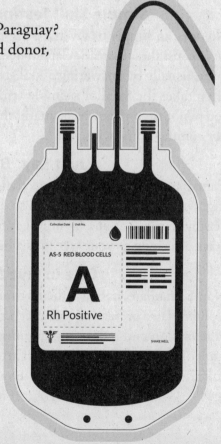

* According to South Korean law, traffic officers must report all bribes they receive from motorists.

* An Australian regulation makes it illegal for fax modems to pick up on the first ring.

* Members of the British Parliament are not allowed to enter the House of Commons in full armor. They can't die in Parliament, either.

* Farmers in France, be aware—you may not name your pig Napoleon. Alas.

* In Israel it's illegal to pick your nose on the Sabbath.

* The head of any dead whale found on British shores automatically becomes the property of the king. The queen gets the tail.

* Be careful to check the clock—it's illegal to flush a toilet after 10 P.M. in Switzerland.

* Bad for business: In Sweden, prostitution is legal. Hiring the services of a prostitute, however, is not.

* All males in England who are older than 14 must spend at least two hours per week practicing firing a longbow.

Chapter 11

Fumbling Felons

Even crime has its dimmest, least glamorous moments. This chapter contains a collection of crime-related gaffes that put the "dumb" in dumbfounded.

✳ ✳ ✳ ✳

It Pays to Follow the Styles

A 54-year-old man in San Francisco robbed several banks just seven days after being released from prison—for bank robbery. In February 2007, the man's probation officer took a photo of him on the day he was released. Still wearing the 1980s-style clothes and Members Only jacket in which he strode away from prison—but adding a new hairnet—the man proceeded to rob a bank. Authorities weren't able to positively identify the robber's face from the surveillance photos, but they were able to clearly distinguish his Members Only jacket, his hairnet, and the 1980s-era clothes he wore. He wasn't wasting any time, however, and robbed two more banks before police caught him. The images from the later robberies were widely distributed to police agencies—the bank robber's probation officer instantly recognized him and immediately contacted authorities with the man's name and address. The bank robber was apprehended later that night. He was identified due to the fact that he was still wearing the same clothes.

Half-Baked

After robbing two convenience stores in an hour, a man went for a third caper just a few hours later on September 30, 2007, in Delaware. The thief used a note that read, "Give me your money I'll shoot you." It was the same note used in the previous robberies. This time, however, the 25-year-old robber left his demand behind, and it just so happened to be written on the pay stub from his job at a local bakery. Along with fingerprints, the stub included the thief's full name. Bail was quickly set at $31,000.

Funny Money

In Gary, Indiana, a cafeteria worker broke up a money-counterfeiting scheme when she was handed a fake $20 bill. The culprit: a ten-year-old boy. He aroused her suspicion when he paid for lunch with the large bill, so she turned it in. Police say the boy enlisted the help of two of his friends and created the money on his home computer. In December 2005, the children faced charges of forgery and theft. The boys were the youngest counterfeiters the FBI had ever come across. Reportedly, the counterfeits were even pretty good.

Choose Your Designated Driver Carefully

Many people drink alcoholic beverages responsibly. If they do have a little too much, most designate a capable driver. In November 2007, however, a 41-year-old man in Clio, Michigan, made a few key mistakes in his choice. Despite the fact that the man selected his son as his designated driver, the two ended up stuck in the mud where police arrested them both. What happened? His son was only 13 years old and also drunk.

He Was Only Reporting a Robbery

A man in south Texas called police to report a theft. Nothing unusual about that, right? Yet, the man told police that two masked gunmen had kicked in his door and stole 150 pounds of marijuana. He then explained to police that he was wrapping the drugs for shipment when the gunmen arrived. When police investigated the "crime," they found 15 pounds of the stuff lying on the man's floor. Not only did police charge the man with felony possession of marijuana, but he also turned out to be an illegal immigrant.

Choose Your Location Carefully

Perhaps he thought the lot was still vacant, or maybe he believed that no one would think to look for marijuana in such a place. Regardless of his reasoning, a 17-year-old male was arrested for growing nine marijuana plants in a wooded area of Ocala, Florida. Unfortunately for the teen, that wooded area belonged to the deputy chief of police. Neighbors noticed the teen acting suspiciously and asked why he was on the chief's property. He replied that he'd come from a skate park, but they didn't buy it. One neighbor went to where the teen had been spotted and found the illegal crop. The deputy chief was immediately notified.

Safety Goggles Wouldn't Have Helped

Two 19-year-olds were treated for minor burns and arrested after shoplifting gunpowder and PVC pipe from a Wal-Mart in Bayou Black, Louisiana. The youths had successfully gotten away from the store, but they didn't follow all the safety precautions that they should have. One of them subsequently set off the black powder when he flicked cigarette ashes near the open bottle. Following up on reports of a bang, police arrived to investigate. They found damage from an explosion in the kitchen and dining room. The duo was charged with shoplifting and possessing or making a bomb.

Smile!

A man decided to steal a camera from a store in Connecticut. His technique might have been perfect except for the surveillance camera that caught him on tape. The criminal seems to have remembered to keep his face well-hidden from that camera. The surveillance camera, however, caught the would-be thief taking a picture of himself with another display model, which he put down and left behind in the store, just before walking out with a different $400 camera in hand. Brilliant!

Don't Call Us...

A man in St. Charles, Missouri, stole a computer and printer from a driver's license facility. The printer could be used to produce fake driver's licenses or other identification, but only with the software found on the PC. That's thinking ahead! The computer, however, was inoperable without a special key to unlock it. Summoning all his cunning, the thief called tech support two days later asking to buy the software for the make and model of the printer he'd stolen from the driver's license facility. He ingeniously used his middle name, but he provided a phone number he'd previously given to the FBI in an unrelated identity theft case.

A Quick U-Turn

A man accused of drug possession successfully eluded police after being chased from Ontario, Oregon, into the neighboring state of Idaho. Shortly after crossing the state line, however, the criminal decided to turn around and go back to Oregon. He quickly made his way to the parking lot of a Wal-Mart, where he surrendered to the authorities. He reportedly told the arresting state trooper that he had done this because he didn't want to go to jail in Idaho.

Drunk Dialing

A man in Germany stole a cell phone and made a clean getaway. Police decided to call the stolen phone, figuring it was worth a shot to see if they could get any information. The thief answered. The officer on the other end told him, "You've won a crate of beer," but they needed the thief's location to drop it off. He happily gave his full address. Police believe the man was drunk.

Now It Can Be Told

In 2003, a jewelry heist occurred at a department store in Temecula, California. Two armed men and a getaway driver all got away—until the driver got in touch with his inner muse. In 2005, Colton Simpson published a memoir, *Inside the Crips:*

Life Inside L.A.'s Most Notorious Gang. Touting its author as the mastermind, Colton's book described details uncannily similar to the actual jewelry heist. Colton discussed waiting outside while two others robbed the store and the fact that he scouted out the jewelry section two days prior. As a result of California's "Three Strikes You're Out" law, Colton received 126 years in prison for his literary spirit!

Do You Have Change for a Bill?

Since 1969, the largest U.S. bill in circulation is the $100 bill. Despite this fact, on October 6, 2007, a man walked into a Pittsburgh supermarket and attempted to pay for his purchase with a one-million-dollar bill! When the cashier refused to accept it and the store manager confiscated the bill, the customer flew into a rage. He was held in the county jail.

Sorry, Wrong Number

A man in Escatawpa, Mississippi, intended to call the local TV station after watching a news story. Angry, he apparently wanted to complain about not receiving a FEMA trailer after Hurricane Katrina. Meaning to dial 411 for the station's number, the man accidentally dialed 911. Panicking, he hung up on the dispatcher. The dispatcher, concerned, requested police to check if anyone needed assistance. When police arrived at the address from where the phone call was made, no one answered the door. Thinking the residents might be in trouble, police broke in and found the 56-year-old caller and four others in a full methamphetamine lab.

Next Time, Carry a Flashlight

A burglar broke into a German sports club around 3:00 A.M. Needing to see what he was about to steal, he turned on the first light switch he could find. That turned on the floodlights and sprinkler system for the football field outside. The groundskeeper for the sports club could see the light from his nearby home and immediately contacted the police. The man was quickly arrested.

Reruns Are Always Annoying

A convenience store supervisor in Edinburgh, Scotland, conspired with a friend to rob his store of more than three thousand dollars and to beat him up for good measure. Their plan seemed foolproof. Police arrived at the store to find the safe open and the supervisor bleeding from repeated blows to the head and body. Upon further investigation, however, the security camera footage showed the supervisor opening the door on his day off and walking in with his friend. The 20-year-olds, known to gamble together, admitted to staging the whole thing.

Don't Drink and Mow

A Martinsburg, West Virginia, man was accused of drunk driving on his riding lawn mower—a mile from his home. After an officer—still in his police car—asked the man to pull over, the man "sped" away on his mower. The officer then jumped out of his car, chased the mower on foot, and caught up to it after a short jog. The officer allegedly found a case of beer strapped to the front of the riding mower. When the driver refused a field sobriety test, the authorities held him on $7,500 bond.

Man of a Thousand Faces

A disguised man robbed a bank in Manchester, New Hampshire. That may not be so unusual, but unfortunately for him, the man had disguised himself as a tree. He walked into the bank with leaves and branches duct-taped to his face and body and demanded money. Despite his face being somewhat obscured, someone recognized the robber after seeing footage released from a bank security camera. An anonymous tip led police straight to the man later that night.

Always Know Your Customer

In Charleston, West Virginia, a 19-year-old sent a text message to his friend asking if he "wanted to buy some reefer." The teen received a text message back saying simply "yes," and a meeting was arranged. What the young man didn't know was that his friend had changed his cell phone number and that the number to which he sent the text belonged to a state trooper. Oops. The teenager was charged with delivery of a controlled substance and possession with intent to deliver marijuana.

When You're Hungry, You're Hungry

In Appleton, Wisconsin, a burglar reportedly entered an unlocked apartment but didn't steal any of the "valuables" within. No, this thief had a particular goal in mind and took six eggs, a container of beef ravioli, a pizza, a can of peaches, and a Hot Pocket (chicken-and-broccoli variety). The crime apparently occurred sometime between 8:30 A.M. and 12:30 P.M.—prime snacking hours!

Taking the Credit

In Britain, two 18-year-olds were arrested for vandalizing a children's campsite. They apparently broke into the facility late one night, smashed plates and dishes, and discharged fire extinguishers. One of the boys decided to write his name in black permanent marker on the wall, boasting that he "was here!" The two wrote the name of their gang, as well. Police simply entered the vandal's name into the computer system for all the information they needed. The boys were quickly arrested. As punishment, they were fined and ordered to perform community service.

The Lap of Luxury

In an attempt to help pay for her and her boyfriend's drug-dealing debts, a woman in Providence, Rhode Island, rented a limo and attempted to rob a bank. The woman hired the driver to take her to the airport, but she asked him to stop at a bank's drive-through lane, where she got out of the limo and handed a teller a note. The note demanded money and claimed that there were two bombs inside the bank. In response, the teller hit the panic button. The would-be bank robber immediately got back in the car without any money, and the limo driver pulled off, unaware of what had occurred. Police eventually arrested the woman and charged her with attempted bank robbery.

It Works in the Movies

In Silver Springs Shores, Florida, a man was charged with commercial burglary, possessing tools for burglary, and felony criminal mischief. The enterprising criminal had a plan to break into a drugstore by removing an air-conditioning cover and gaining access to the air vent. He was going to crawl through it to get into the store, but instead he got stuck until the store opened the next day—ten hours later! In his defense, the man claimed he "heard a cat" and was trying to "chase" it.

Three Times Is No Charm

An unmasked man in Frisco, Texas, attempted to break into three different ATM machines at three different locations with an ax! The machines are apparently built to withstand such an attack. Meanwhile, security cameras at each of the locations captured the incidents on tape. Television news quickly broadcast the footage, and the man, who saw how easily he'd be recognized, turned himself in shortly afterward. His bond was set for $20,000—for each ATM.

There's Nothing Like a Good Disguise

In Ashland, Kentucky, a man tried to rob a liquor store with his face completely wrapped in gray duct tape. Claiming to have a knife, the man threatened to harm the clerk if she didn't give him the money out of the cash register. The clerk complied, but as the robber tried to leave, the store manager pulled out a wooden club and chased him into the parking lot. Several employees joined in and tackled the robber. During a later interview, the suspect—who's since been indicted—claimed that he wasn't the robber, that he had no memory of entering the store, and that he couldn't remember police removing the duct tape.

Driving Through Adversity

A 40-year-old man with no arms and one leg received five years in prison in New Port Richey, Florida, for felony driving. The man once held a valid license, but it had been suspended several times in the previous 20 years. He had previously spent three years in prison for other offenses, such as habitually driving without a license and kicking a state trooper. (Details on how he kicked a state trooper were not forthcoming.)

Going to the Dogs

A woman and two men attempted to steal copper wiring and pipes from an abandoned nursing home in Gainesville, Georgia. The trio apparently ignored signs declaring that the property was owned by the Gainesville police department. And it wasn't just police property—it was a K-9 training facility (also clearly marked). Police dog handlers arrived and discovered the thieves, who dropped their tools and took off running. Naturally, the handlers released the entire K-9 unit to go after them. One thief ended up with a superficial dog bite on the buttocks. All were caught and charged with burglary.

Keep Your Pants On

A police officer in Spokane, Washington, took her van to the dealership for servicing. Later that day, a witness reported a naked man driving by repeatedly and pleasuring himself in a van. Turns out it was the officer's van. After the witness provided the plate number, police found the van back at the dealership—where the naked driver worked. He had apparently gone on a 16-mile test-drive! The man was charged and jailed for taking a motor vehicle without permission as well as for lewd conduct. We just hope the van got cleaned thoroughly.

A Successful Robber Must Be Taken Seriously

A man in Inwood, West Virginia, attempted to rob a store with a gun-shape cigarette lighter. He disguised himself by wearing a pair of blue women's panties over his face. The store clerk, not surprisingly, thought it was a joke and refused to give up any money. Realizing that his plan was falling apart, the man hopped into a Jeep and fled into the night. Within a matter of minutes, the police stopped a vehicle matching the description given by the clerk. After searching the driver and the area, they found the pistol-shaped lighter and recovered the blue under-wear nearby. Unlike the clerk, the police didn't treat the matter as a joke.

In the Driver's Seat

Apparently suffering from a powerful craving, a six-year-old boy in Colorado attempted to drive to Applebee's. He grabbed his grandmother's keys and placed his booster seat in the driver's seat. Although he managed to start the car, he couldn't get it out of reverse. The child backed up about 47 feet, cross-ing the street and hitting the curb. The car continued rolling an additional 29 feet before taking out a transformer and com-munications box. Fortunately, no one was injured. But it's still a mystery to investigators how the boy reached the gas pedal.

The Immovable ATM

In Milwaukee, three men tried to steal an ATM from a gas station. They smashed their SUV through the mostly glass wall where the ATM stood and then yanked on the machine. Discovering that it was bolted to the floor, they decided to wrap a rope around the ATM and tie it to the truck's bumper. But although the driver gunned the accelerator, the ATM refused to budge. They soon gave up completely. The ATM, although badly scratched, still stands where it always did.

Keep It to Yourself

A 60-year-old man in Duisburg, Germany, decided to appeal his court conviction for streaking at a girls' soccer match. Perhaps believing it might help his case, the man stripped off all his clothes in the courtroom when the jury adjourned for deliberation. Needless to say, it did not help his case, as new charges were immediately filed.

Don't Display Your Own Evidence

An Italian university student was arrested for marijuana charges after dropping his cell phone. Apparently, the student had taken a picture of himself in front of a marijuana plant and then inexplicably used that picture as a screen saver on his phone. That wasn't so bad, until he lost the phone. A retiree found it and turned it over to the police. Upon seeing the picture, police called the student in, where he promptly broke down and confessed to everything, including the location of his crop. He was immediately arrested.

The Internet Knows Everything

Two burglars broke into an indoor amusement center in Colorado Springs, Colorado. Police suspect that they had inside help, as the felons had keys, pass codes, and combinations. What they didn't have, however, was information about the safes—which took them more than 75 minutes to open. Security footage showed them fumbling with the dials. In an attempt to obscure the lens of a security camera, the bungling duo sprayed it with WD-40 lubricant, which cleaned the lens instead. Eventually, one of the burglars left the room. Police later checked a computer in a nearby office and found that the thief had performed Google searches for "how to open a safe" and "how to crack a safe." It must have helped. The two easily opened the safes after that, escaping with cash, a laptop computer, and a PlayStation, totaling more than $12,000.

Take Your Name Tag with You

A man who was admitted to a Newark, New Jersey, hospital was arrested for vandalizing the hospital's helicopter. He apparently left the emergency room and walked onto the helipad. Perhaps searching for drugs, the man entered the helicopter and ransacked it. Damages were estimated around $55,000. The vandal, however, left behind his grocery store name tag in the helicopter. Police swiftly arrested him.

Sometimes You Just Need a Hug

Crime scenes can often be confusing places, with victims and onlookers in a state of shock, not sure quite what has happened. But some crimes have a stronger sense of surreality than others. One early summer night, a man crashed the patio of a private party at a Capitol Hill home in Washington, D.C. He held a gun to the head of a 14-year-old guest and demanded money, or he would "start shooting!" The remaining five guests froze for what they later said seemed like minutes; everyone looked at each other in shock. Finally, one guest suggested to the gunman, "Why don't you have a glass of wine with us?"

The robber agreed, took a sip, and replied, "Damn, that's good wine." He proceeded to take another sip, then ate some Camembert cheese that was on the table. Looking around, he put away his gun and apologized. "I think I may have come to the wrong house...I'm sorry...Can I get a hug?" One by one, the guests took turns giving him a hug. The gunman mumbled to himself, "That's really good wine," then asked for a group hug. With arms outstretched, the guests complied. Apparently satisfied, the would-be robber left the patio and walked off with a wine glass full of the expensive wine. The guests—unsure of what exactly had just happened—simply walked in the house, locked the door, and stared at each other in silence. One guest called the police, and when the officers arrived, they found the empty crystal wine glass sitting in the alley behind the home— unbroken. No fingerprints were found. Nothing was stolen. There were no reports of an arrest.

Driving Lessons Not Included

Two car thieves envisioned pulling a "gone in 60 seconds" type robbery. Their heist, however, took a little longer. With their eyes on a red Ford GT, the criminals busted into a California car dealership and pillaged offices until they found the key safe. After busting it open, they hopped in the sporty number, turned the ignition, and listened to the quiet of a dead engine. Thinking quickly, the pair jump-started the car from a battery charger and again they were off—until they reached the locked gates outside. They grabbed the keys to a Lincoln Navigator and smashed down the gates. Apparently, the criminals never learned how to handle the 550-horsepower monster. The Ford GT was found only a few miles away with $30,000 in damage.

Be Prepared

A man decided to rob a safe in an Illinois post office. After realizing that his personal safe-cracking tools weren't up to the job, he decided to burglarize a nearby grain elevator for larger, more powerful tools. When he failed to find the necessary equipment there, he burglarized a house close by but still found nothing useful. Continuing on his way, he burglarized the Town Hall—still nothing. He even burglarized a local church—dead end. He returned to the post office but soon realized he had cut himself at some point, leaving blood across the post office floor.

Concerned about being identified by the DNA, the would-be safe-cracker burned the post office down. Unfortunately, even that wasn't enough to cover his tracks. Police cracked the crime through the footprints he left in the new-fallen snow from one crime scene to the next. Remarkably, there had been a way the burglar could have avoided all this trouble—he had apparently failed to notice the note stuck to the front of the safe revealing the combination.

There's No Place Like Home

A robber in Salisbury, North Carolina, was arrested but quickly escaped custody, eluding police by running through the woods. It quickly turned into a full-out manhunt, with the help of search dogs and a police helicopter, but officers simply could not find the fugitive. The search spread out beyond the woods. Despite the fact that this trick never worked for preschoolers or during a game of peek-a-boo past the age of one, police found the man hiding at his home in his own bed. Apparently it doesn't work for escaped prisoners, either.

Stay Alert!

As gas prices skyrocketed, it's no wonder a man in Muncie, Indiana, attempted to siphon gasoline from a gas station's underground tank. The clever thief installed a 55-gallon tank with a battery-operated pump inside his white van. One night, he attached a hose to that pump and tank and plunged the other end into a gas station's tank under the pavement. He would have been fine if he hadn't fallen asleep. The next morning, the gas station manager saw the van parked on the lot and immediately called police. When officers opened the van, they found the man next to the tank and pump—still sleeping. The authorities charged him with theft and possession of a firearm without a permit.

Man Assaults Police, Steals Squad Car

For Walter J. Brois, it all went downhill in a hurry. In January 2008, two sheriff's deputies in Florida stopped Brois for doing wheelies on his motorcycle. He fled, crashed his bike, then pepper-sprayed the officers. Once apprehended and subdued in the police car, Brois complained of chest pains. The officers let him out, whereupon he stole the squad car, dragged the two officers for approximately 75 feet, then drove the car through three fences before fleeing on foot. Soon after, a local resident reported his truck stolen, and Brois was apprehended three days later.

Come with the Lights and Sirens—I Dare You

A 50-year-old Florida woman was charged with three counts of aggravated assault after chasing paramedics down the street with a rolling pin. A woman called 911 to report chest pains but told the fire department to show up quietly. Instead, they came with lights and sirens, which prompted the woman to grab her rolling pin and go on the attack. No one was injured.

Armed Burglar Becomes Too Relaxed

Evidently it was a hard day at work for burglar Patrick Hazell, who took so many muscle relaxants that he fell asleep on the job. Hazell was worn out after breaking into two cars and two houses in Bonifay, Florida, so he laid down on one homeowner's bed. Finding Hazell asleep in his bed with a pistol in his hand, the resident called 911. Deputies disarmed, awakened, and arrested the intruder.

Socking It to the Car Wash

Twice in late 2007, J. L. Walker was caught on surveillance cameras with socks on his hands burglarizing the Sunshine Car Wash in Clearwater, Florida. Evidently drawn to the establishment, he later dropped off an employment application there. The manager recognized Walker from the video footage and reported him to the police. Officers arrested him at home—his address was on the application—and charged him with burglary and theft.

Woman Shoplifts, Flees with Puppy in Shirt

All ended well for a Chihuahua puppy stolen from a pet store in Plantation, Florida. Surveillance cameras caught a 26-year-old woman stuffing the dog into her shirt and fleeing the store without paying. She soon brought the tiny dog back and turned herself in to police. The woman was taken into custody, but had she remained at large, the outlook was not promising—the $1,600 dog had a tracking microchip.

Digitized Dummy

They say a picture is worth a thousand words. Sometimes it's worth even more. In 2003, when a Wal-Mart in Long Island, New York, discovered that $2,000 worth of digital cameras had been lifted from their store, they went straight to the videotape. There they found images of a male and female suspect but couldn't identify either due to the tape's grainy nature.

Then they spotted something of interest: At one point during the heist, the female accomplice had taken pictures with a demonstration camera. Her subject? Her partner in crime, of course. When the digital information was fed into a printer, out popped a high-quality color image of a balding man with a mustache. The 36-year-old crook was subsequently identified through a tip line and charged with grand larceny. Like Narcissus, the love of his own image brought him down.

Leave Only Footsteps

Sometimes, ambition can impede the job at hand. According to prosecutors, a 23-year-old man filled out a job application while waiting for a pie at a Las Vegas pizza parlor. Then, out of nowhere, the man flashed a gun and demanded that the cashier give him all the money inside her cash drawer. He fled the scene $200 richer. A witness recorded his license plate, and the robber was arrested at home shortly thereafter. But this lucky break wasn't really necessary because he'd jotted down his real name and address on the job application.

Statute of Style Limitations

A security guard working at Neiman Marcus in White Plains, New York, apprehended a young woman for shoplifting. He caught up with the 19-year-old outside of the store and accused her of stealing a pair of $250 jeans. While he waited for police to arrive, the accused railed bitterly against the guard. According to the police report, she was convinced that she was immune from prosecution based on a legal technicality, stating triumphantly, "It's too late. I already left the store!"

Big-Time Loser

Some criminals don't know when to stop. A New Yorker was pulled over for a traffic stop and racked up a bunch of criminal infractions in the process. He was intoxicated; not wearing a seat belt; driving toward oncoming traffic lanes with an open beer container by his side; driving with an expired inspection sticker and with license plates from another car; operating an uninsured vehicle; and transporting his two-year-old daughter without benefit of a car seat or a fastened seat belt.

Indiscriminate Crook

An ex-con pulled a fake handgun on two victims and demanded their cash. The only problem was, they were two uniformed New York City police officers. The officers responded by drawing their real weapons, and the mugger surrendered after a brief, but tense, standoff.

Crime Doesn't Pay

A thief entered a Fairfield, Connecticut, Dunkin' Donuts. Intent on snaring the contents of its cash register, the would-be crook handed the clerk a note stating that he was carrying a gun and a bomb, and he would use both if he didn't receive cash. With that, the robber grabbed the entire machine from the counter and made his getaway. But there was one significant problem: The hapless criminal had made off with an adding machine instead of the cash register.

Dazed and Confused

In McAllen, Texas, police discovered a home with its door bashed in and entered to investigate. They learned that the residence had been burglarized, and they found nearly 15 pounds of marijuana lying on the floor. In a bizarre twist, the home's occupant (who had escaped while the intruders went about their robbery) later returned to talk to deputies. He casually explained that he had been wrapping the marijuana for shipment when the bad guys showed up. He was subsequently charged with felony possession of marijuana.

Shop at Slip 'n' Save!

If you're a scam artist in the 21st century, you're going to have to try a little harder than the Florida woman who tried the old "slip 'n' sue" scam in a convenience store. Surveillance cameras recorded her pouring a bottle of olive oil on the floor before returning to the spot a few minutes later to "fall." She even tried falling a second time, but when authorities watched the video, they saw she was actually falling incorrectly—slips usually take you down bottom first, not face first. Needless to say, the camera didn't lie, and the woman didn't get away with her scam.

Anger Mismanagement at the Golden Arches

Had he asked nicely, McDonald's employees would have gladly just given David Spillers his fries. But when he opened his bag and found them missing, drive-thru rage took over. In January 2008, Spillers plowed his car through the play area and into the

Jacksonville, Florida, store before fleeing the scene. No one was injured, but Spillers left a trail of shattered glass, which enabled police to track him down and arrest him.

Take That, Christmas!

Sometimes one more Christmas decoration is just one too many. A home security camera in Calgary, Alberta, captured footage of a man slashing through a couple's outdoor Christmas decorations with a machete. The huge inflatable Santa, polar bear, and train belonged to a mild-mannered couple. The camera didn't get a very good look at the grinch who also destroyed the sound system playing holiday classics, and the masked bandit responsible wasn't brought to justice.

Hold Up 101

There are beginner books for knitting, marketing, and just about any other hobby or profession. Perhaps there should be one for criminality as well. Two would-be robbers from Palm Beach, Florida, could have certainly used such a primer to learn whom *not* to rob. They walked into a local police station and demanded cash from the receptionist. To complete their tough-guy illusion, they held their hands in their pockets to indicate that they were holding guns. The crooks—finger guns and all—were quickly apprehended.

A Matter of Perspective

An obviously drunk man was driving a van that had already sustained considerable damage. The Georgia police officer that stopped the van discovered several outstanding warrants on the driver. When the drunkard was brought in to the police station, he told the cops he didn't even have change for a phone call. Incredibly, though, the man had won $3 million in a lottery five months previous!

As the man told it, he had so far received an initial payment of $94,000. First he dropped $30,000 in the Atlantic City casinos. Next he spent another $30,000 on the van, which he later rolled because he had drunk copious amounts of expensive

French wine (approximately $10,000 worth). Curious, the cop asked what had happened to the other $24,000. "Oh," the guy replied. "I spent the other $24,000 foolishly."

The Not-So-Great Escape

Some criminals need a really big wall calendar. This was certainly the case with the Rhode Island man who was sentenced to 90 days in jail. Determined to show that no Big House could hold him, he labored on an elaborate escape scheme. He finally put his plan into action—on the 89th day of his sentence. Initially, everything went according to plan; he actually escaped for all of five minutes. After his recapture, he was sentenced to 18 months in prison, which gave him more than enough time to learn how to keep an accurate tally of the passing of days.

It's Not Easy Being Pink

Picking a good hiding place is like shooting dice: Sometimes you roll lucky sevens, and sometimes you crap out.

When police raided the house of a suspected drug dealer, the guy decided to hide inside a large roll of fiberglass insulation to elude the search. A cop spotted him in his pink cave; the officer decided that the distinctive sound of a shotgun being loaded would force him out of hiding.

The cop loaded the gun, and the suspect quickly scrambled out of the insulation. But it wasn't the sound of the shotgun loading that drew him out. Lying in the fiberglass material had irritated his skin, making him itch like mad. The scratching suspect was hauled off to the police station, desperately wishing for some hydrocortisone cream.

Animal Passion

Some criminals are hard cases. Then there are some that are just hard-shelled. After an Indiana man and woman met, the attraction wasn't mutual: He had fallen in love big-time, but the sparks just weren't there for her. She tried to let him down easy, but he didn't want to hear it. He burst out of her home and into the night, but moments later he was back, brandishing . . . a snapping turtle.

Yes, somewhere he had found a snapping turtle, and now he proceeded to chase his former flame around her kitchen with the creature, trying to make the turtle bite her. But the turtle was no fool. It wanted nothing to do with this domestic disturbance and wouldn't cooperate. Finally the woman managed to call the police, who arrived and were able to separate the man from his reptilian weapon.

The man was charged with assault. The turtle was let off with a warning not to engage in any more shell games.

Whipped and Witless

Some criminals consider themselves masters of disguise. Not this guy. A Louisiana man decided that he had devised the perfect way to mask his features while robbing a bank. He would cover his entire head in whipped cream. After all, the topping was easy to apply, quickly wiped off, and covered his face beautifully. Never mind that he resembled a walking marshmallow.

One spring day, the man, looking like a small cloud with feet, strode into a Louisiana bank. The laughter among the employees erupted almost as soon as he entered the building. In fact, by the time he walked up to a teller and demanded money, the bankers could barely stand up from laughing so hard.

And what of the robber's brilliant disguise? Unfortunately, he had neglected to consider the fact that whipped cream needs to stay cold to stay solid. With the combination of warm weather and jittery nerves, the cream was beginning to melt and run down his body. The police, having been summoned by a silent alarm, quickly arrested the gooey criminal.

Return to Sender

It seemed to be the perfect crime: A man had walked into a crowded Florida liquor store and handed the busy clerk a note demanding money. The clerk complied, and in the confusion of the hold-up, the man managed to slip away virtually unnoticed. When police arrived, it seemed they had no evidence and no clues to help them find the robber.

That is, until they looked at the robber's note. In his haste, the criminal had scrawled his stick-up note onto the back of a letter he had received from his probation officer. Neatly printed on the front of the letter was the man's name and home address.

The case quickly went from perfect crime to laughable attempt as the cops cruised to the listed address and nabbed the unthinking crook, who by then probably wished his probation officer had simply used e-mail.

Helping Hands

A robber in England broke into a local supermarket, but the police arrived quickly and apprehended him. Despite the handcuffs, however, the man somehow managed to break free before the cops could bundle him off to the station. The crook had pulled off a near-miraculous escape and should have thanked his lucky stars. But there was still something that didn't feel right to him—he was still wearing the handcuffs. The dim-witted robber went to the nearest police station, hoping that the cops would help him get the handcuffs off. After all, they were the only things marring a perfect escape. Not surprisingly, the cops didn't see it his way and quickly rearrested him.

The Flasher

Kids love those sneakers with the lights in the heels, because every time they put their foot down, the lights flash. Good for kids; bad for crooks.

A Kansas criminal found this out after he robbed a convenience store at night. Fleet of foot, he knew the area well and was confident in his ability to elude the cops that were chasing him. But to the bandit's dismay, every time he darted down another dark alley to elude a cop, more would show up right behind him to continue the pursuit. No matter how much he hopped fences and cut through darkened yards, there was always an officer hot on his trail.

All good things come to an end, and ultimately, so did the crook's stamina. The cops corralled their man, who was amazed that all of his fancy footwork had gone for naught. It was then he learned how the cops had always been able to find him: They had merely followed the flashing lights in the heels of his athletic shoes, which gave them clear pursuit in the dark. Unfortunately for the crook, the next red flashing lights he saw were on the police car he rode in to the station.

Hands Up! This Is a Confession!

Sometimes it just doesn't pay to volunteer—just ask the two crooks who were on trial for armed robbery and assault. In the courtroom, the female victim took the stand, and in a quavering voice, proceeded to tell her story. Then the prosecutor asked her the jackpot question: "Are the two men who committed this horrible crime in the courtroom today?"

Before she could say anything, the two defendants helpfully raised their hands. Even the judge cracked up at the sight of the two crooks aiding their own conviction.

It's Always Something

We've all had one of *those* days—a flat tire, kids late for school, boss yelling for no good reason, grocery bag shreds on the way out of the supermarket. Even criminals have bad days.

An Ohio crook walked into a local café, waved a gun, and demanded money from the proprietors. The waitress obligingly filled a paper bag with cash. So far, so good, right? But as the thief was escaping across the parking lot toward his pick-up truck, the bag ripped open, and the money spilled out onto the concrete. The crook grabbed as much money as he could with his hands. Then, fists stuffed with greenbacks, he got to his pick-up, fished his keys out of his pocket, and thrust them into the door lock.

The key broke off in the lock.

Not wanting to admit defeat, the criminal still tried desperately to open the door. He twisted, turned, jiggled, and rattled the lock, but to no avail. However, his gyrations did accomplish something—he shot himself in the foot with his gun.

Finally realizing that this wasn't his day, the thief gave up and limped from the parking lot. But when he hobbled into a hospital emergency room a few minutes later, the staff notified police, who took him to the station without further mishap.

Her Number Was Up

Forgery is one of those criminal techniques that takes considerable skill. It also helps to have an iota of common sense. For one Oregon woman, the time to try her hand at forgery had come. Standing in a convenience store with a state lottery ticket in her hand, she knew her ticket was a loser—just one number away from winning $20—but she didn't care. She wanted that money. The woman slipped to the back of the store, where she furtively altered the wrong number on the ticket into the winning one with a ballpoint pen.

The alert store clerk immediately spotted the forgery and called the police. The woman was arrested and charged with fraud. But then the arresting officer looked closer at the forged ticket. Squinting, he could just make out the original number underneath the pen mark. When he looked up at the chart of winning lottery numbers, he discovered that the original ticket had, in fact, been a winner—of $5,000.

(Try to) Drive My Car

At least the crook in this story had the right idea—getaway cars are for getaways. Of course, it's ideal if the car can actually be entered before the getaway takes place. Call us crazy, but it seems to work better that way.

At a Honolulu mall, a shoplifter grabbed several expensive ladies' handbags. He sprinted out of the store and headed for his car in the parking lot. Alerted by the store clerk, security guards gave chase.

For a moment, it seemed like the story had all the classic cliffhanger elements: a crime, a chase, and a getaway car ready for action. But when the thief dashed to his car, he stopped short. Seconds later, the guards caught up to him. Baffled, they asked why he had stopped when it seemed as if he was going to beat them to his car. The crook pointed inside the car: Dangling in the ignition were the thief's car keys. He had accidentally locked himself out.

Bear Facts

For someone to shift the blame for their criminal behavior is one thing, but it always works best if the other person or thing happens to be alive. Police are sort of quick to catch on otherwise. A police officer in Florida saw this firsthand when he stopped a van that was driving erratically. As he approached the van, he saw the driver was now sitting in the passenger seat. When the cop asked for the man's license and registration, the man indignantly informed him, "I wasn't driving. The guy in the back was." When the officer looked in the back of the van, all he saw was a huge stuffed teddy bear. However, since the teddy refused to bear all, the man was taken into custody.

The Eyes Have It

Two teenage thieves in Liverpool, England, had been quite successful at their previous scheme: driving around, then suddenly stopping at a random parked car. One would break into the auto while the other drove around the block. By the time he came back, his buddy would be waiting for him with the car radio, CD player, and whatever else they wanted. After successfully fencing the goods, the two hoods would be back on the street, looking for another victim. The case was a difficult one for police to solve, particularly because of the random nature of the crimes. All the cops could do was increase their patrols of the area.

One night two cops were slowly cruising down the street when their squad car's back door opened. In hopped a youth holding a car radio. "Hit it!" he yelled.

Obediently, the cops did; they raced the squad car around the block, and they handcuffed the unwitting thief. Quickly returning to the scene of the crime, the officers caught the hoodlum's accomplice as well. When they inquired why the boy with the radio had jumped into their vehicle, they discovered that he was nearsighted and had forgotten his glasses that evening. He had simply picked out a car that he thought was his friend's and hopped in.

Paper or Plastic?

Disguises can be tricky things—sure, they're great if they work, but every little detail has to be taken into account for that to happen. Especially details like, say, breathing.

An Arkansas thief found this out when he broke into an electronics store. He had forgotten his disguise, so he grabbed the first thing he could find—an opaque plastic bag. But not only did the bag prevent him from seeing where he was going, it also didn't allow in any air. The robber spent several minutes stumbling and tripping through the store, then finally collapsed and crawled away. However, not willing to throw in the towel just yet, the hardy crook was back a few minutes later with yet another plastic-bag disguise. This time, though, he had cut two eyeholes into the bag, which presumably let in some air as well. Fortified by fresh air, the crook managed to grab thousands of dollars worth of electronic equipment.

When the cops reviewed the surveillance footage, they found that in his haste, the thief had neglected to remove the nametag from his clothing—a security guard's uniform from the mall where the store was located. The cops quickly corralled the crook, and took him to a place where he was issued a number to go with his name.

Criminal Quickies

A police department in Ottawa, Canada, had to expel a cadet from its officer training school when they discovered he'd stolen a car to get to class on time.

In Benecia, California, two armed robbers stuck up a credit union only to discover it was one of many "cashless" credit unions in the state. It would've paid to do some research first.

When Long Beach, California, armed robber James Elliot's revolver misfired, he peered down the barrel to check out the problem. He didn't survive.

A mugger robbed a couple visiting a zoo in Blomfield, South Africa. Fleeing the scene, the mugger ran inside a tiger enclosure. The couple's belongings were recovered. The mugger was not.

When Honesty Is the Worst Policy

A clerk at a New Zealand food store was describing to police the man who had just robbed the store at gunpoint. Since the clerk had said that the man wasn't wearing a mask, the cop asked him to describe whatever he remembered to a police sketch artist.

As the clerk worked with the artist, it was clear that he had an amazing eye for detail. He noted specific features of the robber's face—a remarkable feat, especially for someone who had been held at gunpoint.

At last the artist finished and handed the picture to the investigating officer. The officer did an immediate double take. The clerk had described himself! When confronted with the fact, the clerk confessed that it was indeed he who had robbed the store. When the cop asked him why he had so accurately described himself to the sketch artist, the clerk responded: "I was just being honest!"

Wedding Bell Blues

An Alabama female police officer had previously worked prostitution stings, and she had seen a lot of odd things in her time. So she didn't think much of it when, while she was working undercover, a man dressed in a tuxedo pulled up in a car alongside her and propositioned her. The officer played along, and soon the man found himself under arrest. Then the cop discovered why her "john" was dressed so nice: It was his wedding day. He had gotten married just a few hours before and had dashed out from the reception to buy more beer. But once out he apparently decided that booze wasn't enough to quench his thirst.

It's a good bet that her husband's arrest warrant was the one "gift" the bride didn't expect to receive on her wedding day!

No Sale

Sometimes you have to know when to walk away. A man from South Carolina bought substandard cocaine from his dealer. But instead of just feeling burned, he indignantly stormed into a police station. Throwing the bag of drugs disdainfully onto an officer's desk, the man demanded that the police arrest the dealer who had sold him the mediocre coke.

A Developing Crime

Two boys from Louisville, Kentucky, stole a woman's Polaroid camera as she strolled through the park. Alerted by the woman's screams, a police officer gave chase, but the two thieves already had a head start.

Fortunately for the cop, the two boys had stopped and were taking pictures of one another. But much to their chagrin, the pictures that emerged from the Polaroid were all black, which, as many people know, is simply how Polaroid pictures look before they develop. Muttering about broken cameras, the boys continued on their way, occasionally stopping to take a photo. Each time a picture emerged from the camera all black, the thieves discarded it. All the pursuing cop had to do was follow the trail of rapidly developing photographs to find the technology-challenged crooks.

Who Ya Gonna Call?

With all of the informational resources available today, such as the Yellow Pages and the Internet, it's surprising that some people still have trouble finding the right person to contact for a particular task.

This was certainly the case for an Arizona woman who decided that she just couldn't stand her husband anymore. But instead of taking the obvious road and asking for a divorce, she contacted a company called "Guns for Hire" that staged mock gunfights for Wild West theme parks and the like. The woman asked them if they could kill her husband for her.

Now, while advertising is supposedly a key to a successful business, it's unlikely that a hired killer would go about broadcasting his or her services. After all, it tends to make the whole anonymity thing a bit difficult. On the plus side, however, at least the woman's prison sentence gave her a years-long vacation from her husband.

Wisconsin Women Get Revenge

They say they were the victims, but in this case of lover's revenge, four Wisconsin women may have gone a bit too far. Therese Ziemann, who met a Fond du Lac man online through Craigslist, says she fell in love with him and gave him $3,000 before finding out that he was married and had at least two other girlfriends. (And this info came from his wife!)

The four women devised a plan to embarrass the philanderer. They began by luring him to a motel. Hoping for a little action, the man agreed to be bound and blindfolded by Ziemann, who then texted the other women to join her. That's where the plot went awry: Instead of just chatting, Ziemann hit the fella in the face and glued his penis to his stomach with Krazy Glue. The women were charged with varying degrees of felony false imprisonment, and Ziemann had the added charge of 4th degree sexual assault. Who's embarrassed now?

Apologetic Bank Robber Gets Caught

Donteh Smith, a Century College student and father, was very nice when he tried to rob the TCF Bank in St. Paul, Minnesota. He handed the teller a note apologizing and asking for money to feed his kids. Smith was also very helpful—he even wrapped the note around his college ID. The clerk smiled and passed the man his money, which contained a dye pack. When the dye exploded, Smith knew the jig was up. He flagged down a police car responding to the robbery and turned himself in.

Impersonating an Officer...Badly

An Oakland, California, man was arrested in July 2009 when he picked the wrong target. Antonio Fernando Martinez was impersonating a police officer and driving down the road in a Crown Victoria car complete with flashing lights and speakers. Unfortunately for Mr. Martinez, he pulled over a real policeman in an unmarked car. Already on probation for car theft, Martinez had his probation revoked.

Just Change the Oil

Not knowing anything about cars proved to be the downfall of a woman from San Antonio, Texas. After hiding 18 bags of marijuana under her hood, she went in for an oil change. The mechanic discovered the stash and called police who promptly arrested the woman on drug charges. She said she didn't realize they'd have to open the hood in order to change her oil.

Don't Move!

In Detroit, Michigan, two would-be robbers charged in to a store, waving guns in the air. One of them shouted, "Nobody move!" Just then the second robber made a sudden movement, surprising his buddy—who shot him.

Paying with Pot

When a customer at a McDonald's restaurant in Vero Beach, Florida, realized he didn't have enough cash to pay for his order, he offered to trade the clerk some marijuana for the food. The cashier declined the offer and called the police instead, describing the car in question. Police stopped the vehicle soon after and found—surprise, surprise—a baggie of weed. Now he'll be eating his Big Mac in the Big House.

Don't Ask and Certainly Don't Tell

On trial for a convenience store robbery in Oklahoma City, Dennis Newton fired his attorney and decided to represent himself in court. The alleged robber actually was handling the defense pretty well until the store manager took the stand. She identified him as the robber, and Newton blew up, shouting, "You're lying! I should have blown your head off!" Realizing his gaffe, he quickly added, "If I'd been the one who was there." But it was too late—the jury found him guilty within 20 minutes and recommended 30 years in jail.

Call It Multitasking

Apparently no one told Efe Osenwegie of Ontario, Canada, that he should keep his eyes on the road. When he was pulled over for speeding on Highway 401, police discovered he was watching a porn movie on a portable DVD player in the front seat. Osenwegie was charged with speeding and operating a motor vehicle with a television visible to the driver.

Old Enough to Drink

A man walked into the corner store intending to rob it, and he started by asking for all the money in the register. It doesn't sound particularly strenuous, but the effort must have made him thirsty, because he added a bottle of scotch to his order. The clerk refused, saying she didn't think he was over 21, the legal drinking age. The robber swore that he was and pulled out his driver's license to prove it. She looked it over thoroughly and gave the man a bag filled with the cash and the liquor. As soon as he left the store, the clerk called the police with the robber's name and address. He was arrested two hours later.

Two Times—No Charm

John Millison, of Drexel Hill, Pennsylvania, is very loyal to the PNC Bank in Marmora, New Jersey. He was convicted of robbing the bank in August 2003 and served six years in jail for the crime. Just nine months after his release, Millison chose the same bank for a repeat robbery. A surveillance tape showed some similarities in the crimes, and authorities quickly deduced it was the same man. See, although Millison wore pantyhose over his face, and what many criminals don't realize is that face (albeit mashed looking) is still identifiable under nylons.

The Wrong Bar

An 18-year-old Janesville, Wisconsin, man got into trouble at a local bar—but it wasn't for underage drinking. In August 2009 at 11:00 P.M., he burst into Quotes Bar and Grill with a bandana covering his face. Although he didn't actually have a weapon, he had his hand placed in his pants pocket as though he was armed. But the teen picked the wrong night and the wrong bar: The Wisconsin Professional Police Officers Association was in town for their annual golf outing, and Quotes was full of cops from around the state. On the bright side, police responded so quickly to the robbery that the man didn't have time to demand money. He claimed he wasn't planning to rob the bar, but that he sported the mask so no one would recognize him. He was charged with disorderly conduct.

If Only He Could Have Stayed Awake

After a Campbelltown, Australia, man allegedly stole a car, he drove it to a local car wash. Maybe he wanted to wash off any evidence, or perhaps he was hiding out. Heck, maybe the guy just needed a nap. After an hour passed with him sleeping inside the stolen vehicle, the attendant called the police. The sleepy fella was charged with car theft and illegal use of a motor vehicle.

Where Are Those Keys?

When a Texas man robbed a pharmacy of hydrocodone and Xanax, he left his car running for a faster getaway. There was just one problem: He discovered that he had locked the keys inside the car. To add insult to injury (or vice versa in this case), when the man tried to flee the scene on foot, the police, who thought he was armed, shot him in the shoulder. Now he's really going to need those painkillers.

It Doesn't Pay to Lie

Sandy Hamilton of Lincoln, Nebraska, presumably left his house with no criminal intent whatsoever but managed to wander into trouble along the way. The 19-year-old was arrested after he was spotted walking around an area park with no clothes on. When the police stopped him, Hamilton claimed that a man had tried to rob him at gunpoint; when he said he had no money, the robber took his clothes instead. Police eventually concluded that Hamilton took off the clothes because he was hot. Unfortunately, after walking around naked for a while, he forgot where he left his clothes and concocted the story about the robbery. As a result of the lie, Hamilton was charged not only with indecent exposure, but also with suspicion of making a false statement to police.

Look Before You Leap

Jermaine Washington was so focused on his goal—robbing someone in New York City's Riverside Park—that he didn't even register what his victims looked like. If he'd taken a closer look, he would have realized that they were two of New York's finest, in uniform, no less. Washington pulled a fake gun; the officers pulled real guns, and Washington was promptly taken into custody.

Better to Use OnStar

There must be a lesson here. If you drive a stolen car, don't ask police for roadside assistance. Dean Gangl of Richmond, Minnesota, did just that. After the vehicle he stole went into a ditch, he flagged a passerby for help. Unfortunately for Gangl, the motorist passing by just happened to be an off-duty deputy sheriff. The officer recognized the car as one that had been reported stolen in St. Cloud a few hours earlier. Then during the routine arrest for auto theft, the deputy discovered Gangl was also in possession of a white crystal substance—methamphetamine.

Not For Sale

Have you ever gone to a garage sale and thought to yourself, "Oh, I have one of these I could sell"? Well, that happened to a woman in Severn, Maryland—literally. When she attended a yard sale three doors down from her home, she found almost $25,000 worth of stuff that previously had been stolen from her. She immediately called the police.

When they arrived, they arrested David Perticone, who admitted that he had taken the items. His excuse: He needed money to purchase cocaine and heroine with his girlfriend. Oh, and he thought the house was abandoned, and that he may as well clear it out before the stuff was thrown in the dump. See? He was just trying to help!

Overdrawn Check

A Texan named Charles Fuller said he planned to start a record company when he tried to cash a personal check for $360 billion at a Fort Worth Bank. He said his girlfriend's mother had given him the check. She denied it. Guess who police believed?

Click It and Ticket

If you're going to break the law by purse snatching, speeding, and leading the police on a high-speed chase, you may as well go all the way and break one more law by not wearing a seat belt. At least that's how Lawrence Neal of Detroit must have felt after his adventure. He committed the first three crimes, but it was the car seat belt that proved his undoing. During the chase, Neal tried to ditch the car on a front lawn and flee on foot, but got his foot tangled in the seat belt. He was dragged a few hundred feet and broke his leg in the process. Police caught up with him and brought him in on several charges.

Where Do You Find Emma Christ in the Bible?

Emma Kim-Tashis Harrison sometimes goes by her married name: Emma Christ. Or rather, Mrs. Jesus Christ, the name she recently used when attempting to buy a $70,000 car in Jacksonville, Florida. Apparently when you write a check that large, the car dealership feels obligated to run an inquiry on it right away. And surprise, the check and the names on it were bad. The sheriff was called in and charged her with three felonies, including organized fraud. Harrison said her husband, Jesus Christ, would be stopping by the next week to sign papers and pick up the car.

Shoplifting Seagull Chooses Chips

Here's one thief that's actually popular with the locals. His name is Sam—Sam the seagull. No one knows how he got started on his life of crime, but he has been seen (and videotaped) walking into RS McColl Newsagents in Aberdeen, Scotland, and snatching a bag of Doritos with his beak. There's no breaking and entering; the bird simply strolls into the store while the door is open. Maybe it's the proximity of that brand of "crisps," or perhaps it's the look of the bag, but Sam steals the same type of chips each time. He's a savvy little thief, waiting until the coast is clear to make the grab. Then he walks right out and shares his loot with his bird buddies. People are so amazed and entertained by the fowl convict that they have begun to pay the 55 pence for his treat.

Thirsty Thief

Store employees caught a man stealing two bottles of liquor at a store in Boynton Beach, Florida. The workers called the police, and when officers arrived on the scene, the thief was guzzling alcohol out of one of the bottles. His explanation? He said if he had to go to jail anyway, he might as well drink.

Don't Hold the Ketchup

In 2009, a Surprise, Arizona, woman surprised a Kentucky Fried Chicken employee, resulting in her own arrest. Monique Aguet was upset when she didn't get condiments with her order at the KFC drive-through, so she took matters into her own hands. She walked into the store boiling mad and confronted an employee who asked the irate woman to leave. The employee even followed her out to the parking lot. Aguet may not have gotten the food her way, but she did get her way in the fight: She started her car and backed up over the startled employee. Aguet was arrested on suspicion of assault with a deadly weapon and disorderly conduct.

Kitty Porn

A Jensen Beach, Florida, man accused of downloading more than 1,000 pictures of child pornography has an unusual claim—he says his cat did it. Keith R. Griffin said that when he left his computer after downloading some music, the cat leaped onto the computer keyboard. Griffin returned to his computer with unusual images on the screen. Oddly enough, officers on the scene didn't buy his story. He was arrested with bail set at $250,000.

Crime Really Stinks

Some people steal money or jewelry or even electronics. A few criminals have even stolen pedigree dogs. But a skunk? That's what a Sarasota, Florida, couple took from the Animal Crackers Pet Store in 2009. It's bad enough that the pair stole the $400 baby animal, but the real kicker is that the man tried to return the skunk the next day. Suspicious employees called the police, who charged the man with grand theft and the woman with accessory to the crime.

Give Her a Break

Ohio police pulled over 42-year-old Nancy M. Lang's van after they noticed her driving erratically. They suspected that she might be driving under the influence, so they submitted her to the usual sobriety tests. Lang couldn't stand on one leg or walk in a straight line when asked, but she voluntarily performed several jumping jacks and a cartwheel to show she could still drive. Lang was charged with a DUI, driving with an expired registration, and driving with a suspended license. Her excuse? According to police reports, she offered, "Please, give me a break. I'm drunk."

Burglary and Ethics

Two burglars in North Yorkshire, England, committed a crime when they stole a laptop computer owned by 24-year-old Richard Coverdale. All went well until the pair took a look at the computer. They were surprised to see videos and pictures of child abuse and pornography disturbing enough that they decided to turn it over to the police. Coverdale confessed to several counts of sexual offenses and was sentenced to 3½ years in jail. The original perpetrators got a little leniency for their belated honesty: They both got one year of community service.

It's Not a Field Trip

An undercover policeman in Toronto, Canada, was a little surprised when a suspected drug dealer met him for an arranged drug deal—with his five children in tow. That's right: The guy brought along his two teenagers, a 10 year old, an 11 year old, and a toddler while he sold cocaine. After buying the drugs, the detective followed the man back to his car where he found additional cocaine and two knives. The dad was arrested and charged with selling cocaine, possession with the intent to sell, and possession of a weapon. The Children's Aid Society took the kids into protective custody. Apparently, this was not an appropriate way to participate in Bring Your Kids to Work Day.

No Dancing Matter

It all began on Andrew Singh's 2009 wedding day in Preston, Lancashire, England. A coach bus from Manchester was hired to transport three loads of wedding guests to the ceremony. On the way there, a car swerved into the bus causing a small collision. Oddly, the groom decided this was the perfect opportunity to come away with a bit of cash. He and his family sued the motor coach company, claiming that they had suffered injuries such as bruising and whiplash. But the case had no legs: It was soon discovered that Andrew and his father were not actually passengers on the bus during the accident. A judge threw out their claim, and a police investigation was launched. The final straw was a video taken at the wedding reception, showing Andrew, his family, and festive wedding guests dancing, clapping, and cheering—and not looking very injured at all. The groom and his parents were convicted of conspiracy to defraud and perjury, and they were sentenced to a year in jail. Wisely, the bride ditched them all. Who's dancing now?

Con Man Quickies

In November 2006, a jail inmate in Austria climbed into a cardboard box and mailed himself to freedom. Two months later, a prison inmate in neighboring Germany did the same.

In 2008, Reginald Peterson called 911 to lodge a complaint. The charge? Apparently, a Jacksonville, Florida-based Subway sandwich shop employee left the sauce off his spicy Italian sub. In fact, he called 911 twice—first to complain about the lack of sauce and later to complain that police were slow in responding.

Boss Expands Bonus Package
to Include Pick-Me-Ups

Employees always appreciate a bonus for a job well done. It's always nice to have your hard work confirmed and appreciated. Some people like perks on the job, but an auto-body shop in Mankato, Minnesota, was handing out something much different than paychecks.

Jesse Michael Seifert, the owner of Clear Choice Auto Body Repair, was arrested after an employee said that he was handing out methamphetamine for bonuses. Seifert's incentive plan didn't turn out the way he thought it would.

Seifert and his girlfriend, Nancy Jean Loehlein, allegedly handed out a half-gram of meth to each of the shop's six employees.

Agents of the Minnesota River Valley Drug Task Force investigated the shop and also found syringes and a digital scale with traces of the drug.

Seifert had previously been arrested for marijuana possession and drunken driving.

Would-Be Dumb Driver Can't Drive

Many of us who grew up with automatic-transmission cars are thrown for a loop when we encounter a manual transmission. But one would-be car thief in Phoenix, Arizona, got confused when the car she tried to steal was an automatic.

According to police, a man dropped his kids off at a house one evening and left his car running while he went inside. Meanwhile, Jasmine Hernandez hopped into the running car to make a quick getaway. But when the owner heard his car engine revving, he ran outside to find the woman using the levers that work the headlights and windshield wipers, trying to put the car into drive.

Apparently Hernandez didn't realize that many cars have their transmissions located in the center console. The car owner was able to detain her until police arrived.

Woman Joyrides in Police Car

In less than an hour, Kassandra Ellis managed to steal and completely destroy a University of North Dakota police cruiser.

UND Police received reports of a drunk woman wandering around the Hamline Square Apartments, and arrived to the complex in two cruisers. While they were trying to locate the woman, she managed to jump into one of the cars and drive away. UND Police Sergeant Danny Weigel said, "Officers responded to that area, attempted to locate that person, and were unable to do so. A short time later they left the building and noticed that one of the patrol vehicles had been stolen."

Officers say that after stealing the car, Ellis rolled it into a ditch off Highway 2 near the University of Minnesota Crookston campus.

"It's totaled, there's heavy front-end damage and heavy rear-end damage," Sgt. Weigel said.

Ellis was treated for minor injuries.

A Criminal's Profile

There are certain situations where using social media is okay—like when you're bored at home or on the train—and there are other situations in which it isn't. A man from Minneapolis, Minnesota, James Wood, came home one evening to find a wet pair of pants on the floor, a strange Facebook account logged in on his computer, and his home burglarized. Wood noticed credit cards, cash, and other valuables missing from his home, along with a general mess from the broken glass and rain coming in from outside. Wood had been burglarized, and lucky for him, he had everything he needed for justice.

The dimwitted thief left his Facebook account open on Wood's computer, giving Wood the opportunity to express his anger and seek justice. Wood wrote a scathing message with his phone number on the criminal's wall, and—surprisingly—the criminal texted him a few hours later.

Wood told the thief that he had left a few things at his house, and that they should meet so Wood could return the thief's belongings. The next day they met to exchange the left behind goods, but before the thief got his items, he got what he deserved. Upon arriving to the rendezvous point, Wood recognized the criminal from his Facebook photo and immediately called the cops, who arrested the man and charged him with second-degree burglary.

Car Thief Looking to Make Some Fast Cash

A car thief in Albany, New York, made away with a PT Cruiser and the car owner's cell phone in hopes to make some fast cash. The car owner began to call his phone frantically after realizing the fate of his car and his belongings in it. After several tries, the car thief, fifty-five-year-old David Moore, finally answered, ready to make a deal.

Moore knew that the car would—if it wasn't already—be reported to the police as stolen, and that it would only be a matter of time before the law caught up with him. Moore wanted to make a deal. He told the owner of the car that he would return the car in exchange for $20, and that they should meet to do the exchange.

Maybe a little outside of Moore's strategic foresight, the owner of the car had no plans to pay Moore the $20 they had agreed upon. Probably a predictable situation for most, but Moore didn't see what was coming.

The car owner stayed true to his word by meeting Moore, but he didn't bring the money with him. Instead, the owner had Albany's finest escort him into the situation to arrest this short-sighted car thief. It's no joke when people say that crime doesn't pay, especially when it's only $20.

Got to Catch Them All

It seems like thieves have a problem with keeping track of their possessions while stealing from other people. A comic book store in Festus, Missouri, was recently robbed of two Kiss action figures, Pokemon cards, a laptop, $35 in cash, and the store's cash register.

Jason Hughes and Brandon Williams, the store owners, told police that the store was broken in through the back entryway and that the burglar had left behind—in true geek-fandom fashion—a calling card of sorts. They had found a pack of cigarettes and the criminal's phone that rang multiple times—

flashing the criminal's face on the locked screen—as the police investigated the scene.

The cell phone eventually led to the arrest of the criminal and the return of the merchandise to the store. All Pokemon were returned safely into the care of the storeowners.

Google Search: Police Near Me

Horatio Toure was on a bike ride in the Market neighborhood of San Francisco, California, looking for an unlucky victim he could snatch a phone from. He found his target and began to pedal his way toward her location, waiting for the perfect time to cruise by and swipe her phone from her hands.

Unlucky for Toure, the woman was working for her company, testing a real-time GPS tracking application. Toure snatched the phone and fled, but didn't get far before he was caught.

The application was the only application running on the phone, making it awfully easy to see where he went to hide with his smart-phone loot. The police followed the application to Toure, who was logging into his email account on the phone. Toure was booked in jail for suspicion of grand theft and possession of stolen property.

Ice Cold Fugitive

Most of the time, it's a standup thing to raise money for fundraisers, but maybe it isn't too smart to do so on social media when you're a wanted fugitive. A man from Omaha, Nebraska, Jesean Morris, should have known better than to film himself participating in the ALS Ice Bucket Challenge and post it on Facebook, but he didn't.

Wanting to be a part of this philanthropic online sensation, Morris led police right to his door with the evidence found in his ice-bucket video. Police examined the video and determined the area in which Morris had been living under the radar of the law. Police began to hone in on their fugitive's location.

With the help of an informant who knew of Morris' past, police were given the exact address where Morris had been staying. They watched Morris and his house for some time until they made their move as he entered the back of a friend's car that then drove off. The officers pulled the car over and arrested Morris, who was still not thrilled by the prospect of cold cells and showers in the local penitentiary. One thing is obvious, not even ice can cool down the hot trail of evidence found on the social-media profiles of criminals.

Christmas Light Catastrophe

The Montrose Shopping Park in Glendale, California, dealt with a string of unusual thefts during the 2016 Christmas season. Instead of taking merchandise or breaking into any stores, the thieves were making off with thousands of dollars' worth of Christmas lights!

The lights were taken from the trees that line Honolulu Avenue, the main thoroughfare through the shopping center. Dale Dawson, the business administrator for the shopping center, says this is the first time anything like this has happened, and he suspects that some of the thefts occurred in broad daylight, because lights that were on trees in the afternoon were gone by evening. "It's a head-scratcher that someone could be so bold," he said. Dawson thinks the thieves may have sold the stolen lights.

Even though the stolen lights added up to more than $2,000, the shopping center replaced all of them, wanting to continue to provide a festive holiday location for shoppers.

Bad Santa

Santa Claus is supposed to be a symbol of peace and joy. So when someone dressed like Santa robs a bank, it's even more startling than a regular bank heist!

Just before Christmas in 2016, a man dressed in a Santa mask walked into a bank in Memphis, Tennessee, and handed a teller a note demanding money. After the teller turned over some money, the robber fled on foot (not by sleigh!).

But that's not the strangest part of the story. Before robbing the bank, the man had been passing out candy and wishing every-one in the bank Merry Christmas. Surveillance video posted on the Memphis Police Department's Facebook page shows the Kris-Kringle-masked man calmly walking through the bank, offering tellers and customers candy canes. He then walks back to one of the tellers and gives her his demand note.

At least the robber spread some holiday cheer before breaking the law!

The Most Wonderful Time of the Year

It's not unusual for family arguments to break out around holiday time; but it is unusual to use the Christmas tree as a weapon. But that's what one woman in York County, Pennsylvania did during a family scuffle.

Karen Harrelson was at her grandmother's house when another guest in the house, Kayla Still, asked her not to light a cigarette in the home. Harrelson argued with Still, verbally threatening her, and the fight escalated until Harrelson picked up her grandmother's Christmas tree and hurled it at Still. Police were called, and Harrelson was charged with assault.

This wasn't Harrelson's first offense: in 2013 she was arrested for stabbing Gregory Stambaugh when they argued over who should win *American Idol*. But it's likely that she'll now be remembered as the woman who wielded a Christmas tree as a weapon!

They'll Be Home for Christmas?

If you were in prison, your idea of a Christmas miracle would probably be the perfect opportunity for a prison break. For six inmates in the Cocke County jail in Newport, Tennessee, their holiday wishes came true on Christmas Day.

The group broke out of the prison after they removed an old toilet from the wall and crawled out through the hole behind it.

The inmates benefitted from an old plumbing system with a history of repairs, weak spots, and rust, which made tunneling through the concrete wall easier. They also, it would seem, had nothing better to do. "It's the product of them having nothing to do 24 hours a day for seven days a week except think of how to tear things up," said Cocke County Sherriff Armando Fontes. Their freedom was short-lived, however. All six of the escapees were back in prison three days later, just in time for the New Year.

Reindeer Games

A little girl in Australia was heartbroken when her favorite decorations, a pair of light-up reindeer, were stolen from her yard one evening in December 2016. The girl, nine-year-old Chiara Velardi, was interviewed on the news after the incident, which resulted in something unexpected: an apology from the thief.

The robber wrote Velardi a note by hand, which began, "To whoever's Christmas I destroyed. I'm very sorry for taking your Raindeer. I was unaware of my actions due to being drunk." Despite not knowing how to spell "reindeer," the thief seemed to be genuine in his remorse, adding, "I hope this letter makes you feel better. I'm so sorry once again I promise to never do this again. Please feel safe and have a nice Christmas!" He also enclosed $100, so Velardi can buy new decorations.

In the spirit of the Christmas season, the little girl forgave the robber. And next year, maybe he'll try a little harder to avoid Santa's "naughty" list!

The High Point of Christmas

A man thought he was being clever when he found a unique way to transport thousands of dollars' worth of marijuana across state lines: he wrapped the drugs like shiny new Christmas presents!

But unfortunately for Daniel A. Yates, of Eureka, California, he was stopped by state troopers on interstate 80 in Ohio for following the car in front of him too closely. The troopers thought that Yates was acting suspicious, and a drug-sniffing dog alerted them to something in Yates' rented Ford Expedition. In the back, the troopers discovered 10 gift-wrapped boxes, which were found to contain 71 pounds of marijuana, 360 THC pills, and a pound of hash wax oil.

Needless to say, Yates did not have a merry Christmas—he was incarcerated in an Ohio county jail and charged with possession and drug trafficking. A conviction could mean 16 holidays in prison for the crafty Christmas criminal.

Smugglers Might Not Be Getting Smarter

A woman trying to enter the United States was arrested by Customs and Border Protection when her innocent-looking burritos turned out to be hiding nearly a pound of methamphetamine.

Susy Laborin was carrying a bag stuffed with what looked like delicious burritos. But when a drug-sniffing dog alerted handlers to a controlled substance, officers found the meth, according to the reports. The meth burritos were worth about $3,000.

Laborin said that she "was supposed to be paid $500 to transport the drugs via shuttle from Nogales, Arizona, to Tuscon where she would deliver them to an unknown third party."

Local Wants to Stop
Domestic Violence but Can't

What is the definition of irony? Perhaps it's being arrested for domestic violence while wearing a t-shirt that says, "Stop Domestic Violence."

That's what happened to Emily Wilson, from Sangerville, Maine. Wilson, a social studies teacher at Piscataquis Community High School, allegedly fired a gun and grabbed her husband during an argument in their bedroom.

Wilson believed her husband was having an affair, and in her anger, she fired a shot from a .45-caliber handgun into the mattress of the bed.

Wilson was charged with domestic violence, reckless conduct with a dangerous weapon, and domestic violence assault.

And if she doesn't already regret her actions enough, her booking photo clearly shows that she was wearing a shirt that reads "Stop Domestic Violence."

Locals Turn to DIY Dentistry

No one likes going to the dentist. But we still appreciate knowing the person we go to has a license to practice dentistry.

For two years, Elda Graciela Margez de Zamora, of Phoenix, Arizona, ran an unlicensed dental practice out of her apartment. She was charged with two felony counts, including fraudulent schemes and practices.

Zamora turned her apartment into a dentist's office, converting a bed into a dental chair and setting up a waiting room in her living room, complete with chairs and magazines.

Police say she also branched out into orthodontics, and even fitted her apartment manager with braces.

Some neighbors noticed that Zamora had lots of visitors, but didn't think much of it.

"There was just a lot of people going in and out, but I guessed they were friends and family," said one neighbor.

Fortunately, Zamora is not accused of physically harming her "patients," and court documents made available shortly after her arrest make no mention of the quality of her care.

Local Pageant Winner Ditches School

A teenage beauty queen was arrested after she allegedly faked doctor's notes to skip school.

Madison Cox, Miss South Carolina Teen International 2015, was arrested after she used a pad from Parris Family Chiropractic, in Lyman, to write fake doctor's notes explaining her absences from Byrnes High School, the Duncan Police Department told reporters.

Cox was never at the clinic on the dates she used in her notes, and on some of the dates, the clinic was closed, police said.

After she was arrested, the teenager took to Twitter to express her annoyance at her new-found fame.

"Did they really just put me on the news BC I went to jail for a DOCTORS NOTE???" one Tweet read, which was later deleted. But she followed it up with, "It's sad that I'm the only entertainment in y'alls lives," complete with crying and laughing emojis. She added, "I've got to learn to stop being so childish and keep my mouth closed."

Cox was crowned Miss South Carolina Teen International in 2015.

Inebriated Bear Bait

A man in Minot, North Dakota, snuck into a zoo after hours and was bitten by a bear.

David Shepard, and his friend Kody Nelson Kage, were under the influence of alcohol when they climbed the fence surrounding the Roosevelt Park Zoo. Shepard approached the bear enclosure and attempted to lure a bear closer to him by sticking his arm through the bars. The bear, of course, interpreted this as an invitation for a midnight snack.

Fortunately, Shepard was able to escape the jaws of the bear, and was taken to the Trinity Hospital Emergency Trauma Center, where he was treated for his injuries.

Because he was injured, police did not immediately arrest Shepard, but he was eventually charged with criminal trespassing. Considering he still has all his limbs, he got off pretty easy.

The Crime That Wasn't

A man in Texas called police to report that he'd been shot. But it turns out he was just bitten by his dog.

The man had been smoking marijuana on his porch as a thunderstorm passed through the area. Apparently a clap of thunder startled one of his dogs, which then nipped the man in his buttock. The alarmed man then called the police to report the alleged "shooting."

An officer from the Groesbeck Police Department, near Waco, responded and discovered the man had been smoking marijuana and the "shooting" was simply a dog bite.

"During the course of the investigation, it was determined that the 'victim' had been smoking marijuana on the porch as the thunderstorm passed through the area," Groesbeck Police Chief Chris Henson said in a Facebook post. "The loud thunder scared one of the dogs causing it to nip the 'victim' in the left buttock. He believed he'd been shot and subsequently called the police."

Henson posted about the incident on Facebook because there had been rumors of a shooting in the area. The dog bite victim was treated at the scene and released.

Student Turns into Indecent Trash Man

In case you need more examples to prove why taking drugs is a bad idea, here's the story of Benjamin Abele. The University of Georgia student took PCP one night in May 2016, and then proceeded to dive naked into a garbage truck.

A police officer saw Abele running naked toward the truck, which was stopped during its usual route at about 2:30 A.M. Abele then hopped right into the "dirty and foul liquid" in the back of the truck, and the officer found the student curled up in the trash with "a dazed look on his face," according to reports.

When the officer attempted to pull Abele from the trash, the student became combative, burrowing deeper into the trash while punching and kicking the officer. Eventually, Abele was struck with a Taser, which had little effect on the PCP-addled man. It took four police officers to finally subdue Abele.

He was charged with felony obstruction and public indecency and released on bond, jail records show.

Abele, a senior in management information systems, recently won a $10,000 prize during the school's entrepreneurship competition for designing an ecommerce startup for art sales. Hopefully he learned his lesson and will steer clear of PCP and garbage trucks from now on!

Local Saves Money on Gas

Apparently, Daniel C. Guthrie of West Fargo, North Dakota, likes to push his luck. Guthrie is facing charges for driving off from a gas station without paying. But not just once or twice— he went to the same station thirteen times before he was finally arrested. Between April and May of 2016, Guthrie repeatedly visited the Little Duke's station in Fargo. The smallest charge he skipped out on was $11.25, and the largest was $29.01.

He faces thirteen counts of theft. According to City Attorney Erik Johnson, all of the drive-offs were documented by surveillance footage.

Mother and Daughter Like to Party Together

A mother from England, Nicola Austen, went too far when it came to planning her soon to be eighteen-year-old daughter's birthday party. Austen had invited all of her daughter's friends, rented a limo to take them to London, and bought twelve bags of cocaine—weighing 8.65 grams—in order to insure that she, her daughter, and all of the partygoers had a good time.

The day before the party, Austen had a bit of bad luck when police came by to question her, halting her plans for the narcotics ridden party. Austen had several counts on her record already, including methamphetamine possession, which led to the police showing up that day. But the police didn't come alone; they had a drug-sniffing dog with them that picked up on the scent of narcotics.

Austen admitted to possessing cocaine and that it was for her daughter's birthday party. All they wanted was to have a good time, but no fun was had. Austen was made to serve a nine-month suspension and unpaid work time instead of jail time. The judge decided not to jail her because she had a young son who would suffer if Austen were incarcerated.

Mother and Daughter Duo Not the Perfect Team

It's pretty bad when you get your eleven-year-old daughter to shoplift for you, but it's even worse when you ditch her after the cops pick her up. A mother from Troy, Michigan, allegedly convinced two children—one being her eleven-year-old daughter—and an older woman to help her shoplift from an Old Navy store in town. Her daughter was taken in by the police but the mother refused to pick her daughter up from jail that very night.

The forty-nine-year-old woman had convinced her eleven-year-old daughter, a young boy, and a sixty-one-year-old woman to be accomplices in her Old Navy merchandise heist. The four entered the store around 8:00 P.M. and made their way to different departments to begin stuffing merchandise into various bags. Security cameras caught all of the action, while the security guards were only able to catch the eleven-year-old daughter and the sixty-one-year-old woman. The mother of the daughter and the young boy were able to get away before the police arrived.

The eleven-year-old was found with $123.95 worth of stolen baby clothes, jewelry, and women's shirts. She told investigators that her mother had instructed her to steal the items and then meet her back by the car, but she never made it to the parking lot. Instead, she made it to the local police station.

Authorities later called the mother to come and pick her child up, but she—in a paranoid manner—denied that she had been at the store earlier, claiming she knew nothing of the incident. She said she would not be picking up her daughter. The Michigan woman then called a few hours later to admit that she lied about the situation because she was scared, so scared that she still never came to pick up her daughter. An aunt came to pick the child up later that night, and the mother was then wanted for retail fraud, child neglect, and contributing to the delinquency of a minor.

What a Long and Strange Trip It's Been

A Michigan man, Phillip Englem, from Mukegon Charter Township, had a hell of a trip when he was arrested for shooting a gun at a local pizzeria while freaking out on LSD. Not only is that bad, but he was reportedly only wearing a towel and accompanied by his three children.

Engle, who lives next door to Happy's Pizza in Muskegon, is known to cause some trouble about town, but this incident definitely breaks all of his personal records. Wearing just a towel, Engle walked to the pizzeria with a gun in hand and began using the butt of the gun to bang on the glass entryway. The glass shattered and the gun then fell and discharged.

An employee at Happy's Pizza reports that Engle was screaming, "No one will help me! No one will feed my kids!" Then, followed by a deep moment of self-awareness, he muttered, "I'm tripping out."

It might seem funny, but the children were awfully scared. Police were called. They arrived at Engle's house where he sat on the porch with a handgun—supposedly a different gun than before. As ordered, he threw the gun into the front yard and then revealed that he had three more guns—that were loaded—inside the house.

While being interviewed, Engle revealed that he had ingested four hits of LSD earlier that day and that he had been having a rough trip. One of Engle's children told officers that he had also shot the dashboard of his car because it wouldn't stop beeping. They found a spent casing and a bullet hole to confirm the story.

Engle was arraigned on four misdemeanor charges: malicious destruction of property, careless discharge of a firearm, reckless use of a firearm, and possession of a firearm while under the influence.

The Mayor's Bag of Dirty Tricks

The mayor of an upscale town in Southern California resigned after he was caught on tape messing with some dirty business. No, he wasn't caught having an affair or embezzling money or any of that dirty mayor stuff that happens regularly. He was filmed throwing a bag full of dog poo (eww!) onto his neighbor's front porch. Surveillance cameras on the San Marino home caught footage of the town's beloved mayor, Dennis Kneier, finding a bag of dog poo hung on a light-post, picking it up, and then flinging it into the residents' yard. After the homeowners found the footage, they originally didn't know that it was their mayor who was the offender, but authorities quickly identified the mayoral mischief-maker.

Sorry for his inappropriate misuse of refuse, Kneier publicly apologized to the residents, but they had a hard time getting over the offense. The resident claims that the mayor's action was not a mistake but retaliation in response to the resident opposing the mayor's plan for a city dog park. If so, this is the mayor's clear-cut message as to why there should be a dog park in the city.

Kneier's actions garnered national attention and enraged enough people to show up at the next city council meeting to call for Kneier's resignation. Kneier didn't put up a fight. He knew he should have left the bag where he had found it or thrown it away properly. Kneier claimed that he would pay a littering fine and resign from his position as mayor, but he wanted to remain a member of the city council. He vouched that he will not let the city down by throwing anymore dog poo around.

Broken Door, Use Front Entrance

A man trying to break into a Rent-A-Car facility in Brockton, Massachusetts, got stuck for nearly nine hours under the roll-up metal door he was trying to crawl under. The owner of the store came to work in the morning to find Manuel Fernandes' head sticking out from the bottom of the door. Fernandes' looked like he was just about ready to give up on everything. He had been lying there for nine hours, so his seeming lack of ambition or drive makes sense.

The owner called the cops and snapped a few photos—and a video—of the would-be burglar lying there with nowhere to go. He told Fernandes to hold tight until the cops got there. The cops figured it all out and clarified Fernandes' story for him. Fenandes told the cops he got stuck as he was trying to fix the door, but the cops didn't buy it. He was charged with attempted robbery, and his embarrassing situation became very popular amongst the online community.

Eleven-Year-Old Thieves Not Found To Be Funny or Cute

In 2011, dozens of young men in Philadelphia, Pennsylvania, ran into a Sears department store as part of a flash-mob and stole thousands of dollars' worth of merchandise.

Police believed that the group organized their activity through social media, traveling together on public transportation and arriving at the store at the same time.

Police Superintendent Michael Chitwood said that about forty boys between the ages of eleven and nineteen arrived at the store and began to "rob, steal, and pillage."

Officers were able to catch sixteen of the suspects. Most of them were juveniles who were released to the custody of their parents, but a nineteen-year-old was charged with retail theft and corrupting the morals of a minor.

Chitwood said, "When this mob mentality comes to a community and robs a village, there has to be consequences. That's the only way you're going to stop this."

He added, "People have to realize this is not condoned, funny, or cute. It's criminal. Period. If you've got an eleven-year-old involved in this type of mob mentality, what are they going to be doing when they are sixteen?"

You Can't Make a Horse Drink, But You Can Make It Take You Home

Louisiana cowboy Jack Williams was almost charged with a DWI when he was pulled over along Highway 16 near Baton Rouge, but was only given a ticket because he was riding his horse home.

Williams had been towing some horses around with his truck that day when he decided to stop in a local bar for some daiquiris. After putting a few down and visiting the restroom, it was time for him to hit the road home. Williams realized how inebriated he had become from the deceivingly sweet yet strong drinks, stumbling into the parking lot towards his truck and trailer full of horses.

Williams is an upright guy with good values, and he knew he was in no condition to be driving himself and his horses back to the ranch. So he decided to saddle up his favorite horse.

A little worried about the cowboy and his horse, Sugar, on the side of a busy highway, a deputy stopped the two to make sure they were okay, soon realizing Williams had had a little too much to drink. Although they couldn't charge him with a DWI, he was still cited for public intoxication. He later reported that it was the safest option for him to get home because the horse still knew the way when he didn't.

Gone Fishin'

Wisconsin is known for its beer, country roads, and fish fries. What happens when you add the three together? You get an everyday situation with an outlandish explanation. A seventy-six-year-old Wisconsin man, John Przybyla, faced his tenth charge of operating a vehicle while intoxicated because of—as he claimed—the beer battered fish he had eaten earlier that night for dinner.

A deputy had noticed Przybyla's car swerving across the centerline of a county road while patrolling the Wisconsin countryside. The deputy approached the car and immediately smelled alcohol on Przybyla's breath. A field sobriety test was conducted.

Przybyla failed and explained that the reason why he smelled and acted like he was under the influence was because he had eaten beer battered fish for dinner. The deputy laughed and asked how much beer battered fish one would have to eat to act and smell the way Przybyla did that evening. Apparently, Przybyla had eaten so much beer battered fish that his blood alcohol level was nearly .06, which is under the legal limit in

Wisconsin unless you are a repeat offender—which he obviously was.

Even in court, Przybyla continued to claim that he had not had a single beer that evening, and that his blood alcohol level was so high due to the fact that he had eaten beer battered fish. The jurors found his explanation a little fishy and concluded that he was guilty of his tenth offense of operating a vehicle while intoxicated.

Woman Exposes More Than She Wanted To

A woman from Elyria, Ohio, forty-nine-year-old Elizabeth Johnson, thought she might be able to get out of a traffic stop by showing a little skin, but she ended up exposing more than she wanted. What turned out to be a normal traffic stop turned into a peep show and then a drug bust.

Reports say that early that morning, Johnson was pulled over for a standard traffic violation, but the officer became suspicious after he watched her reach into her shirt as if she were stashing something in her bra. The officer ordered Johnson out of the car, but she did not cooperate.

Johnson locked the doors of her car and rolled up her windows, refusing to come out to speak to the officer. She became erratic, yelling at the officer and still not cooperating.

Reports claim that the officer eventually convinced Johnson to come out of her car, but she was no calmer than before. She screamed and screamed, finally saying, "Fine, you want to see what I have," as she lifted up her shirt. Johnson pulled her shirt and her bra up over her head, exposing her breasts to the officer, trying to prove that she wasn't hiding anything. But her plan didn't go as she suspected, because she forgot to secure what she was actually hiding in her bra.

The bra and shirt went up, but her crack pipe fell to the ground. The officer told her to cover herself and immediately picked up the pipe to collect as evidence against Johnson.

Johnson was arrested and charged with possession of cocaine, obstructing official business, and possession of drug paraphernalia.

Firing on All Cylinders

Having your car towed is one of the worst surprises we can encounter in this day and age. There is nothing like coming out of a concert or restaurant in the most trendy part of town—laughing and enjoying your time thoroughly—to find that you had parked your car illegally, and it had been towed away while you were gone. There might not be much you can do once your car is up on the tow-truck but there is one thing you can do to bring it back down to the street.

A forty-year-old Manchester, New Hampshire, man thought of a brilliant way to stop the tow-truck driver from towing his car away. Shad Badeau had illegally parked his car, and by time he came back, the tow-truck driver already had his car on the truck and was ready to drive off. Badeau thought about how to stop this from happening and came up with the perfect idea: light the car on fire so it couldn't be towed.

The car went up in flames fairly quickly, causing the tow-truck driver to drop the car back down and unhitch it. Badeau put out the fire after the car was back on the street, but his plan didn't go down without a hitch. The Manchester Police arrived and charged Badeau with arson. No word has been given whether the car was later towed away or not.

Broadcast Yourself Doing the Dumbest Things

I think we all—or most of us—know better than to associate any illegal activity we might participate in with our social media accounts, but eighteen-year-old Robert Kelley didn't. Kelley was so proud of his reckless driving that he posted the video of his joyride to social media as he lay hospitalized from it.

The video of the Smyrna Beach resident weaving between cars, blowing red lights and stop signs, speeding, and jamming out to some hardcore techno music is almost as good as the latest *The Fast and the Furious* movie except it ends with a crash.

Kelley drove ceaselessly like an idiot, not letting anything—including traffic laws—stand in his way. He crashed into one car, but that didn't stop him. Speeding down the Florida roads, Kelley then ran into three more cars in one accident that left him injured and his car totaled. Kelley had to be cut from his car and then airlifted to the hospital. Others involved in the crash were also injured.

The next day while he was in the hospital, Kelley posted the video of his reckless driving—which he apparently filmed in true idiocy—to YouTube, giving officers a few more offenses on their list of charges. Kelley was ultimately charged with fleeing the scene of an accident with injuries, reckless driving, and driving without a license.

Drug Trafficking in Traffic Court

Sometimes the line between bravery and stupidity is awfully obscure, and you just can't tell if criminals are truly fearless or if they're truly clueless. A Glenshaw, Pennsylvania, man, Christopher Durkin, was in traffic court for one count of driving on a suspended license and ended up leaving that day with a few more counts against him.

Durkin sat patiently through his court hearing, waiting for his punishment. After the conclusion of his hearing, Durkin remained in the courtroom to talk with an unnamed man during the next hearing. The deputy asked Durkin to leave after he noticed Durkin still sitting there and causing somewhat of a disturbance in the courtroom.

Durkin left peacefully and everyone thought that was the end of that, but the unnamed man then confessed that Durkin had just tried to sell him the narcotic Suboxone —a prescription used to help opioid addicts deal with withdrawal symptoms.

Durkin hadn't gotten far when the deputy stopped him and searched him, finding two doses of the prescription drug on him and charging him with intent to distribute and possession of a controlled substance. Although Durkin was dreaming of hitting the open road with a valid license, he was unable to work his way around this traffic jam.

Too Young for a Tattoo

Terry Hardy, a gymnastics coach at Park High School in Cottage Grove, Minnesota, was placed on administrative leave after he tattooed a fifteen-year-old girl.

Hardy tattooed the girl without her parents' permission, and was cited for two counts of assault. At the time, Minnesota law required written authorization from parents before anyone under eighteen could get a tattoo. The law has since changed, requiring that anyone who gets a tattoo be eighteen years of age, regardless of parental permission.

The girl also received a tongue piercing from Hardy. In an interview, she recalled that halfway through the tattoo, Hardy asked "Is your dad going to be mad?"

"In the middle of a tattoo that's kinda a dumb question," she added.

According to the girl, Hardy told her he has a license to perform tattooing, but he doesn't.

And the girl's dad is none too pleased with the conduct of the coach. "Why is he bringing fifteen-year-old girls to his house?" the father said to reporters. "That's just not right behavior." The father reported his daughter's tattoos to the police.

Hardy's school district released a statement that said: "Allegations have been made against Park High School Gymnastics Head Coach Terry Hardy. Upon learning of the allegations, he was placed on paid administrative leave by the district. He is on administrative leave pending further investigation as the head coach of Park High School gymnastics, but has been dismissed as a gymnastics coordinator for District 833s community education program."

Nothing Says South Like Armadillos and Guns

A man in Georgia accidentally shot his mother-in-law as he attempted to kill an armadillo. Authorities say the bullet ricocheted off the animal's hard shell, hit a fence, traveled through the back door of the mother-in-law's home, and hit the recliner where she was sitting, striking her in the back.

Larry McElroy's mother-in-law, Carol Johnson, suffered non-life-threatening injuries, and was able to walk and talk after the shooting. McElroy was about one hundred yards away from the home when he shot the armadillo, which he managed to kill. But perhaps McElroy will be more apt to leave them alone from now on.

Staying at Grandma's House

An eighty-year-old Pennsylvanian woman thought she had been living alone in her two-story house in Bedford, but it turns out she was mistaken. Police on the case claim that a forty-nine-year-old man was secretly living upstairs in the woman's house for weeks before he was found. His little holiday was truncated when the woman's daughter came to visit and heard a suspicious noise coming from upstairs. Upon further investigation, Mark Allen Potts was found hiding away in a closet.

Police found duffel bags, suitcases, personal belongings, and a handgun in the upstairs room where Potts was staying, and then charged him with criminal trespassing. The gun was supposedly Potts' protection from trespassers, but it did no good in protecting him from the investigative mother and daughter team. During the arrest, the woman recognized the trespasser as her former caretaker's boyfriend. It might not be good to find people squatting in your house, but one thing is for sure, it's never a good thing when you get to know your caretaker's boyfriend.

Florida Woman's Name Just a Random String of Words

A group of fraudulent shoppers were charged with buying a spear gun and a digital camera from a local surf shop in Jupiter, Florida. Paying for their merchandise with a declined credit card, the group of three twenty-year-olds were later detained by police for fraud.

The report was later shared on the Florida Woman Twitter account because of the name of the woman who took part in the crime. Cherries Waffles Tennis was charged with her two male friends for fraud and was then made a mockery of because of her seemingly random-string-of-words name.

Cherries Waffles Tennis is now part of the Florida elite who are talked about on the ridiculous-but-true social-media sites of Florida Man and Florida Woman. Although Cherries Waffles Tennis might not be the most absurd story this entertainment site has talked about, she sure has the most absurd name anyone has seen.

Two Tickets to Ride

Some people have a need for speed, and some people just never learn. Royalton, Vermont, resident Seth Tichenor is a person who falls neatly into both categories.

Tichenor was running late for traffic court to resolve a speeding ticket. He started on his way and hit the interstate, but he just couldn't catch up to his schedule. He kept adding a little more pressure to the gas pedal every time he passed someone, eventually making his way up to 112 mph in a 65 mph zone.

He was getting closer and closer and faster and faster every second, cutting his time down to the bone, until he saw those red and blue lights flashing in his rearview mirror.

The interstate patrolman didn't only issue a ticket this time; Tichenor was nearly going double the speed limit! He wasn't charged with a petty moving violation but severe speeding charges and time spent in a jail cell. Tichenor was charged with excessive speed and negligent operation. He was later released to take care of his original speeding ticket.

Pancaking the Waffle House

A Florida woman drove into the side of a Waffle House restaurant as she tried to park her car in the surrounding parking lot. The forty-four-year-old woman—with a pretty good buzz going that evening—was obviously very excited to get breakfast for dinner at this roadside staple. Her hunger, excitement, and inebriation caused her to jump the curb and crash into the outside wall of the restaurant.

She would have been able to get away from the wreckage and flee if it weren't for two nearby sheriff's deputies who had heard the crash. Upon their arrival, they stopped the woman from fleeing the scene and soon realized her condition.

As they told her to exit the vehicle, they noticed her lack of pants and how much difficulty she had standing on her own. The deputies had a pretty good idea of what was going on by that point, but first took her to the hospital to treat the injuries she sustained during her close encounter with the Waffle House. After her condition stabilized, the deputies charged her with a DUI for a blood alcohol level of .295 and property damage for pancaking the Waffle House.

Okay, Now Keep Both Paws on the Wheel!

A woman was recently reprimanded for letting her Yorkshire terrier take the wheel of her Toyota sedan while driving on a road near Llanelli, South Wales. Passengers in passing vehicles were awestruck and astonished to see a feisty terrier with both paws on the wheel of a car moving at 30 mph.

The passing cars snapped photos of the terrier at the wheel and sent it to local officials because of the danger it posed to the public. For one thing, there is no need for dogs to be driving cars, let alone hyperactive terriers with aggression problems.

Using the photos, local authorities were able to track the car's registration and address to investigate the situation further. The owner of the car and motor-skilled dog confessed to letting the dog take the wheel and now promises to keep the dog in the back of the car while driving.

Uprooted and Smashed

This story might take the cake for most totally unaware driver ever. A Chicago-area woman wasn't pulled over for swerving in between lanes, running stop signs, or speeding, but because of a glaring anomaly the officer had spotted: the fifteen-foot tree sticking straight up from the hood of the woman's car.

The fifty-four-year-old, Maryann Christy, was pulled over on January 23, 2016 when the officer spotted her and her tree-stand of a car driving down Spruce Court in the Chicago suburb of Schaumburg. Police had received a report of a vehicle driving with a tree embedded in its grill, but it was hard to believe until it was seen.

Deputy Chief Roman Tarchala pulled Christy over when the strange reports materialized before his eyes. Obviously though, the tree in the woman's car was not the biggest problem. Christy admitted that she had run into the tree, but she couldn't remember exactly where the incident had occurred. Maybe the alcohol had something to do with Christy's forgotten adventure. She was charged with several offenses off the bat, including two counts of DUI, operating an uninsured vehicle, and driving with an obstructed windshield.

After scanning the area to find where the accident had occurred, the Schaumburg Police located the site where the tree had been hit, separated, and inserted into the grill of Christy's car—nearly five miles away from where she had been pulled over. On top of her DUI charges, she was also charged with failure to report property damage and damage to village property. We be-leaf it.

How Much, Really, Is That Deal Worth?

One woman was so desperate for a discounted video game console that she sprayed her fellow shoppers with pepper spray. The incident happened in 2011 at a Walmart in the Porter Ranch area of Los Angeles, California.

Firefighters treated ten people who were exposed to the spray at the scene, and no one required hospitalization.

The woman sprayed the crowd as people were grabbing for Xbox video game consoles. But according to Officer Robert Chavira, a police spokesman, the suspect was actually able to sneak away from the crowd, pay for her purchases, and leave the store before police arrived.

A witness who was looking at a Wii video game, Juan Castro, said he and other customers were hunting for "deals," when the woman began spraying shoppers.

"I don't know if she felt threatened or she felt she had to do that to get what she wanted," Castro told reporters. "I didn't see her personally, but I sure got the scent of the mace. I got it in my throat. It was burning. I saw people around me, they got it really bad," Castro said.

"I tried to get away as quickly as possible because I didn't think it was worth it. No deal's worth that," he said.

A Shopper's Guide to Self-Defense

An armed shopper who pulled out a handgun during a 2012 Black Friday scuffle at South Park Mall in San Antonio, Texas, was within his rights, according to police.

An hour after the store opened for Black Friday shoppers, police were dispatched to the Sears in the mall after receiving a call about a shooting, according to an incident report. When they arrived, they detained Jose Alonzo Salame, thirty-three, who was holding a black 9-mm semi-automatic handgun.

"We don't see this very often," Officer Matthew Porter said, adding that Salame did not break the law by displaying the weapon. "He was within his rights."

Salame had a concealed handgun license, and he told officers that he pulled the gun out to defend himself after he was punched in the face by Alejandro Alex, thirty-five, who had tried to cut in line. Salame said he feared further injury by Alex, so he held the gun as a deterrent.

Some witnesses reportedly had a different story, telling police that Salame had provoked the situation by behaving rudely, and then pulling the handgun out and pointing it at Alex. But San Antonio Police Sgt. Rob Carey said that Salame had actually pointed it at the ground.

A witness at the Sears store, Roger Rivera, said Salame was punched and then pulled a gun. Customers immediately ran, "tumbling over things, dropping boxes," Rivera said.

After the situation was resolved, Salame was released from police custody and he and his family were asked to leave the store. The report states that a manager gave him a store voucher.

"We're glad the incident was resolved peacefully," said Sears spokeswoman Kim Freely. "The safety of our customers and associates are our No. 1 priority."

Chapter 12

Money, Money, Money

It's Probably a Con If...

From shell games to e-mail scams, nearly all con games are played the same way: The "mark" gives up something of value to get a reward that never comes. Here are a few surefire signs that you're being conned.

✳ ✳ ✳ ✳

✳ You trade money for something with questionable value. "The swap" is the heart of most cons. For example, a con artist might pose as a bank examiner, standing outside a bank. He flashes a badge, "inspects" a customer's withdrawn cash, and seizes the bills, claiming they are evidence in an embezzling case. He gives the customer a receipt and sends him or her back into the bank for replacement bills. When the mark goes back in, the con artist escapes.

✳ You pay for future money. This basic recipe is a con staple: You hand over your own money to access much more money. For example, in one scam, an e-mail asks you to put up thousands of dollars to pay administrative fees that will unlock millions of dollars held overseas. Of course, after you wire your money, it disappears.

✳ You're running out of time. Con artists fog a mark's decision making by saying time is limited. The mark doesn't want to miss the opportunity and so throws caution to the wind.

* A stranger trusts you. One way to earn someone's trust is to trust them first. For example, a con man might trust you to hold onto a diamond necklace he "found," if you put up a small fraction of what the necklace is worth (say, $200). A great deal . . . except the necklace is really a $5 knockoff.

* Someone else trusts the stranger. Many con games involve a "shill," a co-conspirator who pretends to be like the mark. Seeing that someone else believes the con artist, the mark follows suit.

* You're misbehaving. When the mark breaks societal rules, like taking found valuables rather than turning them in, he's less likely to go to the police after figuring out the scam.

True Tales of the Counterfeit House

On a hill overlooking the Ohio River in Monroe Township, Adams County, sits a house that isn't what it seems. Its modest size and quiet exterior hide countless architectural and historical secrets— secrets that have earned it the nickname "The Counterfeit House."

✳   ✳   ✳   ✳

IN 1850, OLIVER Ezra Tompkins and his sister, Ann E. Lovejoy, purchased 118 acres and built a rather peculiar house to suit the needs of their successful home-based business. Tompkins and Lovejoy were counterfeiters who specialized in making fake 50-cent coins and $500 bills. They needed a house that could keep their secrets. Although passersby could see smoke escaping from the house's seven chimneys, only two of those chimneys were connected to working fireplaces; the others were fed by ductwork and filled with secret compartments. The front door featured a trick lock and a hidden slot for the exchange of money and products, and the gabled attic window housed a signal light.

The counterfeiting room was a windowless, doorless room in the rear of the house, accessible only through a series of trap-doors. A trapdoor in the floor led to a sizeable tunnel (big enough to fit a horse) that provided an escape route through the bedrock of the surrounding hills to a cliff. Although no records exist to support the imagined use of these features, local historians believe the reports to be true.

Visitors Not Welcome

While Lovejoy was in Cincinnati spending some of her counterfeit money, she was noticed by the police. A Pinkerton agent followed her home and watched as she opened the trick lock on the front door. He waited until she was inside, then followed her in.

Immediately past the door, in a 10-foot by 45-foot hallway, Tompkins was waiting—he beat the agent to death. To this day, bloodstains are still visible on the walls and floor. Tompkins and Lovejoy buried the agent's body in one of the nearby hills, and Tompkins used the hidden tunnel to escape to a friendly riverboat, collapsing the tunnel with explosives as he went. Lovejoy held a mock funeral for Tompkins and inherited his estate, although shortly after the incident she went into debt and moved away.

Keeping Up the Counterfeit House

Although Tompkins never returned to the house, both his ghost and that of the agent are said to haunt it. Tourists have reported seeing a man's shape in the front doorway and have complained of unexplained cold spots and an unfamiliar spooky "presence."

In 1896, a great-great uncle of Jo Lynn Spires, the later long-time owner, purchased the property. It passed to Spires's grand-parents in the 1930s, and Spires and her parents lived in the house with her grandfather. Although privately owned, the house was a tourist attraction, and Spires regularly kept the house clean, repaired, and ready for the stream of visitors that would trickle in each weekend. Unable to keep up with the repairs on the house, however, Spires moved into a trailer on the property in 1986. She continued to welcome approximately 1,000 tourists each summer.

In February 2008, windstorms caused severe damage to the house. One of the false chimneys blew apart, and the roof ripped off. Although Spires was able to prevent damage to the antiques and furnishings within the house, she was not able to prevent future dilapidation. After Spires passed and the house was inherited by her daughter, the attraction was closed, and the house drifted further towards ruin. Perhaps someone will find the money to someday restore—or, in keeping with the history of the house, they'll print some!

Did You Know?

Creative bookkeeping has not gone out of fashion—it's just gone corporate. In a 2005 scandal nicknamed "Coingate" by the Toledo Blade, a rare coin investment fund reported missing two coins worth more than $300,000. Coin dealer and GOP fundraiser Thomas Noe was trusted with investing Ohio taxpayer dollars in coins—$50 million worth—and made most of it disappear, covering his crime with a second set of books. Lacking any secret passageways, Noe was convicted in 2006 and sentenced to 18 years in prison.

The Franklin Syndicate

What does it take to fleece the public? Confidence, a believable lie, and something everybody wants: money. Take a closer look at the first big American pyramid scheme.

✳ ✳ ✳ ✳

I N 1898, A low-wage clerk named William F. Miller was working at a New York brokerage firm, desperately trying to support his family on meager earnings. At only 19 years old,

Miller was tantalizingly close to the world of financial success but lacked the funds to participate. One evening while leading his Bible study class, Miller hit upon the idea of inviting the men in his group to invest $10 each in return for a 10 percent return every week. Though skeptical at first, the men eventually agreed, knowing that their friend had some sort of job on Wall Street.

Robbing Peter to Pay Paul

Although Miller originally conceived his scheme as a means to raise quick money to speculate in the stock market, he quickly realized that it was far easier to simply find new investors and pocket the profits. These investors, convinced by the returns being paid to the current investors, gladly contributed money and most often chose to reinvest their dividends. Miller named his new enterprise "The Franklin Syndicate" and set up a Brooklyn office. Because he promised a 10 percent return every week (520 percent per year), he quickly became known as "520% Miller."

144 Floyd Street

All of the syndicate's advertising featured the visage of Benjamin Franklin and his quotation: "The way to wealth is as plain as the road to the market." Indeed, many were beguiled into believing that the road to wealth lay in Miller's office located in a house at 144 Floyd Street. Miller soon began hiring clerks to accommodate the crush of eager investors.

At the peak of the syndicate's popularity, the house was a beehive of financial activity with 50 clerks working into the night. Miller, sitting at the top of the front porch stoop, received the cash, distributed receipts, and seemed to hardly notice as the money piled up behind him. His clerks opened correspondence, distributed dividends, and mailed advertisements. It was reputed that investors could receive or drop off money in any of the rooms, including the kitchen, parlor, or laundry.

People from as far away as Louisiana and Manitoba, Canada, sent money. The activity and evidence of so much money easily enticed even the delivery men and postal carriers to deposit their cash as well. The press of people eager to hand over their hard-earned wages was so great on one particular Friday that the stoop collapsed. At the end of each day, Miller and his clerks literally waded through knee-high mounds of cash.

Overwhelmed, Miller added Edward Schlessinger as a partner. Schlessinger helped open the Franklin Syndicate's second office in Boston. In return, he took a third of the profits away in a money-filled bag every evening.

Enter the Colonel

When the newspapers, particularly the *Boston Post* and a New York financial paper edited by E. L. Blake, began to cast doubts about the syndicate's legitimacy, Miller's advertising agent introduced him to an attorney named Colonel Robert A. Ammon. Charismatic, compelling, and utterly corrupt, Ammon incorporated the company, did battle with the press, and increasingly became the syndicate's chief behind-the-scenes operator.

When the *Post* alleged that the Franklin Syndicate was a swindle, Ammon and Miller took $50,000 in a bag to the paper's office to prove their liquidity. When a police chief referred to the Franklin Syndicate as a "green goods business" the two men repeated the display, whereupon the police chief apologized.

The Swindler Is Swindled

Miller, Ammon, and Schlessinger knew that the end was near, but only Ammon knew just how close it really was. Having fully duped Miller into believing he was acting in his best interest, Ammon prodded the young man to squeeze every last dollar from the enterprise before it collapsed.

On November 21, 1899, Miller placed $30,500 in a satchel and went to Ammon's office. Ammon advised his client to give him the money to protect it from the investors. Ammon also convinced Miller to surrender securities, bonds, and a certificate of deposit, all of which totaled more than $250,000. On Ammon's advice, Miller opened the Floyd Street office the following day, a Friday and the last best chance to gather additional funds. After work, Miller was pursued by a detective but eluded his pursuer by ducking through a laundry and fleeing to Ammon's office. Upon learning that Miller had been indicted in Kings County for conspiracy to defraud, the lawyer convinced his client to flee to Canada.

Die in Prison or Let Your Family Suffer?

It's unclear whether Miller returned two weeks later because he missed his wife and baby or because Ammon, nervous about scrutiny being cast on his own role in the syndicate, convinced him to come back. What is certain is that, with Ammon acting as his counsel, Miller was sentenced to the maximum ten years in Sing Sing prison. Knowing that Miller was the only man capable of implicating him, Ammon gave his client's family $5 a week and reminded Miller that without the allowance his family would starve. After three years, the District Attorney finally convinced Miller, sick from his years in prison and tempted by the possibility of a pardon, to turn evidence against Ammon.

Just Desserts?

Ammon served five years—the maximum penalty for receiving stolen goods.

Schlessinger fled with $175,000 in cash to Europe where he gambled and lived well until his premature death in 1903.

Miller was released after five years in prison. He moved his family to Long Island where he operated a grocery until his death. When a man named Charles Ponzi was being tried for running a pyramid scheme 20 years later (turn the page for that story), a reporter from the *Boston Post* located Miller and asked him to compare his scheme to Ponzi's. Though there is no record that Ponzi knew of "520% Miller," the reporter concluded that the two men's schemes were remarkably similar.

Ponzi: The Man and The Scam

Do you want to get rich quick? Are you charming and persuasive? Do you lack scruples? Do you have a relaxed attitude toward the law? If so, the Ponzi Scheme may be for you!

* * * *

YES, THERE WAS a real Mr. Ponzi, and here's how his scam works. First, come up with a phony investment—it could be a parcel of (worthless) land that you're sure is going to rise in value in a few months or stock in a (nonexistent) company that you're certain is going to go through the roof soon.

Then recruit a small group of investors, promising to, say, double their money in 90 days. Ninety days later, send these initial investors (or at least some of them) a check for double their investment. They'll be so pleased, they'll tell their friends, relatives, neighbors, and coworkers about this sure-fire way to make a fast buck.

You use the influx of cash from these new investors to pay your initial investors—those who ask for a payout, that is. The beauty part is that most of your initial investors will be so enchanted with those first checks that they'll beg to reinvest their money with you.

Eventually, of course, your new investors will start to wonder why they aren't getting any checks, and/or some government agency or nosy reporter might come snooping around . . . but by then (if you've timed it right) you'll have transferred yourself and your ill-gotten gains out of the country and out of reach of the authorities.

Like related scams that include the Pyramid Scheme and the Stock Bubble, financial frauds like this one have been around for centuries, but only the Ponzi Scheme bears the name of a particular individual—Charles Ponzi.

Mr. Ambition Learns His Trade

As you might imagine—given that he was a legendary con man—Ponzi gave differing accounts of his background, so it's hard to establish facts about his early life. He was likely born Carlos Ponzi in Italy in 1882. He came to America in 1903 and lived the hardscrabble existence of a newly arrived immigrant. While working as a waiter, he slept on the floor of the restaurant because he couldn't afford a place of his own. But the handsome, suave Ponzi was determined to rise in the world—by fair means or foul. The foul means included bank fraud and immigrant smuggling, and Ponzi wound up doing time in jails in both the United States and Canada.

The Check is (Not) in the Mail

While living in Boston in 1919, the newly freed Ponzi more or less stumbled across the scheme that would earn him notoriety. It involved an easily obtained item called an International Postal Reply Coupon. In simple terms, the scam involved using foreign currencies to purchase quantities of a kind of international postal stamp, then redeeming the stamps for U.S. dollars.

This brought a big profit because of the favorable exchange rate of the time, and it actually wasn't illegal. The illegal part was Ponzi's determination to bring ever-growing numbers of investors into the scheme . . . and just keep their money. Until the roof fell in, Ponzi became a celebrity. Before long, people across New England and beyond were withdrawing their life savings and mortgaging their homes to get in on the action.

The end came in the summer of 1920, when a series of investigative reports in a Boston newspaper revealed that the House of Ponzi had no foundations. By that time, he'd taken some 40,000 people for a total of about $15 million. In 21st-century terms, that's roughly $150 million. Ponzi spent a dozen years in prison on mail fraud charges. Upon release, he was deported and continued his scamming ways abroad before dying, penniless, in Brazil in 1948.

Gambling

Most people would cheat Las Vegas blind if they could get away with it—but few bother to try. We asked an expert some questions about the fine art of betting, and its shady side.

Q: How would someone mark cards?

A: You need two things: very sharp eyes and a deck with a repeating pattern on the back—Bicycles, Bees, and Aviators are great, but corporate logo decks are terrible. Ideally, use cards with backs printed in a color matching a fine-tip permanent marker. Then decide what mark will encode each suit and rank, and very carefully mark the cards. Since cards can be upside-down, and since most people fan them so as to view the upper left corners, mark both the upper left and lower right of each card. Wear prescription sunglasses so people can't see you staring at the backs of the cards they're holding.

Q: Does card counting really work in blackjack?

A: Depends how many decks there are, first of all. The more decks are used at once, the less fruit card counting can bear. There are two types of card counting: in your head and mechanically assisted. The casino can't stop you from counting cards in your head; it can only make it more difficult for you. Some states have laws against mechanical assistance, and if you're caught with it, expect a quick blackball from every casino in the region.

Q: Is anyone getting away with counting cards?

A: Have no doubt of that. You'll never hear of them, because they will never be caught. Pigs get fat; hogs get slaughtered, as tax accountants say. They make reasonable money, they go to different places, they lose sometimes, they act like your every-day gambling addict or hobbyist. They don't give the game away by placing suspicious bets; they know how to behave, be friendly, flirt with employees. They stay under the radar. When the numbers are in their favor, they bet more; when numbers aren't good, they bet less, but they don't overdo it.

Q: How do casinos battle card counters?

A: First of all, from the pit boss to the security office, people are watching. When gambling you should consider yourself under surveillance from head to toe. I wouldn't put it past casinos to have night-vision cameras underneath the tables. They have a lot of experience and know what to look for. Free drinks are another tool, because hardly anyone's counting skills improve with alcohol intake. If the boss thinks you're counting, he or she may "flat bet" you—ask you to make the same wager on every hand, which is the opposite of what a counter is trying to do. What they're looking for is your reaction to that request. If you don't follow it, they'll ask you to leave.

Q: What are the best and worst games in terms of payout?

A: Casino poker, blackjack card counting, and video poker generally pay best. Slot machines are terrible, as are live keno and Wheel of Fortune. House payouts tend to range from 85 to 95 percent overall, so on the whole, the game favors the casino. Do you think all those pyramids, sphinxes, complimentary buffets, and neon lights come from the money people have won?

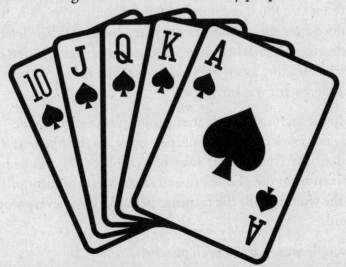

French Assurance

A break-and-enter scene in Calgary, Alberta, had all the signs of a real crime scene—missing electronics and jewelry, a hysterical victim, smashed windows, and dirty footprints leading away from the scene. Everything seemed to add up to a robbery that left the victims with nothing, but as the case unraveled, the victims turned out to be the criminals.

✳ ✳ ✳ ✳

EVERYTHING AT THE scene started to make sense as Constable Charanjit Meharu arrived and began interviewing one of the victims. The victim's phone rang, and she asked the constable to excuse her while she answered a call from her father.

The victim spoke Quebecois French to her father, explaining everything that had happened, but what she was telling her father was not what she had told the constable. Const. Meharu spoke seven different languages, and that day, his French lessons were paying off.

The victim—not knowing the constable was a polyglot and well versed in French—began explaining her and her boyfriend's plot to make a fraud insurance claim for some extra cash. She explained over the phone how they had hid all of their jewelry and electronics, smashed their windows, and even planted fake footprints leading away from the home. She reassured him that law enforcement was buying it.

Slowly, the victims' machinations unraveled, revealing the couple not as victims but as perpetrators. As the phone call ended, Const. Meharu put away his ten pages of notes he had just taken from the phone call and said, "Merci beaucoup," startling the woman with the fact that he understood every word she said.

The couple was charged with mischief.

Con Artists, Fake Stocks, and Federal Agents: ABSCAM

What do a convicted con artist, fake Arab sheikhs, U.S. politicians, and the FBI have in common? They were all a part of a sting operation called ABSCAM in the late 1970s and 1980s.

✳ ✳ ✳ ✳

An Elaborate Setup

IN JULY 1978, the FBI set up an undercover operation in order to catch thieves dealing in stolen art. To help with the logistics, they brought a convicted con artist and swindler, Melvin Weinberg, and his girlfriend, Evelyn Knight, in on the plan. In exchange for their help, Weinberg and Knight—who were both facing prison sentences—were let out on probation. Weinberg helped the FBI create a fake company called Abdul Enterprises – the "AB" in ABSCAM. To make it look legitimate, Weinberg told the FBI to set up a million-dollar account under the name of Abdul Enterprises at the Chase Manhattan Bank.

Next, FBI employees posed as fictional Arab sheikhs named Kambir Abdul Rahman and Yassir Habib. The "sheikhs" were said to have millions of dollars to invest in the United States and were looking for profitable oil companies and rare art.

Weinberg suggested art thieves who might be willing to do business with Abdul Enterprises, and within a few weeks, the FBI had recovered two paintings worth $1 million. The operation then switched focus to criminals who were dealing in fake stocks and bonds: thanks to the FBI's efforts, they halted the sale of approximately $600 million worth of fraudulent securities.

Political Targets

At this point, ABSCAM began taking aim at political corruption. A forger who was under investigation approached the fake sheikhs with the idea that they invest in New Jersey casinos, saying they could obtain licensing for the "right price." So for the first time in American history, the FBI began videotaping government officials as they were approached by the sheikhs' representatives and offered money in exchange for building permits, licenses, and "private immigration bills": proposed laws that would allow foreigners working for Abdul Enterprises into the country.

Thirty-one political officials were targeted during ABSCAM, and when it was all over, one senator and six congressmen were found guilty of bribery and conspiracy. Also convicted were three Philadelphia city councilmen, and Angelo Errichetti, the mayor of Camden, New Jersey.

Errichetti was the first to be caught during the ABSCAM sting, when he accepted money in exchange for a casino license for Abdul Enterprises. Errichetti then introduced the "sheikhs" to Senator Harrison Williams and congressmen Michael Myers, Raymond Lederer, and Frank Thompson. All would later be convicted.

Entrapment?

In February 1980, ABSCAM was made public. Some had an ethical issue with the secretive videotaping employed by the FBI, as well as the fact that Weinberg was paid $150,000 and avoided prison thanks to his part.

Many felt that the FBI was overzealous in its tactics and ABSCAM amounted to nothing short of entrapment. Still, all of the convictions due to ABSCAM were upheld in court.

Following the controversy, however, Attorney General Benjamin Civiletti issued "The Attorney General's Guidelines for FBI Undercover Operations," which formalized procedures to be used during sting operations, in an effort to avoid future debates about FBI tactics.

Coupon Schemes Similar to Drug Cartels

These criminals took "extreme couponing" very seriously. A little too seriously.

✳ ✳ ✳ ✳

PHOENIX POLICE ARRESTED forty-year-old Robin Ramirez, forty-two-year-old Amiko Fountain, and fifty-four-year-old Marilyn Johnson after the trio took extreme couponing too far. The three were running a counterfeit coupon scheme, the Associated Press reported. Police recovered $40 million dollars of fake coupons from the women's homes, according to a local TV station.

Yahoo Finance reported that up to forty major manufacturers, including Proctor & Gamble, were affected by the illegal operation. The manufacturers joined the Phoenix Police Department and the FBI to investigate and ultimately stop the illegal ring.

The fake coupons were allegedly sold through sites that eventually helped coordinate the investigation.

Police also seized $2 million in assets from the three homes, which included vehicles worth $240,000, 22 guns, and a 40-foot speed boat, according to reports. Sgt. David Lake of the Phoenix Police Department described the women's lavish lifestyles as the "equivalent of drug cartel-type stuff," according to reports.

The three suspects were charged with illegal control of an enterprise, forgery, counterfeiting, fraudulent schemes, and artifices and trafficking in stolen property.

A Charlatan of Epic Proportions

"Greed is good," said Gordon Gekko in Oliver Stone's 1987 hit movie Wall Street. *Greed resides at the center of the financial industry. For the powerful real-life stockbroker Bernie Madoff, greed knew no boundaries.*

Madoff, a well-respected broker who became chairman of the Nasdaq in 1990 and served in the position in 1991 and 1993, orchestrated the largest Ponzi scheme in history: an estimated $65 billion fraud. He conned thousands of investors and would later pled guilty to 11 felony charges—including money laundering, perjury, and fraud—and earn a prison sentence of 150 years.

Bernie Madoff was, according to the New York Times, *a "charlatan of epic proportions, a greedy manipulator so hungry to accumulate wealth that he did not care whom he hurt to get what he wanted."*

✳   ✳   ✳   ✳

Small Beginnings

MADOFF FOUNDED Bernard L. Madoff Securities in 1960. He started his firm with a paltry $5,000 he saved from lifeguarding. His wife's father allowed Madoff to work out of his Manhattan accounting firm. A market maker, Madoff dealt in over-the-counter penny stocks. He was also, Madoff would later recall in an interview, a "little Jewish guy from Brooklyn" who felt like he was on the outside looking in.

Madoff steadily grew his business—and reputation—as he embraced new trading technology and crafted friendships with industry regulators. While traders described him as obsessive, paranoid, secretive, and manipulative, Madoff earned the trust of employees, investors, and Wall Street. At the same time, Madoff was overseeing a massive con involving fraudulent transactions on an epic scale.

He later claimed that a handful of powerful clients known as the "Big Four" forced him into a Ponzi scheme beginning in the early 1990s.

A Confession

In the late 1990s, Frank Casey, an investment firm executive, asked a colleague to look into Madoff's trades. The colleague, Harry Markopolos, quickly became suspicious and suspected a Ponzi scheme. Casey told PBS FRONTLINE that Markopolos compared Madoff's returns to a baseball player "hitting .925 straight for 10 years in a row." Markopolos sent an eight-page memo to the SEC, but the agency did not follow up with an investigation. He wrote additional memos to the SEC, and in January 2006, the SEC launched an investigation. Finally, at the height of the 2008 financial crisis, Madoff's jig was up.

On December 10, 2008, Madoff allegedly confessed to his sons that his business was a massive Ponzi scheme. The next day, authorities arrested Madoff on one count of securities fraud, and he was released on $10 million bail. In June 2009, a federal judge sentenced Madoff to 150 years in prison. He did not appeal the sentence.

Taking Responsibility?

The Department of Justice announced in December 2017 that it had begun to return money to Madoff's many thousands of victims, such as thousands of respected individuals and institutions. The initial distribution included $772.5 million, a fraction of the more than $4 billion in assets recovered for the victims. An additional $504 million was announced in April 2018.

In a 2011 interview with Barbara Walters, Madoff said he has no fear because, "I'm no longer in control of my own life." He told Walters that he took full responsibility for his crimes, but he said, "Nobody put a gun to my head. I never planned to do anything wrong. Things just got out of hand."

Even prison hasn't keep Madoff's profit-motivating instincts at bay, however. At one point, the aging criminal reportedly purchased hot chocolate packets from the commissary and sold them for a profit in the prison yard.

Just Don't Stick Those Bills in the Washing Machine

If only the black art of money laundering were as simple as putting your cash through a spin cycle or two.

✳ ✳ ✳ ✳

Hiding the Loot

YOU KNOCK OVER an armored car and suddenly your mattress is overflowing with cash. But if you enjoy your ill-gotten gains by treating yourself to something big—a solid-gold yacht, say—the Feds will want to know where the money came from. And if you can't point to a legitimate source, it's off to the big house with you.

When faced with this dilemma, criminals turn to money laundering, the process of making "dirty" money look "clean"—in other words, making it appear that the money is legitimate income. For relatively small amounts of dirty cash, the go-to trick is to set up a front: a business that can record the cash as profit. For example, Al Capone owned laundromats all over Chicago so that he could disguise the income from his illegal liquor business as laundry profits (how appropriate). There wasn't any way to know how much money people really spent at the laundromat, so all the profit appeared to be legitimate.

On a larger scale—like when drug traffickers take in millions—the laundromat scheme doesn't really work, and things get more complicated. But no matter how elaborate the scheme, you can usually break it down into three basic steps: placement, layering, and integration.

Step One: Placement

In the placement stage, the goal is to get the hard cash into the financial system, which usually means depositing it into accounts of some kind. In the U.S., banks report any transaction greater than $10,000 to the authorities, so one placement strategy is to deposit money gradually, in smaller increments, across multiple bank accounts. Another option is to use a bank in a country with lax financial monitoring laws.

Step Two: Layering

The goal of the next stage—layering—is to shift the money through the financial system in such a complicated way that nobody can follow a paper trail back to the crime. In other words, the criminals are trying to disguise the fact that they are the ones who put the money into the financial system in the first place. Every time launderers move money between accounts, convert it into a different currency, or buy or sell anything—particularly in a country with lax laws—the transaction adds a layer of confusion to the trail.

Step Three: Integration

Finally, in the integration stage, the criminals get the money back by some means that looks legitimate. For example, they might arrange to have an offshore company hire them as generously paid consultants; this way, the money that they earned from their crimes enters their bank accounts as legitimate personal income.

Money laundering is big business, and it's a key foundation for drug trafficking, embezzling, and even terrorism. Many nations have enacted stricter laws and boosted enforcement in order to crack down on money laundering, but they can't put a stop to it unless everyone is vigilant. As long as there are countries with lax financial regulations that trade in the world economy, criminals will have a way to launder their funds. So, if you've been scrubbing your ill-gotten cash in the sink and hanging it on the line to dry, stop it now. You're doing it wrong.

The Fall of the Crooked E: Who Killed Enron?

For a company that seemed to have everything going its way, the end sure came quickly.

✳ ✳ ✳ ✳

IN THE 1990S, the U.S. Congress passed legislation deregulating the sale of electricity, as it had done for natural gas some years earlier. The result made it possible for energy trading companies, including Enron, to thrive. In effect, the law allowed a highly profitable market to develop between energy producers and those local governments that buy electricity—a system kept in place because of aggressive lobbying by Enron and other such firms. By the turn of the 21st century, Enron stock was trading for $80 to $90 a share.

Trouble in the Waters

All was not smooth sailing, however, for the energy giant. Its new broadband communications trading division was running into difficulties, its power project in India was behind schedule and over budget, and its role in the California power crisis of 2000–2001 was being scrutinized.

Then, on August 14, 2001, CEO Jeffrey Skilling announced he was resigning after only six months in his position. He also sold off 450,000 shares of Enron stock for $33 million.

Ken Lay, the chairman at Enron, affirmed that there was "absolutely no accounting issue, no trading issue, no reserve issue, no previously unknown problem" that prompted Skilling's departure. He further asserted that there would be "no change or outlook in the performance of the company going forward." Though he did admit that falling stock prices were a factor behind Skilling's departure, Lay decided he would assume the CEO position.

Don't Worry, Everything's Under Control

Enron's financial statements were so confusing because of the company's tax strategies and position-hedging, as well as its use of "related-party transactions," that Enron's leadership assumed no one would be able to analyze its finances. A particularly troubling aspect was that several of the "related-party" entities were, or had been, controlled by Enron CFO Andrew Fastow (who may or may not have realized that he was being groomed as a scapegoat).

Sound confusing? Good, then the plan worked. And if all this could confuse government regulatory agencies, think of how investors must have felt. Stock prices slowly started sliding from their highs at the beginning of 2001, but as the year went on, the tumble picked up speed. On October 22, for instance, the share price of Enron dropped $5.40 in one day to $20.65. After Enron officials started talking about such things as "share settled costless collar arrangements" and "derivative instruments which eliminated the contingent nature of restricted forward contracts," the Securities and Exchange Commission (SEC) had a quote of its own: "There is the appearance that you are hiding something."

Things Fall Apart

The landslide had begun. On October 24, Lay removed Fastow as CFO. Stock was trading at $16.41. On October 27, Enron began buying back all of its shares (valued around $3.3 billion). It financed this purchase by emptying its lines of credit at several banks.

On October 30, in response to concerns that Enron might try a further $1–2 billion refinancing due to having insufficient cash on hand, Enron's credit rating was dropped to near junk-bond status. Enron did secure an additional billion dollars, but it had to sell its valuable natural gas pipeline to do so.

Enron desperately needed either new investment or an outright buyout. On the night of November 7, Houston-based energy trader Dynegy voted to acquire Enron at a fire-sale price of $8 billion in stock. It wasn't enough.

The sale lagged, and Standard & Poor's index determined that if it didn't go through, Enron's bonds would be rated as junk. The word was out that Lay and other officials had sold off hundreds of millions of dollars of their own stock before the crisis and that Lay stood to receive $60 million dollars if the Dynegy sale went through. But the last, worst straw was that Enron employees saw their retirement accounts—largely based on Enron stock—wiped out.

By November 7, after the company announced that all the money it had borrowed (about $5 billion) had been exhausted in 50 days, Enron stock was down to $7.00 a share. The SEC filed civil fraud complaints against Arthur Andersen, Enron's auditor. And on November 28, the sky fell in: Dynegy backed out of the deal to acquire Enron, and Enron's stock hit junk-bond status. On December 2, 2001, Enron sought Chapter 11 protection as it filed for the biggest bankruptcy in U.S. history. Around 4,000 employees lost their jobs.

So Who Killed Enron?

* There was blame aplenty.

* Ken Lay and Jeffrey Skilling were indicted for securities and wire fraud. Lay was convicted on 6 of 6 counts, and Skilling on 19 of 28. Skilling was sentenced to 24 years and 4 months in prison. Lay avoided prison time by dying of a heart attack before he was sentenced.

* Arthur Andersen accountants signed off on this fraud. Why? They were getting a million dollars a week for their accounting services. The firm was convicted of obstruction of justice for shredding documents related to the Enron audit and surrendered its licenses and right to practice. From a high of more than 100,000 em-ployees, Arthur Andersen is now down to around 200. Most of them are handling lawsuits.

* Investors bought stock in a company they didn't understand for the greedy promise of quick money.

* Stock ratings companies said it was a great investment, even though they had no idea what shape Enron was in.

* Investment bankers who knew that Enron was shaky bought in for a shot at quick and easy profits. They, too, are being sued by investors.

* And we can't forget the Enron employees, some of whom knew that something was fishy yet stayed silent because they were getting paid. There were a few whistle-blowers, but the ones who knew and said nothing earned their places at the unemployment office.

✳ Chapter 13

One for the History Books

Murder in The Vatican

As head of the Catholic Church, they serve as the Vicar of Christ and are among the world's most respected leaders. Yet over the centuries, this hasn't always been the case for the popes of Rome. Dozens have met untimely fates at the hands of pagan oppressors, rivals to their papal throne, scheming cardinals, plotting aristocrats, and outraged husbands.

✳　✳　✳　✳

Early Days Under the Empire

MANY OF THE first 25 popes are believed to have been martyred by the Romans. Pontian (230–235) is the first pope recorded by history as having been murdered for his Christian beliefs. Arrested under the orders of Emperor Maximinus Thrax, Pontian was exiled to Sardinia—then known as the "island of death"—where he is believed to have died from starvation and exposure. Sixtus II (257–258) was another early martyr, killed in the persecutions of Emperor Valerian, who condemned all Christian priests, bishops, and deacons to death. Sixtus was arrested by Roman soldiers while giving a sermon and may have been beheaded on the spot. Martin I (649–653) began his papacy on bad terms with Emperor Constans II, who refused to recognize his election. Martin made matters worse by condemning the doctrines of the Monothelite heretics, whose tenets were followed by many powerful Roman officials, including Constans II. Ordered to Constantinople, Martin I was sentenced to death and exiled to the Crimea, where he died of starvation.

The Middle Ages and Beyond

The martyrdom of popes passed into history with the fall of the Roman Empire, but the ascendancy of the Catholic Church was accompanied by endless papal intrigues. From the 9th to the 20th centuries—when popes served not only as head of the church but as rulers of the Papal State, a substantial kingdom in central Italy—rumors abounded that many had been murdered.

Most documented murders occurred during the Middle Ages, particularly between 867 and 964, the so-called Iron Age of the Papacy, when the politically powerful families of Rome had pontiffs elected, deposed, and killed to advance their own ambitions. Seven popes died by violence during this period.

The first to receive this dubious honor was Pope John VIII (872–882), who was so concerned about plots swirling around him that he had several powerful bishops and cardinals excommunicated. Unknown conspirators convinced a relative to poison his drink. When the poison failed to kill him, he was clubbed to death by his own aides. According to some accounts, however, Pope John was actually Pope Joan—a female pope who was erased from the historical record when her true identity was uncovered. Though some historians believe Pope Joan is a myth, others point to an obscure Church ritual that began in the late 9th century, in which a papal candidate sat in an elevated chair with his genitals exposed, prompting passing cardinals to exclaim in Latin, "He has testicles, and they hang well!" Lacking a similar endowment, Pope Joan may have paid with her life.

The papal carnage continued over the next few hundred years. Adrian III (884–885) was allegedly poisoned. Leo V (903) was allegedly strangled. John X (914–928) may have been smothered with a pillow. Both Stephen VII (928–931) and Stephen VIII (939–942) met similar untimely ends due to various palace intrigues.

John XII (955–964) was only 18 years old when elected pope. A notorious womanizer, he turned the papal palace into something resembling a brothel. He either suffered a heart attack while with a mistress or was murdered by a cuckolded husband. Pope Benedict V (964–966) raped a young girl and fled to Constantinople with the papal treasury, only to return to Rome when his coffers were empty. He was killed by a jealous husband, his corpse bearing a hundred dagger wounds as it was dragged through the streets.

Benedict VI (973–974) and John XIV (983–984) had strangely parallel fates. Intriguers rebelled against Benedict VI after the death of his protector, Emperor Otto the Great. Benedict VI was strangled by a priest on the orders of Crescentius, brother of the late Pope John XIII. Boniface Franco, a deacon who supported Crescentius, became Pope Boniface VII but fled Rome due to the people's outrage over Benedict's murder, becoming Antipope Boniface. John XIV was chosen as a replacement by Emperor Otto II without consultation of the Church. When Otto suddenly died, another new pope was left without allies. Antipope Boniface returned and had John XIV thrown in prison, where he starved to death.

Popes Gregory V (996–999), Sergius IV (1009–1012), Clement II (1046–1047), and Damasus II (1048) were all allegedly poisoned or met otherwise convenient ends. Boniface VIII (1294–1303) died from beatings by his French captors while held prisoner in Anagni. Benedict XI (1304–1305) may have also been poisoned.

Much Milder Modern Days

Officially, no pope has been murdered in the modern age, though rumors held that Pope Clement XIV was poisoned in

1771, following his disbandment of the Jesuits. Two hundred years passed before such allegations arose again in 1978 with the sudden death of Pope John Paul I, who had reportedly planned such reforms as ordaining women as priests and welcoming gays into the church. In both cases, coroners and investigators found no evidence of foul play. John Paul's successor, John Paul II, was nearly murdered in St. Peter's Square in 1981 by Mehmet Ali Agca, a Turkish gunman who was part of a conspiracy involving the KGB and Bulgarian secret police.

Cold Case: The Cadaver Synod

The Cadaver Synod—or Cadaver Trial—is considered the lowest point in papal history. How low? Try six feet under.

✳ ✳ ✳ ✳

V as in Vengeance (and Stephen VII)

THE MASTERMIND BEHIND what became known as the Cadaver Synod was Italy's King Lambert, who sought revenge for Pope Formosus's actions against his father, Guido, the duke of Spoleto. Previously, Formosus's predecessor Pope Stephen V had crowned Guido and Lambert co-Holy Roman Emperors in A.D. 892. But Formosus favored the German king Arnulf, and he convinced Arnulf to invade Italy and usurp the crown. Guido died before he was forcibly removed from office, and in February 896, Arnulf was crowned emperor.

Physical paralysis ultimately cut short Arnulf's reign; he returned to Germany, leaving Lambert to take over and exact his revenge on Formosus. The pope died before Lambert got a chance to strike, but that didn't stop Lambert: He ordered Formosus's successor Pope Stephen VI—himself a Spoletian sympathizer—to dig up the pope's body and put it on trial for perjury, violating church canons, and coveting the papacy.

(Technially, Formosus was immediately succeeded by Boniface VI, whose papacy lasted all of two weeks before he either died of gout or was murdered to make way for Stephen VI, and his election was later ruled invalid.)

A Trial of the Grotesque

No transcript of the Cadaver Synod exists, but historians agree as to how it probably went down: In January 897, the rotting corpse (it was only nine months after Formosus's death) was exhumed, carried into the courtroom, dressed in elaborate papal vestments, and propped in a chair, behind which cowered a teenage deacon, who was in charge of speaking for the dead pope. Stephen ranted and screamed at Formosus's body, who, of course, was found guilty of all charges.

As punishment, Stephen ordered that all of Formosus's papal ordinances be overturned, that the three fingers on his right hand used to give papal blessings be hacked off, and that his body be stripped of its papal vestments, dressed in peasant's clothes, and reburied in a common grave. After the sentence was carried out, the pope's body was dug up yet again and tossed in the Tiber River, from which a monk retrieved it and buried it. Again.

The Cadaver Synod caused a public rebellion and within a few months, Stephen was deposed, stripped of his vestments, and sent to prison where he was strangled to death in 897.

Return of the Synod

In 897, Pope Theodore II held a synod to annul the Cadaver Synod—one his few actions as pope, since his pontificate lasted only 20 days. Formosus's body was dug up once more and carried back to St. Peter's Basilica, where it was redressed in papal vestments and returned to its tomb. The next pope, John IX, held another synod to confirm Theodore II's decision. He also declared it illegal to put a dead body on trial.

But John's successor, Pope Sergio III, who participated in the Cadaver Synod and was a "violent hater of Formosus," held his own synod to reverse the decisions made by the previous two popes. Maybe because it was finally illegal to dig up and put dead bodies on trial, he simply had an epitaph made for Stephen's tomb that heaped insults on Formosus. Sergio's ruling was never overturned, however; it was just ignored.

* Formosus means "good-looking" in Latin.

* From A.D. 896 to 904, there were nine popes—the same number of popes throughout the entire 20th century.

* Pope Sergio III was quite the controversial figure. His papacy has been called "The Rule of the Harlots."

* Though Formosus has been unanimously vindicated and cleared of all charges, there has never been a Pope Formosus II. Cardinal Pietro Barbo apparently thought about taking the name in 1464 but was talked out of it. He took the name of Paul II instead.

Dracula Impales in Comparison

The origins of Dracula, the blood-sucking vampire of Bram Stoker's novel (and countless movies, comics, and costumes) are commonly traced to a 15th-century Romanian noble, whose brutal and bloody exploits made him both a national folk hero and an object of horror.

✳ ✳ ✳ ✳

The Real Dracula

VLAD III TEPES (1431–1476) was born into the ruling family of Wallachia, a principality precariously balanced between the Ottoman (Turkish and Muslim) and Holy Roman (Germanic and Catholic) empires. His father, Vlad II, became known as Dracul ("Dragon") due to his initiation into the knightly Order of the Dragon. As a part of Dracul's attempt to maintain Wallachia's independence, he sent Vlad III and his brother Radu as hostages to the Turks. When Dracul was assassinated in 1447 and a rival branch of the family took the throne, the Turks helped Vlad III to recapture it briefly as a puppet ruler before he was driven into exile in Muldovia. Eight years later (1456), Vlad III, known as Dracula, or "son of Dracul," regained the throne with Hungary's backing and ruled for six years.

Dracula faced several obstacles to independence and control. The Ottoman Empire and Hungary were the largest external threats. There was also internal resistance from the boyars (regional nobles), who kept Wallachia destabilized in their own interests, as well as from the powerful Saxon merchants of Transylvania, who resisted economic control. Lawlessness and disorder were also prevalent.

A Reign of Might and Terror

Dracula's successes against these obstacles are the source of the admiration that still pervades local folklore, in which there are many tales of his exploits. Locally, he is portrayed as a strong, cunning, and courageous leader who enforced order, suppressed disloyalty, and defended Wallachia. Not only did Wallachia remain independent and Christian, but, as the story goes, Dracula could leave a golden cup by a spring for anyone to get a cool drink without it being stolen—no one was above the law.

His methods, however, are the source of his portrayal elsewhere as a sadistic despot who merited an alternate meaning of Dracula, namely "devil." He eliminated poverty and hunger by feasting the poor and sick and, after dinner, burning them alive in the hall. He eliminated disloyal boyars by inviting them to an Easter feast, after which he put them in chains and worked them to death building his fortress at Poenari. Ambassadors who refused to doff their caps had them nailed to their heads. Dishonest merchants and bands of Romani travelers suffered similarly grisly ends.

Vlad's favorite method of enforcement was impaling (a gruesome and purposefully drawn-out form of execution in which victims were pierced by a long wooden stake and hoisted aloft), though he also found creative ways of flaying, boiling, and hacking people to death. When the Turks cornered him at Tirgoviste in 1461, he created a "forest" of 20,000 impaled captive men, women, and children, which so horrified the Turks that they withdrew. They called him *kaziklu bey* ("the Impaler Prince"), and though Vlad himself did not use it, the epithet Tepes ("Impaler") stuck.

Twists, Turns, and The End of the Story

The Turks then backed Radu and besieged Vlad in Poenari. Dracula escaped to Hungary with the help of a secret tunnel and local villagers, but was imprisoned there. Dracula gradually ingratiated himself and, upon Radu's death, took back the throne in 1476. Just two months later, Dracula was killed in a forest battle against the Turks near Bucharest. Tradition has it that his head was put on display by the Turks and his body buried in the Snagov Monastery, but no grave has been found.

Bram Stoker, while researching for a vampire story about "Count Wampyr," discovered in a library book that "Dracula" could mean "devil" and changed his character's name.

Connecting Stoker's Count to Vlad III has been popular in the press (starting with the 1958 *In Search of Dracula*) and in the tourist industry. However, Stoker's character probably has little basis in Vlad Dracula.

The Bloody Countess

In the early 1600s, villagers in the Carpathian region of Hungary whispered amongst themselves about a vampire living in the local castle. An investigation brought to light the brutal atrocities of Countess Elizabeth Bathory, who was accused of torturing hundreds of young girls to death and bathing in their blood.

✳ ✳ ✳ ✳

The Best Sort of People

ELIZABETH BATHORY (BORN Erzsébet Báthory in 1560) was the daughter of one of the oldest and most influential bloodlines in Hungary. Her wedding in 1575 to Ferenc Nadasdy was enough of an event to warrant written approval and an expensive gift from the Holy Roman Emperor himself.

Of course, there were rumors that a streak of insanity ran in Elizabeth's family; some rumors hint that she may have been related to Vlad the Impaler. However, nobles of the time were given wide latitude when it came to eccentric behavior, even when that eccentric behavior resulted in pain for others.

Ferenc would go on to become one of the greatest Hungarian military heroes of the age. He was a battle-hardened man, but even so, his own wife made him nervous. He was aware that she treated the servants even more harshly than he did—and he had no reservations when it came to punishing the help. He was known to place flaming oil-covered wicks between the toes of lazy servants. But Elizabeth's punishments far exceeded even this brutality. Ferenc saw evidence of this when he discovered a servant who had been covered with honey and tied to a tree to be ravaged by ants as punishment for stealing food.

Still, Ferenc spent a great deal of time away at war, and someone had to manage his castle. Elizabeth took on the task willingly; in turn, he turned a deaf ear to complaints about her more gruesome activities.

From Punishment to Atrocity

Initially, Elizabeth's punishments may have been no more harsh than those imposed by her contemporaries. However, with her husband's lengthy absences and eventual death, Elizabeth found that she had virtually no restrictions on her behavior. A series of lovers of both sexes occupied some of her time. She also dabbled in black magic, though this was not uncommon in an age when paganism and Christianity were contending for supremacy.

She spent hours doing nothing more than gazing into a wrap-around mirror of her own design, crafted to hold her upright so that she would not tire as she examined her own reflection. The exacting fashion of the day required Elizabeth, always a vain woman, to constantly worry over the angle of her collar or the style of her hair.

She had a small army of body servants constantly by her side to help maintain her appearance. They were often required to attend to their mistress in the nude as an expression of sub-servience. If they failed in their duties, Elizabeth would strike out, pummeling them into the ground. On one notable occasion, a servant pulled too hard when combing Elizabeth's hair; Elizabeth struck the offender in the face hard enough to cause the girl's blood to spray and cover the countess. Initially furious, Elizabeth discovered she liked the sensation, believing her skin was softer, smoother, and more translucent after the experience.

A Taste for Blood

The incident led to the legends, which cannot be confirmed, that Elizabeth Bathory took to bathing in the blood of virgins to maintain her youthful appearance. One rumor has her invit-ing 60 peasant girls for a banquet, only to lock them in a room and slaughter them one at a time, letting their blood run over her body. Though that incident may be apocryphal, it is certain that the countess began torturing girls without restraint. Aided by two trustworthy servants who recruited a never-ending supply of hopeful girls from the poor families of the area, she would beat her victims with a club until they were scarcely recognizable. When her arms grew tired, she had her two assistants continue the punishment as she watched. She had a spiked iron cage specially built and would place a girl within it, shaking the cage as the individual bounced from side to side and was impaled over and over on the spikes. She drove pins into lips and breasts, held flames to sensitive regions, and once pulled a victim's mouth open so forcefully that the girl's cheeks split.

Perhaps most chillingly, allegations of vampirism and cannibalism arose when Elizabeth began biting her victims, tearing off the flesh with her bare teeth. On one occasion, too sick to rise from her bed, the countess demanded that a peasant girl be brought to her. She roused herself long enough to bite chunks from the girl's face, shoulders, and nipples. Elizabeth's chambers had to be covered with fresh cinders daily to prevent the countess from slipping on the bloody floor.

Justice for the Countess

Eventually, even the cloak of nobility couldn't hide Elizabeth's atrocities. The situation was compounded by the fact that she got sloppy, killing in such numbers that the local clergy refused to perform any more burials. Thereafter, she would throw bodies to the wolves in full view of local villagers, who naturally complained to the authorities. The final straw was when Elizabeth began to prey on the minor aristocracy as well as the peasants; the disappearance of people of higher birth could not be tolerated. The king decided that something had to be done, and in January 1611, a trial was held. Elizabeth was not allowed to testify, but her assistants were compelled to—condemning themselves to death in the process—and they provided eyewitness accounts of the terrible practices of the countess. Especially damning was the discovery of a list, in Elizabeth's own handwriting, describing more than 600 people she had tortured to death.

Elizabeth Bathory was convicted of perpetrating "horrifying cruelties" and was sentenced to be walled up alive in her own castle. She survived for nearly four years but was finally discovered dead on August 21, 1614, by one of her guards who had risked a peek through a tiny food slot. The countess was unrepentant to the end.

The Mysterious Death of Christopher Marlowe

Who exactly is responsible for the death of Christopher Marlowe?

❊ ❊ ❊ ❊

IN 1593, CHRISTOPHER Marlowe, the most famous playwright in London, was killed when he accidentally stabbed himself during a tavern brawl. His premature death is one of the greatest tragedies in English literature, snuffing out a career that may have still been in its infancy—Shakespeare, who was Marlowe's same age, was just coming into his own as a writer at the time. But some people continue to doubt the official story (i.e., that Marlowe accidentally stabbed himself while fighting over the bill). After all, Marlowe and some of the others in the room with him had ties to the Elizabethan underworld. Was his really an accidental death—or could it have been murder?

Rise of a Shoemaker's Son

Born to a shoemaker the same year that Shakespeare was born to a glove maker, Marlowe attended Cambridge University, where he posed for a portrait that showed him in a black velvet shirt, smirking beside his Latin motto, *Quod met nutrit me destruit* ("What nourishes me destroys me.") He was a distinguished enough scholar that he seems to have been recruited, as many Cambridge scholars of the day were, to work as an undercover agent. Letters from the government excusing him from missing classes seem to back up the widely held theory that he went on spy missions in Spain. When he returned to

London, he found fame as a playwright, churning out "blood and thunder" shockers such as *Doctor Faustus* that helped pioneer the use of blank verse, and were some of the first great pieces of secular theatrical entertainment produced in the English language.

Walk on the Wild Side

But to say that Marlowe had a wild side is to put things mildly. He was imprisoned twice, once for his role in a fight that left a tavern keeper dead (he was acquitted when a jury determined that he'd acted in self-defense), and ran with an underground group of atheists who called themselves "The School of Night." They hung around in graveyards, reading poetry and having the sort of blasphemous debates that were illegal in Elizabethan England, where everyone was required to be a member of the Church of England. Breaking somewhat from her predecessors, Queen Elizabeth generally didn't care too much if people doubted religion in their minds, as long as they kept their mouths shut and kept attending church services. But for someone as famous as Marlowe to be a heretic was potentially very dangerous.

Richard Baines, a professional snitch, wrote a letter to the government containing a bunch of blasphemous things that he claimed to have heard Marlowe say, such as that Moses was really just a juggler, that people in the New World had stories and histories dating back 10,000 years (which went against the "official" view that the Adam and Eve had lived "within six thousand years,"), and that the Virgin Mary was "dishonest." Around the same time, the government arrested Thomas Kyd, Marlowe's former roommate, for possessing atheist literature, and Kyd said under torture that it was Marlowe who had turned him on to atheism in the first place.

And so, at the height of his fame, Marlowe was arrested for blasphemy. He was released on parole and ordered to check in every day until he was brought to trial, at which he faced a possible sentence of death. If lucky, he would just get his nose chopped off.

Marlowe never once checked in with authorities, so far as is known, and he was killed in Deptford only a couple of weeks later, while awaiting trial.

An Accident, or...?

The exact circumstances of his death are still not quite agreed upon, though a detailed coroner's report exists. Official documents state that Marlowe and a few other men had spent the day in an establishment owned by "The Widow Bull," but what sort of business this was is a matter of some mystery—it's been variously described as a tavern, a brothel, or a sort of bed and breakfast. The fact that the investigations into what happened that day mention a "reckoning" (bill) is about the only evidence we have that it was any sort of business at all, not just a house owned by Ms. Eleanor Bull.

However, according to official reports, a bill of some sort was presented to Marlowe and his friends. A fight broke out over who should pay it, and in the scuffle, Marlowe (reportedly) accidentally stabbed himself just below the eye and "then and there instantly died."

A Cover Up?

Now, most fights over bills ("I shouldn't have to pay an equal share, because I just had water and appetizers, not steak and beer....") don't end in knife fights, but this explanation seems sensible enough on the surface: The theatres were closed at the time due to a plague outbreak, and Marlowe was probably hard up for money. Perhaps he had taken up an offer of going to dinner thinking that his meal was being paid for, and when he was asked to kick in for the bill, his hot temper got the best of him. He reached for the dagger of one of the other men present— one Ingram Frizer—and stabbed himself while the other men tried to stop him from attacking.

The death was officially determined to be the result of an accidental, self-inflicted wound, but more and more scholars now believe that Marlowe was murdered to make sure he didn't reveal sensitive information at his upcoming trial.

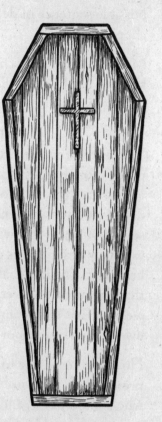

It does seem that a lot of people may have had a reason to want Marlowe to be killed before he could go to trial. Frizer, for example, had been working for Thomas Walsingham, a relative of Queen Elizabeth's secretary of state, and had Marlowe been convicted of atheism, Walsingham himself would have been disgraced, and financially ruined, for having once been Marlowe's patron. Perhaps Frizer was acting on his boss's orders and killed Marlowe to ensure his own future.

But others believe that the "political murder" theory doesn't go far enough, and that the body on the coroner's slab wasn't Marlowe at all, but the body of a man named John Penry who had been hastily hanged. According to this theory, Marlowe wasn't killed at all, but instead escaped to the continent, where he kept on writing. Some of the wildest theories in this vein hold that he was the true author of Shakespeare's plays.

It seems far-fetched, but then again, if anyone could have pulled off faking his own death, it was Christopher Marlowe. And while conspiracy theorists have tried to claim several people as the "true" author of Shakespeare's works, Marlowe is the only one who was a good enough author that he could have rivaled Shakespeare for the title of greatest dramatist of the English language.

The Purveyor of Poisoned Potions

Although it sounds like a perfume or face cream, "Aqua Tofana"
was a lethal poison developed in the 17th century. And its creator
may have been one of the most prolific serial killers the world has
ever seen.

✳ ✳ ✳ ✳

Divorce Italian Style

THE CONCEPT OF legal divorce is a rather modern notion.
For hundreds of years, unhappy couples found ways around
their marriage vows, or simply ignored them, to quell their dis-
satisfaction. In 1533, King Henry VIII even created an entirely
new church, the Church of England, when the pope refused to
allow an annulment of his marriage to Catherine of Aragon so
he could marry Anne Boleyn.

England eventually enacted a divorce law in 1857. The United
States was even more lenient. But in Italy, where the Roman
Catholic Church holds great influence, divorce was not legalized until 1970. Hundreds of years earlier, in the 17th century,
Italian women were rarely given a choice when it came to marriage. Oftentimes, young women with no financial means were
married off to older men and forced to live out their lives in
loveless, and sometimes abusive, marriages. Women in poorer
classes had few options: They could stay single and work as
prostitutes (the only "profession" available to them); they could
marry and risk abuse; or, if they were already married, they
could wait for their husband to die and inherit his estate.

A Cunning Cosmetic

For women trapped in abusive marriages, option three often
seemed best. But waiting for a husband to die of natural causes
could take years, maybe decades. That's where Guilia Tofana
stepped in. Little is known about Tofana's early life, although
she is believed to have been born in Palermo in 1620. She was
widowed at a young age, and she and her daughter, Girolama

Spara, moved to Naples and then Rome. Tofana was known to spend time in apothecaries, where she observed the creation of compounds and potions, and she began to devise a potion of her own. The resulting lethal concoction is believed to have been a mixture of arsenic, lead, and belladonna. Tofana named it "Aqua Tofana" and packaged it in a cosmetics bottle labeled "Manna of St. Nicholas of Bari." This was a popular healing ointment of the time, so the bottle would look at home on any woman's dressing table.

Tofana began selling her Aqua Tofana to women who were desperate to escape their marriages. Just a few drops of the deadly poison added to a glass of wine or a bowl of soup would cause a man to feel ill; a few more drops the next day would cause vomiting, stomach aches, and dysentery; a final dose would be the end, with the death appearing to be the result of a severe illness. The poison was so undetectable that a widow could even "demand" a post-mortem examination to preserve the illusion of her innocence.

The Beginnings of a Legend

Tofana gained a reputation as a friend to troubled women, and for almost two decades, her daughter and three employees helped her keep up with her booming business. But it was only a matter of time before one of her clients had a change of heart. In 1650, a woman confessed to buying the poison, and named Tofana as the seller. Tofana took refuge in a church, but authorities soon closed in, arresting her, her daughter, and her three helpers.

Tofana confessed to providing the poison that killed at least 600 men, making her the mastermind of one of the biggest murder sprees in history.

She, her daughter, and her three employees were executed in 1659, but that was not the end of her legend. Even more than a century later, as composer Wolfgang Amadeus Mozart lay dying, he proclaimed, "I am sure that I have been poisoned...

Someone has given me acqua tofana and calculated the precise time of my death."

While historians have found no evidence that Mozart was actually poisoned, it is a testament to Tofana's notoriety that her poison was still famous, long after her own demise.

A Jewel of a Heist

The Crown Jewels of the United Kingdom are a collection of royal ceremonial objects that are so valuable they are considered priceless. So it's surprising that there has been only one attempt to steal them; and even more surprising that the thief was pardoned for his crime.

✳ ✳ ✳ ✳

War and Aftermath

THOMAS BLOOD IS believed to have been born and raised in Ireland in the early 17th century, and was educated in Lancashire, England. When the First English Civil War broke out in 1642, Blood initially joined the Royalists who were loyal to King Charles I. But as the war progressed, it appeared that Oliver Cromwell's Roundheads might win the war, and Blood switched sides.

Charles I was indeed defeated in 1653, and Cromwell rewarded Blood for his services by granting him land and appointing him a justice of the peace. But Blood's good fortune didn't last long, as the monarchy was restored in 1660 when King Charles II ascended the throne. Blood fled back to Ireland with his wife and son. The land he'd been granted was confiscated under the Act of Settlement 1662, leaving him financially ruined.

In Ireland, Blood joined a group of disgruntled Cromwell supporters who attempted to seize Dublin Castle and kidnap James Butler, 1st Duke of Ormond and Lord Lieutenant of Ireland. When their plan went awry, Blood managed to flee, but several of his coconspirators were captured and executed.

Now holding a grudge against Lord Ormond, Blood and the remaining Cromwell supporters made one more attempt to kidnap and kill him, but the duke escaped. Blood hid out for six months while he planned his next move.

A Bold Plan

And his next move was a big one: Blood decided to steal the Crown Jewels. The jewels were kept in the basement at the Tower of London and were overseen by the Master of the Jewel House, a man named Talbot Edwards. Edwards and his family lived in an apartment on the first floor of the Tower, where he could easily access the jewels when needed. One day, Blood arrived to the Tower of London disguised as a parson, with a woman pretending to be his wife. They requested to view the jewels, but as Edward led them through the basement, Blood's "wife" complained of stomach pains. The gracious jewel keeper invited the duo upstairs to his apartment, where Mrs. Edwards kindly tended to the "ill" woman.

Several days later, Blood returned to thank Mr. and Mrs. Edwards for their help, and the fake "parson" struck up a friendship with the couple. He eventually even offered to arrange a marriage between Edwards' daughter and his own wealthy nephew, which Edwards gladly accepted. Blood soon returned to the Tower with his "nephew" and two other men, who requested to see the Crown Jewels. Edwards, assuming he was entertaining his future son-in-law, led the men down into the basement.

Crime and No Punishment

But suddenly, Edwards' hopes of a wealthy suitor for his daughter were dashed when Blood and the three other men attacked him. One man hit Edwards with a mallet to knock him out, and then the poor jewel keeper was tied up and stabbed. Blood and his accomplices removed the Crown Jewels, but the bulky items proved difficult to hide, even underneath his fake "parson" robes. So he flattened the crown with the mallet, while another man sawed the scepter in half. But by this time, Edwards had woken up, and began shouting, "Treason! Murder!" The thieves barely made it out of the tower before they were apprehended.

Blood had heard that King Charles had a reputation for respecting daring scoundrels, and so refused to answer to anyone else. When he was at last brought before the king, his hunch was confirmed: the king was amused by Blood's audacity, and not only pardoned him for the crime, but granted him more land in Ireland.

A Final Switcheroo?

Blood died in 1680, owing the Duke of Buckingham thousands of pounds. His body was exhumed by authorities to confirm that he really was the man in the grave. And it's hard to blame them: after his dishonesty, who would've been surprised if "Parson Blood" had faked his death to pull off one last heist?

Pirates!

As long as cargo has been carried across the sea, there have been pirates who have tried to plunder the goods, or "booty." Learn more about what it meant to be a pirate in the good ol' days of privateering.

✳ ✳ ✳ ✳

The Genuine Arrr-ticle

MOST CONSIDER THE golden age of piracy to be from the 16th to 18th centuries. Pirates at this time could be found primarily sailing their ships around the Caribbean Sea, off the coasts of Arabia and North Africa, and in the South China Sea. These were major sea trade routes at the time, and the huge cargo ships there routinely transported everything from gold and silver to ivory, spices, and slaves.

Anything of worth was desirable to the pirate, who could either use what he stole or sell it at a profit wherever his ship landed next.

Worth the Risk?

Being a pirate was a big gamble. Piracy was illegal, and punishment often meant torture and death by hanging. Basically, if you were caught pirating, you were toast.

But if you could remain free, privateering was a better occupation than many available on land. You could say that pirates were equal opportunity employers: blacks, West Indians, Arabs, and everyone in between were welcome to "go on the account," in other words, to sign up to work a pirate ship.

Discrimination was almost nonexistent: If you could sail, steal, and keep a secret, you were in. Many black men enlisted, since their only other option was often forced slavery in Europe and in America. Criminals on the lam, as well as people who opposed their government, found asylum on a pirate ship (which numbered around 100 men, depending on the size of the vessel). Piracy was a refuge for many, but remember, if they were caught, they faced death.

Another Day at the Office

Many jobs were onboard the ship. There was the role of the captain, who acted as the commander of his onboard army. Captains, while indisputably in charge, were just as vulnerable as the rest of their men when it came to justice. If one pirate ship attacked another, the captain of the victorious fleet would ask the captured crew if their captain was a fair man. If he was, he lived. If not, he'd likely be thrown overboard. Famous pirate captains include "Black Sam" Bellamy and Blackbeard.

For others, most of their time privateering was spent like that of any mariner. The daily grind of mending the ship's ropes and sails, repairing rowboats, and swabbing the decks kept the sailors busy between attacks. Life onboard was much more lenient than that of, say, the British Royal Navy, but there was still a lot of work to be done, and each man was expected to pull his own weight.

There were specialty jobs, too. A surgeon (or someone with at least a little medical experience) was usually kept onboard, as well as a quartermaster, who dealt with counting money and keeping the peace. Other positions aboard a pirate ship included the cook, master gunner (in charge of ammunition), and boatswain (head of the cables, anchors, and such).

A Pirate's Life for Me

Food was scarce on the ship, though pirates tended to eat better than most other sailors. Dolphin and tuna meat was supplemented with yams, plantains, and other fruits. Life onboard was crowded, dirty, and smelly, but the pirates kept their sense of humor. They were known to put on plays, play cards and dice, sing songs, and dance all day long, reveling in the freedom they enjoyed. There were even some crews that held mock trials, entertaining themselves with hypothetical scenarios of being caught and put on trial.

But what about all that booty? The notion of buried treasure has been debunked, unfortunately—when pirates had money, they spent it. When on land, the crew of a pirate ship could be found carousing in pubs and indulging in wine, women, and song until it was time to board the ship and sail in search of more treasure.

Myths and Truths

Pirates were just drunken debauchers. Yes, these guys tended toward drunkenness and debauchery; it's the "just" part that's inaccurate. They were also violent, womanizing scoundrels—but for the most part, they restricted these unseemly behaviors to shore. Rules governing their conduct often stipulated a lifestyle better suited to Boy Scouts than to bloodthirsty thieves. To avoid shipboard violence among the crew, captains frequently banned women and gambling, forbade drunkenness while on duty, and strictly enforced early "lights out."

All pirates talked the same way. If for a period in the 1950s it seemed like every movie pirate had the same accent, it's because they did, or rather, they shared an accent with Robert Newton, the actor who portrayed both Blackbeard and Long John Silver several times on big and small screens. Newton was born in Dorset, England (as were many famous pirates), and his rough accent and trilled "r" fit the public's image of pirates nicely. But pirate ships were melting pots, pulling sailors in from all over Europe, the Caribbean, and the Americas, so there was no "typical" pirate accent. What's more, Ol' Chumbucket and Cap'n Slappy, the aspiring-pirate masterminds behind International Talk Like a Pirate Day, would like to point out that no pirates—fictional or otherwise—ever said, "Arrrgh," though they might have said, "Arrr."

Pirates were lawless criminals. Who says there's no honor among thieves? Pirates had few qualms about liberating a treasure-laden merchant ship of its burden, but they operated under strict codes of conduct on their own ships. Called Articles of Agreement, these pirate codes varied from ship to ship and governed elections and management, division of booty, disability compensation, shipboard safety, ethics, and responsibilities. Each pirate was required to sign the agreement before embarking on a voyage, and those who violated the rules found themselves marooned—that is, left on a remote island with as little as a flask of water and a weapon. Here are a few of the provisions in the Articles of Agreement drawn up by Captain John Phillips for the crew aboard his ship *Revenge*:

✻ If any Man shall steal any Thing in the Company, or game, to the Value of a Piece of Eight, he shall be maroon'd or shot.

✻ That Man that shall strike another whilst those Articles are in force shall receive Moses's Law (that is 40 Stripes lacking one) on the bare Back.

✻ If at any time you meet with a Prudent woman, that Man that offers to meddle with her, without her Consent, shall suffer present Death.

Dread Pirates of History and Their Fates

Here are some of the most notorious rascals of the era, plus noteworthy pirates from other times.

✳ ✳ ✳ ✳

John Taylor: Taylor , an English pirate, earned his fame capturing the Portuguese carrack Nossa Senhora do Cabo in 1721. It was one of the richest prizes of its time, consisting of diamonds and other portable loot. No idiot, Taylor then bought a pardon in Panama, where he likely retired wealthy.

Edward Teach: More infamously known as Blackbeard, Edward Teach (active 1713–1718) was a privateer turned pirate whose success and reputation for cruelty made him a legend across the Caribbean. From his ship, *Queen Anne's Revenge*, Blackbeard terrorized the commercial lanes and coastal waters of the West Indies and the American Atlantic coast for four years. Never one to run from a fight, Teach gained immense fame among his fellow pirates by successfully fighting off a Royal Navy ship, an encounter that he could have, and that most other pirate captains would have, completely avoided.

The infamous Blackbeard was a full-time drunkard who terrorized the Carolina coast, racking up captures and loot. But it wasn't all about money and rum: He once raided Charleston and took hostages until townsfolk gave him much-needed medicine for his venereal disease.

Blackbeard was well aware that his public image of wickedness was a key to his success, and he took pains to cultivate the impression. Before battle, he embedded match cord in his beard and set it alight, wreathing his head in smoke and giving his enemies the impression that he had arisen from the depths of hell.

His unfortunate crews sometimes bore the brunt of his attempts to reinforce his image; on one occasion Teach shot his chief gunner, crippling the man for life. When asked his reason, Blackbeard replied that if he didn't kill one of his men now and then, they would forget who he was.

Despite this capriciousness, Teach's achievements in plunder and his seeming invincibility made men eager to sail with him. Aware that he was being sought for capture, Blackbeard briefly retired in January 1718 and was pardoned by the governor of North Carolina, a man to whom Teach paid a number of bribes. However, Edward Teach wasn't temperamentally suited to retirement, and soon returned to his old ways.

Blackbeard's career came to an end in November 1718, when two Royal Navy sloops commanded by Lieutenant Robert Maynard came athwart of the outlaw. Although outnumbered by more than two to one, Blackbeard and his crew chose to give battle to their pursuers, fighting hand to hand on the deck of *Queen Anne's Revenge*. Teach had snapped Maynard's sword and was on the verge of killing the British officer when one of Maynard's men slashed his throat. Teach continued to fight viciously until his body succumbed to blood loss. Maynard decapitated the famous pirate and hung his head from the bowsprit—the spar that projected from the bow of *Queen Anne's Revenge*—for all to see.

Thomas Tew: His 1692–1694 Indian Ocean rampage made English pirate Tew rich enough to retire in New York under the protection of his friend, Governor Benjamin Fletcher. In 1695, his former crew talked him into one more voyage to raid Moghul ships. Piracy was a little like gambling: Most people lose, and winners should probably quit. Tew didn't, and in 1695 he was disemboweled by cannon fire.

Jean-David Nau: A French pirate also known as François l'Olonnais, Nau was a psycho in a sick line of work. Nau whittled prisoners with his cutlass, once allegedly eating a beating heart.

Let us all thank the Native Central Americans for tearing him apart alive in 1668.

Charles Vane: When the reformer Woodes Rogers showed up to clean out the Caribbean pirates' favorite lair (New Providence, now Nassau), the wily English pirate Vane was the only captain to reject the proffered amnesty. He kept marauding—losing ships and gaining them—until his luck and cunning finally ran out. He was captured and hanged in 1720.

Edward Low: Low was hideously scarred by a cutlass slash to the jaw, but the tortures he inflicted upon others would have nauseated a Stalin-era KGB interrogator. It's said that he once forced a man to eat his own severed ears—with salt. According to some sources, he was last seen running from a Royal Navy warship; good thinking on his part, given his record. It is believed that this English pirate was hanged by the French after 1723.

George Lowther: Lowther, an English pirate, was elected captain after a mutiny aboard a slave ship. This pirate's hobbies were torture and rape. In 1723, while his ship was beached for hull maintenance, the Royal Navy showed up. Lowther decided he'd rather not dangle from the gallows and shot himself instead.

Henry Morgan (active 1663–1674) Captain Morgan was one of the most successful pirate leaders, as well as one of the few who managed to retire with his fortune intact. At the time, Spain was the dominant colonial power in the Americas, shipping home gold and silver by the boatload. Morgan served English foreign interests by raising merry hell with Spanish shipping and colonial interests.

Ostensibly acting under authority given him by the British crown to make war against Spain, the Welsh pirate's actions frequently exceeded the bounds of a privateer's commission, not to mention human decency. Remarkable in that many of his successful raids targeted towns rather than ships, Henry Morgan showed a ruthlessness that respected little but the pursuit of treasure. On one occasion, he locked captured enemy soldiers in houses, then blew up the buildings with gunpowder. He would routinely torture prominent residents of captured towns, looking for treasure whether it existed or not.

Most infamously, during an attack in Panama, Morgan took advantage of the Catholic beliefs of his foes by forcing priests and nuns to the front of the assault, ensuring that the Spanish could not fire on his troops without killing the clergy.

Morgan made a fortune during the course of his career, sacking Puerto Principe, Portobelo, Maracaibo, the coast of Cuba, Panama City, and other hapless targets. He pocketed more than 100 million dollars, but when Morgan's actions became so egregious that they threatened a peace treaty between England and Spain, he was briefly arrested by his benefactors. The British had no real wish to punish Morgan, however, and he was released and knighted, after which he retired from the sea.

Moral of his story: If your piracy serves the national interest and makes you rich, your country may reward you with a knighthood and a governorship. In this case, the British government eventually saw to his appointment as Lieutenant Governor of Jamaica. Morgan died in 1688 of natural causes exacerbated by a life of hard drinking.

Ironically, a fanciful version of his image lives on as the mascot of a popular brand of rum.

Olivier "la Buze" Levasseur: The French pirated nicknamed "The Buzzard" collaborated with John Taylor and actually wore an eye patch. Unlike Taylor, though, Levasseur didn't quit while he was ahead but kept up his piratical career until his capture by French authorities at Madagascar in 1730. He was hanged.

Gráinne ni Mháille: The Irish pirate was also known as Grace O'Malley. Rebel, seagoing racketeer, admiral—she was all these and more, engaging in piracy to champion the Irish cause against England. Gráinne didn't even kowtow to Queen Elizabeth I, though she did visit for tea and chitchat. She died of old age in 1603.

Howell Davis: This sneaky Welsh rogue once captured two ships in one encounter. After the first catch, he forced the captives to brandish weapons at the second, inflating his apparent numbers. Davis was planning to seize a Portuguese island governor when the local militia recognized him and shot him in an ambush in 1719.

Rachel (Schmidt) Wall: This American woman turned pirate with her husband, George, luring likely prizes with convincing distress cries. After George drowned in a storm, Rachel forsook the sea for petty thieving along the Boston docks. In 1789, she was arrested for trying to steal a woman's bonnet and was then accused of murdering a sailor. She stood trial, confessed to piracy, and was hanged.

William Kidd: The famous Captain Kidd (active 1695–1701) may have been the most misunderstood pirate of all time. A prominent citizen of New York, Kidd was on friendly terms with several colonial governors. In 1695, he was commissioned to hunt down some of the more well-known pirates of the day. Kidd dutifully outfitted a ship, the *Adventure Galley*, and set out for the pirate haven of Madagascar.

Shortly after his voyage began, however, many of his handpicked crew were pressed into service by a British naval ship, and Kidd was forced to replace them with common criminals and ex-pirates. Discipline immediately suffered, and Kidd struggled to maintain control over his men, eventually killing one in a heated argument. With no luck at finding pirates, the *Adventure Galley* took a number of merchant ships as prizes over the protest of Kidd himself, who finally acceded to his crew's demands for adventurous plunder.

On encountering their first pirate ship, the *Adventure Galley* crew mutinied and joined the outlaw vessel, leaving Kidd and

13 loyal men to make their way back to the Americas, where Kidd was astonished to find that he was wanted as a pirate. He was charged with murder and the illegal seizure of English ships. Captured and sent back to England for trial, Kidd was found guilty and sentenced to be hanged.

More ignominy was in store: The executioner's rope broke on the first drop and required a second, successful attempt. Subsequently, Kidd's corpse dangled from a gibbet over the River Thames for several years, as a warning to other pirates.

Mary Killigrew: Female pirates date back at least as far as the fifth century, but the most notable figures appeared long after that. Mary Killigrew, a lady under Queen Elizabeth I, operated in the late 16th century.

In her most celebrated outing, Killigrew and her shipmates boarded a German vessel off of Falmouth, Cornwall. Once on deck, they killed the crew and stole their cargo.

When later brought to trial for the murders, Killigrew was sentenced to death. With some well-placed bribes and a queen sympathetic to her plight, however, she was eventually acquitted. Her bold tale is said to have inspired female pirates yet to come.

"Calico" Jack Rackham, Anne Bonny, and Mary Read: Two remarkable women earned their places in the annals of the profession. Coincidentally, both were found on the same ship, the *Revenge*, captained by Calico Jack Rackham.

The fancy-dressing Rackham got his buccaneering start under the notorious Charles Vane, whom he soon deposed in a mutiny. Rackham fell in love with an Irish lass, Anne Bonny, who was stuck in an unhappy marriage in the Bahamas. They eloped and began a new piratical career aboard the sloop *Revenge*, where Bonny's hard-living, hard-fighting style earned her respect in a male-dominated business.

Bonny was the daughter of a wealthy Charleston planter, and had a reputation as something of a wild child. At 13, she was rumored to have stabbed a servant girl with a table knife. She eventually left decent society behind to run away with the dashing Calico Jack. Though she may have initially tried to conceal her gender, secrets were hard to keep on a small ship.

Mary Read had a long history of crossdressing, having posed as a boy to trick a relative out of an inheritance and also serving as a man in the British military. Read was on board a ship that was taken by Calico Jack and was pressed into service with his crew.

One day, Anne Bonny happened to walk in on Read while she was undressing, and Mary's secret was out. The two naturally gravitated to each other and lived openly as women accepted by the crew, donning men's clothes only in times of battle. The two women became friends and peers in the fine arts of fighting, swearing, and drinking.

When pirate hunter Jonathan Barnet caught up with *Revenge* in 1720, Read and Bonny were among the few crewmembers sober and/or brave enough to fight.

Accounts of the capture say that Bonny and Read fought ferociously with cutlasses and pistols while the men of the ship cowered below decks. Tried and sentenced to hang, the two women achieved a nine-month reprieve by "pleading their bellies"—both were pregnant.

As Rackham was marched off to hang, Bonny showed her contempt: "If ye'd fought like a man, ye needn't hang like a dog." (One suspects that history has omitted a volley or two of choice profanities.)

Mary Read eventually died in prison, possibly in childbirth. Anne Bonny disappears from the history books; one popular legend claims she escaped justice through the auspices of her estranged father, who bought her freedom before she could be executed.

Bartholomew "Black Bart" Roberts: The "Great Pyrate Roberts" (active 1719–1722) was a man of contradictions. Although initially reluctant to sail under the black flag, he was forced into the role when brigands captured the vessel he was on.

Bartholomew Roberts had one of the greatest careers in history, capturing an estimated 400 ships and pocketing treasure beyond reckoning. Black Bart's reputation was such that many authorities refused to tangle with him, but his success ended in 1722 when pirate hunters surprised his ship, the *Royal Fortune*, as its crew lay drunk from celebrating the capture of a prize the day before. Roberts died in the battle, his throat ripped open by grapeshot as he defiantly stared down his enemies from astride a gun carriage during the exchange of cannon fire—a pirate to the end.

Walking the Plank

The myth is persistent, but did pirates really force people to walk the plank? Let's look at the evidence.

✳   ✳   ✳   ✳

Plank-Walking: Myth or Reality?

ONE OF THE earliest definitions of the phrase "walking the plank" appears in the 1788 book *A Classical Dictionary of the Vulgar Tongue*, which explains it as "a mode of destroying devoted persons or officers in a mutiny on ship-board." The victim was bound and blindfolded and forced to walk on a board that was balanced on the ship's side until he fell into the water. This way, "as the mutineers suppose," they might avoid the penalty for murder. Since no record exists of charges being brought against anyone who forced their officers to walk the plank, maybe those old scalawags were right.

On the other hand, it's possible that plank-walking was an extremely rare occurrence—if it ever really happened at all. In fact, some experts scoff at the notion, saying that the practice existed only in the work of novelists and illustrators. But journalists wrote about it, too. In 1821, a Jamaican newspaper reported that pirates from a schooner had boarded the English ship *Blessing*. When the pirates were unable to get any money out of the *Blessing's* captain, the lead marauder made him walk the plank. The buccaneers then shot the ousted captain three times as he struggled to stay above the water before musket-whipping the captain's teenage son, pitching him overboard, and setting the entire ship aflame. (Now that's a thorough job!) Another sailor, George Wood, confessed a similar crime to a chaplain just before being hanged for mutiny in 1769. No other documentation exists to validate either story.

A Wacky Idea

Where did the notion of walking the plank originate? It's possible that it was conjured by the pirates who plagued the Mediterranean Sea when it was dominated by the Roman Empire. Yes, there were pirates in those days, and when they captured Roman ships, they would mock the sailors by telling them that they were free to walk home. Of course, at sea, there's no place to walk without sinking like a stone.

But if walking the plank wasn't actually used as a form of maritime punishment, how were unwanted men dealt with at sea? Marooning—leaving a man on a desert island to die—was a popular practice among both pirates and mutineers. In addition, prisoners were tied up and tossed overboard to drown or be eaten by sharks. Eyewitness accounts of hanging, shooting, whipping, and torturing prisoners abound. Pirates had a number of unpleasant punishments for prisoners and rule breakers, including twisting cords around an offender's head until his eyes popped out, forcing him to eat his own ears, or tying him to a mast and throwing glass at him or burning him with matches.

What pirates didn't do was make prisoners walk the plank (how nice of them). Only one reputable, first-hand account of plank walking exists, and it took place 100 years after the peak of piracy. The idea that this was a common practice comes primarily from J. M. Barrie's play *Peter Pan* and old Hollywood movies in which walking the plank was one of the few forms of torture that would get past the censors.

Beaten on the Senate Floor

After Massachusetts Senator Charles Sumner's speech got personal, a South Carolina representative took matters into his own hands—literally.

✳   ✳   ✳   ✳

RAW EMOTION AND angry exchanges can often come to dominate a political debate, and at times it can be downright dangerous. In the tension-filled years that led up to the secession of the Southern states, the U.S. Senate was a frequent setting for passionate, and often bitter, oratory in which the adversaries were North versus South, slaves states versus free.

An Acrid Address

It can be argued that no speech in the history of the Senate has been more provocative than the address made by Massachusetts Senator Charles Sumner on May 19 and 20, 1856. For two days, the fervent abolitionist delivered his blistering "Crime Against Kansas" speech. It was an attack on proslavery forces in the Kansas territory and beyond that was loaded with personal invective directed toward the supporters of that peculiar institution. Sumner made a number of personal insults against senators who advocated slavery, calling them imbeciles and immoral. He referred to Illinois Senator Stephen Douglas, one of his political enemies on the slavery question, as a nameless animal unfit to be an American senator.

Sumner also specifically singled out South Carolina Senator Andrew Butler for scorn. Butler was ill at the time and therefore not present in the Senate chamber to hear the address himself. Sumner identified Butler as a prominent example of hypocrisy on the slavery question and repeatedly disparaged South Carolina as a state whose contributions to the Union were so historically insignificant that it would be immediately overshadowed by the admission of a new territory such as Kansas. He also made a number of pointed personal attacks against Butler, the most graphic of which was his repeated suggestion that Butler kept a "harlot, Slavery."

A Personal Attack

The fallout from this incendiary speech was far more than merely political. The response from Butler's camp came two days later when Preston Brooks, a member of the House of Representatives from South Carolina and the nephew of Senator Butler, offered his reply. He had heard the Sumner speech from the Senate gallery and, incensed by its tone, was determined to avenge the honor of both his uncle and his state.

Brooks entered the Senate chamber during a recess. Seeing Sumner sitting at his desk, Brooks began to denounce the senator for the insults he'd made two days earlier. Before Sumner could reply, Brooks suddenly struck him with his hollow, metal-tipped cane, delivering a series of vicious blows to Sumner's head and body that left the senator battered and semiconscious. When his cane broke after 30 blows, Brooks walked away from the crippled Sumner and returned to his business in the House of Representatives.

In many contemporary reports of the attack, Southern senators present in the chamber were said to have laughed as Sumner was beaten. It took three years for Sumner to fully recover from the injuries he received.

Although a motion to expel Brooks from the House of Representatives for dishonorable conduct was defeated when representatives from the South refused to support it, the House did vote to censure him. He resigned from office, but his South Carolina district elected him right back into Congress. Brooks became a hero in the South, a symbol of a man who was prepared to defend principle and honor when challenged. Sumner became a heroic figure in the North, where he was characterized as both a victim of Southern brutality and an example of how proslavery forces attempted to suppress free speech through violent acts.

John Wesley Hardin—the Old West's Deadliest Gun?

Some credit this Texan with as many as 50 kills. Some call him a misunderstood Southern folk hero. What most obscures the facts about John Wesley Hardin is Hardin himself. He wrote a self-serving autobiography late in life, taking responsibility for many killings and painting himself as a sort of avenging angel against wrong. Some of his statements have been corroborated; others can't be.

✳ ✳ ✳ ✳

✳ Hardin was born a minister's son in Bonham, Texas, in 1853. His parents named him for Methodism's founder, John Wesley.

✳ As a child, he was outdoorsy even by rural Western standards. John was an adventuresome young man, hunting and exploring with guns and dogs at an early age. This would later stand him in good stead when he spent several years with large numbers of people from Kansas, Indian Territory, or Texas chasing him around the bush and all the way to the Florida panhandle.

✳ John was 12 when the Civil War ended, and postwar Texas bred desperadoes and made them into folk heroes: The average white Texan of the day looked most leniently upon anyone who showed hostility to the Yankee occupiers.

✳ Hardin killed his first man when he was 15. After volleys of bragging, he and a crony wrestled with a local freedman named Mage Holshousen, a mature fellow with a brawny reputation. Two teens against a big strong guy wasn't as uneven as it sounds. Hardin murdered Holshousen the next day with a .44, point blank. The spree was on.

* Though a white jury at the time probably wouldn't have convicted John, he still went on the lam. At 16, he had a brief stint teaching school while the heat died down.

* Hardin claims to have done some killing—two white soldiers, one African American soldier—in his early adult life while working as a cowboy for relatives. During this time, he also mastered the fine arts of spitting chew, gambling, and drinking—habits that would work against him for the rest of his life.

* Hardin's killings, alleged and claimed, followed a pattern: A situation would arise involving gambling and drinking, and someone would say the wrong thing. Given the opportunity to escalate things or calm them down, Hardin would do the former. All evidence says he was the epitome of pistol wizardry, a brilliant quick-draw artist and dead shot. Likewise, no one doubts his homicidal temper. He had allegedly killed 12 men by the time he was 17.

* How did Hardin get away with so many murders? Chalk it up to the times. There was little legal infrastructure in the West during his youth, but there was a lot of vigilante justice. If you kept moving, you could probably duck the consequences. He also had an uncanny ability to make friends with law enforcement; it seems he could be a likeable guy when he wasn't drunk and losing at cards. He could also be a dangerous man to pursue—sneaky and willing to lay in wait rather than run.

* The cattle business led Hardin through Indian Territory (now Oklahoma), with more alleged killings along the way, and up to Abilene, Kansas. Abilene was a wild cattle

trailhead, and J. B. "Wild Bill" Hickok was its marshal. A town full of rowdy, drunken gamblers? John Wesley Hardin? This would not end well.

* The story goes that Hickok at one point tried to confront and disarm Hardin, and that Hardin proffered the pistols, then did the "border roll" (reversing the firearms in his hands to point them, loaded and ready, at Marshal Hickok). It's possible. Reliable accounts say that Hardin was a master of this trick, which was mostly a way for kids to shoot themselves by mistake while trying to impress their friends. We can only be sure that Hickok never disarmed Hardin, because John later shot someone and hurried out of Abilene.

* By the time Hardin got back to his home state, he'd supposedly ended 23 lives, and he was 18 years old.

* Hardin married and had children. His descendants naturally still take an interest in their kinsman. That's more than can be said for Hardin, who mostly neglected his entire family. That he was usually hiding out from the law isn't a great excuse; the law might have stopped bothering him had he stopped putting holes in people.

* Back in Texas, Hardin finally killed enough people to interest the law in hunting him down. He fled across the South to Florida with a big price on his head, using the name John Swain.

* Lawmen subdued him in a passenger rail car at Pensacola and hauled him back home to stand trial for murder. He was convicted of second-degree murder in 1877, and the jury sentenced him to 25 years of hard labor.

* Texas governor James Hogg released Hardin several years early. Why? Hardin's wife and the mother of his children had died while he was imprisoned, and he had kept his nose clean during the later part of his sentence. Hardin had done 17 years, and at the age of 42, he was now free.

* Unfortunately, he was also free to resume his habits of drinking and gambling. This led to more confrontations, more killings, and a rapid downward spiral. A constable finally shot John Wesley Hardin dead in 1895 without warning as he played dice in the Acme Saloon in El Paso.

* According to legend, the constable who killed Hardin, John Selman, did so over an unpaid debt. Apparently, Hardin had actually hired Selman to kill another man, allegedly the husband of a woman with whom Hardin was having an affair. Although Selman carried out his end of the bargain, Hardin neglected to pay him for the job. As a result, Selman tracked Hardin to the saloon and ended his life as well.

* Hardin's death tally could be as low as 20 or could have exceeded 50. Although he went out of his way in his autobiography to claim kills and paint himself as the ultimate bad guy, there may perhaps have been murders he didn't bother to mention. Was John Wesley Hardin comfortable with or perhaps even addicted to killing? On that charge, the record is fairly clear.

Reality TV: The Saga of the Hatfields and McCoys

About a century after it began, America's most infamous feud spilled onto the boob tube.

* * * *

How It All Began

THINGS JUST AREN'T like they used to be. America has gone from a country of hardworking people to a consumer-based society that is driven by greed and empty entertainment. Even our family feuds have lost their integrity. Nowadays, people go on game shows to battle it out. Back in the good old days— back when America was America—folks just shot each other.

With apologies to Richard Dawson, the former host of the silly game show *Family Feud*, the most notorious family feud in American history is that of the Hatfields and the McCoys. In the mid-19th century, these two Appalachian clans settled on opposite sides of the quaintly named Tug Fork, a stream that forms part of the West Virginia–Kentucky border. On the West Virginia side lived the Hatfields, a logging family of fifteen that was headed by "Devil Anse" Hatfield, a former Confederate officer who was none too happy that his state had joined the Union. The McCoys were equally large, with patriarch "Rand'l" McCoy siring thirteen children, although some sources indicate that he fathered sixteen children. For many years, the two families coexisted somewhat peacefully, working together and intermarrying furiously. But the peace was not to last.

According to some historians, the trouble began when young Harmon McCoy joined the Union army and fought for the North during the Civil War, an offense for which, upon his return to Tug Fork, he was hunted down and killed by a group of Hatfields. Bad feelings simmered through the 1860s and 1870s. They flared up again when a dispute over ownership of a pig led to another murder, this one committed by the McCoys. But the big trouble didn't really ensue until Roseanna McCoy fell in love with a Hatfield. This backwoods version of Romeo and Juliet eventually led to the murders of at least 20 members of the two families.

America Takes Notice

Though there was a great deal of family feuding in Appalachia during the late 19th and early 20th centuries, no squabble captured America's imagination quite like that of the Hatfields and McCoys. Countless folk songs, books, plays, and movies have been written about the two families, and their depiction as violent, poorly educated, incestuous hillbillies has been instrumental in creating the popular perception of Appalachia. Some might say that the Hatfields and McCoys have done more to destroy Appalachia's image than anybody this side of Ned Beatty's "wooer" in *Deliverance*.

From Appalachia to *Family Feud*

But grudges can only last so long. In 1891, after the fighting got so bad that it was making national headlines, the families finally decided to call a truce. Over the next century, they lived in uneasy harmony. Then in 1979, the Hatfield and McCoy families emerged from their remote Appalachian homes to join the rest of the world—by appearing together on *Family Feud*.

The Sutton-Taylor Feud

When disputes fester, they can turn deadly. Such was the case with Texas's version of the Hatfields and McCoys. When the smoke cleared, and this long-standing feud died out, dozens lay dead in its wake.

✳ ✳ ✳ ✳

TEXAS'S FIGHT BETWEEN the Suttons and the Taylors claimed an estimated 30 to 50 people. In one of the state's longest and deadliest disputes, William E. Sutton and Creed Taylor did their hateful best to mow each other down. Eventually, family and friends joined each combatant in their unquenchable quest for revenge. For such loyalty, many paid the ultimate price.

So, What Do We Know?

Hatred between the families may have begun as early as the 1840s, when Sutton and Taylor lived in Georgia. By the 1860s, both families had relocated to Texas's DeWitt County, bringing their loathing with them.

In March 1868, a pivotal event occurred when accused horse thieves Charles Taylor and James Sharp were shot to death. This was followed by the Christmas Eve murders of Buck Taylor and Dick Chisholm. William Sutton was believed to be involved in both episodes.

With the gauntlet thrown down, there was no turning back. The Taylors staged deadly ambushes, claiming a number of Sutton's soldiers. In 1872, Pitkin Taylor was shot and wounded, and he died six months later. His family swore revenge and enlisted kinsman and notorious outlaw John Wesley Hardin. Soon, Hardin and Jim Taylor disposed of Jack Helm, an agent of Sutton.

Settled?

This deadly tit-for-tat continued until the late 1870s, when Texas Rangers arrested eight men from the Sutton camp for killing Dr. Phillip Brassel and his son. By this time, the feud was so widespread and fragmented that no one was sure who fought for what or for whom. With witnesses understandably scared to testify against either side, the legal case fell apart. But the feud appeared to be over. With a whimper instead of a bang, the Sutton-Taylor feud had finally come to an end.

The Legend of Belle Starr

Known as the "Bandit Queen" and the "Female Jesse James," Belle Starr's exploits may not have been quite as colorful as those of some other Wild West outlaws. But her legend, and her unsolved murder, continue to captivate fans of the Old West.

✳   ✳   ✳   ✳

Good with a Gun

BELLE STARR WAS born Myra Maybelle Shirley on February 5, 1848, in Carthage, Missouri. She enjoyed a comfortable upbringing, graduating from the private Carthage Female Academy, a school that her father helped found. But in addition to her classical education, her older brother, Bud, introduced the young Belle to less ladylike activities including shooting guns and riding horses. His influence would go on to shape the rest of her life.

The Shirley family were Confederate sympathizers, and Bud was killed during an altercation with Union soldiers in 1864. Soon after, the family left Carthage and moved to Scyene, Texas, where Belle married her first husband, Jim Reed, and had two children. Reed had a reputation as a thief, stealing horses, cattle, and money throughout the Dallas area. While there is little evidence that Belle joined her husband in his misdeeds, she gained notoriety as an excellent shot with her pistols, and was often seen riding sidesaddle, wearing velvet skirts and a plumed hat.

Consorting with Criminals

Many historians believe that, despite her flamboyance, Belle wanted nothing more than to live a quiet life as a mother and homemaker. But in 1874, a warrant was issued for her arrest for a stagecoach robbery in which her husband had participated. Before the law could close in, Reed was killed by a member of his own gang, and Belle fled north to Oklahoma Indian Territory.

It was there, in 1880, that Belle met and married a young Cherokee man named Sam Starr. Starr ran his own gang of cattle and horse thieves, and Belle began joining the gang on their escapades. The pair also opened their home to criminals on the run, harboring thieves, bootleggers, and fugitives like Frank and Jesse James. The Starrs ran a lucrative criminal enterprise for three years before they were arrested in 1883. Belle and Sam were convicted of stealing horses, and each spent nine months in prison in Detroit, Michigan.

Once they were released, the couple resumed their life of crime. But tragedy struck in 1886, when Sam was killed in a gunfight. On her own again, Belle found companionship with several different men, eventually settling in with a relative of her late husband, Jim July Starr. Fifteen years her junior, Jim July was the last in Belle's string of outlaw relationships. In 1889, he was summoned to Arkansas to face charges for robbery. Belle accompanied him partway, then said goodbye and headed back to Oklahoma.

An Enduring Mystery

On her way back home, just two days before her 41st birthday, Belle was shot in the back as she rode her horse. She fell to the ground, and the murderer shot her again to make sure the job was done. No one witnessed the shooting, but historians believe the primary suspect was a tenant named Edgar Watson who had rented land from Belle. Watson was a fugitive wanted for murder in Florida, and when Belle heard about his past, she kicked him off her land. It seemed a good enough motive, so Watson was arrested on suspicion of murder; but the evidence was so scanty that he was eventually acquitted.

To this day, the murder of Belle Starr remains officially unsolved. But her story immediately became popularized in Richard K. Fox's novel *Bella Starr, the Bandit Queen, or the Female Jesse James*, published the same year as her death. Belle's legend has continued to endure in literature, music, and film for more than a hundred years.

Murder by Rail: It Didn't Just Happen in Silent Movies

Indeed, there are recorded instances of people being tied to railroad tracks—although it wasn't exactly the most efficient way to kill someone.

✳ ✳ ✳ ✳

I've Been Working on the Railroads

EVERYBODY IS FAMILIAR with the scene: the hero, tied to the railroad tracks, struggling desperately as the locomotive charges onward and blows its horn loudly and futilely. Will the train stop in time? Will the hero free himself in time? He will, of course. (Sorry if we wrecked the suspense.)

More interesting, however, is the question of whether this was ever a common occurrence in real life. The scenario is perfect for a melodrama, but come on—aren't there more efficient ways of killing people?

The whole tied-to-the-railroad-tracks cliché has been around for a long time—about as long as railroads themselves. The new means of transportation, coupled with the public's insatiable hunger for unlikely melodrama, prompted a number of playwrights and hack serial writers to use the idea in the latter half of the nineteenth century. By 1913 the set-up had become such a cliché that it was lampooned in one of the first Hollywood parodies, the silent film *Barney Oldfield's Race for a Life*. Of course, for those of us who weren't alive in 1913, it was Snidely Whiplash of the Dudley Do-Right cartoons who ingrained in our prepubescent minds the idea that tying somebody to the railroad tracks was a preferred method of murder.

The Real-Life Story of August Gardner

As it turns out, tying folks to the railroad tracks didn't just happen in Hollywood or cartoons. There are some documented cases of this dastardly occurrence happening in real-life America. Way back in 1874, for example, a Frenchman named August Gardner was abducted and robbed by three men in Indiana who proceeded to tie him to the railroad tracks and leave him for dead. Gardner wrestled with his bonds as the train approached, freeing one hand and then another. As the train drew closer, he loosed one of his feet. It seemed, in classic melodramatic fashion, that our hero was going to escape with his life.

But alas, he fumbled untying the last knot—the train ran over his foot and cut it off. The plucky Gardner spent the night in a culvert, then hobbled on one foot into a nearby town, where he was able to relay his story before dying.

Of course, the number of documented cases of evildoers tying people to railroad tracks is far smaller than silent films and

Dudley Do-Right cartoons would have you believe. But that's okay—we can accept that the real world doesn't always mirror what happens in the movies or on television. Just don't try to tell us that bad guys don't really twirl their handlebar mustaches as they prepare to enact their devious plans.

Pancho Villa: The Man with Two Faces

Hero or criminal? You decide.

✳ ✳ ✳ ✳

THE MAN THE world knew as Pancho Villa led a contradictory life that caused some to venerate him as a saint and others to loathe him as a fiend. Certainly, Pancho Villa was a man of bold action with an uncanny sense of destiny whose exploits—whether actual or mythical, inherently good or evil—have become the stuff of legend. Even in his own time, he was celebrated as a living folk hero by Mexicans and Americans alike. In fact, film companies sent crews to revolutionary Mexico to chronicle his exploits—a circumstance that pleased the wily Villa, if for no other reason than the gold the directors brought with them. Journalists, novelists, friends, and enemies all conspired to create the image of a man whose true nature remained elusive. To the present day, the name of Francisco "Pancho" Villa continues to inspire both admiration and scorn with equal fervor... depending on whom you ask.

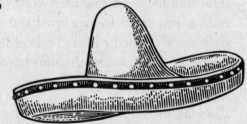

General Pancho Villa: Hero of the People

Pancho Villa was born Doroteo Arango in Durango, Mexico, either in 1877 or 1879. As the son of a peasant family working for a hacienda owner, he realized that he would eventually inherit his father's debt and work the land until the day he died. At age 16, however, Doroteo returned home to find his sister fending off the lecherous advances of a local don. Unable to countenance the dishonoring of his beloved sister, Villa obtained a pistol, shot and killed the offending "gentleman," and escaped to the hills. For nearly ten years, he lived as a bandit, robbing from the rich and giving to the poor men who joined him. With the start of the Mexican Revolution, Villa came down from the mountains to form an army in support of the populist platform espoused by Francisco Madero.

As a general, Villa staged bold cavalry charges that overwhelmed his opponents even at great risk to his own life. General Villa was very popular with the ladies (purportedly marrying 26 times) and loved to dance. However, he did not drink and once famously choked on a dram of brandy offered him by fellow revolutionary General Emiliano Zapata. As the Mexican Revolution ground through a series of corrupt leaders, Villa remained true to his populist ideology.

When his political rival, Venustiano Carranza, came to power, Villa became a wanted man again, this time in both Mexico and the United States. As in his youth, he took to the mountains, evading capture for several years until, weary of life on the run, he surrendered in 1920. Villa purchased a former hacienda known as La Purísima Concepción de El Canutillo and moved there with about 400 of his soldiers and their families. Rather than become like the wealthy landowners he despised, however, Villa used the hacienda to form an agricultural community that soon swelled to approximately 2,000 men, women, and children who received an education and shared in the profits.

Pancho Villa: Murderous Thug

When American President Woodrow Wilson chose to support the presidency of Villa's rival Venustiano Carranza, Villa retaliated. On January 11, 1916, Villa and a group of his men stopped a train in Santa Ysabel, Mexico, and brutally killed

18 Texas businessmen. Murder and banditry were nothing new to Villa; as a young man he had made his living stealing cattle and was a murderer before he reached 20. As a revolutionary general, he ordered executions for specious reasons, robbed herds of cattle to sell north of the border, and shot merchants who refused to take the money he had printed for his army. His cattle thieving incensed powerful newspaper magnate William Randolph Hearst, who conducted a long-term smear campaign against the bandit, which, among other things, led to the criminalization of marijuana in the United States.

Pancho Villa's greatest moment of infamy, however, came at 2:30 A.M. on March 9, 1916, when he led a band of 500 horse-mounted followers against the 13th U.S. Cavalry and then into Columbus, New Mexico, where the bandits killed indiscriminately and destroyed property. When the Villistas departed at 7:00 A.M., 14 American soldiers, 10 civilians, and scores of bandits lay dead.

President Wilson ordered Brigadier General John J. Pershing to lead a punitive cavalry expedition into Mexico to capture Villa but multiple, costly attempts to corner the cunning outlaw proved fruitless. Soon, the nuisance of Pancho Villa was replaced in the national consciousness by the United States' entry into the war raging in Europe.

The End of the Man, the Start of the Legend

Pancho Villa was assassinated by unknown persons while visiting the village of Parral in 1923. After Villa's death, one of his officers allegedly opened his tomb in Parral and removed his head to sell to a Chicago millionaire who collected skulls. Villa's body was later moved to Mexico City and interred in the Tomb of the Illustrious, but many believe that it was simply a headless decoy and his true resting place remains in Northern Mexico. Thus, even the final resting place of Villa's body has become obscured by speculation and doubt.

Gregorio Cortez—Texas Folk Hero

The trend of lionizing fighters against lawful authority goes back to the days of Robin Hood and perhaps even earlier. More than a century ago, Tejanos (Texans of Hispanic origin) had their own legendary figure: Gregorio Cortez.

✳ ✳ ✳ ✳

✳ Cortez was born in Matamoros, Mexico, in 1875. His family moved across the border when he was 12, and he began learning how to farm and be a cowboy.

✳ To understand why the legend of Gregorio Cortez matters today, one must realize the context. When he came to the United States, it had only been some 50 years since Texas had gained its independence from Mexico. Spanish-speaking people had lived in Texas for centuries before it joined the United States, but they now found themselves playing second fiddle to English-speaking Texans.

✳ Cortez's affable nature contributed to the way his story unfolded, and it definitely affected his esteemed place in Texas folklore. Unlike reviled outlaws such as John Wesley Hardin, Cortez was not a habitual criminal and was liked and trusted by both English- and Spanish-speakers.

✳ Everything went downhill for Cortez in 1901, when two county sheriffs and two deputies went hunting for a horse thief. In those days, people took a dim view of horse thieves, and if the law didn't string them up, vigilantes would do so without a second thought. Calling a man a horse thief was like calling him a liar: an insult not easily wiped away without bloodshed.

✳ The sheriffs contributed this precise description of the culprit: "medium-size Mexican." In Kenedy, Texas (50 miles southeast of San Antonio), in 1901, that description could have applied to virtually anyone. However, a nearby resident told the deputies he had recently traded horses with Cortez and revealed where they could find him.

* According to legend, one of the deputies mistranslated Cortez's statement from Spanish to English. Cortez had said something like "you have no reason to arrest me," but the deputy believed he said, "No white man can arrest me."

* It's unclear if the sheriffs took this bad translation as a "you'll-never-take-me-alive" threat or as simple disrespect for the law. Regardless, one of the sheriffs shot and wounded Cortez's brother Romuldo. Cortez then drew his gun and killed his brother's assailant.

* Now Cortez was really in hot water. He managed to escape, but his mother, wife, and children were captured. However, there is no evidence that sheriffs had any legal grounds to detain them. Cortez grew even more distrustful of law enforcement.

* County sheriffs eventually cornered Cortez at a neighboring house. By this time, Cortez probably didn't expect anything but a long rope and a short drop if he were captured, so he fought back. One deputy and the property's owner died in the resulting gunfight, but Cortez escaped again.

* Cortez then walked about a hundred miles to the home of a friend, who gave him a saddled horse and some supplies so that Cortez could proceed to the border town of Laredo.

* By now the law was after Cortez in full cry. Authorities even offered a $1,000 bounty for his capture, an enormous sum of money at the time. Hundreds of people became part of the posse to chase down the fugitive.

* As Cortez's reputation spread throughout Texas, an odd thing happened: The English-speaking press and public took a shine to him, admiring his ability to lead the authorities on such a wild chase. To elude the famous Texas Rangers was

no small feat. Cortez was becoming not just a Tejano folk hero but a folk hero for all Texans.

* Even with this newfound multicultural popularity, the chase of Gregorio Cortez provoked some ugly racial violence in several Texas counties.

* A posse captured Cortez near Laredo on June 22, 1901, just ten days after the chase had begun. When he was sent back north to face trial, it became clear that not everyone admired Cortez, and the police had to face down at least one lynch mob.

* For killing the landowner in the second fight, a Gonzales County jury sentenced Cortez to 50 years in jail. Although this sentence was thrown out, he was sentenced to life in prison for killing the sheriff's deputy during the same shootout.

* While Cortez was jailed, his wife of 13 years, Leonor Díaz, divorced him, claiming that he had abused her, both physically and verbally. Less than two years later, while still imprisoned, Cortez married Estéfana Garza.

* In jail, Cortez was a model prisoner, popular with his jailers and fellow inmates of all backgrounds. Outside the walls of the jail, sentiment began to build for his release.

* Gregorio Cortez served 12 years in prison, and in 1913, Governor Oscar Colquitt pardoned him. Following his release, he went back to Mexico to fight in the Mexican Revolution. He died of pneumonia in 1916.

* Why did an accused killer and horse thief inspire such admiration from so many Texans? Surely it helped to be liked. As word spread about Cortez, many people believed that he was a good person in an unfortunate situation, rather than just a bad person. People also admired his resourcefulness. Certainly, notions of fairness played a part, as Cortez's story

is one of hasty and unwarranted accusation. Most important, Cortez didn't set out looking to start a fight, but when one began, he dared to finish it.

✳ Gregorio Cortez has lived on in ballads, books, and film. Américo Paredes explored the legend in his 1958 book, *With His Pistol in His Hand: A Border Ballad and Its Hero*, which challenged some of the stereotypes that had surrounded the story.

✳ In the early 1980s, Edward James Olmos starred as Cortez in the film *The Ballad of Gregorio Cortez*.

New York City?!

Legendary western outlaw Billy the Kid was born in New York City! His family followed a common path out west during the twilight of the Manifest Destiny era.

✳　✳　✳　✳

Lonely Boy

HENRY MCCARTY WAS born and baptized in Manhattan before moving with his family first to Indianapolis and then to New Mexico. After his mother died, he took a job working in exchange for room and board at a boardinghouse in town. But before long, he had begun committing petty thefts and crimes in town and was unceremoniously escorted out and unwelcome to return. Billy stayed briefly with his stepfather, whom he also stole from before absconding. He continued to alternate working, losing money, fighting, and stealing.

21 Kills?

The legend does that Bily the Kid killed 21 men, one for each year of his life. Was that true? Here's what we know. In 1877, at Fort Grant in Arizona Territory, Billy the Kid was repeatedly slapped and then thrown to the ground by a burly blacksmith named F. P. Cahill. Because he'd been bullied by Cahill for months, the slightly built 17-year-old pulled out a revolver and fatally wounded him. Then, in a Fort Sumner saloon early in 1880, the Kid was challenged by gunman Joe Grant. When Grant's six-gun misfired, the Kid pumped a slug into the man's head. The following year, the Kid shot his way out of jail in Lincoln, New Mexico, and gunned down guards J. W. Bell and Bob Olinger in the process.

Cahill, Grant, Bell, and Olinger are the four men who are known to have fallen under the revolver fire of Billy the Kid. But the Kid was also a central figure in New Mexico's bloody Lincoln County War. Early in the conflict, the Kid and several comrades, lusting for vengeance, blasted two prisoners, Frank Baker and William Morton. Then the Kid led an ambush on Lincoln's main (and only) street, and the bushwhackers killed Sheriff William Brady and Deputy George Hindman.

During the five-day Battle of Lincoln in July 1878, the Kid was blamed for killing Bob Beckwith, though there is a strong case that Beckwith fell to friendly fire.

Eventually, a sheriff named Pat Garrett, who'd sought Billy for months or even years, found Billy and shot him to death. Billy was 21.

The Legend Begins

A conspiracy theory sprang up almost immediately that Sheriff Garrett had been in the wrong to kill Billy or that the killing had been dishonorable, which seems ludicrous given Billy's crimes. As with Bonnie and Clyde and other true-crime legends, Billy's actions were more egregious and capricious than they're painted in hindsight.

Fame and Legacy

Billy appears in a cameo role in the 2014 video game *80 Days*, in which an adapted Phileas Fogg and Passepartout make their way around the world from an array of transit options between major cities. He boards their train in the American west, more like a Doolin-Dalton outlaw gang member than his own biography. But no other outlaw has the level of recognition that Billy has. If Bill Doolin boarded the train, no one would bat an eye.

The contrast between New York and the Old West was less pronounced in Billy's lifetime than it is today—think of the clashing gang culture immortalized in *Gangs of New York* or the relative anarchy in Mark Helprin's novel *Winter's Tale*. But today, when this biographical tidbit makes many of us think of the "New York City?!" commercial for Pace picante sauce, Billy's birthplace and life's work seem at odds.

The Cast of Characters at the O.K. Corral

The most notorious gunfight in the Wild West featured an array of people—from the good to the bad to the ugly—who were perfectly suited for a Hollywood movie.

✳   ✳   ✳   ✳

The Setting

FIRST, THE FAMOUS showdown in Tombstone, Arizona, didn't take place in the O.K. Corral—it happened in the city's vacant lot No. 2. Somehow, "The Shoot-out in Vacant Lot No. 20 doesn't have quite the same ring to it, so a savvy journalist or scriptwriter must have moved the action a few yards over.

Second, despite what the movies may suggest, it wasn't a simple tale of white hats versus black hats. The real story has as many twists and turns as a warren of prairie dog tunnels, with a roundup of suspects that includes carousing cowboys, contentious lawmen, corrupt politicians, card sharks, cattle rustlers, a dentist named Doc, and Doc's lady friend (the appropriately named Big Nose Kate).

The Characters

What do we know for sure? On October 26, 1881, at around 3:00 PM, four men entered the lot behind the O.K. Corral: Wyatt Earp, his brothers Virgil and Morgan, and John Henry "Doc" Holliday. There, they encountered Ike Clanton, his brother Billy, Frank and Tom McLaury, and Billy Claiborne. Thirty seconds later, both of the McLaury brothers and Billy Clanton were dead. Virgil and Morgan Earp sustained serious wounds, Holliday suffered a minor injury, and Wyatt walked out without a scratch.

What brought them there? Trouble had been brewing between the Earp and Clanton factions for quite some time. Doc Holliday, a Philadelphia-trained dentist, preferred playing cards to pulling teeth, and this habit often left him short of cash. Earlier in 1881, he had been accused of stagecoach robbery by his own girlfriend, Big Nose Kate. The Earp brothers suspected that Ike Clanton had put her up to it to deflect suspicion from Clanton's friends. When four of those friends turned up dead, Clanton accused the Earps, and the bad blood began to boil.

The Gunfight

Who fired first? Most historians agree that Holliday and Morgan Earp started it, one wounding Frank McLaury and the other Billy Clanton. With that, as the locals say, "the ball had begun." An estimated 30 shots were fired within half a minute. Wyatt claimed that 17 were his, though he is only thought to have killed one man, Tom McLaury.

The Earps and Holliday were ultimately acquitted of any wrongdoing. Several months later, Morgan Earp was shot to death by unknown assailants. Wyatt spent the next two years tracking down everyone he thought was connected with his brother's death. Was he "brave, courageous, and bold," as the song says? Or was he just a ruthless vigilante? The jury is still out. One thing is certain, though: Wyatt Earp was an American original, and his story will be told for generations to come.

Tragedy at the Haymarket

What began as a campaign for an eight-hour workday ended with a bloody event Chicago will never forget.

✳ ✳ ✳ ✳

IT WAS THE mid-1880s, and Chicago was in a state of transition. Industry was growing more and more mechanized—good news for the corporations that were able to increase profits and lower wages, but bad news for workers who were putting in 12 to 14 grueling hours a day, 6 miserable days a week. In October 1884, the Federation of Organized Trade and Labor Unions set a goal to make the eight-hour workday standard, even if nationwide strikes were necessary to make that goal a reality. The stage was set.

The Calm Before the Storm

On May 1, 1886, hundreds of thousands of workers across the country took to the streets in support of an eight-hour workday. The first few days of the strike were relatively peaceful, but all hell broke loose on May 3, when police killed several unarmed strikers near Chicago's McCormick Reaper Works.

Workers gathered in a light rain in Haymarket Square on the West Side on May 4. Mayor Carter Harrison Sr. stopped by in a show of support for the workers, then left early when it appeared that all was peaceful. The rest, as they say, is history—and a somewhat murky history at that, as many questions remain about what unfolded in the incident now known as the Haymarket Riot.

Every Man for Himself

Once the mayor left, the police inspector sent in the riot police to disperse the crowd. At the same time, a bomb blasted the ranks of the police force. The police opened fire. Workers reportedly returned fire. A few short minutes later, eight policemen were dead, and scores of workers and bystanders had been injured. The *Chicago Tribune* later quoted an unnamed police officer, who reported, "a very large number of the police were wounded by each other's revolvers . . . It was every man for himself, and while some got two or three squares away, the rest emptied their revolvers, mainly into each other."

The Fallout

Chicago police immediately swept across the city in search of the bomber. They arrested eight known anarchists (August Spies, Samuel Fielden, Oscar Neebe, Michael Schwab, Louis Lingg, George Engel, Adolph Fischer, and Albert Parsons) and charged them with the crime. After a well-publicized trial, the jury (which included a Marshall Field's sales rep and not a single industrial worker) returned guilty verdicts for all eight, even though only two of the men were even at the Haymarket the night of the incident. The men had clearly been tried for their incendiary speeches leading up to the Haymarket incident, not for anything they had actually done. Seven of the men were sentenced to death, and the show trial resulted in protests around the world.

Seriously, Who Threw the Bomb?

Spies, Fischer, Engel, and Parsons were hanged on November 11, 1887; Lingg had committed suicide in prison one day earlier. Governor Altgeld pardoned Schwab, Fielden, and Neebe in 1893. To the present day, no one is absolutely sure who threw the bomb, but most historians believe it was one of two anarchists who were present at the protest that day: Rudolph Schnaubelt or George Meng—neither of whom was ever arrested for the crime.

Historians consider Haymarket one of the seminal events in the history of labor, and its legacy resonates to this day. The Haymarket defendants stand as icons of the American labor movement and are remembered with rallies, parades, and speeches around the world on the anniversary of the bombing. But most important is the spirit of assembly that can be traced back to Haymarket. Today, monuments stand at the corner of Des Plaines and Randolph streets (near the spot where the bomb was thrown) and in Forest Park, Illinois, at the grave of Spies, Fischer, Engel, Parsons, and Lingg. These symbols are poignant reminders of Chicago's critical place in labor history.

Jack the Ripper and Royalty

Between 1888 and 1891, he brutally murdered at least five women in London's East End. But was there really a connection between Jack the Ripper and the British royal family?

❋   ❋   ❋   ❋

IT'S ONE OF the most famous cold cases in history. The serial killer known as Jack the Ripper is one of history's most famous murderers. He breathed terror into the gas-lit streets and foggy back alleys of the Whitechapel area of London and became renowned the world over. Despite the countless books and movies detailing his story, however, his identity and motives remain shrouded in mystery. In the absence of hard evidence, speculation abounds. One of the most popular theories, espoused by the 2001 movie *From Hell* (starring Johnny Depp), links the killer to the British royal family.

The Crimes

Five murders are definitively attributed to Jack the Ripper, and he has variously been connected to at least six other unsolved slayings in the London area. The body of the first victim, 43-year-old Mary Ann Nichols, was discovered on the morning of August 31, 1888. Nichols's throat had been cut and her abdomen mutilated.

The subsequent murders, which took place over a three-year period, grew in brutality. The killer removed the uterus of his second victim, Annie Chapman; part of the womb and left kidney of Catherine Eddowes; and the heart of Mary Kelly. All of his victims were prostitutes.

The Name

A man claiming to be the murderer sent a letter (dated September 25, 1888) to the Central News Agency, which passed it on to the Metropolitan Police. The letter included the line, "I am down on whores and I shant quit ripping them till I do get buckled." It was signed, "Yours truly, Jack the Ripper." A later postcard included the same sign-off. When police went public with details of the letters, the evocative name "Jack the Ripper" stuck.

The Suspects

Officers from the Metropolitan Police and Scotland Yard had four main suspects: a poor Polish resident of Whitechapel by the name of Kosminski, a barrister who committed suicide in December 1888, a Russian-born thief, and an American doctor who fled to the States in November 1888 while on bail for gross indecency. Since there was little or no evidence against any of these men, the case spawned many conspiracy theories, the most popular of which links the killings to the royal family.

The Royal Conspiracy

The heir to the British throne was Prince Albert Victor, grandson of Queen Victoria and son of the man who would later become King Edward VII. The prince, popularly known as Eddy, had a penchant for hanging around in the East End, and rumors abounded that he had a daughter, Alice, out of wedlock with a shop girl named Annie Crook. To prevent major embarrassment to the Crown, Eddy sought assistance from Queen Victoria's physician, Dr. William Gull, who institutionalized Annie to keep her quiet. However, her friends, including Mary Kelly, also knew the identity of Alice's father, so Dr. Gull created the persona of Jack the Ripper and brutally silenced them one by one.

A variation on this theory has Dr. Gull acting without the knowledge of the prince, instead driven by madness resulting from a stroke he suffered in 1887.

Royal involvement would certainly explain why the police were unable to uncover the identity of the Ripper or to even settle on a prime suspect. There *was* a shop girl named Annie Crook who had an illegitimate daughter named Alice, but there is nothing to connect her to either the prince or the murdered prostitutes. In fact, there is no evidence to suggest that the murdered women knew one another. Until the identity of Jack the Ripper is settled beyond doubt, these and other conspiracy theories will likely persist.

Mother Knows Best

You might think that someone with a nickname like "Ma Barker" would spend her time baking pies and graciously entertaining guests. But this matriarch is known for actions that were much less wholesome.

✳ ✳ ✳ ✳

Boys Will Be Boys

BORN ARIZONA CLARK on October 8, 1873, in Ash Grove, Missouri, the child later known as Ma Barker regularly attended church with her family but was also known for her headstrong attitude and quick temper. One day when she was a young girl, she witnessed the outlaw Jesse James and his gang riding through her hometown. Some historians believe that it was this moment that shaped the rest of her life.

After marrying George Barker in 1892, Barker had four sons: Herman, Lloyd, Arthur, and Fred. While most mothers try to teach their children right from wrong, Barker tended to be lenient with her sons, rarely disciplining them and getting angry at anyone else who did. Consequently, all four boys ran wild and got into trouble with the law from a young age. Herman, the oldest, was the first to be arrested, in 1910; the other three soon followed, with charges ranging from petty theft all the way up to murder.

The family eventually left Missouri and moved to Tulsa, Oklahoma, where the boys continued to find trouble. In 1927, Herman committed suicide to avoid prosecution for murdering a police officer, and by the next year, Lloyd, Arthur, and Fred were all imprisoned. George, fed up with his sons' lawlessness and his wife's "loose morals," moved out, and Barker was left alone, living in poverty with no children, husband, or job.

Joining the Gang

In 1931, Fred was released from prison, but he certainly hadn't learned any lessons. He immediately joined up with a former cellmate named Alvin Karpis, and the two began pulling off robberies throughout the Midwest. Barker, fully approving of the newly formed Barker-Karpis Gang, often traveled with them and allowed them to hide out in her Tulsa home. After Fred and Karpis murdered a Missouri sheriff named C. Roy Kelly, Barker was featured on a wanted poster as an accomplice to the crime.

But this didn't deter Barker or slow down the Barker-Karpis Gang. In fact, their next robbery was their biggest yet, when they made a clean getaway from the Northwestern National Bank in Minneapolis with more than a quarter of a million dollars, an amount that would be worth more than $4 million today! By September of 1932, Arthur had been released from

prison, and the gang was stronger than ever. They traveled between Minnesota and Wisconsin, where they moved on from robbing banks to kidnapping wealthy businessmen for ransom. Barker stayed in various hotels and apartments, remaining hidden while her sons committed crimes and laundered the ransom money.

Downfall

But a new technology—finger-print identification—was help-ing the authorities close in on the Barker-Karpis Gang. Barker and Fred fled to Florida, where they rented a house as a hide-out. Unfortunately for them, Arthur, who had stayed behind in Chicago, was arrested and found to be in possession of a map that gave away their loca-tion. On January 16, 1935, the FBI surrounded the house and ordered the occupants to surren-der. But Barker and Fred refused to go down without a fight. Fred opened fire with a machine gun, sparking an hours-long gunfight. When the bullets finally stopped flying, both Barker and Fred were discovered in an upstairs bedroom of the house, dead from gunshot wounds.

While Ma Barker's legend as a notorious gang leader has been portrayed in films, television, and music, some historians believe she has been unfairly maligned. While there is no question that her sons participated in criminal activity, there is little evidence that she joined them or actually helped to plan their exploits. Still, her role as the gang's matronly caregiver has been enough to cement her name in history as an unlikely criminal sympathizer.

Chapter 14

So Sue Me

One of the benefits of living in a democratic country with a well-established judicial system is the opportunity to use the courts to achieve justice and set wrongs right. But there is a drawback—some folks go to court about things that make most of us shake our heads. Take a look at the odd cases found in this chapter and judge for yourself.

✳　✳　✳　✳

Bubbles Aren't Always Fun

Early on the morning of July 7, 2001, a prankster dumped detergent into a public park fountain in Duluth, Minnesota, creating a mountain of bubbles. A few hours later, passerby Kathy Kelly fell down and suffered several injuries. She sued the city because it had not cleaned up the suds (on Saturday morning) or posted warnings to citizens urging them not to walk through the slippery wall of bubbles. A jury in March 2004 found the city 70 percent responsible for Kelly's injuries—leaving her with only 30 percent of the blame—and thus awarded her $125,000.

Fingered as a Scam

In March 2005, Ann Ayala filed a claim against a Wendy's franchise owner, asserting that she had found a fingertip in a bowl of chili. But authorities found no evidence of missing fingers at the accused restaurant. Suspicion turned on Ayala, who dropped the suit when reporters discovered that she had previously accused several other companies of wrongdoing.

No Good Deed Goes Unpunished

In July 2004, two teenage girls in Colorado baked cookies and delivered them to their neighbors. But the door-knocking apparently scared resident Wanita Young, who had an anxiety attack, went to the hospital, and sued the girls' families. A local judge awarded Young almost $900 for medical expenses but denied her half-baked demand for nearly $3,000 in itemized expenses, including lost wages and new motion-sensor lights for her porch.

All Toys Are Not Equal

Jodee Berry, a Hooter's waitress in Florida, won the restaurant's sales contest and thought she'd just won the new Toyota that her bosses said the champion would get. The prize was actually a toy Yoda, not a Toyota, so she left her job and sued the franchisee for breach of contract and fraudulent misrepresentation. The force was with Berry—the out-of-court settlement in May 2002 allowed her to pick out any Toyota car she wanted.

Trespass at the Owner's Risk

Let's say you're illegally sneaking onto a railroad's property so you can get a view from the top of a boxcar—and then an electrical wire above the car electrocutes you. What do you do? Obviously, you sue the railroad! In October 2006, a jury awarded more than $24 million to two young men who were severely burned while atop a parked railroad car in Lancaster, Pennsylvania, in 2002. The jury said that, although they were trespassing, the 17-year-old boys bore no responsibility. Instead the blame fell entirely on Amtrak and Norfolk Southern for failing to post signs warning of the danger from the electrified wires that power locomotives. For medical costs, pain and suffering, and "loss of life pleasures," one boy received $17.3 million and the other $6.8 million.

Sue the Pants Off Them

In 2005, in one of the most outrageous lawsuits of recent times, Roy Pearson, a Washington, D.C. judge, sued a small mom-

and-pop dry cleaner for $54 million for misplacing his pants. The shop's owners, Jin and Soo Chung, returned the pants a week later, but Pearson refused them, saying they were not his $800 trousers but a cheap imitation. He also sued the Chungs and their son $1,500 each, per day for more than a year, claiming that the store's signs, which read "Satisfaction Guaranteed" and "Same Day Service," were fraudulent. In 2007, a judge ruled in favor of the Chungs and ordered Pearson to pay the couple's court costs, and possibly their attorney fees as well.

Spilling the (Coffee) Beans

Then there's the most notorious of lawsuits. Stella Liebeck, of Albuquerque, sued McDonald's in 1992 after spilling a cup of the restaurant's coffee, which burned her lap severely and hospitalized her for a week. Two years later, a jury awarded her $160,000 in direct damages and $2.7 million in punitive damages, which a court later reduced to $480,000. Both parties appealed, and they eventually settled out of court for an undisclosed amount—surely enough for her to buy McDonald's coffee for the rest of her life. Liebeck inspired the creation of the Stella Awards, which highlight particularly "wild, outrageous, or ridiculous lawsuits."

What the Devil Is Wrong with This Fellow?

A Pennsylvania man filed a claim against "Satan and his staff," alleging that the "Prince of Darkness" had made the plaintiff's life a miserable failure. He also claimed that "Old Scratch" had "deprived him of his constitutional rights" and, since he was poor due to the devil's work, he couldn't afford the court costs. The court had to deny the claim, on a technicality, as no directions had been supplied as to the known whereabouts of Satan for U.S. marshals to serve him the papers.

From Soup to Nuts

A Florida man stopped by a chain restaurant and ordered a bowl of potato soup. Served clam chowder by mistake, the man claimed he suffered an allergic reaction and subsequent nightmares from the experience. He sued the chain for more than $55,000 for medical costs and pain and suffering. Refusing an out-of-court settlement for $1,000, he went to trial. The jury found the man 90 percent responsible for his damages and awarded him only $407 for his claim. But he wasn't finished yet—the restaurant chain also sued him to recover their legal costs.

You Just Have To Hand It To Him . . .

When a carpenter grabbed his circular saw one morning, he noticed a strange marking on his hand. It was 666—the mark of the Devil! There was only one thing to do—he had to cut off his hand. Fellow workers packed the severed hand in ice and sent it with the carpenter to the hospital. A physician almost convinced him that two hands were better than one, but the carpenter insisted that the hand not be reattached. Several months later, the carpenter sued the doctor for $144,000 for listening to his demand. The jury, throwing up its hands, threw the case out.

Sometimes Life Stinks

A maintenance worker for a mobile home trailer court was asked to investigate an awful odor emanating from one of the homes. His inspection revealed a rotting, maggot-infested opossum, which he quickly removed and dumped. But it seems the smell was too much for him, and he suffered a heart attack as a result. The insurance company refused his worker's compensation claim, saying his weak heart was a preexisting condition. The jury didn't agree and awarded the man his full compensation benefit.

He Should Have Stuck with Being a Snack Parent

Many youth league baseball coaches manage their teams with their hearts on their jersey sleeves. They live and die for their kids, so what could be worse than a losing season? How about getting sued for a losing season? One coach finished the season 0–15 and was then served with a lawsuit for $2,000 from the father of his team's catcher. The suit claimed poor coaching cost the team a trip to a tournament. A judge found the claimant was way off base and dismissed the case.

Goosed Out of a Job

Many strange things can happen when starting a new job. A man tried to enter his office building on only his second day with the company when he found himself under attack by swooping wild Canadian geese. In trying to escape their wrath, he fell and broke his wrist. He sued his company, claiming they had built their offices in a dangerous "high-goose" area, complete with short grass and a pond to attract the feathered fowls. A jury found in the plaintiff's favor, awarding him more than $17,000 for his injury.

A-Wunerful, A-Wunerful

A young man paid plenty for the new high-tech sound system installed in his truck. Bass rumbling, he motored down his neighborhood streets—until a police officer arrested him for playing his loud music with the truck windows down. A judge offered the guilty offender a choice—he could pay a $100 fine or listen to four hours of polka music. He chose the polka music and can now sing "Who Stole the Kishka" with the best of the polka kings.

He Ought to Get Some Credit for Trying

During the 1990s, a prisoner doing time in Virginia for breaking and entering and grand larceny came up with a novel way of getting someone else to pay for his troubles. Noting that his civil rights had been abused, he sued himself for violating his own religious beliefs by getting drunk. Suffering from the effects of drinking too much, he maintained, he failed to exercise good judgment and had committed the acts that had led to his arrest and incarceration. The prisoner believed he was owed five million dollars for all this: three million for his wife and children for pain and suffering, and two million to make up for the salary he'd fail to earn during his 23-year sentence. Since he was behind bars, however, he had no money to pay in case the judgment went against (or would that be for?) him. But he had a solution: As a prisoner, he was a "ward of the state," so that meant the government should be responsible for his debts. Alas, he neither won nor lost, as the judge threw the case out of court.

Fear of Flying

An airline was found liable when a flight was too bumpy. Flying into a thunderstorm in 1995, a pilot for a large commercial jet failed to turn on the "fasten seat belt" signs, and passengers were caught by surprise in what they claimed was extremely violent turbulence. Not wearing seat belts, of course, some of the passengers were thrown from their seats, and many thought the plane was going down and that they were all going to die. Particularly traumatized, the suit claimed, were the children aboard the plane. In part, the lawsuit argued that the flight crew and those on the ground could have used radar to detect and avoid the storm. At the very least, the seat belt sign could have served as a warning. A jury granted the 13 passengers who sued a total of two million dollars for their emotional distress.

His Reputation Was at "Steak"

Who doesn't like a nice steak now and then? One man went to his local steak house, ordered a thick and juicy slab, and asked for the senior-citizen discount. There was one problem—he was only 31 years old, so the discount didn't apply. He sued the restaurant chain for age discrimination. Not only did the judge throw the claim out like a spoiled sirloin—he fined the man more than $8,500 for abusing the legal system.

Swept Under the Carpet

Two carpet layers were doing their job in a basement when a hot-water heater kicked on, igniting a nearby three-and-a-half gallon container of carpet adhesive and severely burning the men. Apparently, cautionary statements on the can's label such as "Flammable" and "Keep Away from Heat" meant nothing to them. They filed a lawsuit against the adhesive company, claiming the warnings on the label weren't sufficient. A jury agreed—the men received $8 million for their ignorance.

Seeking the "Plane" Truth

A prominent food company ran a promotion offering all sorts of prizes to contestants who collected points by buying the company's products. A TV commercial emphasized the magnitude of the prizes by showing a full-size fighter jet and flashing "7,000,000 points" on the screen. One clever participant accrued the 7,000,000 points and filed suit for fraud when the company refused to award the jet. A judge ruled that no "reasonable person" could believe a company would actually offer a $22 million jet in exchange for seven million points and dismissed the case.

Barefoot Book Boy Banned

A young man seeking knowledge entered an Ohio library shoeless and was turned away, as the library's policy required patrons to wear shoes. For the next four years, the man tried to enter the library barefoot only to be sent away. Fed up, library officials finally handed the man a banning for one day. He filed a lawsuit, claiming his First Amendment rights had been violated. The suit was denied—first by a federal district court and then by a court of appeals, which noted that the safety of the public, as well as the individual's feet, was at risk.

I Saw It First!

After-holiday sales often result in spirited shopping, as customers compete for bargains. Sometimes too spirited. In one case, two women grabbed the same crystal figurine bears at the same time, which turned into a fight. One of the women sued the store, saying they should have protected her from other customers. Her husband also sued, claiming loss of income, "company and consortium" due to the incident. Seeking $600,000 in damages, the couple was disappointed when the lower court and court of appeals each turned the suit down.

Doing It for the Kids

Basketball Town, a sports and recreational facility for kids in California, was forced to shut down as a result of $100,000 in legal fees because of a lawsuit filed by a wheelchair-bound man. The plaintiff claimed he couldn't attend a party on the mezzanine level there because it wasn't wheelchair accessible. Even the offer of a $35,000 wheelchair lift wasn't enough to mollify the plaintiff. The legal wrangling and countersuits led most to believe the only solution would be to close the facility.

Just Put It on His Tab

After several break-ins, a bar owner decided to set a trap, along with a warning sign around his windows, to convince wannabe burglars that it just wasn't worth it. But a drunken and drug-crazed robber tried anyway and set off the trap, electrocuting himself. The district attorney chose not to pursue murder charges, but the burglar's family sued the bar owner anyway. A jury awarded the family $150,000, but that amount was later cut in half when somebody realized that the burglar should have to take at least some of the responsibility.

What Does That R on the Gear Shift Mean Again?

After a night of hard drinking, a young woman accidentally backed her car off a dock. Although her passenger managed to get out and escape, the inebriated driver couldn't get out of her seat belt and didn't survive. The driver's parents sued the carmaker for making a seat belt their daughter couldn't operate underwater, even though her blood alcohol level was 0.17—almost twice the legal limit. A jury found the car company mostly responsible for the woman's fate and awarded her family $65 million. Cooler heads prevailed when an appeals court tossed the verdict out.

Staying on Track

After a woman was struck by a metropolitan subway train in a major city, she was awarded $14.1 million. While these dreadful events happen all the time, this one was a bit different.

Further investigation by the city's police force revealed that the woman had been attempting suicide and was lying across the tracks when the train ran over her. The conductor was warned of the situation and slowed the train down but did not stop it. Yet, when the court learned of the suicide attempt, the ruling wasn't thrown out. It was instead reduced by 30 percent, to $9.9 million.

The Fruit of the Suit

Back in 1893, in the case of *Nix v. Hedden*, the U.S. Supreme Court was called upon to solve a question that had plagued salad-eaters for centuries: Was the tomato a fruit or a vegetable? The decision was important because, at the time, imported vegetables were taxed while imported fruit was not. Chief Justice Melville Fuller and his associates ignored botanical evidence that established the tomato as a fruit—rather, they considered dictionary definitions and expert testimony. The result? The court unanimously found the tomato to be a veggie.

Yourself for the Defense

Under the Sixth Amendment to the U.S. Constitution, everyone accused of a crime is entitled to legal representation. If someone can't afford a lawyer, a public defender is appointed. The accused may choose to defend himself or herself—sometimes with less than successful results. In one such case, the defendant questioned the victim, asking, "Did you get a good look at my face when I took your purse?" The defendant was found guilty and sentenced to ten years in jail for robbery.

Turn the Other Cheek

A woman teaching catechism filed suit against her archdiocese after her pastor punched her. She sued the church for emotional distress, defamation, and battery following a disagreement on how she was teaching the lessons of the Lord to her grade-school-age students. When the archdiocese refused to acknowledge or investigate her complaint, the woman felt she had no alternative but to file the lawsuit. A jury found in her favor and awarded her nearly one million dollars for the assault. The guilty priest may have gotten off easy—he died three weeks into the trial.

Landlord Lands a Legal Lulu

An apartment landlord acknowledged that he had committed 70 out of more than 400 alleged building-code violations. The judge gave him a choice of sentences—he could either spend up to 17 years in jail and pay up to $21,000 in fines, or he could live in one of his own apartment buildings for two months. Seeking to demonstrate that the conditions in his buildings weren't as bad as they had been portrayed, he chose to live amid the rats and filth in an apartment that had no heat or functioning refrigerator. His first day in his new home? Christmas Eve.

She'll Drink to That

A woman employed by a drug and alcohol treatment center as a teacher for recovering abusers was fired after her third conviction for drunk driving. She sued the center for wrongful termination, claiming she hadn't corrupted any students and her ability to teach hadn't been affected (even if the same thing couldn't be said for her driving). The state's education chief upheld the firing, citing a zero-tolerance statute. The state courts agreed, leaving her (it's hoped) not too high and dry.

What a Drag

Two young men headed out on a Friday night for a beer-filled evening of fun. They took things a little too far by hurling empty bottles at a woman in her car. Caught by the police, they were found guilty of criminal damage, fined $250, and given a choice of spending two months in jail or walking through downtown for one hour dressed as women. The men chose to don dresses and wigs.

Piercings Get to the Point

The big retailer hired a young lady, knowing she had four ear piercings and several tattoos. Within several years, however, the woman had joined a religious group that encouraged body piercing, and she had her eyebrow pierced. Since the retailer had a policy against facial piercings, the employee was terminated. The Equal Employment Opportunity Commission found she had been discriminated against, and she filed a $2 million claim against her former employer. But the District Court and Court of Appeals denied the claim of discrimination, leaving the woman's claim as full of holes as her ears.

Gimme an S! Gimme a U! Gimme an E!

Nearly 100 high school cheerleaders decided to file a suit against their district administrators after that organization banned many of their cheerleading moves and routines— including pyramids, mounts, and tumbling—as "dangerous and unnecessary." The girls claimed that grounding their activities was like asking a football team to stop tackling. In protest, the cheerleaders tossed around cardboard cutouts of themselves at that season's football games. A judge went along with the kids, issuing an injunction against the ban and leaving the cheerleaders jumping for joy.

She Let Her Fingers Do the Walking

Troubled by the unsightly bulge around her midsection, a woman decided to get liposuction. Consulting her local phone book, she chose a physician—not bothering to determine whether the doctor was board certified in plastic surgery. In fact, the doctor she selected was actually a dermatologist. That, however, didn't stop him from performing the surgery. When the botched procedure left scars across her belly, she sued—the phone book company, blaming them for not noting whether the doctor was properly licensed in cosmetic surgery. A jury found in her favor, awarding $1.2 million to her and an additional $375,000 to her husband for loss of spousal services.

Now Don't Blow a Fuse

A young lady was sure she had uncovered a conspiracy that threatened all of humankind: The U.S. government was preparing to reinstate slavery around the world. She knew this because, of course, she was a cyborg, and being a cyborg allowed her to discover these threats telepathically. She sued two former U.S. presidents, a presidential candidate, and many top-level government agencies. It was suggested that the judge established a new world record in the fastest case dismissal of all time.

What—No Tip?

A tourist in a West Coast city was accosted by a mugger, who grabbed her purse and ran. A cabbie witnessed the whole thing and chased down the thug, pinning him to a wall and courageously making a citizen's arrest. The mugger didn't like the rough treatment (his leg had been broken), so he sued the cabbie and the taxi company for using excessive force. A jury gave the ruffian more than $24,000 for injuries suffered in the commission of the crime, but a judge later overturned the verdict.

Got Milk?

As a boy, he had done what Mom always said—"Be sure to drink your milk every day." But, as a grown man, he suffered a mild stroke and was sure his lifetime "addiction" to milk was to blame. So he sued the state's dairy commission, along with the grocery chain where he bought most of the milk. The man's claim sought punitive damages, as well as warning labels for "dangerous" dairy products and a fund to care for other suffering addicts with "a cow on their back." The judge quickly dismissed the suit, calling the whole affair "udderly ridiculous."

Give the Lady a Hand

Everyone thought she was a sweet little old lady. But the granny turned into a tiger when she brought a lawsuit against the inventor of a popular device that controls electrical appliances by the clapping of hands. She received the gadget as a holiday gift, but when the lady repeatedly clapped her hands, the only reaction she got was inflamed arthritis. During the trial, it was discovered that the woman had set the sensitivity control too low to react to her claps. The court "handed" down a dismissal.

A Shocking Verdict

The view from the top of the rocks was breathtaking. Having trekked to the summit of the national park's tallest peak, the man enjoyed the vista with no notice of the approaching storm clouds. Without any warning, he was blasted by the swift crackle of a lightning bolt. When he recovered, he sued the park service, believing they were negligent in not posting warnings or instructions about the dangers of lightning strikes. The court didn't go along with that theory and struck the claim down like...well, like a bolt of lightning.

Thongs of Pain

They may not be the most comfortable things, but it turns out thongs can also injure you—at least, according to a 2008 lawsuit filed against Victoria's Secret. A woman claimed her thong snapped while she was putting it on and ended up hitting her in the eye. The underwear apparently had metal links holding a jewel in place on its waistband, which, upon contact caused her "excruciating pain."

Bathroom Explosion

A bank president sued a construction company after the toilet in his executive bathroom flooded. The water "came blasting up out of the toilet with such force it stood him right up," the man claimed, and the resulting media coverage wiped away his good reputation. A judge didn't buy it.

Reality Show Regurgitation

Sure, bad reality TV is painful to watch, but is it bad enough to warrant a $2.5 million lawsuit? In 2005, Austin Aitken sued NBC over its *Fear Factor* program. The man said the show's disgusting displays caused him to become lightheaded, then vomit and run into a doorway. The courtroom tribunal voted him off the stand, and he didn't get a dime of NBC's dough.

Beer Disappointment

Getting a buzz wasn't enough for one Michigan beer drinker. In 1991, he decided to sue Anheuser-Busch for $10,000, saying the company's Bud Light commercials provided false and misleading advertising. His beef? The ads depicted regular guys having a grand time with beautiful women while drinking the beer, and no matter how many cold ones he pounded back, this kind of "unrestricted merriment" just wasn't occurring. It's probably no surprise that this lawsuit fell flat.

Killer Whale Confusion

The killer whale really needs to make its intentions more clear. In 1999, a man snuck past security guards at SeaWorld Orlando to take a late-night swim. He was later found naked and dead in a killer whale's tank. His parents sued the park, saying there was no kind of "public warning" that the killer whale might be inclined to, well, kill someone. SeaWorld described the lawsuit as being "as crazy as they come."

Mistaken Celebrity

Most people would love to be mistaken for a successful celebrity. But in 2006, Allen Heckard from Oregon found the fact that he looked like Michael Jordan insulting—so much so that he sued both Jordan and Nike, the shoe company he blamed for making Jordan a household name. Heckard said he'd experienced emotional pain and suffering from people noticing his resemblance to the NBA star. He asked for $832 million, leading one news agency to say the case was "so outrageous that it actually [gave] frivolous lawsuits a bad name."

Bathroom Bother

What does a guy have to do to use the bathroom in peace? A man attending a 1995 Billy Joel and Elton John concert in San Diego claimed to have seen women in every restroom he tried to use at the stadium. The fellow said the sightings caused him emotional distress, and he sued the stadium and city for $5.4 million. Probably even more distressful to him: He lost.

Chapter 15

Grab Bag

Con Talk

As long as there has been greed, there have been con artists. In fact, these games cons play have a language all of their own.

✳ ✳ ✳ ✳

✳ The shill is important to many con schemes because he's the confederate who draws the sucker to the bait. The shill is also called the roper or stooge.

✳ Cooling the mark—This remains the most important part of any confidence game, as it allows the victim, or mark, to depart the scene feeling like he got lucky, when in fact, he's been taken.

✳ The Big Store con made famous in the movie *The Sting* was based on reality. Involving high overheads and multiple confederates, this con is directed at a single mark—often another con man—for a big payoff. One Chicago-based con man, Yellow Kid Weil, staffed a fake bank with prostitutes and fellow con artists in order to take a corrupt businessman. Most cons aren't that elaborate.

Smaller Scale Cons

Short cons come in all sizes and flavors. They're the bread and butter for many con artists because they can be carried out quickly and inexpensively. Among these are the following.

* Chugging—Hustling donations to a fictitious charity. Currently used for fake disaster relief donations.

* True Believer Syndrome—Fake swamis, palm readers, and psychics love naïve marks afflicted with this "syndrome," because it means they keep coming back for more. Repeat business is always better than a one-time con.

The King Is Dead . . . Wait, Not Yet

On January 20, 1936, England's beloved King George V— grandfather of Queen Elizabeth II—died in his sleep. Or was it actually murder? You be the judge.

✳ ✳ ✳ ✳

Case Files

ON JANUARY 17, 1936, Queen Mary called the royal physician, Lord Bertrand Dawson, to attend to her 71-year-old husband, King George V, who couldn't seem to shake his bronchitis. Over the next three days, the king slipped in and out of consciousness. On the morning of January 20, the king held a ten-minute meeting with his counselors and, at some point, summoned his private secretary, Wigram, to discuss the nation's business. "How is the Empire?" he asked, in what would allegedly be his final words. Exhaustion overcame him before the conversation could continue.

That night after dinner, Dawson gave the king a shot of morphine to help him sleep. At 9:25 P.M., Dawson issued a brief medical bulletin to prepare the nation for the inevitable: "The King's life is moving peacefully towards its close," it said. An hour and a half later—five minutes before midnight—the king was dead.

For half a century, this is the story that the public (and biographers) believed. But some startling details later came to light, revealing what may in fact be a case of murder in the first degree—and regicide.

Stop the Presses!

November 28, 1986, was a day that literally rewrote history. It was on this day, nearly 50 years after the king's death and 41 after Dawson's, that the physician's personal diary was published in the Windsor archives. The sordid truth about the king's demise was exposed.

According to the doctor's notes, the king simply wasn't dying quickly enough. Around 11:00 P.M. on January 20—an hour and a half after Dawson released the bulletin announcing the king's imminent passing—he realized it was not going to be a speedy process. "The last stage might endure for many hours," he wrote, "unknown to the patient but little comporting with the dignity and serenity which he so richly merited."

What's worse, the king's delay would mean that his obituary wouldn't run in the morning edition of the London *Times*, the paper considered most appropriate for national news, but rather in some "less appropriate" evening publication. How very bourgeois!

Taking matters into his own hands, Dawson called his wife and asked her to contact the *Times* to have them hold publication; there was going to be some big news coming yet that night. Then, at 11:25 P.M., Dawson prepared a lethal cocktail of three-quarters of a gram of morphine and one gram of cocaine, and he injected it into the king's jugular vein. Thirty minutes later, King George was dead—just in time to make the morning news. "A Peaceful Ending at Midnight," read the *Times* headline.

In his notes, Dawson describes his actions as "a facet of euthanasia or so-called mercy killing," done to protect the reputation of the king. He also claims that both the queen and Prince Edward were in agreement that the king's life should not be prolonged if his illness was fatal. That said, his notes say nothing about his efforts to consult them of his decision. Most likely, he made it on his own.

Murder or Mercy?

Euthanasia is defined as "the intentional killing of a dependent human being for his or her alleged benefit." Euthanasia by action means "intentionally causing death by performing an action such as giving a lethal injection," while nonvoluntary euthanasia means doing it without the patient's consent. Murder, on the other hand, is to "kill unlawfully and with premeditated malice."

If the question is intent, then it's hard to argue that Dawson's actions make him a murderer, even though many in England, including the medical community, believe that's just what the prominent physician was. From a legal perspective, euthanasia is and always has been "unlawful" in England, as it is in most places throughout the world.

In fact, Dawson himself opposed euthanasia as a legal practice. Just ten months after the king's passing, Dawson spoke against a bill that would have legalized it, arguing that it should be a choice left to the individual doctor, not the federal government. In what can now perhaps be seen as an attempt to excuse his own actions, Dawson went on to say that a doctor "should make the act of dying more gentle and more peaceful, even if it does involve the curtailment of the length of life."

Although Dawson died in 1945 with a glowing reputation for his years of service to the royal family, today his name is a source of anger and disgrace. In 1994, the *British Medical Journal* published an article deriding him for his selfishness and "arrogance," claiming that he committed a "convenience killing" of the king in order to return to his own busy private practice in London.

And About Those Last Words . . .

Now, it's true that King George asked Wigram, "How is the Empire?" and then drifted into sleep. But those words actually weren't the last ones spoken by the dying king. According to Dawson's notes, the king's last worst words were uttered just as the doctor injected him with the first dose of morphine: "God damn you."

In Switzerland, assisted suicide has been legal since the 1940s. According to a 1997 Reuters UK article, many terminally ill people from other countries travel to Switzerland to end their lives.

In 1994, Oregon passed the Death with Dignity Act, becoming the first state to legalize physician-assisted suicide, in which a patient voluntarily enlists the help of a doctor to end his or her life. (Think Dr. Jack Kevorkian.) The law didn't go into effect until 1997.

Speaking of Dr. Kevorkian (aka "Dr. Death"), the physician was released from prison in June 2007 following an eight-year sentence for second-degree murder, of which he was convicted after administering a fatal injection to Michigan patient Thomas Youk, who suffered from Lou Gehrig's disease. Prosecutors had previously failed on four different occasions to convict Kevorkian for assisting in the suicides of terminally ill patients.

Broadmoor's Most Famous Residents

In Britain, the criminally insane wind up in Broadmoor mental hospital. Here one has a wide variety of neighbors, from artists and lexicographers to "rippers" and cannibals.

✳   ✳   ✳   ✳

Welcome to Broadmoor

COMPLETED IN 1863, this imposing collection of brick structures stands on the Berkshire moors about 30 miles from London. The Broadmoor "criminal lunatic asylum" was the first institution dedicated specifically to the detained treatment of those deemed too mentally ill to be guilty but too dangerous to be free. Conceived as a hospital (not a prison), Broadmoor opened with a farm, 57 staff cottages, and a school. Its first patients were women, many of whom most likely suffered from what would now be identified as postpartum depression. Within a year, however, a block for men opened.

Patients of Note

Long the repository of some of England's most notorious individuals, over time Broadmoor has been identified with the violence committed by outwardly normal men whose minds compel them to perform horrific acts. Here are some of the Broadmoor's more notable inmates.

Richard Dadd (painter): On August 28, 1843, a young aspiring painter named Richard Dadd became possessed with the notion that his father was the devil, and so Dadd killed him with a razor. Committed to the Bethlehem Hospital (aka "Bedlam") asylum, Dadd was allowed to continue his painting and spent nine of his years there completing his most well-known work, *The Fairy Feller's Master-Stroke*, which would later hang in the Tate Gallery. In 1864, he was among the first male patients transferred to Broadmoor; there he prepared the stage scenery for the hospital's theater and painted murals and portraits for then-Superinten-dent Dr. William Orange. Dadd died in Broadmoor in 1886 of "an extensive disease of the lungs."

Thomas Hayne Cutbush (Jack the Ripper?): In 1888, young Thomas Cutbush began to act increasingly mentally unstable. His days were spent sleeping, and at night he could be found prowling the streets. Then Cutbush took to drawing anatomical portrayals of dissected women. Curious habits, particularly in light of the Jack the Ripper killings occurring in London at the time. When Cutbush's name appeared on a list of possible sus-pects, his uncle, a superintendent at Scotland Yard, had the name removed. Detained as a wandering lunatic, Thomas escaped, pur-chased a knife, and tried to kill two women before being appre-hended. Deemed unfit for trial, he was sent to Broadmoor, where he spent the rest of his life. But was Cutbush Jack the Ripper? Consider the following:

The Jack the Ripper killings, which targeted prostitutes, lasted from April 3, 1888 to February 13, 1891. Cutbush reportedly contracted syphilis in 1888 (indicating his involvement with prostitutes, as well as a possible explanation for his madness) and was arrested on March 5, 1891.

When Cutbush's name later appeared in the papers in connection with the attempted stabbings, his uncle was devastated and committed suicide two years later.

Recently released Broadmoor documents include a description of Cutbush's piercing blue eyes and limp, both physical characteristics noted by Jack the Ripper witnesses.

Robert Maudsley ("Hannibal the Cannibal"): Born in 1953, young Maudsley was subject to frequent and violent physical abuse at the hands of his parents. Cast in the streets, he turned to prostitution to survive. After strangling a man who showed him pictures of abused boys in 1974, Robert was sent to Broadmoor, where in 1977 he and another psychopathic inmate barricaded themselves in a cell with a pedophile. After torturing the man for nine hours, they strangled him and then allowed the staff to enter. It was observed that part of the victim's skull had been cracked open and a spoon inserted into the brain material. Maudsley admitted to consuming the brain matter. He was sent to Wakefield Prison, known as "Monster Mansion," where in 1978 he killed two inmates. Afterward, Maudsley was imprisoned in a two-room specially made cell of hard plastic featuring cardboard furniture.

Graham Young ("The Teacup Murderer"): In 1961, Graham Young began a lifelong fascination with poisons, which the 14 year old tested in small doses on his family. A year later, his stepmother died from these "experiments." Young confessed his hobby to a psychiatrist, who had him arrested.

He served nine years of a 15-year sentence at Broadmoor, where he researched poisons in the library and tested his concoctions on his fellow inmates.

After his release in 1971, Young went to work for a photographic supply store in Bovingdon where he prepared tea for clerks and customers. Over the course of several months, Young administered nonfatal doses of poison to more than 70 people.

He kept a detailed journal of the poisons and their effects; he also noted which coworkers he ultimately planned to kill. When two employees at the shop died similarly agonizing deaths, the police launched an investigation into the so-called "Bovingdon Bug." Young helpfully suggested to the police that they should consider thallium poisoning as a possible cause. Not being stupid, the police searched Young's apartment, found his notebook and a small pharmacy of poisons. Young received a life sentence; he died of a heart attack in Parkhurst prison at age 42.

The Mad Bomber

Sure, he wanted revenge, but he also wanted to protect New Yorkers from their utility company.

❊　❊　❊　❊

NINETY MILES NORTH of New York City, George Metesky, an amiable-looking middle-aged man in a business suit, drove his car 80 feet from his driveway to the garage workshop at his family's house. He changed into coveralls and used gunpowder extracted from rifle bullets to craft what he called "units." He wanted New Yorkers to know that he had been wronged. When he meticulously packed away his tools at the end of the day, Metesky's bomb was ready.

The man who would become familiar to New Yorkers as the Mad Bomber nursed a grudge against his former employer, Consolidated Edison (Con Ed), New York's utility company. While working for Con Ed in 1931, Metesky suffered an accident and came to believe that he had been gassed and contracted tuberculosis as a result.

Some of that may have been fanciful thinking, but two things were indisputable: The illness left him unable to work, and Con Ed denied him workman's compensation. Metesky was angry.

A Little Attention, Please

More than 900 letters sent by Metesky to elected officials and newspapers failed to bring Con Ed to account. Frustrated, he devised an alternative plan. In November 1940, he left a pipe bomb outside a Con Ed plant on Manhattan's Upper West Side. A note read, "CON EDISON CROOKS, THIS IS FOR YOU." He signed it, "F.P." The bomb didn't go off, but Con Ed—and New York—had been warned.

The following September, an unexploded pipe bomb wrapped in a sock with a note signed "F.P." was discovered near Con Ed's headquarters. However, before Metesky could scare the city a third time, the nation entered World War II. New York City police received a letter from "F.P." outlining his patriotic intentions:

"I WILL Make no more BOmB UNITS for the Duration of the WAR . . . Later I WILl bring The con EDiSON to JUSTICE—THEy will pay for their dastaRdLy deeds."

New York saw no more bombs from "F.P." for nearly ten years, although the threatening letters continued. Then, in March 1950, an intact bomb was found in Grand Central Station. "F.P." was back.

Clues

Metesky rapidly escalated his Con Ed war. A bomb blew up in the New York Public Library in April 1951, and another hit Grand Central. Between 1951 and 1956, Metesky placed at least 30 bombs. Although 15 people were injured by 22 that exploded, no one was killed.

The lead detective turned to a criminal psychiatrist. Dr. James Brussel studied the case and concluded that the "Mad Bomber," as the press now called him, was of Slavic descent, Catholic, and was burdened with an Oedipal complex. Detectives could find him outside the city living with a female relative. The NYPD was dubious, but Dr. Brussel assured them that when they found "F.P.," he wouldn't come along until donning a buttoned double-breasted suit.

To trap "F.P.," the *New York Journal-American* encouraged him to submit his story. Metesky bit, and the story was printed. A Con Ed clerk had previously sifted through files of "troublesome" former employees and discovered Metesky. All this information added up to an identification. In January 1957, the cops drove to Waterbury, Connecticut, where Polish Catholic Metesky lived with his sisters. He opened the door in his pajamas and cheerfully admitted to being "F.P.," explaining that the initials stood for "Fair Play." Before he was arrested, he changed into a doubled-breasted suit.

Just What Is Insanity, Anyway?

Metesky grinned throughout his arraignment. He was sent to Bellevue Hospital for evaluation and ruled insane. He was committed to Matteawan State Hospital for the Criminally Insane without trial.

On his release in 1973, Metesky told the *New York Times* that he wished he had stood trial. "I don't think I was insane," he said. "Sometimes . . . I wondered if there was something wrong with me, because of the extreme effort I was making." He reminded reporters that he was trying to help others. "If I caused enough trouble, they'd have to be careful about the way they treat other people."

George "Fair Play" Metesky died in Waterbury in 1994 at age 90.

Super Speakeasy: '21'

Prohibition didn't inhibit the alcohol consumption of habitués of New York's most famous watering hole.

✻ ✻ ✻ ✻

IN JANUARY 1920, the United States government attempted to banish public consumption of alcohol by instituting Prohibition. (Previous "temperance" movements, led by religious groups and fed-up women, had been confined to the state level.) The manufacture or distribution of liquor was prohibited, nationwide. Americans could possess alcohol, but it was only to be consumed at home, indoors, with family and guests.

As everybody with half a brain predicted, the law failed miserably and spawned an underground Jazz Age society that delighted in thumbing its collective nose at the law. The government's wet blanket was going to be wetter than the "drys" could ever have imagined.

The City That Never Sleeps Also Likes Its Drink

New Yorkers in particular have never appreciated being told what to do, and the city's eating and drinking establishments had no intention of folding just because the Constitution said so. Thus was born the "speakeasy" (as in, keep your voice down): Food might be served as a cover, but booze was the *raison d'être*.

At the height of Prohibition, New York had an estimated 100,000 downstairs dives, uptown haunts, and midtown hoocheries. Would-be patrons needed to know the guard at the door and/or a special password. This was risky business. There was money to be made, but first people had to be paid off. In an atmosphere in which respectable businessmen mingled with bootleggers, many police and others in positions of authority were known to be "on the take."

Take Us to the '21' Club

Named after its address on West 52nd Street between Fifth and Sixth avenues (the block's generous number of saloons earned it the nickname "Swing Street"), '21' was the classiest gin joint in Manhattan. The food was reliably delicious, the place's genteel clientele adhered to a strict dress code, and an alert doorman kept out gangsters and other undesirables—including the Feds. Owned by cousins Jack Kriendler and Charlie Berns and operating out of an 1872 townhouse that had previously been home to a bordello, '21' opened on New Year's Eve 1929. Later that year, the club's alleged and inexplicable ban of all-powerful newspaper and radio gossip Walter Winchell sparked a vengeful column wondering why '21' hadn't yet been raided. The police, predictably, arrived the next night.

The Secret Wine Cellar

Kriendler and Berns promptly hired architects and engineers to redesign '21.' Four alarm buttons were installed in the vestibule; if the doorman pressed any one, stashes of booze were locked behind secret doors by switches designed to automatically short-circuit. Bar shelves were rigged to collapse and ditch bottles down a brick-lined chute, where they would shatter and their contents drain directly into the sewer. And in the basement, behind smoked hams hanging from the ceiling and a shelf of canned goods, stood a cement wall camouflaging an airtight door weighing 2.5 tons, which opened only when a meat skewer was inserted into the appropriate crack. The doorway led into a basement located next door at 19 West 52nd, where the comfortably appointed wine cellar housed 2,000 cases of wine—and frequently, New York Mayor Jimmy Walker, who sipped in seclusion while his police department searched in vain above.

Eat, Drink, and Be Merry

On December 5, 1933, the 21st Amendment repealed Prohibition, and people drank openly once more. Still standing at its original location, the '21' Club invokes its past with

"Speakeasy" Steak Tartare. Patrons can't help but remember that this is where Bogart and Bacall once billed and cooed, where presidents and moguls made deals and policy, where Groucho Marx ordered and returned a single bean ("Undercooked!") to the kitchen.

As for the wine cellar, it's now a meticulously restored private dining room that can hold up to 22 free-spenders who come for costly three-course lunches or seven-course dinners. If you ask nicely, they may even show you Mayor Walker's favorite corner.

Queen of the Bootleggers

New York wasn't the only state with Prohibition stories. In Wisconsin, the "Queen of the Bootleggers" was popular in the press, beloved by the public, and pursued by G-men.

Jennie Justo's family came to Wisconsin from the east coast, allegedly fleeing gang warfare and assassination. Besides producing booze, they set up several illegal Madison bars, or "speakeasies," during Prohibition. The press loved the idea of a woman gangster, and by all accounts, Justo was quite a charming woman.

Despite her reputation as a ladylike Robin Hood for liquor lovers, at least as reported at the time in *Esquire* magazine, Justo was arrested by the FBI in 1932. She received two federal sentences and went to prison. After her release, Justo returned to Madison and, in 1939, opened a popular steakhouse that today survives as Smoky's Club on University Avenue. In later years, she flatly refused to speak of her past career. Justo died in 1991.

Crockefeller

What began as a search to find a missing girl uncovered 30 years of fraud, fake identities, and possible foul play. Before Christian Karl Gerhartstreiter was a convict, he was a con artist.

✳ ✳ ✳ ✳

IT STARTED AS a case of parental kidnapping not uncommon in custody battles: In July 2008, Clark Rockefeller, a descendant of the moneyed oil family, absconded with his seven-year-old daughter during a court-supervised visitation in Boston.

But oddly, FBI databases showed no record of a Clark Rockefeller, and the Rockefeller family denied any connection. His ex-wife, millionaire consultant Sandra Boss, confessed he had no identification, no social security number, and no driver's license. *So who was this guy?* The FBI released his picture, hoping for information. And that's when the stories—and aliases—began pouring in.

Fake Foreign Exchange

His real identity was that of Christian Karl Gerhartstreiter, a German national who came to the United States in 1978 at age 17, claiming to be a foreign exchange student. In truth, he showed up unannounced on the doorstep of a Connecticut family he'd met on a train in Europe, who'd suggested he look them up if he ever visited the States.

After living with them briefly, he posted an ad describing himself as an exchange student in search of a host and was taken in by the Stavio family. They threw him out after it became clear he expected to be treated like royalty. During this time, Gerhartstreiter allegedly became enamored with the *Gilligan's Island* character Thurston Howell III, the ascot-wearing millionaire, and even adopted Howell's snobbish accent.

Bogus Brit

In 1980, "Chris Gerhart" enrolled at the University of Wisconsin-Milwaukee as a film major and persuaded another student to marry him so that he could get his green card (they divorced as soon as he got it). Shortly after the wedding, he left school and headed to Los Angeles to pursue a film career—this time posing as the dapper British blue blood Christopher Chichester (a name that he borrowed from his former high school teacher).

He settled in the swanky town of San Marino, living in a building with newlyweds John and Linda Sohus. The couple went missing in 1985, around the same time Chichester moved away; allegedly, he went back to England following a death in the family.

Chichester resurfaced in Greenwich, Connecticut, as former Hollywood producer and business tycoon Christopher Crowe. It was under this name that, in 1988, he tried to sell a truck that had belonged to the Sohuses. Police investigators traced the Sohus's missing truck to Connecticut, and they soon realized that Crowe and Chichester were the same person. But by then, he'd already vanished.

Mock Rock

Now he was Manhattan's Clark Rockefeller, the new darling of the elite. It was here that he met and married the Ivy League-educated business whiz Sandra Boss. For most of their 12-year marriage, Sandra believed his elaborate stories. She even believed he'd filed the paperwork for their marriage to be legal (it appears he hadn't).

Eventually, however, Sandra grew suspicious. She filed for divorce and won full custody of their seven-year-old daughter, Reigh, and the two moved to London. Clark was limited to three court-supervised visits per year. It was on the first of these visits that he kidnapped her.

Conclusion

In August 2008, the con man was arrested in Baltimore, and Reigh was returned to her mother. In June 2009, a judge sentenced him to four to five years in prison.

In 2011, Gerhartstreiter was charged in California for the Sohus murders. He was tried and convicted in 2013. He will be eligible for parole in 2030.

Gerhartstreiter says he has no recollection of his life before the 1990s. And he insists on being called Mr. Rockefeller because that's his name, thank you very much.

Heidi Fleiss and the World's Oldest Profession

Imagine an entrepreneur who is so successful in her profession that she earns a million dollars in her first four months on the job, and she eventually starts turning away prospective employees because so many people want to work for her. Sounds like an ambitious company, right? No doubt a booming industry.

In the 1990s, that entrepreneur was Heidi Fleiss. And her profession was, well, the world's oldest.

✳ ✳ ✳ ✳

Ring Management

FLEISS WAS BORN in Los Angeles in 1965, and by the time she was 13, was already showing a penchant for management. Perhaps a foreshadowing of her criminal future to come, a teenaged Fleiss ran a "babysitting ring" for her neighborhood, assigning different friends to different sitting jobs, but taking a cut of the money for herself.

In 1987, Fleiss was dating film director Ivan Nagy, who introduced her to a well-known Beverly Hills madam named Madam Alex. Alex dealt exclusively with wealthy clientele, and took young Fleiss under her wing. Alex's prostitutes were mostly middle-aged women wanting to leave the business, so Alex felt that Fleiss was the perfect fresh face to revamp the operation. Fleiss became a prostitute for a short time to learn about the profession, and by 1990, she set her sights on recruiting new women and starting her own prostitution ring.

A Quick Rise and Fall

By 1993, Fleiss was known as the "Hollywood Madam," and she was bringing in thousands of dollars a night from her working girls. She bragged that on a "slow" night she could still make $10,000, and a good night would bring in $100,000. But the profitable venture wouldn't last forever: In June 1993, Fleiss was arrested and charged by the state of California with five counts of pandering, and in 1994, federal tax evasion charges were filed against her.

The media was fascinated by the revelation of a "black book" which Fleiss supposedly maintained, with names and details of her clients. Fleiss refused to give up any names, but when she was arrested, she happened to have traveler's checks in her purse that belonged to actor Charlie Sheen. Sheen became the most prominent name to be connected to the Fleiss prostitution scandal, and he testified during her trial that he'd hired her call girls on at least 27 occasions.

A Troubled Life

Fleiss was convicted on the state charges, but they were later overturned. But in 1996, she was convicted of tax evasion and sentenced to seven years in prison. She served 20 months, and she was released to a halfway house in 1998, where she was ordered to perform 370 hours of community service. She was released from the halfway house in 1999, but she has lived a troubled life since then. After her release, she dated actor Tom Sizemore, who she later accused of domestic abuse—Sizemore was convicted and sentenced to 17 months in prison. Fleiss has also struggled with drug addiction, and was arrested on drug charges in 2008. She attended a substance abuse program in 2009, and appeared on *Celebrity Rehab* with Dr. Drew, ironically, with her ex, Sizemore.

Fleiss has never completely extracted herself from the world of prostitution. She makes her home in Pahrump, Nevada—one of the few areas of the country where prostitution is legal, and she proposed to open a brother in 2005. It didn't pan out; she later said that she didn't want to deal with the logistics of it. She did open a laundromat called "Dirty Laundry" in 2007, however, and later became the owner of a private use airport for ultralight aircraft in Pahrump.

She dated and was briefly engaged to Dennis Hof, the owner of the brothel called the Moonlite Bunny Ranch. She also has a lot of parrots, owning dozens of them at a time.

A Criminal Behaving Nicely?

It's amazing what a quick smile and a few block parties can do for one's popularity.

✳ ✳ ✳ ✳

John Gotti

LABELED THE "TEFLON Don" for his uncanny knack at evading prosecution, John Gotti, the Gambino family crime boss was beloved by his Queens, New York, neighbors. Each year, the cheerful don would stage an elaborate Fourth of July celebration, free of charge, solely for their benefit.

When the Teflon finally wore off in 1992 and Gotti was convicted on murder and racketeering charges, no one defended him more passionately than his neighbors. But their faith was misplaced. In 2009, informant Charles Carneglia testified that Gotti had neighbor John Favara "dissolved in a barrel of acid" after the man accidentally killed Gotti's 12-year-old son in a car accident. So much for Gotti's good neighbor policy.

11 Terms Used by Spies

Spies have their own secret language to keep from being discovered. By spying on these spies, we've managed to uncover the meaning of some of their terms.

✻　✻　✻　✻

1. **Black Bag Job:** A black bag job, or black bag operation, is a covert entry into a building to plant surveillance equipment or find and copy documents, computer data, or cryptographic keys. The name is derived from the black bags spies used to carry the equipment for such operations. In 1972, the Supreme Court declared black bag jobs unconstitutional, but are bags of different colors okay?

2. **Brush Contact:** A brush contact is a brief and public meeting in which two spies discreetly exchange documents, funds, or information without speaking to each other, except perhaps to utter "Excuse me" or other pleasantries. To the average person, the interaction would seem like an accidental encounter between two strangers.

3. **L-Pill:** An L-pill is a lethal pill carried by spies to prevent them from revealing secrets if captured and tortured. During World War II, some L-pills contained a lethal dose of cyanide encased in a glass capsule that could be concealed in a fake tooth and released by the agent's tongue. If he bit into the capsule and broke the glass, he would die almost immediately. But if the pill came loose and was swallowed accidentally while the agent was sleeping or chewing gum, it would pass through his system without causing any harm, as long as it didn't break and release the poison.

4. **Window Dressing:** The best spies are able to blend into any situation. To accomplish this, they use window dressing—the cover story and accessories they use to convince

the authorities and casual observers that they are everyday people and not spies. For example, if a spy is disguised as a construction worker to cover the fact that he is planting a listening device, his window dressing might include official-looking work orders, tools, and knowledge of the people who would have authorized his presence.

5. **Sheep Dipping:** In farming, sheep dipping is a chemical bath given to sheep to rid them of bugs or disease or to clean their wool before shearing. In CIA terminology, sheep dipping means disguising the identity of an agent by placing him within a legitimate organization. This establishes clean credentials that can later be used to penetrate adversary groups or organizations. Similar to the real sheep, the agent is cleaned up so that nobody knows where he's been, kind of like money laundering.

6. **Canary Trap:** Do you suspect a leak in your organization? Even if the leakers aren't small yellow birds, you might be able to catch them by setting a canary trap—giving different versions of sensitive information to each suspected leaker and seeing which version gets leaked. Although this method has been around for years, the term was popularized by Tom Clancy in the novel *Patriot Games*.

7. **Dangle:** In spy terminology, a dangle is an agent who pretends to be interested in defecting to or joining another intelligence agency or group. The dangle convinces the new agency that they have changed loyalties by offering to act as a double agent. The dangle then feeds information to their original agency while giving disinformation to the other.

8. **Honeypot:** A honeypot is a trap that uses sex to lure an enemy agent into disclosing classified information or, in some cases, to capture or kill them. In the classic Hitchcock film *North by Northwest*, Eva Marie Saint's character was both a honeypot and a double agent. In real life, in 1961, U.S. diplomat Irvin Scarbeck was blackmailed into provid-

ing secrets after he was lured by a female Polish agent and photographed in a compromising position.

9. **Camp Swampy:** Camp Swampy is the nickname of the CIA's secret training base. That's about all that is known about it, except that it was named for the Camp Swampy in the *Beetle Bailey* comic strip.

10. **Uncle:** Uncle is a slang term referring to the headquarters of any espionage service. One such headquarters is the United Network Command for Law and Enforcement or U.N.C.L.E., the headquarters on the 1960s spy series *The Man from U.N.C.L.E.*, starring Robert Vaughn, David McCallum, and Leo G. Carroll.

11. **Starburst Maneuver:** How does a spy lose someone who is tailing him? One way is by employing a starburst maneuver—a tactic in which several identical looking vehicles suddenly go in different directions, forcing the surveillance team to quickly decide which one to follow. A classic example of this strategy was utilized in the 2003 film *The Italian Job*. Similar-looking agents can also be used instead of vehicles. Kids, don't try this with your parents.

The Judith Coplon Case: Muse of the Nursery

How one beautiful American spied for the Russians and used promiscuity, patience, and the U.S. Constitution to best the FBI at the start of the Cold War.

✳   ✳   ✳   ✳

A Mother's Sorrow

IN THE SPRING of 1949, Mrs. Rebecca Coplon sat in a New York courtroom sobbing into a handkerchief. The cause of Mrs. Coplon's grief: Her beautiful and talented 27-year-old daughter Judith was on trial for international espionage.

Judith Coplon had come from a respectable family in upstate New York. Her father, a retired toy merchant, was known as the "Santa Claus of the Adirondacks" for his yuletide generosity to needy children. Judith herself had shown great promise at New York City's Barnard College and, more recently, as an analyst for the Department of Justice in Washington, D.C.

Sadly, Mr. Coplon died of a cerebral hemorrhage shortly after hearing of his daughter's arrest. Mrs. Coplon was completely unnerved by both her daughter's arrest and her husband's sudden demise. She could only sit sadly on the sidelines of one of the most sensational trials of the 20th century.

A Sloppy Arrest

Judith Coplon had been arrested in New York City, ostensibly on her way to visit her family. In her possession were confidential documents that had been fed to her by FBI agents. The FBI suspected that Russian engineer and U.N. liaison Valentin Gubitchev, whom Coplon met with regularly, was more than he appeared to be. In fact, Coplon began gathering information for the Soviet Union in her college days, with Gubitchev acting as her case manager in the newly formed New York bureau of the KGB. Moreover, Coplon and Gubitchev were lovers.

The FBI already knew all of this. Following information gleaned from a secret decryption project codenamed "Verona," they conducted extensive wiretapping and surveillance of the pair to gain further information. However, the FBI arrested Coplon before she had actually handed the confidential documents to Gubitchev. What's more, they failed to obtain a warrant for her arrest, despite having had ample time to do so.

A Burlesque Trial

For her trial in Washington, D.C., Coplon hired the first lawyer she could find who agreed to work pro bono—the inexperienced, comedic, and essentially inept Archie Palmer. Despite his professional shortcomings, Archie turned out to be a genius at creating an aura of sensational wrongdoing and soon won public sympathy for Coplon's cause. The FBI alleged that, in addition to Gubitchev, Coplon was involved in a sexual relationship with a lawyer (who would end up serving as one of the prosecutors in a second trial in New York). However, Palmer's courtroom clowning and Coplon's hedged denials effectively downplayed the issue. Palmer sneered, laughed, and sarcastically poked holes in the FBI's case. He argued that the "confidential source" named by the FBI was nothing more than an illegal wiretap, which was true. One FBI agent even admitted that the details of the meeting between Coplon and Gubitchev were only known because of tapped phone conversations.

America's Evil Darling

The lurid details of Coplon's promiscuous and traitorous life made their way to the front pages and gossip columns of newspapers and magazines across the United States. The public was entranced by stories of the so-called "sexy spy," who giggled throughout her trial, and by the antics of her sensationalistic lawyer. Nevertheless, the juries in both the Washington, D.C., and New York trials found Coplon guilty. Both cases were appealed. The dubious legality of the wiretaps and the lack of an arrest warrant created a legal quagmire. As a result, Coplon never served a day in jail and lived to see both cases against her dismissed.

To Catch a Soviet Mole

When people get bored, they often take up hobbies–something to pass the time and bring a bit of excitement to life. Those seeking adventure might explore skydiving or mountain climbing; but Hanssen took a different route: he became an FBI mole, passing information to Soviet and Russian intelligence services.

✳ ✳ ✳ ✳

BY ALL APPEARANCES, Robert Hanssen was a typical American. Born and raised in Chicago, Hanssen graduated from William Howard Taft High School in 1962; he then graduated from Knox College with a degree in chemistry in 1966. He dabbled with the idea of becoming a dentist, and he met his wife, Bonnie, in dental school. After they married in 1968, Hanssen dropped out of dental school and decided to pursue business instead, earning an MBA in 1971. After working as an internal affairs investigator for the Chicago Police Department, he got a job as a special agent with the FBI in 1976. He and his growing family—Hanssen and his wife eventually had six children—moved from Gary, Indiana, to New York City so he could work in the field office there. A staunch Catholic, he was known as a quiet family man and a hard worker. Robert Hanssen's life, it would seem, was so stable it was almost boring.

Secrets and Lies

Hanssen's double life began in 1979, just a few years after joining the FBI. After being transferred to counterintelligence and tasked with compiling a list of Soviet agents, he volunteered his services to the Soviet military intelligence agency, GRU. He began leaking information to them, including the identity of CIA informant Dmitri Polyakov, who was later executed by the Soviets. A year later, in 1980, Hanssen's wife caught him with some suspicious documents, and he admitted to her that he'd been spying for the Soviets. He claimed that he'd given them nothing of importance, but Bonnie insisted he confess to a priest and immediately cease his espionage activities.

In 1981, Hanssen was transferred to Washington, D.C., where he worked in the FBI's budget office and had access to information about wiretapping and electronic surveillance, and three years later he was transferred to the Soviet analytical unit. True to his word, he had no contact with the Soviets during these years; but in 1985, Hanssen sent a letter to the KGB, once again offering his services as a spy. This was the beginning of an on-and-off espionage career that would last more than fifteen years. Hanssen gave the Soviets—and, after the dissolution of the Soviet Union in 1991, the Russians—thousands of pages of classified materials over the years. These included identities of Soviets spying for the U.S., information about the U.S. nuclear program and details about American spying methods.

Red Flags

Throughout the years he was spying, occasional concerns would be raised about Hanssen. In 1990, his own brother-in-law, also a member of the FBI, recommended that Hanssen be investigated for possible espionage after spotting a pile of cash in his home; however, no action was ever taken. Several years later, another FBI mole who had been spying for the Russians, Earl Edwin Pitts, told the Bureau he suspected that Hanssen was also a spy. But once again, no action was taken.

But Hanssen couldn't keep dodging bullets forever. The FBI expressed confusion about how certain information was leaking to the Russians even after they'd caught several moles within the organization. So in 1994, they organized a mole-hunting team to locate "Graysuit"—the codename for the suspected spy. After years of false leads and dead ends, the FBI finally found an ex-KGB agent who was willing to share information—for a price. They paid $7 million for a file that included an audiotape of Hanssen speaking with KGB agent Aleksander Fefelov, and their investigation was finally on a roll. With Hanssen now under surveillance, the FBI "promoted" him in order to keep an eye on him. On February 18, 2001, Hanssen drove to Foxstone Park in Vienna, Virginia, and taped a bag full of classified information to the underside of a footbridge. FBI agents immediately rushed in to arrest him, and Hanssen, apparently unsurprised, commented, "What took you so long?"

The End of the Spy Game

Interestingly, Hanssen was never motivated by any political or ideological beliefs, but rather by good, old-fashioned financial gain. He was paid around $1.4 million in cash and diamonds by Moscow throughout the course of his espionage career. Hanssen also wrote in a letter to the Russians that he was inspired to be a spy when he was only 14 years old, after reading the memoirs of Kim Philby, a British double agent.

Whatever his motivations, the outcome for Hanssen was dire: he was sentenced to 15 consecutive life sentences with no possibility of parole, and is living out his days at a Colorado federal supermax prison.

To his credit, he apologized for his behavior when he was sentenced, stating, "I am shamed by it." He was especially remorseful for the pain he caused his family, saying, "I have opened the door for calumny against my totally innocent wife and our children. I hurt them deeply. I have hurt so many deeply."

The First Case

If you have an interest in true crime stories but not the patience to read a long book or watch a movie, how about listening to a podcast? While there are many to choose from, including My Favorite Murder *and* Crime Junkie, *the podcast that started it all is the award-winning* Serial.

✳ ✳ ✳ ✳

The First Case

ON JANUARY 13, 1999, a Baltimore, Maryland, high school student named Hae Min Lee was seen driving away from Woodlawn High School in her gray Nissan. That was the last time she was seen alive. When she failed to pick up her young cousin from daycare that afternoon, a police search was conducted near the school, but to no avail. Sadly, on February 9, a passerby discovered Lee's partially buried body in Leakin Park, one of the largest parks in the city. On February 28, police arrested Lee's ex-boyfriend, Adnan Syed, and charged him with her murder. But did they have the right man?

That is the question posed by the first season of the podcast *Serial*, an investigative journalism show hosted by Sarah Koenig. Koenig, who has worked as a journalist for ABC

News, *The New York Times*, and *The Baltimore Sun*, spent a year investigating the case of Lee's murder and Syed's subsequent trial. Koenig questioned Syed's guilt in the case, and her resulting podcast became so popular and garnered so much attention that Syed was almost granted a new trial.

Lee and Syed

So what did Koenig discover during her year-long investigation? Let's start at the beginning: Lee, a Korean immigrant who moved to the United States with her family when she was 12, was a popular student at Woodlawn High School who played lacrosse and field hockey and hoped to become an optician. After she disappeared, her family hoped the responsible student would return, but tragically, it was not to be. When her cause of death was determined to be strangulation, authorities at first assumed that her murder could be connected to another murdered Woodlawn girl, who had been found a year earlier.

But then police received an anonymous phone call pinning the murder on Lee's ex-boyfriend, Syed. Police subpoenaed his wireless phone records and interviewed a friend named Jay Wilds, who eventually confessed that he helped Syed bury Lee's body and get rid of her car. Syed was arrested, tried, and, on February 25, 2000, convicted of Lee's murder. According to prosecutors, Syed, who had dated Lee until December 1998, was angry when he found out she had begun dating other men.

Open and Shut?

It may have seemed like a cut-and-dried case, but Koenig's investigation uncovered several potential problems. First and foremost, Syed vehemently denied killing Lee, and maintained his innocence throughout his trial. Second, Koenig questioned Wilds' "confession," which she believes may have been coerced. Wilds changed his story several times, and may have been motivated by the promise of a reward that authorities were offering for information. Finally, and perhaps most important, Koenig spoke to a former classmate of Syed's named Asia

McClain, who insisted that she saw Syed in the library at the time the murder is believed to have occurred.

In 2016, a judge granted Syed a new trial, but the ruling was overturned by the Maryland Court of Appeals. It is still unknown whether Syed is truly guilty, and even Koenig says she is unsure about his innocence or guilt. But thanks to Lee and Syed's story, *Serial* became an instant phenomenon when it debuted in 2014, ranking #1 on iTunes and earning a Peabody Award in April 2015. Subsequent seasons have focused on Sergeant Bowe Bergdahl and an examination of the criminal justice system, but they may never live up to the first season, which cemented *Serial* as podcasting's benchmark hit.

Yep, Moonshine and NASCAR Are Kin

White lightning, hooch, mountain dew, hillbilly pop—whatever you called it, it was the lifeblood of the South. It was illegal, and it was the juice that jump-started NASCAR.

✳ ✳ ✳ ✳

Model "T" for Tripper

HENRY FORD WAS an adamant teetotaler, but without him, the South's illicit moonshine business could never have been so successful. The mass production of Ford's Model T, and later his V-8, coincided with the dawn of 1920s Prohibition. Southerners demanded bootleg booze, and "whiskey trippers" were now equipped to deliver as many as 100 gallons a night, at 30 cents a gallon. To crack down was futile: Local cops often had kinfolk in the biz and, in any case, appreciated "corn likker" as much as anybody else.

Despite the end of Prohibition in 1933, there was still a demand for moonshine. Alcohol was technically legal but only from legitimate, tax-paying distilleries. Selling untaxed liquor, or moonshine, was illegal (as it is today). Moonshine was also cheaper and stronger than the legal stuff. People certainly weren't going to stop make it.

Federal tax agents were sent in to hunt down the shiners, who learned speed was their best defense. For an extra leg up, shiners sought the help of "whiskey mechanics," who specialized in souping up V-8s, sawing cylinders to boost horsepower, and tweaking the rear suspension with heavy-duty springs and steel wedges to keep liquor bottles in place while driving on twisty mountain roads.

Shiners vs. Shiners

Informal races soon cropped up among the shiners to see who had the fastest cars and meanest driving skills. Tracks were plowed in the red dirt fields; crowds dropped coins in a hat for the winner's purse. Local entrepreneurs started cashing in as well, sponsoring races at horse tracks and fairgrounds across the South.

The appeal was clear: Until then, car racing had been the domain of the American Automobile Association (AAA) and the wealthy Northern elite. But stock car racing's everyman appeal is what struck driver and race promoter Bill France as a golden opportunity.

NASCAR Is Born

Southern stock car racing picked up momentum after World War II, and several regional organizations formed. AAA had been flirting with stock car racing for years, and it now decided it wanted to control the action, but France wanted races for regular working folk.

In late 1947, he called a meeting of representatives from every southern stock car group. Within three days, they had united as the National Association of Stock Car Auto Racing (NASCAR), named France president, and agreed to uniform racing rules. To gain respect as a legitimate organization, France felt they must distance NASCAR from its moonshine roots.

Easier said than done, since most of his drivers had cut their teeth running whiskey. What he could do was make the races "strictly stock," meaning no souped-up cars allowed. Several drivers showed up at the first race in February 1948 with no car to drive, looking for willing spectators to hand over their keys.

Glenn Dunaway was one such driver. He finished first in a borrowed Ford coupe—that is, until a post-race inspection showed signs of "bootlegger souping," and he was disqualified. Sure enough, the car's owner had delivered a load of moonshine just a few days earlier.

Keep Shining

Many of NASCAR's earliest stars traced their roots to moonshining. Legendary driver Junior Johnson was eight years old when he started running whiskey in 1939; he gave it up in the late '50s, after a yearlong prison stint interrupted his racing career. Curtis Turner, another great, claimed he started running hooch at age ten.

Today, NASCAR is a multibillion-dollar industry with a family-friendly image. Yet glimmers of its traditional whiskey-soaked history still "shine" through: As recently as March 2009, retired driver Carl Dean Combs was arrested in North Carolina for making and selling hooch.

Subway Vigilante!

Bernhard Goetz shot four young men he said tried to rob him. The result was a national debate on vigilantism that still rages today.

❋ ❋ ❋ ❋

I T WAS LIKE a scene out of the Charles Bronson thriller *Death Wish*. Three days before Christmas in 1984, Bernhard Goetz, a mild-mannered, white electronics expert, shot four youths he claimed tried to rob him on a crowded Manhattan subway car. He then fled the scene, eventually turning himself into police in New Hampshire.

The incident was headline news for weeks. Some hailed Goetz as a hero and commended him for standing up to thugs; others considered him just as bad as the young men he said tried to rob him.

Instinct or Malice?

According to accounts, it all went down quickly. The youths—Barry Allen, 18; Troy Canty, 19; James Ramseur, 19; and Darrell Cabey, 19—told police they were just panhandling money to play video games. Goetz, who had been mugged previously, claimed he felt threatened and believed the youths, all of whom were black, were going to rob him. When Canty demanded five dollars, Goetz rose, pulled a gun from beneath his windbreaker, and quickly fired five shots, striking each of his alleged assailants. All survived, though Cabey was left paralyzed and brain damaged when a bullet severed his spinal cord.

In the aftermath of the shooting, Goetz found himself a reluctant public figure. He gave only one interview, to the *New York Post*, in which he said, "I'm amazed at this celebrity status. I want to remain anonymous." But that was not to be.

In 1987, Goetz was acquitted of attempted murder and assault but found guilty of criminal possession of an unlicensed weapon. He spent 250 days in jail. Nine years later, Cabey and his family won a $43 million civil-court judgment against Goetz, who declared bankruptcy.

Cities of Refuge

Family vendetta was the law of the Israelites in the early days, but then Mosaic Law set up six cities of refuge, where a person accused of murder could find protection and get a fair hearing.

✳   ✳   ✳   ✳

AS IN MANY early societies, the Israelites who lived before the time of Moses had no laws to regulate punishment for criminal acts. If a person was a victim of a crime, he or a near relative took it upon himself to exact retribution. Because that retribution was often more excessive than the original crime, the precept of "eye for eye, tooth for tooth" (Exodus 21:23–25) was brought into play. Although this concept sounds brutal, it was actually moderating. The punishment should fit the crime, not go beyond it. If someone steals your chicken, you should not take three of his cows in retaliation. If someone blinds you, you are not justified in taking his life.

Blood Vengeance

When one person deliberately took another's life, the stakes were higher. The victim's nearest male relatives were expected to act as "redeemers" and seek revenge. Under the old law, "anyone who kills a human being shall be put to death" (Leviticus 24:17). Even if the killing was an accident, it was considered the duty of the victim's relatives to find the killer and take his life. There was nowhere an innocent person could reside without fear of blood revenge. All he could attempt to do was to claim sanctuary by holding on to an altar. But how long could a person remain in such a position?

Something needed to be done to prevent the shedding of innocent blood, as such acts generally led to more and more violence. One man might kill another whom he mistakenly believed murdered his father, then a brother of the innocent man would seek revenge for his brother's wrongful death, resulting in still another act to be revenged. In the end, one accidental death could result in the annihilation of an entire family. This clearly had to be stopped.

Hope for the Innocent

In response to the excesses of blood vengeance, the Law of Moses established six so-called cities of refuge, where a person responsible for someone else's death could find asylum. A person who killed another intentionally was still executed, but if he unintentionally caused another's death, he could flee to one of six cities: Golan, Ramoth-Gilead, or Bezer on the east side of the Jordan River, or Kedesh, Shechem, or Hebron on the west side of the river.

There were still loopholes. If the avengers caught the suspect while he was traveling to a city of refuge, they could legitimately kill him without a trial. Consequently, according to Jewish rabbis of the first few centuries A.D., the Sanhedrin, the official Jewish governing council, had the job of keeping the roads to the cities of refuge in good repair, allowing the suspect a fair chance of reaching sanctuary. The rabbis wrote that the roads were wide and smooth and without hills, that bridges spanned all the rivers, and that guideposts displaying the word "Refuge" were placed at every turn. Furthermore, the rabbis claimed, two students of the law accompanied every fleeing man to attempt to pacify the avenger should he overtake them.

Bad Santa!

Yes, it's true. Some people have ended up on Santa's naughty list by committing crimes while impersonating the jolly old elf himself. They're sure to get coal for Christmas.

✳ ✳ ✳ ✳

APPARENTLY LOOKING LIKE Santa doesn't make one always act like Santa. Over the years, many crimes have been committed by individuals dressed as Santa Claus. Here's a partial rundown:

✳ **December 23, 1927** Marshall Ratliff and three accomplices held up the First National Bank in Cisco, Texas, triggering one of the largest manhunts in state history. Ratliff was known in Cisco, so he dressed as Santa Claus to disguise his identity. The robbers were barely out the door when a wild shoot-out and chase ensued. Ratliff and two accomplices were captured; the third accomplice died from his injuries.

✳ **December 10, 2004** Santa-bedecked Elkin Donnie Clarke, 49, of Atlanta, struck Annie Ruth Nelson in the head with a board outside a shopping mall, knocking her unconscious. When a passerby came to Nelson's aid, police said, Clarke threatened her with the board as well. Clarke was charged with two counts of aggravated assault.

✳ **December 24, 2008** Bruce Pardo, 45, of Montrose, California, arrived dressed as Santa Claus to a holiday party at his ex in-laws' house. Once inside, Pardo opened fire on the crowd, killing nine and wounding several others. He attempted to set the house on fire, burning himself in the process. Pardo later took his own life.

✳ **December 22, 2009** A man wearing sunglasses and a Santa suit robbed the SunTrust Bank in Hermitage, Tennessee. According to witnesses, the armed man said he was robbing the bank to "pay his elves."

Tree Thief

It's the unkindest cut of all! The holidays are stressful. Between buying gifts, planning dinners, and visiting relatives, it's understandable that some things get pushed off to the last minute. Maybe the tree hasn't been bought yet, and the ones remaining are spindly little things. Alas, some people went for a somewhat unusual solution.

✳   ✳   ✳   ✳

Idiot Ruins Christmas

ONE SCROOGE SNUCK onto Seattle's Washington Park Arboretum in December 2009 and cut down a rare Chinese keteleeria tree worth over $10,000. David Zuckerman, the horticulturist for the University of Washington Botanic Gardens, was shocked that this particular tree was cut. "It's a Charlie Brown tree," he said. Many firs, which are more traditional Christmas trees, are prevalent throughout the arboretum. The keteleeria is a sparsely branched tree, not as bushy as firs. It's also much more rare.

The keteleeria tree, native to China, is endangered. It was planted at the arboretum in the hopes that its seeds would be used to help propagate the species.

The theft wasn't even a last-minute panic decision on Christmas Eve. The perpetrator cut down the tree sometime on December 9. That's 15 solid tree-shopping days that don't necessitate cutting down the nearest endangered keteleeria.

Those who worked at the arboretum to cultivate the tree from a sapling to a fine seven-foot specimen were particularly hurt by the act. The local botanic gardens might have to watch their flowers around Mother's Day.

This was not even the first time a tree had been stolen from the Washington Park Arboretum. Several Christmases ago, a fir was cut down and displayed in a restaurant. The perpetrator was caught, but trees that are cut down are dead and can't be repaired. Staffers at the arboretum are considering covering the trees with bright, nontoxic paint during December that can be washed off after the— apparently deadly—holidays are over.

Old Dog Learns New Trickery

Capitalizing on tragedy is bad enough, but life got especially "ruff" for a dog trainer who pocketed funds that were meant for homeless pets.

✳   ✳   ✳   ✳

WHEN AN AMHERST man who called himself "Don the Dog Guy" promised to care for 28 dogs made homeless by Hurricane Katrina, a rescue group decided to throw him a bone—worth more than $37,000.

In 2006, Donald Chambers agreed to care for pets rescued by the Utah-based Best Friends Animal Society and vowed to find permanent homes for his four-legged wards. Chambers kept the ruse going—and the checks coming—by sharing photos of happily adopted dogs and their heartwarming stories on the organization's Web site. The problem? Not a bit of it was true.

Where Are the Dogs?

The fraud wasn't discovered until after Best Friends Animal Society had already paid thousands for the dogs' care. The organization quickly sent Amherst police to fetch Chambers, but it was too late: The money had disappeared, and so had most of the dogs. It turns out that as he bilked funds meant for the Hurricane Katrina survivors, Chambers was unceremoniously dropping dogs at the local pound, where they were killed. In the end, only three were adopted.

Chambers didn't have to face the harsh fate he'd shown the dogs, but he did receive comeuppance. After a series of court appearances in 2009, 40-year-old Chambers received a year in prison, a fine of $1,000, and an additional $62,000 to pay in restitution.

Although he'd previously operated a boarding and instructing facility for dogs in Lorain County, as news of Don the Dog Guy's misdeeds spread, life became (ahem) ruff. His dog-training facility closed, and Chambers received some training of his own—as a tow truck operator.

From the Vaults of History

Treason

IN THE MIDDLE Ages and beyond, the crime of treason was considered the most momentous transgression of its day. People found guilty of disloyalty to their monarch, spouse, or country were often hanged, drawn, and quartered—not necessarily in that order—in a trilogy of torture techniques that went on until the 1800s. The criminal was dragged to his place of execution on a wooden rack, hanged until he was "almost" dead, then dumped on a table where his entrails and genitals were extracted and his frame pruned into four quarters. Only men were subjected to such sectioning. Women found guilty of treason were hanged or burned. In 1814, an effort was made to reduce the barbaric nature of the proceedings, but the offender who led that charge was hanged until dead before his corpse was filleted into fourths. He got off easy: At least he wasn't breathing when he was butchered.

That's Gotta Hurt!

Captain Jonathan Walker (no relation to the liquor) was the last person to be branded as punishment for a crime in the United States. He was convicted of aiding seven slaves in their attempt to escape from Florida to the Bahamas in 1844. Walker was branded on the palm of his right hand with the letters SS, signifying "Slave Stealer." In his poem "The Branded Hand" two years later, John Greenleaf Whittier suggested that it might instead mean something else:

"Then lift that manly right-hand, bold ploughman of the wave! Its branded palm shall prophesy, 'Salvation to the Slave!'"

Starting a Trend

On October 6, 1866, Frank Sparks, with brothers Simeon and William Reno, pulled off the first train robbery in U.S. history. The trio boarded the eastbound Ohio & Mississippi train at the Seymour, Indiana, depot. Brandishing guns and wearing masks, the criminals emptied one safe and pushed the other out the window to pick up later. The robbers got away with $12,000. The three were later arrested but never stood trial.

Notorious Buckeyes

Every state has a long list of famous sons and daughters and an equally long list of the infamous. Ohio is no exception. For every Orville and Wilbur Wright, there's a Jeffrey Dahmer or Harry Pierpont—individuals who are famous for all the wrong reasons.

✳ ✳ ✳ ✳

Charles "Cadillac Charley" Cavalarro: After sneaking into the United States from Italy in the 1920s, Cavalarro rose through the ranks to become one of Ohio's most powerful mobsters. Based in Youngstown, he claimed to be a simple produce merchant, but his ties to the Licavoli/Detroit mob family were well known. Cavalarro and his 11-year-old son were killed in a car bombing in November 1962, just one in a series of violent, mob-related crimes that shook Ohio in the late 1950s and early 1960s.

Bruce Ivins: Ivins was a microbiologist at the U.S. Army's defensive biological laboratory at Fort Detrick, Maryland, where he worked with a variety of lethal substances. Investigators believe Ivins was responsible for the rash of post-9/11 anthrax attacks that killed five people and sickened several others. A native of Lebanon, Ivins took his own life on July 29, 2008, after learning that federal prosecutors were about to arrest him on murder charges.

Jeffrey Lundgren: A self-proclaimed prophet who believed God spoke to him directly, Lundgren was the leader of a bizarre religious cult based in Kirtland. In 1990, he was convicted of killing cult members Dennis and Cheryl Avery and their three children, ages 15, 13, and 7, because he believed the family lacked sufficient faith. He was sentenced to death and executed by lethal injection in October 2006.

Harry Pierpont: After John Dillinger helped him escape from an Indiana prison, Pierpont repaid the favor by helping to spring Dillinger from jail in Lima, killing Sheriff Jess Sarber in the act. Pierpont was tried for the murder and sentenced to death, but he attempted a daring prison escape using a fake gun made out of wood. Severely wounded by prison guards in the attempt, he lived long enough to get the electric chair.

Gerald Robinson: Robinson was a Catholic priest in Toledo who was tried and convicted of the 1980 strangling and stabbing death of Sister Margaret Ann Pahl nearly 26 years after the heinous act. The case had grown cold when new forensic technology helped link Robinson to the grisly crime, which took place just before Easter in the chapel of Mercy Hospital. Robinson was sentenced to 15 years to life in prison.

Author O. Henry, less well known by his real name, William S. Porter, changed his name for good reason: a felony conviction. Henry started writing around 1900 while doing hard time for embezzlement. Some believe that the pen name was taken from a guard named Orrin Henry at the Ohio State Penitentiary.

While **Mildred Gillars** was not born in Ohio, she attended Ohio Wesleyan University. She is better known to history as "Axis Sally" for her propaganda broadcasts in support of the Nazis during World War II. Imprisoned for treason, she was paroled in 1961. Her grave is in Columbus.

No Strangers to Fiction

Here are two bloody blockbuster movies supposedly based on real-life events. In both cases, Hollywood didn't let facts get in the way of profitable fiction.

✳   ✳   ✳   ✳

The Texas Chain Saw Massacre

THE MYTH THAT Tobe Hooper's 1974 bloodbath has any semblance to real-life events can be dispelled by the movie's opening narrative, which states that the "real" events took place on August 18, 1973. But the movie was in the can by August 14, 1973, so the actual events on which it was allegedly based hadn't even happened yet. There is speculation that the movie is loosely based on the life of Wisconsin serial killer Ed Gein, who, like his cinematic cohort, wore a mask made of human skin and left behind a cornucopia of corpses.

Fargo

In Joel and Ethan Coen's masterpiece of modern film noir, two wayward kidnappers/murderers wreak havoc on the citizens of Brainerd and Minneapolis, Minnesota. Again, the real events depicted onscreen are fictitious, despite claims to the contrary.

The plot does, however, contain references that are similar to a pair of well-known Minnesota crimes. The first occurred in 1962 and involved an attorney, T. Eugene Thompson, who contracted a man to kill his wife. That man contracted another man to do the deed, and in the confusion that followed, calamity and chaos converged. Mrs. Thompson died, Mr. Thompson lied, and the feebleminded felons were fried, legally speaking. Ten years later, another crime took place, this one involving the kidnapping of Virginia Piper, the wife of a wealthy banker. A million-dollar ransom was paid, and Mrs. Piper was found alive, tied to a tree in a park. The two men convicted of the crime were later acquitted, and only $4,000 of the ransom money was recovered.

Creepy, Catchy Murder Ballads

Sometimes you're singing along to a song. Then you think to yourself, "Wait, what did the lyrics just say?" Such is sometimes the case with a murder ballad.

✳ ✳ ✳ ✳

"Mack the Knife"

PERHAPS THE MOST well-known murder ballad, "Mack the Knife" tells the tale of dashing, but murderous, highwayman Macheath as portrayed in the musical drama *The Threepenny Opera*. It was popularized by Bobby Darin in the late 1950s.

"Lizie Wan"

Taking an incestuous turn, this ballad tells the tale of poor Lizie, who is pregnant with her brother's child. He kills her, then tries to pretend the blood is from an animal, but finally confesses before setting sail on a ship, never to return.

"Nebraska"

Before he cemented his place in musical history with "Born in the U.S.A.," Bruce Springsteen put a modern spin on the murder ballad with his 1982 song "Nebraska," based on the late 1950s killing spree of Charles Starkweather.

"Frankie & Johnny"

This song is based on an 1899 murder case in which a prostitute named Frankie kills her teenage lover after finding out that he's cheating on her. Frankie was acquitted but died in a mental institution in the 1950s. The writer and origin of the song are debatable, but the tale led to a number of films, including a 1966 musical starring Elvis Presley.

"Banks of the Ohio"

Around since the 19th century, "Banks of the Ohio" tells the story of Willie, who proposes to his young love during a walk by the river. She turns him down, so he murders her. The song has been recorded by a variety of musicians, from Johnny Cash to Olivia Newton-John.

"Hey Joe"

Penned by Billy Roberts in the early 1960s, this song of love gone murderous was immensely popular among rock bands of the decade. One of the most popular versions was recorded by Jimi Hendrix and was played by the influential guitarist at the Woodstock Music Festival in 1969.

"Tom Dooley"

Based on the 1866 murder of Laura Foster, this tune tells the story of her boyfriend, Tom Dula, a former Confederate soldier from North Carolina. Dula was convicted and hanged for the girl's brutal stabbing death, but there is speculation that he had another lover named Ann Melton, who may have killed Foster in a fit of jealous rage. The story inspired a number one hit for the Kingston Trio in 1958 and a movie starring a young Michael Landon the following year.

"Lily, Rosemary and the Jack of Hearts"

Bob Dylan has performed numerous murder ballads in his career and has incorporated their musical style into his own songwriting. In 1975, he released his own take on the genre with this complex narrative song about a bank robber and the people of the town he has stumbled upon.

"Stagger Lee"

This song is based on the slaying of William Lyons by Lee Shelton, a black cab driver and pimp, on Christmas night 1895. The two men were friends, but after a night of drinking and gambling, things turned deadly. The tune became a staple of blues musicians, but the 1928 record by Mississippi John Hurt is considered the definitive version.

"Jellon Grame"

Drawing the story out over years, the song tells the tale of a man who kills his pregnant lover and removes the still living baby. He raises the child as his own, and, one day, when his son wants to know the truth about his mother, the man explains what happened and shows him the scene of the crime. The boy kills his father on the spot. The tale is intertwined with the history of the British Isles and has been retold for generations.

"Omie Wise"

This murder ballad is based on an 1807 murder case in which Naomi Wise, an orphaned servant and field hand, became pregnant by her boyfriend, Jonathan Lewis. He drowned her but was found not guilty of the crime. In 1820, Lewis confessed to the murder on his deathbed.

"El Paso"

Written and performed by Marty Robbins, "El Paso" tells the fictional saga of love turned deadly in Mexico and was Robbins's best-known song. The ballad relates the story of a cowboy who falls in love with a cantina dancer and kills another man defending her honor. Originally, it was thought the song would be a flop because of its nearly five-minute running time, unheard of during the late 1950s. Incidentally, the song was covered by the Grateful Dead and became one of their most popular tunes, performed live more than 380 times.

"The Twa Sisters"

Stepping away from the love triangle or murderous lover scenario, this song explores "sororicide"—sister killing sister. Dating back to at least 1656, "The Twa Sisters" is thought to be the inspiration for a number of other ballads. In a strange twist, the body of the dead sister is made into a musical instrument that sings of its own murder—in some versions at the wedding of the guilty sister.

"Jack the Stripper"

A foray into the modern murder ballad, "Jack the Stripper" was a serial killer who murdered prostitutes in London in the 1960s and dumped their naked bodies around the city. Modern heavy metal and hard rock bands have performed this song about his dirty deeds.

"It's Not Illegal If You Don't Get Caught"

Americans made many sacrifices during World War II, but for some, forgoing sugar, meat, or gasoline was too much. Instead, they turned to the black market.

✳ ✳ ✳ ✳

SINCE THEIR COUNTRY'S founding, Americans have generally enjoyed the benefits of a free market economy. During the Second World War, however, the Roosevelt administration realized it would need to control the consumption of many basic goods in order to effectively fight a two-front war.

The World War II-era rationing and price-control system was the brainchild of Wall Street financier Bernard Baruch. He first suggested the scheme in early 1941, arguing that the government should apply rationing vertically (for example, rationing would affect not only automobiles, but also the steel, rubber, and cloth used to make them).

To curb inflation, price controls would be needed. Americans would learn to sort through their ration books for items such as gasoline and meat. What Baruch did not take into account, however, was the rise of a vast black market fueled by many ordinary and otherwise law-abiding citizens.

Dumping Directive No. 1

The modern American black market is said to have been born on January 27, 1942. On that day, the Office of Price Administration (OPA) was given authority to enact civilian rationing and price control under Directive No. 1 of the War Production Board. Among the list of items classified as "scarce" were sugar, automobiles, tires, gasoline, and typewriters. Violators could face up to a year in jail and a $5,000 fine, but that was hardly a deterrent. Manufacturers, distributors, retailers, and consumers soon found ways to evade and sometimes profit from the price controls and rationing systems. Consumers learned that with enough money, they could readily find what they wanted—regardless of government regulations. By some estimates consumer industries such as department stores, meat packers, and leather tanners realized profits as high as 1,000 percent during the war.

The subterfuge took many forms: trimming less fat from meat, counterfeiting gas vouchers, processing livestock through unregulated channels, and ignoring rent controls. Counterfeit vouchers, often sold through organized-crime syndicates, were the most common form of black-market exchange. One arrest in Detroit yielded 26,000 counterfeit vouchers that had been sewn into the lining of gang members' coats.

Public Support for the Black Market

The black market could not have existed, however, if a large number of Americans had not been willing to engage in illegal trade. To most citizens, the transactions seemed so innocuous that they probably never thought twice about the corner gas station owner selling a few extra gallons for a bit more money or their friend the butcher providing them with a larger cut of meat for the same price.

Efforts to enlighten the public did little. In February 1944 Patricia Lochridge wrote an article for *Woman's Home Companion* titled "I Shopped the Black Market." In it, she detailed how homemakers, ministers, bankers, and other average Americans willingly engaged in illegal activity. Realizing the effect of this trade, the OPA launched campaigns that equated purchasing black market meat with doing "business with Hitler." For the most part, however, Americans ignored the pleas of the ineffective bureaucratic agency. In fact, many sympathized with those who were punished for transgressing the price controls.

Many of the items bought through black market channels had their origin in the military, which was where the goods had been funneled. While the penalty for selling goods within the armed services was severe, even rumors of executed transgressors did little to slow the brisk business. In the final months of the war, cigarettes were more valuable abroad than any country's currency. Robert F. Gallagher remembers that while serving as an MP in Belgium, he and his friends often used intermediaries to sell their cigarette rations to locals for a hefty profit. Another common form of profiteering involved the illegal sale of currency. Some soldiers claimed to have made thousands of dollars buying and selling foreign currencies in the confusion and economic depression of postwar Europe. Gallagher: "It's not illegal if you don't get caught."

How Big Was It?

It is nearly impossible to quantify the amount of black market activity that occurred in the United States during the war. Some have claimed that at the height of the price controls, a majority of the citizens of New York engaged in black market exchanges, and 90 percent of the meat being shipped from San Antonio, Texas, came from black market sources. The black market flourished in part because Americans mistrusted the goods' regulation. Equally important, the OPA was relatively powerless to enforce its controls: Popularly elected officials were reluctant to take measures of which the majority of their constituents would disapprove. Any society that has attempted to overregulate its market has had to increase its security and monitoring forces in kind. The police states engendered by Nazi Germany, Soviet Russia, and scores of Third World dictatorships did exactly that to secure the sanctioned exchange of goods and defend government property. Ironically, it was the war against Fascism and the police states of Nazi Germany and Imperial Japan that gave rise to regulation in America—and to the black market.

Groomzilla: The Very Married Signor Vigliotto

"Love 'em and leave 'em" could not have been a more appropriate motto for serial bigamist Giovanni Vigliotto, who wed 105 ladies without bothering to divorce any of them.

✳   ✳   ✳   ✳

VIGLIOTTO SAID "I do" in ten different countries as he traveled the world hawking tchotchkes and furniture at flea markets. Although he was short, paunchy, and something less than Romeo-esque, the raven-haired Vigliotto had no trouble attracting ladies. Starting in 1949 at age 19, Vigliotto perfected a method that brought in a bride every time.

Something Borrowed, Something Boo-hoo'd

Vigliotto began each con by choosing an alias that seemed appropriate to whichever country or neighborhood he found himself in. (He later claimed he used too many aliases to remember them all.) After he carefully selected a woman of financial means, who also appeared lonely and vulnerable, he preyed on her sympathy by confessing that he was lonely, too. A proposal soon followed, but before the ink was dry on the marriage license, he'd find some reason to convince his new bride to sell her home and move. That left him in a position to zoom off in a moving truck laden with all his bride's possessions while she trailed behind in her car. He would then sell her purloined belongings at the next flea market.

Walter Mitty of Love

It was a profitable setup, but his luck ran out in November 1981. Earlier that year, he'd abandoned wife Sharon Clark of Indiana, leaving her in Ontario, barefoot, alone, and $49,000 lighter. With all the stubborn rage of a woman not only scorned but robbed, Clark reasoned that if she went to enough flea markets, she would eventually find her runaway groom. Sure enough, she tracked him down in Florida and caught him peddling her possessions. By that time, he was wanted in Arizona for taking Patricia Ann Gardiner, wife number 105, for $36,500 worth of goods plus another $11,474 in profits from the sale of her house. He was hauled back to Phoenix, where he stood trial in early 1983. The 53-year-old Casanova spent his time before the trial researching the history of bigamy.

Vigliotto played the wounded victim in court, asking plaintively why it was so wrong of him to open doors for women and bring them flowers, insisting that most of his wives actually proposed to him. He also painted himself as a sort of Walter Mitty of love, innocently acting out fantasies of marriage. He never did admit that it was wrong to rob the ladies after he married them.

I Do...Find You Guilty!

In less than a half hour, a jury found Vigliotto guilty on 34 counts of bigamy and fraud; the judge subsequently fined him $336,000 and slapped him with 34 years in prison, the maximum.

Vigliotto served eight years in a state prison in Arizona before dying of a brain hemorrhage in early 1991. Local papers reported various grandiose schemes hatched by Vigliotto during that time, such as a made-for-TV movie based on his life and a million-dollar deal to become the poster boy for a male virility drug, but his plans invariably fizzled, ensuring that Vigliotto's legacy will remain that of a record-setting bigamist.

Quotes about Crime

"Indeed, history is nothing more than a tableau of crimes and misfortunes."

—VOLTAIRE

"Capital punishment is as fundamentally wrong as a cure for crime as charity is wrong as a cure for poverty."

—HENRY FORD

"It's a proven fact that capital punishment is a detergent for crime."

—CARROLL O'CONNER AS ARCHIE BUNKER IN ALL IN THE FAMILY

"The murdered do haunt their murderers, I believe. I know that ghosts have wandered on earth. Be with me always—take any form—drive me mad!"

—EMILY BRONTË, WUTHERING HEIGHTS

"Crime is common. Logic is rare. Therefore it is upon the logic rather than upon the crime that you should dwell."

— SIR ARTHUR CONAN DOYLE, THE ADVENTURE OF THE COPPER BEECHES

"It is worse than a crime, it is a blunder."

—MULTIPLE ATTRIBUTIONS

"Whatever the punishment, once a specific crime has appeared for the first time, its reappearance is more likely than its initial emergence could have been."

—HANNAH ARENDT

"Crime like virtue has its degrees; and timid innocence was never known to blossom suddenly into extreme license."

—JEAN RACINE

"Successful and fortunate crime is called virtue."

—LUCIUS ANNAEUS SENECA

Chapter 16

Prisons and Punishment

Medievally Executed

In contrast to popular belief and medieval myth, crime and punishment in the days of yore wasn't all guts and gore.

※ ※ ※ ※

ALTHOUGH EXECUTIONS MAY be uncommon these days, they were regular events until the late 20th century. Humankind even invented "humane" ways of sending a convicted criminal to the eternal prison, methods that include the gas chamber, electric chair, and lethal injection. Culprits from medieval times were escorted off this mortal coil by more macabre methods, none of which could be considered morally acceptable by today's standards. Here's the story behind the history.

Lightweight Laws

Common criminals weren't drawn and quartered for petty insults, nor were they sentenced for their transgressions by mob justice without the benefit of a formal inquiry. There were judges and there were trials, and though justice was swift, it was rarely sudden. Hearings lasted less than half an hour, and judges often deliberated and delivered the verdict themselves. In today's system, prison terms are handed out like traffic tickets, but offenders in medieval times were subjected to a "three strikes" policy. If a person was caught committing a crime for a third time, he or she was ushered out of town, which kept the jails uncluttered and the streets safe. The malcontent was sent elsewhere to transgress in a new location. Banishment, not beheading, was the rule of the day. Considering that most common people spent their entire lives within 10 to 15 miles of where they'd been born, being sent away from everything they'd ever known was serious punishment.

Sentences Fit the Crimes

Significant offenses such as murder and arson were treated seriously, often resulting in capital punishment. Most of these wrongdoers met their fate at the end of a rope, which was the preferred method of execution.

Being burned at the stake was the designated demise for pagans and heretics. It was a common punishment in the earlier years of the Protestant Reformation, and the definition of a heretic changed depending on who was in power. In England, Henry VIII split from the Catholic Church, but he still burned Protestants such as Anne Askew. His son, Edward VI, was a devout Protestant, however, and being Catholic during his reign could lead one to the stake. This Catholic/Protestant persecution switched once more after Mary I was crowned, and then back again with Elizabeth I.

The rack was one of the stake's partners in criminal justice. It was used to extract confessions and to "persuade" those already judged guilty to accuse others. Being put to the rack was a torment for commoners only, since it was considered uncouth to torture a member of the nobility. However, jailers had few compunctions about racking a commoner in order to get him to implicate a noble.

Nobles convicted of high treason were spared the traditional drawing and quartering. Instead, they were beheaded—having one's head lopped off with a swift swipe of the blade was considered a "privileged" way to die. The honor was dubious, though, since the ax was usually dull, and it often took several swings before the head was severed.

The First Decapitation Machine

Execution by removing a person's head from his or her body was all the rage a few hundred years ago. Executioners were always looking for a better way to perform the task. The world's first machine developed for this purpose was the Halifax gibbet, used in its British birthplace since 1286. It differed from the later French guillotine in that it had a huge horizontal ax blade, whereas the guillotine had a slimmer profile and a blade whose leading edge was at a 45-degree angle.

The guillotine was allegedly invented in 1792 by Joseph-Ignace Guillotin. In reality, he simply proposed the idea. The actual design was by a Parisian surgeon, Dr. Antoine Lewis. The prototype was built in 1792 by pianomaker Tobias Schmidt and first used that year on a highwayman named Nicholas-Jacques Pelletier. The crowd, accustomed to the entertainment value offered by a hanging body jerking around in its death dance, found this swift method of execution lacking and lustily called for the return of the gallows. There's just no pleasing some people.

Law and Disorder: The Finer Points of an Insanity Plea

No, judges don't keep a "You must be this nuts to get out of jail" sign hidden behind their benches. But you can be found not guilty by reason of insanity if you're cuckoo in just the right way.

✳ ✳ ✳ ✳

A Murky Defense

Criminal insanity doesn't refer to any specific mental disorder, but it is related to mental illness. The reasoning behind the insanity defense is that some mental disorders may cause people to lose the ability to understand their actions or to differentiate between right and wrong, leaving them unable to truly have criminal intent. Intent is an important element of crime. If you intentionally burn down a house by dropping a lit cigarette in a trash can, we'd call you an arsonist. But if you do exactly the same thing accidentally, we'd probably just call you an inconsiderate (and perhaps a criminally negligent) jerk.

Similarly, the reasoning goes, you shouldn't be punished if a mental illness leads you to break the law without really comprehending your actions. Now, this doesn't apply to just any run-of-the-mill murderer with an antisocial personality disorder. A lack of empathy may lead someone to commit crimes, but if he understands what he's doing and he realizes that what he's doing is wrong, he's not insane.

How to Be Considered Legally Insane

You can only be found not guilty by reason of insanity in two cases: if mental illness keeps you from understanding your actions and deprives you of the ability to tell right from wrong, or if mental illness leaves you unable to control your actions and you experience an irresistible impulse to commit a crime. Details vary from state to state (and some states don't recognize the insanity defense at all), but these are the general criteria.

Some form of the insanity defense seems to date back to the sixteenth century, but early versions were awfully hazy. The 1843 trial of Daniel M'Naghten helped to clear things up. Thinking that the pope and English Prime Minister Robert Peel were out to get him, M'Naghten went to 10 Downing Street to kill Peel but ended up killing Peel's secretary. Witnesses claimed that M'Naghten was delusional, and the jury found him not guilty by reason of insanity. Queen Victoria was none too pleased, so a panel of judges was convened to clarify the rules governing the insanity defense as it involved the inability to distinguish right from wrong.

The definition has been controversial ever since, and every high-profile case in which it is invoked seems to throw the idea into question. Patty Hearst and Jeffery Dahmer both tried to use the insanity defense unsuccessfully, while David Berkowitz (Son of Sam) and Ted Kaczynski (the Unabomber) seemed ready to pursue the defense but ultimately decided against it. But a jury did acquit John Hinckley Jr. of all charges related to his assassination attempt on President Reagan after it determined that he was insane.

It's No Sure Thing

A successful insanity plea is rare. In the 1990s, a study funded by the National Institute of Mental Health found that defendants pleaded insanity in less than 1 percent of cases, and that only a quarter of those pleas were successful. Those who are successful hardly ever get off scot-free—they're simply committed to mental institutions rather than sent to prisons. On average, those who are found insane end up spending more time confined to an institution than they would have in prison if they had been found guilty.

So unless you really love padded rooms, it's probably best to try another defense.

Last Meal Requests

U.S. prisoners on death row traditionally have the chance to order a special last meal on the night before they are to be executed. Last meals over the years have been a bizarre mix of ice creams, cigarettes, fried chicken, and—in one case—a single olive with a pit in it. Here are some of the more memorable last meals ordered by prisoners.

✳ ✳ ✳ ✳

VELMA BARFIELD, WHO killed five people, made history when she was executed by lethal injection at Central Prison in Raleigh, North Carolina, in 1984. She was the first woman in the United States to be executed after capital punishment was reinstated in 1977. Barfield, who became a devoted Christian while in prison, had simple tastes: She ordered a bag of Cheez Doodles and a can of Coca-Cola for her last meal.

Timothy McVeigh, a veteran of the U.S. Army, was responsible for 168 deaths when he bombed the Alfred P. Murrah Federal Building in Oklahoma City. Prior to September 11, 2001, the Oklahoma City bombing ranked as the deadliest terrorist attack in the United States. McVeigh was executed on June 11, 2001. He ordered two pints of mint chocolate chip ice cream as his last meal.

No one knows exactly how many victims serial killer **Ted Bundy** claimed, but the estimates range from 26 to 100. Bundy did not request a last meal before he was executed on January 24, 1989, in Florida. Instead, he was given the traditional last meal of steak, eggs over easy, hash browns, toast, milk, coffee, juice, butter, and jelly.

The crimes of **John Wayne Gacy** shocked the nation. Gacy was arrested in 1978 and was ultimately convicted of murdering 33 boys and young men in Illinois. He was executed on May 10, 1994, at Stateville Correctional Center in Crest Hill, Illinois. Before the execution, Gacy ate a last meal of a dozen deep-fried shrimp, a bucket of Kentucky Fried Chicken, French fries, and a pound of strawberries.

Serial killer **William Bonin** was known as the Freeway Killer and is thought to have killed as many as 36 young men and boys. He was convicted for 14 of those killings. Bonin, who was put to death on February 23, 1996, in San Quentin State Prison, was the first person executed by lethal injection in California. For his last meal, he ordered two sausage-and-pepperoni pizzas, three servings of chocolate ice cream, and 15 cans of Coca-Cola.

Philip Workman was convicted in 1982 of murdering a police officer during a failed robbery of a fast-food restaurant in Memphis. Workman's conviction was controversial, with many doubting that he was the man who fired the shot that killed the officer. Before he was executed on May 9, 2007, Workman made an unusual request for a last meal: He asked that a large vegetarian pizza be donated to a homeless person in Nashville. Prison officials denied this request, and Workman subsequently ate nothing for his last meal. However, many other people across the country donated vegetarian pizzas to homeless shelters in the state on the day Workman was executed, honoring his final request.

Victor Feguer killed a doctor in 1960 in Illinois, after picking him at random from the phone book. He was arrested in Montgomery, Alabama, after trying to sell the doctor's car. On March 15, 1963, Feguer was hanged at the Fort Madison Penitentiary in Iowa. Feguer requested one of the more unusual last meals—a solitary olive with a pit in it. Feguer was buried with the olive pit in his suit pocket.

The Hangman's Noose

Hanging can be one of the most painless ways to be executed. Unless, of course, you're at the mercy of an incompetent hangman. Then, you're out of luck.

❋ ❋ ❋ ❋

A SKILLED HANGMAN KNOWS exactly how far to drop a prisoner to kill him instantly. Chicago, Illinois, kept the identity of the local hangman a closely guarded secret—perhaps in part because whoever he was, he was really terrible at his job. Chicago hangings tended to take 15 to 20 minutes, and sometimes even longer.

Tough Breaks

Prisoner Michael McNamee held the dubious honor of being one of the first men to endure a hanging Chicago-style. On the first attempt, the rope broke, and McNamee dropped ten feet to the ground. When asked if he could stand, the prisoner seemed not to understand the question (he *had* just taken a nasty hit on the head). "I can stand that and twice that!" he barked. He was led back to the scaffold and hanged again.

Which just goes to show that if at first you don't succeed, you should try, try again. There's no need to get hung up on perfect execution!

About 100 people were hanged in Chicago between 1840 and 1927, when Illinois switched to the electric chair. Only three men were hanged publicly (the state banned public executions in 1871). One such hanging was held in a field near what is now 26th and the lake, and the others were held in the middle of Reuben Street (now Ashland) near Taylor, a West Loop site that thousands drive over every day. Most of the other hangings took place in the prison behind the criminal court building on Hubbard; the location of the gallows was inside the jail (near the corner of Dearborn and Illinois), where the fire station is now. Few Chicagoans know the history of these places, and that's just as well. Chicagoans today are so used to efficient and skilled city officials that they'd probably have a hard time believing that incompetence was once allowed to run rampant!

A Shocking Invention: The Electric Chair

Electrocution was meant to be a more humane form of execution, but things didn't exactly work out that way.

✳ ✳ ✳ ✳

Alfred Southwick's Lightbulb Moment

D R. ALFRED SOUTHWICK was a dentist in Buffalo, New York, but he was no simple tooth-driller. Like many of his contemporaries in the Gilded Age of the 1870s and 1880s, he was a broad-minded man who kept abreast of the remarkable scientific developments of the day—like electricity.

Though the phenomenon of electric current had been known of for some time, the technology of electricity was fresh—lightbulbs and other electric inventions had begun to be mass produced, and the infrastructure that brought electricity into the businesses and homes of the well-to-do was appearing in the largest cities.

An Unexpected Application

So Southwick's ears perked up when he heard about a terrible accident involving this strange new technology. A man had walked up to one of Buffalo's recently installed generators and decided to see what all the fuss was about. In spite of the protests of the men who were working on the machinery, he touched something he shouldn't have and, to the shock of the onlookers, died instantly. Southwick pondered the situation with a cold, scientific intelligence and wondered if the instant and apparently painless death that high voltage had delivered could be put to good use.

Southwick's interest in electrocution wasn't entirely morbid. Death—or more specifically, execution—was much on people's minds in those days. Popular movements advocated doing away with executions entirely, while more moderate reformers simply wanted a new, more humane method of putting criminals to death. Hangings had fallen out of favor due to the potential for gruesome accidents, often caused by the incompetence of hangmen. While the hangman's goal was to break the criminal's neck instantly, a loose knot could result in an agonizingly slow suffocation; a knot that was too tight had the potential to rip a criminal's head clean off.

Messy Progress

To prove the worth of his idea, Southwick began experimenting on dogs (you don't want to know) and discussing the results with other scientists and inventors. He eventually published his work and attracted enough attention to earn himself an appointment on the Gerry Commission, which was created by the New York State Legislature in 1886 and tasked with finding the most humane method of execution.

Although the three-person commission investigated several alternatives, eventually it settled on electrocution—in part because Southwick had won the support of the most influential inventor of the day, Thomas Alva Edison, who had developed the incandescent lightbulb and was trying to build an empire of generators and wires to supply (and profit from) the juice that made his lightbulbs glow. Edison provided influential confirmation that an electric current could produce instant death; the legislature was convinced and a law that made electrocution the state's official method of execution was passed.

Enter William Kemmler

William Kemmler was an illiterate street peddler in Buffalo, New York, who possessed a jealous streak and a penchant for drinking—a dangerous combination. His common-law wife, Tillie Ziegler, suffered the consequences of these demons in March 1889, when a drunk Kemmler brutally killed her with a hatchet. He confessed to a neighbor, saying that he would willingly "take the rope" for his intentional actions. But instead of swinging for his sins, Kemmler went down in history as the first person ever to be executed by electrocution.

An Undercurrent of Rivalry

Given his guilty admission, Kemmler's trial was swift. By May 13, he was sentenced to death by electrocution—a manner of capital punishment the New York legislature had recently deemed to be "less barbarous" than the noose.

Then a high-price lawyer mysteriously materialized in time to appeal Kemmler's death sentence on the grounds that electrocution was cruel and unusual punishment. When the appellate court upheld the electric chair as humane, another high-profile attorney argued Kemmler's case to the U.S. Supreme Court—again, unsuccessfully.

Although Kemmler's attorneys professed to be acting out of purely humanitarian interests, they were thought to be bankrolled by George Westinghouse, a pioneer in the burgeoning electric industry. Westinghouse, an alternating-current proponent, was desperately trying to defend the merits of AC so that it would gain public favor as the preferred mode of electrical transmission. Thomas Edison, his direct-current rival, hoped to solidify DC's market share by vigorously publicizing the dangers of AC's high-voltage currents.

Sparks Fly

To secure the subliminal link between AC-generated electricity and death, Edison's allies made certain the electric chair would be powered with Westinghouse generators. This was no easy feat, since Westinghouse attempted to block all generator sales suspected of connection with Edison or the electric chair.

Electrician Harold Brown was commissioned to create the first deadly device. Rumored to be an Edison agent, Brown favored AC as a power source. He also cunningly sidestepped Westinghouse: By orchestrating the shipment of Westinghouse "dynamos" to Brazil, Brown rerouted the generators back to the United States for use in developing the electric chair.

Onlookers Shocked

Sober and reborn as a Christian, Kemmler calmly approached the electric chair on August 6, 1890. As the warden shakily attached electrodes to Kemmler's body, the prisoner advised him to take his time and keep calm. In fact, according to an eyewitness, Kemmler was the coolest person in the room.

Accounts of the day vary, but all agree Kemmler's electrocution was badly bungled. The executioners seemed unclear on the amount of time the electricity was to be administered, volleying suggestions ranging from a few seconds to fifteen. Finally, ten seconds was agreed upon, and the switch was flipped. Kemmler's body convulsed and turned bright red, but to the horror of onlookers, he appeared to remain alive, groaning and gasping. Additional shocks were applied until at last he succumbed.

By some accounts, Kemmler died instantly. His latent reactions were thought involuntary, compared to the phenomenon of a chicken running around after its head has been cut off. By other accounts, Kemmler suffered a slow, painful, and torturous death. Whatever the story, the Westinghouse and Edison camps placed their spin on the event, using Kemmler's death to further their own ambitions.

In the long run, neither side prevailed. Although alternating current became the standard, financial woes eventually caused Westinghouse to lose control of his company. Bankers later took over Edison's companies, which ultimately became General Electric.

Old Sparky

For the 104 electrifying years that it remained in service, "Old Sparky" shocked Ohioans—literally and figuratively. Most of them never knew that the invention of the electric chair had direct connections to their state.

✳   ✳   ✳   ✳

FROM 1897 TO 1963, 315 men and women died in Ohio's electric chair, nicknamed "Old Sparky," which would remain on call for three decades after its final use. The chair was moved into the Ohio Penitentiary's new Death House in Columbus in 1913. Seventeen-year-old Willie Haas, convicted of raping and murdering a farmer's wife near Cincinnati, was the first and youngest criminal to die.

An Impressive Resume

Nationally, electric chairs killed many famous 20th-century criminals including: Bruno Hauptmann, killer of the Lindbergh baby; Julius and Ethel Rosenberg, the atom bomb spies; and serial killer Ted Bundy. Chillingly effective, the chairs sent 2,000 volts surging through their victims via an electrode on the head. The current was typically applied for one minute, but when performed correctly, the charge would stop the heart in a fraction of a second.

As we learned on the previous pages, native Ohioan Thomas Edison was involved in the story, and some historians credit Dr. David Rockwell, who lived in Edison's hometown of Milan, with building Ohio's chair, as he believed it was faster and more humane than the rope.

Old Methods Die Hard

In Ohio, the demise of "Old Sparky" came slowly. After the mid-1960s, the state allowed death row prisoners a choice— strap on the electrodes or take a lethal injection. Every one of them chose the needle. Then came John W. Byrd, convicted of killing a convenience store clerk near Cincinnati in 1983. Appeals delayed his execution, slated for 1994. That year, prison officials tuned up their aging death chair by hiring an electrician to design, build, and install a modern control panel, a high-voltage transformer, new cables, and body electrodes. When Byrd's appeals ran out in 2001, he requested the chair, which prompted lawsuits by death-penalty opponents and raised awareness of punishment by electrocution. Ohio's legislature banned the chair before Byrd could sit on it. He died by lethal injection the next year.

By then, Old Sparky was gathering dust in a Lucasville prison, which relieved Reginald Wilkinson, director of the Department of Corrections. None of his employees had ever executed anyone in the chair. "In modern society," Wilkinson told a reporter, "we shouldn't have to depend on technology that's over 100 years old."

The chair went to the Ohio Historical Society in Columbus in 2002, while a replica of the chair was donated to the Mansfield Reformatory Preservation Society (Ohio's death row was moved to the Mansfield Correctional Institution in 1995). These days, museum visitors need not worry if they stand too close to Old Sparky. Unplugged and unrepentant, the dreaded chair has a more quiet and efficient role—illustrating death-penalty history.

Did You Know?

Prisoner Charles Justice was sentenced to death and executed at Ohio Penitentiary on November 9, 1911, courtesy of "Old Sparky," for the crimes of robbery and murder. Now here's the ironic part: Justice had been a prisoner in the same prison in 1900, where he helped clean the area where the electric chair was kept. Originally, the condemned prisoners would be bound to the chair by leather straps; if they strained under them and their skin broke contact with the chair's electrodes, the charge would jump the gap and severely burn their flesh. Justice made the helpful suggestion of using metal clamps to better secure prisoners. His ideas were put to use, and he was paroled for his efforts but ended up right back where he had been 11 years later.

When One Life Sentence Isn't Enough

How can someone be sentenced to multiple life sentences? What purpose does the ruling serve?

✳ ✳ ✳ ✳

LOGICALLY ENOUGH, JUDGES hand down multiple sentences in order to punish multiple criminal offenses. Multiple charges may be decided in the same trial, but they are still considered separate crimes and often yield separate punishments. Even in cases of life imprisonment, multiple sentences can end up being very important in the rare instances in which convictions are overturned on appeals.

Let's say a jury finds a man guilty of killing five people. The judge might sentence him to five life sentences to address the five charges. Even if any one of the convictions is overturned (or even if four of them are overturned), the murderer still has to serve a life sentence. To walk free, he would have to be exonerated of all five murders.

Furthermore, "life" doesn't always mean an entire lifetime. Depending on the sentencing guidelines of the state, the judge may sentence a man to life imprisonment with the possibility of parole. In this instance, life is the maximum length of the sentence, meaning that the defendant could conceivably go free if a parole board releases him after he's served the minimum time (thirty years, for example).

If, however, a defendant is convicted on multiple charges, the judge may hand down multiple life sentences with the possibility of parole—but the judge can also specify that those sentences are to be served consecutively rather than concurrently. This way, the prisoner will not get a parole hearing until the minimum time for all the sentences put together has been served, which might equate to a single lifetime.

The Rock

When people discuss famous prisons, you can bet your bottom dollar that "The Rock"—Alcatraz Island, or just Alcatraz for short—is nearly always mentioned.

✳ ✳ ✳ ✳

FOR THOUSANDS OF years, Alcatraz Island sat peacefully off the coast of California—until Spanish explorer Lieutenant Juan Manuel de Ayala sailed into San Francisco Bay in 1775. For a long time, the island's only inhabitants were pelicans, rocks, grass, and more pelicans. Ayala named it *Isla de los Alcatraces*, which means "Island of the Pelicans."

A Less Peaceful Future

The island evolved into a military fortress, then during the Civil War, it served as a prison for enemy soldiers, insubordinate army personnel, and Confederate sympathizers, thus beginning its long and illustrious history.

A new prison complex was built on Alcatraz Island in 1912. The U.S. Army turned Alcatraz into a 600-cell military prison—the largest reinforced-concrete building in the world. But getting food, water, and supplies to the island became too expensive for the military.

New Trends in Lockups

Before long, a new kind of criminal emerged: mobsters. The public needed a place to put these much-feared lawbreakers, and "escape-proof" Alcatraz provided the perfect solution. In 1934, the federal government took over Alcatraz from the military and redesigned it to strike fear in the heart of any public enemy. Significantly fortified buildings, combined with the jagged rocks of Alcatraz Island and the icy waters and strong currents of San Francisco Bay, made escape from Alcatraz seem virtually impossible.

No prisoners were sentenced directly to Alcatraz. Instead, the facility was populated with the "worst" inmates from other prisons. It was not until prisoners got in trouble elsewhere in the penitentiary system that they were sent to the Rock. This included inmates with behavioral issues, those who had previously attempted to escape, and the most notorious criminals of the day, including such people as Al Capone, George "Machine Gun" Kelly, Doc Barker (of the Ma Barker Gang), and Alvin "Creepy" Karpis.

James A. Johnston was hired as warden of Alcatraz. Under his administration, prisoners received only basic necessities. Life on "The Rock" was anything but luxurious. Each cell measured five feet by nine feet and featured a fold-up bunk, desk, chair, toilet, and sink. Each day was exactly the same, from chow times to work assignments. The routine never varied and was completely methodical. Compliance was expected, and the tough guards sometimes meted out severe punishment if rules were not followed.

When extreme discipline was warranted, prisoners were placed in a "strip cell" or "hole"—a dark, steel-encased room with a hole in the floor in which the inhabitant could relieve himself.

Guards controlled the ability to flush. This institution took the concept of solitary confinement to a new level. The strip cell got its name because inmates were stripped naked before entry. They were also placed on severely restricted diets. The room was kept pitch-black. A mattress was allowed at night but taken away during the daytime.

Prisoners might spend as long as 19 days in complete isolation from other inmates. Time spent there usually meant psychological and physical abuse from the guards as well. Screams from hardened criminals could be heard echoing throughout the entire building in a stark warning to the other prisoners.

Men often came out from these strip cells with pneumonia or arthritis after spending days or weeks on the cold cement floor with no clothing. Others came out devoid of their sanity. Some men never came out of alive.

A Mental Cost

Perhaps its most famous resident, Al Capone arrived at Alcatraz in August 1934. He was fairly well behaved, but life on "The Rock" was not easy for the ex-crime boss. He was involved in a number of fights during his incarceration, was once stabbed with a pair of scissors, and spent some time in isolation while at Alcatraz.

Attempts on his life, beatings, and the prison routine itself took their toll on Capone. Seeking a diversion, he played the banjo in a prison band. Some legends say that Scarface spent most of his time strumming his banjo alone, hoping to avoid other prisoners. In reality, after more than three years in Alcatraz, Capone was on the edge of total insanity. He spent the last year of his federal sentence in the hospital ward, undergoing treatment for an advanced case of syphilis.

Al Capone was not the only inmate to lose his grip on reality at Alcatraz. While working in the prison garage, convicted bank robber Rufe Persful picked up an ax and chopped the fingers off his left hand. Laughing maniacally, he asked another prisoner to cut off his right hand as well. An inmate named Joe Bowers sustained a superficial wound when he tried to slash his own throat with a pair of broken eyeglasses. Ed Wutke, who was at Alcatraz for murder, managed to use a pencil sharpener blade to fatally cut through his jugular vein. These were not the only suicide attempts, and many other men suffered mental breakdowns at Alcatraz.

Getting Out

During Alcatraz's 29 years as a federal prison, more than 30 different men tried to escape the island in many separate attempts. In almost every case, the escapees were killed or recaptured. Two escape attempts are particularly infamous.

In May 1946, six inmates captured a gun cage, obtained prison keys, and took over a cell house in less than an hour. Unfortunately for them, the only key they did not get was the one that would let them out of the cell building, which effectively grounded the escape plot. The prison break turned into a heated gunfight that led to the deaths of three of the escapees, as well as several guards. When it was over, two of the surviving escapees were sentenced to death and the third received a life sentence.

Though the 1946 incident may have been the most violent escape attempt at Alcatraz, it is not the most famous. That belongs to the attempt that took place on June 11, 1962, when Frank Lee Morris, Allen West, and Clarence and John Anglin executed a clever escape plan. The complex plot involved escape holes made with crude drills fashioned from kitchen equipment, human decoys, and a rubber raft made from raincoats. After a bed check, three of the inmates were never seen again, having escaped through utility corridors and ventilation shafts to the beach. Allen West, however, failed to make his escape hole large enough by the scheduled time and was left behind. The trio's escape was officially deemed to be unsuccessful—there was no evidence that any of the three survived the attempt—but the television show *MythBusters* proved that escape was indeed possible with the materials they had at hand. The story of the escape was brought to the silver screen in the 1979 film *Escape from Alcatraz*, starring Clint Eastwood.

Alcatraz closed in 1963. In 1972, Congress created Golden Gate National Recreation Area, which included the island. In 1973, Alcatraz reopened as a tourist destination and is now an ecological preserve.

The Haunted Prison?

In the daytime, the former prison bustles with the activity of tour guides and visitors, but at night, the buildings play host to some unexplainable phenomena. Many believe that some of those who served time on "The Rock" linger for all eternity.

Accounts of hauntings have been widely reported since Alcatraz first shut its doors. Park service employees and visitors to Alcatraz report weird, ghostly encoun- 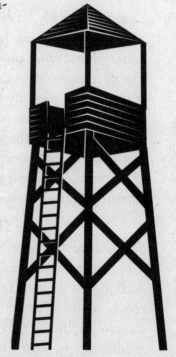 ters in the crumbling, old buildings. Unexplained clanging sounds, footsteps, and disembodied voices and screams are commonly heard coming from the empty corridors and long-abandoned cells. Some guides have reportedly wit- nessed strange events in certain areas of the prison, such as the infamous "holes," where prisoners suffered greatly.

But perhaps the most eerie sound is the faint banjo music sometimes heard in the shower room. Is it the broken spirit of Al Capone that creates this mournful melody on his phantom instrument? Or is it another ghostly inmate, unable to escape, even after death?

A Condemned Man
Leaves His Mark

Did a condemned man protest his innocence beyond the grave?

✳ ✳ ✳ ✳

IN 1877, CARBON County Prison inmate Alexander Campbell spent long, agonizing days awaiting sentencing. Campbell, a coal miner from northeastern Pennsylvania, had been charged with the murder of mine superintendent John P. Jones. Authorities believed that Campbell was part of the Molly Maguires labor group, a secret organization looking to even the score with mine owners. Although evidence shows that he was indeed part of the Mollies, and he admitted that he'd been present at the murder scene, Campbell professed his innocence and swore repeatedly that he was not the shooter.

The Sentence

Convicted largely on evidence collected by James McParlan, a Pinkerton detective hired by mine owners to infiltrate the underground labor union, Campbell was sentenced to hang. The decree would be carried out at specially prepared gallows at the Carbon County Prison. When the prisoner's day of reckoning arrived, he rubbed his hand on his sooty cell floor then slapped it on the wall proclaiming, "I am innocent, and let this be my testimony!" With that, Alexander Campbell was unceremoniously dragged from cell number 17 and committed, whether rightly or wrongly, to eternity.

The Hand of Fate

The Carbon County Prison of present-day is not too different from the torture chamber that it was back in Campbell's day. Although it is now a museum, the jail still imparts the horrors of man's inhumanity to man. Visitors move through its claustrophobically small cells and dank dungeon rooms with mouths agape. When they reach cell number 17, many visitors feel a cold chill rise up their spine, as they notice that Alexander Campbell's handprint is still there!

"There's no logical explanation for it," says James Starrs, a forensic scientist from George Washington University who investigated the mark. Starrs is not the first to scratch his head in disbelief. In 1930, a local sheriff aimed to rid the jail of its ominous mark. He had the wall torn down and replaced with a new one.

But when he awoke the following morning and stepped into the cell, the handprint had reappeared on the newly constructed wall! Many years later Sheriff Charles Neast took his best shot at the wall, this time with green latex paint. The mark inexplicably returned. Was Campbell truly innocent as his ghostly handprint seems to suggest? No one can say with certainty. Is the handprint inside cell number 17 the sort of thing that legends are made of? You can bet your life on it.

Mansfield Reformatory

North of the Lincoln Highway, outside of Mansfield, is an imposing medieval-type castle that seems very much out of place in Ohio's heartland. This site has been home to more than 150,000 inmates, a set for four major motion pictures, and a midnight location for numerous paranormal television shows, including Scariest Places on Earth. *It even holds a place in* Guinness World Records.

✳   ✳   ✳   ✳

MANSFIELD REFORMATORY (AKA Ohio State Reformatory) was built to hold juvenile first offenders. Given the population, it did not have an electric chair or a gallows, but, over the years, prisoners, guards, and the family of staff died within its walls—and not always by disease or natural causes.

Two guards were killed during escape attempts, one in 1926 and the other in 1932. In both cases, the killers were convicted and executed in the electric chair at the Ohio Penitentiary in Columbus. The wife of Warden Arthur Glattke accidently shot herself in 1950 when she knocked a loaded revolver off a closet shelf. She died three days later of pneumonia. Arthur followed in 1959, dying of a heart attack in his office. There are also other, less documented stories that circulate of unnatural deaths within the walls of the prison.

Mansfield in the Movies

In an early scene of the 1994 movie *The Shawshank Redemption*, the character Andy Dufresne (Tim Robbins), convicted of killing his wife and her lover, is on a bus headed to prison. The bus turns down a tree-lined street, heading toward a large stone building. The camera slowly glides toward and over the building, panning down on a massive prison yard filled with inmates. This and a number of other scenes from the movie were filmed in Mansfield.

Closed only four years earlier, the almost 100-year-old prison boasted the world's largest freestanding cell block, six stories high, noted in *Guinness World Records*. Prior to the prison's closing in 1990, portions of two other movies were filmed within its walls. James Caan and Elliott Gould visited the prison during the making of *Harry and Walter Go to New York* in 1976, and Sylvester Stallone and Kurt Russell were in the prison filming *Tango & Cash* the year before it closed. By the time *The Shawshank Redemption* was filmed, all inmates had been transferred out. The prison yard, captured by the aerial view at the start of *Shawshank Redemption*, had been torn down when small parts of *Air Force One* were filmed on the site in 1997.

Ghostly Activities

While no major pictures have been shot there in recent years, several minor movies, music videos, and television programs have continued to bring attention to the Gothic castle. Paranormal studies of the location have discovered several "hot spots" where researchers have experienced strange visions, noises, and even the scent of perfume from the living quarters where Helen Glattke was shot. Ghost tours have become a popular means of visiting the remaining structure. Some explorers even stay overnight to better their chances of communicating with the spirits of those who once inhabited the prison. Visitors to the Ohio State Reformatory may not run into Sylvester Stallone or Tim Robbins, but there is a chance Arthur or Helen Glattke or one of the many deceased inmates or guards may make their presence known. Not a bad addition to an afternoon tour.

Convict Corral

At the Oklahoma State Penitentiary, hardened criminals— cowboy convicts—risked life and limb while competing in a prison rodeo.

✳ ✳ ✳ ✳

Spectator's Sport

BETWEEN 1940 AND 2009, hotel rooms were hard to come by on on particular weekend in McAlester, Oklahoma (population 18,000). In late August, or on Labor Day weekend, masses of people visited the town, or more precisely, the maximum-security Oklahoma State Penitentiary, to watch an odd competition. The curious watched and cheered from behind a thick, razor wire-topped chain-link fence within the prison's walls, as inmates from ten state prisons competed in classic rodeo events such as steer wrestling and bull riding.

The top crowd-pleasers, though, were the prison's own signature events. In the Money the Hard Way competition, inmates attempted to grab a ribbon from between the horns of a 2,000-pound bull for a prize of $100 (about ten times what they made in a month laboring behind bars). In another event, four convicts sat around a card table and wait for the bull to charge them. The last man sitting won.

Dressed in borrowed Western wear and often lacking real-world rodeo experience, the inmates compete in teams of ten, and only the well behaved were eligible. Even so, armed guards stood at the ready in watchtowers above the arena.

A Dangerous Game

Despite the convicts' checkered pasts, the real danger came from the livestock: Injuries ranged from minor scrapes to ruptured groins and, yes, the occasional goring. Nevertheless, inmates clamored for the chance to prove themselves on the back of a bronco. Afterward, they shared a celebratory meal of hamburgers and milkshakes before it was time to return to their cells.

Oklahoma is said to have modeled its prison rodeo after that of its neighbor and rival, Texas, which held the nation's first "behind the walls" rodeo at Huntsville in 1931. A lack of funding forced that rodeo to close down in 1986, leaving the Okie competition the distinction as the world's only behind-the-walls prison rodeo.

The McAlester rodeo, too, fell prey to funding gaps. In 2006, women were permitted to compete, but they only did so for a few years, before the rodeo shut down after the 2009 event.

Angola

Visitors seeking a similar event now need to travel to Louisiana, where prison rodeos at "Angola," the Louisiana State Penitentiary, began in 1965 and still run twice a year, in April and in October. It was opened to spectators in 1967, and thousands attend each year, though there was a break in 2020 due to COVID-19.

At the rodeo, prisoners man concessions stands that sell food. Rodeo events include bareback riding, bull-dogging, and bull riding. Inmates also sell handmade crafts, furniture, and art. The rodeo raises money for religious educational programs for the prisoners.

Audacious Prison Escapes

When you have nothing to lose, you might have everything to gain. Such appears to be the mind-set behind these wild and woolly escapes.

✳ ✳ ✳ ✳

Libby Prison, Virginia

AFTER DIGGING A 50-foot tunnel, 109 Union soldiers broke free on February 9 and 10, 1864. Over half made it to safety behind northern lines.

Brushy Mountain State Prison, Tennessee

The convicted killer of Martin Luther King Jr., James Earl Ray used a makeshift ladder to scale the prison's 14-foot-high walls in 1977. He eluded authorities for 54 hours in what's been described as "one of the greatest manhunts in modern memory."

Colditz P.O.W. Camp, Germany

During World War II, British inmates built a glider to escape from this Nazi P.O.W. camp. Before they could use it, they were liberated. Tests later proved that the contraption could indeed fly.

Pascal Payet, French prisoner

Payet pulled off not one but two daring prison escapes, both times with the use of accomplices flying hijacked helicopters. After a 2007 escape from France's Grasse Prison, the fugitive underwent cosmetic surgery. Despite his proactive attempt at eluding authorities, Payet was soon recaptured.

Salag Luft III, Germany

Immortalized in *The Great Escape* (1963), the March 24, 1944, escape from the Nazi P.O.W. camp featured three tunnels (Tom, Dick, and Harry) that reached beyond the prison's fences. In all, 76 men crawled to freedom. Sadly, only three evaded recapture.

Prison by the Numbers

✳ In the United States, escape attempts generally add to the prisoner's sentence. In some other countries, including Germany, Sweden, and Austria, the drive to escape is considered natural, and escape attempts that do not include violence or property damage do not incur additional time.

✳ The United States has the highest incarceration rate in the world. In 2020, the United States was imprisoning more than 2.1 million people, a quarter of the world's prisoners.

✳ In the United States, about 737 people per every 100,000 people are incarcarated, the highest rate in the world. Russia incarcarates 615 people per every 100,000 people. Every other country imprisons less than 400 people per every 100,000.

✳ The "War on Drugs" that begin in the 1980s caused a large surge in prison populations.

✳ The World Prison Brief said in 2018 that approximately one quarter of the prison population consisted of pre-trial detainees and remand prisoners.